AS LONG AS THE SUN SHINES AND WATER FLOWS

AS LONG AS
THE SUN SHINES
AND WATER FLOWS

A Reader in
Canadian Native Studies

Edited by

Ian A. L. Getty and Antoine S. Lussier

Nakoda Institute Occasional Paper No. 1

UNIVERSITY OF BRITISH COLUMBIA PRESS
Vancouver

AS LONG AS THE SUN SHINES AND WATER FLOWS:
A READER IN CANADIAN NATIVE STUDIES

This book has been published with the
help of grants from the Nakoda Institute
and the Canada Council.

Canadian Cataloguing in Publication Data

Main entry under title:

As long as the sun shines and water flows

  Includes bibliograpies.
  ISBN 0–7748–0181–6 (bound). — ISBN
0–7748–0184–0 (pbk.)

  1. Indians of North America — Canada —
Government relations — History — Addresses,
essays, lectures. 2. Indians, Treatment of —
Canada — History — Addresses, essays, lectures.
I. Getty, Ian A. L., 1947–   II. Lussier,
Antoine S.

E78.C2A82   323.1′197′071   C83–091270–3

International Standard Book Number 0-7748-0181-6 (cloth)
0-7748-0184-0 (pbk)

This book is printed on Acid Free Paper

Printed in Canada

CONTENTS

Foreword

The Nakoda Institute Occasional Papers series is sponsored under the auspices of the Stoney Indian Tribe at Morley, Alberta.

The Nakoda Institute is a learning centre which provides adult and advanced educational opportunities for the local and off-reserve communities. The Institute recognizes the importance of encouraging Indian people to achieve self-determination and to enhance their economic, social, and cultural development. Its philosophy represents an Indian way of life and thinking, and it provides a tangible educational facility for people to use in their learning and spiritual development. The Institute is open to all who share a sincere interest in the advancement of Indian culture and quality of life in Canada.

Acknowledgements

The Institute will, from time to time, publish materials which reflect its goals and aspirations.

Further information regarding the Nakoda Institute and its publications programme may be obtained from the Stoney Tribe, Morley, Alberta, Canada T0L 1N0.

Chief John Snow
Stoney Indian Tribe,
Morley, Alberta

Recognizing the cultural heritage and historical role of native people in Canada, the Nakoda Institute is proud to undertake the publishing of this reader focusing upon Canadian Native Studies. The main body of articles were originally read before a native studies conference hosted by the Native Studies Department, Brandon University; and in addition, grateful acknowledgement is made to the authors and publishers for their kind permission to reprint the following articles:

"Clifford Sifton and Canadian Indian Administration 1896–1905" by David J. Hall. From *Prairie Forum* 2, no. 2 (November 1977). Reprinted by permission of the Canadian Plains Research Center, University of Regina, Regina, Saskatchewan.
"Herman Merivale and Colonial Office Indian Policy in the Mid-Nineteenth Century" by David T. McNab. From *The Canadian Journal of Native Studies* 1, no. 2 (1981). Reprinted by permission of the author and publisher.
"The Politics of Indian Affairs," abridgement from Chapter 17 of *A Survey of the Contemporary Indians of Canada*, Part 1, edited by H. G. Hawthorn (Ottawa, 1966). Reprinted by permission of Queen's Printer.
"Canada's Indians Yesterday: What of Today?" by D. Jenness. From *Canadian Journal of Economics and Political Science* 20, no. 1 (February 1954).
"The Tragedy of the Loss of the Commons in Western Canada," a revised version of "The Great Transformation: The Disappearance of the Commons in Western Canada" by Irene M. Spry. From C.P.R.C. publication no. 6, *Man and Nature on the Prairies*, edited by Richard Allen. Reprinted by permission of the Canadian Plains Research Center, University of Regina, Regina, Saskatchewan.
"Protection, Civilization, Assimilation: An Outline History of Canada's Indian Policy" by John L. Tobias. From *Western Canadian Journal of Anthropology* (now the *Canadian Journal of Anthropology*) 6, no. 2 (1976). Reprinted by permission of the author and the editor.
"The Inuit and the Constitutional Process: 1978–81" by Simon McInnes. From *Journal of Canadian Studies* 16, no. 2. Reprinted by permission of the journal.
The opinions and views expressed herein are those of the individual authors and are not necessarily accepted by the Nakoda Institute.

Preface

This collection of essays and articles focuses upon Canadian native history since the passage of the Royal Proclamation of 1763, the original document in which Britain recognized the prior sovereignty of the Indian nations. This reader is comprised of original research papers given at a native studies colloquium hosted by Brandon University in November 1981 and a selection of published articles on aspects of native history. This arrangement is intended to provide a broad overview of the official Canadian Indian Policy, its effect on the Indian, Inuit, and Metis, and their responses to it. The papers demonstrate varied approaches to native studies and reflect a number of the major issues and themes currently under analysis in Indian history — colonial Indian policy, constitutional and legislative developments, Indian treaties, policy and government decision-making, native responses reflecting both persistence and change, and the broad issue of aboriginal and treaty rights. Regrettably there remain many emerging areas of research left untouched in this anthology — Indian philosophy, spirituality and medicine, educational issues, native identity, reserve life, oral tradition and local history, pan-Indian movements, and provincial Indian organizations. Our desire at the Brandon Conference was to encourage and stimulate the growth and awareness of native scholarship across Canada.

The book opens with a broad historical review of Indian-white relations presented as a keynote address by Professor George Stanley at the Brandon conference. By its title, the essay suggests the firm commitment and importance of the historical relationship between native people and the non-native population in Canada. For half a century, Professor Stanley has done a great deal to include the native people in Canadian historiography. In his survey of Indian–white relations from the earliest contact with European explorers to the current parliamentary debates over aboriginal rights in Canada's recently patriated constitution, he touches upon many of the themes in native history which receive detailed scrutiny in the following studies. The challenge to historians, Stanley states, is to understand the values and philosophies of the respective cultures under study. More scholars are now aware of the vital contribution of Indian oral tradition towards a more balanced understanding of the written records. ˙

Stanley offers a critical look at some of the turning points in Indian history — notably the Royal Proclamation of 1763. Following the procedure outlined in the Proclamation, the creation of Upper Canada in 1791 led to a series of land purchases. After 1818 the practice of paying for Indian lands with annuities was adopted and has continued to the present. Stanley traces how Indian policy evolved through successive phases of imperial management to Canadian control at mid-nineteenth century, until Confederation placed the Indians under the exclusive jurisdiction of the federal government under Section 91 (24) of the British North America Act. The treaties were signed and set the stage for the current debate on the recognition and entrenchment of "existing" aboriginal and treaty rights in the Canadian constitution.

Section I concerns the evolution of British Indian policy and Canadian Indian administration since the Royal Proclamation of 7 October 1763. The papers in this section suggest collectively that over time there has been a notable continuity in British Indian policy and later Canadian legislation which originates from the philosophy first articulated in that document. The Proclamation unequivocally recognizes aboriginal title and declares that unceded lands can be surrendered only to the Crown in a prescribed manner, that is, through negotiated agreements or treaties. Consequently, it is regarded as a key document by the courts in defining aboriginal rights and by historians in tracing the roots of Indian sovereignty and nationhood. As a legal document and a statement of policy, the Proclamation spells out several provisions to ensure crown sovereignty and to regulate relationships between Indian Nations and the Crown. The Proclamation recognized the sovereign rights and special status of Indian Nations and imposed strict constraints on Indian-white relations. It remains to be decided whether the Proclamation applies throughout Canada or only in those territories designated in 1763. Moreover, is the concept of crown sovereignty mutually compatible with the concept of Indian nationhood based upon self-government and self-determination?

In the following essays, it is generally agreed that British colonial policy in the early nineteenth century set the tone and style for Canadian policy in the latter half of the century. The fundamental issue was land ownership. Once this was initially resolved through peace treaties and surrenders as set forth in the Royal Proclamation of 1763, the discussion of the best means to "civilize" and to "Christianize" the indigenous population began.

John Tobias, who was research director with the Federation of Saskatchewan Indians (1972–75) and is currently an instructor of history, Red Deer College, Alberta, provides a succinct analysis of Canada's Indian policy and the various pieces of legislation designed to "protect, civilize, and assimilate" native people. While the general goal was clear, often-times the policies and legislation were apparently contradictory, a dilemma elaborated upon in the succeeding papers of this section.

The first paper on early nineteenth-century British North America Indian policy looks at "Indian Land Cessions in Upper Canada" from 1815 to 1830. Robert Surtees, the author of *The Original People* (1971) and presently teaching at

Nipissing College, documents how the War of 1812 between British North America and the United States prompted several changes in British colonial Indian policy. A deep schism was created between Indian tribes living north and south of the Great Lakes (notably the Six Nations or the Iroquois Confederacy which had originally split in the American War of Independence). After the War of 1812, new settlement patterns prompted a series of peace treaties and land cessions covering much of present-day southern Ontario. Concomitantly, the military and political influence of the Indians decreased just as the Indian population of Upper Canada was steadily decreasing in proportion to the settler population, which demanded more and more agricultural land. Once their homeland was reduced, the Indian population came under successive schemes by church and state to "christianize" and "civilize" them, a policy sanctioned and officially implemented in 1830.

David McNab's analysis of "Herman Merivale and Colonial Office Indian Policy in the Mid-Nineteenth Century" indicates that British Indian policy was not uniform. Rather, there gradually evolved a series of regional Indian policies centred on the Atlantic colonies, central British North America, Rupert's Land under Hudson's Bay Company control, and Vancouver Island (before its union with British Columbia). A key imperial policy maker was Herman Merivale, permanent under-secretary of state at the Colonial Office from 1847 to 1860, who brought new ideas to Indian policy. On the two coasts, the prevailing objective was to "insulate" the Indians from white settlement until they were ready for assimilation. In central Canada and the northwest, the goal was to "amalgamate" the Indian quickly through education and assimilation. In the Atlantic region, Indian-white relations went through all these phases until a concerted attempt was made to assimilate the native population.

John Milloy analyses the early Canadian period of Indian policy at mid-nineteenth century. Through his examination of the various pieces of Indian legislation beginning in 1857 (when the Enfranchisement Act was passed), Milloy identifies a shift in policy from that of "civilizing" the Indians to that of "assimilating" them through enfranchisement. The policy was a failure since only one Indian enfranchisement occurred during a nineteen-year period; still, it remained the essential thrust of the Enfranchisement Act of 1869 and the Consolidated Indian Act of 1876. The Canadian government later resorted to coercive legislation when the policy of persuasion followed by the British had failed. The new legislation instituted "a system of wardship, colonization and tutelage" in place of Indian self-government. The legacy of 1857–76 remains the basis of constitutional and legislative goals today — the assimilation of the Indian through the force of the law.

Once in place, the Indian Act was implemented with sternness and aggressiveness by the bureaucrats in the Department of Indian Affairs, established as a separate government branch within the Department of the Interior in 1880. Lawrence Vankoughnet served as deputy superintendent-general of Indian Affairs from 1874 to 1893. Historian Douglas Leighton regards Vankoughnet as the epitome of the dedicated nineteenth-century bureaucrat, zealously carrying out the government's policies, regardless of the realities on Indian reserves. Vankoughnet's implementation of economy and centralized control during the early 1880's were critical factors in the events leading to the violent confrontation of 1884–85. It was evident that the Indian Affairs Department rated a low priority and consequently received little support, from either senior government officials or other departments. Political partisanship reached the senior ranks when Vankoughnet was forced into early retirement in 1893 to make way for new incoming civil servants, notably the long-serving Duncan Campbell Scott.

Following the 1896 federal election, the new Liberal minister of the interior, Clifford Sifton, introduced a more repressive system since the assimilation of the western Indian population was not proceeding rapidly enough. Professor David Hall, author of a recent biography of Clifford Sifton, summarizes the Liberal government's new Indian policy at the turn of the twentieth century, of favouring land surrenders, assimilation through education, and stricter enforcement of regulations under the revised Indian Act of 1906. The staff reductions and departmental reorganization resulted in centralized control by Ottawa bureaucrats "who were more concerned with ledger books [to reduce expenditures] than difficulties on the reserves." The next major shift in policy directions would not occur until the 1940's, which culminated in the Indian Act revisions of 1951.

The 1870's were a crucial turning point in relations between the government of Canada and the Indian Nations of western Canada where seven treaties covering most of present-day Manitoba, Saskatchewan, and Alberta were signed between 1871 and 1877. David McNab's paper on the "Administration of Treaty No. 3, 1873–1915" discusses the political, cultural and economic implications of one of these numbered treaties. By 1873, when Treaty No. 3 was signed (and coincidently, when a separate Indian affairs branch was created within the Department of Secretary of State), federal Indian policy was essentially developed, and, clearly, the British attempt to establish a uniform policy from sea to sea had failed. This was in part the result of provincial interests in land and resource ownership. McNab's paper documents the negotiations concerning the demarcation of reserve boundaries from the time the treaty was signed until the federal-provincial agreement of 1915. The protracted negotiations had enormous consequences for the Ojibway people in northwestern Ontario. Today, the Nishnawbe people continue to press the federal and provincial governments to be sensitive to and respectful of their traditional lifestyle, and they seek firm assurances that their land and resource base will not be arbitrarily compromised. The issues discussed in McNab's historical analysis concerning the legal complications and interpretations of the meaning or intent of the treaty terms are shared by many Indian tribes throughout Canada.

In a paper presented at a meeting of the Canadian Political Science Association in 1953, Canada's distinguished anthropologist, Diamond Jenness, described the inferior living conditions of the Canadian Indians as he observed them in the 1920's during his field trips. The government neglected the political and economic welfare of the Indians and failed to provide them with adequate educational facilities. Jenness, born in New Zealand and educated at Oxford, came to Canada in 1913 and spent three years in the Arctic with the Canadian Arctic Expedition. He was appointed chief of the Anthropology Division of the National Museum in Ottawa, and he conducted fieldwork among several tribal groups across Canada as well as undertaking archaeological work in Newfoundland and Alaska. He is best known for his volumes on Eskimo administration and his *Indians of Canada*, first published in 1932, still remains an invaluable, although somewhat outdated, study. What is obvious from Jenness's text, delivered with such frankness, is his sympathy and concern with Canada's native peoples. He clearly wanted Canadians to consider the country's first inhabitants as equal citizens. At the same time, his paper contains the central message of Canadian Indian policy-makers since the mid-nineteenth century — the desire to assimilate the Indian and eventually to terminate their reserves.

The concluding chapter in this section is an abridgement from the first comprehensive scientific survey of the social, political, economic, and educational needs and policies of the contemporary Indian scene. The Hawthorn Report, commissioned in 1958, has become the benchmark for contemporary studies on Canada's Indian population. The report notes the growing involvement of provincial governments in delivery of services traditionally provided by the federal government to Indian people. The study provides the context for understanding why the federal government formulated its infamous termination policy presented in the White Paper of 1969.

Section II focuses on native responses as they came in confrontation with Euro-Canadian society.

In the opening paper, Professor Laurie Barron examines alcohol use among the Indians living on missions in Upper Canada during the early decades of the nineteenth century. The temperance movement which swept North America in the 1820's prompted a concerted effort to ban the sale of liquor to Indians (before the idea of government intervention was acceptable to control sobriety in the wider society). Ironically, the governing legislation passed in 1835 "strictly prohibited the sale, barter, exchange or gift — of any distilled spirituous liquors to any Indian man, woman or child," but no corresponding law was passed to make the actual consumption by an Indian punishable by law. This paternalistic legislation treated the Indian "as a child-like ward of the state [who] was not required to assume any responsibility for his actions." Inevitably, the law proved unenforceable. The alien standards imposed by the temperance movement — the ideas of thrift, punctuality, industry, and discipline which reflected middle class norms — probably had more to do with accentuating the drinking problems than with ameliorating the social consequences of drunkenness.

In an essay reprinted from the Canadian Plains Research Center's *Man and Nature on the Prairies*, Irene M. Spry documents the social and economic upheaval that resulted among the Indian tribes and the Metis people during "the great transformation" following 1870. The decisive changes occurred during the 1870's with the signing of the treaties, soon followed by the disappearance of the buffalo which had been the mainstay of both Indian and Metis. Now dependent upon government assistance, the demoralized, starving tribes had no alternative but to accept their reserves. Their effective removal as a political or military factor in the West opened the way for the white man's concept of exclusive ownership of formerly commonly held property and resources. Now private ownership controlled access to land, water, grass, wood, and shelter which had formerly been freely shared and utilized. Wide open access to hunting and trapping territories was replaced by the confined requirements of agriculture. The Indian reserves set aside under treaty were operated more along the lines of confinement camps to protect the surrounding private interests. The legacy of bitterness and resentment toward the dominant white society remains at the root of much of the conflict in race relations today.

Robert Allen focuses upon the infamous Cypress Hills Massacre of 1873 to portray the differences in attitude between American and Canadian authorities towards the Indian people of the great plains. He suggests that the Canadian officials were earnest and sincere in their efforts to demonstrate that the "medicine line" along the 49th Parallel made a real difference. The first challenge in gaining the confidence of the native residents was to apply the principles of justice equally to all inhabitants in the Queen's territory. Allen's thorough sifting of the conflicting evidence given at the American hearings and during the Winnipeg trial demonstrates the difficult task historians face not only in reconstructing the actual events, but also in delineating the different perceptions of American frontiersmen and Canadian settlers towards the Indian people. The symbolic gestures of British justice, upheld by the North West Mounted Police and Canadian officials, were instrumental in convincing the western tribes to sign peace agreements with the treaty commissioners in 1876 (Treaty 6) and in 1877 (Treaty 7).

The following three articles deal with specific aspects of Metis history and its most significant figure, Louis Riel. In "Louis Riel and Aboriginal Rights," Tom Flanagan, chairman of the Political Science department at the University of Calgary, presents a dimension of Riel's capacity to politicize an issue to which few people in western Canada had given any thought — the issue of compensation for Metis lands not from a position of aboriginal rights but from the perspective of *international law*. Those who believe in Riel's prophetic abilities will probably agree with Flanagan that "Riel's theory of aboriginal rights is an intermediate position between the government doctrine, which is still held by Canadian courts, and the emerging view of the native community." The present Metis leaders seem to be following in Riel's footsteps when they claim that the extinguishment of Metis aboriginal title must be done in a collective fashion instead of settling individual claims.

"A Parting of the Ways," by Raymond Huel, an historian from the University of Lethbridge, is a most interesting account of how Louis Schmidt (a Metis colleague of Riel) evaluated his leader during the trials and tribulations of 1884–85. The confrontations that occurred between Schmidt and Riel over the issue of Metis identity deserve careful analysis, for they are still a major source of contention among Metis people. Perhaps Schmidt was not aware that Riel had his own concept of a superior race. In a letter addressed to a M. Lavallée of St. François Xavier in 1883, Riel gives reasons why French-speaking Metis and French-Canadians should inter-marry. The good qualities and virtues of both would certainly create a strong race of Metis-Canadien Français, so Riel thought.

"La conquête du Nord-ouest, 1885–1985/The Imperial Quest of British North America, 1885–1985," by Jean Morisset from the Université du Québec à Montréal is a most intriguing argument that attacks the conventional "founding myths upon which the British North American State has built itself." According to Morisset, the victim has been the native population, and today, given government activities in the Northwest Territories, the cycle is repeating itself. One may not necessarily agree with Morisset's analysis of native-government relations from 1885 to the present, but it is a provocative analysis. Morisset's paper was an oral presentation given at the Native Studies Conference. Though the conference was to have had papers presented in French, 99 per cent of the assembly was English-speaking. Perhaps one of Morisset's conclusions is worth noting: "The fact that we can hold here a Métis symposium without simultaneous translation is meaningful enough, and is indeed only possible because we all tacitly agree to speak the language of the conqueror."

The next three papers analyse from different perspectives the native people's response when they confronted white society. Two substantive issues are addressed — incarceration for violating the white society's laws, and the relatively successful response of the Inuit to modernization in the Canadian Arctic. The first two papers portray how the colonial position of Canada's Indians has contributed to the social dilemma of Canada's native people. Part of the solution may be a greater willingness by government to allow native communities real local control at the reserve and community level. The partial introduction of self-government in the 1960's and 1970's demonstrated that the administrative constraints placed upon local band government did not provide the necessary latitude — culturally, politically, psychologically, spiritually, or otherwise — to allow real Indian self-determination. As Professor Roberts points out with reference to the Inuit people, modernization *per se* is not the issue for the rising generations — it is the right of self-determination and recognition of Indian self-government, as so eloquently outlined in the concluding document to this section.

The exorbitantly high number of native people in correctional institutions indicates the high degree of failure of many native people to adjust to non-native society. One of the first scholars to analyse the structural limitations of the criminal justice system is Don McCaskill, chairman of the Department of Native Studies at Trent University. The high incidence of native incarceration is rooted in the same ambiguities which the temperance movement faced: "For the government to assume they could replace Indian authority structures with a foreign value system simply through the individual efforts of educators, government agents, and others was simply naive. Civilizing the Indian with an eye to eventually assimilating them did not, and could not, occur." Indians living on isolated reserves remained unaware of the social norms expected in white society, and, instead, native people developed "adoptive strategies" to regulate their interaction with white society to avoid serious conflict.

McCaskill's analysis of the pattern of criminal activity identified two types of crime: theft (usually the property of a non-Indian situated on the reserve or in a town nearby) and assault (normally involving another native person). The crimes were usually unpremeditated and the vast majority of offences involved the influence of liquor. These patterns are "characteristic of minority groups which consider themselves excluded from participation in the dominant society." The real issue, and challenge, is to appreciate the right of self-determination and social-cultural equality which can accommodate differing values and modes of behaviour.

Lance Roberts's paper on current social and cultural developments among the Canadian Inuit provides an interesting contrast to similar developments among the Indian people of southern Canada. Like the Indian, the Inuit has been exposed to European culture contact for centuries — with whalers, fur traders, missionaries, and government officials. By the mid-twentieth century the Inuit had been transformed. Their lifestyle rapidly changed from a nomadic family-oriented camp life (partly sustained by hunting and trapping) to a largely sedentary settlement pattern complete with modern forms of education, social agencies, and government officialdom. In several communities under study, the Inuit have successfully adapted to wage employment in the oil and mining industries. The key factor was community control in which the Inuit have not been overwhelmed and dominated by non-natives. This adaptive strategy is being increasingly adopted by Indian bands across Canada — living on their home reserve and commuting to off-reserve jobs. The issue remains the same for all native communities: How can the Inuit become "modern" in a manner that preserves their self-identity and minimizes social disorganization? Ultimately, the resolution of the social forces of modernization must come for each local community in its own unique fashion.

From 1978 to 1982 Canada's political leaders vigorously debated constitutional change and the patriation of Canada's constitution, the British North America Act of 1867. Under Section 91(24) of the BNA Act the federal government has a special constitutional responsibility towards Indian people which, since a Supreme Court of Canada decision delivered in 1939, includes the Inuit of Canada. During public hearings held by a special Joint Committee of the Senate and House of Commons in 1980–1981, various native organizations and individual tribes proposed ways of recognizing and entrenching their aboriginal and treaty rights. This description by Simon McInnes of the interplay between "The Inuit and the Constitutional Process" from 1978 to 1981 points out the complexities of developing a compatible legal and political framework that the native people may operate within. The implications of patriation are far-reaching because under the new amending formula for constitutional reform, the provinces are directly involved in the entrenchment process. Under the Charter of Rights and Freedoms (specifically sections 25 and 35), the "existing" aboriginal and treaty rights are recognized and affirmed but not defined, and under the amending formula, the entrenchment of any native rights will require the consent of seven or more provinces representing at least 51 per cent of the national population. It may very well prove true that real and meaningful acknowledgement of aboriginal and treaty rights will best be implemented through the parliamentary legislative process if the constitutional process is deadlocked.

The final document in this section, "A Declaration of the First Nations," was adopted by the Indian chiefs of Canada to reaffirm their national rights and to attain recognition for their special status in Canada. The Indian people mounted a massive campaign in 1980–81 in opposition to patriation of the Canadian constitution in order to have their special rights entrenched and protected from future amendment without their consent. They did not achieve the latter goal, but aboriginal people (meaning Indian, Inuit, and Métis) did attain constitutional recognition and the opportunity to define the meaning and extent of their aboriginal and treaty rights at a first ministers' conference held in March 1983. Patriation may prove to be the turning point in resolving the outstanding legal and constitutional claims of Canada's Indian people along the terms and conditions outlined in their declaration. The major significance of the declaration is its emphasis on the right of self-government and self-determination in their own tribal lands. The First Nations demand equal and shared powers with the federal government in accordance with the principles of the Proclamation of 1763. The declaration is a landmark document asserting their inherent rights as sovereign peoples.

Although full consideration was not given to native rights issues at the meeting held between the prime minister of Canada and the first ministers of the provinces on 15 and 16 March 1983, it was agreed that future conferences would be held to discuss these matters, and that representatives of native groups, and of the Yukon and Northwest Territories, be invited to take part in these conferences. Further, the government of Canada proposed the following schedule for an amendment to Canada's new constitution, which the first ministers agreed to put before Parliament and the provincial legislatures prior to 31 December 1983. Quebec was not a signatory to this agreement.

SCHEDULE

Motion for a Resolution to authorize His Excellency the Governor General to issue a proclamation respecting amendments to the Constitution of Canada

Whereas the Constitution Act, 1982 provides that an amendment to the Constitution of Canada may be made by proclamation issued by the Governor General under the Great Seal of Canada where so authorized by resolutions of the Senate and House of Commons and resolutions of the legislative assemblies as provided for in section 38 thereof;

And Whereas the Constitution of Canada, reflecting the country and Canadian society, continues to develop and strengthen the rights and freedoms that it guarantees;

And Whereas, after a gradual transition of Canada from colonial status to the status of an independent and sovereign state, Canadians have, as of April 17, 1982, full authority to amend their Constitution in Canada;

And Whereas historically and equitably it is fitting that the early exercise of that full authority should relate to the rights and freedoms of the first inhabitants of Canada, the aboriginal peoples;

Now Therefore the [Senate] [House of Commons] [legislative assembly] resolves that His Excellency the Governor General be authorized to issue a proclamation under the Great Seal of Canada amending the Constitution of Canada as follows:

PROCLAMATION AMENDING THE CONSTITUTION OF CANADA

1. Paragraph 25(b) of the Constitution Act, 1982 is repealed and the following substituted therefor:

"(b) any rights or freedoms that now exist by way of land claims agreements or may be so acquired."

2. Section 35 of the Constitution Act, 1982 is amended by adding thereto the following subsections:

"(3) For greater certainty, in subsection (1) "treaty rights" includes rights that now exist by way of land claims agreements or may be so acquired."

(4) Notwithstanding any other provision of this Act, the aboriginal and treaty rights referred to in subsection (1) are guaranteed equally to male and female persons."

3. The said Act is further amended by adding thereto, immediately after section 35 thereof, the following section:

"35.1 The government of Canada and the provincial governments are committed to the principle that, before any amendment is made to Class 24 of section 91 of the Constitution Act, 1867, to section 25 of this Act or to this Part,

> (a) a constitutional conference that includes in its agenda an item relating to the proposed amendment, composed of the Prime Minister of Canada and the first ministers of the provinces, will be convened by the Prime Minister of Canada, and
>
> (b) the Prime Minister of Canada will invite representatives of the aboriginal peoples of Canada to participate in the discussions on that item"

4. The said Act is further amended by adding thereto, immediately after section 37 thereof the following Part

"PART IV.I

CONSTITUTIONAL CONFERENCES

37.1(1) In addition to the conference convened in March 1983, at least two constitutional conferences composed of the Prime Minister of Canada and the first ministers of the provinces shall be convened by the Prime Minister of Canada, the first within three years after April 17, 1982 and the second within five years after that date.

(2) Each conference convened under subsection (1) shall have included in its agenda constitutional matters that directly affect the aboriginal peoples of Canada, and the Prime Minister of Canada shall invite representatives of those peoples to participate in the discussions on those matters.

(3) The Prime Minister of Canada shall invite elected representatives of the governments of the Yukon Territory and the Northwest Territories to participate in the discussions on any item on the agenda of a conference convened under subsection (1) that, in the opinion of the Prime Minister, directly affects the Yukon Territory and the Northwest Territories."

The concluding historiographical essay, "The Indian in Canadian Historical Writing, 1971–1981," by Professor James Walker, continues the discussion he initiated in "The Indian in Canadian Historical Writing," presented in the 1971 *Report* of the Canadian Historical Association. It is a fine documentary analysis of stereotypical images presented of native people in historical literature and standard educational texts. Ten years later, Walker acknowledges the tremendous growth in specialist and general studies on native topics. However, Walker notes that little of this revisionist research has filtered through to the scholarly historians writing general Canadian survey texts. Walker identifies a common pattern in Canadian writings before 1971 and concludes that it has continued into the surveys written in the 1970's: "Once a white presence is firmly established the Indians are allowed to drift out of historical consciousness, returning only occasionally but always in the role of client or problem." Individual Indian leaders or tribal events are rarely mentioned, the notable exception being when they sign treaties with the government to make way for peaceful settlement. Most books have successfully purged the term "savages" from their lexicon, but this has simply led to a noticeable reduction in Indian content in the majority of general texts. He concludes by analysing why the stereotyped treatment and neglect of Indian history persists in Canadian historiography. It is hoped that this reader will make a number of the new critical assessments of Canada's native past available to a larger audience, to complement the general texts discussed in Walker's article.

The Native Studies Conference held at Brandon was made possible by the efforts of individuals in the Native Studies Department, the president of Brandon University, Dr. Jack Perkins, the Social Sciences and Humanities Research Council, the Multiculturalism Section of the Department of the Secretary of State, and the Province of Manitoba.

The business community of Brandon donated the wine and cheese, and SAGA Foods catered the banquet. To all the speakers who showed and those who substituted for the "no-shows," we say thank you. To Margaret and little D'Arcy who probably wondered why Daddy was always at the office, a special acknowledgement. Thanks to Dr. L. Clark of the History department, Brandon University, whose advice and encouragement was always appreciated, and to Dennis Bérubé, the accountant at Brandon University, who listened and gave encouragement and direction during the on-going preparations for the conference. Lastly, we thank the staff of the Nakoda Institute of the Stoney Indian Tribe in Alberta for their enthusiastic support and technical assistance in producing this publication.

To all, a sincere thank you.

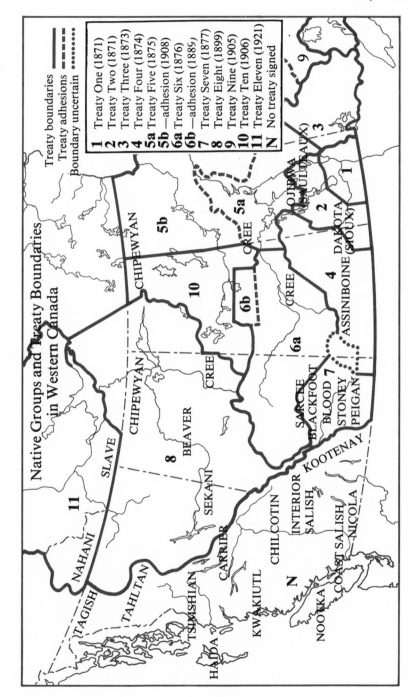

Native Groups and Treaty Boundaries in Western Canada

Treaty boundaries
Treaty adhesions
Boundary uncertain

1   Treaty One (1871)
2   Treaty Two (1871)
3   Treaty Three (1873)
4   Treaty Four (1874)
5a   Treaty Five (1875)
5b   —adhesion (1908)
6a   Treaty Six (1876)
6b   —adhesion (1889)
7   Treaty Seven (1877)
8   Treaty Eight (1899)
9   Treaty Nine (1905)
10   Treaty Ten (1906)
11   Treaty Eleven (1921)
N   No treaty signed

Abbreviations

AO	Archives of Ontario
CHR	*Canadian Historical Review*
CO	Colonial Office
PAC	Public Archives of Canada
PAM	Provincial Archives of Manitoba
PRO	Public Record Office
RG	Record Group

As Long as the Sun Shines and Water Flows:
An Historical Comment

George F. G. Stanley

I

Anyone embarking on a discussion of Indian-white relations in Canada is faced, from the outset, with a virtually insoluble dilemma. Since every man is the product of the culture into which he is born and in which he is nurtured and educated, of necessity his thinking will follow certain well-defined lines. To change the direction of thinking is as difficult as changing the colour of skin, and probably more painful. Few achieve it, even if they get to the point of wanting to do so. When I undertake to comment on the interaction of the two cultures, Indian and European, I must, inevitably, adopt a viewpoint within my own tradition. To do otherwise would take a very special effort of imagination. It might come easier to me were I a poet rather than an historian.

The problem which I face is not merely a matter of linguistics. It is rather a problem of values, of philosophies. To take a simple example: the educated white man is taught to rely upon written records for the story of his past, records which were long transcribed by hand, but which, since the invention of the Gutenburg press, are now to be found in print. The Indian, possessing no written records, has relied upon oral tradition, or upon strings of wampum to serve as *aides-mémoire*.[1] Interestingly enough, the uneducated white man of earlier generations, who could recite his genealogy covering several centuries,[2] would probably have understood the Indian's method of recording past events. But the educated white man, the missionary, the trader, the government official, the school teacher, tied to written records, is critical of oral tradition.

Because the Indian had no written records when the first white man reached this continent, he was dismissed by the white man as having no past. The pre-white era was regarded as an age of darkness. And darkness, remember, is equated with danger. It is something inimical. And the people of darkness were the Indians, the savage antagonists of the white man. Even today the darkness of the forests frightens many sophisticated white townspeople. Like the history of the past, it is peopled with distorted images of lurking dangers.[3]

I am not prepared to argue whether written or oral history, law or tradition, is the more reliable. Certainly, men's memories are frequently faulty; but documents may be incomplete or ambiguous, or, at the worst, forgeries or outright lies. Who, then, has the whole truth and nothing but the truth? The Indian with his memory, or the white man with his documents? Perhaps both are struggling in the darkness of the past. Whence cometh the light?

II

From ancient times, those people who were self-consciously "civilized" regarded their less fortunate neighbours as morally and intellectually inferior. The Greeks called the Egyptians "barbarians" because they had not had the good fortune to be born Greeks. The Romans called the Goths "barbarians." The Normans referred to the Irish as "wild men," the "savage Irish, our enemies."[4] The English applied the same term "savages" to the Scottish highlanders even as late as the seventeenth and eighteenth centuries. It is hardly surprising, therefore, that the first Europeans to reach North America should use the same dichotomy when they encountered the autochthones. The Europeans saw themselves as apostles of civilization, bringing light to enlighten the darkness of ignorance and savagery. In fact, these apostles of civilization were invaders. Columbus, Cabot, Cartier, each of them believed that he had discovered a "new world," when what he really did was "establish contact between two worlds, both already old."[5]

Because they found the "new world" occupied, the Europeans had to answer the moral questions: were the occupants men, and did these men possess any right to the land they occupied? The Spanish theologian, Francisco de Vitoria, in 1532 argued that Spain could not claim the lands of the natives by right of "discovery," since this doctrine applied only to lands that were unoccupied. And clearly America was not unoccupied. True, the occupants were not Christians, but idolatry was, by the sixteenth century, no longer considered a just cause for war. Vitoria was backed by Pope Paul III who, in his bull, *Sublimus Deus*, issued in 1537, stated that "Indians are truly men . . . they may and should, freely and legitimately enjoy their liberty and the possession of their property; nor should they be in any way enslaved; should the contrary happen, it shall be null and void."[6] That meant that the Spaniards and the Indians should be regarded as equals. But papal bulls invariably lacked horns. And what good Englishman would give credence to any Spanish theologian, or pope, for that matter. Certainly not Elizabeth I, who in 1583 authorized Humphrey Gilbert to seize "remote heathen and barbarous lands" in North America, by which she meant Newfoundland.[7] That there might be Indians there did not matter very much.

European expansion to North America was prompted by a variety of factors. Evangelization of the native peoples was one. The fur trade was another. And the acquisition of lands for settlers was another. As far as the fur trade was concerned, the Indian was a necessary and not unwilling collaborator; in the matter of land for settlement, the Indian was an unwitting dealer in real estate — his own real estate, that is. But in the early history of Canada, the Indian was most frequently a subject of evangelization and a partner in the fur trade. There was never much demand for land for settlement. And for the two and a half centuries between the arrival of Cartier and the coming of the United Empire Loyalists, no conflict developed between the Indians and the Whites over the possession of land. However, it was otherwise in the English Colonies to the south, where colonists came in great numbers to escape religious persecution, to establish plantations, or to engage in the fur trade.

At the outset, the Anglo-Americans experienced little trouble with the native peoples. Both the Virginians and the New Englanders went through the motions of recognizing the Indian claim to the land by purchasing what they required from the Indians. The Virginians did not bother to obtain deeds for the land they obtained, unlike the careful, businesslike New Englanders. But then the Virginians never really considered that deeds were necessary. Did not Samuel Purchase argue that God intended the land to be cultivated and not left as "that unmanned wild Countrey" in which the native peoples "range rather than inhabite."[8] This argument, although it could not be found in the writings of the international lawyers such as Hugo Grotius, became virtually axiomatic in English-speaking North America. And it fitted very well with the argument of John Winthrop of Massachusetts, who took the view that North America was an "unoccupied" land, a *vacuum domicilium* which the native peoples had never "subdued" because they did not till the soil. Because they ranged over and did not farm the land, they could not be said to "occupy" it.[9] These were the arguments used to justify the seizure of Indian lands by squatting, or by force of arms when necessary. In other words, the Anglo-Americans looked upon the land as "free" — free to be taken by the immigrant invaders when and where required. Even at the end of the nineteenth century, Americans were still talking about free land: Frederick Jackson Turner is a case in point.

But whatever pseudo-legal or philosophic arguments might be trotted out to confound the Indians, the Anglo-Americans were sufficiently pragmatic to realize that it would be easier and less costly to go through the motions of negotiating for the transfer of Indian lands to the Whites than to have recourse to bloody combat. However, the various purchase agreements between the Whites and the Indians that were part of the history of colonial America did not imply any recognition that the Indians were "nations" in the political sense of the word or that they possessed "sovereign rights" of ownership of the land. The purchase agreements implied no more than a recognition that the Indians were the actual occupants. But as occupants they could not sell to whomsoever they might choose. They could sell only to the Crown or the state authorities representing the Crown who reverted to the old doctrine of "discovery." Such, at least, is how the Chief Justice of the United States Supreme Court saw it in the early part of the nineteenth century. Delivering his judgement in the cases of *Johnson v. McIntosh* (1823) and *Worcester v. the State of Georgia* (1832), John Marshall stated that three options had been open to the "discovery" nations: to abandon their so-called discoveries, proceed by armed conquest, or acquire land by negotiation. The first was unfeasible, the second was undesirable; the third was acceptable. According to Marshall, the Indians were free to sell or not to sell; but in either case they would lose their lands.[10] The original land purchases in the Thirteen Colonies were the genesis of the so-called treaty system which subsequently became the basis of Indian-white relations in land, both in Canada and in the United States.

III

The first Canadian Indians to come into contact with the Whites (after the Vikings) were the Micmacs of Nova Scotia. These Indians had had over a century of experience in dealing with white men — even longer if we take into consideration the early European fishermen and the explorers — before the arrival of the British in Nova Scotia after the Treaty of Utrecht in 1713. During that period of contact the Whites were so few in number that they constituted no threat to the Indians. However, the white presence was not without its impact on Indian Culture. French religion, French men, French trade goods — none of them could be totally ignored by the Indians; the only thing they ignored was the French claim that the region was the property of Louis XIV and that the king could dispose of the lands as he willed. Because the French never recognized anything in the nature of an Indian title and because the Indians were not alarmed at the presence of the few French settlers, there was never any question of instituting negotiations for the surrender of Indian lands to the Whites. Even if the Indians had understood the nature of the French seigneurial system — which they did not — it is doubtful if the Micmacs and the Malecites would have cared very much. The realities of life in the Maritime region made any theoretical claim on the part of the French king quite meaningless. And so, without bothering about theories of land tenure, the Micmacs accepted the French presents and French muskets and helped the French fight their Anglo-American enemies. And in the meantime Acadian settlers acquired Indian lands and Indian wives.

In the fighting for empire indulged in by France and England during the seventeenth and early eighteenth centuries, the French came off second best. In 1713, the whole of Acadia, within its ancient limits, was ceded to Great Britain. To the lawyers, the Treaty of Utrecht was simply the legal instrument by which His Most Christian Majesty transferred his title to the land of Acadia to His Britannic Majesty. Because the Anglo-Americans had adopted the practice of negotiating once-and-for-all-time land settlements with the Indians of the Thirteen Colonies, they were prepared to do the same thing with the Micmacs in Acadia, now called Nova Scotia.[11] But this idea of negotiations was strange to the Indians; even stranger was the demand that they should make their "submission" to the British king, give undertakings to trade only with people approved by the government of Massachusetts, agree that disputes between the Indians and the Whites should be settled "according to His Majestie's laws," and share their land with the Whites who were expected to flock into the newly acquired colony. This was just too much to swallow. The French had never imposed conditions like these.

For some years the Micmacs tried to play off the two imperial powers of France and England against each other. But it was clear that their sympathies were generally with the former, and when war was resumed in 1744 the Indians came out openly on the French side. The white men's war ended with the Treaty of Aix-la-Chapelle in 1748, but the Indians kept on fighting, and in so doing still further discouraged white settlement. Finally, in 1752, Governor Peregrine Hopson concluded a treaty of "Peace and Friendship Renewed" with the Micmacs.[12] This was no one-sided affair. The treaty stipulated, for instance, that the Indians were to have "free liberty of hunting and Fishing as usual." It provided also that the British government would furnish the Indians with "a Quantity of bread, flour and such other Provisions, as can be procured, necessary for the Familys and proportionable to the Numbers of the said Indians . . . half Yearly for the time to come." This treaty, apparently never fulfilled, at least to the letter, was followed ten years later (1762) by a proclamation issued by Lieutenant-Governor Jonathan Belcher of Nova Scotia, promising to "protect the Indians in their just Rights and Possessions" and enjoining all squatters to quit any lands reserved for or claimed by the Indians or be "prosecuted with the utmost Rigour of the Law."[13]

It is obvious from the evidence available that the Indians were already running into difficulties with Whites who were prepared to ignore native land, and native fishing and hunting rights, when this proclamation was issued. But no steps were taken to mollify the Indians until the outbreak of the American Revolutionary War. In an effort to ensure Indian neutrality, the British authorities promptly offered presents and promises to the Indians. But when the war was over, the earlier disputes between the Whites and Indians doubled and trebled. The end of the war saw thousands of Whites, United Empire Loyalists, flock to Nova Scotia. They came in such numbers and spread so widely over the Maritime region that it was considered necessary to divide Nova Scotia into three provinces to ease administrative problems: New Brunswick, Cape Breton, and Nova Scotia. And, of course, there was also the Ile St-Jean, soon to be re-named Prince Edward Island.

From 1784 onwards the Indians of the Maritimes were in deep trouble. Their rights had never been defined, if only because the British had slipped into the old French pattern of claiming the land of the provinces as crown land and not bothering about negotiating land surrender treaties with the Indians. From time to time the provincial authorities of both Nova Scotia and New Brunswick were prepared to recognize that certain areas were occupied by and therefore belonged to the Indians; and from time to time moneys were voted by the provincial legislatures for Indian welfare. There were also the inevitable committees appointed by the legislature to consider Indian complaints and to suggest remedies for such ills as might be diagnosed. But little of any consequence appears to have been done. Squatters continued to settle on lands occupied by the Indians, and Indian complaints went unanswered, regardless of Belcher's proclamation of 1762. The Indian commissioners appointed by the government were largely ineffective.[14] One of them, Abraham Gesner, prepared a report in 1849, in which he painted a gloomy picture of the Indians' future.

> To use a phrase of their own, "their resources have gone to the graves of their fathers," their fisheries are obstructed, their game which once afforded them subsistence has disappeared, they cannot procure furs, and their most advantageous camping grounds are occupied by British settlers.

After noting the failure of the potato and wheat crops and the high mortality rate among the native peoples, Gesner concluded

> Should any malignant epidemic arise, like that which destroyed 4000 Indians in Nova Scotia in 1746, its ravages among the tribe are even now manifest, and instead of the "Last of the Mohicans," the historian will have to record the "last of the Micmacs."[15]

The New Brunswick story is no more cheerful. Inertia seems to have been the rule in all matters relating to Indian affairs. Unauthorized settlers occupied Indian lands; others stole Indian timber. Occasionally, members of the executive council uttered bleats of protest but did nothing. Nor could they do anything in the face of the pro-settler, anti-Indian lobby and the inadequate funds provided by the government for Indian affairs. When, by mid-century, the provincial authorities did get around to dealing with the Indian problem, they found it convenient to conclude that since the natives were a dying race, Indian lands might as well be put up for auction to the highest white bidders. On 12 April 1847, the assembly agreed that "in all cases where portions of the Indian Reserves in any parts of the Province may be advantageously sold, they should be disposed of for actual settlement so soon as practicable."[16] When, in 1867, Indian affairs became a federal rather than a provincial responsibility, the new master of the Indians' fate discovered that not only had the provincial governments pretty much ignored the Indians, but also that there were no Indian treaties and no body of provincial jurisprudence dealing with aboriginal rights.

The same situation existed in Quebec. During the *Ancien Régime*, relations between the Indians and the Whites were strictly military and economic. There never was any question of France recognizing an Indian land title which should be extinguished by treaty. Admittedly, lands were set aside for the use of Indians, such as the reserves at Lorette, Sault St-Louis, Lac des Deux Montagnes, St. François, and St-Régis, but these lands were not granted in any recognition of aboriginal rights, but rather as a matter of grace.[17] Whatever rights the Indians could claim in these reserves flowed from the generosity of the king or the Jesuits and not from any abstract theory of natural right. The surrender of New France to Great Britain in 1763 did not place the British government under any legal obligation to do more for the Indians than the French government had done; nevertheless, the British authorities were prepared to give some recognition to Indian rights. General Amherst willingly accepted article 40 of the Capitulation of Montreal in 1760 requesting that the Indian allies of New France should be "maintained in the lands they inhabit."[18] Even more significant was the promise in the Proclamation of 1763 expressly establishing a separate Indian Territory west of the Appalachians and the Thirteen Colonies and east of the Mississippi and south of the height of land dividing the waters flowing into the Arctic from those flowing into the Atlantic Ocean. Within this territory there was to be no squatting by Whites or any land purchases other than by the Crown. Elsewhere, in the established colonies, namely, Newfoundland, Labrador, Quebec, Nova Scotia (including New Brunswick, Prince Edward Island, and Cape Breton), and the Thirteen Colonies, existing squatters on Indian lands were to be removed and no private purchases of lands occupied by or reserved for the Indians were permitted. All purchases of Indian lands in the colonies named were to be made only by the Crown in the presence of the assembled Indians.

The importance of the proclamation of George III was underlined by the instructions sent to Governor Murray from London in December 1763.[19] The injunction against purchases of Indian lands was repeated. British policy was designed to impose a freeze on white immigration and white settlement beyond the limits of the established colonies. The new Indian Territory was to be an Indian homeland, where the native peoples would be free to live according to their traditions without pressures from white farmers. All very idealistic, but not very realistic. The impossibility of controlling the activities of the Whites in the Indian Territory was apparent within a few years. Accordingly, in 1774, a large portion of the Indian Territory, namely that portion north of the Ohio River, was restored to Canadian jurisdiction by the adoption of the Quebec Act by the Imperial Parliament in 1774. The old rule about land purchases remained unchanged, and Governor Guy Carleton was told that he should continue to exercise control over land purchases and over the Indian trade in such a way as to avoid exciting the "enmity" of the Indians.[20]

After the conclusion of the American Revolutionary War, Carleton found himself faced with the same problems in Canada as those which faced his opposite numbers, John Parr in Nova Scotia, and his younger brother, Thomas Carleton, in New Brunswick, namely that of finding homes for the displaced United Empire Loyalists. Grants of land in Lower Canada were made to the Loyalists without any reference to the Indians. After Confederation, additions were made to the Province of Quebec (formerly Lower Canada) in 1898 and 1912 of federally owned lands which had formerly belonged to the Hudson's Bay Company. In each of these instances provision was made for compensation to be paid to the Indians for those lands required for white settlement. The provision for compensation was clear enough to be recognized by the Dorion Commission, which stated in 1971 that aboriginal rights did exist in the newly acquired territories, although not within the boundaries of the original French colony.[21]

Upper Canada came into existence in 1791. Formerly part of New France, it had been included within the boundaries of the Indian Territory as defined by the Proclamation of 1763. In 1774 it became part of the old Province of Quebec, and during the Revolutionary War the region served as a base of operations for those Indians who actively supported the British cause, particularly the members of the Confederacy of the Six Nations. When, in 1783, Great Britain was forced to accept defeat and sign the Treaty of Versailles, the British delegates agreed to the cession of all British territory south of the Great Lakes to the successful United States. However, the ceded area included the former homeland of the Six Nations south of Lake Ontario. The Indians were incensed. They had never regarded themselves as subjects of the British Crown and thus denied that the British authorities had any rights in their lands to cede to the United States. Fearing that his allies might soon become his enemies, the governor of Quebec, Sir Frederick Haldimand, set about to find new lands for his Iroquois refugees.[22] He needed land, too for those loyalists who chose to settle along the St. Lawrence front. Where could he find it? How was he to obtain it? The answer was obvious. Buy it from the Indians. Was not this the policy which had been followed, more or less successfully, in the Thirteen Colonies, in happier days? True, the principle of recognizing Indian ownership had not been adopted either in the Maritimes or in Quebec. But in neither instance had the need to obtain land been as pressing, or the Indians as numerous. Accordingly, as early as 1781, Haldimand entered into negotiations with the Mississaugas of southern Ontario and obtained from them the surrender of their land rights in that region. Thus, he was in a position to provide land both for the Mohawks of John Deseronto at Kingston and the Six Nations Indians who followed Joseph Brant, along the Grand River, north of Lake Erie. In this way Haldimand mollified his Indian allies.[23]

Haldimand's precedent was followed by his successors. Between 1781 and

1836, twenty-three such land cessions were negotiated with the Mississaugas, Chippewas, Ottawas, Potawatomis, and other Indians living in the region bounded by Lakes Huron, Erie, and Ontario. These land surrenders were not properly treaties. Rather, they were simple real estate deals, paid for on a once-and-for-all-time basis with goods and later with money.[24] In 1818 the practice was adopted of paying the Indians for their lands with annuities at the rate of £2.10s. for each man, woman, and child. Some years later (1829) the annuities were applied towards the cost of building houses and purchasing tools and farm stock. The government bureaucracy was beginning to take over. This was then followed by the establishment of the "band fund" system, a financial device with which most present day Indians are familiar.

In 1836, at the instigation of the lieutenant-governor of Upper Canada, Sir Francis Bond Head, it was proposed to establish a large reserve in Lake Huron, by attracting to Manitoulin Island Indians who were willing to surrender their land claims elsewhere.[25] The scheme collapsed largely because the Indians refused to move. They would not leave the regions that were familiar to them. Disappointed as the provincial authorities were, they were not prepared to go the full way (as the Americans did when they adopted a similar policy) of compelling the Indians to move. Accordingly, the reserved lands on Manitoulin were sold and the moneys distributed to the Chippewas and Ottawas in 1862.

Meanwhile, in the 1850's new land deals were made with the Indians of Upper Canada for the surrender of the Indian land title to lands north of Lake Superior and Lake Huron. These were the so-called Robinson treaties, named after the chief negotiator, William B. Robinson.[26] They are known as the Robinson-Huron and the Robinson-Superior Treaties of 1850. Robinson's procedures in many ways set the pattern for the subsequent treaties negotiated by the federal government of Canada after Confederation. Robinson, it should be noted, was guided by the principles laid down in the Proclamation of 1763; his negotiations were conducted in the presence of the assembled Indians; the lands were transferred directly to the Crown and were not disposed of to private individuals; provision was made for the establishment of Indian reserved areas; payment was made by annuities; and the Indians were given the promise that they would retain the "full and free" aboriginal privilege of hunting over the lands they were ceding and fishing "in the waters thereof."

The story of treaty negotiations in British Columbia is quite different from that in Upper Canada. In some ways it more closely resembles that of Quebec in the sense that treaty-making was not part of the British Columbian method of dealing with the Indians. Admittedly, there was a brief period, between 1850 and 1854, while the administration of Vancouver Island was still in the hands of the Hudson's Bay Company, when the Songhees, Sooke, and Cowichan Indians were asked to surrender their land claims in return for a monetary consideration, while at the same time retaining their traditional villages and fishing stations. These treaties were the work of the governor and chief factor, James Douglas.[27] It was not because he or the company was ever impressed with the idea of aboriginal rights; but rather that he felt that such negotiations were a measure of fairness, nicely calculated to meet the company's and the colony's special interests. However, the Douglas treaties are the sole instance of the Indian land title in British Columbia being extinguished by negotiation. It is true that, from time to time, the provincial authorities have set up land reserves for the Indians; but these reserves, like those in Quebec, were reserves of grace and charity, not reserves of natural or legal right.

From this brief summary of the negotiations between the Indians and the officials of the various British North American colonies, it is clear how difficult was the problem facing the new federal administration in Ottawa as far as aboriginal land rights were concerned. In 1867 there was no uniformity of policy, no precedents to be followed. How were the various provincial policies to be reconciled? The answer to that problem still evades us. And it is of no assistance that the administration of lands within each province is a provincial and not a federal responsibility. It was (and still is) only on federal territory acquired from the Hudson's Bay Company by the extinction of the company's charter, or acquired from Great Britain in 1870, that a distinctly federal Indian policy could be devised. And the nature of that policy may be seen by a glance at the numbered treaties concluded with the western and northern Indians between 1871 and 1921.

Prior to the entry of Red River and Rupert's Land into Confederation in 1870, the Canadian northwest was administered by the Hudson's Bay Company. To keep a steady flow of furs into the company vaults, the company had to maintain the goodwill of the Indians. The standing orders of the company stated that the Indians were to be treated "with kindness and indulgence . . . and liberally supplied with requisite necessaries, particularly articles of ammunition, whether they have the means of paying for it or not."[28] It was in accordance with company policy that, in 1817, Lord Selkirk, having obtained an extensive area of land along the Red River for the establishment of a colony of indigent Scottish Highlanders, entered into an arrangement with the Cree and Saulteaux Indians of the neighbourhood for the extinction of the Indian title in the area concerned.[29] However, after the entry of Manitoba into Confederation, following negotiations in Ottawa with the representatives of Louis Riel's Metis provisional government in 1870, the federal government considered it advisable to obtain from the Indians the surrender of their aboriginal land rights in the territories purchased from the Hudson's Bay Company. The object of Rupert's Land purchase had been to forestall the Americans, who were pushing towards the northwest, and to fill the country with settlers who would owe their allegiance to the British Crown. The Indians were aware of the pressures which had been on the company for many years to surrender their political and territorial rights, and they were concerned about their own future. At least, they were familiar with the company; the Canadians, they did not know. That is why they told Colonel Garnet Wolseley, who commanded the Canadian expedition sent to Red River in 1870 that, although they were willing to let the white soldiers pass through their country, they did not want any of them "to live amongst us . . . until a clear understanding has been arrived at, as to what our relations are to be in the time to come."[30] Accordingly, during the summer of 1871, Treaties 1 and 2 were concluded with the Indians for the surrender of their title to the area of southern Manitoba west of Lake of the Woods, and including south-eastern Saskatchewan. The form followed during the negotiations was that of the Robinson treaties, and thus derived from the Proclamation of 1763. Without going into the details of these and other treaties which followed, it is sufficient to say that between 1873 and 1877 Treaties 3, 4, 5, 6, and 7 were negotiated and signed, covering the whole area west of Thunder Bay to the Rocky Mountains; that is, including what is now northern Manitoba and the southern half of Saskatchewan and Alberta. A second group of treaties — 8, 9, 10, and 11 — were concluded between 1899 and 1921. They were concerned with the cession of northern Ontario, northern Saskatchewan, and northern Alberta, and the Mackenzie River Valley in the Northwest Territories.[31] To date, treaty negotiations have not been carried out with the Indians and Inuit of the Yukon, the District of Franklin, or the Arctic Islands.

All these treaties followed much the same pattern. All designated the area to be ceded; all mentioned, by name, the chiefs and headmen who served as spokesmen for the Indians; all specified the monetary consideration to be paid, although the amounts varied from one treaty to another; all provided that the payments take the form of annuities, "interest money," paid to each member of the signatory bands; all stipulated that reserves would be provided; all reserved to the government the right to acquire such portions of the reserves as might be required for roads, railways, or other public works; all provided for the maintenance of schools for the education of Indian children; most of them promised supplies to help the Indians make their living on reserve lands; some promised to place a medicine chest at the agent's house for the use of sick or injured Indians; and, to use the words of the Ojibway chief who acted as Indian spokesman for Treaty 3, Mawe-do-penais, the treaties were to last "as long as the sun goes round and the water flows," words already spoken by Alexander Morris, the lieutenant-governor of Manitoba and principal government negotiator.[32]

IV

What, basically, was the Canadian government's motive in entering into these Indian treaties? Was it because the government formally recognized that the Indians were, in fact, the aboriginal owners of the land with which the negotiations were concerned? In a legal sense, no. Neither the British nor the French ever departed from the view that the land belonged to the Crown. The British, at least, simply accepted the fact that the Indians occupied the land and that it would be convenient if the Indians could be persuaded to surrender their right of occupancy in order to avoid hostilities or bloodshed with white immigrants. It would be better, for the Indians as well as for the Whites, if the process of white settlement could proceed in peace. The imperial authorities were, of course, dealing from a position of strength, and they recognized strength on the part of the Indians, whenever they saw it. That is why the provincial governments in the Maritimes did not bother to negotiate with Indians whose economy and numbers were traditionally weak. In Upper Canada, the well-organized and militarily experienced Iroquois were able to obtain a land grant at Grand River larger than anything in the Maritimes or Quebec, despite the fact their own homeland was outside British jurisdiction. The large reserves allotted the Blackfeet and Blood Indians in Treaty 7 were a reflection of the strength of their numbers. So, too, were reserves given the refugee Sioux in Manitoba and Saskatchewan. Like the Six Nations, the Sioux had no aboriginal land rights in Canada, but they did have a vigorous warlike tradition.

The Metis people, the offspring of the early fur traders and the Indians, form a separate group. They have always had a strong sense of their own identity, particularly those born and raised in western Canada. As a people they combined the qualities of both the Indians and the Whites, and as such they were better able than the Indians to understand and to work within the cultural framework of the Whites. In the prairie region they found a well-defined place in the eighteenth and nineteenth centuries in the economy of the fur trade. They were buffalo hunters, freighters, and boatmen, the men who kept the fur trade alive and moving. They even occupied a specific geographical area which became their homeland. In Red River, they developed their own lifestyle, vividly described by fur traders such as Alexander Ross and Daniel Harmon and by travellers such as Viscount Milton and Dr. Cheadle. It was these Metis, or half-breeds, who, under the leadership of one of their own, Louis Riel, were responsible for the creation of Manitoba and its entry into the Canadian Confederation in 1870. Following the establishment of the new province, the Metis, the legatees on the maternal side to a share in the aboriginal right to land, received, from the federal government, scrip for some 565,000 hectares of land. Unfortunately, much of the scrip passed into the hands of clever and unscrupulous Whites. Scrip was issued again in Saskatchewan in 1885, with much the same result. The last Metis land reserve, established in northern Alberta in the late years of the nineteenth century, was not granted to the Metis. It was placed in the hands of the Oblates in trust for indigent Metis, following the model of the grant of Sault St. Louis to the Jesuits in trust for the Mohawks in 1680.[33]

It would be unfair not to point out that the Indian treaties and Metis land grants were inspired by a sense of goodwill on the part of the white authorities. To the present day cynic, any hint of altruism on the part of the Whites in their relations with Indians has a hollow sound. But it was there, nonetheless. Up to 1830, the only purposes the Indians served, as far as the Whites were concerned, other than souls to be saved for God, were as military auxiliaries and purveyors of furs. However, during the early and mid-nineteenth century the people of Great Britain were attracted by the "Humanitarian" movement. This movement was marked by a revival of religion as evidenced by the growth of Methodism, Evangelicalism, the Clapham Sect, and the Puseyites. This was no make-believe piety. Even the black-coated unction of Exeter Hall was real and sincere.[34] In England, it found expression in the factory acts for improving working conditions and the spread of missionary societies to carry the gospel and civilization to the benighted heathen and to help the lot of the poor natives.

In Canada, it was reflected in the transfer of responsibility for Indian affairs from the military to the civil authorities. It was the civil authorities who talked about helping the Indian to adjust to the changing world in which he was living, of educating Indian children, of saving the native peoples from ethnic extinction by helping them survive in what was becoming a white man's world. In brief, their motivation was honest and well-intentioned; their means, cultural assimilation.

Cultural assimilation was part of the concept of imperialism which dominated the history of the nineteenth century, particularly in Great Britain and France. The theory of empire, cultural and political, was one in which every white man believed, in those countries at least; empire as an instrument for the betterment of mankind; empire as an instrument through which the more fortunate white man would assume the burden imposed on him by God; empire as an instrument not of oppression but of freedom, freedom from ignorance. Of course, there was always a gap between theory and reality. But the currency of the idea of empire as a means for good cannot be explained away as self-deception.

Assimilation of the native peoples had become the declared purpose of Canadian Indian policy by the 1830's. It was unquestionably in the minds of the men who directed the Indian Affairs Department after Confederation in 1867, and it was given impetus by the decline in the numbers of the native population in the later years of the nineteenth century. The native peoples were moving rapidly towards extinction; at least, that was what many Whites believed. In the 1930's Diamond Jenness of the National Museum of Canada wrote:

> Doubtless all the tribes will disappear. Some will endure only a few years longer. Others like the Eskimo may last for several centuries. Some will merge steadily with the White race, others will bequeath to future generations only an infinitesimal fraction of their blood.[35]

Social Darwinists argued, therefore, that the Indians must be helped to adjust themselves to their inevitable fate; they would have to adapt themselves to the white man's economy by learning to live and think like white men. The school teacher, the missionary, the farm instructor would make the Indians of Canada into dark-skinned white men.

Interestingly enough, the decline of the numbers of natives was halted not by cultural assimilation but by improvements in medicine, inadequate and limited though they were. After the turn of the century the number of Canadian Indians slowly increased; it increased, in fact, to such an extent that by the mid-twentieth century, the reserves were too small to accommodate them, and Indians were compelled to move into the urban communities in every province of the country. All the better from the standpoint of those who believed in the idea of assimilation. Forced to compete with the Whites in a white man's environment, the Indians would have to adopt the white man's techniques of thought and action. The time might even come when the reserves could be done away with, all special status discarded, and the Indians given complete equality with white man: equal services and equal political rights would be available for all Canadians. Jenness was thinking along these lines in 1947. Twenty-two years later it became federal policy when Pierre Elliott Trudeau stated in Vancouver that two courses of action were open to the federal government in the field of Indian administration, either to retain the conventional way of "adding bricks of discrimination" around the ghetto in which the Indians lived or to discard the old system and give the Indians full status in white Canadian society. The prime minister's leanings were obvious. "It's inconceivable," he said, "that in a given society, one section of the society have a treaty with another section of the society. We must be all equal under the laws."[36]

The Indian response to Prime Minister Trudeau's suggestion came as a surprise to federal authorities. The principle of segregation had become unpopular in many quarters of the white man's society, and the idea that the Indians would eschew equality in favour of maintaining treaty rights was hard to understand. What was not really clear to many Whites was that to a minority group struggling to maintain their own identity, equality was a negative concept, self-defeating, equivalent only to the extinction of the weaker and the smaller society. Unorganized though the Indians were, and unable to produce a consensus as to what future government policy should be, they were agreed at least upon three basic points: they wanted their special rights honoured, their treaties maintained, and their grievances dealt with in an equitable manner. Another thing they wanted was a louder and more effective voice in the formulation of policies affecting their future. In other words, what the Indians wanted was an affirmation, not of equality, but of their special status. They did not want to become a segment of the dominant cultural group but to retain their own cultural uniqueness. Trudeau could talk all he wanted about participatory democracy. But what did that mean, when Whites were in the vast majority and Indians constituted only a small minority? Better to be big frogs in a small puddle, than little frogs in a big puddle, especially one filled with predators.

In the end, the government's 1969 White Paper was dropped, and the federal government bent to the force of the Indian wind. The responsible minister, Jean Chrétien, while asserting that the White Paper had served a useful purpose in stimulating discussion, conceded that it no longer figured in government policy. Even Pierre Trudeau admitted that his proposals had been "short-sighted and misguided."[37] Both Trudeau and Chrétien were honest. They carried the assimilative policy to its rational conclusion; but they abandoned it when they realized that however popular it might be with white sociologists, it was not what the Indians wanted. Henceforth the Indian Department would have to pay more attention to the Indians themselves and less to the ideologues. Cultural assimilation manifested through equal status was dead, because the imperial humanitarian idea which was behind it had died earlier in the century.

The dominating idea of the century in which we live is nationalism. The old imperial idea has withered away; the empires of Great Britain and France have collapsed, and imperialism has become a bad word. Perhaps it was Woodrow Wilson, at the peace conference after World War I, who popularized nationalism and the doctrine of self-determination for subject peoples. But whoever was responsible, the idea of nationalism spread all over the world, even overcoming the setback received as a result of the excesses of the Hitler regime in Germany. Even Canada, a country struggling to assert its own national identity against the American republic to the south, unexpectedly found itself cast in the role of an imperialist power by the demands placed upon it by the cultural and ethnic minorities within its frontiers. The French Canadians and Acadians are obvious examples; so, too, to a lesser extent are the Ukrainians, and, of course, the native peoples. It is this idea of cultural nationalism which has provided the motivation for the establishment and development of the various native organizations now in existence in Canada, and the vigour with which the native peoples assert their land claims, criticize the treaties, and insist upon the recognition of a new role for the native peoples in a new Canadian constitution.

V

During the discussion on the White Paper, many native peoples took the stand that the government's proposals were in direct violation of the undertakings given by government representatives at the time the treaties were negotiated. Charges were also made that there was a long history of such violations, and that Canadians should not point a finger at the United States and thank God that they were not as Americans were. Perhaps the breaches of treaty obligations were not as serious or as blatant as they were in the United States; but they existed nonetheless. The critics were not referring to the way in which Indian claims had been so cavalierly dismissed in the Maritimes and in British Columbia or to Quebec, where, until the James Bay agreement in 1974, there had never been any recognition, even nominally, of aboriginal rights. In fact, they were referring to the western and northern treaties in which the obligations of Indians and government alike were specifically outlined.

To accuse the government of breaches of faith was a serious matter. And yet the Indians, and some white men as well, have adamantly claimed that such breaches have occurred. This being so, what is the explanation? Deliberate intent to deceive the Indian peoples can, I believe, be discarded. Deliberate, wholesale dishonesty has not, in my mind, been part of the Canadian tradition. Such an explanation is also too simplistic. Misunderstanding of the meaning of the treaty terms, or misinterpreting those terms, seems to me to be the more likely explanation. And this takes me back to remarks I made earlier, concerning the problems attending oral and written accounts of historical events. There is, I believe, evidence to show that the obligations inherent in the signed treaties were not always carefully set forth. Promises and assurances were given orally by the commissioners. And it is over the extent and significance of these unwritten promises that most of the disputes between the Indians and the government have arisen. The Indians, with their long tradition of oral history, are in a stronger position to argue about the oral promises than the Whites, many of whom have disappeared from the scene without leaving accounts of what actually happened at the various treaty negotiations. The probability that promises were made to the Indians, which they remember and the Whites have forgotten, seems strong. Part of the problem arose from the fact that the negotiators for the government usually attended the meetings with the Indians with draft treaties already prepared. They did not expect any Indian input and had no authority to alter the documents given them. They knew, and they knew that the Indians knew, that, treaty or no treaty, white settlement would soon spill over into the Indian country and that it would be better for the Indians to accept than to refuse the treaties. In this sense, the treaties were hardly negotiated agreements. To the surprise of the negotiators, some Indians did insist upon making their views heard, and in order to obtain Indian signatures, oral assurances had to be given. This is clear from letters written by the commissioners to their superiors in Ottawa. In some instances the government agreed to modify the treaties to meet Indian demands. When the terms of Treaties 1 and 2 became generally know, so great was Indian dissatisfaction that the Indian Department in 1875 and 1876 agreed to their revision in the direction of greater generosity to the Indians.[38]

A study of Treaty 3 also reveals an insistence by the Indians upon the inclusion of terms not contained in the draft treaty, namely that steps be taken by the government to protect the wildlife, which seemed always to diminish whenever white settlers appeared. There is also evidence to suggest that some Indian bands were shortchanged on the size of their reserves owing to incorrect head counts by government officials. Such was the case with South Quill's band in Manitoba. Furthermore, an examination of Louis O'Soup's grievances in 1911 reveals not only a laxity on the part of the government officials to provide adequate facilities for Indian education, contrary to promises made in the treaty, but also the department's failure to provide care for the orphans and aged despite Commissioner Morris's assurances that this would be done. [39]

There are numerous instances of complaints by the Indians of Treaty 8 and Treaty 11 with respect to promised hunting and fishing rights and undertakings to protect the Indians against encroachments by white hunters and trappers. In this instance David Laird, the government commissioner, admitted that he had assured the Indians there would be no curtailment of their hunting and fishing rights. The Indians, he said, would be as "free to hunt and fish after the treaty as they would be if they never entered into it," and any laws imposed on the territory would be such as were "in the interest of the Indians."[40] Laird was not being dishonest. He could not foresee, for instance, that the province of Alberta would be formed in 1905, with boundaries extending to the 60th parallel of latitude, thus including much of the land covered by Treaty 8. He did not foresee that land would be allotted to settlers before the Indian reserves had been surveyed or that provincial laws with regard to a closed season on hunting would be imposed on the Indians, which would severely restrict the freedom he had promised. Nor could he anticipate all the delays on the part of the Indian Department in implementing those sections of the treaties dealing with schools, land surveys, rations, even in handing out annuities. So bitter were the Dogribs, Chipewyans, Slaveys, and Yellowknives about these delays that they boycotted the treaty payments at Fort Resolution in 1920.[41]

But there were still greater problems which arose in the Mackenzie River region covered by Treaty 11. These included the discovery of oil at Fort Norman, the collapse of the fur market, the expansion of water transportation, the extension of the railway towards Fort McMurray, and, of course, the development of air travel. The Indians could scarcely comprehend what was happening to their country. The one thing they did understand was that the government was supposed to protect them from the white man; and now the white man was moving in. Some were prospectors from the Yukon, others attracted by the oil strike, others, alleged sportsmen, anxious to enjoy hunting and fishing in wilderness regions. The Indians, under the pressure of competition from the Whites, complained to Ottawa. So, too, did the missionaries, the Mounted Police, and Hudson's Bay Company men. Ralph Parsons, fur trade commissioner of the Hudson's Bay Company, asserted that the white hunter and white trapper "will go into a territory and not be satisfied until he has cleaned it out, the Indian will only take what he requires to see him through from day to day."[42] Perhaps it can be argued that the government officials were guilty of deliberately breaking the terms of the treaty; but no one will deny that they ignored the spirit of both Treaties 8 and 11. Unfortunately, but inevitably, the Indians and the Whites looked upon the treaties from different standpoints. The former interpreted the treaties in a broad and generous sense; the latter in a narrow legalistic sense. And even in a strict legalistic sense, the government was inclined to favour the Whites rather than the Indians of whose welfare it was supposed to be the guardian. Until there is a meeting of minds on the extent of the obligations imposed upon the Department of Indian Affairs and Northern Development by Treaties 8 and 11, needless hardship and suffering is bound to be inflicted on the native peoples.

VI

What, in simple terms, is the nature of the Indian treaties as legal documents? In international law a treaty is a pact between two or more sovereign nations, usually subject to ratification before it goes into effect. In private law a treaty is a discussion of the terms which precede the conclusion of a civilian contract. The early arrangements made between the Indians and the white men in what is now Canada were classified as "Indentures" and "Surrenders." The Robinson Treaties were specifically designated as "Agreements." The Manitoulin Island Treaty was officially called an "Agreement and Convention." The first treaty specifically so called was Treaty 1 in Manitoba.[43]

There is some question as to whether the designation "treaty" is accurate. It is a moot point whether any one of the Indian treaties or surrenders is technically a treaty in the strict sense of international law. The Indian bands or tribes were never regarded, in British law, as independent sovereign entities: the agreements they concluded with the white governments were never ratified by the British Parliament or by the provincial legislatures. There is some question in the minds of white lawyers whether the Indians should be referred to as nations. That they may be cultural "nations" is not contested. But in the political sense, the Indians have always been classified as subjects of the Crown: subjects possessing special status, but subjects nonetheless. According to Lieutenant-Governor A. G. Archibald and Lieutenant-Governor Alexander Morris of Manitoba, both of whom served as treaty commissioners, the subject status of the Indians was always emphasized during the negotiations with the Indians.[44] The British Parliament also took the view that the Indians were subjects and not sovereign nations. This is shown by the fact that the Indians were placed by Parliament under federal jurisdiction in the B.N.A. Act in 1867. And up to 1970, the Canadian courts never questioned the precedent established by the case of *Rex v. Syliboy* (1929), which stated that the treaty of 1752 between Nova Scotia and the Micmac Indians did not meet the requirements of a treaty in international law because neither Nova Scotia nor the Micmacs could be regarded as independent nations, and their agreement had not been ratified by Parliament.[45] However, in 1966, on an appeal to the Supreme Court of Canada in the case of *Regina v. White and Bob*, one of the so-called Douglas treaties in British Columbia was upheld as an enforceable obligation, but no statement was made as to whether the Indians could be regarded as a sovereign nation. This decision was reaffirmed in the case of *Regina v. Cooper* in 1969, which ruled that one of the Douglas treaties was a binding agreement within the meaning of the Indian Act. Unfortunately, case law dealing with Indian treaties in Canada has been limited, and it is hard to produce positive statements or principles as to what the law really is. At the very least, it seems clear that Indian "treaty" obligations are enforceable by the courts.

The legal cases referred to above deal specifically with the validity of the treaties and the undertakings made in those documents. Another and more fundamental question also arises, with which the courts trying these cases did not concern themselves. That is the legal validity of the doctrine of aboriginal rights. Do such rights exist in law? The very fact that the government of Upper Canada saw fit to enter into negotiation with the Mississaugas for the cession of their lands would seem to imply a recognition of aboriginal title. But such title is now considered to be no more than a recognition of a right of occupation and use.

The governing case in Canadian courts appears to be *St. Catherine's Milling and Lumber Company v. the Queen* (1889), which involved a dispute between the provincial and federal governments over the issue of timber licences on lands surrendered by the Ojibway Indians to the federal government under Treaty 3. The federal government argued that the Indian title was valid and had been transferred by treaty to it. The province of Ontario took the view that there was no such thing as aboriginal title, nothing more than a personal right of occupancy during the pleasure of the Crown. Lord Watson expressed the opinion of the Judicial Committee to whom the case went on appeal. He stated emphatically that there was no such thing as aboriginal title and that by Treaty 3 the Ojibway Indians had simply surrendered their usufructuary and personal rights in the land in question; the title to the land had always rested in the Crown, and in this instance, now rested with the Crown in the right of Ontario.[46] A subsequent case, brought before the Judicial Committee of the Privy Council in 1897, took the same view, adding only that an Indian treaty was analogous to a commercial contract.[47] Neither of these cases can be considered as giving very much support to the concept of natural rights. Certainly, in the *St. Catherine's* case, both the Supreme Court and the Judicial Committee implied that any Indian title derived from the Proclamation of 1763. A more recent case, *Calder v. the Attorney General of British Columbia* (1973) dealt with the claim of the Nishga Indians of British Columbia that their aboriginal title had never been extinguished. Unfortunately, the judgement was inconclusive. The court was divided, a decision being given by a narrow margin against the Indians on a technicality.[48] But the judges, whether for or against the claim, saw aboriginal rights only as usufructuary rights and rights of occupation. These rights the Indians could assert against the world, but not against the Crown. And that, basically, is and has been the law in Canada. The concept of natural rights embodied in an aboriginal title has received no substantial backing from the courts.

Broadly speaking, it is true to say that the meagre body of jurisprudence in

Canada dealing with native rights does not give substantial support to any theory of natural rights. However, it should be noted that there has been a tendency in recent years for the courts to respond more sympathetically to arguments advanced by Indian litigants. Even so, it is likely that the political, rather than the legal, approach will be the more satisfactory from the native point of view. Perhaps a better instrument for dealing with Indian claims than the courts, which rather than developing special rules for interpreting Indian treaties have applied the rules of interpretation normally used in other areas of law, would be the establishment of a special independent Indian claims commission. This is not a new suggestion. It was advanced in 1963, discussed for several years, but never implemented. Perhaps it is time this should be done.

VII

The efforts of the federal government in recent years to bring about a revision in Canada's constitution, including a Charter of Rights and an amending formula, emphasize the urgency of clarifying the place of the native peoples in Canada. Two options are open to them, co-existence and assimilation. The former, co-existence, would require the entrenchment of Indian rights, including internal self-government, in the constitution; assimilation would mean the acceptance by the native peoples of their absorption by the dominant culture. As far as the Indians are concerned, past history suggests that co-existence would be their choice. Only in this way could they retain their identity as a distinct cultural group. This would require their formal recognition, in the constitutional instrument, as one of Canada's three founding peoples. The Indians were, after all, the first people to occupy the region we call Canada. In fact, the very name of our country, Canada, is derived from the Huron-Iroquois word, *kanata*, meaning a village or place where people live. White French settlers did not arrive here until the seventeenth century, and the British did not arrive until the eighteenth. The Indians, it should be remembered, have fought in defence of our — and their — country, and, although there was never any requirement in any of the treaties for military service, Indians and Metis fought in two world wars and in Korea during the present century. The case for the inclusion of the native peoples along with the French and English as the founders of Canada was a strong one. That explains why the native peoples were included as one of the founding peoples in the new draft constitution in January 1981.

What was lacking in the draft constitution was an affirmation in the Charter of Rights of the sanctity of Indian treaties and the obligation of the federal government to observe both the terms and the spirit of all treaty agreements. It was also essential that all administrative contacts between the Indians and the Whites should be conducted through the federal government. To interpose any provincial government into this relationship would lead only to the kind of confusion that has existed with respect to Indian land rights since pre-Confederation days. Indians and their activities on their own lands should be beyond the reach of provincial laws of general application, while Indians off their reserves should be subject to the same laws as the white men. It seems only fair that in any Charter of Rights appended to the constitution the Indian peoples should be secured in their rights to possession of their existing lands, whether assured by treaty or other agreement, and to all other lands to which the aboriginal title has not been previously extinguished. And, I contend, this should include, in addition to surface rights, all mineral, water, and timber rights.

The agreement arrived at in January 1981 was one of great importance to Canada's native people. Section 34 (now Section 35) of the Charter of Rights recognized, for the first time, the principle that Canada's native peoples have a legal claim to the lands they have always occupied. This section, together with the Supreme Court decision in the Nishga case, placed the native peoples in a strong position. In a symbolic gesture, Justice Minister Jean Chrétien turned to the national leaders of the Indian, Inuit, and Metis associations, inviting them to join him at the table around which the members of the Senate-Commons Committee on the Constitution were sitting. When they did, Del Riley of the National Indian Brotherhood, Eric Taguna of the Inuit Tapirisat, and Harry Daniels of the Native Council of Canada, Chrétien said, "Now, they are my advisers!"[49] Peter Ittinuar, an Inuit member of Parliament for the Northwest Territories, introduced the amendment to the government's constitutional resolution, that aboriginal rights should be included in the charter. All three political parties agreed.

But if the federal government was prepared to accept the principle of aboriginal rights, there were several provinces that were not. Tony Belcourt, the first president of the Native Council of Canada, predicted that such would be the case when he told the members of the Metis and Non-status Indian Constitutional Review Commission,

> I think the greatest sort of opposition is going to come from provincial premiers. They have never recognized our rights . . . I believe strongly that one of the major reasons they are going to be continuously opposing patriation of the constitution is because of the Charter of Rights. Certainly because now in that charter aboriginal people are specifically mentioned.[50]

In 1870 Louis Riel had placed his hopes in the provinces, hence his emphasis upon Red River entering the Canadian Confederation as a province. Probably, he was thinking of Quebec's role as the defender of the special status enjoyed by French Canadians within Confederation. However, only a few years passed before Manitoba was transformed, by the influx of white settlers, from a Metis province into a cultural outpost of Ontario. Because of this change, many of the Metis moved to the North Saskatchewan valley. After the unfortunate events of 1885, they moved again, this time to northern Alberta. Provincial status promised no secure refuge for the mixed-blood people any more than it did for the Indians. The attitude of the provinces had been established as early as 1909, when Richard McBride, premier of British Columbia, argued, "Of course, it would be madness to think of conceding to the Indians' demands. It is too late to discuss the equity of dispossessing the Red Man in North America."[51]

Belcourt was correct in his prediction. The provinces (with two exceptions, Ontario and New Brunswick) opposed the new constitution. And when the final meetings were held in November 1981 between the provincial premiers and the prime minister, seven provincial premiers, it is said, opposed the inclusion of native rights in the proposed Charter of Rights. The three most adamant were British Columbia, Alberta, and Manitoba, the first two of which were faced with extensive native land claims. Oddly enough, the fact that the premier of Alberta, Peter Lougheed, was of Indian descent in no way prompted any sympathy on his part for his grandmother's people.[52] As a result, the amendments, accepted by all federal parties in January, had to be dropped by the prime minister in November, in order to secure provincial consent for the new constitution. For the present, the excision of the native rights' clause appeared to be a defeat for Canada's native peoples. Said the Hon. Jack Austin, the federal secretary of state, "It is a subject of personal agony to me — to see this result of the November 5 decision . . . to see people brought to the brink of expectation, and then be let down like this."[53]

There was not much the prime minister could do in the face of provincial hostility. He had no desire to pick another quarrel with the provinces, particularly with a belligerent René Levesque threatening secession from the Canadian union. The argument advanced by James Fulton, the member of Parliament for Skeena, that the federal government should go it alone, without provincial assent, on the grounds that the BNA Act gave the federal Parliament exclusive jurisdiction over Indians and Indian lands, ignored the fact that the act did not say anything about the Inuit, the non-status Indians, and the Metis.[54] To give these native peoples any leverage to re-open land claim negotiations, they had to be included in the charter. A coalition of native groups managed to hammer out a tentative agreement among themselves calling for the restoration of the clause recognizing native rights but accepting a three-year delay in implementing such rights. This delay would enable native leaders and both levels of government to define the nature and extent of native rights in a series of conferences. If agreement could not be reached on what constituted native rights, then the question should go to the courts.[55] Still, the prime minister seemed reluctant to move as long as the provincial premiers stood against the inclusion of native rights in the proposed charter. It is to the credit of Chrétien, who continued his efforts, and of the native groups that lobbied the provincial premiers, that within two weeks native rights were once more included in the draft Canadian constitution. On 23 November Chrétien told the members of the House of Commons "I am happy to report . . . that all provinces have agreed to enshrine aboriginal rights in the Canadian constitution."[56] Just what "aboriginal rights" would include would be something to be decided at a later date through the courts and as a result of conferences with native leaders. The new clause adopted by the House of Commons was not all that the native leaders wished for — it guaranteed only "existing" native rights — but it was better than nothing at all. Peter Ittinuar congratulated Mr. Chrétien on what he had achieved. The battle had been long and sometimes bitter; but it was, in the end, a victory for Canada's aboriginal peoples.

VIII

But how would Canada's native people make their views known in the event of any future constitutional debate? One possibility would be through a Native Council, structured along the lines of the New Zealand Maori Council. The powers and responsibilities of this body would be set forth in a special federal statute. Another possibility would be native representation in the Senate and the House of Commons. This would be within the competence of the federal Parliament. Critics may argue that group representation is a denial of the well-established conventions of our constitution, based as it is on the British parliamentary system. But is group representation nowhere to be found in our existing parliamentary machinery? Is not membership in the Senate based, not on individual constituencies, but upon regions with their own special interests? Is not membership in the cabinet based upon the principle of group and regional representation? Can it really be argued that ignoring the existence of a cultural collectivity numbering over one million people (1,112,180, including status Indians, Inuit, Metis, and non-status Indians)[57] is democratic? Surely, it is not beyond the wit of Canadians to devise a scheme of representation that would give the native peoples a suitable place in the governmental machinery, both in the Senate and the House of Commons, other than the existing single-member constituency system.

Today, the general public in Canada has become aware of the native fact. The activities of organized native groups, the publications of Indian and Metis organizations, the reports of the Task Force on Canadian Unity, the Metis and non-status Indian Constitutional Review Commission, and others, have stirred the consciousness and the conscience of the white people in Canada and awakened them to the role the native peoples have played in the past and may be expected to play in the future. Native Studies departments are to be found in several Canadian universities, Canadian scholars are examining the contribution of the native peoples to our history, art, and folklore. Indians have become subjects of study for linguists, anthropologists, sociologists, and historians. In 1971, a Canadian writer, Dorothy Livesay, stated that "bit by bit and almost without being aware of it, the Canadian writer has had to find himself by finding the Indian."[58] Another writer has even defined a Canadian as someone forced to choose between being an

American and an Indian. Others have suggested that Canadian Whites are moving slowly towards an acceptance of Indian values in relation to nature and to human contact. Perhaps this is no more than a conscious effort to cash in on a growing public interest: perhaps it is an unconscious response to the threat to Canadian culture from the penetration of our press and our airwaves by an alien culture from the United States. I ask myself if this means that, just as we Whites sought military alliance with the Indians in the eighteenth and nineteenth centuries in order to defend our political identity from invaders from the south, we are today seeking alliance with our native peoples in order to preserve our cultural identity? Is it possible that we need the native peoples more than they need us?

However, let me sound a note of warning. For the native peoples to keep battering away at the government's consititutional proposals, to keep sending delegations to London to seek British support in a matter which has long since ceased to be within the competence of the British authorities, can achieve nothing. I do not mean that pressure within Canada, on Canadian politicians, should be relaxed. On the contrary. The best tactic would be to agitate for a revision of the Indian Act, or rather for the substitution for it of a new Native Peoples Act or an act to clarify the status of the Native Peoples in Canada. Such an act might take the form of an amendment to the charter within the new constitution. To attempt to stall the adoption of the new constitution would be as negative as it would be futile. To make use of the amendment procedures would be positive, and, I believe, ultimately successful. That is the course I would urge on all native organizations, Indian and Metis. Accept the new constitution and make use of it to achieve your own objectives.

NOTES

1. For examples, see E. B. O'Callaghan, ed., *Documents Relative to the Colonial History of New York; procured in Holland, England and France* (Albany, 1855), 8:227ff: Proceedings at a treaty with the Six Nations, the Indians of Canada, etc. . . . July 1770; also ibid., 9:1102: Message of the English to the Five Iroquois Nations sent with four strings of wampum, 26 December 1743.

2. Anthony Wagner, *Pedigree and Progress, Essays in the Genealogical Interpretation of History* (London, 1975), pp. 2–3.

3. Stephen Leacock wrote in his *Canada, the Foundations of its Future* (Montreal, 1941), p. 19, "We think of prehistoric North America as inhabited by the Indians, and have based on this a sort of recognition of ownership on their part. But this attitude is hardly warranted. The Indians were too few to count. Their use of the resources of the continent was scarcely more than that of crows and wolves, their development of it nothing."

4. Francis Jennings, *The Invasion of America: Indians, Colonialism and the Cant of Conquest* (New York, 1975), pp. 6–7. See also J. W. St. G. Walker, "The Indian in Canadian Historical Writing," Canadian Historical Association, *Historical Papers* (1971):21–47.

5. J. H. Parry, *The Spanish Seaborne Empire, The History of Human Society* (New York, 1966), p. 65. See also Jennings, p. 39.

6. Peter Cumming and Neil H. Mickenberg, eds. *Native Rights in Canada*, 2d ed. (Toronto, 1972), p. 14.

7. Jennings, p. 45.

8. Ibid., p. 80.

9. Ibid., p. 82.

10. Cumming and Mickenberg, pp. 16–19.

11. L. F. S. Upton, *Micmacs and Colonists, Indian-White Relations in the Maritimes, 1713–1867* (Vancouver, 1979), p. 37. See also G. P. Gould and A. J. Semple, eds., *Our Land: The Maritimes. The Basis of the Indian Claim in the Maritime Provinces of Canada* (Fredericton, 1980), chapter 1.

12. A copy of this treaty is printed in "Documents Relative to the Maritime Indian Claims," in Gould and Semple, pp. 172–73.

13. Ibid., p. 177.

14. Joseph Howe, the Nova Scotia reformer, was appointed Indian commissioner in 1842. His enthusiasm for Indian reform soon waned, and after writing two reports he resigned.

15. *Journals of the Proceedings of the House of Assembly of Nova Scotia, 1849*, Appendix 36, pp. 337–39.

16. *Journals of the House of Assembly of New Brunswick, 1847*, p. 358.

17. G. F. G. Stanley, "The First Indian 'Reserves' in Canada," *Revue d'histoire de l'Amérique française* 4, no. 2 (1950): 178–210.

18. W. P. M. Kennedy, ed., *Documents of the Canadian Constitution 1759–1915* (Toronto, 1918), p. 12, Articles of Capitulation of Montreal, 1760, no. 40.

19. Ibid., pp. 33–34: Instructions to Governor Murray, 7 December 1763, paras. 61 and 62.

20. Ibid., pp. 156–57: Instructions to Governor Carleton, 1775, paras. 31 and 32.

21. *Rapport de la Commission d'Etudes sur l'Integrité du Territoire du Québec: Le Domaine Indien* (Quebec, 1971), 4:253–55, 392–93. This is known as the Dorion Commission Report.

22. G. F. G. Stanley, "The Six Nations and the American Revolution," *Ontario History* 56, no. 4 (December 1964): 229.

23. C. M. Johnson, *The Valley of the Six Nations*, Champlain Society (Toronto, 1964), pp. xxx-viii–xlii.

24. Canada, *Indian Treaties and Surrenders from 1680–1902*, 3 vols. (Ottawa, 1891–1912), vol. 1.

25. Ibid., 1:112–13.

26. Ibid., 1:147–52. See also Alexander Morris, *The Treaties of Canada with the Indians of Manitoba and the North-West Territories* (Toronto, 1880), pp. 16–21.

27. A. S. Morton, *A History of the Canadian West to 1870–71* (London, n.d.), p. 762. After Douglas's retirement as governor, his successors were men totally ignorant of Indian affairs. See Cumming and Mickenberg, p. 179.

28. G. F. G. Stanley, *The Birth of Western Canada* (Toronto, 1970), p. 197.

29. Morris, pp. 13–15.

30. Stanley, p. 204.

31. A summary of the Canadian numbered treaties will be found in Allan G. Harper, "Canada's Indian Administration: Basic Concepts and Objectives," *America Indigéna*, 5 (April 1945): 119–32; and in the same author's "Canada's Indian Administration: The Treaty System," *America Indigéna* 7 (April 1947):129–48.

32. Morris, p. 75.

33. G. F. G. Stanley, "Alberta's Half-Breed Reserve, Saint-Paul-des-Métis," in A. S. Lussier and D. B. Sealey, eds., *The Other Natives: The Métis* (Winnipeg, 1978), 2:75–107.

34. Arthur Bryant, *English Saga, 1840–1940* (London, 1960), pp. 135 ff. See also G. M. Trevelyan, *Illustrated English Social History* (London, 1952), 4:50 ff.

35. Diamond Jenness, *The Indians of Canada*, National Museum of Canada, Bulletin no. 65, 2d ed. (Ottawa, n.d.), p. 264. On the question of assimilation, see J. L. Tobias, "Indian Reserves in Western Canada: Indian Homeland or Devices for Assimilation," in D. A. Muise, *Approaches to Native History*.

36. Sally M. Weaver, *Making Canadian Indian Policy, the Hidden Agenda* (Toronto, 1981), p. 179.

37. Ibid., p. 185 ff.

38. Morris, pp. 126–42.
39. Delia Opekokew, *The First Nations: Indian Government and the Canadian Confederation*, Federation of Saskatchewan Indians (Saskatoon, 1980), p. 32.
40. René Fumoleau, *As Long as This Land Shall Last* (Toronto, 1973), p. 84. For a full account of the breaches of Treaties 8 and 11, consult Fumoleau.
41. Ibid., p. 124 ff.
42. Ibid., p. 239.
43. The treaties for over two hundred years in Canada are to be found in *Indian Treaties and Surrenders from 1680–1902*. This collection, originally published between 1891 and 1912, has been reprinted in Cole's Canadiana Collection.
44. Morris, pp. 50, 93.
45. Cumming and Mickenberg, p. 59.
46. R. A. Olmstead, *Decisions of the Judicial Committee of the Privy Council relating to the British North America Act, 1867 and the Canadian Constitution 1867–1954*. Ottawa, 1:236–51.
47. *Indian Claims in Canada, an Introductory Essay and Selected List of Library Holdings*, Research Resources Centre, Indian Claims Commission, Ottawa, 1975, p. 19.
48. Ibid., p. 25.
49. Michael Valpy, "The Sellout of Canadian Native Rights," *Globe and Mail* (Toronto), 11 November 1981, p. 7.
50. H. W. Daniels, *The Report of the Métis and Non-Status Indian Constitutional Review Commission, Native People and the Constitution of Canada* (Ottawa, 1981), p. 27.
51. Valpy, p. 7.
52. Peter Lougheed's grandmother, Isabella Christine Hardisty, was a Metisse, the daughter of William Hardisty, an employee of the Hudson's Bay Company. She married James, later Sir James, Lougheed in 1884. Sometimes Sir James was criticized for marrying an "Indian." See Allan Hustak, *Peter Lougheed, a Biography* (Toronto, 1979).
53. *Sunday Star* (Toronto), 8 November 1981, A 11.
54. *Globe and Mail*, 10 November 1981, p. 4.
55. Credit should be given to the Inuit member of Parliament, Peter Ittinuar, for persuading native leaders to agree to this delay. See *Globe and Mail*, 12 November 1981, p. 4.
56. *The Gazette*, 24 November 1981, p. 1.
57. H. W. Daniels, *The Report of the Métis and Non-Status Indian Constitutional Review Commission, Native People and the Constitution of Canada* (Ottawa, 1981), p. 27.
58. Quoted in Leslie Monkman, *A Native Heritage, Images of the Indian in English-Canadian Literature* (Toronto, 1981), p. 3.

Section I

The Evolution of Indian Administration Since the Royal Proclamation of 1763

The Royal Proclamation/Proclamation Royale
October 7/7 Octobre 1763

BY THE KING, A PROCLAMATION

GEORGE R.

Whereas We have taken into Our Royal Consideration the extensive and valuable Acquisitions in America, secured to our Crown by the late Definitive Treaty of Peace, concluded at Paris, the 10th Day of February last; and being desirous that all Our loving Subjects, as well of our Kingdom as of our Colonies in America, may avail themselves with all convenient Speed, of the great Benefits and Advantanges which must accrue therefrom to the Commerce, Manufactures, and Navigation, We have thought fit, with the Advice of our Privy Council, to issue this our Royal Proclamation, hereby to publish and declare to all our loving Subjects, that we have, with the Advice of our Said Privy Council, granted our Letters Patent, under our Great Seal of Great Britain, to erect, within the Countries and Islands ceded and confirmed to Us by the said Treaty, four distinct and separate Governments, styled and called by the names of Quebec, East Florida,

PROCLAMATION PAR LE ROI

GEORGE R.

Attendu que Nous avons accordé Notre considération royale aux riches et considérables acquisitions d'Amérique assurées à Notre couronne par le dernier traité de paix définitif, conclu à Paris, le 10 février dernier et désirant faire bénéficier avec tout l'empressement désirable Nos sujets bien-aimés, aussi bien ceux du royaume que ceux de Nos colonies en Amérique, des grands profits et avantages qu'ils peuvent en retirer pour le commerce, les manufactures et la navigation, Nous avons cru opportun, de l'avis de Notre Conseil privé, de publier Notre présente proclamation royale pour annoncer et déclarer à tous Nos sujets bien-aimés que Nous avions, de l'avis de Notredit Conseil privé, par Nos lettres patentes sous le grand sceau de la Grande-Bretagne, établi dans les contrées et les îles qui Nous ont été cédées et assurées par ledit traité, quatre gouvernements séparés et distincts, savoir: ceux de Québec, de la Floride Orientale, de la Floride

West Florida and Grenada, and limited and bounded as follows, viz.

First — The Government of Quebec bounded on the Labrador Coast by the River St. John, and from thence a Line drawn from the Head of that River through the Lake St. John, to the South end of the Lake Nipissim; from whence the said Line, crossing the River St. Lawrence and the Lake Champlain, in 45. Degrees of North Latitude, passes along the High Land which divide the said River St. Lawrence from those which fall into the Sea; and also along the North Coast of the Baye des Chaleurs, and the Coast of the Gulph of St. Lawrence to Cape Rosieres, and from thence crossing the Mouth of the River St. Lawrence by the West End of the Island of Anticosti, terminates at the aforesaid River of St. John.

And whereas it will greatly contribute to the speedy settling of our said new Governments, that our loving Subjects should be informed of our Paternal care, for the security of the Liberties and Properties of those who are and shall become Inhabitants thereof, We have thought fit to publish and declare, by this Our Proclamation, that We have, in the Letters Patent under our Great Seal of Great Britain, by which the said Governments are constituted, given express Power and Direction to our Governors of our Said Colonies respectively, that so soon as the state and circumstances of the said Colonies will admit thereof, they shall, with the Advice and Consent of the Members of our Council, summon and call General Assemblies within the said Governments respectively, in such Manner and

Occidentale et de Grenade, dont les bornes sont données ci-après.

1e. — Le gouvernement de Québec, sera borné sur la côte du Labrador par la rivière Saint-Jean et de là par une ligne s'étendant de la source de cette rivière à travers le lac Saint-Jean jusqu'à cette rivière à travers le lac Saint-Jean jusqu'à l'extrémité sud du lac Nipissin, traversant de ce dernier endroit, le fleuve Saint-Laurent et le lac Champlain par 45 degrés de latitude nord, pour longer les terres hautes qui séparent les rivières qui se déversent dans ledit fleuve Saint-Laurent de celles qui se jettent dans la mer, s'étendre ensuite le long de la côte nord à la baie de Chaleurs et de la côte du golfe Saint-Laurent jusqu'au cap Rozière, puis traverser de là l'embouchure du fleuve Saint-Laurent en passant par l'extrémité ouest de l'île d'Anticosti et se terminer ensuite à ladite rivière Saint-Jean.

Et attendu qu'il est à propre à faire connaître à Nos sujets Notre solicitude paternelle à l'égard des libertés et des propriétés de ceux qui habitent comme de ceux qui habiteront ces nouveaux gouvernements, afin que des établissements s'y forment rapidement, Nous avons cru opportun de publier et de déclarer par Notre présente proclamation, que nous avons par les lettres patentes revêtues de notre grand sceau de la Grande-Bretagne, en vertu desquelles lesdits gouvernements sont constitués, donné le pouvoir et l'autorité aux gouverneurs de nos colonies respectives, d'ordonner et de convoquer, de l'avis et du consentement de notre Conseil dans leurs gouverne-

Form as is used and directed in those Colonies and Provinces in America which are under our immediate Government; And We have also given Power to the said Governors, with the consent of our Said Councils, and the Representatives of the People so to be summoned as aforesaid, to make, constitute, and ordain Laws, Statutes, and Ordinances for the Public Peace, Welfare, and good Government of our said Colonies, and of the People and Inhabitants thereof, as near as may be agreeable to the Laws of England, and under such Regulations and Restrictions as are used in other Colonies; and in the mean Time, and until such Assemblies can be called as aforesaid, all Persons Inhabiting in or resorting to our Said Colonies may confide in our Royal Protection for the Enjoyment of the Benefit of the Laws of our Realm of England; for which Purpose We have given Power under our Great Seal to the Governors of our said Colonies respectively to erect and constitute, with the Advice or our said Councils respectively, Courts of Judicature and public Justice within our Said Colonies for hearing and determining all Causes, as well Criminal as Civil, according to Law and Equity, and as near as may be agreeable to the Laws of England, with Liberty to all Persons who may think themselves aggrieved by the Sentences of such Courts, in all Civil Cases, to appeal, under the usual Limitations and Restrictions, to Us in our Privy Council.

We have also thought fit, with the advice of our Privy Council as aforesaid, to give unto the Governors

ments respectifs, dès que l'état et les conditions des colonies le permettront, des assemblées générales de la manière prescrite et suivie dans les colonies et les provinces d'Amérique placées sous notre gouvernement immédiat; que nous avons aussi accordé auxdits gouverneurs le pouvoir de faire, avec le consentement de nosdits conseils et des représentants du peuple qui devront être convoqués tel que susmentionné, de décréter et de sanctionner des lois, des statuts et des ordonnances pour assurer la paix publique, le bon ordre ainsi que le bon gouvernement desdites colonies, de leurs populations et de leurs habitants, conformément autant que possible aux lois d'Angleterre et aux règlements et restrictions en usage dans les autres colonies. Dans l'intervalle et jusqu'à ce que ces assemblées puissent être convoquées, tous ceux qui habitent ou qui iront habiter nosdites colonies peuvent se confier en Notre protection royale et compter Nos efforts pour leur assurer les bienfaits des lois de Notre royaume d'Angleterre; à cette fin Nous avons donné aux gouverneurs de Nos colonies sous Notre grand sceau, le pouvoir de créer et d'établir, de l'avis de Nosdits conseils, des tribunaux civils et des cours de justice publique dans Nosdites colonies pour entendre et juger toutes les causes aussi bien criminelles que civiles suivant la loi et l'équité, conformément autant que possible aux lois anglaises; cepedant, toute personne ayant raison de croire qu'elle a été lésée en matière civile par suite des jugements rendus par lesdites cours, aura la liberté d'en appeler à Nous siégeant en

and Councils of our said Three new Colonies, upon the Continent full Power and Authority to settle and agree with the Inhabitants of our said new Colonies or with any other Persons who shall resort thereto, for such Lands, Tenements and Hereditaments, as are now or hereafter shall be in our Power to dispose of; and them to grant to any such Person or Persons upon such Terms, and under such moderate Quit-Rents, Services and Acknowledgements, as have been appointed and settled in our other Colonies, and under such other Conditions as shall appear to us to be necessary and expedient for the Advantage of the Grantees, and the Improvement and settlement of our said Colonies.

And Whereas, We are desirous, upon all occasions, to testify our Royal Sense and Approbation of the Conduct and bravery of the Officers and Soldiers of our Armies, and to reward the same, We do hereby command and impower our Governors of our said Three new Colonies, and all other our Governors of our several Provinces on the Continent of North America, to grant without Fee or Reward, to such reduced Officers as have served in North America during the late War, and to such Private Soldiers as have been or shall be disbanded in America, and are actually residing there, and shall personally apply for the same, the following Quantities of Lands, subject, at the Expiration of Ten years, to the same Quit-Rents as other Lands are subject to in the Province within which they are granted, as also subject to the same

Notre Conseil privé conformément aux délais et aux restrictions prescrits en pareil cas.

Nous avons également jugé opportun, de l'avis de Notredit Conseil privé, d'accorder aux gouverneurs et aux conseils de Nos trois nouvelles colonies sur le continent, le pouvoir et l'autorité de s'entendre et de conclure des arrangements avec les habitants de Nosdites nouvelles colonies et tous ceux qui iront s'y établir, aux sujet des terres des habitations et de toute propriété dont Nous pourrons hériter et qu'il est ou sera en Notre pouvoir de disposer, et de leur en faire la concession, conformément aux termes, aux redevances, aux corvées et aux tributs modérés établis et requis dans les autres colonies, ainsi qu'aux autres conditions qu'il Nous paraîtra nécessaire et expédient d'imposer pour l'avantage des acquéreurs et le progrès et l'établissement de Nosdites colonies.

Attendu que Nous désirons reconnaître et louer en toute occasion, la brave conduite des officiers et des soldats de Nos armées et leur décerner des récompenses, Nous enjoignons aux gouverneurs de Nosdites colonies et à tous les gouverneurs de nos diverses provinces sur le continent de l'Amérique du Nord et Nous leur accordons le pouvoir de concéder gratuitement aux officiers réformés qui ont servi dans l'Amérique du Nord pendant la dernière guerre et aux soldats qui ont été ou seront licenciés en Amérique, lesquels résident actuellement dans ce pays et qui en feront personnellement la demande, les quantités de terre ci-après

Conditions of Cultivation and Improvement; viz.

To every Person having the Rank of a Field Officer — 5,000 Acres.

To every Captain — 3,000 Acres.

To every Subaltern or Staff Officer — 2,000 Acres.

To every Non-Commission Officer — 200 Acres.

To every Private Man — 50 Acres.

We do likewise authorize and require the Governors and Commanders in Chief of all our said Colonies upon the Continent of North America to grant the like Quantities of Land, and upon the same conditions, to such reduced Officers of our Navy of like Rank as served on board our Ships of War in North America at the times of the Reduction of Louisbourg and Quebec in the late War, and who shall personally apply to our respective Governors for such Grants.

And whereas it is just and reasonable, and essential to our Interest, and the Security of our Colonies, that the several Nations or Tribes of Indians with whom We are connected, and who live under our Protection, should not be molested or disturbed in the Possession of such Parts of Our Dominions and Territories as, not having been ceded to or purchased by Us, are reserved to them, or any of them, as their Hunting Grounds. — We do therefore, with the Advice of our Privy Council, declare it to be our Royal Will and Pleasure, that no Governor or Commander in Chief in any of our Colonies of Quebec, East Florida, or West Florida, do presume, upon any pretence whatever, to grant Warrants of Survey, or pass any Patents

pour lesquelles une redevance égale à celle payée pour des terres situées dans la même province ne sera exigible qu'à l'expiration de dix années; lesquelles terres seront en outre sujettes aux mêmes conditions de culture et d'amélioration que les autres dans la même province:

A tous ceux qui ont obtenu le grade d'officier supérieur, 5000 acres.

A chaque capitaine, 3000 acres.

A chaque officier subalterne ou d'état major, 2000 acres.

A chaque sous-officier, 200 acres.

A chaque soldat, 50 acres.

Nous enjoignons aux gouverneurs et aux commandants en chef de toutes Nos colonies sur le continent de l'Amérique du Nord, et Nous les autorisons de concéder aux mêmes conditions la même quantité de terre aux officiers réformés de Notre marine, d'un rang équivalent, qui ont servi sur Nos vaisseaux de guerre dans l'Amérique du Nord lors de la réduction de Louisbourg et de Québec, pendant la dernière guerre, et qui s'addresseront personnellement à Nos gouverneurs pour obtenir des concessions.

Attendu qu'il est juste, raisonnable et essentiel pour Notre intérêt et la sécurité de Nos colonies de prendre des mesures pour assurer aux nations ou tribus sauvages qui sont en relations avec Nous et qui vivent sous Notre protection, la possession entière et paisible des parties de Nos possessions et territoires qui ont été ni concédées ni achetées et ont été réservées pour ces tribus ou quelquesunes d'entre elles comme territoires de chasse, Nous dé-

for Lands beyond the Bounds of their respective Governments, as described in their Commissions; as also that no Governor or Commander in Chief in any of our other Colonies or Plantations in America do presume for the present, and until our further Pleasure be known, to grant Warrants of Survey, or pass Patents for any Lands beyond the Heads or Sources of any of the Rivers which fall into the Atlantic Ocean from the West and North West, or upon any Lands whatever, which, not having been ceded to or purchased by Us as aforesaid, are reserved to the said Indians, or any of them.

And We do further declare it to be Our Royal Will and Pleasure, for the present as aforesaid, to reserve under our Sovereignty, Protection, and Dominion, for the use of the said Indians, all the Lands and Territories not included within the Limits of Our said Three new Governments, or within the Limits of the Territory granted to the Hudson's Bay Company, as also all the Lands and Territories lying to the Westward of the Sources of the Rivers which fall into the Sea from the West and North West as aforesaid.

And We do hereby strictly forbid, on Pain of our Displeasure, all our loving Subjects from making any Purchases or Settlements whatever, or taking Possession of any of the Lands above reserved, without our especial leave and Licence for that Purpose first obtained. And, We do further strictly enjoin and require all Persons whatever who have either wilfully or inadvertently seated themselves upon any Lands within the

clarons par conséquent de l'avis de Notre Conseil privé, que c'est Notre volonté et Notre plaisir et nous enjoignons à tout gouverneur et à tout commandant en chef de Nos colonies de Québec, de la Floride Orientale et de la Floride Occidentale, de n'accorder sous aucun prétexte des permis d'arpentage ni aucun titre de propriété sur les terres situées au-delà des limites de leur gouvernement respectif, conformément à la délimitation contenue dans leur commission. Nous enjoignons pour la même raison à tout gouverneur et à tout commandant en chef de toutes Nos autres colonies ou de Nos autres plantations en Amérique, de n'accorder présentement et jusqu'à ce que Nous ayons fait connaître Nos intentions futures, aucun permis d'arpentage ni aucun titre de propriété sur les terres situées au-delà de la tête ou source de toutes les rivières qui vont de l'ouest et du nord-ouest se jeter dans l'océan Atlantique ni sur celles qui ont été ni cédées ni achetées par Nous, tel que susmentionné, et ont été réservées pour les tribus sauvages susdites ou quelques-unes d'entre elles.

Nous déclarons de plus que c'est Notre plaisir royal ainsi que Notre volonté de réserver pour le présent, sous Notre souveraineté, Notre protection et Notre autorité, pour l'usage desdits sauvages, toutes les terres et tous les territoires non compris dans les limites de Nos trois gouvernements ni dans les limites du territoire concédé à Compagnie de la baie d'Hudson, ainsi que toutes les terres et tous les territoires situés à l'ouest des sources des

Countries above described, or upon any other Lands which, not having been ceded to or purchased by Us, are still reserved to the said Indians as aforesaid, forthwith to remove themselves from such Settlements.

And whereas great Frauds and Abuses have been committed in purchasing Lands of the Indians, to the great Prejudice of our Interests, and to the great Dissatisfaction of the said Indians; In order, therefore, to prevent such Irregularities for the future, and to the end that the Indians may be convinced of our Justice and determined Resolution to remove all reasonable Cause of Discontent, We do, with the Advice of our Privy Council strictly enjoin and require, that no private Person do presume to make any purchase from the said Indians of any Lands reserved to the said Indians, within those parts of our Colonies where, We have thought Proper to allow Settlement; but that, if at any Time any of the Said Indians should be inclined to dispose of the said Lands, the same shall be Purchased only for Us, in our Name, at some public Meeting or Assembly of the said Indians, to be held for that Purpose by the Governor or Commander in Chief of our Colony respectively within which they shall lie; and in case they shall lie within the limits of any Proprietary Government, they shall be purchased only for the Use and in the name of such Proprietaries, conformable to such Directions and Instructions as We or they shall think proper to give for that Purpose; And we do, by the Advice of our Privy Council,

rivières qui de l'ouest et du nord-ouest vont se jeter dans la mer.

Nous défendons aussi strictement par la présente à tous Nos sujets, sous peine de s'attirer Notre déplaisir, d'acheter ou posséder aucune terre ci-dessus réservée, ou d'y former aucun établissement, sans avoir au préalable obtenu Notre permission spéciale et une licence à ce sujet.

Et Nous enjoignons et ordonnons strictement à tous ceux qui en connaissance de cause ou par inadvertance, se sont établis sur des terres situées dans les limites des contrées décrites ci-dessus ou sur toute autre terre qui n'ayant pas été cédée ou achetée par Nous se trouve également réservée pour lesdits sauvages, de quitter immédiatement leurs établissements.

Attendu qu'il s'est commis des fraudes et des abus dans les achats de terres des sauvages au préjudice de Nos intérêts et au grand mécontentement de ces derniers, et afin d'empêcher qu'il ne se commette de telles irrégularités à l'avenir et de convaincre les sauvages de Notre esprit de justice et de Notre résolution bien arrêtée de faire disparaître tout sujet de mécontentement, Nous déclarons de l'avis de Notre Conseil privé, qu'il est strictement défendu à qui que ce soit d'acheter des sauvages, des terres qui leur sont réservées dans les parties de Nos colonies, où Nous avons cru à propos de permettre des établisements; cependant si quelques-uns des sauvages, un jour ou l'autre, devenaient enclins à se départir desdites terres, elles ne pourront être achetées que pour Nous, en Notre nom,

declare and enjoin, that the Trade with the said Indians shall be free and open to all our Subjects whatever, provided that every Person who may incline to Trade with the said Indians do take out a Licence for carrying on such Trade from the Governor or Commander in Chief of any of our Colonies respectively where such Person shall reside, and also give Security to observe such Regulations as We shall at any Time think fit, by ourselves or by our Commissaries to be appointed for this Purpose, to direct and appoint for the Benefit of the said Trade:

And we do hereby authorize, enjoin, and require the Governors and Commanders in Chief of all our Colonies respectively, as well those under Our immediate Government as those under the Government and Direction of Proprietaries, to grant such Licences without Fee or Reward, taking special Care to insert therein a Condition, that such Licence shall be void, and the Security forfeited in case the Person to whom the same is granted shall refuse or neglect to observe such Regulations as We shall think proper to prescribe as aforesaid.

And we do further expressly enjoin and require all Officers whatever, as well Military as those Employed in the Management and Direction of Indian Affairs, within the Territories reserved as aforesaid for the use of the said Indians, to seize and apprehend all Persons whatever, who standing charged with Treason, Misprisions of Treason, Murders, or other Felonies or Misdemeanors, shall fly from Justice and take Refuge in the said Territory, and to send

à une réunion publique ou à une assemblée des sauvages qui devra être convoquée à cette fin par le gouverneur ou le commandant en chef de la colonie, dans laquelle elles se trouvent situées; en outre, si ces terres sont situées dans les limites de territoires administrés par leurs propriétaires, elles ne seront alors achetées que pour l'usage et au nom des propriétaires, conformément aux directions et aux instructions que Nous croirons ou qu'ils croiront à propos de donner à ce sujet; de plus Nous déclarons et signifions de l'avis de Notre Conseil privé que Nous accordons à tous Nos sujets le privilège de commerce ouvert et libre, à condition que tous ceux qui auront l'intention de commercer avec lesdits sauvages se munissent de licence à cette fin, du gouverneur ou du commandant en chef de celle de Nos colonies dans laquelle ils résident, et qu'ils fournissent des garanties d'observer les règlements que Nous croirons en tout temps, à propos d'imposer Nous mêmes ou par l'intermédiaire de Nos commissaires nommés à cette fin, en vue d'assurer le progrès dudit commerce.

Nous autorisons par la présente les gouverneurs et les commandants en chef de toutes Nos colonies respectivement, aussi bien ceux qui relèvent de Notre autorité immédiate que ceux qui relèvent de l'autorité et de la direction des propriétaires, d'accorder ces licences gratuitement sans omettre d'y insérer une condition par laquelle toute licence sera déclarée nulle et la protection qu'elle conférera enlevée, si le porteur refuse ou néglige d'observer les them under a proper guard to the Colony where the Crime was committed of which they stand accused, in order to take their Trial for the same.

Given at our Court at St. James's the 7th Day of October 1763, in the Third Year of our Reign.

GOD SAVE THE KING

règlements que Nous croirons à propos de prescrire. Et de plus Nous ordonnons et enjoignons à tous les officiers militaires et à ceux chargés de l'administration et de la direction des affaires des sauvages, dans les limites des territoires réservés à l'usage desdits sauvages, de saisir et d'arrêter tous ceux sur qui pésera une accusation de trahison, de nonrévélation d'attentat, de meurtre, de félonie ou de délits de tout genre et qui, pour échapper aux atteintes de la justice, auront cherché un refuge dans lesdits territoires, et de les renvoyer sous bonne escorte dans la colonie où le crime dont ils seront accusés aura été commis et pour lequel ils devront subir leur procès.

Donnée à Notre cour, à Saint-James le septième jour d'octobre mil sept cent soixante trois, la troisième année de Notre règne.

DIEU SAUVE LE ROI

1

Protection, Civilization, Assimilation:
An Outline History of Canada's Indian Policy

John L. Tobias

Protection, civilization, and assimilation have always been the goals of Canada's Indian policy. These goals were established by governments which believed that Indians were incapable of dealing with persons of European ancestry without being exploited. Therefore, the government of Canada had to protect the person and property of the Indian from exploitation by the European, which meant that the Indian was to have a special status in the political and social structure of Canada. This distinction was made part of the constitutional structure of Canada through Section 91, Subsection 24 of the British North America Act of 1867, which gave the government exclusive jurisdiction over "Indians and Indian land." However, the legislation by which the governments of Canada sought to fulfill their responsibility always had as its ultimate purpose the elimination of the Indian's special status. The means to achieve this goal was by training, that is, "civilizing," the Indian in European values, to make him capable of looking after his own interests. Eventually, through this training, the Indian identity and culture would be eradicated, and the Indian would be assimilable and no longer in need of special status. However, rather than furthering the ultimate goal of assimilation, such legislation has only served to thwart it. How and why this paradoxical situation arose is the subject of this paper.

Reprinted from the *Western Canadian Journal of Anthropology* 6, no. 2 (1976).

COLONIAL ORIGINS OF CANADA'S INDIAN POLICY

The basic principles of Canada's Indian policy pre-date Confederation. They were a carry-over of policies developed by the imperial government during the century preceding Confederation. Protection of the Indian was the first principle of imperial Indian policy, having its roots in the eighteenth-century European struggle for empire in North America. It evolved from the exigencies of the French-British rivalry for dominion in mid-century and from the difficulties experienced by the British with the Indians when British colonials encroached on Indian lands. Realizing that the lack of a uniform system of dealing with the issue of Indian lands and Indian trade often led to the Indians allying with France, the imperial government decided to make relations with the Indians an imperial responsibility.

The British government adopted the policy of protecting the Indians from European encroachment in the use of their lands and of preventing fraudulent trading practices'that had been characteristic of much of the Indian-white economic dealings. Therefore, Indian superintendents were appointed and made responsible for these matters, as well as for making the Indians allies of the British through annual distribution of presents (Allen 1971:1–8; Alvord 1908:24–26; Scott 1913a:698–99). Later, a boundary line was established between Indian lands and European settlement, which could be altered only by the Crown making treaties to take the surrender of Indian title to the land. Regulations for trade with the Indians were also made. These policies, adopted in the period 1745–1761, were made law when they were incorporated into the Royal Proclamation of 7 October 1763 (Alvord 1908:31–35, 51–52; Allen 1971:17–20).

Adherence to the principles of the Royal Proclamation of 1763 remained the basis of Britain's Indian policy for more than half a century and explains the success of the British in maintaining the Indians as allies in Britain's wars in North America during that period. Even when Britain lost much of its North American territory after 1781, and its Indian allies lost their traditional lands as a result of their British alliance, the Crown purchased land from Indians living within British territory and gave it to their allies who moved north to remain under British protection. The British continued also to purchase Indian title to any lands needed for European settlement and economic exploitation as the population of their North American colony expanded (Scott 1913a:700–719).[1] Such practices became the basis for later Canadian treaties with Indians living in the territories purchased from the Hudson's Bay Company.

It was after 1815 that the British adopted the policy of civilizing the Indian as an integral part of their relationship with the Indians. The policy evolved slowly, as a result of much propaganda in Britain and North America about the need to develop the Indian. Much of the propaganda in North America was made by Protestant sects which were in the throes of Evangelical and Revivalist movements stressing the need to Christianize all men. Many of these sects established missions among the Indians, similar to those the Jesuits and other Catholic orders had been carrying on for generations. Such missions were intended not only to teach the Indian a new religion, but also to encourage him to adopt European or American values. In Britain the Humanitarians, who were responsible for the abolition of slavery in the empire and who supported such causes as the Aborigines' Protection Society, advocated the need to protect and civilize the Indian. Romantic writers on both sides of the Atlantic also joined the chorus which protested the British and American policy of pushing the Indian further into the wilderness, and they tried to induce both governments to instruct the Indian in European civilization (Surtees 1969:87–90; Allen 1971:207–11; Upton 1973:51–61).

These protests were effective, for in the 1830's the British initiated several experiments in civilization. Essentially, they entailed the establishment of Indian reserves in isolated areas. Indians were encouraged to gather and settle in large villages on these reserves, where they would be taught to farm and would receive religious instruction and an education. These endeavours became the basis of the reserve system in Canada (Surtees 1969).[2] The reserve system, which was to be the keystone of Canada's Indian policy, was conceived as a social laboratory, where the Indian could be prepared for coping with the European.

Legislation was passed in the colonial assemblies to facilitate this purpose. In Upper Canada, Indian lands, including the new reserves, were among the crown lands upon which settlers were forbidden by law in 1839 to encroach. By 1850, Indian lands were given special status by being protected from trespass by non-Indians and by being freed from seizure for non-payment of debt or taxes. In fact, Indian lands were designated as being held in trust by the Crown and free from taxation. Finally, to protect the Indian from being debauched by certain accoutrements of civilization, a ban on the sale of liquor to Indians was legislated (Statutes of the Province of Canada 1839, 1840, 1850a). All these protective measures were incorporated into Indian legislation of the Canadian Parliament and were later expanded.

Legislation for Lower Canada differed somewhat from that for Upper Canada. This difference was primarily a result of the fact that there was much less political involvement in new efforts to civilize the Indian, since the Catholic Church had for more than a century been engaged in such work. Some protection was granted to these reserves and Indian lands when a commissioner was appointed to supervise them. What was most remarkable about legislation in Lower Canada was that it defined who was an Indian for the first time. It did so in very sweeping terms, for it included all persons of Indian ancestry, and all persons married to such persons, belonging to or recognized as belonging to an Indian band, and living with that band (S.P.C. 1850b).[3] Subsequent legislation would modify this definition by requiring that ancestry and membership would have to be traced through the male line, and marriage would only grant such status if a non-Indian woman married an Indian. However, this act of 1850 established the precedent that non-Indians determined who was an Indian and that Indians would have no say in the matter.

Disenchantment with the efforts to settle Indians on isolated reserves in Upper Canada became manifest by 1850. An evaluation of the programme led to the conclusion that the reserve system as then constituted was impractical and a failure. However, rather than repudiate the ideal of the reserve as a school or laboratory for civilizing the Indian, blame for the failure was placed on the fact that such programmes were carried out in isolation from centres of European civilization. American experience in Michigan was believed to have shown that where reserves were surrounded by settlement, Indians not only became civilized, but also were being assimilated into the communities bordering on the reserves. Therefore, the decision was made to try working with smaller reserves for individual bands located next to or near European-Canadian communities. With the change in location it was thought that the civilization policy would work (Hodgetts 1955:210), for the Euro-Canadian would serve as an example of what the Indian should become, and the existence of the town, it was thought, would attract the Indian from the reserve and into the non-Indian community where the Indian's newly learned values would supplant his old values and allow him to be fully assimilated.

This alteration in dealing with Indians and their reserves brought about a change in the ultimate goal of British Indian policy. No longer was the end result simply to teach the Indian to cope with persons of European ancestry; he was to become European and to be fully assimilated into the colonial society. In order to achieve such a goal, it was thought necessary to give the Indian special legislative status in order that he could be indoctrinated with European values and thereby made capable of being assimilated. This was the avowed purpose of the law, "an Act to encourage the gradual civilization of the Indians in this Province, and to amend the laws respecting Indians," passed in the legislature of the United Canadas in 1857 (S.P.C. 1857).

The paradox that was to become and remain a characteristic of Canada's Indian policy was given a firm foundation in this act. After stipulating in the preamble that the measure was designed to encourage civilization of the Indian, remove all legal distinctions between Indians and other Canadians, and integrate them fully into Canadian society, the legislation proceeded to define who was an Indian and then to state that such a person could not be accorded the rights and privileges accorded to European Canadians until the Indian could prove that he could read and write either the French or English language, was free of debt, and of good moral character. If he could meet such criteria, the Indian was then eligible to receive an allotment of twenty hectares of reserve land, to be placed on one year probation to give further proof of his being civilized, and then to be given the franchise (S.P.C. 1857). Thus, the legislation to remove all legal distinctions between Indians and Euro-Canadians actually established them. In fact, it set standards for acceptance that many, if not most, white colonials could not meet, for few of them were literate, free of debt, and of high moral character. The "civilized" Indian would have to be more "civilized" than the Euro-Canadian.

CANADA'S INDIAN POLICY

The principles of Canada's Indian policy were thus all established by the time of Confederation. What changed after Confederation was the emphasis placed on these principles. Until Confederation, protection of the Indian and his land was the paramount goal. Civilization of the Indian was gaining in importance but was regarded as a gradual and long-term process. Assimilation was the long-range goal. These priorities were retained for a short period after 1867, for although the British North America Act gave the government of the Dominion of Canada exclusive jurisdiction over Indians and lands reserved for Indians, the first legislation on this subject in 1868 merely incorporated the earlier colonial legislation concerning Indian lands. The only changes were the definition of who was an Indian and the penalties imposed for trespass on Indian lands (Statutes of Canada 1968).[4] In 1869 the goals of civilization and assimilation were formally added by the passage of "an Act for the gradual enfranchisement of Indians" (S.C. 1869).

The title of this piece of legislation demonstrates a change in emphasis. Whereas the colonial legislation was "for the gradual civilization," this new act was "for the gradual enfranchisement" of the Indian. This shift is demonstrated by the power the governor-in-council was given to impose the Euro-Canadian political ideal of elected local government on an Indian band and to remove from band office those considered unqualified or unfit to hold it. The elected band council was empowered to make by-laws on minor police and public health matters, but before such regulations could be enforced they had to be approved by the superintendent general (the minister) of Indian affairs (S.C. 1869). This act, designed for the Six Nations and other Indian people with long contact with Europeans, who were supposed to have received a rudimentary training under earlier legislation and missionaries, was to provide further instruction in Euro-Canadian values. This extensive education in what was regarded as the more sophisticated aspects of European civilization was to be provided by a paternalistic government which would lead the Indian away from his "inferior" political system. It thereby established another criterion of civilization.

The new Dominion of Canada developed its Indian policy during the decade of the 1870's. It extended its authority over the Plains Indian through the treaty system. In doing so, the Canadian government demonstrated its acceptance of the principles established by the old imperial government, for not only did the dominion government purchase Indian title to the land, but also it imposed the reserve system as a laboratory for cultural change on the Plains Indians by means of these treaties (Morris 1971).[5] In addition, through the "Act to amend and consolidate the laws respecting Indians" or, as it was short-titled, "The Indian Act" of 1876 (S.C. 1876; RG10, vol. 1923, file 3007),[6] the foundation for all Canada's future Indian legislation was laid.

The new legislation incorporated all the protective features of the earlier legislation and established more stringent requirements for non-Indian use of Indian lands and for their alienation. It contained slight revisions of the mechanism for enfranchisement which it was thought would facilitate assimilation. However, most of these changes were related directly to furthering the process of civilization and permitting the government to encourage and direct it. Thus, the elective system was no longer to be imposed but was only to be applied if the band asked for it. To encourage this system of government, band councils under the elective system were given increased authority. However, the legislation set out the formula for the number of councillors and chiefs a band could have and who could vote in such elections (S.C. 1876; Debates of the Parliament of Canada, 2 March 1876:342–43; Debates, 21 March 1876:749–53).

The most important innovation of the new Indian Act, in the eyes of the government, was the introduction of the location ticket. This was regarded as an essential feature of the civilization process and a necessity for enfranchisement. It was a means by which the Indian could demonstrate that he had adopted the European concept of private property. The new policy stipulated that the superintendent general have the reserve surveyed into individual lots. The band council could then assign these lots to individual band members. As a form of title the superintendent general would then give the band member a location ticket. Before an individual received a ticket he had to prove his suitability in the same manner as under the earlier legislation. On passing this first test and receiving his location ticket, the Indian entered a three-year probationary period during which he had to demonstrate that he would use the land as a Euro-Canadian might and that he was fully qualified for membership in Canadian society. If he passed these tests, he was enfranchised and given title to the land. If all band members wished, they could enfranchise in this way (S.C. 1876; Debates, 2 March 1876:342–43; Debates, 21 March 1876:749–53).

An alternative means of assimilation was also offered, which required less time and supervision than the one discussed above. An Indian who went to university and earned a professional degree as minister, lawyer, teacher, or doctor could be given a location ticket and enfranchised immediately without going through the probationary period (S.C. 1876). By earning such degrees, the Indian had demonstrated his acceptance of Euro-Canadian values and his ability to function in Canadian Society.

What becomes even clearer is the government's determination to make the Indians into imitation Europeans and to eradicate the old Indian values through education, religion, new economic and political systems, and a new concept of property. Not only was the Indian as a distinct cultural group to disappear, but also the laboratory where these changes were brought about would disappear, for as the Indian was enfranchised, that is, became assimilated, he would take with him his share of the reserve. Therefore, when all Indians were enfranchised, there would no longer be any Indian reserves. The first piece of comprehensive legislation by which the government exercised its exclusive jurisdiction over Indians and Indian lands had as its purpose the eventual extirpation of this jurisdiction by doing away with those persons and lands that fell within the category of Indians and Indian lands.

The new Indian Act, like all previous legislation, was designed for the Indians living east of Lake Superior. The western Indians were excluded from the operation of most sections of the Indian Act until such time as the superintendent general of Indian affairs considered them advanced enough in civilization to take advantage of the act. However, to speed up their advance, and under the guise of protecting them from exploitation, the 1876 Indian Act and subsequent amendments contained provisions which attacked traditional Indian sexual, marriage, and divorce mores and furthered the Christian-European values. Into this category fall the sections relating to illegitimate children, non-band members on the reserve after sundown, non-Indians on reserves and cohabiting with Indians, and Indian women in public houses (S.C. 1879, 1884a, 1887, 1898, 1894; RG10, vol 2378, file 77,190; vol 2004, file 7728; vol. 3947, file 123,264–1; vol 1596; vol 6809, file 470–2–3, vol. 11, part 3; many other examples could be given). In addition, Indian agents were given the powers of a justice of the peace to enforce sections of the criminal code relating to vagrancy, in order that the western Indian could be kept on the reserve where he might be taught to farm and learn the value of work (S.C. 1890, 1895; RG10, vol. 3832, file 64,009; vol. 2446, file 93, 503; vol. 2497, file 102, 950; vol. 3378, file 77,020; vol. 6809, file 470–2–3, vol. 11, part 4).

The eastern Indians who were to be the beneficiaries of the act rejected it, for they knew that if they adopted the elective system, the superintendent general would not only have supervisory and veto power over band decisions, but also, according to other provisions of the act, he could force the band council to concern itself with issues with which it did not wish to deal. Many eastern bands clearly stated that they would never request an elected band council because they did not wish to be governed and managed by the government of Canada (S.C. 1876; RG10, vol. 2077, file 11,432). Such protests were interpreted as demonstration of the fact that the Indian needed more direction and guidance, for subsequent amendments and later Indian acts increased the authority of the superintendent general to interfere in the band and personal affairs of the Indians.

The Indian Act of 1880 provided the means to manage Indian affairs. It created a new branch of the civil service that was to be called the Department of Indian Affairs. It once again empowered the superintendent general to impose the elective system of band government whenever he thought a band ready for it. In addition, this new legislation allowed the superintendent general to deprive the traditional leaders of recognition by stating that the only spokesmen of the band were those men elected according to the provisions of the Indian Act when the elective system was imposed. Otherwise, the Indian Act of 1880 differed little from that of 1876 (S.C. 1880).[7]

The elected band council was regarded as the means to destroy the last vestige of the old tribal system, the traditional political system. The reserve system, other sections of the Indian Act, and missionaries were thought to have dealt effectively with all other aspects of traditional Indian values. The only impediment to civilization and assimilation was lack of training in the Canadian political system. This evaluation was the reason for the stress on the elective system despite Indian opposition to it. It was also the reason for passage in 1884 of "An Act for conferring certain privileges on the more advanced bands of Indians of Canada with the view of training them for exercise of Municipal Affairs" (S.C. 1884). This bill came to be known as the Indian Advancement Act.

The Indian Advancement Act was an ideal tool for directed civilization. It extended slightly the powers of the band council beyond those of the Indian Act by giving the band council the power to levy taxes on the real property of band members. It also expanded the council's powers over police and public health matters. At the same time it greatly increased the powers of the superintendent general to direct the band's political affairs. Election regulation, size of the band council, and deposition of elected officials were all spelled out in the act. Moreover, the superintendent general or an agent delegated by him was empowered to call for the elections, supervise them, call band meetings, preside over them, record them, advise the band council, and participate in the meetings in every manner except to vote and adjourn the meetings. In effect, the agent directed the political affairs of the band (S.C. 1884).[8]

To further encourage the Indians to ask for this form of government, Indians east of Lake Superior were granted the franchise in dominion elections by the Electoral Franchise Act of 1885. Thus, they would be able to participate in the political process off the reserve as well as on it. However, few bands accepted either measure, and in 1896 the franchise was withdrawn from the Indians. Nevertheless, the Advancement Act was retained.

Despite most bands refusing to come under the Advancement Act, the elective system as provided for in the Indian Act was imposed on them. Many bands merely elected their traditional leaders, who were often unsatisfactory to the government and were deposed as being incompetent, immoral, or intemperate, all grounds for dismissal under the act. However, these men were usually re-elected, which thwarted the government's intentions in deposing them. Therefore, in 1884 the Indian Act was amended to prohibit persons deposed from office from standing for immediate re-election (RG10, vol. 3947, file 123,764–2; S.C. 1884).

A decade later, an amendment was added to the Indian Act which allowed the minister to depose chiefs and councillors where the elective system was not applicable. This amendment was included because the band leaders in the West were found to be resisting the innovations of the reserve system and the government's efforts to discourage the practice of traditional Indian beliefs and values (RG10, vol. 6809, file 470–2–3, vol. 11, part 4; S.C. 1895).

Interference in and direction of a band's political affairs led to an increase in the government's control of the band's resources. Because most bands opposed enfranchisement of their members and the alienation of reserve lands that this procedure entailed, they were able to thwart the goal by refusing to allot reserve lands to individual band members. Without a land allotment, no location ticket could be given, and without a location ticket, enfranchisement was impossible. Therefore, in 1879 power to allot reserve lands was taken from the band and given to the superintendent general (S.C. 1879, 1884; RG10, vol. 2378, file 77,190). Because most bands refused to alienate their land, even for a limited period, persons who held location tickets and wanted to lease their land to non-Indians as a source of revenue could not do so, because the band refused to vote for the required surrender. Consequently, the Indian Act was amended in 1884 and 1894 to allow the superintendent general to lease such lands for revenue purposes without taking a surrender. The first was for the purpose of revenue for those holding a location ticket and desiring to lease their land, while the 1894 amendment allowed the superintendent general to lease the land of orphans or aged who held location tickets, but who did not specifically ask to have their land leased. The 1894 amendment was really a device for cutting the cost of government aid to various bands where the location ticket system was well established. By these means, the government thought it was preventing an "unenlightened" band council from holding a "civilized" band member in check (ibid. Also S.C. 1894, 1895; RG10, vol. 6809, file 470–2–3, vol. 11, part 4; vol. 2378, file 77,190). In 1898, as a result of bands refusing to exercise their police and public health powers and not expending their band funds for this purpose, the superintendent general was empowered to make the necessary regulations and expend band funds for whatever expense was entailed in carrying out the regulations (S.C. 1898; RG10, vol. 6809, file 470–2–3, vol. 11, part 4).[9]

While the effort to direct civilization and assimilation of the eastern Indian led to direct involvement in band affairs, legislation for the western Indian was to further the initial process of the civilization programme and was therefore geared much more to the individual. Because the Plains Indians and the Indians of British Columbia attempted to preserve their traditional religious and cultural values, despite pressure from missionaries and the government to repudiate them for being contrary to Christian and European values, the government decided to prohibit many of the traditional practices. The "Sun Dance," "Potlatches," and all "Give Away" ceremonials were banned because they promoted pagan beliefs and were anathema to the development of a concept of private property (S.C. 1884a, 1895; RG10, vol. 6809, file 470–2–3, vol. 11, part 4). A similar purpose, to teach the Indian to husband his resources, was behind the legislated prohibition on the sale of produce and livestock from Indian reserves on the Prairies (S.C. 1884a, 1890; RG10, vol. 2446, file 93,503; vol. 2497, file 102,950).[10]

The ability of many Indians living in Manitoba and the old Northwest Territories to pursue their old form of livelihood, hunting and fishing, was particularly irksome to the government, for it was regarded as a drawback to the Indian's adopting a more settled economic base, farming. Besides, the hunting Indian was retarding the education of his children, because he took them with him into the bush, which meant they did not attend school. These children were regarded as being the first generation which would become civilized and to whom the full benefits of the Indian Act could be extended. However, if they were kept illiterate by their parent's economic pursuits, the government's plans for them would be thwarted. Therefore, in 1890 an amendment to the Indian Act was made empowering the governor-in-council to declare the game laws of Manitoba and the Northwest Territories to be applicable to Indians (S.C. 1890; RG10, vol. 2378, file 70,020; vol. 3832, file 69,009; vol. 2446, file 93,503; vol. 2497, file 102,950).

School attendance was of vital concern to the government, for education of the Indian child was a keystone of the civilizing process the reserve system was to perform. Since schools on the reserve were not well attended by Indian children, they were regarded as ineffectual instruments of this process. Residential and industrial schools, which removed the child from the detrimental influence of uncivilized parents and Indian traditions, were regarded as better instruments of government policy. Indian parents refused to send their children to such schools because they were long distances from the reserve and alienated the child from his culture. Therefore, in 1894 amendments to the Indian Act were made authorizing the governor-in-council to make whatever regulations on the school question he thought necessary and empowering him to commit children to the boarding and industrial schools founded by the government (S.C. 1894; RG10, vol. 3947, file 123,764–3; vol. 6908, file 470–2–3, vol. 11).

The programme of directed and aggressive civilization that was a characteristic of Indian policy and legislation in the period after 1870 had spent its force by the turn of the century. By 1900, the reserve system was being questioned as a means of achieving assimilation. In fact, many had come to regard the reserve as preventing assimilation, and to believe that the existence of reserves was a check on the economic development and growth of areas where they were located. This attitude began to find expression in the new or, rather, consolidated Indian Act of revised statutes of 1906 (S.C. 1906a).[11] Amendments to this act in subsequent years reinforced this view, for most of them were designed to remove the protection the reserve seemed to provide the Indian and to force the Indian people off the reserve. Assimilation was no longer regarded as a long-term goal; it was one that could be attained immediately if the Indian were removed from the protective environment of the reserve.

The initial attack on the reserve began in the 1890's when the superintendent general was given power to lease land for revenue purposes. Shortly thereafter, amendments were made to ease the permanent alienation of reserve land by allowing the government to distribute in cash up to 50 per cent of the value of the land as an inducement for a surrender for sale (ibid.; also S.C. 1898, 1906b; RG10, vol. 6809, file 470–2–3, vol. 11, parts 4, 5). As was expected, much reserve land was made available for sale to non-Indians, particularly on the Prairies. These measures were justified as promoting the economic growth of the country and removing a retarding influence on development of an area. Such arguments were also used when the superintendent general was given the power to lease Indian land without taking a surrender for purpose of mineral exploration, to expropriate for right-of-ways for highways and provincially chartered railways, and to lease for revenue farm lands said not to be used by Indians. These powers were given because Indians had refused to make surrenders for these purposes in the past. Finally, a mechanism was established to deal with situations similar to those of Sarnia, Ontario, and Victoria, B.C., where reserves within the boundaries of a city could be abolished when it was found to be in the Indian and public interest (SC. 1910a, 1910b, 1918; RG10, vol. 6809, file 470–2–3, vol. 2, Part 6; vol. 6810, file 470–2–3, vol. 12, part 10).

Dissatisfaction with the reserve system principally resulted from the fact that it only partially fulfilled its functions. It did civilize the Indian, but it did not complete the process as envisioned by encouraging them to enfranchise. In the period between 1857 when the enfranchisement process was first enacted and 1920, only slightly more than 250 persons were enfranchised (RG10, vol. 6810, file 470–2–3, vol. 12, Part 7; memo on enfranchisement). To remedy this situation the government amended the Indian Act to permit Indians living off the reserve to be enfranchised without the required land. This change resulted in the enfranchisement of 500 people within two years after passage of the amendment (S.C. 1917; RG10, vol. 6809, file 470–2–3, vol. 11, part 6). Subsequent amendments reduced the number of Indians by making it easier for half-breeds who had taken treaty in the West to be enfranchised and for Indian women married to non-Indians to give up entirely their Indian status (S.C. 1914, 1920; RG10, vol. 6810, file 470–2–3, vol. 12, part 7).

The civilized Indian who preferred to live on the reserve was untouched by any of these amendments, but this was the individual the government wanted off the reserve, for otherwise the reserve and the Indian would become permanent features of Canadian society. The government found such a thought abhorrent, for it wanted to do away with the reserve and "make a final disposition of the individuals who have been civilized into the ordinary life of the country" (RG10, vol. 6810, file 470–2–3, vol. 12 part 7; memo on enfranchisement). Therefore, assimilation was not to be a voluntary act on the part of the Indian. The superintendent general, at his discretion, was given the power to establish boards of inquiry to examine the fitness of Indians for enfranchisement, without the people making application, report on their fitness for enfranchisement, and the superintendent general would then recommend to the governor-in-council that they be enfranchised. Such people could then be given title to the reserve lands they occupied, receive their share of the band's monies, and be enfranchised (ibid.; S.C. 1920).

The outcry and protests that resulted from the operation of these procedures was so great that two years later the government modified these sections of the act to appoint such boards only after applications for enfranchisement were received. However, when this change failed to achieve the purpose established for the original amendments, power to create such boards was returned to the discretion of the superintendent-general, and compulsory enfranchisement was re-enacted (S.C. 1922, 1933; RG10, vol. 6810, file 470–2–3, vol. 12, parts 7–9).

Forced or compulsory enfranchisement was designed for the Indians east of Lake Superior. In the West, where the Indians were thought to be less advanced, the policy of directed civilization was applied to hasten their development. Because the existing provisions of the act were thought not strong enough to achieve this purpose, amendments were made to ensure compulsory school attendance and to treat chronic non-attenders as juvenile delinquents (S.C. 1914, 1920, 1930; RG10, vol. 6809, file 470–2–3, vol. 11, parts 5 and 6, vol. 6810, file 470–2–3, vol. 12, parts 7–8). Also, stronger efforts were made to put an end to Plains Indians' practice of old ceremonials, so that prohibitions against these Indians appearing in aboriginal garb and performing their traditional dances at fairs and stampedes under the guise of entertaining the non-Indian community were interpreted as being part of the act. Later this section was amended to prohibit such dances in any type of dress, unless prior approval in writing was given by the Department of Indian Affairs (S.C. 1914; RG10, vol. 3825, file 60,511, vol. 1 and 2). To promote farming on western reserves so that the Indians could become self-supporting landholders, the superintendent general was authorized to use band funds to purchase farm machinery for individual Indians and to establish a fund from which loans might be made to allow Indians to purchase machinery or get started in small businesses (S.C. 1917, 1922, 1938; RG10, vol. 6809, file 470–2–3, vol. 11, part 6; vol. 6810, file 470–2–3, vol. 12, parts 8, 10).

In an effort to reduce the distinctions between Indian and non-Indian communities, the government also incorporated into the Indian Act authority for the superintendent general to regulate the use and operation of amusement and recreational facilities on Indian reserves in accordance with provincial and local laws which forbade opening such facilities on Sundays. Moreover, provincial laws on general matters, such as on motor vehicles, could be declared to be applicable on reserves, and such laws would have the same effect as though they had been incorporated into the Indian Act (S.C. 1922, 1930, 1936; RG10, vol. 6810, file 470–2–3, vol. 12, parts 8, 10).

Enactment of compulsory enfranchisement and the breaking down of the barriers of the reserve boundaries both literally by lease and sale and figuratively by making provincial laws apply there were all to promote more rapid assimilation. However, these acts had only limited success. With the economic crisis followed by a major war in the period 1933–1945, little attention was paid to Indian matters. In fact, in that period the government and the civil servants in what became the Indian Affairs Branch appear not to have had any policy. They left this whole area of government-Indian relations in a state of flux and made only ad hoc decisions. Perhaps this situation was a result of the realization that all previous policies had failed to attain the goal established for Canada's Indian administration. At any rate, there is an obvious lack of policy or policy goal in this period.

This apparent aimlessness changed after 1945, when public interest in Indian affairs was awakened to an unprecedented degree. This interest was largely a result of the strong Indian contribution to the war effort in the years 1940–45. The public was generally concerned with what was regarded as the treatment of the Indian as a second-class person and with the fact that the Indian did not have the same status as other Canadians. In fact, the Indian was not even a citizen. Veterans' organizations, churches, and citizen groups across the country called for a royal commission to investigate the administration of Indian affairs and conditions prevailing on Indian reserves. All wanted a complete revision of the Indian Act and an end to discrimination against the Indian (RG10, vol. 6810, file 470–2–3, vol. 12, part 11).

No royal commission was appointed, but a joint committee of both the Senate and House of Commons was created in 1946 to study and make proposals on Canada's Indian administration and the revision of the Indian Act. After two years, the joint committee recommended (Proceedings 1948:186–90):

1. The complete revision of every section of the Indian Act and the repeal of those sections which were outdated.
2. That the new Indian Act be designed to facilitate the gradual transition of the Indian from a position of wards up to full citizenship. Therefore the Act should provide:
   A. A political voice for Indian women in band affairs.
   B. Bands with more self-government and financial assistance.
   C. Equal treatment of Indians and non-Indians in the matter of intoxicants.
   D. That a band might incorporate as a municipality.
   E. That Indian Affairs officials were to have their duties and responsibilities designed to assist the Indian in the responsibilities of self-government and to attain the rights of full citizenship.

3. Guidelines for future Indian policy were to be:
   A. Easing of enfranchisement.
   B. Extension of the franchise to the Indian.
   C. Co-operation with the provinces in extending service to the Indian.
   D. Education of Indian children with non-Indians in order to prepare Indian children for assimilation.

In essence, the joint committee approved the goal of Canada's previous Indian policy — assimilation — but disapproved some of the earlier methods to achieve it. They assumed that most of the work of civilization was virtually complete, and that therefore many of the protective features of earlier acts could be withdrawn and bands allowed more self-government and less governmental interference. Moreover, since assimilation was soon attainable, the guidelines for the new Indian policy and the new Indian Act stipulated that the dominion government should begin turning over responsibilities for providing services to the provinces. In this way the barriers provided by the reserves and the Indians' special status under the constitution would be further broken down and assimilation made all the easier. Thus, the Indian and the Indian reserve were still regarded as a transitory feature of Canadian society.

In 1951 a new Indian Act was passed which met most of the criteria established by the joint committee. At first glance it appeared to differ greatly from all previous Indian Acts back to 1876. Not since the 1876 Act had the minister's powers been so limited, for under the new act the minister's "powers were reduced to a supervisory role" but with veto power. His authority to direct band and personal matters required band approval. The individual bands, if they desired, could now run their own reserves. As many as fifty sections and subsections were deleted from earlier acts because they were antiquated or too restrictive on individuals or the band. Most of the provisions for aggressive civilization and compulsory enfranchisement were deleted (S.C. 1951).

A closer look at the 1951 Indian Act and a comparison with the Indian Act of 1876 shows that there are only minor differences. In format, content, and intent they are quite similar. Both provide for a co-operative approach between government and Indian towards the goal of assimilation, although enfranchisement is made easier in the 1951 Act by eliminating the testing period and the requirement for location tickets or certificates of possession. However, other provisions are virtually the same. The new act definitely differs from the Indian Acts between 1880 and 1951, but only because it returned to the philosophy of the original Indian Act: civilization was to be encouraged but not directed or forced on the Indian people. Assimilation for all Indians was a goal that should be striven for without an abundance of tests or the compulsory aspects of the preceding Indian Acts. Through the 1951 Indian Act the government managed to extricate itself from the quicksand that a desire to hurry assimilation had mired it in after passage of the 1876 Indian Act.

Speedy assimilation was not repudiated as the goal of Canada's Indian policy — what was repudiated was the earlier means to achieve it. Therefore, when it became obvious that the 1951 Indian Act would not promote the purpose it was designed for any more than earlier acts did, an alternative means to those tried between 1880 and 1950 was sought. This was provided in part by the recommendation by the joint committee to turn over responsibility for services to Indians to the provinces. Therefore, this process was begun in the 1950's and continued in the decade of the 1960's. Then, in 1969, when this transfer was nearing completion, the government announced its intention to absolve itself from responsibility for Indian affairs and the special status of Indians and to repeal special legislation relating to Indians, that is, the Indian Act.[12] By adoption of this policy and by repealing the Indian Act, the Indian would be assimilated by government fiat, and what the Indian Act of 1876 had sought as a long-term goal — the extirpation of the Indian and Indian lands — would be realized.

The announcement of this policy in the 1969 White Paper on Indian Affairs brought such a protest from the Indian people, who had always rejected this goal, that the government was forced to reconsider its policy, delay transfer of services, and in 1973 announce the withdrawal of the policy statement. However, this official withdrawal does not mean that the goal has been repudiated; at least there is no indication of such renunciation to date. It is simply that alternative means to achieve it are being considered. At the moment Canada's Indian policy is in a state of flux, but unlike any earlier period, a more honest effort is being made to involve the Indian and Indian views in the determination of a new Indian policy.[13]

NOTES

1. The best study of Britain's Indian policy is that by Allen (1971). See also Surtees (1971:45–49), Scott (1913b:345–46), Wright (1943:40).
2. For a more detailed study of this policy, see Surtees's unpublished M.A. thesis (1966) on which his article is based. See also Hodgetts (1955:209–10) and Upton (1973:51–61).
3. The Indian reserves which existed in Lower Canada at this time were those that had been established by the various religious orders on lands granted to them during the French regime. These reserves were therefore within or next to non-Indian communities. Thus, there was often intermarriage or non-Indians living on the reserves, which were run by the religious orders and not by colonial officials, as in Upper Canada. For this reason, it was necessary to define who was being protected by this legislation governing Indian lands. The special circumstances of Lower Canada made this definition necessary, for as was stated above, non-Indians were forbidden by law from living on crown lands used for or regarded as being Indian lands in Upper Canada.

4. Incorporated in this act was a law not·mentioned above, which dealt with surrender of Indian lands (S.P.C. 1860).
5. The last chapter of this book provides an excellent summary of the views of the man responsible for making many of the western treaties and his reasons for including the various provisions of the treaties.
6. The latter reference gives some background to this act. From the RG10 series, vol. 1935, file 3589; vol. 1928, file 3281; vol. 3084, file 3608. All provide information as to reasons various provisions of the act were made.
7. Further amendments regarding the minister's power in elections and band government were included in S.C. 1884a. See also RG10, vol. 2378, file 77,190.
8. This amendment included provisions which gave band councils most of the powers, except taxation, provided in the Indian Advancement Act.
9. Earlier acts, such as S.C. 1887, allowed leases for cutting hay and timber without a surrender.
10. The government had found that the Plains Indians disposed of all their agricultural and livestock produce each fall in order to get cash which was, in turn, expended for foodstuffs. However, since other purchases were also made, by mid-winter many of the Indians were destitute, having no food on hand and no means by which to procure it, for their money was completely expended. This situation meant that the government had to provide rations to keep these people alive. Rather than do this, the government thought that the Indian should be prevented from disposing of his crop all at once. It was assumed that the Indian, having seen that husbanding his crop would mean that he would be able to feed himself and have cash at intervals throughout the year, would then voluntarily limit himself to selling only a portion of his produce in the fall and that he would have learned the efficacy of husbanding his resources.
11. See RG10, vol. 6810, file 470–2–3, vol. 12, part 7, for the correspondence concerning the new attitude towards the reserve.
12. See the *Statement of the Government of Canada on Indian Policy, 1969,* presented to the First Session of the 28th Parliament by the Honourable Jean Chrétien, minister of Indian Affairs and Northern Development (Ottawa, 1969).
13. Discussions concerning the development of a new Indian policy between government and Indian leaders have been going on since 1974. The chances of success for these discussions hinge to a large degree on whether the traditional dichotomy between Indian and government understanding of some basic concepts, such as reserves and treaties, can be resolved. This difference in views on the question of reserves and treaties is the subject of a paper that I have written entitled "Indian Reserves in Western Canada: Indian Homelands or Devices for Assimilation," which will appear in the Mercury History Series (National Museum of Man). [See D. A. Muise, ed., *Approaches to Native History in Canada* (Ottawa 1977)]

REFERENCES

Allan, Robert S. 1971. *A History of the British Indian Department in North America (1755–1830).* National Historic Sites Manuscript Report no. 109. Ottawa.
Alvord, Clarence W. 1908. *The Genesis of the Proclamation of 1763.* Michigan Pioneer and Historical Society, vol. 36.
Debates of the Parliament of Canada, 2 March 1876; 21 March 1876.
Hodgetts, John E. 1955. "Indian Affairs, The White Man's Albatross." In *Pioneer Public Service, An Administrative History 1841–1867.* Toronto, chapter 8.
Morris, Alexander. 1971. *The Treaties of Canada with the Indians of Manitoba and the North-West Territories.* Toronto: Coles (Orig. 1880).
Proceedings of the Joint Senate-House Committee on Indian Affairs. 1948.
Public Archives Canada
    Record Group 10 (RG10)
    Indian Affairs Files. Volumes:
    1596

1923, file 3007
1928, file 3281
1935, file 3584
2004, file 7728
2077, file 11, 432
2378, file 77, 190
      file 70, 020
2446, file 93, 503
2497, file 102, 950
3084, file 3608
3378, file 77, 020
3825, file 60, 511, parts 1 and 2
3832, file 69, 009
3947, file 123, 764-1
        123, 764-2
        123, 764-3
6809, file 470-2-3, vol. 11, parts 3, 4, 5, 6
6810, file 470-2-3, vol. 12, parts 7, 8, 9, 10, 11, 12.
Scott. 1913.
Statutes of Canada (S.C.)
    1860 23 Victoria, chapter 151.
    1868 31 Victoria, chapter 42.
    1869 32–33 Victoria, chapter 42.
    1876 39 Victoria, chapter 18.
    1879 42 Victoria, chapter 34.
    1880 43 Victoria, chapter 28.
    1884 47 Victoria, chapter 27.
    1884 47 Victoria, chapter 28.
    1887 50–51 Victoria, chapter 33.
    1890 53 Victoria, chapter 24.
    1895 58–59 Victoria, chapter 35.
    1898 61 Victoria, chapter 34.
    1906 Revised Statutes, chapter 81.
    1906 6 Edward VII, chapter 20.
    1910 9–10 Edward VII, chapter 20.
    1910 1–2 George V, chapter 14.
    1914 4–5 George V, chapter 35.
    1915 6–7 George V, chapter 56.
    1917 8–9 George V, chapter   .
    1918 9–10 George V, chapter 50.
    1922 12–13 George V, chapter 26.
    1930 20–21, chapter 25
    1934 23–24, chapter 42.
    1936 1 Edward VIII, chapter 20.
    1938 2 George VI, chapter 31.
    1951 15 George VI, chapter 29.
Statutes of the Province of Canada (S.P.C.)
    1839 2 Victoria, chapter 15.
    1840 3 Victoria, chapter 13.
    1850 13–14 Victoria, chapter 74.
    1850 13–14 Victoria, chapter 42.
    1857 20 Victoria, chapter 26.
Surtees, Robert J. 1971. *The Original People*. Toronto.
Upton, L. F. S. 1973. "The Origins of Canadian Indian Policy." *Journal of Canadian Studies*.
Wright, Anna Margaret. 1943. "The Canadian Frontier, 1840–1867." Ph.D. diss., University of
    Toronto.

2

The Early Indian Acts: Developmental Strategy and Constitutional Change

John S. Milloy

With the fall of New France, the British government seized the opportunity to consolidate its imperial position by structuring formal, constitutional relations with Canadian natives. In the Proclamation of 1763, it announced its intention of conciliating those disgruntled tribes by recognizing their land rights, by securing to them control of unceded land, and by entering into a nation-to-nation relationship with them. Under this policy of conciliation, the agency charged with conducting relations with the tribes, the British imperial Indian Department, was a foreign office in every sense. Departmental agents could not command; they could employ only the ordinary tools of the diplomat: cajolery, coercion, bribery, or, put more politely, persuasion. The well-known success of the Indian Department-cum-foreign office in maintaining friendly and useful military relations with the tribes and in expediting a peaceful and inexpensive transfer of needed tribal territory should not be misread. It was a sign of talented diplomats and of the coincidence of imperial and Indian interest, not of any sure or constitutional control.

This nation-to-nation status quo was maintained even after 1830 when the imperial government added a policy of Indian civilization to that of conciliation, when it began to offer foreign aid in the form of developmental assistance through training in European skills. Despite the influence of Indian Department agents, now dedicated to social engineering, or of God himself represented by Methodist, Baptist, and Anglican missionaries, it was tribal councils who decided the degree and direction of culture change: whether schools would be allowed on the reserves, the rate and type of agricultural or resource development, and the extent to which Indian finances, composed of the annual payments received by the tribes for lands surrendered to the Crown, would be devoted to projects of development.

In short, in the period in which the British imperial government was responsible for Indian affairs, from 1763 until 1860 when that responsibility was transferred to the government of the United Canadas, Indian tribes were, de facto, self governing. They had exclusive control over their population, land, and finances.[1]

This constitutional status was not destined to survive the subsequent phase of imperial reorganization in Canada — Confederation. Under the authority of section 91 subsection 24 of the British North America Act, the Canadian federal government in the first comprehensive Indian Act, that of 1876, took extensive control of reserves and tribal nations. Traditional Indian government was dismissed and replaced by Indian-agent-controlled models of white government. The ultimate control of finance and land use passed into federal hands. Governmental powers left with the tribes placed them, in the multi-layered Confederation, well below the position of a respectable municipality. That the mid-century change in the constitutional status of native people was dramatic is apparent; the cause of that change is less obvious.

It might be postulated that the full dismantling of tribal independence which occurred in 1876 was related directly to the process and challenge of nation-building: the Indian nations, like former colonies, were to find new low water-marks in the drive for national consolidation. This is an appealing explanation. With respect to the West, for example, the act of 1876 and treaties of 1871–77 served the need to secure a firm grip over the area in the worrisome light of American pretensions and the post-buffalo days of economic and social crisis that faced the powerful Plains tribes. There is evidence, as, well, that some western treaty makers saw their task in just such a political light. Alexander Morris was one. During the negotiations for Treaty Six he explained to Say-sway-kus the government's provision of red coats for chiefs, saying "all the other Chiefs of the Queen wear the coats we have brought, and the good of this is that when the Chief is seen with his uniform and medal, everyone knows he is an officer of hers."[2] Morris's implication that the treaty was more than a land cession but also subsumed tribal authority to that of the Crown was made even more explicit in his subsequent writing on the administration of the treaties. He advised the government that "they [the chiefs] should be strongly impressed with the belief that they are officers of the Crown, and that it is their duty to see that the Indians of their tribes obey the provisions of the treaties"[3] for it is advantageous "to the Crown to possess so large a number of Indian officials, duly recognized as such, and who can be inspired with a proper sense of their responsibility to the Government."[4]

Despite the case that might be made for the foregoing explanation, it can be demonstrated that it was factors other than the varied geopolitical considerations of the 1860's and 1870's which motivated the process of constitutional change. In fact, the events of nation-building are largely irrelevant, for the first step in that process of change was taken by the British with the Gradual Civilization Act of 1857 and was related solely to developmental strategy designed to secure more readily the Christianization and civilization of native people in Ontario, and the destruction of native self-government was completed in the Enfranchisement Act of 1869. Indeed, the path from 1857 to 1869 was marked by a continuing quest for a more perfect developmental strategy in an atmosphere of escalating political conflict involving native leaders and local civilizers, such as Indian agents and missionaries. It was the formulation of what might be termed a developmental logic mainly in the pre-Confederation era which both motivated constitutional change and determined the nature of it. Any understanding of the acts of 1857, 1869, 1876, and no doubt that of 1951, and of the particular constitutional status they forced upon native people is rooted in the historical evolution of that logic — in the deterministic nature of developmental strategy. It is to that evolution one must turn.

The foundations of this constitutionally disturbing developmental logic were put in place by the British with the passage by the Assembly of the United Canadas of the Gradual Civilization Act of 1857.[5] The act was based upon the assumption that the full civilization of the tribes could be achieved only when Indians were brought into contact with individualized property. It had been argued by the Sir Charles Bagot Commission on Indian Affairs in the 1840's[6] and by the Methodist missionaries in the 1850's[7] that this would create industriousness in the breast of the properly educated and thereafter the increasingly self-reliant native farmer. However, there were tactical problems. The fact that in 1846 tribal councils across the colony had firmly rejected the concept of reserve subdivision meant that qualified Indians would have to be brought into the colonial environment where freehold tenure was available; that is, they would have to be enfranchised.[8] Thus, individual tenure and enfranchisement became the heart of developmental strategy, which included the more traditional elements of skill training, education, resource development, and general behavioural modification through conversion to the Christian faith.

The Act of 1857 was designed to facilitate this newly reformed strategy. Any Indian, the act stipulated, adjudged by a special board of examiners to be educated, free from debt, and of good moral character could on application be awarded twenty hectares of land within the colony and "the rights accompanying it."[9] He was thereby enfranchised, enabled to participate equally with his white neighbours in the political life of the colony, and made amenable to the same laws. As a consequence, he would cut his tribal ties, and, according to this new developmental strategy, he would be rescued from the retrograde influence of reserve life, while his possession of twenty freehold hectares would animate his existence with industry.

The impact of this act was profound in at least three ways. First, it created a constitutional inconsistency in that it allowed that the twenty hectares to be awarded to the enfranchised individual was to be reserve land removed from tribal control on the questionable authority of a colonial act. Since the Proclamation of 1763, colonial legislatures had been excluded from involvement in Indian affairs. They had provided legislation supportive of the policy of civilization, but this had been done by restraining the behaviour of their white colonial constituents toward the native population. Such legislation, since it did not apply to native people or their land, was constitutionally correct.[10] The act of 1857 was not. It represented a direct colonial intervention in Indian affairs. Furthermore, the act gave development a higher priority than traditional constitutional relations anchored to the Proclamation of 1763, for it removed exclusive tribal control over reserves for the sake of enfranchisement.

Second, it changed radically the intent of the British policy of civilization and in so doing further threatened the promises of 1763. From 1830 the goal of the Indian Department's effort, though not often articulated, had been the creation of civilized, Christianized, and self-governing native communities seated securely on reserves protected by the British imperial government.[11] The idea that these civilized communities would be amalgamated with the colony was never discussed, and the idea that individual Indians should become colonial citizens was rejected on the only occasion it was suggested[12] before the policy reformation in the late 1840's and the early 1850's. With the act of 1857 a wholly new course was charted. Thereafter, the goal, full civilization, would be marked by the disappearance of those communities as individuals were enfranchised and the reserves were eroded, twenty hectares by twenty hectares.

Third, the developmental strategy at the heart of the act and its constitutional implications created a political conflict — a crisis in the relationship between tribal leaders and local civilizers — which set the stage in the 1860's for more overt encroachment on native independence and for the consequent statutory destruction of tribal self-government. Immediately upon publication of the act, tribal councils recognized its intent and rejected it. Surely, one tribal leader noted accurately, it was an attempt "to break them to pieces."[13] It did not, he continued, "meet their views"[14] since it was inconsistent with their desire to maintain tribal integrity within customary forms most recently expressed by their insistence on group rather than individual tenure of reserve land. On their part, civilizers were coldly unsympathetic to these views. The head of the Indian Department, Civil Secretary R. J. Pennefather, replied to tribal objections with the curt phrase "the Civilization Act is no grievance to you."[15]

This frank exchange of views symbolizes the breakdown of the generally progressive partnership in development which had existed since the 1830's involving the agents of the department, missionaries, and tribal councils. It had been through the efforts of these men that the on-reserve infrastructure for development: housing, schools, mills, roads, barns, and so forth, had been realized, and through their efforts also that the body of Indians had participated in activities designed to achieve the goals of self-sufficiency on the basis of an agricultural economy. As recently as 1849-50 they had co-operated in the formation of two off-reserve boarding schools, manual labour schools teaching the arts and crafts of European life, which all concerned viewed as a marked improvement over ordinary on-reserve common schools.[16]

The 1860's were not marked by continued co-operation in improving developmental systems which were critical in producing candidates for enfranchisement. Accord was replaced by opposition; allies were now enemies. In the eyes of many chiefs, missionaries and officials of the Indian Department were no longer sympathetic purveyors of the benefits of civilization and staunch defenders of native rights but aggressive and disruptive agents of assimilation. Thus, they threw themselves into a campaign to maintain the pre-1857 status quo. Together they petitioned for the repeal of the act and protested the transfer in 1860 of the responsibility for conducting Indian affairs to the government of the United Canadas, which they dismissed as a government of land jobbers. They also announced in a general council that they would sell no more of their land and organized a lobby to lay their grievances before the Prince of Wales, who was then visiting the province.[17] Individual councils took varied action: some removed their children or financial support from schools; other refused to allow the annual band census or reserve surveys.[18]

A general Indian position emerged in the 1860's. Councils across the colony remained pro-development. They wanted education and agricultural and resource development but would not participate in a system designed, as an Oneida petition said, to "separate our people."[19] Civilization, which they might define as the revitalization of their traditional culture within an agricultural context, they would have; Assimilation, the total abandonment of their culture, they would not. The policy of civilization, particularly as it was now centered on enfranchisement, was destined to founder upon the rocks of tribal nationalism.

In terms of changing the traditional constitutional relationship between natives and Whites, it was the new attitude and policy recommendations of departmental agents and missionaries, not the position of the tribes, that were the most critical, for it was the advice of these men which formed the basis of the second substantial act of the period, that of 1869. Facing the failure of co-operation and yet loyal to the developmental logic of 1857, the need for individual landholding and enfranchisement, they placed their trust in a new strategy to remove all the difficulties. Officials and missionaries placed their trust in the coercive power of the law. For example, a missionary, the Rev. J. Musgrove, wanted a law to "make it obligatory upon parents to keep the child at the school until 20 years of age,"[20] and agent J. Gilkison prayed that the government would enact legislation giving the department extensive control over on-reserve activities, from the power to imprison

Indians for drunkenness to that of compelling them to cultivate the land.[21] In this fashion, it was imagined, the whole range of developmental systems could be made to operate effectively again.

To the department, the difficulty of central importance involved both the core of the old constitutional relationship, native self-government, and the heart of the new developmental logic, enfranchisement. Officials had had high hopes for enfranchisement. To them it was much more than a status change necessitated by off-reserve freehold tenure. It was itself an important inducement to individual development. Pennefather's predecessor, L. Oliphant, held that:

> the prospect of one day sharing upon equal terms in those rights and liberties which the whole community now enjoy would operate as the highest stimulant to exertion, which could be held out to young Indians.[22]

All were confident that many Indians would qualify easily and that many were "desirous even now of sharing the privileges and responsibilities which would attend their incorporation with the great mass of the community."[23] These assumptions proved unfounded. Between 1857 and 1876 only a handful of Indians came forward and only one application, that of Elias Hill, was accepted.[24] In fact, as early as 1863 one agent admitted that "the object for which the act was passed is not likely to be attained — for all practical purposes, it is a dead letter."[25]

The department's analysis of the failure of enfranchisement came quickly. The fault was directly attributable to Indian leaders, who had, after all, stated openly, as had the Six Nations' Council, that they were "wholly averse to their people taking the advantages offered"[26] by the act. The chiefs were pictured, perhaps quite accurately, as using the traditional authority of their office to dissuade their members from volunteering for enfranchisement.

This specific critique inspired a general missionary and agent campaign against traditional native government. It was, they claimed, the major block on the road to civilization, as it had prevented the prerequisites for progress: reserve subdivision and enfranchisement. It had frustrated the developmental logic of 1857. In addition, it was inefficient, its form cumbersome, and its members rarely qualified to make wise decisions on the proper use of tribal funds and valuable reserve resources.[27] The department's proposed solution to all these problems was again the coercive force of the law. "Petty chieftainships,"[28] it was recommended, should be abolished and a "Governor, and a sufficient number of magistrates and officers"[29] should be set over the tribes.

The department's argument can be stated succinctly. If the various systems of development were ever to produce the civilized Indian amenable to enfranchisement, then native self-government had to be abolished. It had to be shouldered aside and replaced by new institutions allowing unchallengeable departmental control.

That this argument was accepted by the newly created federal government is evidenced by the 1869 Act for the gradual enfranchisement of the Indians.[30] The Hon. H. Langevin, who piloted the bill through the House of Commons for Sir John A. Macdonald's government, noted in his introductory remarks that though the act also updated the enfranchisement provisions of 1857, its key provision was "in giving them [the Indians] the benefits of municipal government."[31] What was given was not only a municipal institution but that degree of departmental control over this new governmental system for which officials had lobbied throughout the 1860's.

The Act of 1869 allowed the election of chiefs and councillors by all male band members over the age of twenty-one. However, here all meaningful Indian participation ended, for the time, place, and manner of the election was to be determined by the superintendent general of Indian affairs, and, most critically, public officials served at Her Majesty's pleasure: they could be removed from office before the end of their term "by the governor for dishonesty, intemperance or immorality."[32] Apparently, the exact meaning of these terms and the applicability in specific cases would be left to the governor's advisers, departmental agents. Clearly, the problematic independent authority of the chiefs was to be circumscribed.

The intrusion of federal authority did not stop at the electoral system. The newly created "municipal" council was allotted by the act a specific and very restricted list of jurisdictional concerns. It could make by-laws for the care of public health, the observance of order and decorum at assemblies, the repression of intemperance and profligacy, the prevention of trespass by cattle, the maintenance of roads, bridges, ditches, and fences, the construction and maintenance of school and council houses, and, finally, for the establishment of pounds and the appointment of pound keepers. But having given with one hand, the act took back with the other. The council faced an all-encompassing federal power of disallowance, in that all the rules and regulations it made were "subject to confirmation by the Governor in Council."[33]

With the Act of 1869 federal control of on-reserve governmental systems became the essence of Canadian-Indian constitutional relations. In the Consolidated Indian Act of 1876 the political formula of 1869 was repeated, and its accompanying implication, that Indians would lose control of every aspect of their corporate existence, was spelled out in extensive and complex terms. Through its control of native government, the department could now institute all the systems of development it cherished. Under the Act of 1876 it could create, for example, individualized land holding, determine the use of resources, and create particular educational systems.[34] It now had the political and financial control to make enfranchisement a reality, or so at least the minister in 1869, Hector Langevin, predicted.[35]

Standing back from the complexity of the acts of 1869 and 1876, it can be seen clearly that Indian self-government had been abolished for the sake of the department's developmental strategy, and thus tribal nations entered a wholly new relationship with white authority in Canada. For Indians a unique and unenviable position in Confederation was reserved. For the original people there was to be no partnership, no degree of home rule to protect and encourage the development of a valued and variant culture, as was the case with French Canada. Not only were the Indians not a necessary element in the creation of Confederation as French Canadians were, but their cultural aspirations, their desire to create a new Indian culture on the reserves, was rejected. Responsible white authorities, politicians, departmental officials, and missionaries were convinced that their duty towards the Indian was, as Superintendent General David Laird declared in 1876 "to prepare him for a higher civilization by encouraging him to assume the privileges and responsibilities of full citizenship"[36] and that this could only be achieved through a system of wardship, colonization, and tutelage.

NOTES

1. See Chapters 1 and 5 in J. S. Milloy, "The Era of Civilization — British Policy for the Indians of Canada, 1830–1860" (D.Phil thesis, Oxford, 1978).
2. A Morris, *The Treaties of Canada with the Indians of Manitoba and the North-West Territories* (Toronto 1880), p. 226.
3. Ibid., p. 286.
4. Ibid., p. 287.
5. *Statutes of Canada*, 20 Vict., c. 26, 10 June 1857.
6. PAC, RG10, vol. 36, *Report on the Affairs of the Indians in Canada*, 20 March 1845.
7. PAC, RG10, vol. 209, Enoch Wood to Col. Bruce, 22 April 1854. Enoch Wood was the supervisor of Methodist Missions.
8. For tribal reaction to the subdivision request, see: PAC, RG10, vol. 195, T. G. Anderson to Col. Bruce, 29 March 1852.
9. *Statutes of Canada*, 20 Vict., c. 26, 10 June 1857.
10. See for example: Statutes of Canada 1850–51, 13 & 15 Vict., "an Act to provide more summary and effectual means for the protection of such Indians in the unmolested possession and enjoyment of the lands and other property in their use or occupation."
11. PRO, CO 43/27, no. 95, Sir George Murray to Sir James Kempt, 25 January 1830.
12. PRO, CO 42 349/88, Sir Francis Gore to Lord Castlereagh, 4 September 1809.
13. PAC, RG10, vol. 245, part 1, D. Thorburn to R. Pennefather, 13 October 1858.
14. Ibid.
15. PAC, RG10, vol. 519, R. J. Pennefather to Revd. A. Sickles, 11 November 1858.
16. These were the Mount Elgin Ojibway Industrial School at Muncey Town on the River Thames and the Alderville Industrial School. Tribal enthusiasm for this initiative is indicated by the fact that every council agreed to devote 25 per cent of its annuity to support the schools. See, for example, PAC, RG10, vol. 158, Chiefs, Warriors, etc. of the Tribes of Almwick, Rice, Mud and Scugog Indians to Cathcart.
17. Petitions for the repeal of the Act of 1857 can be found in PAC, RG10, vol. 245, Part 1, D.

Thorburn to R. J. Pennefather, 13 October 1858. In the same source one finds tribal objections to the Transfer Act drafted in 1858. Protests continued during the debate in the colonial legislature and when the transfer took effect. Information relative to the general council's position on future land sales is found in PAC, RG10, vol. 247, R. J. Pennefather to Sir E. Head, Draft Annual Report, 11 January 1859, and vol. 256, Bartlett to Pennefather, 25 September 1860, which contains information on the visit of the Prince of Wales.

18. Information on education is plentiful. See, for example, PAC, RG10, vol. 258, J. Musgrove Missionary to F. Talfourd, 2 April 1861. For protests against the census see, for example, PAC, RG10, vol. 258, Geo. Ironside Manitouaning to R. J. Pennefather, 8 March 1861, and in vol. 256, see, Bartlett to R. J. Pennefather, 19 November 1860. An example of the opposition to surveys appears in PAC, RG10, vol. 262, Part 2, Proceedings of a Council assembly at Manitouaning on the Great Manitoulin Island on Saturday the 5th of October 1861.

19. PAC, RG10, vol. 258, Part 2, Memorial to His Excellency Sir Edmund Walker Head from the Oneida Indians of Muncey Town and other Bands on the River Thames, 1858.

20. PAC, RG10, vol. 258, M. Musgrove to F. Talfourd, 2 April 1861.

21. PAC, RG10, vol. 288, J. Gilkison, Brantford, to W. Spragge, 30 September 1861.

22. PRO, CO 42/95, L. Oliphant to Lord Elgin, 3 November 1854.

23. Ibid.

24. PAC, RG10, col. 519, R. J. Pennefather to the provincial secretary, 31 March 1859.

25. PAC, RG10, vol. 287, J. Gilkison to the chief superintendent of Indian affairs, 4 March 1863.

26. PAC, RG10, vol. 242, D. Thorburn to R. J. Pennefather, 27 May 1858.

27. One of the earliest and most complete criticisms of native government is provided by the influential Methodist missionary and departmental adviser the Rev. T. Hurlburt, in PAC, RG10, vol. 239, Part 1, Rev. T. Hurlburt to R. J. Pennefather, 22 December 1857.

28. Ibid. Hurlburt's letter also brings forward the department's solution.

29. Ibid.

30. *Statutes of Canada*, 32–33 Vict., c.6, 22 June 1869.

31. *House of Commons Debates*, 2d session, 1st Parl., 32–33 Vict., vol. 2, p. 83.

32. *Statutes of Canada*, 32–33 Vict., c.6, 22 June 1869.

33. Ibid.

34. *Statutes of Canada*, Revised, the Act of 1876, vol. 1, 1886. See, for example, sections 69–74 on Indian finances, sections 75–76 on Indian government, and section 96 on liquor.

35. *House of Commons Debates*, 2d session, 1st Parl., 1869, pp. 83–85.

36. Annual Report, Department of Indian Affairs, 1876.

3

Indian Land Cessions in Upper Canada, 1815–1830

Robert J. Surtees

In the decade after the War of 1812, the Indians of Upper Canada experienced greatly increased pressure to give up further large sections of land to the Crown. Unfortunately for them, this came at a time when the Indians were themselves more vulnerable than ever. The combination of increased demand and concurrent Indian vulnerability was caused by two sets of decisions taken outside the colony. On the one hand, because of their concern for the defence system of Upper Canada, which had proven inadequate during the war, British officials altered immigration policy. The intent was to bring to Canada persons of British origin who would be more loyal than those who had previously come from the United States. This resulted in a greatly increased white population which, inherently, demanded new settlement lands. The Americans also adopted policies which affected the Indians of Upper Canada. By imposing a series of peace treaties and land cession agreements upon the tribes who occupied the border regions, the American government forced these tribes to remove themselves from the lands immediately adjacent to the Canadian frontier. Likewise, American relations with the United Kingdom included demands that the British cease cultivating the friendship of Indian tribes living within the confines of the United States. Although reluctant, the British did back down somewhat in the face of this American

Prepared for the Annual Meeting of the Canadian Historical Association, University of Ottawa, 4 June 1982.

pressure. Therefore, the Indians of Upper Canada very quickly found themselves cut off to a large extent from their American brethren and facing a rising white population in their own province. The full consequences of these two developments were seen in the seven major land cession agreements of that decade, which saw some 2.8 million hectares of Indian land pass to government control.[1]

The British decisions were made first. The inadequacies of the Upper Canadian defence system were obvious. Among the most glaring was the presence in Canada of American settlers who had entered the colony during and shortly after the Simcoe years and whose record of loyalty was extremely weak. Their location on the long Canadian-American frontier made their presence all the more serious. During the war, many had openly joined the invading American forces, and others had either remained passively neutral or had tended to sympathize with their former countrymen. Those who had not only extended their loyalty to Britain, but who had also fought alongside the British and the Canadians did not impress as much as those who were openly or quietly treasonous. Thus, Americans living in Canada were suspect. It was by no means certain that the War of 1812 would be the last conflict between Britain and the United States, and the colonial secretary, Lord Bathurst, wished to prevent the aliens in Canada from placing Canada in jeopardy simply by their presence. Accordingly, he issued orders that Americans were not to receive grants of land[2] in Upper Canada, and they were, as far as possible, to be prevented even from entering the province.[3] It had the desired effect, for the influx of Americans came to a halt.[4]

But stopping American immigration accomplished only half the job. Bathurst also wanted to bring loyal subjects from the United Kingdom to strategic areas of the province in order to shore up the Upper Canada defences. To this end, soldiers who were serving in Canada during the war were granted land for their use. Upon demobilization, some British regulars were placed on land in Glengarry County, on the Rideau River, and at the head of the Bay of Quinte.[5] This region was one of prime concern, for all observers noted that if the link between the two provinces along the St. Lawrence River were ever broken by the Americans, Upper Canada would be defenceless.[6]

To bring newcomers from the United Kingdom to Canada required planning, and a variety of schemes were broached. Among them was a plan, conceived as early as November 1813 and set into operation in 1815,[7] which called for the transportation of 4,000 emigrants, mainly from Scotland and Ireland, to Canada when peace was secured. In the end, only 699 made the trip.[8] Other plans called for the creation of military settlements in the eastern end of the province. The town of Perth grew from the desire to plant settlers along the route of the proposed Rideau Canal. Other proposals saw the beginnings of the Lanark and Peterborough settlements, and farther west, in the township of London, a second Talbot settlement was begun by Richard Talbot, a relative of Colonel Thomas Talbot.[9]

The population growth was not very rapid in the beginning. A. R. M. Lower recorded that in 1816, 1,250 immigrants came to Canada; in 1817, 6,800 arrived; in 1818, 8,400; and in 1819 there were 12,800.[10] These figures, while small, did constitute a substantial increase in Upper Canada's population; but more significant is the fact that large numbers were expected and preparations had to be made to accommodate them. Apart from the arrangements that had to be made with respect to transportation and the various types of assistance that might be offered to prospective immigrants, there was the more important matter of lands upon which to locate them. None was available.

Thomas Ridout, the surveyor-general of Upper Canada, reported to Sir Gordon Drummond, the administrator of Upper Canada, that apart from the crown reserves, the lands of the Eastern, Johnstown, and Midland Districts were nearly all located, and those in the London District had been placed under the exclusive supervision of Colonel Thomas Talbot.[11] His suggestion that lands be acquired by buying more land from the Indians on the St. Clair River or in the Lake Simcoe region was not at first welcome.[12] Such purchases would not provide lands where they were wanted, on the exposed American frontier, and the government was unable to find suitable locations in the desired regions. Also, conflicts between the lieutenant-governor of Upper Canada, Francis Gore, and Sir Gordon Drummond prevented the two principal executives from co-operating to solve the problem. Thus, government looked to the Indians and their lands for a way to provide for the military settlements and for the expected immigration.

The Indians of Upper Canada had emerged from the War of 1812 much weakened. This was not from heavy losses in manpower as a result of the fighting, although they had certainly suffered both casualties and the destruction of property, especially in the western end of the province.[13] Rather their general position, in terms of numbers and geographic location, had been altered to their detriment. By 1812, their total numbers amounted only to about 10 per cent of the population of the province. While still a substantial minority, they were at that time a greatly reduced proportion when compared to their stature in 1784 or even 1800.

More significant was the situation of the Indians in the United States. Britain had, since 1783, cultivated her ties with the Western Confederacy in the American Old Northwest. This policy had paid rich dividends during the War of 1812. Indian resistance had been largely responsible for British successes at Detroit and elsewhere on the western frontier in 1812; and it had kept the American left flank occupied through most of 1813. Even after Tecumseh's defeat and death at the Battle of the Thames in October of 1813, the American armies in the west did not advance *en masse* beyond Amherstburg during 1814 because they were wary of the Indian threat. Much of the deference paid to the Indians in Upper Canada by the British and by settlers was based on the connections between them and the Western Confederacy centred in the Ohio country.

The War of 1812 shattered the confederacy. The principal chief, Tecumseh, was dead, and after the war his brother, the Prophet, wandered aimlessly without any following of consequence. Throughout 1815, the Americans imposed a series of peace treaties on the several tribes of the Ohio country. And subsequent to the Treaty of Ghent, the United States also secured from the western Indians a number of substantial land cessions. These cessions brought the border lands into the hands of the American government, thereby opening the Canadian-American frontier to American settlement. The effect was not lost on the Indians of western Upper Canada. In 1818 John Norton, a half-breed[14] chief of the Six Nations on the Grand River, observed that the American policy of Indian removal in the Old Northwest would mean that "they [the American Indians] will in a few years be completely separated from us by an extensive population which it [the American Government] will not fail to introduce into that quarter, now that it has entirely extinguished the Native right to that country."[15]

The American government pushed its advantage even further by objecting to Britain's continued efforts to retain friends among the American Indians. Britain's principal method was distributing annual presents to visiting Indians who attended British posts for the annual bounty. Protests from American authorities regarding this practice were longstanding, but after the War of 1812, they became more vehement and more insistent. Because the Indians had been forced, for the most part, out of the borderlands, by continuing to issue the gifts, the British were affecting Indians well within the American border. The most serious complaints came from Michilimackinac concerning the Indians on the Mississippi who travelled to visit the British post at Drummond Island. Although the practice was not halted, the British did relent by sending orders to the commander at Drummond Island to discourage such visits. This marked a difference in style, for previously the act of dispensing gifts had been pursued vigorously and aggressively. The same change occurred at Amherstburg. By 1820 this custom had become merely one of form.[16]

Thus, when representatives of the Crown approached the various tribes of Upper Canada with respect to selling their lands in the years immediately following the War of 1812, the Indians found themselves in a greatly weakened bargaining position. They had declined in numbers in relative terms, and because they were being separated from their American brethren, they were losing a major aspect of their importance in the eyes of British commanders. Moreover, events had conspired to divide them within the province itself for the several separate tribes, and groups within tribes, had grown farther apart since the days when Joseph Brant had attempted to forge an alliance, or at least a closer association, between his followers on the Grand River and the Mississaugas.[17] In part this division was promoted by the British officials, who always tried to keep the Indians divided in order to make each group dependent upon the king. Administrative methods such as a careful use of interpreters, the location of the distribution of gifts, or the assignments of Indian agents were the usual methods adopted to promote that division.

The events of the war had also contributed to the divisions. Rivalries within the Indian Department during the conflict caused specific bands to attach themselves to individual agents. Thus, the quarrel between John Norton and William Claus resulted in the Chippewas and Munseys of the Thames, who followed Norton during the war, being separated from the other tribes — the Ottawas, Wyandots, and Chippewas — of the St. Clair River region who were attached to Claus. This particular rivalry extended beyond the war years and was accompanied by charges of discrimination in the distribution of gifts in 1816–18. Likewise, the Thames River Chippewas apparently resented other bands who had not suffered as many casualties or damages and who were yet being treated as well or better than they in terms of annual presents.[18] Some of these hard feelings can be attributed to the presence of Norton, who appears to have revelled in such quarrels, but regardless of the source, the discord cannot be denied. Even among close neighbours some ruptures were evident. For example, the Wyandots of Amherstburg felt it necessary on one occasion to suggest that they be granted a patent for the Huron Reserve because they feared that the Potowatomies and Chippewas who shared the tract might sell it without their assent.[19] The animosity between the Iroquois of the Grand River and the Bay of Quinte had grown stronger in the years since 1784;[20] and generally the Mississaugas of the eastern end of the province acted independently of their cousins in the western regions. Also, since the Toronto Purchase of 1806, there had developed a tendency for the Chippewas of the Lake Simcoe region to direct their attention to their own areas, thereby separating themselves from their traditional relations with the Rice Lake Mississaugas. These latter divisions were apparent during the War of 1812 since the several bands acted quite independently of each other. No doubt this tendency towards semi-independent enclaves was promoted by the gradual growth of white settlement, which had deleterious effects on the hunting areas, and which tended to encroach on Indian reserved lands and fishing locations in the more settled areas along the lake frontage. This had the effect of encouraging the separate Indian groups to transfer their activities towards the unsettled interior regions. Such redirection tended to draw them away from the traditional meeting points along the shores of Lake Ontario or within the river valleys and to diffuse them over a wider area. This diffusion enhanced the divisions.

These considerations serve to explain much of the ease with which the land surrenders of 1815–25 were made. Another factor was the decision by the British to change the method of paying for the land when it was purchased. Always mindful of costs, the Lords of the Treasury expected that from 1818 on the expenses connected with land purchases from the Indians would be covered by the province of Upper Canada. To provide this revenue, Lieutenant-Governor Maitland proposed to sell a portion of the Indian lands at public auction. Purchasers would be required to pay 10 per cent as a downpayment and carry a mortgage for the balance. However, as long as they paid the annual interest, the principal would not be required. The annual income from interest would then be used to make an annual payment,[21] in perpetuity, to the Indians who sold their land. Therefore, it was in an effort to save money that the British adopted a system of annuities rather than the former method of making a single, one-time payment. The Treasury approved the plan,[22] and although it did not function as neatly as Maitland had envisaged, the system was retained, and Canada's Indians soon grew accustomed to receiving their annual "treaty money." The scheme had an added advantage in that persons who negotiated future land surrenders could advise the Indians involved that by selling their lands they would receive a continuous annual income. It was an enticement that was used extensively in the negotiations of 1817, 1818, and 1819.

However, the first land surrenders of the postwar era were handled under the old rules calling for a single, one-time payment; in fact, they were agreements that had been tentatively reached before the war broke out. These involved a major tract of land, some 100,000 hectares, between Lake Simcoe and Notawasaga Bay on Lake Huron and a much smaller piece of land, some 171 hectares, in Thurlow township on the Bay of Quinte. Both had been arranged in 1811, on Lieutenant-Governor Gore's orders, but they had been delayed because the war intervened.

Gore's primary interest in the Lake Simcoe region apparently was the fur trade.[23] Leading partners in the North West Company represented to the governor and the executive council of Upper Canada that they suffered considerable hardships in conducting their trade along the Great Lakes frontier because of interference by American customs officials. The interference began after the transfer of the western posts, especially Detroit and Michilimackinac, to the United States in 1796. Gore cited in particular the seizure in 1808 by an American revenue officer of "several boats richly laden with goods for the Indian Country."[24] As a result of such "vexatious interference,"[25] members of the firm of McTavish, McGillivray, and Company sent a memorial to the lieutenant-governor that the government should open a route to the western Indian Country farther from the American border.[26] A route via the Toronto Carrying Place, Lake Simcoe, and Penetanguishene Bay, it was felt, would provide security from the American customs and also shorten the route considerably. However, it would also require that a road be built between Lake Simcoe and Penetanguishene, a distance of forty-five kilometres;[27] and that would require purchasing the territory from the Indians of the region. Gore added that the Lake Huron terminus of the proposed road also afforded an excellent harbour, and one which would be safer and more convenient than Amherstburg [28] should a war break out with the United States. He concluded his remarks by noting that the land itself was very suitable for settlement and would, he predicted, show a profit of £2,500[29] over what would have to be paid to the Indians.

Ancillary or circumstantial evidence would suggest that Gore was more interested in settlement, or perhaps military concerns, than his retrospective letter of

1812 would suggest. For example, the memorial of McGillivray et al. reads, "Your Memorialists have been given to understand that it is the contemplation of your Excellency to open a Road and Establishment from Kempenfelt Bay to Penetanguishene Bay,"[30] a statement which would suggest that the North West Company did not provide the first impetus to the scheme as Gore suggested.

Regardless of the exact motivation, Gore sent William Claus, the deputy superintendent general of Indian affairs, to meet with the Chippewas of Lake Simcoe and Matchedash Bay. The council was held on 8–9 June 1811[31] at Gwillembury. Claus advised the Chippewa chiefs that the government wished to purchase the land in question in order to provide for the rapidly growing numbers of settlers and also to build a road through the tract which would provide a safer passage to "his Western children."[32] Also, he said, the king wished to build a town in Penetanguishene Bay and requested that the Indians refrain from removing the surveyors' stakes which would mark out each lot.[33]

In response, Chief Yellowhead observed that the chief agreed to sell the land in return for the £4,000 offered, but he added several requests. Significantly, he desired that the king send a blacksmith to make spears and hoes; he asked that he be permitted to occupy his garden grounds in Penetanguishene Bay until the settlers arrived; he asked also that provisions be sent in the summer to help while the corn ripened; and he also requested that the annual presents be sent out earlier in order to facilitate moving to winter hunting grounds while the weather was not too cold. Claus agreed to the occupation of the garden at Penetanguishene; he promised to ask the lieutenant-governor about the summer supplies; and he promised to give orders that the presents be sent out "in good season"; but he made no reference to a blacksmith.

Although Gore left the colony in October of 1811, the provisional agreement of 8–9 June 1811[34] was fully supported by his successor, Sir Isaac Brock, who strongly recommended its approval[35] and sent the appropriate requisitions for payment in goods.[36] The requisition was approved by the Lords of the Treasury[37] and the goods shipped.[38] The same shipment contained provisions, also approved by the Treasury,[39] to pay for the 171 hectares of Mississauga land in Thurlow township.

That parcel was desired by government in order to build grist mills to serve "a populous neighbourhood"[40] near the mouth of the Moira River. The appropriate council was convened by James Givens, Indian agent for York, on 24–25 July at Smith's Creek (Port Hope).[41] Givens gave no reason for buying the land other than to say that the king wanted it; he added that he expected the Mississaugas, who had often spoken of their love for the king, would cheerfully "comply with his request."[42] As Claus had done at Gwillenbury, Givens distributed rations, termed "your Great Father's Bread and milk,"[43] and some ammunition to the Mississaugas while they deliberated upon the request. Through their spokesman, Indiun-way-way, the Mississaugas agreed to sell the land for £107 worth of goods and apparently signed the provisional agreement calling for the surrender of "lots number four in the first and second concession in the Township of Thurlow."[44] Indiun-way-way also took the opportunity provided by the council to register formally certain concerns that the Mississaugas felt regarding the white settlers who were increasingly pressing against Indian land.

He complained of white people moving onto the islands around the Moira River in the Bay of Quinte. They were doing so, he said, without permission from the chiefs, but claiming that they did so "by order of the Governor at York." He declared that the Mississaugas wished to reserve those islands for their cornfields, and he asked for "a writing to show these people that they may be sent off."[45] He also complained of white men who were cutting timber, without consent, "on the borders of the Rice Lakes, and on each side of the Road leading from Smith's Creek to the Rice Lake"[46] and floating it into the Bay of Quinte. One man in particular, Mr. William Williams, had actually settled on the "Carrying Place from Smith's Creek to the Rice Lake"[47] and was also cutting timber without permission from the Indians.

The chief concluded his remarks by asking that the goods which would serve as payment for the land should include axes, hoes, and spears; and, like Chief Yellowhead at Lake Simcoe, he also requested a blacksmith to repair and to make these items.[48] Givens could make no specific guarantees. He limited himself to saying that he would relay the message to the governor, through the lieutenant-governor, and added that he had no doubt that they would "receive a favourable answer as it is their particular care to do every justice to all their Indian Children."[49]

When the goods intended to complete these purchases arrived in Canada in the summer of 1812, the war had begun. And because of a scarcity of supplies in the general store at Lachine, these goods were applied to the general purposes of the Indian department.[50] However, the lands were no less coveted, for the war underlined the importance of establishing a naval station at Penetanguishene[51] and building a road[52] through the lands of the projected purchase. Both of these were begun during the conflict.[53] To soothe the Chippewas of the region, Claus advised that the goods would be coming to complete the payment and that, although the road was being built, the Indians should continue to consider the land as theirs. He asked them to permit the road to be completed on the promise that the full payment would be received.[54]

Claus transmitted the appropriate requisitions in February 1815,[55] and Francis Gore, who returned to Canada in September, issued instructions that the necessary steps be taken to complete the purchases he had arranged four years earlier.[56] On 18 November 1815, Claus, and others appointed by Gore, met the Chippewas of Lake Simcoe near Kempenfeld Bay of Lake Simcoe. The goods were delivered, the final deed signed, and the land officially transferred.[57] Hoes and spears were included in the list of goods, but again, no mention was made of a blacksmith.

The Thurlow land purchase was completed in August 1816 when James Givens led a delegation to meet the Mississaugas led by Indiun-way-way and other chiefs from the Rice Lake region.[58] Here, too, the goods included hoes and spears, but no mention was made of a blacksmith, or of the complaints of the Mississaugas regarding the islands at the mouth of the Moira, or of the habit of Whites cutting timber on Indian land.

Securing the lands involved in the Lake Simcoe area and in Thurlow was perfectly compatible with the postwar concerns of the British towards Upper Canada. Because these agreements had already been negotiated in 1811 it was a relatively simple procedure to complete them in 1815 and 1816. The desire to provide for the future military security of the province by settling loyal persons in substantial numbers and by building new military establishments at strategic locations meant that further Indian lands were needed. These, in turn, required that new, formal agreements be made. Because of the weakened Indian position in the postwar years, such agreements were obtained easily and quickly. However, the terms of these agreements, and the discussions which preceded them, suggest that the Indians involved were beginning to learn the true nature and meaning of land sales, for they asked pertinent questions and insisted on the inclusion of some specific conditions.

The eastern region of the province was the area of most pressing concern for the government. New immigrants began to arrive for the projected military settlements in 1815, and newcomers arrived yearly. A complicated series of circumstances caused them to be settled in what may be termed the back line of settlement.[59] The absence of available land close to the international border meant that more distant regions had to be used. Also, the importance of having alternate lines of communication through the province had led several officers and officials to note the value of the Rideau waterway system between the St. Lawrence and the Ottawa Rivers and of the Trent River-Kawartha Lakes system between the Bay of Quinte and Lake Simcoe.[60] Likewise, the Toronto Carrying Place route between York and Georgian Bay, already considered important, was stressed again as a valuable alternative route into the western country.

At first it was intended only to use four or five townships to the rear of the townships of Crosby, Burgess, Elmsby, Montague, and Marlborough.[61] William Claus sent John Ferguson, the resident agent at Kingston, to advise the Mississaugas that the government intended to survey the area and to build establishments there. He was to advise them also that the government intended to pay for the land, but because that would take some time, he should also request the Indians to refrain from interfering with surveyors or work crews who might enter the area.[62] In his report on this mission, Ferguson noted several significant points.

First, the Mississauga chiefs agreed fairly readily to desist from obstructing the work in the territory. They also told Ferguson that the land in question was the exclusive domain of the Mississaugas, for "the claims of the Nipissings and

Algonquins do not cross the Ottawa River." The chiefs were less certain "whether the lands were purchased formerly" but were of the opinion that they had not been. However, they were willing to sell them in the event that no previous sale had occurred. Ferguson concluded by observing that his recollections of the Crawford purchase of 1783-84 and Sir John Johnson's purchase of 1787 had included all the land between the St. Lawrence River and the Ottawa River, but he, too, indicated some uncertainty.[63]

Gore attempted to investigate the possibility that the lands had, in fact, been purchased.[64] The decision to acquire a larger area, including lands behind Rice Lake where Peterborough was founded, brought the Rice Lake Mississaugas into the negotiations, and this group was less uncertain than their Mississauga brethren living in the area of the Rideau River. The Rice Lake region was considered valuable also in order to open an inland water communication to Lake Simcoe.[65] As a result, rather than press the issue, the government of Upper Canada decided to pay for the lands required, no doubt as the easiest administrative avenue around the problem, and the plan received approval from the Lords of the Treasury.[66] However, to save money the land would be paid for through perpetual annual payments rather than a single large payment.[67] Two large land surrender agreements resulted from this decision, and both took place almost three years after establishments had been begun in the areas concerned.

On 5 November 1818, William Claus convened a council at Smith's Creek with the Mississaugas of the Rice Lake region.[68] That these chiefs had insisted that no previous surrender existed was clear from Claus's opening remarks.

> Children. . . . My errand is, to put at rest the doubts with respect to the lands in the back parts of this Country which you seem to think were never disposed of to the King, and hope that hereafter none of your young men will be so idle as to remove the Posts or marks which will be put up by the King's Surveyors.[69]

He then produced a sketch of the area and asked the chiefs to show him the bounds of the previous surrender and also to note the area desired by the government at this point.

Claus told the chiefs that the king was buying lands in order to provide for the settlement of "his children." And then he introduced the new method of payment, and stressed its advantage by saying the king "does not mean to do as formerly to pay you at once, but as long as any of you remain on the Earth to give you Cloathing in payment every year, besides the presents he now gives you."[70] Buckquaquet, the principal chief, replied to Claus's offer. His response revealed clearly the vulnerable position of the Rice Lake Mississaugas.

> Father: You see me here, I am to be pitied, I have no old men to instruct me. I

am the Head Chief, but a young man. You must pity me, all the old people have gone to the other world. My hands are naked, I cannot speak as our Ancestors were used to.

Father: If I was to refuse what our Father has requested, our Women and Children would be more to be pitied. From our lands we receive scarcely anything and if your words are true we will get more by parting with them, than by keeping them — our hunting is destroyed and we must throw ourselves on the compassion of our Great Father the King.

Father: Our young People & Chief have always thought of not refusing our Father any request he makes to us, and therefore do what he wishes.

Father: If it was not for our Brethren the farmers about the Country we should near starve for our hunting is destroyed.[71]

Buckquaquet also expressed the hope that his people would be allowed to continue hunting and fishing where they could still find fish and game and that the settlers, when they came, would not mistreat the Indians.[72] Finally, he asked that the islands be reserved to the Indians for purposes of farming. Claus declared that the rivers and forests were open to all and that the Mississaugas had an equal right to them. He made no promise regarding the islands, but he did say that he was sure the governor would accede to that wish.[73]

The written agreement did not mention either the islands or the right to continue hunting and fishing.[74] It was restricted to naming the annuity of £740 per year[75] and to describing the tract north of Rice Lake, estimated to contain 780,400 hectares of land.[76] The method of paying the annuity was clarified to say that each man, woman, and child would received $10 yearly.[77]

Late in the following spring the agent, John Ferguson, was delegated to treat for the tract of land behind Tweed and Perth. At a council held on 31 May 1819,[78] Ferguson met with the 257 Mississaugas of the Bay of Quinte region (159) and the Kingston area (98) who claimed the area of the intended purchase. The enormous tract involved, known as the Rideau Purchase,[79] contained 1,099,200 hectares, which the Mississaugas agreed to sell for an annuity of £642.10.[80] It was stipulated that this sum would be distributed at the rate of 50 shillings per person. This provisional agreement was approved by the Treasury, but because of delays in making some of the annuity payments, a confirmatory surrender did not follow until 26 April 1825.[81] At that time the per capita annuity was designated as £2.10. Apparently, the changes inherent in designating a per capita payment rather than a lump sum had been noted, for this final agreement carried the provision that the number of persons receiving the payment must not be greater than 257,[82] that being the number claiming the land at the time of the original agreement.

By acquiring the area of the Rideau and Rice Lake purchases the government of Upper Canada provided itself with lands to accommodate new settlers from the

United Kingdom and also secured two of the three inland communication systems which were considered desirable for military purposes. The third was secured by two surrenders in 1818 from the Chippewas of Lake Simcoe and the Mississaugas of the Credit River. Each required little effort.

Purchases in 1785, 1798, and 1815 had already provided the government with the bulk of the lands lying between Lake Simcoe and Lake Huron (Georgian Bay). In 1816–17 it was considered necessary only to acquire the portion of the portage route between Kempenfelt Bay and Nottawasaga Bay which still remained in Indian country. The problem with restricting a new purchase to that small area, according to William Claus, who received word of it on 15 March 1817,[83] was that the Nottawasaga River would still remain largely in possession of the Chippewas. The Nottawasaga River was an important line of communication. To secure it, Claus suggested buying either all of the land from 3.2 kilometres west of that river or a piece of territory enclosed by a line running from the western corner of King township to the deepest point of Nottawasaga Bay.[84] He also expressed the opinion that the Chippewas would readily accede to the surrender of their territory.

Perhaps it was this first consideration which determined the government's decision to request an even greater tract. When William Claus met the assembled Chippewas in council on 17 October 1818 at the house of Nathaniel Gamble near the Holland River,[85] he asked them to sell 636,800 hectares of their land to the westward and southward of Lake Simcoe.[86] It was an enormous tract which included the shoreline of Lake Huron between Wasaga and Vail Point and contained more than three times the area of Claus's second option to Gore. In setting forth the proposition, Claus observed that while the ultimate intention was to settle the region, it would be "many years after both of us and most of your people will have left the world before any settlement" would "come near to your villages."[87] At present the land lay idle, he said, and the Chippewas received no benefit from it. But by selling it to the king, they could continue to use it as they always had and still receive yearly clothing, in addition to the normal presents which the king distributed each year. "Consider," he said, "whether it is not better to get some covering for yourselves, your wives and children than letting it lay idle."[88]

Chief Yellowhead, who had led the delegation of Chippewa chiefs at the 1815 surrender, replied that they could "not withhold a compliance with the subject of your request."[89] For that compliance the government agreed to pay an annuity of £1,200 in goods.[90] No mention was included of a method for distributing the annual payment. Presumably, that task would be the responsibility of the chiefs. The refinement of a per capita designation would come in agreements of 1819. Yellowhead did not mention hunting or fishing. However, he did ask that a doctor might be encouraged to live in the area and to tend to the medical needs of his people.[91] Claus replied that his words would "be faithfully communicated" to the governor, "who I have no doubt will attend your wishes."[92] This consideration also escaped mention in the formal agreement for the land surrender. Inasmuch as doctors were subsequently stationed at the Penetanguishene naval base and later were attached to the Indian establishment at Coldwater, this provision can be said to have been honoured.

After Claus had arranged for the sale of 17 October 1818, he turned his attention towards acquiring the lands which lay directly to the southward. This consisted of 259,200 hectares extending to the purchase line of 5 September 1806.[93] The region was recognized as the domain of the Credit River Mississaugas who had, in an 1806 agreement, retained three small pieces of land for their exclusive use at the mouths of the Credit River,[94] Sixteen Mile Creek,[95] and Twelve Mile Creek.[96] This band had found itself under steady pressure from white settlers because of their location between the provincial capital of York and the Niagara River frontier. Despite proclamations to the contrary and despite efforts by the Indian Department officials, the Credit River Band suffered encroachments on its lands and fisheries; and it also found itself the victim of such evils as liquor and disease. In addition, the advancing settlement had, as usual, served to drive the game from the Mississauga hunting areas.[97] The beleaguered band declined drastically in both numbers and self confidence, and it was, as a result, in an extremely weakened position by the time the War of 1812 ended.[98]

This weakened state was evident when William Claus met them at a council at the Credit River on 27, 28, and 29 October 1818.[99] After adhering to the customary greetings, Claus remarked that the band appeared to him to be "thin and miserable" and deriving no benefit from their land, which was "lying dead." To help them, the king proposed buying that useless land from them and giving them "Goods yearly to cover" their "Women and Children" in addition to the regular annual presents.[100] The response to this proposal was delivered the following day by Ajetance, who had been elected chief of the Credit River band in 1810.[101] Ajetance agreed to surrender the land as Claus requested and asked only that his band be allowed to retain their land at the mouth of the Credit River, adding that "it is but small and we will not have it long; it is all we have to live upon."[102] By this agreement, the Mississaugas of the Credit were to receive goods to the value of £522.10 annually.[103] They also retained their three reserves.

One scholar has interpreted Ajetance's sad words as an indication that the Mississaugas believed "that they would soon disappear."[104] The proceedings of the council, including Claus's response, could well have that meaning. However, it could also have meant that they expected yet another assault on their remaining land. If so, they were prophetic words. The three reserves occupied strategic locations which were desired for roads, mill-sites, and harbours.[105] Accordingly, Claus held councils with the Mississaugas in June 1819 to prepare for further cessions, and on 18 February 1820[106] he concluded an agreement which claimed all of the Mississauga reserve lands, except for 80 hectares on the Credit River which were retained. Upon this small parcel was to be built a village for the use of the Indians; and presumably it would be at that village that the money emanating from the proceeds of the sale of the reserves would be used to "make provision for the maintenance and religious instruction of the people of the Mississauga Nation of Indians and their posterity."[107] These agreements with the Mississaugas of the Credit River secured virtually all of the lands of the Home District for the government of Upper Canada.

In the western portion of the province, the need for land was not quite as urgent. However, there was a desire to settle loyal subjects in an area where loyalty had been tested during the war and often found wanting. This was especially the case along the Thames River between London and Chatham, an area which was being developed, but which had not yet been purchased from the Indians.

The first approach was made by John Askin, the superintendent of Indian affairs at Amherstburg. Acting on instructions from Lieutenant-Governor Maitland, through William Claus, on 16 October 1818, Askin met the chiefs of the Chippewa bands of the Chenail Ecarte, the St. Clair River, Bear Creek, the Sable River, and the Thames River.[108] He advised them that the king wished to purchase all of their lands on the Thames River and on Lake Huron just north of the Sable River and extending inland as far as the Grand River tract[109] and asked the chiefs "to state on what terms they would dispose of the said Tract."[110]

After deliberating on the question, Chief Chawne replied for the assembled chiefs. They agreed to sell the land and left it to the king's representative, Maitland, to assess its value with payment to be made annually for fifty years. This payment, they said, was to be above and beyond the annual presents; furthermore, part of the new annuity was to be used to furnish them with a blacksmith and a husbandman[111] who were to be stationed near their reserves. The blacksmith they expected to service their axes, traps, and guns; the husbandman would be expected to instruct them "in the art of Husbandry."[112] These reserves, they stipulated, should be located:

1st.   Four miles square at some instance below the Rapids of the river St. Clair.
2nd.   One mile in front by four deep bordering on the said river and adjoining to the Shawanoe Reserve (Sombra Township).
3rd.   Six miles at Kettle Point, Lake Huron.
4th.   two miles Square at the River au Sable.
5th.   two miles square at Bear's Creek, also a reserve for Tomico and his band up the Thames which he will point out when he arrives.[113]

They added that they expected that reserves would be enlarged at the time the final agreement would be made if the king's representative felt that they were too small.

As a result of Askin's exploratory mission, it was decided to seek this enormous area by two separate agreements.[114] Of greater interest to government was the section known as the Long Woods, extending on the north bank of the Thames River between the Delaware Village in London Township and the Moravian Village in Orford Township. The Chippewa owners were invited, independently of their brethren of the Chenail, St. Clair, and Ausable rivers, to meet Askin in February of 1819.[115] It was unusual to convene a council at that time of year, for most bands dispersed to small camps during the winter. Therefore, it was with some difficulty that Askin managed to gather them for a council held on 9 March in Malden Township.

In the provisional agreement that grew out of that council, the chiefs of the Chippewas agreed to sell the prescribed tract of land estimated at 220,876 hectares for an annuity of £600, half of which was paid in specie and the other half in goods.[116] The agreement also called for two areas of reserved land for the Chippewas. About 6,144 hectares were reserved on "the northerly shore of the Thames River, nearby opposite the Township of Southwold."[117] This, it would seem, was the reserve called for the previous fall for Chief Tomico. A second reserve was described as "two miles square distant about four miles above the rapids near the source of Big Bear Creek where the Indians have their improvements."[118] Both reserves were shown on the sketch of the proposed purchase sent to Askin before the agreement was made.[119]

At the end of March, the Chippewas of the Chenail Ecarte, Ausable River, and the St. Clair River, having been sent for some weeks earlier, met Askin at Amherstburg to discuss the sale of the remainder of the lands desired by government. Known as the Huron Tract and containing some 1,102,784 hectares of land, this area was sold by its owners for an annuity of £1,375, half to be paid in specie and half in goods.[120] The reserved areas called for in October were duly made by this agreement of 30 March 1819 and shown on the sketch of the proposed surrender.

However, neither of these two agreements stood up, for objections were raised regarding the proposal to make payment in cash.[121] As a result, new agreements had to be made and the Indians had to agree to the proposed alterations. This was done, but it was accomplished with some difficulty, [122] and it required several years to complete the purchase agreements. Some interesting alterations occurred in the process. The Long Woods annuity was altered to provide a per capita payment of £2.10, to a limit of 240 persons, that being the number of persons who claimed and inhabited the area at the time of the original surrender.[123] This alteration is easy to understand in view of the arrangements which had been made for the Rideau Tract and the Rice Lake (or Adjutant) Surrenders. More difficult to comprehend is the omission of any mention of the two areas reserved in the original agreement.[124] More difficult still is the fact that the reserve set aside for the Chippewas in Caradoc township continued to be recognized as Indian land (indeed a portion of it remains today), while the reserve on Bear Creek seems never to have been established.

The Huron Tract took longer to settle. At first the delay was occasioned because Maitland saw no urgency for pushing its conclusion, since so much other land had become available to the government.[125] After John Galt's scheme to form the Canada Company began to take shape the question of the Huron Tract became more urgent, since the 400,000 hectares[126] to be given to the company were to come from the Indian territory. Finally, on 25 April 1825 a second agreement was made with the Chippewas of the Chenail Ecarte, the St. Clair River, and the Ausable River. It provided for the four reserves called for in 1818 and 1819 below the St. Clair River rapids, at Sombra Township, at Kettle Point, and at the Ausable River.[127] These totalled 9,222 hectares, which was no more nor less than called for at the 1818 council. For this, the several bands were to receive an annuity of £1,100, to be divided equally among the 460 persons said to inhabit the tract in 1825.[128] This sum was £275 less than the 1819 provisional agreement, and the 1825 agreement also provided that, should the total population decline by half, the annuity would be reduced by the same amount. And it would continue to be reduced in like amounts if the population decline continued.[129] There was no mention of a schedule to increase the annuity in the event of an increase. Clearly, no one expected that to happen. A final point in connection with these Indian lands in the Western and London Districts is that the tract of land known as Walpole Island was not included in any of the land cessions of 1790, 1796, 1819, 1822, or 1825.[130] It remained Indian land.

The first postwar decade witnessed seven major land cession agreements made by the Indians of Upper Canada. These agreements, and others for smaller parcels of land, were somewhat different than those made in the prewar years, in that the principal method of payment changed to the annuity system, and also in that the Indians began to request some specific conditions for the sale of their lands. Reserved areas had been arranged before, in 1806, but requests for blacksmiths, husbandmen, and doctors were new. Also the rights to continue hunting and fishing were discussed, apparently for the first time.

If there was a predominant characteristic common to all of the postwar land sales it was the ease with which the government was able to conclude the arrangements. The meetings were brief; the demands were minimal; and the government agents appear to have anticipated no trouble as they prepared for the formal surrender councils. And they received none. The picture one receives from these arrangements is one of a demoralized, even docile, race of people submitting to the will of government. The land cessions, taken so easily, without any form — or fear — of substantial resistance, add a dimension to the story of the advent of a reserve policy in Upper Canada.

It has been noted, most recently in a doctoral thesis by John S. Milloy, that the 1820's were the decisive decade in the administrative history of Indian affairs. In that time, a number of plans for the amelioration of the Indians were set forth; several were actually begun; and in 1830 a programme to promote the civilization and Christianization of the Indians was officially adopted. All schemes, whether promoted by Methodists, Catholics, the New England Society, The Society for the Propagation of the Gospel, or the government, were remarkably sanguine.

The optimism of the philanthropists can be traced to many roots, including the conviction that they were superior and that the Indians would recognize that superiority and accept the tenets of civilization and Christianity as it was presented to them. While that conviction of superiority was inherent in the European view of aborigines everywhere, it was no doubt reinforced in Upper Canada by the experience of land cessions. The Indians of the southern regions surrendered their lands, which every commentator then and since had observed had very special importance to the native people. Such actions served as an indication that the native peoples had lost their confidence in survival. In such circumstances, the presentation of an alternative lifestyle, it was felt, would be gratefully, even eagerly, embraced. It was this situation which encouraged philanthropists to suggest and promote an alternative: a programme that would lead to a settled and civilized way of life. The land cessions of the postwar decade, therefore, can be seen as encouraging the advent of the programme, suggested in the 1820's, that would be adopted in 1830.

NOTES

1. Before the war, a series of land surrender agreements had secured the lands along the shores of the upper St. Lawrence River, Lake Ontario, and Lake Erie. In addition, a small tract at Penetanguishene had been purchased, as well as St. Joseph and the island of Michilimackinac. See J. L. Morris, *The Indians of Ontario* (Toronto, 1946).
2. H. J. M. Johnston, *British Emigration Policy 1815–1830* (Oxford, 1972), p. 16.
3. George C. Patterson, *Land Settlement in Upper Canada 1783–1840; Sixteenth Report of the Department of Archives, Province of Ontario* (Toronto, 1921), p. 112.
4. Johnston suggests that American emigration to Canada might have been slowed in any case, because of the lands that were being opened up in the old northwest, p. 16.
5. Ibid., p. 19.
6. Ibid., p. 16; G. S. Graham, "Views of General Murray on the Defence of Upper Canada, 1815," *CHR* (June 1953): 158–65; G. M. Craig, *Upper Canada: The Formative Years* (Toronto, 1963), p. 76.
7. Helen I. Cowan, *British Emigration to British North America* (Toronto, 1967), p. 41.
8. Johnston, p. 21.
9. The story of immigration schemes and military settlement has been told elsewhere: A. C. Casselman, "Pioneer Settlements," in Adam Shortt and Arthur G. Doughty, eds., *Canada and Its Provinces*, vol. 17 (Toronto, 1914), pp. 72–84; A. R. M. Lower, "Immigration and Settlement in Canada, 1812–1820," *CHR* 3 (March 1922): 37–47; Craig, pp. 85–89; Johnston, pp. 10–31; Cowan, pp. 40–64.
10. Lower, pp. 46–47.
11. Lillian F. Gates, *Land Policies of Upper Canada* (Toronto, 1968), p. 87.

12. Ibid.
13. PAC, RG8, vol. 260, p. 481, John Norton to Addison, 6 December 1816.
14. There is some controversy surrounding Norton's heritage. His biographers state that he was half Cherokee (C. Klinck and J. J. Talman, eds., *The Journal of John Norton* [Toronto, 1973]).
15. PAC, RG8, vol. 262, p. 2, Norton to Addison, 9 January 1818.
16. James A. Clifton, " 'Visiting' Indians in Canada," manuscript on file in Canadian Ethnology Service, National Museum of Man, Ottawa, 1979, p. 35.
17. This interesting episode is recounted in C. M. Johnston, ed., *The Valley of the Six Nations* (Toronto, 1964).
18. Norton to Addison, 6 December 1816, pp. 481–83; Norton to Addison, 9 January 1818, pp. 1–2.
19. PAC, Claus Papers, vol. 11, pp. 144–45, Askin to Claus, 3 March 1819.
20. M. Eleanor Herrington, "Captain John Descrontyou and the Mohawk Settlement at Deseronto," *Queen's Quarterly* 29 (1921): 165–80.
21. PAC, RG8, vol. 262, p. 306, Maitland to Duke of Richmond, 9 April 1819; Gates, p. 159.
22. PRO, T-29, vol. 192, pp. 711–12, Treasury Minute #13902, 28 December 1820; PRO, T-29, vol. 176, p. 486, Treasury Minute #15967, 20 August 1819.
23. PAC, Q316, pp. 38–41, Gore to Robert Peel, 10 March 1812.
24. Ibid., p. 39.
25. PAC, Q314, pp. 142–46, Memorial of William McGillivray et al., 5 November 1810.
26. Ibid.
27. PAC, Q317, p. 40, Gore to Peel, 10 March 1812.
28. Ibid, p. 41.
29. Ibid.
30. Memorial of William McGillivray et al.
31. PAC, Q314, pp. 157–63, Proceedings of a Meeting with the Indians of Matchdash and Lake Simcoe at Gwillembury on the 8th and 9th June, 1811.
32. Ibid.
33. Ibid., p. 160.
34. PAC, Q314, pp. 155–56, Provisional Agreement regarding the Lake Simcoe Land, 8 June 1811.
35. PAC, Q314, pp. 140–41, Brock to Liverpool, 23 November 1811.
36. PAC, Q314, pp. 150–51, Requisition for . . . Articles . . . As Payment for the Tract of Land . . . purchased of the Chippewa Indians.
37. PRO, T-28, vol. 45, Harrison to Peel, 24 April 1812.
38. PAC, RG10, vol. 27, pp. 1255, 1260–66, Barker to Harrison, 8 August 1812.
39. Harrison to Peel, 24 April 1812.
40. Brock to Liverpool, 23 November 1811.
41. PAC, Q314, pp. 166–70, Proceedings of a meeting with the Mississauga Indians of the River Moira, at Smith's Creek, 24 July 1811.
42. Ibid., p. 166.
43. Ibid., p. 167.
44. PAC, Q314, p. 164, Provisional Agreement with the Mississaugas for 428 acres (171 hectares) in Thurlow, 24 July 1811.
45. Ibid., p. 186.
46. Ibid., pp. 168–69.
47. Ibid., p. 169.
48. Ibid.
49. Ibid., p. 169–70.
50. PAC, RG10, vol. 3, p. 1624, Claus to MacMajor, 29 December 1814.
51. PAC, Q128, Part 2, p. 332, Prevost to Bathurst, no. 204, 5 November 1814. PAC, Q128, Part 2, pp. 425–26, Prevost to Bathurst, no. 211, 8 November 1814.
52. PAC, Q128, Part 2, p. 336, Prevost to Drummond, 29 October 1814.
53. PAC, RG10, vol. 3, p. 1624, Claus to MacMajor, 29 December 1814.
54. Ibid.
55. PAC, RG10, vol. 4, p. 1651, Claus to Loring, 22 February 1815.
56. PAC, RG10, vol. 4, p. 1791, Halton to Boulton, 23 October 1815; PAC, RG10, vol. 4, p. 1802, Gore to Beaman and Proctor, 14 November 1815.

57. Canada, *Indian Treaties and Surrenders from 1680 to 1890*, 3 vols. (Ottawa, 1891 and 1912; Coles reprint, 1971), 1, no. 16:42–43.
58. Ibid., no. 17, pp.45–46.
59. Gates, p. 137.
60. PAC, Q320, pp. 34ff, Gore to Bathurst, no. 9, 23 February 1816.
61. PAC, Q320, p. 45, Claus to Ferguson, 7 February 1816.
62. Ibid.
63. The Crawford purchase was hastily concluded in 1783 by Captain William R. Crawford, on orders from Governor F. Haldimand; because the actual written agreement had been lost, there was uncertainty about its exact extent.
64. PAC, Q322, Part 1, pp. 87–88, Gore to Sherbrooke, 14 January 1817.
65. The Rice Lake region was considered valuable also in order to open an inland water communication to Lake Simcoe.
66. PRO, T-29, vol. 180, Treasury Minute #23894, 10 December 1819.
67. See above, p. 70.
68. Minutes of a Council held at Smiths Creek . . . on Thursday, the 5th of November, 1818 . . . Judgement in the Supreme Court of Ontario Court of Appeal. The Queen vs. Taylor and Williams, 16 October 1981, pp. 4–6.
69. Ibid., p. 4.
70. Ibid., p. 5.
71. Ibid.
72. Ibid., pp. 5–6.
73. Ibid., p. 6.
74. *Treaties and Surrenders*, 1, no. 20:48–49.
75. Ibid., p. 49.
76. Ibid., p. 48; also PAC, Claus Papers, vol. 11, p. 113, Description of Land of Adjutant Purchase, Description no. 7508.
77. *Treaties and Surrenders*, 1, no. 20:49.
78. Ibid., no. 27, pp. 62–63.
79. PAC, RG8, vol. 263, p. 194, Return showing the present scale of Annual Presents . . . on account of the Surrender of Lands . . . commonly called the Rideau Purchase.
80. *Treaties and Surrenders*, 1, no. 27:62.
81. Ibid., no. 27¼, pp. 63–65.
82. Ibid., p. 65.
83. PAC, RG8, vol. 261, p. 130, Claus to Addison, 30 March 1817.
84. Ibid., pp. 131–32; PAC, Claus Papers, vol. 11, p. 33, Sketch of proposed Surrender (Presently Brock's Point).
85. PAC, Claus Papers, vol. 11, pp. 101–4, Minutes of an Indian Council held . . . the 17th October, 1818, with . . . the Chippewa Nation.
86. *Treaties and Surrenders*, 1, no. 18:47.
87. Minutes of an Indian Council . . . 17th October, 1818, p. 102.
88. Ibid., p. 102.
89. Ibid., pp. 102–3.
90. *Treaties and Surrenders*, 1, no. 18:47.
91. Ibid., p. 103.
92. Ibid., p. 104.
93. PAC, RG8, vol. 263, p. 158, Land Purchased from the Indians.
94. PAC, Claus Papers, vol. 12, p. 98, A Statement of Indian Reserves in Upper Canada. The Credit River Reserve contains 3576 hectares.
95. PAC, Claus Papers, vol. 11, pp. 27–29, Description of the Indian Reservation on the Sixteen Mile Creek, Description no. 7486. It held 387 hectares.
96. PAC, Claus Papers, vol. 11, pp. 29–30, Description of the Indian Reservation on Twelve Mile Creek, Description no. 7487. It contained 541 hectares.
97. PAC, RG10, vol. 27, Proceedings of a Meeting with the Mississauga Indians at the River Credit, 3 October 1810.
98. The Credit River band is the subject of an extensive and complete study by Donald B. Smith,

"The Mississauga, Peter Jones and the White Man" (Ph.D. thesis, Toronto, 1975). See particularly chapter 5, pp. 113–37.

99. PAC, Claus Papers, vol. 11, pp. 110–12, Minutes of the Proceedings of a Council at the River au Credit on the 27th, 28th, and 29th October, 1818.
100. Ibid., p. 110.
101. Smith, p. 135.
102. Minutes of . . . a Council at the River au Credit on the 27th, 28th, and 29th October, 1818, p. 111.
103. *Treaties and Surrenders*, 1, no. 19:47–48.
104. Smith, p. 135.
105. Ibid., p. 136.
106. *Treaties and Surrenders*, 1, no. 22:50–53.
107. Ibid., p. 53.
108. PAC, Claus Papers, vol. 11, pp. 95–96, Minutes of a Council at Amherstburg, the 16th October, 1818.
109. PAC, Claus Papers, vol. 11, p. 137, Sketch of Land to be purchased.
110. Minutes of a Council at Amherstburg, p. 95.
111. Ibid., p. 96.
112. Ibid.
113. Ibid.
114. PAC, Claus Papers, vol. 11, p. 195, Askin to Claus, private, 19 February 1819.
115. Ibid., p. 195, Askin to Claus, private, p. 143.
116. *Treaties and Surrenders*, 1, no. 21:49.
117. Ibid.
118. Ibid., p. 50.
119. Sketch of Land to be purchased, p. 137.
120. PAC, Claus Papers, vol. 11, pp. 187–90, Articles of a Provisional Agreement entered into on the 30th day of March 1819.
121. PAC, RG8, vol. 263, p. 104–5, Claus to Hillier, 7 August 1820.
122. PAC, RG8, vol. 263, pp. 76–77, Ironside to Hawkins, 4 May 1820; PAC, RG8, vol. 263, pp. 78–79, Hawkins to Bowles, 10 May 1820.
123. *Treaties and Surrenders*, 1, no. 25:59.
124. Ibid., pp. 58–60.
125. PRO, T-29, vol. 191, Treasury Minute #17042, 3 November 1820.
126. Gates.
127. *Treaties and Surrenders*, 1, no. 27½:65–67.
128. Ibid., p. 66.
129. Ibid.
130. David J. McNab, "Research Report on the Location of the Boundaries of Walpole Island Indian Reserve #46" (Toronto, 2 May 1980).

4

Herman Merivale and Colonial Office Indian Policy in the Mid-Nineteenth Century

David T. McNab[1]

Historians have examined the origins of Canadian Indian policy and have generally agreed that prior to Confederation it was a product of the ideas and actions of
politicians and administrators in the Canadas.[2] This interpretation is partially true,
but it has tended to obscure two important facts. In the first instance, before 1860,
the Colonial Office in London, England, and the colonial governors rather than the
Indian Department were responsible for Indian (that is, Indian and Metis) policy in
British North America. The Indian Department dealt with administrative details,
while the British government still held within its purview questions of policy.
Other colonial governments in British North America had other administrative
mechanisms. The emphasis on the development of this policy in the Canadas and
its transfer in the 1860's and 1870's to the other provinces and to the Northwest
Territories has also given the mistaken impression that there were no other Indian
policies outside of the Canadas before 1867. Such was not the case, for an analysis
of Colonial Office Indian policy reveals that Lord Grey, secretary of state for war
and the colonies (1846–52), and then Herman Merivale, permanent undersecretary from 1847 to 1860, in conjunction with the colonial governors had by the
mid-nineteenth century developed a regional approach to the "native question" in
British North America.[3] This approach was contained within the framework of
responsible government in British North America.

Reprinted from *Canadian Journal of Native Studies* 1, no. 2, 1981.

In the North Atlantic colonies Colonial Office Indian policy attempted to "insulate" the Micmac by confining them to Indian reserves, until they were ready for assimilation. Its aim in the Canadas was "amalgamation": an attempt to reduce the number and extent of Indian reserves and to try to persuade Indian people to mix with the white population, by miscegenation and education. In the West the objective was amalgamation, which would occur if the fur trade continued and if the position of the Hudson's Bay Company could be maintained. The company administered Rupert's Land and was responsible to the Colonial Office for the welfare of the native peoples. On Vancouver Island and on the coast of British Columbia, Merivale and his colleagues relied on James Douglas to develop his own Indian policy. Douglas's policy consisted of insulation for those Indian people who lived close to areas of non-Indian population, and amalgamation for all other areas.

As they faced the problem of the future of the native peoples, imperial administrators in the 1840's and 1850's espoused pragmatic rather than doctrinaire goals. They aimed at all costs to prevent conflicts between the indigenous inhabitants and white settlers concerning specific issues related to land and labour. In this regard Merivale was in an unusual position for, as a commentator,[4] he provided the "best summation of the conventional wisdom of Empire (as it stood)" and, a few years later, had the opportunity as an administrator to test his ideas (Upton 1973:53–55). The Colonial Office did not develop its policies entirely on pragmatic grounds because of the presence of Merivale as its chief civil servant. The responsibilities of a permanent undersecretary in mid-nineteenth century Britain were varied and crucial to the efficiency of the Colonial Office.

Merivale was an unusual permanent undersecretary, if compared with his predecessor, James Stephen, and his successor, Frederick Rogers. Born in 1806 as the son of a poor London lawyer, Merivale became, like his contemporary, Thomas Babington Macaulay, a child prodigy. After attending the best public schools including Harrow (largely because his uncle had been the headmaster of this institution), Merivale went up to Oxford for his B.A. and M.A. and at the age of twenty-two became a fellow of Balliol College. Despite his academic achievements, Merivale decided to become a lawyer and was called to the Bar in 1832. He soon found it exceedingly difficult to live in London and raise a large family on a lawyer's salary, and, accordingly, he eagerly accepted the offer of the University of Oxford to become Drummond professor of political economy in 1837.

For the next five years Merivale was able to continue his study and writing dealing with questions concerning classical political economy, with a new emphasis upon the expansion of European empires overseas. As Drummond professor his chief duties consisted of delivering a series of lectures which were published in 1841 as his *Lectures on Colonization and Colonies*. With his reputation now firmly established, Merivale continued to write on these questions for the Whig periodical, the *Edinburgh Review*. He was, however, unable to attain his next objective, the post of Regius Professor of Modern History at the University of Cambridge, and for the next five years he went back to the law as recorder for the Cornish boroughs of Falmouth, Helston, and Penzance.

In the fall of 1847 Merivale accepted Lord Grey's offer of appointment as assistant undersecretary of state at the Colonial Office. Grey chose Merivale to replace James Stephen because of the latter's sudden physical and mental collapse and Stephen's recommendation that Merivale was the best external candidate. There were in Grey's view no suitable internal candidates. When Stephen was not able to return to his duties, Merivale was promoted to the permanent under-secretaryship in the winter of 1848. Merivale, the intellectual, had become a career civil servant at the age of forty-one, and he remained an imperial administrator until he died in February 1874. Although he was initially greatly influenced by the ideas of Grey and Stephen, Merivale was not a sycophant at the Colonial Office. He introduced new ideas and procedures and frequently found himself far ahead of his more pragmatic colleagues. Nowhere was this more true than in Merivale's views on the "native" question.

In 1841, Merivale pointed out that four alternatives had been put forward to address the "native question": extermination, slavery, insulation, and amalgamation. By the 1840's Merivale and his colleagues considered only insulation and amalgamation to be practicable. The work and the influence of the humanitarians and their organizations had effectively ruled out extermination and slavery. Insulation proved to be unsatisfactory because it led to the alienation of native land and ultimately to economic dependence. Amalgamation, a gradual and ultimately a consciously assimilative policy, entailed in the long term the complete or partial loss of the native culture and economy. However, the native question was not decided entirely by the application of these schemes but rather by a response to other pressures: the demands of the settlers for colonial self-government, the desires of British politicians and the Treasury to rationalize the British Empire in economic terms, the failures of missionaries to "civilize" the natives, and of great significance, the active resistance of the native people against those persons who wanted to change their way of life.

As an imperial commentator, Merivale had advocated the maintenance of metropolitan control over the relationship between the white settlers and the native peoples by a policy of insulation or amalgamation. In 1841 he inclined toward the latter as the "only possible Euthanasia of savage communities."[5] Later, Merivale recognized that neither insulation nor amalgamation would provide satisfactory solutions to the native question in British North America.

By the 1840's British civil servants, politicians, commentators, and white settlers believed that the native population did not fit into any future political or economic plans for the development of the British North American colonies. Although Indian and Metis problems reached the Colonial Office, very little action was taken on them.[6] To a certain extent, Merivale and his colleagues were hampered by their lack of knowledge concerning these people. Merivale's views were representative of his contemporaries, when in 1841 he described the Indian people in the following way:

> they seemed possessed of higher moral elevation than any other uncivilized race of mankind, with less natural readiness and ingenuity than some but greater depth and force of character; more native generosity of spirit, and manliness of disposition; more of the religious element; and yet, on the other hand, if not with less capacity for improvement, certainly less readiness to receive it; a more thorough wildness of temperament; less curiosity; inferior excitability; greater reluctance to associate with civilized men; a more ingovernable impatience of control. And their primitive condition of hunters, and aversion from every other, greatly increases the difficulty of including them in the arrangements of a regular community. (1967:493)

They would not be very easy to absorb by amalgamation, for, except for their religiosity, they were usually regarded as "barbarians" or "savages."[7] In contrast, the Metis, having already experienced amalgamation through the fur trade by miscegenation, were highly regarded. Merivale observed that miscegenation "affords a considerable check to that mutual repulsion which arises merely out of prejudices of colour, and for which there can be no substantial reason where slavery does not exist. And there is strong testimony to the superior energy and high organization of many of these half-blood races."[8] Merivale got some opportunities to test these views at the Colonial Office.

The North Atlantic region, comprising the colonies of New Brunswick, Nova Scotia, Prince Edward Island, and Newfoundland, had been one of the first areas which had experienced Indian-European contacts in British North America. By the mid-nineteenth century the British government was still not any closer to a satisfactory solution. Beothucks in Newfoundland had become well nigh extinct, and the Colonial Office believed that a similar fate would befall the Micmac who inhabited the Island and the other colonies (Upton 1977). The major problem facing native people, colonial governments, and the Colonial Office alike was the development and implementation of equitable policies with respect to land and labour. Although Micmac title to the land had been vaguely defined and acknowledged by the British government as a usufructuary right, non-Indians continued to alienate Micmac land with impunity. No doubt the "ideal Indian was the invisible one," but Micmacs like other persons were not "ideal" and moreover were visible in the nineteenth century.

In the 1850's the Colonial Office believed that the Micmac people should be amalgamated as soon as possible. Hitherto they had not been forced to relinquish their traditional existence as hunters and fishermen, and every attempt to persuade them to turn to agricultural pursuits had failed (Upton 1974:3, 1975:44–54). A variation on the reserve system had been tried in New Brunswick but had proved to be unsatisfactory. The Micmac had been given land only for their occupancy and use. No title in fee simple to the land was granted; nor were they compensated for their aboriginal interest in lands. Indeed, until 1847 very little had been done for the Micmac, despite the ceaseless efforts of Moses H. Perley, the superintendent of Indian Affairs in New Brunswick, to draw the attention of the authorities in the colony and London to problems of the Micmac.

In 1844 Perley succeeded, with the co-operation of the governor, Sir William Colebrooke, in passing an Indian Act. Although the act was passed with the best of intentions it proved to be a disaster for both Micmac and administrators alike. Indian reserve land was alienated, and only twenty hectares of land was given to each Indian family. Moreover, the Micmac were removed to separate villages, and whatever lands they had held previously were to be sold or leased at public auctions, with the proceeds to be placed into a trust fund which was to be used to "civilize" them. Perley and the Micmac soon perceived the inadequacies of this legislation. The Micmac received no compensation for the lands they had relinquished to the Crown by the act because few white settlers could afford to buy the land. Consequently, the land was sold at very low prices, often on credit, and most of the revenue obtained had only paid for the administration of the land sales. The act had also done nothing to prevent another serious problem, the presence of squatters on Indian land. The Micmac complained to Perley, who raised three objections with the governor. The latter argued that he could do nothing as long as the assembly either refused to grant the Micmac an annuity or declined to lease the land on a long-term basis. Colebrooke sent a report on these proceedings to Downing Street (Upton 1974:5–14; 17–19).

This despatch found its way to Lord Grey, secretary of state for war and the colonies, the Land Emigration commissioners, and the permanent undersecretary in 1848. Colebroke had argued that unless the situation was changed immediately the material development of the colony would be considerably set back. Very pointedly he wrote that the Micmac needed less land and the white colonists and entrepreneurs more.[9] Merivale minuted that the Colonial Office should wait until a further report was submitted by the new governor, Sir Edmund Head. In the meantime he observed that the land question was very important: "if the assembly continue to sell Indian land at 4 s. [shillings] an acre there would be only a capital of £12,000 secured for their benefit after all the existing reserves had been parted with."[10]

Head's report was based largely on Perley's original criticisms of the act, but the governor sought to find a compromise between Perley's position and the assembly's assertions that the act had not been given sufficient time to prove its usefulness. In fact, the act had been a failure. The Micmac were left with less land and no money for the land they had relinquished, in addition to the social and economic dislocation caused by their removal to separate villages. Yet, Head proposed to keep the act and simply set up a "new set of instructions," which he believed would ameliorate the condition of the Micmac. Significantly, he also noted that there were only two ways to deal with the native question in a colony of this sort: to recognize that the Micmac had legal rights and let them fend for themselves or to reorganize their rights but make them wards of the imperial government to protect them from the white settlers.[11] With the approval of the Colonial Office, Head proceeded with his plan, but soon he had to confess that he had failed. Gloomily, he reported that it seemed unlikely there would be any "permanent improvement" or any "real advancement" because the assembly, comprised of non-Indians, refused to provide help for the Micmac population, which was declining and did not pose a threat to the settlers. During the remainder of his years in the colony, Head spent little time on Micmac problems because he was preoccupied with the introduction of responsible government. This emphasis boded ill for the Indian people because the settlers were consistently ignorant of and hostile to Indian interests (Upton 1974:20–29). Head also refused to let Perley implement the new instructions to the Indian Act because Perley had supported Micmac objections to it. Technically, Head was correct, but now he had lost the most informed official on Micmac affairs in the colony.[12] Apparently without exhibiting too much concern (McNab 1978, ch. 6), the Colonial Office informed the governor that he would implement and administer the new regulations without Perley's aid.[13]

Head's scheme failed because it had done nothing to prevent the alienation of Micmac land. The white settlers continued to ignore the Indian Act.[14] Squatting remained a fundamental problem.[15] In the 1850's the Indian fund never became large enough to provide relief, and no additional financial aid was forthcoming from the colonial Assembly or from the British government. Ironically, the Micmac, although suffering economically, survived partially because a dearth of financial resources prevented Head's policy of "improvement" from being implemented (Upton 1974:22; 25–26). The situation in Prince Edward Island and Nova Scotia was similar, although there were some differences. In Newfoundland the Micmac were not considered to have any special status because they lived in isolated communities on the western and southern coasts of the island, and there was no pressure on their lands until the twentieth century. No treaties or any other similar agreements were signed with them. They were almost invisible.

An incident occurred in the mid-nineteenth century which epitomized the Colonial Office's neglect of the Micmacs in all of these colonies. Silas Rand, a Baptist minister and one of the few individuals seriously concerned about the welfare of the Micmac in Nova Scotia, sent a petition to Downing Street on their behalf. When it crossed his desk, Merivale noted that he did not believe it was genuine because it "was written and conceived in English" rather than in Micmac. Thus, the Duke of Newcastle, then secretary of state for the colonies, merely referred the claims of the petitioners back to the colonial government, and, as usual, nothing more was done (Upton 1975:22–24, 31). Micmac requests for aid were not taken seriously by the Colonial Office and the local government.[16]

Colonial Office Indian policy in the Canadas was a blend of insulation and amalgamation. The Indian people were to be put on reserves and thus would be protected from the white sttlers. Except for these reserves, Indian lands would be ceded formally by the Indian people through treaties and would be made available for purchase to the ever-increasing number of emigrants from Britain. The civil servants in Downing Street, ever mindful of the Treasury, also assumed that putting Indians on reserves and encouraging them to amalgamate with the white population would lower the cost of Indian administration. Presents, which had been given to the Indian people to secure and maintain the early treaties of peace and friendship and military alliances with the Indian people, would cease to be distributed. By the mid-nineteenth century, if not before, the Colonial Office's primary interest in Indian affairs in the Canadas was economic rather than humanitarian.

Unlike the situation in the Atlantic colonies, the Colonial Office had much more knowledge about the Indian people in the Canadas. It was derived primarily from the writings of travellers, missionaries, and military personnel.[17] Nevertheless, Colonial Office Indian policy in the Province of Canada was always subordinated to the economic and political priorities of free trade and responsible government. Nothing was allowed to stand in the way of the economic and political development of non-Indians in the Canadas. This objective was stated by Lord Grey: "With regard to the Indian Department, as by the arrangement lately made, the extinction of the charge (except so far as some payments for their lives to individuals) is provided for within five years, no further steps are required to be taken." His policy was implemented by Merivale, after Lord Grey left the Colonial Office in 1852 (1853:265–68).

During the 1840's Merivale became aware of the problems faced by the Indian people, particularly the inefficient manner in which they had been, and were still being, administered by the Indian Department (Merivale 1967:494–95). However, while he was at the Colonial Office, he did not attempt to change this state of affairs because he was more concerned about the consequences of responsible government in the Canadas and the relationship between the native population and the Hudson's Bay Company in Rupert's Land and the other Hudson's Bay Company territories. In his *Lectures* he portrayed the problems with which he believed the Indians in the Canadas were confronted. Although the British government had promised to protect their hunting territories when it issued the Royal Proclamation of 1763, their condition was:

a remarkable instance of the mischievous manner in which even the best intentions towards the Indians have been carried into execution. After declaring in the most solemn language the perpetuity of the cession of the lands, it ends with the saving clause, "unless the Indians shall be inclined to part with them." By virtue of this proviso, every art has been introduced to obtain their consent to the usurpations made upon them; bit by bit they have been deprived of their magnificent hunting-grounds, which are not altogether possessed by whites (1967:506).

Later, instead of attempting to correct this problem, Merivale supported a policy which exacerbated it.

From 1856 to 1860 the Colonial Office debated the feasibility of giving the government of the Provinces of Canada the power to control Indian affairs and the methods to be adopted to facilitate this change. A commission was appointed in 1858 to inquire into these problems (Clarke 1953:164–66). After reading the commission's report of 1858 and Head's suggestions, Merivale concluded that it would be advantageous to "get rid of the responsibility of the Home Government"[18] in Indian affairs, and his view prevailed in the Colonial Office. He prepared the despatch which gave effective control over Indian affairs in the Canadas to the local government as long as its actions were "consistent . . . with the full preservation of the faith of the Imperial Government so far as it may be pledged to the natives."[19] This decision was an abrogation of responsibility because the Colonial Office was now relinquishing effective control over Indian affairs to non-Indian colonial interests. The Indian people or their representatives were not consulted concerning this change. In 1860 responsibility for their affairs was delegated to the government of the Province of Canada. After 1860, the Colonial Office was replaced by colonial politicians, administrators, and, after 1867, the Department of Indian Affairs (Upton 1973:59–60; Leighton 1975:218–19).

In the Canadas, the Colonial Office's land policies were also inconsistent. Merivale had argued in 1841 that white settlers should have control over their land (1967:433), but he failed to reconcile the difference between the colonists using the land for agricultural and other purposes, such as mining and lumbering based upon European forms of proprietary rights, and the native population's subsistence economy based on hunting and fishing and their aboriginal title to the land (1967:114). Before this time the problem had not been of great concern to governments, and there had been no "systematic regulation" for the disposal of lands. There had been plenty of land for all of the inhabitants to use for whatever purpose, while the "danger from Indians" kept the colonists from straying too far into the wilderness (1967:96). However, by the 1840's land hunger was increasingly evident, and, in response, the Colonial Office attempted to implement new theories concerning land and labour, based largely upon the theories of classical political economy. Thus, by these canons, a colony was deemed to be developing satisfactorily if it was gradually becoming self-sufficient in land, capital, and labour. Of the three, Merivale argued, as a classical political economist and a follower of Edward Gibbon Wakefield, that labour was the most important because "land and capital are both useless unless labour can be commanded."[20] Clearly, Merivale and his colleagues valued the labour of the white settlers far more than that of the native people. They believed the Indian economy would eventually disappear and the Indians would either become extinct or assimilate with the non-Indian population.

To Merivale and his colleagues, the native question appeared to be very different in Rupert's Land because of the presence of the Hudson's Bay Company and its monopoly. The fur trade was still an important economic activity, although it was beginning to decline in the southern areas. The Indian and Metis people were the chief source of labour and participated directly in or supplied goods to the fur trade.[21] At the Red River colony there was a small agricultural settlement. Already, by the mid-nineteenth century there were signs of a shift from the fur trade and the buffalo hunt to a commercial agricultural economy (Ray 1974:195–216).

In this area Merivale's primary concern was with the conflict between the Hudson's Bay Company and the subsistence economy and the rights of use and occupancy to the land and resources by the native people. Merivale believed paradoxically that despite the company's monopoly, the company's presence was generally in the economic interests of the native peoples. The future of the native people here would be developed by amalgamation, particularly miscegenation, because of the impact of the fur trade. The presence of the Metis was a sign that this process of amalgamation had already begun. Consequently, Merivale always defended the *status quo ante bellum* and the Hudson's Bay Company.

In 1848, soon after he had taken up his new position in Downing Street, Merivale had to deal with the complaints of a Metis spokesman based in London, Alexander K. Isbister, who had charged that the Hudson's Bay Company was contributing to the decline of the native people in Rupert's Land by its use of alcohol as a trading item.[22] In responding to Isbister's allegations, Merivale placed great weight on the report of Major John Crofton, who was then governor of Assiniboia and military commander to the Hudson's Bay Company and in this particular matter was influenced by Sir George Simpson, governor of the Hudson's Bay Company in British North America. Crofton's report exonerated the company of all the allegations made by Isbister. The Colonial Office subsequently dismissed them as well. Merivale concluded that the company's rule was "very advantageous to the Indians" and warned the secretary of state for war and the colonies, as he was to continue to do throughout the 1850's, that if the company's control ceased then the fur trade would be thrown open to all traders, there would be increased competition, prices would rise, and liquor would be used indiscriminately. The situation would therefore become much worse for the native people than it was.

However, Isbister was not content to "let sleeping dogs lie," a tactic used frequently by the Colonial Office itself, and he bombarded Downing Street with letters of protest and petitions in the next few years. Merivale suggested to Lord Grey that the only way to prove or to disprove Isbister's allegations was to appoint a military officer or English traveller to check on these complaints and then have that individual report directly to the Colonial Office. Another possibility was to appoint a commission in England, the members of whom could be sent to Rupert's Land. These alternatives were not followed because of their cost and also because, as Merivale warned Grey, a direct investigation of the company's activities would lead eventually to the Colonial Office having to replace the company with a crown colony.

The Colonial Office, adopting the advice of its permanent undersecretary, refused to contemplate the difficult and expensive alternative of establishing and administering a crown colony in Rupert's Land. Isbister, who claimed (in his letters to the Colonial Office) to be a representative of the native population, had advocated this course of action. He claimed that Rupert's Land was their homeland and that the native people should have the right to colonial self-government like non-Indians in the eastern British North American colonies. But Merivale also believed that the native people of British North America were not ready for British institutions (McNab:1978b:21–38). The Indian people were, of course, still viewed by the British government as warlike savages and therefore not to be trusted at all. Consequently, Merivale fell back on the rationale that establishing a crown colony would simply cost too much. Moreover the Hudson's Bay Company had one important advantage:

> their power of dealing on a regular system with inferior or less powerful races. The Hudson's Bay Company have converted for trading purposes an immense region into a fur preserve, with a success which is perfectly astonishing, and could not be believed were it not in evidence from the supply of furs. Of course, this was simply for their own interest. But it could only be done through introducing a strict and vigorous discipline, which nothing but self-interest would have introduced, and which forms the best possible basis of dealing with savages.

In the same minute Merivale also compared the situation in Rupert's Land to that of the American west and concluded that there was no "alternative between the present system and perfect freedom, that is, such a state of perpetual war and pillage as subsist in the American prairies." Rather frankly he wrote that "Mr. Isbister would have us destroy a regular government on account of its corruption, when the only alternative for it is anarchy." Grey followed Merivale's suggestions and sent out a despatch based on his minute.[23] For the Colonial Office, law and order and economy were more important priorities than the problems and demands of the native people in Rupert's Land in the mid-nineteenth century. In the years that followed the Colonial Office refused to be deterred in its support of the Hudson's Bay Company.

In 1858, after a select parliamentary committee submitted its report on the Hudson's Bay Company and the future of Rupert's Land,[24] Merivale received a letter from the Reverend Griffiths Owen Corbett, a "popular" Anglican clergyman from Headingly (Pannekoek 1979), which asked that the rights of the Indian and Metis people be considered and dealt with by the British government. Merivale's response was important because he was the most knowledgeable civil servant in 13 and 14 Downing Street on this subject:

> I mean the claims of the Indian Tribes over portions of Lord Selkirk's land and generally over the territories comprised in the Charter. The Americans have always taken care to extinguish such rights however vague. We have never adopted any very uniform system about them. I suppose the H.B.C. had never purchased from such claimants any of their land. And I fear (idle as such claims really are, when applied to vast regions of which only the smallest portion can ever be used for permanent settlement) that pending discussions are not unlikely to raise up a crop of them.[25]

However, there were no formal land claims made at this time. Except for the Selkirk "Treaty" of 1817, the Indian interests were initially dealt with in the 1870's when the numbered Treaties were signed.

Despite being rebuffed, the native people and their spokesmen did not stop sending their letters of protest and petitions to the Colonial Office. In December 1859, William Kennedy again raised the issue of Indian and Metis claims in Rupert's Land. Merivale advised the secretary of state to answer Kennedy, Isbister's uncle and a spokesman for the Metis (Sealey and Lussier), with great caution because the matter was one of the "considerable importance." Again he observed that the British government had never recognized the "territorial rights" of the native population in this area. He believed there had been no conflict in the past because of the reciprocal self-interest of the Hudson's Bay Company and the native people in the fur trade and the modicum of land hunger. He advised Newcastle to do nothing "until the question of the Company's rights to the soil are terminated" because "it might be pretty safely assumed, that no right of property would be admitted by the Crown as existing in mere nomadic hunting tribes over the wild land adjacent to the Red River Settlement. But the agricultural Indian settlements (if any such exist) would be respected and that hunting ground actually so used by the Indians would be reserved to them or else compensation made."[26] However, the land question remained unresolved and continued to cause conflict. It was a factor in the armed resistance of the native people in 1869–70 and in

1885.[27] These difficulties became the responsibility of the government of Canada after the Hudson's Bay Company had surrendered and sold its land to Canada in 1869–70.

In the Pacific Northwest the native population was very different from the other regions of British North America. The Indian people lived by and from the sea. Their economic and cultural life was relatively rich, and they were in a position to resist the encroachments of fur traders, gold miners, and white settlers on their land and labour. Moreover, they outnumbered their white counterparts until the late nineteenth century and were considered by the latter to be extremely warlike.[28] Not surprisingly, there was more evidence of armed conflict in the Pacific Northwest than elsewhere in British North America, but it never matched the degree of violence south of the 49th parallel in the Washington Territory. In the Pacific Northwest, Colonial Office Indian policy was largely dictated by the ideas and actions of James Douglas, colonial governor of Vancouver Island and British Columbia, because the armchair administrators at the Colonial Office knew very little about the region or its indigenous population.

Merivale was the only person in the Colonial Office who had any knowledge, however deficient, of the Pacific Northwest. In 1843 he had written that this region of North America was "the last corner of the earth left free for the occupation of a civilized race." The Indians were, he concluded confidently and erroneously,

> few in number, chiefly subsisting by salmon fishing and on roots, and very inferior in physical power and in ferocious energy [compared] to their brethren of the Prairies. But, for this very reason, they offer the less obstructions to the operations of the colonist, and, it must be added, that their simple, inoffensive habits of life are found to be accompanied in many cases with a moral elevation, which ranks them in the scale of humanity far above most savages, and forms but too striking a contrast to the morals and habits of the wandering white and half-breeds who visit them from the East (1843:185–188).

At the Colonial Office, Merivale discovered that these Indian people were not "inferior," "simple," or "inoffensive." Moreover, he was confronted with the problem of dealing with conflicts between these people and the "wandering whites and half-breeds" during the gold rush on the Fraser River.

At least until the 1860's Vancouver Island and British Columbia did not have the same problems associated with land as did some of the other British North American colonies. There was little demand for agricultural land. James Douglas avoided conflict over land by signing fourteen "treaties" with the Indian people on Vancouver Island between 1850 and 1854 and setting aside Indian reserves for Indians elsewhere.[29] There were few white settlers on the Island or the mainland. The Hudson's Bay Company had been responsible for colonization, but it had accomplished little as it was hampered by the great distance from Britain and the high price of land set by the British government in 1849.[30] Thus, land was not the most important cause of Indian-White conflict; labour problems were much more significant. The Colonial Office did not understand these circumstances or their implications and relied on Douglas and the commanders of the ships of the Royal Navy to maintain law and order (Gough 1971:88–89). Primarily preoccupied with avoiding the cost of warfare, which was occurring in southern Africa at the same time, Colonial Office Indian policy was characterized by great quiet and, of course, reliance on James Douglas. As the Fort Rupert incident in 1850 reveals, this objective was sometimes difficult to attain.

The first governor of Vancouver Island was the inexperienced Richard Blanshard. Initially, Blanshard had supported the Hudson's Bay Company's Indian policy, particularly that which opposed the "importation and manufacture of ardent spirits" and had dismissed allegations of "barbarous treatment of the Indians by the Company's employees" as "entirely without foundation." In the summer of 1850 he was confronted with a crisis when reports of the murder of three white deserters from a company ship at Fort Rupert were received at Fort Victoria. The Newitty, a Kwakiutl group which inhabited the northern part of Vancouver Island, had apparently been responsible. By the time Blanshard's despatch reporting the incident had reached London he had taken matters into his own hands and, using men and ships of the Royal Navy, had punished the Newitty. Blanshard assumed that his actions, taken without the sanction of the Colonial Office, would be applauded by the mandarins in Downing Street. However, the Colonial Office was already disenchanted by Blanshard's quarrels with the company's employees. After reading Blanshard's despatch Merivale minuted acidly that the "Governor's account is so meagre it leaves everything unaccounted for." He advised Lord Grey to ask the company for more information thereby short-circuiting the governor. It was more than six months before the Colonial Office discovered what had occurred at Fort Rupert, and, even then, their account was based entirely on Chief Factor James Douglas's report, which was supported by the Hudson's Bay Company.[31]

The company concluded that the murder of the three men made it imperative that Vancouver Island receive better military protection. Acting on Merivale's advice, the Colonial Office dismissed the incident because it was "only that of the murder of three seamen who were trying to escape from their ship, in a part of the island distant from that occupied by the Company." There had been no direct threat to the colony by the Newitty. For his actions Blanshard received an official rebuke from Lord Grey.[32] Although Blanshard had attacked the Newitty with the approval of the company, including Douglas, he had acted without specific instructions from London. He had made little impact upon the Newitty, who had suffered few casualties. Blanshard, a victim of his own inexperience, in ill-health, disillusioned, and hounded by the company, resigned and was replaced by Douglas. After the debacle at Fort Rupert the Colonial Office let its new governor handle all aspects of Indian policy.

The Colonial Office had learned very quickly that in the Pacific Northwest its power to control Indian-white relations was, as Merivale put it, limited:

> To give orders from hence as to the conduct to be observed towards Indians in Vancouver Island seems rather unlikely to be of much service. If the colony is to maintain itself, as was the condition of its foundation, the local government much needs to be left very much to its discretion as to dealings with the natives in the immediate neighbourhood of the settled parts, although distant excursions against them may be discouraged.[33]

During the 1850's the Colonial Office completely supported Douglas when he acted in cases involving Indians. He avoided provoking open hostilities between Indians and white settlers, traders and miners. Thus, Merivale was able to console himself with the fact that Vancouver Island did not have "anything like the fearful massacres and fighting of which we receive occasional accounts from the American side of the frontier."[34] The Colonial Office's Indian policy in the western colonies of British North America was greatly influenced by distance and its reaction to what it believed were the inadequacies of American Indian policy.

During the 1850's James Douglas was given the opportunity to conduct Indian policy almost without any interference from either the Hudson's Bay Company or the Colonial Office. The latter repeatedly responded to Douglas's actions rather than initiating any policy from Downing Street.[35] Merivale was acutely aware of Douglas's power for, as he wrote in 1856: "there can be no doubt the safety of the little British settlement here depends wholly on the firmness and discretion of the governor's conduct toward the Indians: military defense there is none."[36] Douglas was fully in command of every situation. He was able to mount a successful expedition against the Cowichan on Vancouver Island with the aid of men and ships of the Royal Navy[37] and also to provide financial help to Governor Isaac Stevens when an Indian-white war occurred in the Washington Territory in 1857.[38] His greatest challenge came in 1858.

The Colonial Office feared the worst after it received reports of the discovery of gold and when, in the spring of 1858, thousands of miners arrived on the mainland. With his jurisdiction extending only to Vancouver Island, Douglas consulted the Colonial Office. Lord Stanley, then secretary of state for the colonies, reacted by leaving the whole matter to "Mr. Merivale's judgment." Merivale immediately gave Douglas power to govern the area that became the colony of British Columbia until a lieutenant-governor's commission could be sent.[39] Although there was one clash between the miners and the Indians, Douglas kept the situation well under control until the winter of 1859 when most of the miners left the area.[40]

By 1858 the Colonial Office had become completely dependent upon Douglas for an effective Indian policy. Merivale's minute on a petition from the Aborigines' Protection Society in 1858 reveals the extent of this reliance:

> I would acknowledge civilly and do nothing more. These gentlemen are well meaning — at least many of them — and they represent a common and healthy British feeling: but the worst of it is that "protection of the aborigines" has become with them a "technical profession." They never see, or pretend to see, two sides of a case: consequently their practical suggestions, when they make any at all (which I must do justice to say, is very seldom) are of a character which would probably cause some astonishment to people to the spot.[41]

Sir Edward Bulwer Lytton, then secretary of state for the colonies, concurred with Merivale's assessment and instructed him to send a copy of the petition to Douglas as a matter of form, with no specific instructions to reply to the charges. By March 1860, when Merivale left the Colonial Office to become permanent undersecretary at the India Office, he was comparatively optimistic concerning the future of Indian-white relations in Vancouver Island and British Columbia, especially since the Hudson's Bay Company had given up its futile attempts at colonization. The most important problems of Indian-white relations had not been solved. The Indian people remained a military threat, and as Merivale put it, "it seems to be a very attractive region: and likely to prosper greatly, if the settlers can be secure against the Indians: at present (thanks to Hudson's Bay Company management) these seem very tractable." In order to avoid the experience of wholesale massacre prevalent in the United States, Merivale again advocated that Indian-white relations be regulated by the "occasional use of the Queen's naval and military force," although he knew that the latter had an effect "more by shew than even by execution."[42] After Douglas retired in 1864, his Indian policy deteriorated rapidly, and Indian land and labour became increasingly alienated by non-Indians.[43]

In the 1830's and 1840's imperial commentators like Herman Merivale believed that metropolitan control of Indian-white relations in British North America was absolutely essential for economy and the maintenance of law and order, which were their primary objectives, as well as to protect and civilize the native population. By the mid-nineteenth century this ideal had been eroded because the Colonial Office had committed itself to a policy of colonial self-government. After the departure of Grey in 1852, largely influenced by the permanent undersecretary, this policy of the Colonial Office meant that the white settlers would be allowed to control their own domestic affairs. Eventually, all internal aspects of a colony's development would be given to the local legislature, including Indian policy. Potentially, here was the "dark side" of responsible government. By the 1860's formal or informal control over Indian policy passed from the Colonial

Office, which was at times an impartial if distant master, to the colonial politicians who represented the interests of the settlers and other non-Indians.

In 1860, ensconced in Leadenhall Street, in his new position as permanent undersecretary for the India Office, Merivale published the second edition of his *Lectures* and reflected on his administrative career at the Colonial Office and the ideas which he had advocated twenty years previously. His judgement of "native" policy in all parts of the British Empire, including British North America, was an honest lament for the lack of metropolitan control:

> The subject, in short, is one which has been dealt with by perpetual compromises between principle and immediate exigency. Such compromises are incidental to constitutional government. We are accustomed to them: there is something in them congenial to our national character, as well as accommodated to our institutions; and, on the whole, we may reasonably doubt whether the world is not better managed by means of them than through the severe application of principles. But, unfortunately, in the special subject before us, the uncertainty created by such compromises is a greater evil than errors of principle (1967:521).

In the mid-nineteenth century the Colonial Office bequeathed to the Dominion of Canada the legacy of an Indian policy which was regional in its approach, was characterized by "perpetual compromises between principle and immediate exigency," and which continually vacillated in its purpose and implementation in all parts of British North America. With this Indian policy, or more correctly, these regional Indian policies, the Colonial Office established the framework for Canadian Indian policy after 1867.

NOTES

1. I would like to thank Professor Barry Gough, Wilfrid Laurier University, for his comments on earlier versions of this manuscript. All statements expressed in this article are those of the author and not those of the government of Ontario or the Ontario Ministry of Natural Resources. Research grants from the Interuniversity Centre for European Studies and a Canada Council Doctoral Fellowship made it possible for me to complete the research and the writing of this article, originally presented at the Canadian Historical Association Annual Meeting in June 1978.
2. See for example L. F. S. Upton, "The Origins of Canadian Indian Policy" *Journal of Canadian Studies* 8, no. 4 (November 1973): 51–61; D. Leighton, "The Development of Federal Indian Policy in Canada, 1840–1890" (Ph.D. diss., University of Western Ontario, 1975); J. E. Hodgetts, *Pioneer Public Service* (Toronto, 1955), pp. 205–25.
3. For a complete analysis of Merivale's life and imperial career, see D. McNab, "Herman Merivale and the British Empire, 1806–1874" (Ph.D. diss., University of Lancaster, 1978), and specifically

for his ideas on the "native question," see "Herman Merivale and the Native Question, 1837–1861," *Albion* 9, no. 4 (Winter 1977): 359–84.

4. H. Merivale, *Lectures on Colonization and Colonies* (New York, 1967), p. 521. All further references will be to this edition.

5. Ibid., p. 511. See also D. T. McNab, "The Colonial Office and the Prairies in the Mid-Nineteenth Century," *Prairie Forum* 3, no. 1 (Spring 1978): 23–24.

6. For example, see Upton, "Colonists and Micmacs," *Journal of Canadian Studies* 10, no. 3 (August 1975): 53–56.

7. Merivale, pp. 526–30; "British Mission to Shoa," *Edinburgh Review* 80 (July 1844): 56. Also see R. Fisher, *Contact and Conflict, Indian-European Relations in British Columbia, 1774–1890* (Vancouver, 1977), pp 73–94.

8. Merivale, pp. 538, 554–56. Also see S. Van Kirk, "Women and the Fur-Trade," *The Beaver* (Winter 1972): 4–21; *"Many Tender Ties," Women in Fur-Trade Society in Western Canada, 1670–1870* (Winnipeg, 1981), pp. 28–52.

9. C.O. 188/104 ff. 375–87.

10. Ibid.; pp. 135–37; C.O. 188/107 ff. 169.

11. C.O. 188/106 ff. 192–200.

12. Ibid., W. A. Spray, "Moses Henry Perley," *Dictionary of Canadian Biography*, vol. 9, pp. 628–31.

13. C.O. 188/107 ff. 305.

14. C.O. 188/106 ff. 202–22. Compare with Upton, "Indian Affairs in Colonial New Brunswick," *Acadiensis*, 3 (1974) pp. 21–22 and the situation in Nova Scotia, Upton, "Indian Policy in Colonial Nova Scotia," *Acadiensis*, 5, No. 1 (Autumn 1975): 4.

15. C.O. 188/109 ff. 278.

16. C.O. 217/224 ff. 338.

17. Upton, "Canadian Indian Policy," pp. 51, 54, 59–60. Upton's interpretation of Merivale's view of Indians is misleading, see *Lectures*, pp. 487–563, for Merivale's view changed from 1841–1861. Upton attributes his ideas in the second edition of his *Lectures* in 1861 to his views in 1841.

18. C.O. 42/603 ff. 201–2.

19. C.O. 42/603 ff. 205–6.

20. Ibid., 256. See also McNab, ch. 3 concerning Free Trade and the British Empire.

21. H. Merivale, "Mexico and the Great Western Prairies," *Edinburgh Review* 78 (July 1843): 176; "Macgregor — American Commerce and Statistics," 86 (October 1847): 394. For a more thorough analysis see McNab, "Colonial Office and the Prairies," pp. 21–38.

22. A. K. Isbister, et al., *A Few Words on the Hudson's Bay Company, with a Statement of the Grievances of the Native and Half-caste Indians* (London, n.d.), pp. 1–24. This petition was sent to the Colonial Office. For Isbister's background see D. B. Sealey and A. S. Lussier, *The Metis, Canada's Forgotten People* (Winnipeg, 1975).

23. C.O. 42/551 ff. 24–29. See also C.O. 323/243 ff. 328; C.O. 6/23 ff. 11; C.O. 6/23 ff. 55.

24. Parliamentary Papers, *Report from the Select Committee on the Hudson's Bay Company; together with the Proceedings of the Committee, Minutes of Evidence, Appendix and Evidence* (London, 1857), pp. iii-iv, 120–50.

25. C.O. 6/27 ff. 261–62.

26. C.O. 6/31 ff. 201–2.

27. See also Pannekoek, "The Reverend Griffiths Owen Corbett and the Red River Civil War of 1869–1870," *CHR* 51, no. 2 (1976): 133–49; and Desmond Morton, *The Last War Drum* (Toronto, 1972).

28. Fisher, pp. 49–72. Fisher has not adequately dealt with the role of Merivale and the Colonial Office in this study.

29. C.O. 305/9 ff. 361–63. For Douglas's Indian land policy see Robert E. Cail, *Land, Man, and the Law* (Vancouver 1974), pp. 171–72, 247, and Wilson Duff, "The Fort Victoria Treaties," *BC Studies* 3 (Fall 1969): 3–57.

30. National Library of Scotland, Ellice Papers, E. 91, Edward Ellice to Henry Labouchere, 30 September 1856, ff. 94–95. See also J. S. Galbraith, "Fitzgerald versus the Hudson's Bay Company: The Founding of Vancouver Island," *British Columbia Historical Quarterly* 16 (July–October 1952): 191–207. For Merivale's view see C.O. 6/5 ff. 549–50.

31. C.O. 305/2 ff. 36–37, 41–42.
32. C.O. 305/3 ff. 360.
33. C.O. 305/3 ff. 108.
34. C.O. 305/4 ff. 80.
35. C.O. 305/6 ff. 156; C.O. 305/7 ff. 106.
36. C.O. 305/7 ff. 144.
37. Provincial Archives of British Columbia, B 40–1, James Douglas to Admiral Bruce. See also C.O. 305/8 ff. 47 for Merivale's view.
38. C.O. 305/8 ff. 257.
39. C.O. 305/9 ff. 66. See also Gough, "'Turbulent' Frontiers and British Expansion: Governor James Douglas, The Royal Navy and the British Columbia Gold Rushes," *Pacific Historical Review* 41, no. 1 (February 1972): 15–32.
40. Merivale's assessment is in C.O. 6/26 ff. 455–56. W. P. Morrell, *The Gold Rushes,* 2d ed. (London, 1968), pp. 123–25. See also Fisher, pp. 95–103 for a very different interpretation.
41. C.O. 6/26 ff. 297–98.
42. C.O. 305/10 ff. 186–87, 283–84.
43. This interpretation is substantially different from that put forward by Robin Fisher.

REFERENCES

Cail, Robert E. 1974. *Land, Man, and the Law.* Vancouver.
Clarke, D. P. 1953. "The Attitude of the Colonial Office to the Working of Responsible Government, 1854-1868." Ph.D. diss., University of London.
Duff, Wilson 1969. "The Fort Victoria Treaties." *BC Studies* 3:3–57.
Fisher, Robin 1977. *Contact and Conflict: Indian-European Relations in British Columbia, 1774–1890.* Vancouver.
Galbraith, J. S. 1952. "Fitzgerald versus the Hudson's Bay Company: The Founding of Vancouver Island." *British Columbia Historical Quarterly* 16: 191–207.
Gough, Barry M. 1971. *The Royal Navy and the Northwest Coast of North America, 1810–1914.* Vancouver.
———· 1972. "'Turbulent' Frontier and British Expansion: Governor James Douglas, The Royal Navy and the British Columbia Gold Rushes." *Pacific Historical Review* 41:15–32.
Grey, Lord. 1853. *The Colonial Policy of Lord John Russell's Administration.* London.
Hodgetts, J. E. 1955. *Pioneer Public Service.* Toronto.
Kerr, D. G. G. 1954. *Sir Edmund Head, A Scholarly Governor.* Toronto.
Leighton, D. 1975. *The Development of Federal Indian Policy in Canada, 1840–1890.* Ph.D. diss., University of Western Ontario.
McNab, David T. 1977. "Herman Merivale and the Native Question, 1837–1861." *Albion* 9:359–84.
———· 1978a. "Herman Merivale and British Empire, 1806–1874." Ph.D. diss., University of Lancaster.
———· 1978b. "The Colonial Office and the Prairies in the Mid-Nineteenth Century." *Prairie Forum* 3:21–38.
Merivale, H. 1843. "Mexico and the Great Western Prairies." *Edinburgh Review* 78.
———· 1844. "British Mission to Shoa." *Edinburgh Review* 80.
———· 1967. *Lectures on Colonization and the Colonies.* New York.
Morrell, W. P. 1968. *The Gold Rushes.* 2d ed., London.
Morton, Desmond 1972. *The Last War Drum.* Toronto.
Pannekoek, Fritz. 1976. "The Reverend Griffiths Owen Corbett and the Red River Civil War of 1869–1870." *CHR* 51:133–49.
———· 1979. "Some Comments on the Social Origins of the Riel Protest of 1869." In Antoine S. Lussier, ed., *Riel and the Metis.* Winnipeg.
Ray, Arthur J. 1974. *Indians in the Fur Trade.* Toronto.
Sealey, Bruce, and Antoine S. Lussier 1975. *The Metis: Canada's Forgotten People.* Winnipeg.
Upton, L. F. S. 1973. "The Origins of Indian Policy." *Journal of Canadian Studies* 8:51–61.

———· 1974. "Colonists and Micmacs: Indian Affairs in Colonial New Brunswick." *Acadienis* 3.

———· 1975. "Indian Policy in Colonial Nova Scotia." *Acadiensis* 5.

———· 1977. "The Extermination of theBeothuck of Newfoundland." *CHR* 58:133–53.

Van Kirk, S. 1972. "Women and the Fur Trade." *The Beaver,* 303, 3:4–21.

———· 1981. *"Many Tender Ties"; Women in Fur Trade Society in Western Canada 1670–1870.* Winnipeg.

5

A Victorian Civil Servant at Work:
Lawrence Vankoughnet and the Canadian Indian
Department, 1874–1893

Douglas Leighton

Transition, according to Walter Houghton, was the hallmark of the Victorian age.[1] It was a time of change. Forms that were perceived as medieval gave way to others perceived as modern: a new scientific spirit displaced blind faith, just as steam displaced sail and factories absorbed ancient cottage industries. New forms were evident in politics too: Parliament was gradually transformed by a series of reform bills; territories that had previously been colonies began to assume some responsibility for themselves as they embarked on the journey to dominion status. These political and imperial alterations in turn produced great changes in administrative practice, in the ways which government conducted its day-to-day operations. The Victorian period was one of great transition in governmental administration.

The people who effected and who were affected by these changes — the Victorians themselves — possessed a "frame of mind" marked by several distinct characteristics.[2] Among these were rigidity — a stern adherence to fixed standards — and earnestness, which found one of its principal expressions in the doctrine of hard work. Narrow-minded self-confidence, coupled with a "high and serious"[3] attitude towards life's tasks, made many Victorians intolerant of cultural differences.

Missions and the attack on slavery were inspired by religious motives, but

Paper presented to the Canadian Historical Association, London, Ontario, 30 May 1978.

even Americans and Europeans who were not particularly religious were apt to believe that what they had to offer was better than anything to be found outside their culture, and they could do nothing better for non-Europeans than to bring them into its ambit.[4]

These events and attitudes had repercussions in British North America during the third quarter of the nineteenth century, as Britain gradually reduced her role in colonial defence and administration. In the case of the Canadian Indian Department, the matter of transition became acute after Britain relinquished her control over Indian matters in 1860. A permanent chief officer was not found until 1862: over the ensuing thirty years, the department had to cope with vast geographical expansion, political and constitutional change, and the difficulties of its own internal organization. During much of this period, it was controlled by men who accepted Victorian ideas or standards. They transformed an obscure provincial government department into a large and important government agency by the end of the century. Their priorities did much to determine the nature of government-Indian relations in the twentieth century. The administration of Lawrence Vankoughnet, deputy superintendent general of Indian affairs 1874–93, was crucial in this respect.

Lawrence Vankoughnet was born at Cornwall, Upper Canada, on 7 October 1836.[5] The Vankoughnets, an old Loyalist family, were firmly Tory in their politics, and they possessed good connections with those in power, both Oliver Mowat and John A. Macdonald being numbered among their friends.[6] After receiving his education at the Cornwall Grammar School and Trinity College, Toronto, Lawrence joined the Canadian civil service on 13 February 1861, as a junior clerk in the Indian Department.[7] In the summer of 1873, a year before William Spragge's death, Vankoughnet had become chief clerk, so he was the logical choice to succeed his late chief as deputy superintendent general in 1874.

Because his family was long acquainted with John A. Macdonald and because of his own sense of personal gratitude, Lawrence Vankoughnet made the prime minister his lifelong political hero. This became a particularly important element in the administrative relationship of the two men after 1878, when Macdonald was Vankoughnet's minister. The civil servant was always careful to defer to the wishes of the politician. Macdonald found the arrangement convenient in another way. He was notorious for paying scant attention to the day-to-day operations of the government departments in his charge. In Vankoughnet, he knew he had a loyal and conscientious deputy who could manage the Indian Department with a minimum of supervision. Accordingly, Macdonald's intervention was usually confined to problems with distinct political overtones.

Macdonald's confidence in Vankoughnet was justified. He was exceedingly regular in his habits and excessively conscientious in administrative practice. However, his zeal to oversee every facet of the department's operations caused serious difficulties at times. Vankoughnet's desire to read everything personally considerably slowed all important correspondence with agents in the field. Decisions were not made as quickly as they might have been had the office been less centralized. On more than one occasion, Vankoughnet became the victim of his near perfectionism, suffering ill-health and consequent absences from work. Early in 1883, he collapsed from overwork, and his doctor diagnosed "a disordered nervous system."[8] An immediate change to a warmer climate was suggested as the only cure. When a two-week stay in Charleston, South Carolina, did not produce the expected improvement, Vankoughnet moved to Jacksonville, Florida, until the end of April.[9] This long absence must have galled him, for he considered himself indispensable, and the feeling probably retarded his recovery to full health. Certainly, the department was adversely affected by the three-and-a-half-month absence of its permanent head.

Other personal problems beset Vankoughnet during this period, putting him under even greater strain. He had become estranged from his brother, Salter Vankoughnet, who became fatally ill late in 1887. The emotional impact of this family situation greatly affected Vankoughnet, as a private letter to Sir John Macdonald in June 1888 indicated.[10] Such personal pressures probably contributed to the rigidity so characteristic of the department's decision-making processes just when it needed to be as flexible as possible, particularly in regard to the Plains Indians. Not all the blame for the department's lack of sensitivity to local needs can be laid at Vankoughnet's feet: he inherited a tradition of centralized authority which stretched back to the Johnson regimes. But he cannot be completely absolved of responsibility for the department's failings either. His personal inflexibility, his attitude of administration "by the book" left too little room for common humanity.

The administration of Indian affairs in the Prairies felt the effects of Vankoughnet's personality and policies most fully. The early 1880's were a time of great hardship for most western Indian bands, when the buffalo disappeared and white settlers continued to multiply.[11] Administrators in the field often were strongly sympathetic to the Indians' plight, but they seemed able to get little cooperation from Ottawa.[12] The early 1880's were marked by a general economic depression which, combined with Vankoughnet's tendencies towards economy and centralized control, meant that serious western needs often were ignored.

Vankoughnet cut back expenses wherever possible, keeping staff and salaries to a minimum. He was particularly emphatic that the telegraph should be used only in cases of emergency, so that communication costs would be minimal.[13] The arrangement was adequate for Ontario and Quebec, because mail service to Ottawa was fairly quick. But for officers stationed in the Maritimes, and especially in the West, mail communication was entirely inadequate. By the time Vankoughnet had dispatched orders dealing with a given situation, conditions had frequently altered, making the instructions obsolete. Consequently, departmental

employees in the West were allowed greater freedom than their eastern counterparts in their use of the telegraph.[14] Nonetheless, communications remained a
great barrier between Ottawa and its representatives in the field.

Even more significant was the department's handling of relations with Indians
in need. The disappearance of the buffalo and the lean crop years in the early
1880's meant large quantities of supplementary rations frequently had to be issued,
and abuses sometimes crept into this practice. Indians sometimes even got more
than they needed and sold or wasted the surplus. Vankoughnet was fearful that the
department was being propelled into excessive expenditure, and he imposed strict
quotas for supplementary rations. Per diem allowances for individuals of thirteen-
and-a-half ounces of flour, three-and-a-half ounces of bacon, and six ounces of
beef were ordered reduced.[15] This niggardliness regarding food quotas did more to
alienate western tribesmen before the North-West Rebellion than almost anything
else.

Parsimony was evident elsewhere as well. Various learned societies in the
1880's had expressed interest in the cultures of the Plains Indians and approached
Vankoughnet to make contact with leading Indian figures.[16] Other persons asked
the department for help in assembling and studying Indian artifacts as well.[17]
Before 1885 help was given only grudgingly; Vankoughnet allowed one of his
clerks to assist a collector of Indian artifacts — but only outside the regular office
hours.[18] The department was interested only if such projects cost nothing in time
and money.

The events of 1885 brought a pronounced change in this pernicious, secretive
attitude. Responding to criticism over its Indian policies before the rebellion, the
government after 1885 was anxious to give wide publicity to Indian leaders who
had remained loyal during the unrest. When Father Lacombe suggested a trip east
for Chief Crowfoot, the authorities were happy to comply, especially as the noted
missionary thought he could arrange free return passage on the Canadian Pacific
Railway, which had its own reasons for favouring the proposal.[19] Vankoughnet
was so enthusiastic over the latter condition that he authorized the trip without
even waiting for the prime minister's approval. He urged Lacombe to choose the
members of the party making the trip with great care lest they become "saucy" on
their return home.[20] Crowfoot, Three Bulls, Red Crow, Star Blanket, and several
other chiefs travelled east in the autumn of 1886 and visited several eastern Indian
reserves as well as Ottawa before they returned home. The Indian Department in
the same year represented the adventure as being its own reward to the chiefs for
their loyalty.[21]

This episode did not mean that Vankoughnet had changed his views on the
expenses question. A proposal that some of the western chiefs should visit
England at departmental expense was curtly and unceremoniously dismissed. "I
do not see that much good would come of such a scheme. . . . It would cost a very
large amount of money."[22] Clearly, the C.P.R.'s offer of free transportation

accounted for Vankoughnet's permission for the trip to eastern Canada.

It is tempting to explain away Vankoughnet's narrow views regarding the Indian problems in the West as the result of his ignorance of conditions there. But Vankoughnet did make efforts to familiarize himself with prairie conditions, including undertaking an extensive western trip in the late summer and early autumn of 1883.[23] He was personally acquainted with most of his senior western officers, such as Edgar Dewdney and Hayter Reed, who were in a position to advise him closely on matters there. Yet, despite such knowledge and personal acquaintance, he made incredibly wrong-headed decisions. In 1883, for example, he suggested that one way of cutting western expenses was to release all unnecessary help on the model farms during the winter months.[24] This might have been fiscally sound for the department, but it did nothing to alleviate the faltering economy of a reserve. One is forced to the conclusion that for Vankoughnet, fiscal considerations came ahead of human ones.

Not all his ideas were impractical or devoid of human concern. Realizing that language was often a great barrier between Indians and department officials, Vankoughnet supported two dictionary projects, one a Blackfoot-English volume prepared by Father Lacombe, the other a Cree-English work.[25] Individual Indians whom Vankoughnet considered deserving could count on his help. When Thomas D. Green, a Six Nations Indian who had obtained a diploma in civil engineering from McGill University and was employed in the drafting room of the Dominion Lands Branch, expressed interest in obtaining a position with the C.P.R., Vankoughnet gladly endorsed him to the prime minister, asking Macdonald to put in a good word with George Stephen in Montreal.[26]

These concerns in the field were matched by those of the "inside service." Proper quarters for the Indian Department's head office had always been a sore point with its senior officers. As a subordinate and small agency during much of its existence, the Indian Department usually received scant attention when office space was allocated. Its staff, too, was kept to a minimum. In the 1840's, for example, the chief superintendent for Upper Canada had to carry out his duties with the assistance of only a single clerk. Forty years later, to administer some 100,000 Indians scattered over half a continent, the head office at Ottawa boasted a total staff — including part-time clerical help — of thirty-eight.[27] Proper quarters still remained something of a problem. Housed in the East Block of the Parliament Buildings at Confederation, the Indian Department became the temporary victim of government overcrowding in the early 1880's. Deputy Minister of the Interior Lindsay Russell, needing more office space, roused the alarm and ire of Vankoughnet when he suggested that the older records of the Indian Department be removed and burned to provide the required space. Vankoughnet's twelve-page reply to Sir John Macdonald, at that time the ministerial superior of both deputies, suggested Russell could solve his own problem merely by sharing an office with his personal stenographer.[28] The upshot was that the Indian Department moved for a year to the former offices of the St. Lawrence and Ottawa Railway until additional government accommodation became available.[29] Eventually, the department found itself back in its East Block home.

The incidents surrounding this episode revealed several things about the Indian Department. Civil servants who worked outside it had little notion of its functions or importance and held it in low professional esteem. Even Lindsay Russell, who worked in the same ministry and, indeed, in the same building for some time, blithely assumed that Indian Department records were of no real consequence — certainly not on a par with his branch's land survey and other records. Ministerial decisions frequently displayed low regard for the needs of the Indian Department. Thus, no one in authority seems to have been unduly concerned over the difficulties that two moves in a short period inflicted on the department, or about the effects of isolating the department from other government offices. The prime minister himself worried only that the costs of the moves be kept as low as possible.[30] Clearly, in the eyes of the government and most federal employees, the Indian Department remained as it had been in the past, the "White man's albatross."[31]

This low regard meant the Indian Department did not attract the best candidates from among those who joined the federal civil service. The Ottawa office was headed by the deputy superintendent general, assisted by a chief clerk, an accountant, and a small clerical staff. Many of the more than thirty positions in the office during the 1880's were filled by unskilled persons: messengers, box-packers, and janitors, who did not need any special training to carry out their assigned tasks. Most of the clerks did little more than copy voluminous correspondence into letter-books, a process carried out in time-consuming long-hand until the advent of the typewriter in the mid-1880's. The real power of decision-making was firmly entrenched in the hands of the deputy superintendent general. Whenever he was absent from the office for any period, important matters were held in abeyance to await his decision. When Lawrence Vankoughnet took his holidays in August or September — as he usually did — all major decisions were deferred until his return.[32] Only rarely was a matter of extreme urgency referred to his ministerial superior. Hence, the lesser personnel in the Ottawa office occupied themselves daily with inconsequential and boring routine matters.

Employees reacted to this stultifying existence in a variety of ways. Absences were not infrequent. In 1885, for example, F. R. Byshe, the messenger and box-packer in the office, requested a leave of absence on medical grounds. After Byshe had been granted leave, Vankoughnet found that he really wanted the time to build an addition to his house.[33] Two years later, when Byshe tried to take an extra day off, claiming he needed to write civil service examinations, Vankoughnet deducted his pay for one day.[34] Byshe appealed directly to the prime minister against this extreme treatment, but his appeal was not granted.[35] However, he was kept on the Indian Department payroll; evidently Vankoughnet feared that any replacement might be worse.

Feigning sickness was the usual method employed to obtain illicit time off work. Senior department officials, aware of this, demanded medical certificates on such occasions. Their efforts to reduce the amount of lost time were not helped by the presence of practitioners like a certain Dr. A. Church who readily signed such documents.[36] One of Vankoughnet's clerks, J. T. Coffey, who had a drinking problem, was frequently absent under such questionable "medical" circumstances. "I know that Coffey's habits are most unsteady," wrote Vankoughnet during one such episode, "and I have not the least doubt in my mind that he has been on a debauch since the 16th instant."[37] Such incidents occurred with sufficient frequency to hamper the Ottawa office from dealing efficiently with the volume of business which confronted it.

At times the department showed surprising concern for government employees. Michael Corrigan, who was responsible for the furnaces in the winter, was usually released each spring by the Department of Public Works as his services were not required until the succeeding autumn. In 1883, when he was in dire financial straits, Corrigan pleaded with Vankoughnet to keep him employed during the summer months in some other capacity. Corrigan was duly employed as a temporary messenger, though a telegram to the deputy minister of public works was needed to complete the arrangement.[38]

So eager was head office to secure competent, efficient employees that serious shortcomings sometimes were overlooked in order to obtain such persons. A certain William Richardson had been forced to resign his post over suspected financial irregularities. Vankoughnet was anxious to rehire Richardson, for he was an exceptionally able employee, and Richardson, too, was willing. When some of Richardson's friends later made good the loss and helped clear his name, Vankoughnet enlisted Prime Minister Macdonald's aid in obtaining Richardson's reinstatement.[39] Macdonald endorsed Vankoughnet's request and urged Mackenzie Bowell, the minister responsible for the Treasury Board, to "push Richardson through."[40]

Politics, too, played their part in Indian Department appointments. The Tory outlook of the department, so marked in its earlier history, did not disappear in an age which felt that government should be served by its friends and vice versa. The case of the Ross brothers illustrated how political influence operated in the area of hiring employees. W. R. Ross, a Conservative of good standing, had two sons who received probationary appointments in the Ottawa office. The senior Ross asked that his son Frank be given a permanent post without having to write the regular civil service tests. Vankoughnet refused to accede to the request because he had found the young Ross unsatisfactory. However, he was prepared to appoint his brother Thomas, who had proved a model employee, to a second-class clerkship.[41]

Obviously, politics could be an important aid in obtaining employment in the Ottawa office, but just as obviously, there were limits to political patronage in appointments.

The Indian Department also had to deal with an extensive outside service. By 1890, its far-flung operations required the services of some 460 employees in the field. Many of these people were part-time workers who worked for the Indian Department during its busy seasons when presents were being distributed or various funds were being disbursed. Since the department usually employed clergymen as agents in the Maritimes and Quebec, agents there were usually part-time employees. The total costs of such widely extended operations were high. In 1890, travel expenses totalled $25,812.96 while salaries accounted for $211,-421.02, and total operational expenses for the year came to slightly more than $2,106,000.[42]

Barely one-tenth of this over-all amount was met from Indian funds. The capital in the Consolidated Indian Fund in 1890 of just over $3,345,000 generated an annual income of $328,000. From this annual increment the Indians' share of the department expenses — some $281,000 in 1890 — was met. The remainder of the total amount — some $1,778,000 — had to be raised by government grant.

A regional breakdown of total expenses reveals much about the Indian Department's priorities. The table for 1890 was as follows:

Prince Edward Island	$ 2,490.84
Nova Scotia	6,216.03
New Brunswick	6,518.47
Ontario and Quebec (together)	50,262.81
Manitoba and the North-West	940,261.72
British Columbia	102,074.44

The western provinces were clearly uppermost in departmental thinking at this period. The eastern provinces, where fundamental problems had been worked out long before, did not require the massive expenditure of the West.

Lawrence Vankoughnet's desire for economy is more readily understandable in the light of these figures. Cutting expenditures saved both the government and the Indian Fund considerable sums. Vankoughnet's compulsion to economize, always evident, could sometimes produce rather strange appointments in the Outside Service. The hiring of Indian Agent W. M. Tyre at St. Regis, near Cornwall, Ontario, was a good example. When the post became vacant in 1884, Tyre applied for it, though he already acted as customs agent at St. Regis and evidently was nearly eighty years old.[43] Though the prime minister had grave doubts about the appointment, Vankoughnet supported it, citing Tyre's spryness — he arose each morning at 5:00 A.M. to inspect the Montreal-bound steamer — and the money the Indian Department would save through not having to erect its own buildings. Tyre was appointed and served in his dual capacity until his death early in 1887.[44]

Other changes were made in the 1880's in attempts to streamline departmental operations. William Plummer, who had served as central superintendent in Ontario from 1873 to 1882, was brought to Ottawa as commissioner of Indian lands when his former post was abolished.[45] Though there was work for Plummer in Ottawa, his title was largely honorific, being designed to cushion the loss of his former position in Toronto.[46] By 1885, Plummer's health had broken, even under his reduced workload, and he finally retired in 1887.[47] Jasper T. Gilkison, the long-time Six Nations superintendent, also was clearly incapacitated by the later 1880's, and efforts were made to dislodge him. When some Indian funds went astray, Vankoughnet ordered a thorough investigation into the Brantford office over Gilkison's strenuous objections.[48] He thought the department "would be well rid of [Gilkison]." The prime minister seemed to agree and instructed the Six Nations superintendent that he was in danger of being discharged without superannuation.[49] Despite this pressure, Gilkison did not retire on pension until 1891.[50]

Politics was an important consideration in the letting of Indian Department contracts. As with departmental appointments, political loyalty was not sufficient by itself to guarantee a successful tender, though it often helped. To avoid collusion between prospective bidders, tenders were usually kept open as long as possible.[51] Firms that were known to have opposed the government were likely to find their bids rejected unless they were far below those of other more favoured suppliers. In 1891, for example, when the department called for tenders on large quantities of farm machinery, a number of Ontario companies responded, among them the Brantford Mower Company, Frost and Wood of Smiths Falls, the American Plough Company of Ayr, Massey Manufacturing Company of Toronto, and the Toronto Mower Company. Before compiling his final list, Lawrence Vankoughnet discreetly enquired of the prime minister's secretary whether any of these firms had opposed the government at the last election.[52]

These examples demonstrate the departmental emphasis on economy, efficiency, and political loyalty in operations as well as two other qualities. Great difficulty was encountered in discharging incompetent employees who possessed substantial amounts of seniority or who had rendered political services in the past. The obduracy of Jasper T. Gilkison in the late 1880's is a case in point; despite his advancing senility, he kept his post though under some pressure to resign from both the ministerial and civil service levels of administration. Gilkison possessed nearly thirty years' seniority, and he had a longstanding connection with Upper Canadian Toryism, having begun his career as a protegé of Sir Allen Napier MacNab in the 1840's and 1850's. Rather than create undue administrative or political disturbance, Vankoughnet and Macdonald simply left Gilkison alone, realizing he would soon have to retire in any case because of physical incapacity. Though events seemed to prove the wisdom of this decision, the Indian Department's operations in the important Brantford area were nonetheless hampered for some five years. At times, the interests of the department and its Indian clients seemed to be secondary factors in the eyes of those who made decisions in Ottawa.

The second factor these examples illustrate was the pre-eminence the deputy superintendent general had attained by the 1880's. During this period all decisions of consequence, whether great or small, tended to become the prerogative of one man. Centralized authority had been the logical outcome of the changes occasioned by the transfer of the Indian Department to Canadian authority in 1860, and by Confederation. But the chief reasons for the growth of such authority lay in the personalities and aims of the two successive deputy superintendents general after 1862. William Spragge, after his accession to office in 1862, had set out to make the Indian Department a model of civil service bureaucracy. His successor, Lawrence Vankoughnet, was temperamentally incapable of allowing autonomous decision-making by subordinates. This has led one authority to dismiss him as a "niggling administrator."[53]

Vankoughnet's attitude towards Indians seems to have been the typical one for that time. He was more than willing to help individuals, as in Thomas Green's case, when he had reason to feel they would make good use of any opportunity they were given. Indians who settled down to farming, worked hard, and became respectable self-supporting members of society deserved any help the department could give them. Vankoughnet believed that successful Indian farmers should enjoy the same rights as their white neighbours, especially the franchise.[54] Whatever his failings, he was no racial bigot. Like most nineteenth-century Europeans, he simply could not understand why some Indians preferred the old ways, when white society offered them a more comfortable and rewarding lifestyle. The only explanation of such behaviour that he could accept was that of Indian indifference or laziness. And then he wiped his hands of them — if such Indians would not help themselves, there was nothing the department could do for them.

Here was the root of the Indian Department's difficulties at the close of the nineteenth century, for such attitudes were widely shared at the time. Though there were occasional expressions of public concern and sympathy, there was no great public understanding of the Indian situation. The public saw the Indian as a "brown White man," assuming the factors which made for white advancement would meet Indian needs too. White institutions, notably the Christian religion, with their innate sense of superiority, sanctioned such attitudes. In any case, the Indian's difficulties were scarcely of prime public interest. As western Canada was opened to white settlement, exploitation and development were the dominant forces in the minds of both government and people. The image of the Indian in the popular mind was usually that of the noble red man, the romantic mounted warrior of Sir Walter Scott's medieval novels transferred to a different time and place; or the hapless, menacing nuisance, a hindrance to orderly development who had to be removed humanely but expeditiously for the nation's good and the higher ends of civilization. Once the rebellion of 1885 had passed and the fear of Indian attacks disappeared, Indians became little more than objects of curiosity for academics or romantics. There is an air of pathos about the eastern trip of Crowfoot and his colleagues in 1886.

If Indians remained far in the back recesses of the popular mind, so did the Indian Department. It must have irked Vankoughnet that his department remained very much a governmental backwater, occupying a very lowly position in contrast to public works or railways and canals. Other divisions of government often paid little heed to the needs of the Indian Department, encumbering its administrative machinery despite the most valiant efforts of its head. It was not uncommon, for example, for other departments to misplace Indian Department correspondence. The prime minister's office frequently did this, even though Macdonald's ministerial responsibilities for a time included the Indian Department. In one extreme case, a departmental file remained misplaced among Sir John's papers for thirty-two years.[55]

By Vankoughnet's retirement in 1893, the Indian Department was both better and worse than it had been half a century before when the United Province of Canada had come into being. It was far more efficient and enjoyed the services of many competent persons. But it had become much less sensitive to local situations and needs than the old provincial department had been. In its attempt to seek greater economy and efficiency, the Ottawa office had become insulated against local realities. The pattern for twentieth-century government-Indian relations in Canada had been set.

During his thirty years in the Indian Department, Lawrence Vankoughnet's passion for efficiency had earned him more than a few enemies. He was particularly unpopular with some of the senior western administrators who had borne the brunt of departmental economies in the middle 1880's. Hayter Reed, Cecil Denny, and Edgar Dewdney had sharp disagreements over various issues with the deputy minister. With the advent of Sir John Thompson's administration in 1892, this western group formed powerful ties to the government through the new minister of the interior and member of Parliament for Selkirk, Manitoba, Thomas Mayne Daly.

Born in Stratford, Canada West, in 1852, Daly had served briefly on the town council there before moving to Brandon, Manitoba, in 1881.[56] The following year, he was elected mayor and held that office until 1896. In addition he was a member of Parliament from 1887 until the defeat of the Tupper government. Sworn in as minister of the interior on 17 October 1892, Daly immediately began to restructure the department for reasons which remain unclear, but which appear to have been chiefly political. One of his first targets was Lawrence Vankoughnet. "It has become necessary," wrote Daly in July 1893, "in view of impending changes in the Department over which Vankoughnet presides, and in the interests of public economy and efficiency, that he should now be retired."[57] Vankoughnet was offered a pension inducement to retire early: if he did so, he would receive full retirement benefits, even though he was more than three years away from the normal thirty-five years of service required.

Lawrence Vankoughnet refused all such suggestions, leaving Daly little choice but to discharge him. Even this was difficult, for Daly had to find grounds that would seem sufficient for such action to outside observers. The result of the minister's determination and his deputy's stubbornness was the following remarkable exchange of letters in the early summer of 1893.[58]

Ottawa, 28th June, 1893.

Private.

Dear Mr. Vankoughnet,

In watching closely the affairs of the Indian Department, and the management of its branches for some time past, I have come to the conclusion that some radical changes are needed, and I have contemplated making such changes as will reduce the staff and consequently the expenses. Now while thinking these matters over I cannot help stating that I also have for some time noticed that your health is failing and that you have no longer the vigor of intellect which has characterized you in the past. I may say hitherto, when the question of your superannuation was mooted I took care to speak of you as you deserved, in as fair and friendly a light as I could, for that you have been a most zealous and faithful officer no one who knows you well can deny; but I am forced to the conclusions I have come to after a very calm and full review of the whole circumstances as regards the Indian Department. Your long services entitle you to full superannuation, and I know Council will willingly grant the same.

In making this intimation I desire to say that our relationship has been most cordial, and I reciprocate your kind offices to me since my occupancy of the position of Superintendent General. I really think that what I now write you is in your own interest, and that especially from a health point of view your retirement from office will be beneficial to you.

I must say that my convictions are firm in this matter, and not arrived at without mature consideration. In stating, therefore, in this friendly and private way that I am prepared to accept your request for superannuation, I am quite sure you will not disturb our cordial relations by refusing to act in accordance with my wishes — a course which would really be of no benefit to you. I also desire to say that I would like you to take the necessary steps in the matter with as little delay as possible; and whatever Memoranda to Council are necessary I would be glad if you would have prepared at once.

Again assuring you that this letter is not dictated with any hostile feeling or unfriendliness, and trusting that you will regard my request in a right spirit,

Believe me,

Yours faithfully,

(Sgd.) T. Mayne Daly.

Ottawa, 29th June, 1893

Dear Sir,

Yours of the 28th instant received and contents fully considered.

In reply I would state as respects any measures which you may consider it advisable, in the interests of economy, to adopt in the future management of this Department, I shall be happy to assist you.

With regard to your statement that for some time you have noticed that my health was failing, and that I had no longer the vigor of intellect which characterized me in the past, I have to say that I never was in better health than I am now, and have been for the past nine months — since in fact I returned to duty last Autumn, after an absence of sick leave, the same having been only the second of such absences during the long term of thirty years service.

The vigor of my intellect is amply proven by the immense volume of work that receives attention at my hands daily, as well as by the numerous reports on important matters made to you by me, also by the many reports made by me for your signature, addressed to His Excellency in Council.

Moreover, the general management of the Department, both in the Outside and Inside Service of it, of which I challenge fair criticism, shows that a vigorous intellect must be the possession of the one who is presiding genius over it.

As far as age is concerned I am only in my fifty-sixth year; being therefore four years short of the age for superannuation.

And as for service I have had but thirty-two years and four months, being two years and eight months less than the term required by the Act, to admit of superannuation.

I could not, therefore, truthfully apply on the grounds of impaired physical or intellectual condition, age, or length of service, for superannuation — even were I otherwise disposed to make such application.

I must, therefore, respectfully decline to comply with your request.

I reserve for myself the liberty of making such use of this correspondence as circumstances may seem to me to justify.

Yours sincerely,

(Sgd.) L. Vankoughnet
Deputy Supt. General
of Indian Affairs

Despite Vankoughnet's protests, he was unable to withstand such ministerial pressure. He conducted departmental business until 27 July 1893, when the poet Duncan Campbell Scott, the departmental accountant, was made acting deputy superintendent general.[59] The retirement was not made official until the end of September when the government's actions were roundly criticized in some newspapers.[60] Vankoughnet later removed to England with his wife and died at Tunbridge Wells on 21 March 1898.[61]

Lawrence Vankoughnet's career had been in many ways a distinguished one. His earnestness, capacity for hard work and painstaking attention to administrative detail made him a model Victorian civil servant whose superiors implicitly trusted him. But those very qualities brought him into conflict with a new administration after 1892 and ultimately caused his dismissal in a particularly cavalier and shabby fashion. There was some irony in his removal, for he was forcibly retired in the name of efficiency and economy, qualities which he himself had long endorsed.

Vankoughnet's legendary attention to detail perhaps gave him the final word in his power struggle at the end of his career. His last official letter to the Indian Department noted that the government had failed to pay him for his last official day at his regular salary and requested a cheque for the missing amount.[62] Duncan Campbell Scott checked his accounts, found that Vankoughnet was correct, and approved payment.[63] The amount in question was $8.43.

NOTES

1. Walter E. Houghton, *The Victorian Frame of Mind* (New Haven, 1957), p. 1.
2. Houghton's phrase.
3. Houghton, p. 222.
4. G. S. R. Kitson Clark, *An Expanding Society: Britain 1830–1900* (Cambridge, 1967), p. 72. See also, Christine Bolt, *Victorian Attitudes to Race* (Toronto, 1971).
5. C. H. Mackintosh, ed., *The Canadian Parliamentary Guide and Annual Register* (Ottawa, 1881) pp. 30–31.
6. D. G. Creighton, *John A. Macdonald: The Young Politician* (Toronto, 1953), pp. 257, 279, 303. Lawrence Vankoughnet's niece later became Hugh John Macdonald's second wife. Toronto *Globe*, 28 March 1898. PAC, RG10, vol. 9178, p. 1.
7. Mackintosh, pp. 30–31.
8. PAC, Macdonald Papers, Vankoughnet to Macdonald, 13 January 1883.
9. His first correspondence with Macdonald after his return is dated 8 May.
10. PAC, Macdonald Papers, vol. 292, Vankoughnet to Macdonald (private), early June 1888.
11. See J. D. Leighton, "The Development of Federal Indian Policy in Canada, 1840–1890" (Ph.D. diss., University of Western Ontario, 1975), chapters 10 and 11, for a detailed account. Other recent dissertations dealing with the plains area include A. J. Looy, "The Indian Agent and His Role in the Administration of the North-West Superintendency, 1876–1893" (Ph.D. diss., Queen's University, 1977); John L. Taylor, "The Development of an Indian Policy for the Canadian North-West, 1864–79" (Ph.D. diss., Queen's University, 1975). Studies from the imperial perspective include D. T. McNab, "Herman Merivale and the British Empire, 1806–1874" (Ph.D. diss., University of Lancaster, 1978), and J. S. Milloy, "The Era of Civilization — British Policy for the Indians of Canada, 1830–1860" (Ph.D. diss., Oxford University, 1978).

12. L. H. Thomas, *The Struggle for Responsible Government in the North-West Territories, 1870–79* (Toronto, 1956), p. 103.
13. PAC, Macdonald Papers, vol. 293, Macdonald to Vankoughnet, 7 March 1882.
14. Ibid.
15. PAC, RG10, Black Series, file 33711, marginal notation.
16. PAC, Macdonald Papers, vol. 290, Sinclair to Macdonald, 17 September 1886.
17. Ibid., Vankoughnet to Macdonald, 27 January 1885.
18. Ibid.
19. PAC, Macdonald Papers, vol. 291, Vankoughnet to Macdonald, 17 September 1886.
20. Ibid.
21. *SP*, 1887, no. 6, Macdonald's introduction.
22. PAC, Macdonald Papers, vol. 291, Vankoughnet to Macdonald, 6 February 1886; Sir John Carling to Macdonald, 19 February 1886.
23. Ibid., vol. 289, Vankoughnet to Macdonald, 4 August 1883.
24. Ibid., Vankoughnet to Macdonald, 10 December 1883.
25. PAC, Macdonald Papers, vol. 291, Vankoughnet to Macdonald, 6 July 1886.
26. Ibid., vol. 290, Vankoughnet to Macdonald, 11 March 1884.
27. *SP*, 1886, no. 4.
28. PAC, Macdonald Papers, vol. 293, Vankoughnet to Macdonald, 26 January 1882.
29. Ibid., D. Daly to Macdonald, 4 February 1882.
30. Ibid., Macdonald to Vankoughnet, n.d. (February 1882).
31. J. E. Hodgetts, *Pioneer Public Service* (Toronto, 1955), p. 205.
32. PAC, Macdonald Papers, vol. 289, Vankoughnet to Macdonald, 24 July 1883.
33. Ibid., vol. 290, Sinclair to Vankoughnet, 3 June 1885.
34. Ibid. See the exchange of letters between Vankoughnet and Macdonald in May 1887.
35. Ibid.
36. Ibid., Vankoughnet to Macdonald, 17 April 1884.
37. Ibid., Vankoughnet to Macdonald, 24 April 1884.
38. Ibid., vol. 289, Vankoughnet to Macdonald, 19 July 1883.
39. Ibid., vol. 292, Vankoughnet to Macdonald, 31 December 1887.
40. Ibid., Macdonald's marginal notation.
41. PAC, Macdonald Papers, vol. 291, Vankoughnet to Macdonald, 29 May 1886.
42. *SP*, 1891, Auditor-General's Report, pp. C195-C202.
43. PAC, Macdonald Papers, vol. 290, Vankoughnet to Macdonald, 30 July 1884.
44. Ibid., vol. 292, Vankoughnet to Macdonald, 5 March 1887.
45. *SP*, 1883, no. 5. By an order-in-council of 27 July 1882, the central superintendency was abolished and replaced by a system of local agents.
46. PAC, Macdonald Papers, vol. 292, Vankoughnet to Macdonald, 2 February 1887.
47. Ibid., vol. 290, J. D. McLean to Pope (private), 9 May 1885; vol. 292, Vankoughnet to Macdonald, 2 February 1887.
48. Ibid., vol. 290, Vankoughnet to Macdonald, 29 June 1885.
49. Ibid., vol. 292, Vankoughnet to Macdonald (private), 3 February 1887.
50. PAC, RG10, *Preliminary Inventory* (June 1951), v.
51. For example, see PAC, Macdonald Papers, vol. 290, Vankoughnet to Macdonald, 10 May 1884.
52. Ibid., vol. 292, Vankoughnet to Pope, 9 March 1891.
53. P. B. Waite, *Canada, 1874–1896: Arduous Destiny* (Toronto, 1971), p. 147.
54. PAC, Macdonald Papers, vol. 293, Vankoughnet to Macdonald, 3 February 1879.
55. Ibid., vol. 290, Pope to D. C. Scott, 4 April 1916, enclosing file RS 52, 378.
56. The outline of Daly's career may be found in J. K. Johnson, ed., *The Canadian Directory of Parliament*, p. 150. I would like to thank David Hume of the Public Archives of Canada for drawing my attention to the exchange of letters between Vankoughnet and Daly.
57. PAC, RG10, Red Series, file 20692, memo of 3 July 1893.
58. The letters are found in PAC, RG10, vol. 2, 111, Red Series, 20692.
59. PAC, RG10, vol. 4737, contains the transfer of signatures.
60. See, for example, the *Ottawa Free Press*, 2 October 1893.

61. PAC, RG10, Red Series, file 20692, telegram, Indian Department to Mrs. Lucy Vankoughnet, 23 March 1898.
62. Ibid., Vankoughnet to Scott, 4 October 1893.
63. Ibid., Scott's notation of 5 October. See also PAC, RG10, vol. 4741, Scott to Vankoughnet, 14 October 1893.

6

Clifford Sifton and Canadian Indian Administration
1896–1905

D. J. Hall

"The Indians," observed Clifford Sifton in December 1896, "were the wards of the government and when he settled down to work he would see that we either had more Indians to look after or less officials, for at present there were nearly as many officials as Indians."[1] Undoubtedly an appreciative ripple of applause and laughter flowed through his attentive audience of Liberal supporters. Sifton recently had been appointed minister of the interior and superintendent general of Indian affairs in the Laurier government, and was on a speaking tour of the West before assuming his duties in Ottawa. That Sifton's remarks merely reflected conventional wisdom among Liberals is scarcely surprising, for his main concern was with the Interior Department, and with western development generally.

There appears to be little evidence that Sifton ever had anything but the most casual interest in Indian affairs before being called to Ottawa. He did recall the events of 1885 when, as a member of the home guard in Brandon, he had paraded "the street with a six shooter and a shot gun four or five evenings in succession,"[2] but he did not seem to have been profoundly affected by the Indian and Metis uprising. In 1882, aged only twenty-one, he had begun to practice law in Brandon, and he was elected to the provincial legislature in 1888. In 1891 he entered the Greenway government as attorney-general where he gained provincial and national notoriety as the able defender of Manitoba's "national" school system.

Reprinted from *Prairie Forum* 2, no. 2 (1977).

Sifton's great talents as an organizer, administrator and politician were very evident by 1896 when Laurier made him the youngest member of his cabinet and placed him in charge of western development.

Indian affairs had long been closely associated with the Department of the Interior, which was the principal instrument through which the federal government attempted to implement its developmental policies for the prairie West. The dominion authorities were charged with responsibility for all of Canada's Indians, but it was the prairie Indians who created the greatest problems for the government, and to whom the government had the most obligations. Indian affairs was still a branch of the Department of the Interior when most of the numbered treaties were signed in the 1870's. Although created a separate department in 1880, it thereafter normally retained its association with the Department of the Interior by coming under the aegis of the minister of the interior until 1936. Thus, the Indians were viewed always in the context of western development; their interests, while not ignored, only rarely commanded the full attention of the responsible minister.

Sifton illustrates these problems well. There is plenty of evidence of his desire to serve what he believed to be the best interests of the Indians. Yet he shared some pretty conventional prejudices and misconceptions about them, was heavily influenced by his officials, and always had an eye on the political repercussions of his policies. He further obscured the already hazy separate identity of Indian affairs by placing it and the Interior Department under a single deputy minister. During Sifton's tenure, furthermore, the national budget more than doubled, the Department of the Interior budget nearly quintupled, but that of Indian affairs increased by less than 30 per cent.[3] The fact was that the government — and, indeed, Parliament — had an unvaryingly parsimonious attitude toward the Indians.

By 1896 the western Indians had for some years been settled on reserves which, it was hoped, would serve both to protect and ultimately to acculturate them. The general philosophy of the department, which Sifton shared, seemed to be that the Indians should be quietly maintained on reserves, where they should create as little political difficulty as possible. There they should be prepared for assimilation to white society, or at least become willing and able to achieve a state of economic independence. In the meantime, the government would act as a sort of guardian to prevent exploitation of the Indian, while the various leading Christian denominations were aided in the task of giving him a moral and general education. "Great progress" had been made in this direction, Sifton assured the House of Commons in 1901:

> In the organized portion of the country there is no Indian population that may be considered dangerous so far as the peace of the country is concerned. The Indians are becoming rapidly a peaceful population and self-sustaining. The expenditure we are making is large, but it is made in the pursuance of a policy

favoured by parliament for many years based upon a belief that it is better —
aside from the justice of the question — to bring the Indians into a state of
civilization or comparative civilization, than to take any chance of their
becoming a disturbing factor in the community. Generally the results have
been satisfactory.[4]

I

Upon arriving at Ottawa late in 1896 Sifton plunged into departmental reorganization. Indian affairs had for years been a splendid source of patronage and
sinecures for the Conservative party faithful, and Sifton was determined that
Liberals would now share the spoils of power. Beyond that, the government was
under much pressure to slash budgets because for years the Liberals had de-
nounced the lavish spending of the Tories.[5] Sifton applied the knife to Indian
affairs as thoroughly as it was used on any department. Personnel were dropped,
the western agencies reorganized, and salaries generally reduced.

The first and most serious battle which Sifton fought in order to bring about a
thorough reorganization was to remove the deputies of the Interior and Indian
affairs departments, A. M. Burgess and Hayter Reed respectively, and to place
both departments under a single deputy of his own choosing. Firing of deputies by
an incoming minister was not accepted practice. Sifton was the only Liberal
minister to do so and had to overcome opposition from within the cabinet and from
the governor general.[6]

Placed over the two departments was a political ally from Brandon, James A.
Smart. Like Sifton a former Ontarian who had moved west, Smart had operated a
hardware business in Brandon and served as minister of public works and provincial secretary in the early years of the Greenway administration in Manitoba. He
certainly left his mark on the Department of the Interior, where he served until the
end of 1904, but it is questionable how much influence he had on Indian affairs.
Under Reed even the trivial matters of the daily operation of the office were dealt
with by the deputy; under Smart, almost all letters went out over the signature of
the departmental secretary, J. D. McLean.[7] Smart in fact dealt with only the more
politically sensitive matters of general policy or patronage.

Of the Indian affairs officials, Sifton worked most closely with James Andrew
Joseph McKenna, a second-class clerk who was promoted to be the minister's
private secretary for the department.[8] In reality this was a highly political position.
Through McKenna, Sifton probably had more input into departmental policy-
making than is apparent from the written record, where he appears to have
confined himself largely to making recommendations to the governor general-in-
council, usually based on the advice of his officials. Furthermore, McKenna had
Sifton's ear, and he was placed in charge of some delicate and important activities,
ranging from investigation of local squabbles over patronage, to treaty and

half-breed scrip commissions, to negotiations with the British Columbia government. From 1 July 1901, McKenna was assistant Indian commissioner and chief inspector for Manitoba and the Northwest Territories.

Sifton did not institute these changes in order to effect any drastic new Indian policy. He was interested in efficiency and economy of operation and in political considerations. Yet the changes were a wrench with the past, and they prepared the way for more drastic changes in the future. Not only was Indian affairs placed in a position inferior to the Interior Department, but the traditional policy-making structure was thoroughly shaken up. The new men had had little direct contact with the Indians, and most were relatively unsympathetic, if not "hard-line," in their attitudes.[9] Smart knew nothing of the Indians. Prior to going to Ottawa he was directed to familiarize himself with the western operations of the Department of the Interior; almost incidentally Sifton suggested that he also tour all the Indian schools in Manitoba.[10] McLean, thoroughly experienced in the operations at Ottawa, seems to have had little or no direct experience in the outside service. Despite his later fame in Indian affairs, the chief accountant, poet D. C. Scott, had the outlook of an economizing bookkeeper, expressing concern for cutting costs, living within budgets, and demonstrating absolutely no sympathy for the realities of administration at the reserve level. Finally, as will be seen, McKenna had an uncompromising attitude which clearly found favour with the minister.

Only in Manitoba and the Northwest Territories could Sifton hope to effect significant savings. While perhaps less than one-quarter of Canada's Indians lived in this region, about three-quarters of the Indian affairs budget was expended there.[11] This was mainly because of government obligations, contracted when the treaties were signed, to provide assistance in education and agricultural instruction, food for the destitute, annuities, and medical services. During the 1880's most Indians were settled on reserves, agents assigned to supervise and assist them, farm instructors and schools established to instil new ways and ideas.[12]

Necessarily the service had been somewhat decentralized in early years when communications were poor. The commissioner of Indian affairs, located at Regina and the chief administrative officer in the West, had been empowered to make many vital decisions on the spot.

Shortly after his arrival in Ottawa, Sifton received from A. E. Forget, then commissioner of Indian affairs, a recommendation for a drastic restructuring of the western administration. It called for centralization of the administration at Ottawa, the removal of the commissioner's office from Regina to Winnipeg, reduction of the commissioner's staff from fourteen to three, the creation of six inspectorates (three in the Territories and three in Manitoba), and the closing down of several agencies.[13] Such a course had been suggested within the department as early as 1888, but had been rejected by the government.[14] The new superintendent general had little hesitation in approving the proposed changes with only slight modifications.[15] The basic effect was to change the commissioner's office "very largely from a transmitting office to . . . an inspectoral one.''[16] That is, until 1897 the commissioner's office was occupied principally with checking accounts and reports, a procedure which was repeated in Ottawa and also was the instrument through which western operations were carried out. Such duplication of effort was henceforth to be substantially reduced, and the commissioner was expected to occupy himself with overseeing the inspection of western agencies and schools, making recommendations, and helping in the preparation of estimates for western operations. The agencies and schools were now to receive their directions mainly from Ottawa.

One of the expected benefits of this change was reduced manpower. The changes were drastic. When Sifton took over the department there were 144 employees; within two years some 57 had been dismissed or resigned from the northwest service alone.[17] Naturally, there was not a proportionate decrease in the service because Liberals were appointed to many of the vacancies. In 1897–98 the department budgeted for 115 officers, and by 1904–1905 it had increased to 133.[18] Still the reorganization, which resulted initially in dropping 29 officials, could be said to have been successful in effecting a reduction in the size of the department.

Closely associated with this was Sifton's decision to institute widespread reductions in salaries for many of those fortunate enough to retain their positions. In 1896–97 the average annual salary was $712.33; in 1897–98 this became $683.32, or a drop of about 4 per cent. The salaries of Indian agents had ranged up to $1,400; all were to be cut to $1,000 or $900. The salaries of departmental clerks were reduced, none to exceed $600. Farm instructors, who had drawn up to $600, were reduced to a range of $300 to $480.[19] Some in this way found their salaries reduced as much as $300, or 25 per cent.[20] Undoubtedly, these drastic reductions encouraged some employees to resign or seek superannuation; and it is unlikely that departmental morale was much improved. The department claimed a saving in salaries of $27,189 in the reorganization of the northwest service, but there was a gradual recovery in rates of pay, so that by 1904–1905 the average was $725.67[21]

Whatever the political benefits of a $27,000 saving in salaries and of a flurry of dismissals and resignations, the Indian department budget continued to grow steadily.[22] The changes were instituted in the name of greater efficiency, which of course meant speed in bringing the Indians to self-sufficiency and ultimately assimilation.[23].

One change which did not last long was the attempt to combine two departments under one deputy. The rapid expansion of immigration and settlement made the combined responsibility too heavy, and in 1902 the Indian Department was again given its own deputy superintendent general. Sifton appointed Frank Pedley, a Toronto lawyer who had become superintendent of immigration in 1897. Althouh he had had no experience in Indian affairs, Pedley had proven himself to be an excellent administrator, and he would remain at his new post until 1913.[24]

The effectiveness of these administrative changes was debated heatedly within the department in 1904.[25] The evidence which emerged suggested that they were probably justified, but that they had never been as effective as they should have been because of incredibly lax inspection procedures. Most agencies were inspected less than once a year, and several were well over two years between inspections. The inspectors were responsible for schools as well. Some had been over-burdened, while others simply had not been doing their job.[26] With an average of four or five agencies and a few schools per instructor, there seems to be little reason why the inspections could not have been done at least once a year, if not every six months as recommended. But hard work was rarely demanded of most officials, whether in the outside service or at Ottawa.[27]

The administrative changes, in sum, did result in a slightly smaller staff and a lower cost in salaries. As an economy measure the effect was not marked, because most departmental expenditures were on items over which Sifton had little or no control: schools, annuities, feeding the destitute, and so forth. As an attempt at improving administrative efficiency the effect was marginal. But by centralizing control in the hands of the Ottawa bureaucrats, who were much more concerned with ledger books than difficulties on the reserves, the potential for a much more rigorous prosecution of departmental goals was created.

II

"Next to the solution of the problem of immigration to the Northwest, there is nothing that will add greater lustre to Mr. Sifton's administration than the solving of the problem of teaching the Northwest Indians to live like human beings."[28] Such was the opinion of the *Manitoba Free Press*, which claimed that an effective method of educating the Indians had yet to be devised. Few problems claimed as much time or money from the Department of Indian Affairs.

Once the last treaties were signed and the Indians largely settled on the reserves, the federal government faced the problem of how to fulfil its obligations to provide education to the Indians.[29] In 1879 Nicholas Flood Davin produced a report for the government which recommended continuation of existing mission schools and establishment of denominational industrial boarding schools on the American model.[30] However, the government did not begin its experiment with industrial schools until 1884 and ignored Davin's strictures about the need for high salaries to attract good teachers and the dangers of allowing religious denominations a free hand. It established the principle of sharing the costs with various denominations (Roman Catholic, Anglican, Presbyterian, Methodist) which shouldered the major burden of running the schools. The result of parsimony, low standards, poor enforcement, and inadequate inspection was both white and Indian discontent with the system.[31] Plainly, it was substantially a failure.

Rigorous inspections and higher expenditures might have done something to salvage the situation. Neither was undertaken. As a result of the departmental administrative reorganization, the position of school inspector was abolished, for a time at least, and the duties handed over to agency inspectors. Sifton was unequivocal that increases in education costs could not be contemplated: "the expenditure upon Indians, and particularly upon Indian education, has reached the high water mark, and we must now look to reducing rather than increasing it in any way."[32]

"The object of Indian education," he explained, was "to try and get them to take care of themselves as rapidly as possible." The difficulty was greatest among the Indians of Manitoba and the Northwest Territories, which were "the hardest Indians in Canada to deal with, because of the fact that they are the farthest removed from the ordinary type of the working-man. They are the hardest to get settled down to work."[33] Indians educated for years seemed to revert quickly to the old ways once back on the reserves, and the sentiment was widespread that attempting to educate the Indians was a hopeless cause. Frank Oliver, the aggressive independent Liberal from Alberta, and Sifton's eventual successor, argued that educating Indians in industrial schools was self-defeating: "we are educating these Indians to compete industrially with our own people, which seems to me a very undesirable use of public money, or else we are not able to educate them to compete, in which case our money is thrown away."[34] Sifton scarcely disagreed. He believed that a highly specialized education was generally a waste of time. "I have no hesitation in saying — we may as well be frank — that the Indian cannot go out from school, making his own way and compete with the white man. . . . He has not the physical, mental or moral get-up to enable him to compete. He cannot do it."[35]

When Sifton first came into office, he seems to have believed that the goal of making the Indians "self-supporting citizens" could be achieved only "by persistent and patient effort along the lines followed in the past." The system which had evolved contained basically three kinds of schools. The first was the day school, the oldest and most widespread, but probably least effective, where poorly paid and usually underqualified teachers laboured with Indian children on or near reserves.[36] The second type was the boarding school, also on or near reserves, but where Indian children were more removed from the tribal atmosphere and given "a general and moral education." The third type was the industrial school, which was well removed from the reservations and gave the most varied and specialized curriculum. The day schools were poorest in Sifton's view because "the Indian children are not removed from the surroundings which tend to keep them in a state of more or less degradation" The industrial school, by contrast, removed the child from the reservation and tried to make him competitive with Whites, which the Indian was incapable of becoming. Besides, the cost of these schools was very high. The best solution, he concluded, would be to expand the number of boarding schools, "which would give not so great an amount of education, but a reasonable education, to a much larger number of Indian children, [and] the result would be better on the whole for the Indian population."[37]

That he believed he had made important changes in the system was the burden of Sifton's remarks to the House of Commons in 1904:

> My own belief is that the system of industrial schools as I found it in operation when I took office, is not the best, or the most effective, or the most economic way of improving the condition of the Indians. I thought the system adopted was an artificial system. I found that Indian boys and girls were being kept in these schools in some cases until they were 23, 24 and 25 years of age. The Dominion of Canada is not under any obligation to conduct a system of education for an Indian tribe, under which the education of each child becomes so expensive and so artificial. I put in force a rule that children were not to remain in the schools after the age of eighteen. . . . We have substituted a less elaborate system; a system of what we call boarding schools where a larger number of children can for a shorter time be educated more econom- ically and generally more effectively. What we desire to do is not to give a highly specialized education to half a dozen out of a large band of Indians, but if possible to distribute over the whole band a moderate amount of education and intelligence, so that the general status of the band would be raised.[38]

During Sifton's term as superintendent general there was no serious attempt either to reform the school system or to enforce attendance regulations. The number of Indian children registered in the schools grew slightly from 9,700 in 1896 to 10,000 in 1905, the average attendance rising over 7 per cent.[39] He refused, however, to offer any inducements to Indian parents to send their children to school.[40] And he told the House of Commons that much of his time in the Indian Department was spent resisting demands for more money for schools. "Our position with reference to the Indians is this," he said: "We have them with us, and we have to deal with them as wards of the country. There is no question that the method we have adopted of spending money to educate them is the best possible method of bringing these people to an improved state." To those who objected that little progress was being made, Sifton countered with emphatic denial. He added that the schools were perhaps less efficient than white ones, because "you cannot press the Indian children as you can the children of white people, you cannot require so much from them." He also admitted the difficulty of getting competent teachers. In theory they were required to have a third-class certificate, but "when you pay $300 a year and send a young woman, or a young man, out to a lonesome place where there are no social advantages it is very difficult to get a competent teacher under those circumstances."[41] That $300 was less than half what teachers could expect to make in the city must have been known to most members of Parliament. Yet the chief criticism directed at Sifton concerned the rising cost of

Indian education, not whether better salaries might secure better teachers.[42]

There was indeed a strong tendency within the department to blame the churches for the weaknesses and failures of the system. Wrote Inspector Martin Benson in 1903,

> The Indians do not appreciate the instruction in religion and manners their children receive at these schools. What would impress them would be a practical education that would fit them to earn their own living and assist them to better their condition. That they do not receive such an education is generally admitted.[43]

Religious and moral instruction was naturally of central importance to the churches. The government, on the other hand, wanted the Indians to receive a straightforward practical education leading to self-sufficiency. Departmental officials upbraided the churches for not taking greater responsibility for placing graduates of the schools in jobs, for not securing fully qualified teachers, for teaching too much religion and not enough practical training for an agricultural life on the reserves. But churches then, as always, had limited funds and depended upon the government. The government, in its turn, refused to take the full responsibility.[44] The objective of Indian education was to change completely the moral and spiritual values of the primitive societies, a function widely regarded as properly the province of the churches.[45] Thus, a continuing role in Indian education for the churches simply was not disputed.

If standards were not improved, nor attendance regulations enforced, the government still had made some important decisions. The industrial school was considerably diminished in importance. Some pressure was exerted to make Indian education more practical and relevant to life on the reservation. But, as will be seen, this was not always to be done through formal educational institutions; the schools had not been a great success, and the way was opened to consider alternatives.

III

The policy of the Department of Indian Affairs, wrote Deputy Minister Frank Pedley in 1904, was "to bring the Indians as near the status of the white man as can be and make them a moral, industrious and self supporting class."[46] This was a comprehensive purpose of which formal education could fulfil only a part.

However, certain attitudes tended to hamper the desired development. Rarely was the opinion of an Indian taken seriously unless corroborated by some white man. To one correspondent who was inquiring about Indian protests over a medical officer, Sifton replied that the department found considerable difficulty in arriving at facts where the Indians were concerned. "That difficulty," he wrote, "is such that it is almost impossible for a person who has not had experience with the Indians to understand! It is possible for persons to get the Indians to sign almost any kind of statements, if a little excitement and agitation be got up beforehand, and we are unable therefore to rely to any extent upon written statements that come in signed by Indians."[47] This attitude was reflected time and again in departmental dealings with correspondence from local chiefs and petitions from Indian bands.

A similar attitude prevailed with respect to band funds. Theoretically, interest from Indian trust funds was to be distributed to the tribes to promote a sense of responsibility and self-government. In practice the department was reluctant to release the money and did so only for projects of which it approved. The reason, explained Hayter Reed, was that "the money distributed as interest is a positive deterrent to individual improvement amongst the Indians; they learn to depend too largely upon these payments, and frequently they squander them." Department policy forced the Indians to rely "upon their own resources," which "cannot fail to promote self-reliance."[48]

The government attitude was forcibly demonstrated when the government dismissed for political partisanship a doctor attending the Mohawk Indians of the Bay of Quinte Reservation. Not only was the gentleman in question popular with the Indians, but he had also been paid entirely out of band funds. When the dismissal was protested by the Indians, they appealed first to the department and then to the Queen. Governor General Lord Minto attempted to use his influence to correct what he viewed as an injustice, but he was firmly rebuffed by Sifton:

> it is quite clear that the officials who are paid out of Indian funds are regarded as officials of the Department of Indian Affairs and are fully responsible to the Department in the same way as any other departmental officers and while the views of the Indians are properly considered whenever possible the right of the Indians to control the action of the Department is not under any circumstances recognized. . . . It is as Your Excellency remarks quite correct that the Indians have always looked upon Her Majesty as a final Court of appeal for any complaint which they may wish to make. As a matter of practice however the actual discharge of such functions has for many years been confined to recommending the representations which may be made by the Indians, to the careful attention of the advisers of the Crown.[49]

The paternal grip of the department was in no way to be relaxed. It was felt in innumerable ways, from everyday administrative trivia to issues of band politics. For years the department had assumed the power to depose chiefs who "retarded progress" on the reserves, and there seems to have been little hesitation in using it. One such headman, described as "Tom, alias Kah-pah-pah-mah-am-wa-ko-weko-chin" of Moose Mountain Agency, was said to have brought up his children "to think that any thing in the way of work at farming, cattle keeping or schools is not good for Indians," and his example therefore hindered progress on the reserve.[50]

It was indeed the hope of the Canadian government to change within a generation or two a nomadic hunting society into independent self-supporting agriculturalists. The reasons for the difficulty in making the transition were complex. Departmental planning was often poorly related to the realities of the local conditions and tribal attitudes. Not all farm instructors were either competent or conscientious. Tribal customs were deeply entrenched; and the point must never be forgotten that to change a society from a hunting to a settled agricultural existence meant fundamental adjustments in values and outlook. These could not be altered overnight.

At times the department seemed very far removed from the practical difficulties encountered upon the prairie reserves. It was proposed at one point to impose sheep raising upon the Indians, despite objections from agents, farm instructors, and Indians. But the deputy was convinced it would be good for the Indians, particularly the women; "In connection with this industry will be carding, spinning, and weaving of this wool, for there is no reason why the women, who are greatly in need of constant and useful employment, should not make all the cloth required by the Indians for wear."[51] It was an industry which understandably never seems to have succeeded.

Under Sifton the Indians encountered much greater pressure to farm for themselves. "I may say," wrote J. A. J. McKenna, "that I am convinced that the Indians can only be advanced through labour [that is, being taught, and even virtually forced, to grow grain and raise cattle] and that I propose doing what I can to hasten the day when ration houses shall cease to exist and the Indians be self-supporting. That day will never come if officers continue the system of handling Indians through bribing them with food."[52] The Indians were gradually taught principles of cattle breeding, were discouraged from concentrating on ponies, and were taught also the value of growing grain for profit. This paternalism, Sifton pointed out, was likely to be required for some time. But he did want the Indians to receive a practical agricultural education, and both Indians and farm instructors who were successful were encouraged by the department.

One of the farm instructors, for example, was being supported in an experiment in which several young Indian couples, graduates of the schools, were settled away from their tribes and urged to produce beyond their immediate needs, not sharing with the tribe, and keeping the profits for themselves. "As a matter of practice," stated Sifton, "one of the most serious difficulties in improving an Indian band is that just as soon as an Indian couple show an inclination to thrift and gather a little property around them, all their Indian relations think it is not necessary for them to work just in proportion as this couple is prosperous. Their relations take their supplies, and consequently they have no encouragement to accumulate property." He hoped more and more to see Indian school graduates settled separately, "where they can have [a] much higher type of civilized life than they could if they settled amongst the other Indians."[53]

The department's effort did have some effect, nonetheless, and it could demonstrate some impressive figures showing agricultural progress amongst the Indians of the Territories. In later years Sifton believed that the system which he had initiated was working out very well.[54]

The department had also been engaged in breaking down tribal customs and structures in other ways. Particularly important was the question of tribal cere- monies and dances, crucial for the maintenance and survival of the tribal entity. Shortly after Sifton assumed his duties at Ottawa, the British Columbia govern- ment appealed against the prohibition of the potlatch.[55] After investigation Sifton concluded that the prohibition was justified. The potlatch, he argued, had a demoralizing effect upon the Indians, and the consensus of those working amongst the Indians was that judicious or prudent enforcement of the law would cause no difficulty. A younger generation was rising to power and was opposed to the customs. Finally, "the repeal of the law now . . . would be viewed by the Indians as an evidence on the part of the Government of weakness and vacillation and would produce disrespect and want of confidence in the source from which it emanates."[56]

The traditional discouragement of the sun dance among prairie tribes was also maintained. Although the dance was not proscribed by law, except where torture, mutilation, or giving away of property was involved, the department opposed it because it meant that the Indians abandoned their farm work, left the livestock to starve, and so forth. The department was willing to allow dances involving no torture, no compulsion to attend, where children were not withdrawn from school, which had a fixed time limit, and on occasion provided that tribes or bands from other reserves did not attend. Of course, all these qualifications precisely under- mined the social and spiritual meaning of the dance to the Indian collectively.[57]

In 1902 Lord Minto toured the West and decided to take up the issue of the sun dance, which he believed was unreasonably prohibited.[58] The governor general might have considered the dance to be harmless, but unfortunately the Indians for whom he was so concerned happened to be in the Qu'Appelle Agency under Indian Agent Graham, who ran a model agency from the point of view of the department. His methods, while firm, had made the Indians much more "pro- gressive." Defending his prohibition of the sun dance at some length, Graham argued that the dances were one of the most important mechanisms of reinforcing tribal authority and of undoing all the work of years in the schools to "civilize" the Indians.[59] Once again Minto's appeal had fallen upon deaf ears.[60]

Apart from prohibiting or strongly discouraging a few such activities, the department took only limited action in the area of Indian morality. Revisions of the

Indian Act in 1898 included some controls on immorality, particularly with respect to delinquent parents and parents of illegitimate children, who would no longer be eligible to receive the government allowances for their children.[61] The sale of liquor to Indians on reserves was stringently forbidden by the Indian Act, but the fact that only $500 was voted by the government to enforce the law in central and eastern Canada reflected a very limited concern with the problem. "It is hopeless," wrote J. D. McLean, "to expect that this traffic with the Indians can be entirely suppressed."[62] Naturally, drunkenness on the part of civil servants working with the Indians was not long tolerated.[63] On the reserves, the Indian agent had considerable powers as prosecutor and judge in dealing with the alcohol problem. McLean commented,

> There are many reasons why it is often best to let the Agent exercise the powers conferred upon him by the Indian Act, to hear and determine such cases — as for instance the desire to avoid unnecessary trouble and expense, the fact that he is probably in the best position to weigh the value of Indians' evidence, and to judge as to the nature of the punishment likely to have the best effect upon individual culprits, and because the meting out of justice by the Agent direct, tends to instil proper respect for his authority.[64]

Sifton himself did not favour strong government initiatives, for he believed that the power of the law in enforcing morals was very limited. The government could discourage, but not prohibit, Indian camp meetings, he told one correspondent, and when they were held, it could only "take all possible steps to preserve order and decorum." Before he introduced his amendments to the Indian Act of 1898 he commented, "The question of immorality among Indian women on reserves is one that the Department has made efforts to cope with, but it finds it very difficult to adopt any method that will wipe out the evil. The Department has gone to great lengths in procuring legislation with this end in view . . . but I fear that statutory enactments will be slow in effecting reform, and that we must place our hope mainly on Christianising agencies."[65]

Such complacency extended also to an area of vital concern to the Indians, that of medical attendance. Most of the western treaties included provision for such attendance as required by the Indians, a government responsibility which was extended in varying degrees to Indians across the country. It was beyond question that the standard of these services was poor. When Sifton took office, the decline in the general Indian population was continuing, though it levelled off and began a slow recovery early in the twentieth century. Reports from agents and others constantly made reference to the poor state of health of the Indians, a situation largely taken for granted by the government. For example, one of the problems which exercised the department was the high mortality rate among graduates of the industrial schools. However, the concern was not with improving conditions but with selecting healthier students so that the investment in their education would not be wasted.[66] In a scathing attack on conditions in the Territories, a doctor from Fort MacLeod observed that the mortality rate among the Bloods and Piegans was "over *ninety* per thousand."[67]

The doctor's suggestions for reform were not followed up, because as always the members of Parliament were most concerned with reducing costs.[68] Sifton hoped to minimize costs by instituting a policy of paying a fixed stipend, rather than fees for actual attendance.[69] He claimed that it was a continual struggle to effect economy in medical expenses: "When an Indian gets medicine one day, he imagines he cannot get along unless he gets more the next, and there are bound to be increases from time to time, but we are doing the best we can to keep down the expenditure."[70] "You never can satisfy Indians that they are being properly attended to medically," he declared. "The more medical attendance that is provided the more they want."[71]

Mounting criticism was such that in 1904 Sifton appointed a "medical inspector of the Department of the Interior and Indian Affairs," Dr. P. H. Bryce. His duties would be to supervise the medical attendance of immigrants and Indians, and in this capacity Bryce conducted the first systematic survey of the health of Canadian Indian tribes.[72]

Ungenerous and inadequate as this policy appears in retrospect, it must be admitted that the government believed that the Indians receiving free medical attendance were obtaining services denied to the average Canadian. The very fact that the Indians were wards of the government tended, in Sifton's view, to render them more dependent unless a firm line were taken pressing them to independence.

The government was at great pains to prove that there was progress in this direction. Tables prepared for Sifton demonstrated a decline in the amount of government rations to Indians, a decline which, according to Frank Pedley, was "in a large measure, due to the growing ability of the individual Indians to support themselves."[73] It was departmental policy, he added, "not to pauperize the Indian but to make him furnish as near as possible an equivalent in labour for the assistance rendered." The intent of the department was to make "a strenuous effort in all directions . . . to make all Indians self-sustaining."[74]

IV

The administration of Indian lands was one of the least understood functions of the department.[75] To many speculators, businessmen, and settlers the situation seemed quite clear. The Indians were sitting on valuable land which could be used more profitably by Whites; accordingly the Indians should give way or be removed. Others conceded the Indians' right to some land, but contended that the reserves, originally based on calculation of a certain number of acres per capita or head of family, were unrealistically large when the number of Indians had been dwindling steadily. As the Prairies began to fill with white settlers, pressure on the government to obtain some or all of these lands for efficient exploitation increased. Such attitudes had been present almost since the treaties were signed — indeed in one form or another since the very arrival of Europeans in North America — and had if anything hardened in wake of the 1885 rebellion.[76] It was the influx of settlers in the twentieth century, however, which would help to generate very different policies, particularly when Frank Oliver came to office in 1905. The Indians would thenceforth come under every inducement and pressure to sell their lands and become assimilated.

Publicly, at least, Sifton refused to accede to these pressures and was thus the last superintendent general who operated even superficially on the basis of the old philosophy. His was not a wholehearted commitment to the Indian cause, but to pleas that he open up Indian lands, whether for agricultural, timber or mineral exploitation, he made the same dogged response throughout his term of office. The government acted as trustee for the Indians. "The law," he told Frank Oliver, "is very specific and clear." The Alberta member wanted a reserve at Stony Plain thrown open for settlement. He was firmly informed that "in no case in which the Indians are in possession of a reserve can the same be taken from them without their consent and the money placed to the general credit of all the Indians in the country. . . . This system makes it . . . impossible to throw land held by the Indians open for settlement immediately on a proposition to that effect being made, even in cases in which it is clear to the Department that it is in the general interest as well as in the interest of any particular band themselves that such land should be thrown open."[77] Annually, Sifton had to explain to Parliament that very little could be done without the consent of the tribes concerned and that sometimes that was difficult to obtain. "Whatever may be deemed desirable or otherwise," he told A. A. C. LaRivière, M.P., "the fact of the matter is that the Indians own these lands just as many as my hon. friend (Mr. LaRivière) owns any piece of land for which he has a title in fee simple. The faith of the government of Canada is pledged to the maintenance of the title of these Indians in that land." The government would seek Indian consent to exploitation of their lands, "when we think it will not interfere with the means of livelihood of the Indians."[78]

The problems, and Sifton's approaches to them, are best illustrated with specific examples. The Dokis Indians' refusal to accede to the exploitation of pine timber on their reserve in Ontario particularly exercised departmental officials. The forest was mature, and if it was not lost to fire, it would soon begin to rot and lose its value. Even taking only those trees over nine inches at the base, it was calculated that some 45,000,000 board feet of timber could be harvested. In this case Sifton had the power and was quite prepared to legislate to impose an arrangement whereby the band, consisting of eighty people, would receive some

$250,000 cash bonus, and a royalty of $1 per 1,000 board feet. That the deal was perfectly logical and advantageous for the Indians seemed obvious to the department. But there was some impatience with the attitude of the aged Chief Dokis who was unimpressed with the prospect of monetary gain; he believed he had a moral or spiritual obligation to preserve the forest intact for his successors.[79]

In another case, the Canadian Northern Railway promoters, Mackenzie and Mann, wished in 1904 to obtain a townsite for a divisional point, to be located on the Coté Reserve in northeast Assiniboia. It was, they claimed, the best site in twenty miles. The Indians were willing to surrender the land because of the high cash value, and they were supported by the local agent. But Sifton believed that the town (Kamsack), being located on the reserve, would create serious social problems. Only reluctantly did he agree to the sale, after ensuring that the Indians would profit from the arrangement as would any ordinary landowner. Unhappily, the adverse effects foreseen by Sifton were realized in the future.[80]

A different problem had faced the department in the early 1890's at the Roseau River Reserve, located on first-class agricultural land. By 1898 the population had declined to 261, and much of the land was not being used. There was pressure from the surrounding areas and from Indian Department officials to obtain a surrender of at least part of the lands. By 1900 the population was reduced to 244, and by 1902 to 209. The Indians simply were making no progress; as the districts around the reserve were settled the Indians seemed unwilling to work and were tempted to drift into nearby settlements. Their numbers depleted by disease and their spirit sapped, the agent believed that the only hope was to obtain a surrender and use the money to purchase a more isolated reserve where they could be relocated. This was done, after some difficulty in persuading the Indians, in 1903.[81]

In southern Alberta the Blackfoot Indians refused all methods of persuasion by the ranching community to obtain grazing leases on the reserve. There was nothing the department could do in face of such intransigence.[82] On the other hand, the Blackfoot tribe could only have been reinforced in their position by observing the nearby Blood Reserve, where the chiefs had agreed to a lease. When a group of the tribe protested to Ottawa, they claimed that the chiefs had not been representative of the tribe and that each man should have been consulted in a tribal vote, that the leaseholders had not taken up their leases promptly as prescribed in the leases, and that promises of money and free trips to Ottawa for the chiefs (obviously not in the lease) had not been fulfilled. In this case Sifton flatly rejected the tribal contentions.[83] Unquestionably, he saw the issue simply in terms of a legal contract, the obligations of which the Indians must fulfil.

The most extended case involving Indian lands in these years concerned the Songhees Reserve which was located precisely where the city of Victoria, B.C., wished to expand. In British Columbia the province had reversionary rights to any Indian lands sold or funds arising therefrom. The local government viewed the land as a potential source of public money, insisting that the Indians were only entitled to the original value of the land, not the tremendous increment to its value caused by its being in an urban setting. The provincial government hoped through this subterfuge to buy the land for a song and then parcel it out at high prices to various urban interests. It also wanted the federal government to assume the costs of obtaining a new reserve and removing the Indians. Sifton absolutely refused such terms. He was as desirous as anyone to remove the Indians from the "contaminating influences of city life with the worst and most demoralizing features of which they are constantly brought in contact."[84] But the Indians must, he insisted, obtain the full value of the lands.[85]

Land surrenders and leases could serve many purposes. They could be a source of funds to repay tribal debts or to provide capital for new equipment or enterprises. Timber, grazing, or mineral leases in particular were designed to produce income, and sometimes work, for Indians over a number of years. On occasion it was desirable, at least to the department, to remove the Indians from demoralizing urban influences. Similarly, when a reserve declined in population, Indians began to drift to other reserves, and the lands could be sold and the money put to use for the benefit of the other bands.[86] Undeniably, the department was sometimes wrong in its judgment and also induced some Indians in questionable ways to give up their lands. There seemed to be a belief that the Indian population would continue to dwindle, so that large tracts of land on some reserves simply would never be required; why not sell the land, or lease it, when the monetary benefits seemed so obvious? The government also made the assumption that all Indians could and should become agricultural, even in some unsuitable districts, influencing its attitude to non-agricultural lands.[87]

Indian land surrenders were by no means new when Sifton came to office.[88] It is not clear how much land was surrendered during Sifton's term of office, but Frank Oliver claimed that 289,807 hectares of Indian lands were sold between 1 July 1896 and 31 March 1909.[89] Generally speaking this was seen positively by the white community. Any criticism was directed at the government's failure to obtain more land from the Indians; the Indians, it was said, must not be allowed to stand in the way of progress and the Indians' general well-being.[90] But no serious attempt was made to change the law to facilitate the appropriation of Indian lands by Whites.[91] As to what the Indians themselves thought, the department tended to be impatient. Old Indian concepts of land and ownership were considered simply vestiges of a passing culture which was of itself inferior and inevitably giving way to "civilization" and "progress." The government quite sincerely believed that this was in the best interest of the Indians.

V

Clifford Sifton's tenure as superintendent general of Indian affairs did not occasion dramatic changes in Canadian Indian policy. He had almost no creative new ideas to offer, and most of his policy statements and administrative reforms appear to have been generated substantially within the department. It is arguable that his administrative reforms made the service more efficient, more highly centralized, and that he made a fairly steady effort to minimize the number of incompetent officials. He left his stamp on the department in many of the leading personnel and indeed in the drastic upheaval at all levels of the staff. The changes tended to bring to power men who were if anything less sympathetic to the Indians and to place expenditure under the control of a cost-conscious bureaucracy.

Disillusionment with the reserve system was already present in the department when Sifton came to office, and before long it would become more widespread. "Experience does not favour the view that the system makes for the advancement of the Indians," McKenna told Sifton in 1898.[92] The education system in particular was much slower in breaking down old customs than had been hoped. Yet there was no movement toward fundamental change, and Sifton tried to alter the existing reserve administration and the method of education to make them more efficient. Assimilation of individual Indians came to be regarded as the longer-term goal because of the difficulty of educating Indians to compete with Whites or to make their way individually off the reserves. In the short run the emphasis was to be on a practical, limited education for entire bands, to make the Indian self-sufficient agriculturalists on the reserves, and to "wean" them from dependence upon the government. With this end in view the department also encouraged examples of progress among the Indians by special attention to successful Indians and agents.

In these years the Indians seemed at long last to be making the adjustment to reserve life; the decline in population was arrested, and, perhaps with the aid of a programme of vaccination for all Indian children, slight increases in population began to be noticed early in the twentieth century. Government officials could point to some improvements in agricultural progress on the reserves. Although Sifton accepted the widespread belief that Indians could not compete in white society and would require continued government assistance, he resisted complete acceptance of the policy of paternalism. He endeavoured to reduce Indian dependence upon the government. In the long run he hoped to see the Indians self-supporting, civilized, and accepting the competitive and individualistic values of his own society. But continued parsimony in the administration reflected his view that Indians were not a major priority. They were a responsibility to be lived with, not likely to contribute significantly to the progress of the country.

This is to state the obvious: how else did men of Sifton's day regard Indians? Even Lord Minto, no admirer of Sifton and critical of certain details in the Indian administration, concluded by the time he left the country in 1904 that "Canada's management of her Indians has been excellent and something to be proud of for it's a very difficult question, or rather has been, for it is practically worked out now."[93]

Not all of Minto's contemporaries would have agreed. With Sifton's successor, Frank Oliver, and a new Indian Act in 1906, a different era of greater firmness and of serious efforts to assimilate the Indians and obtain their lands was ushered in. By comparison Sifton's term of office appears to be but a mild transition from the practices of early administration, an effort to make past policies more efficient. But in a sense it was also a period which helped to make possible the more drastic change realized under his successors.

NOTES

1. *Winnipeg Daily Tribune*, 12 December 1896.
2. PAC, Sir Clifford Sifton Papers, vol. 242, pp. 231–32, Sifton to Walter Scott, M.P., 5 March 1901.
3. Canada, Parliament, *Sessional Papers*, 1898, #1 (Auditor General's Report for 1896–97), pt. A, p. 4; pt. G, pp. 2–3; pt. H, p. 2; 1906, #1 (Auditor General's Report for 1904–05), pt. C, p. 5; pt.J, p. 2; pt. L, p. 2. The national budget increased from $43,174,000 in 1896–97 to $88,584,111 in 1904–05; the Department of the Interior budget from $817,394 to $4,175,000; and the Department of Indian Affairs from $962,977 to $1,248,000.
4. Canada, House of Commons, *Debates*, 1901, col. 2763, 10 April 1901.
5. *Tribune*, 12 April 1897. Even by Liberal calculations the total saving in government estimates for 1897 was only about $1.5 million, despite claims while in opposition that savings of $3 million or $4 million could be effected.
6. For greater detail on this issue, see D. J. Hall, "The Political Career of Clifford Sifton, 1896–1905" (Ph.D. diss., University of Toronto, 1973), pp. 140–42. Hayter Reed was a former militia officer who had entered the interior service in 1881 and became an Indian agent and then assistant Indian commissioner for the Northwest Territories in 1884. In 1893 he was promoted to the post of deputy superintendent general in Ottawa. See H. J. Morgan, *The Canadian Men and Women of the Time*, 2d. ed. (Toronto, 1912), p. 931; John Frederick Lewis Prince, "The Education and Acculturation of the Western Canadian Indian 1880–1970, with Reference to Hayter Reed" (M.A. thesis, Bishop's University, 1974), esp. p. 38ff.
7. Sifton must have realized that this would be the case; see *Debates*, 1897, cols. 1709–21, 4 May 1897. McLean was promoted from head of the land and timber branch to become secretary and chief clerk. Sifton had a high regard for his ability; but a perusal of McLean's correspondence suggested a man of short temper, concerned with picayune detail in day-to-day matters, and very impressed with his own importance. On more than one occasion he complained to the deputy that he was not being treated with due deference by other employees. When Sifton took over the department, McLean sent him a long screed complaining of gross inefficiency in the department (PAC, Sifton Papers, vol. 7, 3880–4025, 31 December 1896, and encl.). McLean, grandson of a Liberal MP at the time of Alexander Mackenzie, one John Farris, had been appointed to the department in October 1876, rising to the position of first class clerk by 1896 (see memo in ibid., 3973–87).
8. The appointment was effective 1 February 1897. McKenna was an Irish Catholic, born in Prince Edward Island in 1862. He had been private secretary to the superintendent general in 1887–88, and a clerk thereafter. PAC, RG10, Department of Indian Affairs (DIA) Records, vol. 3853, file 77144; Morgan, p. 775.
9. In fairness it must be conceded that a hard line was not new. Certainly Reed, and sometimes his predecessor as deputy, L. Vankoughnet, could be inflexible and unwilling to consider the Indian

viewpoint. Reed, nevertheless, had had at least two years' experience as an Indian agent. On his attitudes, see Prince, pp. 64, 66, 74, 85. He admitted in 1895 that he was "necessarily out of touch, to a great extent, with the Indians."

10. PAC, Sifton Papers, vol. 214, pp. 692–94, Sifton to Smart, 28 December 1896; see also vol. 33, file "Smart, J. A. 1897."

11.

	Total	Manitoba and Northwest Territories
1896–97	$ 962,977.25	$701,503.83
1897–98	$1,001,304.93	$734,919.82
1898–99	$1,037,531.04	$776,192.92
1899–1900	$1,093,429.01	$823,951.34
1900–01	$1,075,849.22	$798,908.30
1901–02	$1,115,271.94	$822,444.00
1902–03	$1,141,099.08	$818,576.54
1903–04	$1,159,712.24	$804,098.55
1904–05	$1,248,305.00	$869,980.95

Source: *Sessional Papers*, 1898–1906, Auditor General's Reports. British Columbia Indians accounted for about one-tenth of the budget, and Ottawa office expenditure for about 6 or 7 per cent, which obviously did not leave much for Indians in the rest of the country.

12. See J. B. D. Larmour, "Edgar Dewdney, Commissioner of Indian Affairs and Lieutenant Governor of the North-West Territories" (M.A. thesis, University of Saskatchewan, Regina, 1969), ch. 1–4, pp. 276–77. On the earlier period, see H. D. Kemp, "The Department of the Interior in the West 1873–1883; An Examination of Some Hitherto Neglected Aspects of the Work of the Outside Service" (M.A. thesis, University of Manitoba, 1950), pp. 12–32.

13. PAC, Sifton Papers, vol. 19, 12029–40, Forget to Sifton, 20 January 1897. The figures were those of Forget; in fact the reduction was from nineteen employees to six in the commissioner's office. The agencies abolished were Clandeboye, Portage la Prairie, Rat Portage, and Savanne. PAC, RG10, vol. 3877, file 91839–1.

14. PAC, Sifton Papers, ibid.; and PAC, RG10, vol. 3635, file 6567, D. C. Scott to the deputy superintendent general of Indian Affairs, 3 March 1904.

15. PAC, Sifton Papers, vol. 19, 12059–60, Sifton to Forget, 21 May 1897; PAC, RG10, vol. 3877, file 91839–1. It should be noted that when Reed was deputy minister the administration had been centralized in practice in Ottawa, as he had been unwilling to delegate any authority. Seen in this light, Sifton's changes simply gave legal sanction to a situation which already existed; but it also permitted a reduction in manpower which redounded to the political credit of the Liberals. I am grateful to Dr. John Tobias of Red Deer College for pointing this out.

16. Ibid., vol. 3635, file 6567, Frank Pedley (deputy superintendent-general) to Sifton, 24 March 1904; Sifton Papers, vol. 221, pp. 346–47, Sifton to J. W. Smith, 10 July 1897.

17. PAC, RG10, vol. 3984, file 168921, James A. Smart, Return to the House of Commons concerning dismissals, June 1896 to 25 April 1898; vol. 3635, file 6567, D. C. Scott to the deputy superintendent general, 3 March 1904, pp. 17–18. Apart from those who resigned, twelve found their positions abolished and were not rehired, eight were removed for political partisanship, and eleven were removed for incompetence, disobedience, insubordination, drunkenness, and related problems. (See also ibid., vol. 3877, file 91839–1.) Those dismissed received gratuities on the following schedule: up to five years' service, 1 month's salary; 5 to 7 years' service, 2 months' salary; over 7 years' service, 3 months' salary (ibid., Sifton to Forget, 6 July 1897). To one correspondent who complained of the treatment meted out to civil servants, Sifton replied, "I can assure you that it has been no pleasure to me to dispense with the services of officials in the West, but in the public interest it was absolutely necessary to bring the expenditure on the Indian service within reasonable bounds, and this could not be done without dismissing some of the staff. Every effort was made in the reorganization to provide for as many of the old hands as possible." PAC, Sifton Papers, vol. 220, pp. 619–20, Sifton to Dr. Hardy, 29 May 1897.

18. PAC, RG10, vol. 3635, file 6567, D. C. Scott to the deputy superintendent general, 3 March 1904, pp. 17–18.

19. PAC, Sifton Papers, vol. 278, file 12; vol. 279, file 13; vol. 280, 18576–7.

20. PAC, RG10, vol. 1120, p. 467, Sifton to Governor General-in-Council, 7 July 1897. One group of eleven employees had their salaries cut an aggregate of $2,200.
21. PAC, Sifton Papers, ibid.; RG10, vol. 3635, file 6567, D. C. Scott to the deputy superintendent general, 3 March 1904, p. 18.
22. See above, n. 11.
23. See Sifton's explanation of the changes in *Debates*, 1899, cols. 5722–5, 22 June 1899. There were also changes in administrative structure at Ottawa, though less change in personnel. Sifton consolidated some seven branches of the department (land and timber, accountant's, correspondence, registry, technical, statistics and supply, and school) into three branches (secretarial, accountants, land and timber).
24. Morgan, p. 893; *Debates*, 1902, cols. 3035–37, 8 April 1902; *Sessional Papers*, 1904, #27, p. xvii. It should be added that petty rivalries among the leading officials in the Indian affairs department were perhaps an important factor in Sifton's decision to appoint someone from outside.
25. PAC, RG10, vol. 3635, file 6567, J. A. J. McKenna to the superintendent general, 12 January 1904; and passim.
26. Ibid., F. Pedley to Sifton, 24 March 1904, pp. 26–28.
27. At Ottawa the office hours were from 9:30 A.M. to 4:00 P.M., with one and a quarter hours for lunch. Nevertheless, J. D. MacLean was complaining about all the correspondence imposed on the office by the centralization, with a reduced staff; he claimed that they actually had to write some 75 to 100 letters a day, and this with a staff of over forty (mostly clerks) at headquarters. PAC, RG10, vol. 1122, pp. 332–33, McLean to Smart, 1 December 1898; vol. 1125, p. 549, McLean to Miss Yielding, 25 July 1902.
28. *Manitoba Free Press*, 29 December 1896.
29. On the question in general, see J. W. Chalmers, *Education behind the Buckskin Curtain: a History of Native Education in Canada* (Edmonton, 1974); H. J. Vallery, "A History of Indian Education in Canada" (M.A. thesis, Queen's University, 1942); Kathryn Kozak, "Education and the Blackfoot, 1870–1900" (M.A. thesis, University of Alberta, 1971); Jacqueline Gresko, "White 'Rites' and Indian 'Rites': Indian Education and Native Responses in the West, 1870–1910," in A. W. Rasporich, ed., *Western Canada, Past and Present* (Calgary, 1975), pp. 163–81.
30. PAC, RG10, vol. 3674, file 11422, "Report on Industrial Schools for Indians and Half-Breeds," Ottawa, 14 March 1879; C. B. Koester, "Nicholas Flood Davin: a Biography" (Ph.D. diss., University of Alberta, 1971), pp. 77–78.
31. PAC, RG10, vol. 3920, file 116751–B, Martin Benson to the deputy superintendent general, 23 June 1903.
32. "My present impression," he told one of his Liberal colleagues in 1897, "is that there will be no substantial increases in these items [Indian education] in the next four years." PAC, Sifton Papers, vol. 264, pp. 258–60, Sifton to Rev. A. Sutherland, general secretary, Methodist Church, 10 January 1898; vol. 220, pp. 777–78, Sifton to J. G. Rutherford, MP, 4 June 1897. See also vol. 224, p. 435, Sifton to Rev. G. M. Grant, 14 January 1898.
33. *Debates*, 1899, cols. 5725–26, 22 June 1899.
34. Ibid., 1897, col. 4076, 14 June 1897.
35. Ibid., 1904, cols. 6946–56, 18 July 1904; see also 1903, cols. 7260–61, 23 July 1903.
36. Salaries ranged from $200 to $300; many teachers were not even required to have a teaching certificate.
37. *Debates*, 1899, cols. 7480–99, esp. 7483–86, 14 July 1899. With the hope that greater economy and better results might be achieved, there was a proposal made in the department that a hierarchy of schools be established. Children were then expected to attend school between the ages of six and sixteen. All children, under this plan, would begin in day schools, though there was no upper age limit. The more promising and healthy students would attend boarding school between the ages of eight and fourteen, and the best of these would be selected for industrial schools. PAC, RG10, vol. 1121, pp. 511–13, J. D. McLean to A. E. Forget, 8 March 1898; pp. 692–99, memorandum, J. D. McLean, 20 July 1897; vol. 1121, pp. 689–91, J. A. Smart to Rev. A. J. Vining, 30 May 1898.

    Sifton also opposed "transferring girls from the boarding [to the industrial] schools. In their case the domestic work in which they can assist at the schools in the later years of their pupilship is the best sort of industrial training that they can obtain." Sifton Papers, vol. 265, pp. 403–5, Sifton to Bishop Legal, 22 March 1901.

38. *Debates*, 1904, cols. 6946–56, 18 July 1904. A case in point occurred in 1903–1904 when the Oblate fathers were given permission to acquire the land and buildings of the St. Boniface Industrial School, in return for which they were to build and help support three new boarding schools, in addition to a fourth which was already nearing completion. While the industrial school could not teach agriculture adequately, it would be taught to the boys at each boarding school, while the girls would be trained "to do house work." PAC, RG10, vol. 3920, file 116751–B, passim, esp. order-in-council, 8 January 1904.

39. *Sessional Papers*, 1897, #14, pp. 416–7; 1906, #27, pt. ii, pp. 54–55.

40. PAC, Sifton Papers, vol. 265, pp. 403–5, Sifton to Bishop Legal, 22 March 1901. He wrote, "I would infer from your Lordship's letter that we would in some way have to make good to the Indians what they lose in service through the absence of their boys and what they would get as marriage gifts from prospective sons in law if the girls were at home and eligible for marriage from their twelfth year. Action in that direction would come pretty close to a system of purchase of Indian children, and, it strikes me, would be more open to objection than even the compulsory method." It should be added that years earlier the department had begun the practice of giving the children in Manitoba and Territorial schools a noonday meal as an inducement to attend, and this practice continued; see Chalmers, pp. 162–63; PAC, RG10, vol. 1120, pp. 692–99, memorandum, J. D. McLean, 20 July 1897.

41. *Debates*, 1902, cols. 3043–46, 18 April 1902.

42. Several times proposals for increased pay for teachers were made within the department. In 1887 the deputy superintendent general, L. Vankoughnet, proposed such action to Prime Minister Macdonald, but it was ignored. In 1891 another proposal was buried, as was a proposal from an Indian agent and backed by the Indian commissioner in 1903. This latter suggestion apparently never reached the ministerial level. Only once, and then put obliquely and unsympathetically, does the idea seem to have reached Sifton's desk. Not until about 1912 or 1913 was there a substantial increase in salaries over levels of the 1880's, but they were still too low to compete very effectively for good teachers. PAC, RG10, vol. 3965, file 1500000–8; vol. 1120, pp. 692–99, memorandum, J. D. McLean, 20 July 1897.

43. Ibid., vol. 3920, file 116751–A, Benson to the deputy superintendent general, 23 June 1903. Concerning similar sentiments about education expenditure among the Yukon Indians, see vol. 3962, file 147654–1, vol. 2, esp. F. T. Congdon to F. Pedley, April 1903; and John Ross to Congdon, 6 July 1903.

44. Sifton did make two small concessions in extending departmental obligations, expending up to $5,000 for education among Yukon Indians, an area ignored by the government prior to the gold rush; and permitting half-breed children residing on Indian reserves to attend the Indian schools. Ibid.; and vol. 3931, file 117377–1C, D. Laird to J. D. McLean, 27 August 1900.

45. See Sifton's speech of 17 November 1902 to the General Assembly of the Methodist Church (Toronto *Globe*, 18 November 1902). Although he was not speaking about Indian education, the points made are applicable.

46. PAC, RG10, vol. 3635, file 6567, Pedley to Sifton, 24 March 1904, p. 4.

47. PAC, Sifton Papers, vol. 238, pp. 635–36, Sifton to Rev. S. D. Chown, 29 August 1900.

48. PAC, RG10, vol. 1119, pp. 625–28, H. Reed to Sifton, 26 December 1896; vol. 1120, pp. 36–37, Reed to Sifton, 26 January 1897.

49. Ibid., and pp. 734–37, Sifton to Governor General-in-Council, 30 December 1896; Sifton Papers, vol. 68, file "Minto, Lord 1899," passim.; Lord Minto Papers, vol. 10, pp. 3–5, Minto to Sifton, 1 May 1899, and reply, pp. 6–8, 11 May 1899; pp. 9–10, Minto to Sifton, 15 May 1899.

50. PAC, RG10, vol. 1121, Sifton to Governor General-in-Council, 11 September 1897; see also vol. 1125, p. 164, same, 4 September 1901 (concerning Chief Paul of White Whale Lake), and p. 379, same, 11 March 1902 (concerning Chief Piapot of the Qu'Appelle Agency).

51. Ibid., vol. 3877, file 91839–1, H. Reed to A. E. Forget, 9 July 1896. For another example, see S. Raby, "Indian Treaty No. 5 and The Pas Agency, Saskatchewan N.W.T.," *Saskatchewan History* 25 (1972):108–9.

52. PAC, Sifton Papers, vol. 106, 83483–92, McKenna to Sifton, 10 December 1901.

53. *Debates*, 1902, cols. 3054–56, 18 April 1902; 1903, cols. 6422–24, 10 July 1903; 1904, cols. 6942–45, 6954–57, 18 July 1904. There was also encouragement for Indians to work with white farmers where "they learn much more than they would on the reserves," particularly "manners,

morals, customs and ideas of earning a living in a civilized way" (PAC, RG10, vol. 3920, file 116751–1A, Martin Benson to deputy superintendent general, 23 June 1903, p. 6). Sifton, however, never went as far as suggested by J. D. McLean, who believed that "it might be advisable . . . in the case of graduates of Industrial Schools to provide for their *ipso facto* enfranchisement, and give them locations on their reserves as enfranchised Indians" (ibid., vol. 1120, pp. 692–99, memorandum, McLean, 20 July 1897.)

54. PAC, Sifton Papers, vol. 201, 159135, Sifton to Laurier, 19 November 1914; PAC, RG10, vol. 3635, file 6567, Pedley to Sifton, 24 March 1904. The figures supplied by Frank Pedley were as follows:

	1897–98	1902–03	Increase
Cattle	15,767	21,291	5,524
Cleared and natural pasturage (acres)	1,917,019	2,279,922	362,903
Cultivated and made pasturage (acres)	16,703	32,557	15,854
Crops (staples) in bushels	128,447	288,695	160,248
Increase in value of clearing, cultivating, buildings, agricultural products, etc.	$ 51,006.00	$ 140,678.00	$ 89,672.00
Increase in value Live Stock and Poultry, Implements, real property, General and Household effects, Real and Personal Property, Incomes	$6,339,600.67	$11,636,976.90	$5,297,376.23

55. On the history of the issue, see F. E. LaViolette, *The Struggle for Survival: Indian Cultures and the Protestant Ethic in British Columbia* (Toronto, 1973); Robin Fisher, *Contact and Conflict: Indian-European Relations in British Columbia, 1774–1890* (Vancouver, 1977).
56. PAC, RG10, vol. 1121, pp. 399–400, Sifton to Governor General-in-Council, 18 January 1898.
57. See ibid., vol. 3825, files 60511–1 and 2, passim.
58. PAC, Sir Wilfrid Laurier Papers, vol. 248, 69214–20, Minto to Laurier, 16 January 1903; 69232–8, same, 17 January 1903. Minto claimed that "there is a want in many cases of human sympathy between the white administrator and the Indian," and suggested that "somewhat narrow religious sentiments have not conduced to a sympathetic understanding of the Indian races."
59. PAC, Minto Papers, vol. 6, 30–36, F. Pedley to Laurier, 30 January 1903 (quoting Graham).
60. Minto's sympathy with the Indians reveals considerable innocence about the importance of the dance in Indian life; he saw it simply as a continuing pleasant tradition, in the same way that the Scots wore kilts and played highland games (PAC, Laurier Papers, vol. 252, 70325–9, Minto to Laurier, 17 February 1903). Perhaps important was the comment of Comptroller F. White of the North West Mounted Police that "the objection to Indian dances has changed from the atrocities practiced by the Indians, to the evil influences of the whites and Half breeds who attend the dances and corrupt the poor Indian" (Minto Papers, vol. 29, 38. White to Minto, 25 May 1903).
61. *Debates*, 1898, cols. 5661–62, 6960–65, 17 May 1898.
62. PAC, RG10, vol. 1125, pp. 550–51, McLean to deputy superintendent general, July 25, 1902.
63. After firing one Indian agent for drunkenness, Sifton commented, "I can see no use whatever in endeavouring to elevate the moral tone of the Indian race and sending drunken officials to carry on the work" (PAC, Sifton Papers, vol. 243, p. 528, Sifton to Rev. John McDougall, 14 May 1901).
64. PAC, RG10, vol. 1124, pp. 507–8, McLean to J. Girard, M.P., 2 March 1901.
65. PAC, Sifton Papers, vol. 264, pp. 172–73, Sifton to Rev. J. W. Lawrence, 10 December 1897.
66. PAC, RG10, vol. 1121, pp. 511–13, J. D. McLean to A. E. Forget, 8 March 1898. A very useful survey is G. Graham-Cumming, "Health of the Original Canadians, 1867–1967," *Medical Services Journal, Canada* 23 (1967): pp. 115–66. This article serves to update the basic study by C. R. Maundrell, "Indian Health, 1867–1940" (M.A. thesis, Queen's University, 1941).
67. PAC, Sifton Papers, vol. 102, 80470–3, G. A. Kennedy, M.D., to Sifton, 14 January 1901. This is substantially confirmed by Graham-Cumming, p. 134. Among the Crees the mortality rate had been as high as 137 per 1000. Most of this was caused by tuberculosis. By 1929 the tuberculosis death rate had fallen to 8 per thousand, still twenty times the national average; by 1967 it was less than 10 per 100,000, but still five times the national average.
68. One exception was A. S. Kendall, M.P. for Cape Breton, who angrily termed the low level of

expenditure "simply criminal" and commented that the $3,000 estimate for medical attendance in New Brunswick "would not provide them [the Indians] with coffins in the spring of the year" (*Debates*, 1902, cols. 3051, 3053, 18 April 1902).

69. Ibid., col. 3041, 18 April 1902; PAC, Sifton Papers, vol. 265, pp. 423–24, Sifton to Rev. John Fraser, 29 March 1901. It should be pointed out that most doctors only supplemented their incomes by being available as required by the Indians and did not live on reserves.

70. *Debates*, 1902, col. 3040, 18 April 1902.

71. Ibid., 1903, col. 6329, 9 July 1903. A fairly long debate on aspects of the question is ibid., cols. 6326–52, 6408–9, 9 and 10 July 1903.

72. Ibid., 1904, cols. 6960–64, 18 July 1904; *Sessional Papers*, 1906, #27, pp. xx, 271–78; M. Zaslow, *The Opening of the Canadian North, 1870–1914* (Toronto, 1971), pp. 227–29; Graham-Cumming, pp. 124–25.

73. PAC, RG10, vol. 3635, file 6567, Pedley to Sifton, 24 March 1904. Pedley's figures were as follows:

			Decrease
Indians on the ration list	1890–91	12,155	
	1896–97	8,853	3,302
	1902–03	5,928	2,925
Flour	1890–91	1,745,300 lbs.	
	1896–97	1,286,100 lbs.	459,200
	1902–03	991,050 lbs.	295,050
Beef	1890–91	2,029,697 lbs.	
	1896–97	1,409,783 lbs.	619,914
	1902–03	1,206,715 lbs.	203,068
Bacon	1890–91	245,742 lbs.	
	1896–97	149,266 lbs.	96,476
	1902–03	135,887 lbs.	13,379

74. Ibid., D. C. Scott to Pedley, 3 March 1904.

75. Ibid., vol. 119, pp. 616–18, Hayter Reed to Sifton, 23 December 1896. According to the act, "Indian Lands" included any reserve, or portion of a reserve, surrendered to the Crown, generally to be sold or used for the benefit of the Indians. It also stated, "The expression 'Reserve' means any tract or tracts of land set aside by Treaty or otherwise for the use or benefit of or granted to a particular Band of Indians, of which the legal title is in the Crown, and which remains a portion of the said Reserve and includes all the trees, wood, timber, soil, stones, minerals, metals and other valuables thereon or therein." See also ibid., vol. 3875, file 90, 880–2, L. Vankoughnet to T. M. Daly, 28 June 1893.

76. See Stewart Raby, "Indian Land Surrenders in Southern Saskatchewan," *Canadian Geographer* 17 (1973): 36–52. A case in point is the attitude of Frank Oliver before and after the events of 1885; see W. S. Waddell, "The Honorable Frank Oliver" (M.A. thesis, University of Alberta, 1950), pp. 58–62, 107–8, 133n.101.

77. PAC, Sifton Papers, vol. 264, pp. 87–88, Sifton to Oliver, 5 August 1897. It should be noted that when Sifton went to Ottawa in 1896 he apparently assumed that Indian lands could readily be appropriated by departmental order. It was only after his officials pointed out the difficulties to him and the Department of Justice ruled in favour of the Indians that Sifton took the line of adhering to the law. This did not, of course, prevent him from trying to persuade the Indians to agree to certain surrenders, in which respect he was somewhat more aggressive than his Conservative predecessors. I am grateful for these comments to Dr. John Tobias of Red Deer College, who also generously permitted me to examine some of the work he has done for the Federation of Saskatchewan Indians.

78. *Debates*, 1904, cols. 6952–53, 18 July 1904; see also 1903, cols. 6410–15, 10 July 1903.

79. PAC, Sifton Papers, ibid.; DIA Records, vol. 1125, pp. 124–29, J. D. McLean to Sifton, 13 August 1901. On the concept "of the reserve as a thing to be handed down inviolate and in trust," see Raby, "Indian Land Surrenders," p. 46.

80. Ibid., pp. 42, 44; PAC, RG10, vol. 4015, file 273023, vol. 1, passim; and see T. D. Regehr, *The*

Canadian Northern Railway: Pioneer Road of the Northern Prairies, 1895–1918 (Toronto, 1976), pp. 172–74.

81. PAC, RG10, vol. 3730, file 26306–1.
82. Ibid., vol. 3571, file 130–18.
83. Ibid., vol 3571, file 130–19. This experience probably contributed to later Blood intransigence on land sales from the reserve; see ibid., vol. 1547, deputy superintendent general to W. J. Hyde, 9 August 1911.
84. The quotation is from Premier J. H. Turner in a letter to J. A. J. McKenna, 22 September 1897, in ibid., vol 3688, file 13886–2.
85. The extensive files on this issue are in ibid., vols. 3688–90, files 13886–1 to 13886–4; see also *Debates*, 1899, cols. 5703–9, 22 June 1899.
86. Raby, "Indian Land Surrenders," passim.
87. Ibid., pp. 49–50; and Raby, "Indian Treaty No. 5," pp. 111–12.
88. See Canada, *Indian Treaties and Surrenders*, 3 vols. (Ottawa, 1891 and 1912, reprint 1971).
89. *Debates*, 1909–10, p. 784, 1 December 1909. The money accrued from sales was $2,156,020. In addition some 1020 islands were sold, including 242 islets in Georgian Bay judged to be almost valueless; the sales of all islands realized $74,353.
90. See the comments of R. L. Borden and G. E. Foster in ibid., 1906, pp. 719–20, 27 March 1906; also pp. 948–9, 951.
91. The only change was an amendment in 1898 permitting justices of the peace to certify the validity of land surrenders. There seems to have been no serious thought given to introducing the contemporary American allotment system, intended to speed assimilation. See Raby, "Indian Land Surrenders," p. 37.
92. PAC, RG10, vol. 3848, file 75235–1, McKenna to Sifton, 17 April 1898.
93. PAC, Minto Papers, letterbook (mfm), 4:300, Minto to Lt. Col. F. White, 23 February 1904.

7

The Administration of Treaty 3:
The Location of the Boundaries
of Treaty 3 Indian Reserves in Ontario,
1873–1915

David T. McNab

Recent commentators, following Alexander Morris's *The Treaties of Canada with the Indians*, first published in 1880, have duly noted the importance of Treaty 3[1] with respect to the renegotiation of Treaties 1 and 2 in 1875 and to the other treaties which were signed subsequent to Treaty 3. However, while the making of Treaty 3 has been examined,[2] there has been no comprehensive critical study of its administration. This paper discusses some of the most important aspects of the administration of Treaty 3 between 1873 and 1915, concerning the location of the boundaries of Treaty 3 Indian Reserves in Ontario[3] which has been controversial since the 1880's.

Prior to the signing of Treaty 3 on 3 October 1873, the government of Ontario (formerly Upper Canada and Canada West) had no formal relationship with the Hudson's Bay Company or the Ojibwa people in this area.[4] The Ojibwa perceived themselves to be a "nation." Their subsistence economy consisted primarily, but not exclusively, of hunting, trapping, fishing, and wild rice harvesting. In the late eighteenth and nineteenth centuries, they acquired goods associated with the fur trade. During the summer the Indian people lived adjacent to trading posts, cultivating small gardens, fishing, and supplying their own needs and some of those of the Hudson's Bay Company. They also acted as voyageurs, provisioners,

The opinions expressed in this article are entirely those of the author, and are not necessarily those of the Ontario Ministry of National Resources or the Government of Ontario.

or tripmen in the fur trade. During the rest of the year they pursued a nomadic existence. Before 1870 the interdependent needs of the Indian people and those of the Hudson's Bay Company, although not without conflict, usually complemented one another. This relationship changed gradually after 1870.[5] By 1873 when Treaty 3 was signed, some Ojibwa were becoming increasingly dependent on the company's trade goods.[6]

From 1870 to 1889 the area which became the Ontario portion of Treaty 3 was part of the Northwest Territories. According to the terms of the transfer of the Hudson's Bay Company's territories in 1870, the government of Canada became responsible for the administration of these lands.[7] However, the area was also in dispute. The provisional northwestern boundary of Ontario was adjacent to the Northwest Territories, and it did not include the Treaty 3 area until after the *St. Catherine's Milling* case had been decided in Ontario's favour and the boundary dispute between the governments of Ontario and Canada had been settled by a British imperial statute in 1889.[8] From 1870 to 1873 the government of Ontario was consulted by the government of Canada concerning mineral lands in the area that was to be covered by Treaty 3, but Ontario was not represented at the Treaty 3 negotiations and was not a signatory.[9] The people of Ontario had, from the mid-nineteenth century, felt that the Rainy River and Lake of the Woods areas should eventually become part of Ontario. However, between 1870 and 1889, the exclusion of the government of Ontario from the treaty negotiations subsequently had a significant impact on the Indian and the non-Indian people in what was to become northwestern Ontario.

After Confederation in 1867, Sir John A. Macdonald's Conservative government intended to expand the new nation from sea to sea, initially with roads and a telegraph line, and eventually with a railroad. The area that was to be covered by Treaty 3 in 1873 was directly within and vital to this plan of expansion. The Canadian government sent surveyors to the Northwest Territories in 1869, an action which precipitated resistance in the Red River settlement, and afterwards the government realized the inadequacy of communication and transportation between central and western Canada.[11] At this time at Fort Frances, the Saulteaux Ojibwa first presented their demands to the federal government.[12]

In 1871 the government of Canada also agreed to British Columbia's terms for entry into Confederation, which included, among other things, the promise to build a transcontinental railway to the Pacific within ten years.[13] The right of way of the proposed railroad was to pass directly through the area that would eventually be covered by Treaty 3. In 1871, the federal government appointed three commissioners to negotiate a treaty.[14] However, the Ojibwa people held firm to their 1869 demands, and no treaty was signed at that time. Two other treaties were subsequently signed, known as Treaty 1 or the Stone Fort Treaty (3 August 1871) and Treaty 2 or the Manitoba Post Treaty (21 August 1871).[15] Four years of fitful discussions followed that eventually led to the signing of Treaty 3.

In the summer of 1873 Alexander Morris, the lieutenant-governor of Manitoba and the Northwest Territories, and his fellow treaty commissioners, Simon J. Dawson and Lieutenant-Colonel J. A. N. Provencher, were authorized by the federal government to negotiate a treaty with the Saulteaux Ojibwa. Although Morris was a neophyte, Dawson and Provencher were experienced in Indian affairs, knew the Indian people, and were well suited for this undertaking. After prolonged and difficult negotiations, Treaty 3, also identified as the Northwest Angle Treaty, was signed by representatives of the federal government and the Indian people on 3 October 1873 at the Northwest Angle, Lake of the Woods.[16] Under one of its provisions, the government of Canada undertook to survey lands that were to be identified as Indian reserves which the Ojibwa people were to select in consultation with federal officials. Another provision stipulated that the Ojibwa were to have the right to "pursue their avocations of hunting and fishing" on the lands which they had ceded. The Treaty 3 land entitlement, considered by the federal government and by the Indian people as the most important part of the treaty, was not to "exceed in all one square mile for each family of five, or in that proportion for larger or smaller families."[17] This was four times the maximum land entitlement specified by Treaties 1 and 2, and it provided a model for the renegotiations of those treaties as well as for the signing of future treaties in Canada.

To meet the Treaty 3 land entitlement, the government sent Simon J. Dawson and Robert J. N. Pither to the Treaty 3 area in 1874 to arrange for the selection of the land for the Indian reserves. The lands selected by the Indian bands were in close proximity to their hunting, fishing, and wild rice harvesting areas. A census was also taken of the number of people in each band. However, the reserve lands selected were based on the areas chosen by the representatives of each Indian band rather than on a strict adherence to the maximum Treaty 3 land entitlement. The amount of land selected greatly exceeded, in most instances, the maximum Treaty 3 land entitlement. The boundaries of Treaty 3 Indian reserves were then surveyed by the federal government and set along the shoreline after the Indian people had been consulted. Most, but not all, of the areas identified as Indian reserves were surveyed by 1880.[18]

The federal government had also become involved in a series of disputes with the Ontario government related to provincial rights, which had the effect of, as one commentator has recently put it, "remoulding" the constitution of 1867. One of the most important of these disputes was the location of the northwestern boundary of the province of Ontario. After twenty years of political and legal wrangling, the boundary was settled by British imperial legislation, The Canada (Ontario Boundary) Act, 1889.[19] Since Ontario now included most of the Treaty 3 area and, since the Government of Ontario had the "beneficial interest" in and the underlying title to the land to be set aside as Treaty 3 Indian reserves in Ontario, it would have to concur in their selection, location, and extent. After a meeting in 1890, joint legislation was passed by the two governments in 1891 which provided for an agreement to settle certain questions between the "Governments of Canada and Ontario respecting Indian lands," and in 1894 the two governments entered into the agreement.[20]

In the late 1880's the impact of commercial fishing by Americans in Lake of the Woods became a local issue. Using pound nets, refrigeration techniques, and a large barge based on the American side of Lake of the Woods, an American fishing company was apparently rapidly depleting the supply of fish. This problem was compounded by a series of natural occurrences, including heavy rains and high water levels which led to the loss of wild rice and other food crops.[21] Rollerway Dam, the funding of which was authorized by a federal order-in-council, was built in 1887. It also helped to raise the minimum water level in Lake of the Woods.[22] The Indian people and other people in the area reported that the subsistence economy of the Ojibwas was threatened.

As an interim measure to ameliorate these economic difficulties, the federal government appointed the local Indian agents "Overseers of the Fishery," in addition to their usual tasks.[23] Since one of them, Robert J. N. Pither at Rat Portage, was quite elderly and had a very large area to patrol in his canoe, this method of policing was inadequate. The Indian people also took direct action in 1890, led by Chiefs Powassin and Flatmouth. A number of the Ojibwa, as a warning to American commercial fishermen, raided one of the fishing company barges.[24]

Other actions to ameliorate this situation, were also taken by the federal government. In 1889, E. McColl, inspector of Indian agencies for Manitoba and the Northwest Territories at Winnipeg, was sent to the Lake of the Woods, Rainy River, and Rainy Lake to investigate the economic and social effects of these reported difficulties on the Indian people. He reported that the Lake of the Woods fishery was in no danger and that the Indian people were not suffering undue hardship.[25] Nevertheless, in 1890 the government of Canada, by an order-in-council, prohibited the use of pound nets in Lake of the Woods.[26] The fishery issue was also referred by the government of Canada to the government of the United States, but no further action was taken.[27]

The idea of headland to headland water boundaries for Treaty 3 Indian reserves in Ontario first appeared in the legislation of 1891 and then again in the 1894 agreement in the context of this fisheries question,[28] presumably as a panacea to retain some of the fishery in Lake of the Woods and some areas for the growing and harvesting of wild rice as food sources for the Ojibwa. By extending the existing shoreline boundaries to a line, drawn from headland to headland, the Indian reserves would be greatly increased in size and the Indian bands would have exclusive control of the fishery and wild rice in that area.

The Indian people were not a party to, nor did they participate directly in, the negotiations that led to the agreement of 1894. Instead, they made their views known to the Department of Indian Affairs, and the federal government was supposed to represent their interests. The intention of the 1894 agreement was to provide a formal means by which the government of Ontario would concur in the selection, location, and extent of Indian reserve lands in Ontario selected by the Indian people and allocated by the federal government according to the provisions of Treaty 3. In part, the agreement of 1894 stated that, "the land covered with water lying between the projecting headlands of any lake or sheets of water not wholly surrounded by an Indian Reserve or Reserves shall be deemed to form part of such reserve, including islands wholly within such headlands" and that the water between the projecting headlands "shall not be subject to the common public right of fishery by others than the Indians of the Band to which the Reserve belongs." The 1894 agreement further provided that if Ontario was dissatisfied with the Indian reserves in Treaty 3 which had already been selected then "a joint commission or joint commissions shall be appointed by the Governments of Canada and Ontario to settle and determine any question or all questions relating to such Reserves or proposed Reserves." The two governments also agreed that in the event "that any future treaties with Indians in respect of territory in Ontario which they have not, before the passing of the said statutes, surrendered their claim aforesaid, shall be deemed to require the concurrence of the Government of Ontario." Thus, another purpose of the 1891 legislation and the 1894 agreement was to make certain that the government of Ontario's concurrence was required in any future treaty signed with the Indian people in Ontario. According to this provision, the government of Ontario was a signatory to Treaty 9 in 1905–1906 and its adhesions in 1929–30 and the Williams Treaty in 1923.

After the 1894 agreement was signed and authorized, the two governments understood that the government of Canada had already concurred in the Treaty 3 Indian reserves. Hayter Reed, deputy superintendent general of Indian affairs, stated his views in 1895:

> The gist of this Agreement is that no disposition shall be made of any Reserve in what was formerly known as "The Disputed Territory" until the same has been confirmed by the Government of Ontario, the fee of such lands being in the Province until the Reserves are confirmed and handed over to the Dominion.[29]

For various reasons the government of Ontario was not to confirm the disposition of these reserves until 1915.

From 1894 to 1913, negotiations between the governments of Ontario and Canada on the reserves occurred intermittently but the two governments could not reach any settlement. Both were awaiting the outcome of court proceedings on Treaty 3. The government of Canada had taken the government of Ontario to court over the expenses which Canada had claimed had been incurred by it since the signing of Treaty 3 in 1873. Those court proceedings, the so-called "Treaty #3 annuities case," began in 1895 and eventually were decided in Ontario's favour by the Judicial Committee of the Privy Council in August 1910.[30] In addition, on 26 February 1896, Aubrey White, then Ontario assistant commissioner of crown lands, replied to a letter from Hayter Reed concerning Ontario's confirmation of the Treaty 3 reserves. He wrote frankly that these Indian reserves

> front generally on navigable waters, and it is reported they are injuriously located with reference to the development and opening up of the contiguous territory.
>
> As the Reserves have been made, the Government of Ontario is unwilling, I am to add, to disturb the expectations of the Indians, and therefore would probably be disposed to acquiesce in the selection, on suitable compensation to Ontario, in view of a larger area having been located for Reserves within Ontario than is fair in proportion to the whole territory surrendered by the Treaty and the retardation which may be expected in the settlement of Provincial lands, cut off by the appropriation of lands to purposes which may cause their development indefinitely.

From 1896 to 1915 the government of Ontario used these same arguments to object to the location and the extent of the Treaty 3 reserves, particularly that the maximum land entitlement had been greatly exceeded and that a disproportionate amount of Indian reserve lands had been taken out of Ontario compared to Manitoba, but there was no change in the location of the reserve boundaries. Between 1889 and 1915 most of the lands identified as Indian reserves in Ontario were administered by the federal Department of Indian Affairs as if they were Indian reserve lands. The Ojibwa were not removed or displaced from lands that they had selected, that had been surveyed for them by the federal government, and that they had not surrendered to the Crown.[31]

On 9 December 1913, a meeting was held in Ottawa with W. H. Hearst, Ontario minister of lands, forests and mines, and W. J. Roche, superintendent general of Indian affairs in Ottawa, with their respective deputies, Duncan Campbell Scott and Aubrey White, in attendance. Representatives of the two governments agreed, rather sanguinely, in Scott's words, to reach a settlement concerning "all outstanding Indian matters in Ontario," including the confirmation by Ontario of the selection, location and the extent of Treaty 3 Indian reserves in Ontario. Scott (1862–1941), a Canadian poet of some renown and a career civil servant (1878–1932), then the newly appointed deputy superintendent general of Indian affairs, began to collaborate with White (1845–1915), a professional civil servant, formerly assistant commissioner of crown lands, and, since 1905, deputy minister of the Department of Lands, Forests and Mines for the government of Ontario. White was the more experienced negotiator of the two. There are no joint formal minutes of this meeting. However, White stated in his memo of 9 December 1913:

> They [Department of Indian Affairs] [are] to take a surrender of all Reserves on Rainy River including Wild Land Reserve and they are to be opened for settlers. We reserve the right to object to percentage of Reserves taken in Ontario — which may be too large — They [are] to arrange that small reserve in Quetico [the land identified as Sturgeon Lake Indian Reserve #24C] shall be done away with — We [are] to confirm such percentage of Reserves as we may think reasonable in Ontario.

Scott's draft "Minutes" of 10 December 1913 on this meeting should also be noted since they are not worded (on the subject to Treaty 3) in quite the same way as White's memo:

> Unconfirmed Indian Reserves in Treaty No. 3:

> Ontario shall confirm the reserves in Treaty No. 3, with the exception of Reserve 24C [the land identified a Sturgeon Lake Indian Reserve #24C located in Quetico Provincial Park] which is cancelled. Ontario is to draft for submission a memorandum to his Excellency the Lieutenant Governor in Council, confirming the reserves, which memorandum shall safeguard the legal rights of Ontario, the memorandum to receive the concurrence of the Dominion and to be the basis of joint Orders-in-Council. The Dominion will endeavour to obtain a surrender for sale of the Wild Lands reserve and an amalgamation of the Indian Bands and Rainy River with a surrender for sale of their reserves, with the exception of the reserve at Manitou Rapids.

Scott and White each noted that a separate order-in-council would ratify each issue after agreement had been reached.[32] At this and subsequent meetings prior to the passage of Ontario legislation of 1915 (5 Geo. V, c. 12), neither the Ojibwa nor their representatives participated in any of the discussions. At this time, Indian involvement in such proceedings was not unusual, and Indian interests were supposed to have been represented through the Indian agents to the Department of Indian Affairs' headquarters staff in Ottawa.

Early in 1914, as the negotiations proceeded, Scott's and White's major concern was the extent, rather than the location of Treaty 3 Indian reserves in Ontario, particularly with respect to the acreage which had been selected by the Indian people of Treaty 3 which was more than stipulated.[33] After a number of meetings at the Legislative Buildings in Toronto (where the Department of Lands, Forests and Mines was located at that time), Scott and White agreed, in a fit of administrative housekeeping, to, in Scott's words, "settle all outstanding matters respecting Indian Reserve lands in Ontario." They signed a "Memorandum of Proposed Settlement between the Dominion and Ontario with reference to Treaty 3 Reserves" by which Canada was to pay Ontario $20,672 for 20,672 "excess" acres which was a compromise formula based on the Treaty 3 land entitlement question and the "excess acreage" question (that is, the number of acres Ontario was obligated to provide for Indian reserve lands in comparison with the area ceded in the province of Ontario). The calculations concerning the excess acreage and compromise figure of 20,672 were based on the acreage of each reserve with the boundaries following along the shoreline.[34] The proposed settlement of 26 August 1914 became the basis for the Ontario legislation of 1915:

> The area [sic] of the said reserves so transferred has been computed and settled at 20,672 acres, and payment therefor [sic] at $1 per acre, being the sum of $20,672, is to be made by the Government of Canada to the Government of Ontario.

However, a few weeks earlier, on 4 August 1914, Britain had declared war on Germany. The Great War clearly delayed the results of these negotiations. It was not until 1916 that the government of Ontario received from the government of Canada a credit of $20,672. By then Aubrey White had died.[35]

Negotiations between the two governments also included other issues concerning Indian lands in Ontario, that is, the "Gibson Indian Reserve," a proposed reserve for the Temagami Indian Band, and unconfirmed reserves in the Robinson Superior Treaty area, among others. Both agreed to ratify the agreements on these other issues pursuant to separate orders-in-council. In Scott's memorandum of 27 August 1914, he noted, "we finally closed all outstanding matters between the Governments." Among other things, Ontario was to confirm by an order-in-council the location and extent of Treaty 3 Indian reserves, and it was "part of the understanding that we are to obtain as soon as possible surrenders of the Reserves on the Rainy River and the location of the Indians at Manitou Rapids."[36] As it turned out, this proposed agreement was not the end of the negotiations. Much remained to be done.

Prior to 15 December 1914, Scott and White had not discussed Ontario's concurrence in the location (as opposed to the selection and extent which had been discussed) of the boundaries of Treaty 3 reserves. They had not been concerned whether these boundaries *should be* along the shoreline, as they had been surveyed, or whether they *should be* along a line between the projecting "headlands" as stated in the agreement of 1894. Scott and White were still aware of the implications of agreement. One day after writing a memorandum for his minister (the Honourable W. H. Hearst) on the negotiations to 14 December 1914,[37] White noted the headland to headland clause in his letter to Scott and said that it "left the door open for all kinds of disputes and misunderstandings hereafter," specifically that the

provision is very far-reaching and might seriously cripple our action with respect to the application of Winnipeg for leave to take its water supply from Shoal Lake, and I think you will agree with me that there is much room otherwise for future trouble under the clause as it reads, because in some of the Reserves I find there are rivers of considerable size running through them and it surely never was intended that lands under a river should belong to the Indians.[38]

White also stated that in the meetings with Scott, in August 1914, he and his minister had assumed that Treaty 3 Indian reserves would be confirmed by Ontario "as actually surveyed, leaving nothing open to argument hereafter."[39]

In a letter dated 30 December 1914 Scott agreed with White's propositions. He said that he would recommend to his minister, whom he had not yet consulted, that it would be "advisable to confirm the Reserves as surveyed," that is, along the shoreline.[40] Subsequently, on 1 March 1915, W. J. Roche approved this joint arrangement.[41] It was Scott's opinion that if this course of action were taken then the statute of 1894 [sic] would have to be repealed and "therefor [sic] an enactment which would cover the settlement of the Reserve question, Treaty 3, in all its bearings" would have to be substituted. This "enactment" after meetings and apparently an oral agreement between the minister and deputies of these respective departments led directly to the hasty drafting and the passage of Ontario's legislation on 8 April 1915 after an all-night sitting of the legislature, rather than an Ontario order-in-council as had been previously agreed by staffs of both governments. In this letter, Scott also wrote that it was his "conviction that we should say nothing about water or fisheries, but leave those questions to be decided as the cases arise by the existing law and usage."[42]

There is some evidence that Scott helped White draft the Ontario legislation.[43] This statute was *not* passed arbitrarily. Moreover, all through the negotiating process, the Department of Indian Affairs believed that it was representing Ojibwa interests. The legislation confirmed the location and extent of Treaty 3 Indian reserves in Ontario and signified that the boundaries would be placed along the shoreline, for, as noted above, White had given "good reason" for these boundaries not to be placed along a line between the projecting headlands. Section 2 of *An Act to confirm the title of the Government of Canada to certain lands and Indian lands* states:

> the land covered with water lying between the projecting Headlands of any lake or sheets of water not wholly surrounded by an Indian Reserve or Reserves and islands wholly within such Headlands shall not be deemed to form part of such Reserve, but shall continue to be the property of the Province, and the Bed of Navigable Waters Act shall apply, notwithstanding anything contained in the fourth paragraph of the agreement hereinbefore mentioned.[44]

Thus the government of Ontario confirmed that the boundaries of Treaty 3 Indian reserves would be as they had been selected by the Indians and surveyed by the federal government. In addition, the last section of the agreement of 1894 concerning the Indian people's exclusive right to the fishery between the projecting headlands of each Indian reserve was not included in the legislation of 1915 because, as Scott had stated, this item would be left "as the cases arise by the existing law and usage."[45] And it has been.

For many years after 1915 there was no significant reappraisal of the location of the boundaries of Treaty 3 reserves in Ontario. And, although the Indian people raised the question of headland to headland water boundaries as a land claim with the governments of Canada and Ontario in 1978, there has been no legislative change which has affected the location of the boundaries.[46]

Through negotiation and various court actions on the issues of the northwestern boundary of Ontario and on the location of the boundaries of Treaty 3 Indian reserves in Ontario prior to World War I, the Ontario government had effectively developed its own Indian policy. This policy was essentially reactive. It was initiated as a response to and under the constitutional arrangements made for "Indians, and lands reserved for the Indians" and for the administration and control of lands and other natural resources in the British North America Act of 1867. The provincial government saw this process as another struggle to attain responsible government. Indian issues between the two governments were significant at this time and loomed large in the area of federal-provincial relations between 1867 and 1914. Those issues helped to "remould" the British North America Act and the developing Canadian constitution.

Historically, Ontario's Indian policy was based on the regional Indian policy that had developed in the Province of Canada between 1841 and 1867. Its thrust was confrontation, on constitutional grounds, with the federal government on proposed Indian reserve lands and other resources, within the context of the development of the lands and resources of the province of Ontario. If these constitutional disputes on lands and resources were overcome, then the government of Ontario was usually ready and eager to co-operate with the federal government on the requests of the Indian people.

By 1915, if not before, the federal government's attempt to develop a national Indian policy, through the Indian Act of 1876 and treaty-making process on the Prairies in the 1870's, had already failed, and the legacy of British Indian policy, the existence of regional Indian policies, had become firmly entrenched once again. It is clear that in the 1913–15 negotiations with the Ontario government, D. C. Scott regarded the role of the Department of Indian Affairs as primarily that of a "caretaker" of Indian affairs. This process was greatly influenced by Indian resistance to the federal government's design for a "sea to sea" Indian policy and by the provincial governments' needs and responsibilities, as specified in the British North America Act, for the lands and resources in each province. In the area of Indian policy at least, one of the ironies of Confederation was that it contributed to the *status quo ante bellum*, that is, to the re-establishment of regional Indian policies in Canada after 1867[47].

NOTES

1. D. T. McNab, "Herman Merivale and Colonial Office Indian Policy in the Mid-Nineteenth Century," *Canadian Journal of Native Studies* 1, no. 2 (1981): 277–302. This theme was also developed by Leslie F. Upton in his article "Contact and Conflict on the Atlantic and Pacific Coasts of Canada," *Acadiensis* 9, no. 2 (1980): 3–13. In comparison with historical examples in the United States, the similarities are striking.
2. A. Morris, "Additional notes to How Treaty #3 Was Made," in A. Morris, *The Treaties of Canada with the Indians* (Toronto, 1880, reprint, 1971), pp. 44–76, 320–29. See also G. F. G. Stanley, *The Birth of Western Canada* (Toronto, 1960); J. D. Leighton, "The Development of Federal Indian Policy in Canada, 1840–1890" (Ph.D. diss., University of Western Ontario, 1975); J. L. Taylor, "Canada's North-West Indian Policy in the 1870's: Traditional Premises and Necessary Innovation," and J. L. Tobias, "Indian Reserves in Western Canada: Indian Homelands or Devices for Assimilation," in *Approaches to Native History in Canada*, D. A. Muise, ed. (Ottawa, 1977), pp. 89–110; See also the perceptive articles on the "numbered Treaties" in the Canadian West by John L. Taylor and John Foster in Richard Price, ed., *The Spirit of the Alberta Indian Treaties* (Toronto, 1979). There is very little on Treaty 3 in those articles, but the authors stress the important point that the Indian people were not being "duped" and that they were aware of what was happening in the treaty negotiations and introduced, in Taylor's words, some "necessary innovations" into them. Using different evidence for Treaty 3, this paper reaches basically the same conclusions on this point. See also Jean Friesen, "Alexander Morris" in *Dictionary of Canadian Biography* 11:608–15.
3. I would like to thank Dr. Paul Driben for first allowing me to "inflict" this paper on his native studies students in July 1980. David Hume also spent many hours following up leads and offering valuable suggestions on sources.
4. E. E. Rich, *Hudson's Bay Company, 1670–1870*, 3 vols. (Toronto, 1960), 1: 52–58. D. T. McNab, "The Colonial Office and the Prairies in the Mid-Nineteenth Century," *Prairie Forum* 3, no. 1 (1978): 21–38.
5. OA, Irving Papers, 30/36/6 (1), "Report by Mr. Borron on the North West Angle Treaty No. 3, as affecting the Rights and Interests, of the Province of Ontario, 1891," contained in E. B. Borron to Oliver Mowat, 9 October 1891; Morris, pp. 44–76.
6. C. A. Bishop, *The Northern Ojibwa and the Fur Trade* (Toronto, 1974). Also see A. J. Ray, *Indians in the Fur Trade* (Toronto, 1974), pp. 3–23.
7. E. E. Rich, 3: 932–37.
8. 52–53 Vict., c. 28. See also M. Zaslow, "The Ontario Boundary Dispute," in *Profiles of a Province* (Toronto, 1967), pp. 108–17.
9. PAC, RG2, series 1, federal order-in-council, P.C.164, particularly the memorandum by David Laird, minister of the interior, 11 February 1875.
10. PAC, RG10, vol. 1846, 131, 132, "Treaty No. 3 between Her Majesty the Queen and the Saulteaux Tribe of the Ojibbeway Indians at the Northwest Angle of the Lake of the Woods with Adhesions, 3 October 1873." See also Zaslow, 108–17.
11. See especially H. V. Nelles, *The Politics of Development* (Toronto, 1974), pp. 1–47, and his excellent article "Empire Ontario: The Problems of Resource Development," in *Oliver Mowat's Ontario*, Donald Swainson, ed. (Toronto, 1972), pp. 189–210; C. Armstrong, *The Politics of Federalism*, (Toronto, 1981), pp. 8–32.

12. Morris, pp. 44–46; On the treaty commissioners, Morris and Provencher, see *DCB* 11:608–15 and 716–17, respectively. Clearly, Dawson had the most experience with the Indian people, while Morris's lack of understanding and inexperience is quite apparent.
13. Desmond Morton, *The Last War Drum* (Toronto, 1972).
14. PAC, RG10, vol. 1918, file 2790 B, and Alexander Morris Papers (Lieutenant-Governor's Collection), MG12, B1, 1869–1873.
15. W. L. Morton, *The Critical Years, The Union of British North America, 1857–1873* (Toronto, 1964), pp. 245–48.
16. Morris, pp. 44–46. See also for the Treaty 3 negotiations, McNab, " 'Hearty Cooperation and Efficient Aid,' The Metis and Treaty 3," *Canadian Journal of Native Studies* 3, no. 1 (1983), forthcoming.
17. PAC, RG10, vol. 1846, "Treaty 3"; vol. 1918, File 2790B. Grand Council Treaty 3 presented the "Paypom Treaty," the "real Treaty, held by the Elders" to the Honourable William G. Davis, Premier of Ontario, on 25 May 1982. The Paypom Treaty" or "Nolin's Notes" on the "Terms" of Treaty 3 states, among other things, that "They [the Ojibwa] shall be free as by the past for their hunting and rice harvest." It appears that when the Ojibwa selected the reserve lands in 1874–75, most of their traditional wild rice harvesting areas were included. Although the historical evidence is not unequivocal, this may be the way in which the Ojibwa and the federal government negotiators dealt with the issue of wild rice harvesting at that time.
18. Federal order-in-council, P.C. 841. See also order-in-council, P.C. 164 which provisionally confirmed the reserves. Attached was a schedule signed by S. J. Dawson, dated 17 February 1875.
19. 52–53 Vict., c. 28.
20. The Ontario statute is 54 Vict., c. 3; Canada is 54–55 Vict., c. 5. The Agreement of 1894, signed on 6 April is contained in PAC RG10, Black Series, vol. 3883, file 95,721. See also AO, Irving Papers, 30/31/37, 25 March 1893. The government of Ontario's staff position on Treaty 3 lands is contained in E. B. Borron's Memorandum, "North-West Angle or No. 3 Indian Treaty, Outstanding Accounts, Claims of the Dominion on the Province of Ontario in respect thereof." Also see Borron's "Report on Indian Claims Arising out of the North-west Angle Treaty, No. 3," 30 December 1893, Irving Papers, 30/36/6 (2).
21. "Annual Report on the Department of Indian Affairs," Manitoba Superintendency, 1888, xliii–xlvii; Morris, p. 73.
22. Arthur V. White and Adolph F. Meyer, *Report to International Joint Commission relating to Official Reference re Lake of the Woods Levels* (Ottawa, 1916), pp. 8–10.
23. PAC, RG10, Black Series, vol. 3800, file 48542, L. Vankoughnet, deputy superintendent general, Department of Indian Affairs, to E. McColl, inspector of agencies and reserves, Department of Indian Affairs, 10 September 1890; L. Vankoughnet, memorandum to Honourable E. Dewdney, superintendent general of Indian Affairs, 17 December 1890; R.S.O. 55 Vict., c. 10, R.S.O. 60 Vict., c. 9.
24. Ibid., newspaper clippings of 13 and 14 August 1890.
25. Ibid., vol. 3802, file 50,265, E. McColl, inspector of Indian agencies, Winnipeg, to the superintendent general of Indian affairs, 29 December 1888; L. Vankoughnet to E. McColl, 11 January 1889.
26. Ibid., vol. 3800, file 48542, order-in-council Canada, 20 August 1890.
27. PAC, RG10, Black Series, vol. 3800, file 48542, order-in-council, Canada, 20 August 1890. For the consequences, see William Smith, deputy minister of marine and fisheries to L. Vankoughnet, 8 February 1893.
28. Ibid., vol. 3830, file 62,509, Pt. 2, "Memorandum of Matters discussed at Conference between the Representatives of the Three Governments," 28 November 1890, enclosed in memorandum by L. Vankoughnet to the Honourable E. Dewdney, superintendent general of Indian affairs, 17 December 1890. The orders-in-council authorizing the Agreement of 1894 are contained in this file. The idea of "headland" boundaries was not unusual at that time. It was also used in the context of the Alaska Boundary dispute between Canada and the United States, see N. Penlington, *The Alaska Boundary Dispute: A Critical Reappraisal* (Toronto, 1972). It was also consistent with the manner in which the Indian fisheries were administered at that time.
29. For Hayter Reed's understanding of the agreement, see PAC, RG10, Black Series, vol. 3803, file 50,358, Reed to T. H. Gilmour, 22 November 1895.

30. PAC, RG10, vol. 2314, file 62,509.
31. Ibid.
32. The draft "minutes" and other documentation concerning this meeting are in PAC, RG10, Red Series, vol. 2314, file 62,509, pt. 1, and MNR Indian Lands File, 186214, "Northwest Angle, Treaty No. 3."
33. Ibid., White to Scott, 31 July 1914. Also see "Memorandum for Mr. White re Treaty No. 3," 31 July 1914 from Mr. Rorke, Surveys Branch, Department of Lands, Forests and Mines.
34. PAC, RG10, Red Series, vol. 2314, File 62,509–5, Pt.1. "Memorandum of Proposed Settlement between the Dominion and Ontario with reference to Treaty 3 Reserves," 26 August 1914, signed by White and Scott.
35. "Bill 102," 5 Geo. V., c. 12, 8 April 1915. The required amount was credited to the government of Ontario on 31 October 1916. Ontario "owed" the federal government more than $20,672 for Treaty 9 annuity payments.
36. PAC, RG10, Red Series, vol. 2314, file 62,509–5, Pt.1, Scott, "Memorandum," 27 August 1914.
37. MNR Indian Lands File, 186214, vol. 2, White Memorandum for the minister of lands, forests and mines, W. H. Hearst, 14 December 1915. This memorandum was marked "Approved" and signed by Hearst.
38. Ibid., White to Scott, 15 December 1914. There may be a parallel here between the headland to headland case and the British Columbia "cut-off lands." However, any comparisons made would be superficial since the headland to headland case is connected directly to the issue of the Treaty 3 land entitlement while the B.C. "cut-off lands" dispute is not related to any treaty provision.
39. Ibid., survey plans of most of the Treaty 3 Indian Reserves had been deposited with the Ontario Department of Lands, Forests and Mines prior to 1915. On all survey plans of Indian reserves in the area covered by Treaty 3 in Ontario prior to 1915, the boundaries clearly follow along the shoreline.
40. Ibid., Scott to White, 30 December 1914.
41. PAC, RG10, Red Series, vol. 2314, file 62,509–5, Pt. 1, Roche to Hearst, 1 March 1915.
42. MNR Indian Lands File 186214, vol. 2, Scott to White, 30 December 1914.
43. Ibid.
44. Ibid., 5 Geo. V, c. 12.
45. Ibid., Scott to White, 30 December 1914.
46. See, for example, MNR Indian Lands File, 46450, vol. 1, J. D. McLean to W. C. Cain, deputy minister, Department of Lands and Forests, 15 December 1922; PAC, RG10, Red Series, vol. 2547, file 111,834–3, Pt. 1, Scott to C. R. Fitch, 11 March 1930.
47. See D. T. McNab, Review of R. J. Ponting and R. Gibbons, "Out of Irrelevance," in *Canadian Journal of Native Studies* 1, no. 1 (1981): 243–46. For other historical illustrations, see "The 'Albatross' and Beyond: The Location of the Northern Boundary of Mississaugi River Indian Reserve #8, Robinson Huron Treaty, 1850–1893," and Douglas Leighton, "The Historical Significance of the Robinson Treaties of 1850," Papers delivered at the CHA Annual Meetings, University of Ottawa, 9 June 1982.

8

Canada's Indians Yesterday. What of Today?

Diamond Jenness

Between the years 1920 and 1930 I visited many tribes and bands of Indians on different reserves throughout Canada — in the east, on the Prairies, in British Columbia, and on the upper waters of the Peace River. In every region I found a deep-rooted prejudice against them, a prejudice that was stronger in some places than in others, but one which was noticeable everywhere from the Atlantic to the Pacific. It was strongest in western frontier settlements where the Indian population outnumbered the white and the latter was struggling to uphold its prestige. And it was least apparent in Quebec — probably because the French-Canadians of that province had associated with the Indians longer than had the English-Canadians and because their Latin tradition had made them more tolerant of other races than are we northerners who speak a Teutonic tongue.

CAUSES OF PREJUDICE

One major cause for prejudice was the reserve or apartheid system which separated the Indians from the Whites and conferred on them a special status. It exempted them, for example, from the income and other taxes that their white neighbours paid, released them from any law-suits for debt, prohibited them from

Reprinted from *CJEPS* 20, no. 1, Feb. 1954.

selling or renting any part of their reserves except through the government, and debarred them from the white man's privilege of purchasing alcoholic liquor. Their reserves therefore formed distinct enclaves, which had a life and individuality of their own different from that of the white communities around them. And this difference, this failure to conform to the prevailing pattern, aroused the prejudice of the surrounding majority, as non-conformity always does, whether it be in religion, in politics, or in social customs.

Still another ground for prejudice was the economic status of the Indians, which was generally considerably lower than that of their white neighbours. Their clothes were shabbier and of inferior quality, their houses smaller and more ramshackle, and their motor-cars, when they possessed any, model-T Fords whose clatter was audible half a mile away.

Not merely was their living standard lower, but they lacked the education of their white neighbours. Only a minority spoke fluent English or French: a high percentage could neither read nor write. The average Canadian, himself but half educated, tolerated the immigrant Italian labourers and the Chinese market gardeners and laundrymen because he was vaguely conscious that these foreigners, despite their defective knowledge of English, possessed civilizations of their own comparable to his Canadian one. But the Indians, he thought, lacked any true cultural background: they were but half-regenerate savages. Accordingly, he treated them with hardly concealed contempt. He barred his house against them, associated with them no more than was absolutely necessary, and employed them only when he was unable to dispense with their services.

Lest I be accused of exaggeration, let us run our eyes briefly from British Columbia to the Atlantic. On the Pacific Coast during that period people frequently spoke of the native population as "Siwashes," and, for good measure, they occasionally added the epithet "dirty." As labourers, it was said, the Indians were shiftless and unreliable. They could be stevedores, fishermen, casual labourers; their women might work in canneries, or sometimes as domestics; but everywhere the white population preferred Chinese or Japanese. Chinese and Japanese children were freely accepted in the schools and colleges of the province; but for Indian children there had to be special schools financed by the federal government, even when, as at Duncan, their reserves lay right inside a white community. In the interior of British Columbia one or two villages actually enforced a Jim Crow Law: thus at Hazelton (which in 1926 counted some 300 white inhabitants to perhaps 400 Indians), no Indian might walk beside a white man or woman, or sit on the same side in the village church. Still farther north, on the upper waters of the Peace River, white trappers by threats of violence sometimes expelled Indian families from their traditional trapping grounds; and the Indians had no protection or redress.

The prairie farmers during that same period shared the prejudices of their countrymen beyond the Rockies. In 1921 those around Calgary were paying $4 a day to immigrant harvesters of Polish and Ukrainian nationalities, but to Indians working in the same fields only $2.50.

The situation was somewhat different in the southern parts of Ontario and Quebec. There the Indians had practised agriculture for many centuries, and their economic condition approximated that of their rural white neighbours. Moreover, the primary schools on the reserves were little if at all inferior to those in the surrounding countryside. Nevertheless, any Indian who left the Six Nations Reserve at Brantford or the Mohawk Reserve at Caughnawaga in order to attend high school or university in Toronto or Montreal encountered considerable prejudice which not every youth was fitted to withstand. An Ojibwa Indian of Parry Sound who had won the Military Medal with two bars and the French Croix de Guerre during World War I lived almost as an outcast: he was too modern, too disturbing, to find favour among his own people, and the local Whites were unwilling to receive him into their homes because he was an Indian. In the lumbering districts farther north the Indians were rated indifferent teamsters, and their women considered fair prey for the lumberjacks. A similar attitude prevails even today, apparently, in parts of the Mackenzie River basin, for in 1943 coloured employees of a firm that had contracted to build an oil pipeline in the region openly offered a prize of $500 to the first Indian woman who should give birth to a baby with black kinkly hair.

EFFECT OF APARTHEID ON THE INDIANS

Confined as they were to their reserves, the Indians had little opportunity to acquire any technical training or experience, little or no chance to diversify their activities and improve their economic position. Their main occupations were farming (or ranching) and, in some places, fishing, neither of which offered much more than a bare subsistence. Particularly precarious was the condition of the non-farming tribes of northern Canada, who derived most of their revenue from trapping the fur-bearing animals.

It was the difficulty of obtaining employment (itself, of course, the result of white prejudice) that prevented the Indians from leaving their reserves in considerable numbers. Each year did, indeed, witness a small seepage into the world of Whites, a seepage mainly of young girls who married white men and followed their husbands into white communities. A few young men also drifted away, principally in eastern Canada, where some Iroquois, for example, would cross the international boundary to work in the automobile plants of Detroit, which asked no questions about racial origin. At no time, however, did this seepage overtake the natural increase of the population; and already on more than one reserve the ugly problem of living space had begun to raise its head.

Can we wonder if under these circumstances the older Indians were thrown back upon their past? Their ancient religion had peopled the world with spiritual forces, and our white civilization with its materialistic outlook seemed to them hollow and empty. Knowing, however, that they lacked the strength to resist it, they resigned themselves to its current and ceased to care where it carried them. They could and did retain their ancient pride and dignity, but the upheaval was so drastic that they accepted with apathy whatever fate set in their path.

Totally different was apartheid's effect upon the younger Indians, or at least a considerable percentage of them. They developed what can best be described as a "segregation camp" mentality, the mentality that characterized so many refugees and displaced persons during and after the last war. Fate, the irresistable, had subjected them to the white race, which had scornfully pushed them to one side. It had taken practically all their land, deprived them of their ancient freedom, and denied them political and social equality, or at least made that status almost unobtainable. The knowledge that they were no longer their own masters sapped their enterprise and destroyed their ambition. If their diet was deficient, their health poor, their housing unsatisfactory, it was the fault of the white man, they said, and the white man's government should set things right.

So it came about that an atmosphere of mingled apathy and discontent had settled on the reserves; and it was the apathy that dominated. Only at rare intervals did the underlying discontent send forth an audible murmur. Small delegations of Indians then travelled from British Columbia, from the Prairies, and from southern Ontario to lay their complaints before the government in Ottawa. But the results of these delegations were negligible.

OTTAWA ADMINISTRATION

The Indian administration of that period was a "holding" one, more concerned with preserving the status quo than with improving the economic and social status of the Indians or with raising their living standard. The head of the administration [Duncan Campbell Scott] disliked them as a people and gave a cool reception to the delegations that visited him in Ottawa. Parliament, for its part, contented itself with voting whatever amount of money seemed necessary to fulfil Canada's treaty obligations towards its aborigines and then promptly forgot them, because their number was small and exercised no influence at the ballot box.

What were the obligations of the Canadian Parliament and people? Briefly these: to protect the Indians from exploitation, to safeguard their health, to educate them, and to train them for eventual citizenship. No one ever asked how long the training should endure, how long the Indians should be kept as wards — whether for one century, two centuries, or a millenium. The Indian administration did not ask: its job was simply to administer, and, like many a custodian, it was so involved in the routine of its administration that it forgot the purpose of its custodianship, especially since the fulfilment of that purpose would sign its own death-warrant. Neither did Parliament nor the Canadian people ask how long: their attitude seemed to be that the less heard of the Indians the better. If the churches felt concerned for Indian welfare and wished to set up special schools and hospitals, the government should support their action and aid it with subsidies. In that way it could transfer some of its responsibilities, promote the spread of Christianity, and (*sotto voce*, be it confessed) silence any murmurs or complaints.

Now and again circumstances forced the administration to adopt a more active policy. In 1920, for example, when the number of the Sarcee Indians had declined from roughly 500 to 120 and the tribe was threatened with extinction, the government stationed a medical officer on the reserve to arrest the epidemic of tuberculosis that was carrying off three children out of every four before they reached the age of twenty. A few years later, under pressure from some missionaries, it passed the controversial potlatch law that prohibited certain Indian ceremonies on the Pacific Coast. Furthermore, it promoted an investigation of the reserves in eastern Canada in order to ascertain how many of their occupants were ready for full citizenship; and when the investigation revealed that all but a few old people could qualify, it drew up a law authorizing the administration to enfranchise any Indian who applied for that status. Down to 1930, however, the number of enfranchisements could be counted on the fingers of one hand. Ottawa placidly continued to devote most of its attention to the financial aspects of Indian administration — to the leasing of mining and timber rights, the payment of treaty and other charges; and it let the Indians themselves drift along as best they could within the boundaries of their reserves.

Parallel with this failure to promote the political and economic welfare of the Indians went negligence in providing them with adequate educational facilities. Although the primary schools on some of the reserves, especially in eastern Canada, were reasonably good, there was little or no encouragement for Indian children to go on to technical or high school, and never any thought of helping them to find employment when their school-days ended. In many parts of Canada the Indians had no schools at all; in others only elementary mission schools in which the standard of teaching was exceedingly low. A few mission boarding-schools, subsidized by the government, accepted Indian children when they were very young, raised them to the age of sixteen, then sent them back to their people, well indoctrinated in the Christian faith, but totally unfitted for life in an Indian community and, of course, not acceptable in any white one. We should not blame the missions. They lacked the resources and the staffs to provide a proper education or technical training that would develop special skills; and they were totally unfitted to serve as employment bureaux. It was not the missions that shirked their responsibility, but the federal government, and behind that government the people of Canada.

Nor did we neglect only the education of the Indians, but also their health.

Among the hunting and fishing tribes of northern Canada malnutrition and its accompanying ailments (tuberculosis, pyorrhoea, and so forth) were epidemic in almost every district, and the government paid very little attention to it. The condition of our Hudson Bay Eskimos shocked the Danes of Knud Rasmussen's 1921–24 expedition, so infinitely worse was it than that of the Eskimos of Danish Greenland. Scabies, or some similar disease, was rife on the Upper Peace River, trachoma on the Nass and Skeena; while dental decay was so common everywhere, even in little children, that it seemed to be the rule rather than the exception.

CHANGES SINCE 1930

Such, in outline, was the condition of our Indians between 1920 and 1930. Much water has flowed over the dam since that period, and the Indian administration has undergone a very great change. No longer is it just a "holding" administration, but, under capable and farsighted leadership, it has made notable efforts to improve the economic and social conditions among the Indians and to integrate them gradually into the life of the country.

That integration, however, is still far from complete. It would therefore appear timely for the administration to review what it has accomplished during the last quarter of a century and, in particular, to set before the public clear and straightforward answers to the following questions:

1. What progress has been made in ameliorating home conditions among the Indians, in ending malnutrition and improving health?

2. What progress is being made towards abolishing special schools for Indian children and providing them (through scholarships and so forth) with the same educational facilities as their white neighbours?

3. What measures are being taken to help the Indians find employment of the reserves and to absorb them into our industrial and commercial life?

4. What steps are being taken to liquidate the Indian reserves and to end once and for all that apartheid system which was never intended to endure more than one or two generations, but which in eastern Canada has lasted more than 200 years?

9

The Politics of Indian Affairs

The historical roots of the changing attitude to Indian administration go back to World War II. In Canada as elsewhere the war contributed to an enlarged role for the state in welfare and regulation of the economy. In general, the war, with its striking indication of the obligations of citizens to their national community in times of crisis, stimulated the emergence of the reciprocal assumption that the community, acting through its collective instrumentality of government, had corresponding obligations to its citizenry. These changing attitudes to the role of the state coincided with public revelation of the inadequacies of Canadian Indian policy in the 1946–48 Joint Committee of the Senate and House of Commons. These hearings laid bare neglect and indifference indefensible in the contemporary setting.

The Indian Affairs Branch at the end of the war had primarily a custodial approach to its tasks. It was staffed with few professionals; its financial appropriations were inadequate; many Indian children did not go to school; much of the existing schooling was undertaken by religious orders which provided only half-day teaching for their Indian pupils; the act governing the administration of Indian affairs had been devised in the previous century and had undergone few amendments; the act contained a repressive attitude to Indian cultures. At this time

Abridged from chapter 17 of *A Survey of Contemporary Indians of Canada*, Part 1, edited by H. B. Hawthorn (Ottawa, 1966).

provincial governments played almost no part in contributing their services to Indian communities with the exception of fur and game management.

This history of neglect and indifference was closely related to the apolitical context of Indian administration. C. T. Loram observed in 1939 that there was much more discussion of Indian problems in the United States than in Canada. In Canada, he claimed, "the British traditions of reticence, of letting well alone, of hushing up 'scandals,' of trusting officials, are stronger, so that there is apparently not so much interest on the part of the public in the so-called Indian question."[1]

The apolitical context of Indian administration and the general absence of widespread public concern for Indians which had almost become national characteristics were rudely shattered by the postwar hearings of the Senate and the House of Commons on the Indian Act. The hearings played a major role in stimulating parliamentary interest in Indians. Up until that time the estimates of the Indian Affairs Branch often went through the House of Commons without comment or criticism because of the ignorance and lack of interest of most members. Since those postwar hearings, and stimulated by the extension of the franchise to Indians in 1960 and the second set of Senate-Commons hearings in 1959–61, there has been a desirable increase in parliamentary scrutiny of Indian policies.

The underlying values and expectations of communities change over time. The laissez-faire belief that he governs best who governs least has been put on the defensive in the past forty years. Governments are now expected to perform important welfare functions, to pursue full employment, economic growth, and so forth. These general shifts in values are permissive in the sense that government is allowed to undertake a new range of responsibilities, and potentially demanding in the sense that significant discrepancies between government conduct and community expectations encourage the emergence of organized pressure to create an equilibrium between the two.

An important aspect of the change in values which affects Indians indirectly is the acceptance of a positive state role. The Depression and the war permanently altered the public conception of an appropriate state role with respect to welfare and economic matters. Since World War II there has been a growing social conscience, an increased acceptance of social responsibility, which has markedly enlarged the scope of the minimum amenities of life to which all members of the community are deemed to be entitled. Concurrent with this evolving set of expectations there has been an enhancement of the administrative capacity of government. The combination of changing attitudes to government and changing governmental capacities has resulted in a significant increase in the scope and sophistication of the performance of federal, provincial, and, to a lesser extent, local governments. As long as non-Indian expectations of the role of government were fairly elementary, there was not a striking divergence between the services Indians received from the Indian Affairs Branch, and the services non-Indians received from federal, provincial, and local governments. However, with a growing role for these governments, an increasing gap between the services provided Indians by the Branch and the government services provided to other Canadians was inevitable. This gap could only be defended by denying the egalitarianism which inspired the development of government activity or by denying that such egalitarianism was applicable to Indians. For reasons to be noted below, neither of these courses was possible. In other words, the level of services now deemed appropriate for Indians is basically a spillover of changed citizen-government relationships in white society.

It should be noted that the enlarged role of governments in Canadian federalism places the personnel of the Indian Affairs Branch in an anomalous position. As citizens, Branch personnel are recipients of government services which they are unable to provide, unaided, for the Indians for whom they bear a heavy burden of responsibility. The complications and tensions caused by the dual orientation of Indian Affairs. Branch personnel as Canadian citizens and administrators of a small minority group help to explain the present aggressiveness of the Branch in attempting to involve other federal agencies as well as provincial and municipal governments in direct service provision for Indians.

The spillover has also operated in another area. Since World War II there has been a dramatic change in the relations between the white and non-white peoples of the world. The development of an international interest in dependent peoples which commenced after World War I reached its full fruition after World War II when western imperialism retreated from its positions of control in Africa and Asia. With the liquidation of the great colonial holdings of the European powers, the world was no longer a European preserve. The Commonwealth has become a predominantly non-white institution. The general Assembly of the United Nations has a majority of African and Asian members. These changes have increased the salience of race in international affairs and, as a byproduct, have done the same for the domestic affairs of multiracial states.

The successful assertion by the non-white peoples of the world of a growing control over their own affairs has changed the context of race relations between Whites and non-Whites from hierarchical to egalitarian. This shift in the global distribution of power is brought much more forcibly to the attention of elites than non-elites. Political elites in particular are constantly confronted with these new developments, especially in the realm of international relations.

Coincident with these international developments there has been a parallel development of national and international interest in the relations between different racial groups within individual nation states. It is striking, for example, how frequently parallels are drawn between the position of Indians and the struggle of American Blacks for full participant rights in American society, the apartheid policies of the South African government, or the general developmental needs of the emerging nations. The accuracy of these analogies is irrelevant for our purposes. What is relevant is the clue they provide to understanding changes in attitudes to the minority Indian population of Canada. Particular changes in Canadian attitudes are simply local aspects of global developments in race relations which affect the internal politics of all states which possess non-white minorities who have not gained full social, economic, and political equality with their fellow citizens. The interest in alleviating the conditions of Indians and improving their socioeconomic status are thus reflections of factors operating on a world scale rather than the results of any specifically Canadian developments. The interdependence of internal and external factors in race relations is noted when public reports of *de facto* exclusion of Blacks from the franchise in Alabama lead to increased enquiries of the Indian Affairs Branch with respect to Indians and the franchise. The same kind of conceptual linking is explicitly put forward by the Indian Eskimo Association which states that Canadian "help to underdeveloped peoples abroad, commendable as it is, is rendered ridiculous by the fact that so little is being done about the poverty, squalor and ignorance of our own native citizens."[2]

As a consequence of the preceding, the Indian Affairs Branch is now in politics to stay. In 1961 the senior administrative officer of the Branch, who had been answering enquiries from the public for fourteen years, stated that when he joined the Branch there were very few, if any, general enquiries. "Now we have enquiries daily from school children to organizations, and the interest which has been aroused in citizens of non-Indian status, particularly in the past five years, has been phenomenal."[3]

The manifestations of this new climate of opinion include two major Joint Committee hearings by the Senate and the House of Commons, a major revision of the Indian Act in 1951, the commissioning and publication of two major socioeconomic studies of Indians in British Columbia and Manitoba, the development of two influential organizations devoted to Indian interests — the Indian Eskimo Association, and the Indian and Metis Conference of the Community Welfare Planning Council of Greater Winnipeg — the appointment of an Indian, James Gladstone, as a senator in 1958, the extension of the federal franchise to all Indians in 1960, a serious attempt to establish a national Indian organization — the National Indian Council — and other events too numerous to mention.

The underlying assumption of democratic political system is that what governments do is a response to what the community demands. The source of government action is located in the demands made on the political system by groups and individuals seeking certain responses. This text book model implies that in democracies the responsiveness of governments is a result of the electoral sanctions possessed by the community.

This model is too elementary to provide an adequate explanation of the complicated processes by which the actions of governments are generated and sustained. With respect to Indians two basic assumptions of the model are incorrect: (1) that the political and administrative elite is a passive instrumentality which translates community demands into public policy, and (2) that the main pressures for policy change come from the public, whether viewed as an aggregation of individuals or as congeries of competing groups. The political context of Indian administration historically has been noteworthy in the extent to which Indians have had little influence on the formation of policy affecting their lives and in the extent to which government elites, both political and administrative, have been relatively unhindered in the determination of Indian policy.

The most obvious source of demands would have been from the Indians themselves. However, Indians, have not been politically effective. The reasons for their ineffectiveness constitute an exhaustive catalogue of barriers to the exercise of influence on government policy. This absence of Indian demands provides a partial explanation of the minimum attention Indians received from governments up until World War II and of the fact that the subsequent postwar development of government interest was given little impetus by Indians themselves.

The basic reason for the absence of Indian pressure on governments for most of the post-confederation period is simply that they were formally outside the federal and provincial political systems. They lacked the federal franchise until 1960, and with the exception of Nova Scotia, the provincial franchise until the post-World War II period. As a consequence they lacked even that minimum ability to influence the political authorities which comes from being on the voters' roll. Although there was a certain logic involved in Indian political exclusion owing to the special system of administration to which they were subject and the fact that they did not receive a number of the services provided by federal and provincial governments for other citizens, the result was to place them in virtually a colonial relationship to government. As their capacity to make effective demands was severely restricted, the best they could hope for was benevolence. For many Indians the combination of political exclusion and a special system of administration came to be psychologically coupled with a lack of identification with the political system of the larger society and with a tenacious emphasis on their own unique status. The extent of this was dramatically revealed when the extension of the federal and provincial franchise to Indians was met with little popular acclaim, much suspicion, and occasional hostility.

Not only did the absence of the franchise deprive Indians of a basic incentive to political activity, but it also meant that when it was extended, Indians and political parties had had very little experience of each other. The extension of the franchise constitutes the beginning, not the end, of a process of providing Indians with the same capacity as Whites to influence the content of public policy. The process requires the concomitant extension and adaptation of the party system to the new environment of reserves, and the assimilation by Indians of patterns of political behaviour and understanding from which they were formerly excluded.

As long as Indians were denied the franchise, they had virtually no sanctioned methods by which they could influence the basic political decisions which affected the conditions of their existence. Their impotence was furthered by a basic Branch policy which lasted from the early 1930's to the early postwar years when it was eliminated partly as a result of the awakened public interest in Indians, particularly the 1946–48 Joint Committee of the Senate and the House of Commons. A Branch directive in 1933 stated that Indian complaints and enquiries had to be routed through the agent on the grounds that the practice of Indians attempting to deal directly with headquarters involved an unnecessary waste of time and interfered with efficiency in the conduct of official business. A number of Indian complaints about this policy — which meant that "If we do not get a square deal from the agent how can we report it if we have no recourse except to the agent himself?" — were made to the postwar Joint Committee.[4]

In spite of the legal and administrative barriers to Indians influencing government policy, there has been a long history of Indian attempts to develop their own organizations to advance their cause on either a local or national basis. The development of powerful regional or national organizations has had to contend with Indian poverty and the geographical dispersal of Indian communities, many of which were, and are, isolated. Language difficulties and adult illiteracy hindered the use of written communications to overcome the barriers of distance. To these as barriers to broadly based political organization must be added the parochial identifications of many Indians, who frequently identified themselves with a particular tribe or as adherents of a particular treaty. Throughout most of their period as an administered people, Indians have lacked any strong feelings of national identity or any common objectives they could collectively pursue. There were, and are, important differences in the degree of Indian contact with and acceptance of the standards of the surrounding white society.

Standards of Indian education achievement have been low, and, until recently, few Indians had opportunities to engage in formal political tasks. The Indian submissions to the 1946–48 Joint Committee are noticeable in the extent to which Indians were, at least on the surface, deferential, humble, and shy. In many cases they prefaced their remarks by reminding parliamentarians that they were uneducated, that they spoke and read English poorly, and that in general they lacked the experience to assume a confident demeanour when appearing before M.P.'s and senators.

Some of these problems and barriers might have been overcome by the emergence of a dynamic charismatic leader with a widespread following. This possibility, which has of course also been hindered by the factors of poverty, geography, and so forth, is greatly lessened by the fact that there is no goal of political independence for Indians. No independent state can be created to satisfy whatever desires exist for self-rule. Their geographical dispersal precludes the possibility of "statehood" within the federal system. Their small numbers imply that they can never aspire to becoming a political majority in any sphere beyond the municipal level. Thus, regardless of their wishes, Indians are destined to having only marginal influence in the political decisions of a society from whose embrace they cannot escape. The simple absence of an exciting goal to political activity has denied Indians the possession of the dynamic incentives to participation in a united political organization which have been available to the indigenous inhabitants of the former empires in Africa and Asia.

Partly as a consequence of the preceding factors, there has been a profusion of Indian organizations which have tended to be fragmented and ephemeral, being either called into existence by, or revived by, some particular crisis or opportune occasion such as the joint committees in 1946–48 and 1959–61. Indians have failed to develop truly national and/or provincial organizations that could speak with authority on their behalf. As a consequence, they have lacked one of the basic political tools by which minorities can overcome governmental indifference or can help to ensure that governmental concern is meaningful in Indian terms. The nature of Indian-organizations has been such that the Indian Affairs Branch and the two postwar joint committees of the Senate and the House of Commons have been baffled by the difficulty of determining the following of the spokesmen who have claimed to speak for certain groups. In a number of instances the view presented by one organization before the joint committee was subsequently repudiated by a group of Indians for whom the organization claimed to speak.[5]

The comparative ineffectiveness of Indian organizations and the relative lack of an Indian impact on the political system have been unfortunate. Even if their small numbers and geographical dispersal preclude any possibility of acquiring significant autonomous power within or without the Canadian political system, it is still true that the most important single mechanism for improving the socioeconomic status of the Indian is government, and favourable and positive government treatment on terms deemed acceptable to Indians is related to the expression of Indian demands which it is politically costly for governments to ignore. Of equal importance as a role which Indian organizations can undertake is the translation of existing government concern into channels of activity which reflect the priorities of Indians rather than those established by politicians and administrators.

Advocacy of effective Indian political activity need not be argued solely in terms of the likely material benefits involved. The successful participation of Indians in Canadian society necessarily includes the political sphere in its own right. Politics constitutes one of the most important activities of free societies, exclusion from which whether by formal denial or by the social or other disabilities of the group concerned constitutes an important indicator of low status. Effective political activity can lead to psychic gains in terms of enhanced Indian self-respect and the respect in which they are held by others.

The extension of the franchise has opened up possibilities of influencing government policy which were formerly denied to Indians. Its extension was not the result of aggressive Indian demands for the possession of voting privileges, but rather of the benevolent action of political elites responding to the changed attitude to Indians that developed in the postwar years. It is thus difficult to make categorical statements about the significance of the franchise, for there were, and are, clearly other factors at work leading to a more progressive involvement of governments in Indian affairs independently of the attitudes of Indians themselves.

It should also be noted that even before the franchise was extended, a small number of parliamentarians interested themselves in the problems, needs, and aspirations of Indians.[6] Nevertheless, the general picture was as described by LaViolette:

> Parliament has been grossly neglectful, admittedly so, in failing to give certain kinds of attention to Indian Affairs. Each year an Annual Report was published; each year the estimates for annual appropriations to support the activities of Indian Affairs went through the House of Commons, certainly without any searching questions, as one can now see from Hansard. Until World War II, enfranchised Canadians and their members of Parliament let Indian Affairs coast along.[7]

The combination of changed public and official values with the extension of the franchise has led to a noticeable increase in parliamentary attention devoted to Indians. All officials with whom the question was discussed, as well as those who have written about it, agree that the franchise at both federal and provincial levels has had a beneficial effect on government policies pertaining to Indians.[8]

The extent to which Indians have used the franchise privileges extended to them is not known, except in general terms. From conversations with knowledgeable informants, it appears that the proportion of Indians who vote is about two-thirds that of the non-Indians who vote. It also seems to be the case that the exercise of the federal franchise has been somewhat more widespread where Indians have already had the provincial vote for a number of years. The extension of the franchise is only the beginning of a process of political involvement. It is followed by a necessary transitional period in which Indians and political parties adapt to each other. Given the novelty of voting privileges and the initial suspicion with which they were regarded by many Indians, the actual participation of Indians in the electoral process is remarkably high.

However, even if maximum use is made of the franchise, the Indian impact on federal and provincial political systems will always be marginal. The Indian population is not only small relative to the total population of Canada, but its political impact is further reduced by its youthfulness, which leaves a disproportionate percentage of Indians below voting age. The total number of Indians twenty-one years and above, according to figurers for 31 December 1964, was only 87,384 out of a population of 210,119.[9] The percentage of Indian population of voting age, 41.6, contrasts unfavourably with the 56.8 per cent of the non-Indian population of voting age. Indian voters as a percentage of total voters amount to only 1.1 per cent. There are a number of federal ridings — Algoma East, Cochrane, Port Arthur, Churchill, Springfield, Prince Albert, Kamloops, and Skeena — in which the Indian vote is sizable enough to be courted. Nevertheless, the importance of the franchise probably resides as much in its contribution to the recognition that Indians are an integral part of provincial and national communities as in the actual leverage it gives to Indians in electoral terms.

The main consequence of the dominant philosophy of administration up until World War II, which denied the possibility of any rapid change in the conditions of the Indian people, was to deny the Indian Affairs Branch the funds and personnel which might have speeded up the process of change. Up until that time Indian administration was a version of colonialism. The Branch was a quasi-colonial government dealing with almost the entire life of a culturally different people who were systematically deprived of opportunities to influence government, a people who were isolated on special pockets of land and who were subject to separate laws. Throughout this period a dominating Branch concern was simply to keep the peace and to prevent unruly clientele reactions to Branch policy.

The possibility of a constructive Branch-clientele relationship was further hampered by the deep suspicion in which the Branch was held by many Indians and their feelings of hostility towards it. The immediate postwar situation was graphically described by a senior Branch official in addressing a Conference of Indian agents.

> The biggest problem confronting the Indians in Canada is discovered in the lack of confidence on the part of the Indians in the Department, and in the intentions and sincerity of Departmental officials. If there is an Indian anywhere who speaks words of appreciation about the things we are attempting to do for him, and who displays enthusiasm when referring to the Department and its officials, well, I have never met him. This mistrust and suspicion on the part of the Indian population is, to me, appalling, shocking and frankly, discouraging.[10]

Further indications of the failure of a constructive Branch-clientele relationship to emerge are found in the widespread misunderstanding and ignorance of the Indian Act among Indians. References to Indian confusion were frequently referred to before the 1959–61 Joint Committee[11] and were noted by several of the researchers in this project who spent time in Indian communities. The low level of Indian information which this reveals illustrates the gulf between Indians and the Branch and thus the difficulties in the way of successful joint co-operation.

A final factor in the failure of the Branch to constitute itself into a powerful intragovernmental spokesman for its clientele was its idiosyncratic nature in the federal civil service. For all practical purposes the Branch, until recently, was a miniature government, rather than an ordinary civil service branch. Unlike other civil service departments, it did not deal with white Canadians who possessed the vote, were part of the general community, and possessed the same cultural values as the administrators. Partly for this reason the Branch was able to develop in a unique way unaffected by some of the constraints which moulded the behaviour of other branches of government which dealt with full citizens. The Branch was, and had a widespread reputation for being, a particularly authoritarian organization in a double sense. Within the organization itself, the Branch was characterized by a concentration of decision-making at the top. In the field, many of the "old line" agents in the past were authoritarian in their relations with Indians.

Possibly because of the unique aspects of its task, the Branch has been possessed of a particularly inward-looking orientation. This was reinforced by a grass-roots pattern of career mobility within the Branch which strengthened introspective tendencies. As a consequence, there evolved a mystique of Indian administration which laid great stress on field experience as a basis for knowing the Indian; by extension this implied that Branch personnel who possessed this experience were in touch with "mysteries" which outsiders could not comprehend. Since outsiders had not shared this special experience of administrative contact which was the basis for understanding Indians, and since Indians were excluded by virtue of their dependent status, the Branch presumably saw little need or justification for seeking external allies. The result was an inward-looking parochialism, a partly self-chosen isolation from the overt political system of voters and politicians and the internal political system of the bureaucracy with its competitive struggle for funds and personnel. As a result, the Branch failed to carve out for itself that minimum position of power and influence in the federal government which was a prerequisite for the successful implementation of a progressive Indian policy.

The previous section implicitly assumed that only the national political system was of concern to Indians. Two decades ago this was a reasonable assumption. However, with the increasing involvement of the provinces in service provision for Indians, the existence of pressures to extend that involvement, and the availability of the franchise to Indians in all but one province, this is no longer the case. In the past Indians have had an especially strong relationship with the federal government and a weak and tenuous link with the provincial governments. As Indians move into the provincial framework of administration and services in education, welfare, community development, selected aspects of local government, and resource exploitation, the importance of provincial policy decisions becomes increasingly germane to the terms of their existence. This development raises the whole question of the nature of the provincial political system, the role which Indians and groups which speak on their behalf can play in that system, and whether or not any special sanctions or safeguards are required as Indians become increasingly subject to the decisions of provincial policy-makers who hitherto have had little experience in dealing with them. These questions, it must be said, share the dubious honour of being simultaneously of exceptional complexity and of exceptional importance. Their importance springs from the fact that one of the most basic tendencies in contemporary Indian administration — the relinquishing of the special and exclusive relation Indians have enjoyed with Ottawa — rests on the assumption that normal provincial services are just as appropriate for Indians as for non-Indians and that provincial governments can be trusted to play an honourable and progressive role with respect to Indians. The complexity of these questions relates simply to the absence of empirical data by means of which various hypotheses could be tested.

In contrast to the century-long federal involvement in Indian administration is the fact that the provinces have only commenced to play an important role in service provision for Indians in the past fifteen years. There are certain obvious advantages with respect to innovation, creativity, and flexibility which are implicit in having a growing level of responsibilities for Indians undertaken by governments which have not built up a tradition of viewing Indians from the perspective of long-established policies. On the other hand, the very flexibility which the provinces possess means that their responses to assuming new responsibilities can be highly idiosyncratic and characterized by uncertainty. There are as yet no powerful or large provincial government agencies mainly concerned with Indians, and there are no provincial counterparts of the federal Indian Act to direct the concern of provincial cabinets and legislators to the specific needs of Indians. Thus, a virtually inherent aspect of growing provincial involvement at this early stage of its development is a high degree of unpredictability as to its future orientation. In most of the provinces a handful of men can determine the emphasis, range, and durability of provincial involvement. This is in marked contrast to the federal scene where an established Branch of government with an organizational history extending back for nearly a century plays a continuing role in Indian administration. Here, too, there is change and flexibility but it occurs within the context of a developing tradition which sets limits to the possibility of sudden policy reversals.

The people and governments of the prairie provinces have long had sizable populations of Indian ancestry, the Metis, who in a legal sense are ordinary provincial citizens. On the whole, the treatment of the Metis by the governments of the three prairie provinces has left much to be desired. Now, however, the historical pattern of indifference and neglect is undergoing rapid change under the impact of the same general forces which have invigorated federal policy towards Indians since World War II. In noting the pressures and forces which play on provincial governments, we are led to the belief that historical analogies of past Metis treatment with future treatment of Indians and Metis are false. Some of the reasons for this will become apparent in the discussion of the factors which are leading the provincial governments to interest increasingly themselves in their citizens of Indian status. For the moment, the generalization that the world of the 1960's is a different world from that of the interwar years will suffice. The essential importance of past provincial neglect of the Metis resides less in its capacity to predict future provincial conduct than its relevance as an explanation for the suspicion with which some Indians on the Prairies are prone to regard provincial governments.

A number of factors encourage the belief that even although the nature of provincial involvement differs from province to province, and in spite of the fact that the extension of particular provincial services is often delayed for a number of plausible reasons, the progressive incorporation of Indians into the provincial framework of law and services will continue at an accelerated pace. Accompanying this process will be an increasing acceptance by Indians and both levels of government of the naturalness of a situation which two decades ago seemed only a distant possibility.

Thus, the rapid rate of Indian population growth and the fact that Indian reserves are economically limited in their capacities to support viable communities inevitably increase mobility out of the reserves and force the provinces to acceptance of the view that a hands-off approach is ultimately self-defeating. Even in the absence of significant off-reserve movement, problems are created for provincial governments. The health of surrounding communities and reserves is bound up together. More generally, the trend to regional planning becomes almost self-contradictory if reserves are excluded from the operation of plans in the areas where they are situated. The inexorable pressure of fact thus denies the provinces any real choice in the matter of deciding whether or not they will contribute to the solution of difficult problems of social adjustment which Indians and their non-Indian neighbours will jointly encounter in both off-reserve and reserve environments.

A factor of importance in Quebec and the four western provinces is that the provincial governments of these provinces are all concerned in major programmes of northern development which will increasingly bring provincial officials and white settlements into the midst of areas in which Indian populations have had the least contact with white society and exist by traditional economic pursuits. These developments provide opportunities to offer the more adaptable Indians the benefits of a wage economy. These opportunities are too important to miss, for if Indians are not included in the initial stages in a planned way, the result will either be freezing them out with southern labour imported at high cost or the development of shack and shanty towns which engender racial tensions in frontier communities.

An additional factor is highly relevant in justifying the assumption that an irreversible process of provincial involvement has commenced. While it would be premature to suggest that the concept of the Indian as a provincial citizen has caught the imagination of provincial policy-makers to the extent that they will vie with each other in attempting to make it wholly meaningful in administrative and service terms, it is true that provincial involvement has already acquired a certain snowballing effect in at least three separate ways. A special situation exists in the prairie provinces where Indians and Metis increasingly compare the respective treatment they receive from federal and provincial governments. This results in demands from the least favoured group for improvements in the pattern of services it receives. The same comparisons are implicitly and explicitly made by officials of both jurisdictions with a resultant development of administrative pressure to reduce discrepancies. A second factor is that developments in one province tend to have a demonstration effect leading to similar developments in other provinces. The provincial extension of the franchise is a noteworthy example of the fact that the response of one government in removing restrictions has an important effect in encouraging other governments to do likewise. British Columbia's extension of the franchise in 1949 was noted and discussed in official circles in Ontario before that province decided to do likewise in 1954. It is also clear that the extension of the federal franchise in 1960 was partly related to the increasing anomaly of federal exclusion when 60 per cent of Indians had the provincial vote. The effect of inter-provincial comparisons is also noteworthy in community development pro-grammes, especially in the prairie provinces. In Ontario, when the Leader of the Opposition was attempting to encourage more governmental interest in Indians, he spoke favourably of the Manitoba Community Development Programme and sarcastically suggested to the government: "To you this is something like talking of astronauts. It is away up in the moon or something."[12]

The actual mechanisms by which these interrelated responses in the federal system intertwine and interact with each other are impossible to describe in detail. In some cases the similarities in the responses of governments simply reflect similarities in the climate of opinion to which they respond. In other instances, interaction among elites possessed of policy-making capacities helps to create a consensus about what should be done. In more general terms, it is evident that in an interdependent political system there are underlying political factors at work which tend to reduce the likelihood of major differences in the scope and orientation of government programmes proving durable.

The third aspect of this snowballing effect occurs within each province as developments in one field eventually encounter the interrelatedness of Indian needs and by so doing generate logical arguments for the extension of the process. The obvious example here is the franchise, which creates a political concern for Indians, which tends to increase the general pressure for provincial involvement in ever new areas.

The intraprovincial snowballing effect does not, of course, proceed as a consequence of abstract arguments as to its logical desirability but rather as a consequence of the evolution of administrative and political foci of concern for Indians. From this perspective the extension of any particular service to Indians is important not only in the light of its contribution to the improvement in the quality of the service received by Indians, nor even in its contribution to the progressive elimination of discriminatory treatment, but in terms of its contribution to the creation of a sustained and more knowledgeable understanding at the government level of the needs of Indians. It is patently clear that there is developing at influential levels of provincial governments groups of individuals who on particular occasions constitute themselves as spokesmen for Indians. The extension of each provincial service thus creates allies who can become important factors in further extensions. In the province of Alberta the driving power of one provincial cabinet minister with a strong civil rights interest was an important factor in precipitating a growing cabinet concern for people of Indian ancestry. This cabinet concern manifested itself in the adoption of a community development programme which has attracted to the provincial public service a small number of highly competent personnel who institutionalize provincial interest, give it a prospect of durability, and constitute centres of influence likely to lead to its expansion into other areas of provincial administration. This particular instance is simply an example of the general principle of cumulative involvement which, to a greater or lesser degree, is a likely consequence of increased contact between provincial officials and Indians. This kind of development is particularly significant, for few things are more important for an underprivileged minority heavily dependent on government for its advancement than the existence of a sympathetic concern among administrators and politicians with the capacity to influence policy.

In particular areas of provincial jurisdiction there has been a dramatic increase in provincial involvement in recent years. In 1964–65, 44 per cent of Indian children attending school were enrolled in provincial schools, a marked increase from the insignificant 7 per cent so enrolled in 1949–50. In several provinces, especially Quebec, Ontario, Manitoba, and Saskatchewan, effective arrangements of an informal or formal nature have long existed to develop fur-bearing animals for the benefit of northern Indians. There has, of course, been a striking improvement in the availability of child welfare services to Indians, and it is expected that in the near future Indians will be progressively brought within provincial programmes of social assistance. Finally, there has been the growth of community development programmes, especially in the three prairie provinces and to a lesser extent so far in Ontario and British Columbia, which are specifically designed to stimulate social change in disadvantaged provincial communities, including Indian reserve communities.

In surveying the development of provincial interest and involvement, several striking impressions quickly emerge. It is noticeable that on the whole provincial involvement has not been the result of Indian demands. In only a few cases — such as the Native Brotherhood of B.C. and the provincial franchise — have Indian organizations played any kind of forceful role. In fact, the typical situation is that

Indians have to be persuaded of the benefits of the provinces playing a larger role in their affairs.

A second point is that there are marked differences in the extent to which the depressed conditions of Indians are seen to constitute an important political problem. On the whole, there has been much less public and governmental interest in Indians in Quebec and the Maritime provinces than in the rest of Canada. This is partially explained by the smaller size of the Indian populations in these provinces, and in the Maritimes by a standard of living markedly below the national average, which makes Indian poverty far less noticeable. In Nova Scotia there has been much more government concern about Blacks than about Indians. In Quebec the major reason for less overt public and government interest is doubtless the dominance of the "Quiet Revolution" as a public issue. It is significant that none of these four provinces has mounted a specific community development programme. In all four provinces Indian organizations are weak or non-existent. With the exception of certain frontier towns in Quebec, such as Matagami, there do not seem to be any special problems of urban adjustment arising from the move from reserve to city. There have been no skid road scandals involving Indians in the Maritimes. Further, the general level of provincial services is not as qualitatively distinguished from Branch services to the extent that is true elsewhere. Finally, in the Maritimes and Quebec, non-Indian pressure groups or lobbies seem virtually non-existent, and there are no spokesmen for Indians in the provincial legislative assemblies.

West of Quebec political concern for Indians picks up noticeably. In Ontario the powerful metropolitan press of Toronto has played an important part in stimulating government interest. Toronto is also the headquarters of the Indian Eskimo Association, and a disproportionate amount of the activity of that body has been centred in Ontario. In the three prairie provinces the existence of a large Metis population, a group which possesses Indian ancestry but is not endowed with Indian status, has been an important factor in provincial interest. The identifiable members of Metis exist at a socioeconomic level differing little from their Indian "brothers." They, too, are poor, socially disorganized, inadequately educated, and only marginally involved in the economy. They are, of course, provincial citizens, in no way legally distinguishable from other citizens. They are, therefore, a direct and undeniable provincial responsibility. Their existence, frequently contiguous to reserves, automatically directs provincial attention to all people of Indian ancestry, whether they possess Indian status or not.

The very condensed survey of provincial involvement given in the preceding pages has left out one of the main variables influencing the provinces to extend their services to Indians. This is, of course, the Indian Affairs Branch, which has assumed the role of negotiator for the inclusion of Indians in provincial programmes. It is difficult to distinguish between the relative influence of the Indian

Affairs Branch in stimulating provincial concern and involvement and the normal pressures and demands coming up through the provincial political system.

The Indian Affairs Branch has played a major role in the context of conferences and committees with provincial officials in helping to focus attention on possible changes in the provincial relationship to Indians. As already noted there are certain aspects of the Indian situation that inevitably create provincial concern. Also, provincial officials have been influenced by the changing community values and expectations already discussed. There has also been in some provinces a development of an independent provincial interest. These factors have the combined effect of making the provinces much more favourably disposed to co-operate with the federal government than formerly and much less likely to assert that the Indian is a "ward" of the federal government and, therefore, its exclusive responsibility.

Nonetheless, for historical reasons there is a widespread provincial feeling that in any case Indians are a federal responsibility. We frequently encountered the attitude that provincial governments were in some sense doing the federal government and/or Indians a favour if they extended any of their normal services to Indian reserve communities. Even where the provinces are concerned, the assumption that the Indians are not really provincial citizens in the same way as other citizens dilutes the urgency with which they respond. There is always another government to blame. These attitudes that in normal circumstances Indians are outside the orbit of provincial interest are automatically reinforced by the federal policy of buying normal provincial services which it is desired to extend to Indians. The inclusion of Indians thus becomes a result of federal-provincial bargaining rather than an automatic result of Indian residence within provincial boundaries and their common citizenship with other Canadians. In a sense, it might even be argued that the existence of special arrangements so that Indians are treated by provincial departments in the same way as anybody else merely reinforces the separateness of their identity to provincial policy-makers.

The perception that Indians are not really complete provincial citizens because of their special status and relation to the federal government easily gets transmuted into the argument that if they wish to receive the same government treatment as other provincial citizens, they will have to give up their special privileges under treaty or the Indian Act. Provincial officials and politicians display a much more assimilative and less protective philosophy to Indians than does the federal government. There is, for example, a fairly general provincial antipathy to the reserve system. Indians, we were told on several occasions, cannot have it both ways and retain their special privileges while simultaneously obtaining the full benefits of provincial citizenship.

One of the most important differences between federal and provincial political systems is the presence at the federal level of a career administration with an exclusively Indian orientation and the absence of such a body at the provincial level. The most important sanction for good government treatment of the Indian people at the federal level is neither the treaties nor the Indian Act, although these play a part, but the existence of a professional body of Indian specialists who can see to it that the interests of their clientele are continuously considered in the formation of federal policy. As already noted, the Indian Affairs Branch was not overly successful throughout most of its history in its pressure-group role, although it has increasingly become so in the past decade. In the provincial governments, no administrative body of comparable orientation and power exists, although the emerging community development programmes in some of the provinces and the Indian and Metis Branch in Saskatchewan may come to constitute a partial alternative as administrative power centres devoted to furthering Indian interests.

This absence of administrative restraint or focus of administrative pressure in the provinces strikes us as unfortunate. It is not simply a desire to ensure that the interests of Indians are considered at the governmental level which concerns us, but that such consideration be restrained by knowledge, filtered through an informed, professional understanding of the difficulties of social change and the dangers of crash programmes based on enthusiasm, funds, and naive assumptions about the simplicity with which dramatic improvements can be achieved.

To the extent that provincial involvement occurs through the regular channels of existing programmes in welfare, education, and highways, no particular problem is raised. The problem of the source and competence of the advice which guides provincial policy makers assumes major importance (1) when provincial governments are considering the establishment of new programmes specifically for Indians or people of Indian ancestry, programmes of community development, economic development, or stimulated migration to urban centres; and (2) when basic provincial policy with respect to Indians is in process of formation. In each of these situations there is a high degree of uncertainty about the direction of future policy or the departmental allocation of new responsibilities. This creates a situation in which individual and departmental jockeying for influence and control is almost inevitable. There is, in short, a temporary void which provides an opportunity for personal and departmental ambitions to advance themselves. In those provinces where this kind of power struggle exists, structural opportunities for its manifestation can be found in interdepartmental committees of provincial civil servants, and in some cases in the federal-provincial co-ordinating committees on Indian affairs.

In part these intraprovincial disputes relate to different philosophies and programme approaches. A degree of tension between welfare-oriented departments and development-oriented departments is frequent. Occasionally, the tension expresses itself in dissension over which provincial department will capture the coveted responsibility of administering a prestigious community development programme. Given the frequency with which these situations emerge, they cannot be explained solely by the irrationalities and perversities of the individuals concerned. In all cases these struggles, whatever their idiosyncratic manifestations from province to province, reflect the novelty of provincial interest and the consequent administrative uncertainty generated by impending change, coupled with the inevitable clash of divergent interpretations of the most appropriate content of future policy. These interpretations which reflect basic differences of opinion intertwined with the whole range of organizational factors from which particular administrative perspectives develop and from which administrative self-interest comes to be defined will only be resolved as the momentum of provincial involvement picks up and stabilizes itself.

We are still left, however, with the basic question of the adequacy of the advice which guides provincial policy-makers as they address themselves to the problems of Indian poverty and anomie. The development of some special focus of interest in Indians at the administrative and cabinet level seems inevitable and desirable. The danger springs from the disproportionate influence in provincial policy-making which a small group of individuals will possess, simply because of the absence of alternative sources of advice and information. In the country of the blind, the one-eyed man is king. Whether this is to be deprecated obviously depends on the competence and integrity of the particular one-eyed men involved. All that can be said in a report of this nature is that in some instances the kind of provincial officials who have assumed a predominant role in the formation of provincial Indian policy at various times in the past decade have not impressed us, although in the majority of cases we have no apprehensions on this score.

Canadian Indians are a seriously disadvantaged group, socially, economically, and politically. These disadvantages are interrelated. In general, groups which are impoverished and held in low esteem by the community lack political influence proportionate to their numbers. Any significant breakthrough in this situation of vicious circular causation must come from government. No other institution possesses the capacity to simultaneously affect the broad range of factors relevant to the introduction of major change — education, economic development, welfare, health, housing, communications, and so forth. As noted elsewhere in this report, the nature and size of the Indian problem is such as to allow a generous development programme to take place without noticeable strain on the national income and government revenues. The essential limitations on government responsiveness to Indian needs are thus almost exclusively political. The fact that limits are essentially political does not mean, however, that they are unimportant. There are many sources of competition for government revenues. No government can address itself to more than a small percentage of the multitudinous problems that press for action and that could be alleviated or overcome by a greater expenditure of funds, use of personnel, or revision of regulations. The priorities which governments impose on the range of possibilities that confront them do not reflect a "cool" analysis of the "best" deployment of government capacities for action. In the process of priority determination, certain group needs and problems inevitably get left by the wayside, not because they are intrinsically, or even relatively, unimportant, but simply because it is politically safe to ignore them. The melancholy indifference of governments to Indians from Confederation until World War II provides eloquent testimony to this fact.

The problem of adequate and effective government responsiveness has two aspects. Public concern for Indians which manifests itself in large-scale pro-grammes based on naive assumptions about social change will do little good and indeed will probably do damage by the inevitable disillusion it will bring in its wake. The first prerequisite therefore is to devise policies which are the best available in the light of existing knowledge. No less unfortunate, however, is a situation in which intelligent understanding of an effective role for government is rendered irrelevant by the failure of governments to manifest this understanding in concrete policies. Historically, Canadian Indian administration has been charac-terized by a protective role to see that Indian rights under treaties were respected, to protect Indian land against alienation, and to provide Indians with the enclaves of the reserve system within which they could be partially isolated from the disruptive, intruding forces of an aggressive, expansive white society. On the whole, this protective role has been well performed, as comparisons of Canadian and American Indian policy make clear. At the present time, there is still scope for the performance of a protective role, but it must be supplemented by a more positive role which will enable Indians to stand on their own feet. This is now almost universally recognized, and postwar developments, especially of the past decade, are extremely encouraging with their manifold indications of positive approaches. However, it is necessary and prudent to enquire about the durability of a political climate which encourages the continuing introduction of progressive policies. Earlier it argued that the nature of the changing Indian "fact" in Canadian society inexorably impels the provinces in the direction of greater involvement with Indians. While this is generally true, it must be remembered that the situations to which government policies are addressed are characterized by complex problems incapable of easy solution. In such circumstances the pos-sibility of disenchantment is always present. The interest of political parties and elected officials has an inherent tendency to be erratic and fluctuating over time and may thus prove to be less durable than the problems themselves. The administrative vigour of the Indians Affairs Branch and the less developed administrative interest of some of the provinces are heavily dependent on particu-lar personalities, and both will be affected by the success or failure of the policies to which they give a temporary priority. Given the recency of provincial interest and the complexity of the problems it is not unrealistic to question the durability of any progressive provincial responses, particularly those responses outside the normal programmes extended to the entire provincial community. There is an inherent danger that existing provincial incentives, particularly in supplementary areas of activity such as community development may be eroded by failure. The interest of the general public is highly variable and is far more likely to be aroused by a shocking case of child neglect than by the drab unsensational poverty which affects the overwhelming majority of Indian communities.

In these circumstances the obvious question is what can be done to facilitate the likelihood that governments will prove themselves capable of the long hard haul which will be required. The first answer must be that no attempt to ensure the appropriate durability of government concern can be certain of attaining its objectives. What can be done is to reduce the chances of a too easy failure. This requires the effective utilization of existing forces and pressures which affect government policies to Indians and the creation of supplementary mechanisms to help fill the gap should existing government concern wither away.

An essential aspect of Branch policy must be to take a positive, interested, and sympathetic approach to Indian organizations and to various interested groups that constitute themselves spokesmen for Indians. A quarter of a century ago the question of the relations between the Branch and interested non-Indian or mixed organizations was irrelevant, for they did not exist. This is no longer the case. The change in community values concerning the position of Indians in Canadian society has led to the emergence of two important organizations and an increasing amount of attention and concern among the innumerable general purpose citizen groups which abound in Canada. Two organizations merit brief special attention because of their size, their durability, and their impact on the public.

The Indian Eskimo Association of Canada was formally established in 1960 as an outgrowth of the National Commission on the Indian Canadian which had been set up in 1957 by the Canadian Association for Adult Education. The association is "a non-sectarian, non-political, independent organization dedicated to the cause of Canada's native people." The association, which has a small permanent staff, is educational in the broadest sense. It publishes bulletins, conducts research, submits briefs to governments, organizes conferences, promotes adult education projects for Indians, and provides information and consultation services to over eighty organizations among its members. In its brief existence the association has made an important contribution as a non-governmental focal point for the Indian and Eskimo peoples whose interest it is designed to serve. The association has recently decided to decentralize its operations with the establishment of provincial branches, a policy change which is eminently desirable in view of the increasing role played by provincial governments in Indian affairs.

The Indian and Metis Conference Committee of the Community Welfare Planning Council of Greater Winnipeg was established in 1954 in response to widespread concern about the plight of Indian and Metis people of Manitoba. That year the committee sponsored the first Indian and Metis Conference. Each year there has been a similar conference, the functions broadly being to focus attention on the needs of the people of Indian origin, to provide Indians and Metis with an opportunity to air their views in public and to suggest ways to resolve their social and economic problems, and to foster understanding between Indians and non-Indians. The conferences have been exceptionally successful in fostering community concern, in providing a forum for informed discussion, and in stimulating the provincial government to action. The annual conference, with over five hundred persons in attendance, has in fact become too large to be easily run. In addition to the annual conference, the committee also helps to organize special educational programmes for Indians, aids research, and prepares proposals for government action.

These two organizations illustrate the stimulus which can be given to a generally favourable public opinion when it is given an outlet and focus for its concern. Such organizations supplement the permissive attitudes of the public with positive demands. By so doing they ease the task of government agencies which in a democratic society cannot long operate without public support.

General acceptance of the wisdom and necessity of regarding such outside groups as important allies already exists. It is, however, easy to occasionally relapse into the attitudes that such groups are perhaps unduly critical, often misinformed, and perhaps too prone to take credit for the inspiration of Branch initiatives that would have occurred independently of their existence or support. It is also realized that a certain amount of tension between outside organizations and a government body is a sign of health, of independence, and the inevitable existence of divergent attitudes to policy in areas where the answers are far from self-evident. The role of outside organizations seeking to play a helpful role in the evolution of government policy is not easy. A recent bulletin of the Indian Eskimo Association reveals some of the difficulties.

> Liaison with officials of the Indian Affairs Branch should be strengthened. The habit of blaming all their troubles on the government is deeply rooted in the Indians and dies hard. They tend to ignore the new I.A.B. initiatives. Because their criticisms are voiced in meetings organized by I.E.A., I.A.B. officials sometimes feel that the Association is endorsing them. The "honest broker" role is difficult to fill.[13]

It is particularly important to support Indian organizations by official encouragement, by the provision when asked of resource personnel for conferences, and by serious consideration of resolutions and complaints. This is necessary to avoid the danger of government policies being devised and implemented with the best intentions but without the appropriate degree of sensitivity to the way in which Indians define the problem to which the policy is applied. The fact that Indian leaders and spokesmen may make unjustifiably hostile and critical statements about the Branch does not simplify the task of senior Branch officials, but in the present context of Indian development some such criticism is inevitable and should be quietly accepted as such.

An important attempt to increase the sensitivity of the Branch and Indians to each other has recently been made with the institution of Indian advisory councils.

A number of factors coalesced to produce a need for a more systematic method of Branch-Indian consultation. as the tempo of policy change quickened, the need for more frequent use of consultative machinery became obvious. Further, as the emphasis in Branch-Indian relations shifted from paternal to democratic, the process of consultation came to be viewed as valuable in its own right. Finally, the fact that important shifts in federal-provincial roles pertaining to Indians were possible added particular urgency to the establishment of consultative machinery, for as already noted Indian agreement to the process of increasing provincial involvement was central to this aspect of Branch policy and essential to its success.

In response to these considerations, the Branch established a series of regional Indian advisory councils in 1965, which was capped with a National Indian Advisory Board. The regional councils have been elected, directly or indirectly, by the Indians themselves. Their membership varies from eight to twelve members, including representatives from Indian associations in the region concerned. It is anticipated that the councils will meet at least once a year for a session of two or three days. The National Indian Advisory Board is composed of eighteen Indian members, selected by the regional councils.

These councils are intended to play a major role in the administration of Indian affairs. Their function is clearly advisory, but it is intended that their recommendations will be carefully considered and their viewpoints sought on broad issues of policy, proposed legislation, federal provincial agreements, new programmes, and proposed changes in existing programmes. Although the Indians will be allowed to raise matters, it is official policy that the matters referred to the councils by the government will take precedence on the agenda of any meeting.

Unfortunately, the recency of the councils makes it impossible to appraise their performance or to predict their future evolution. It is clear that their possible role can be of great importance. They can help to overcome the serious difficulties in Indian-Branch communication which have hampered Branch policy. It is hoped that the meetings will provide opportunities for the Branch to become sensitized to Indian views and also for Indians to become more aware of the difficulties faced by the Branch and the sincerity with which it is attempting to overcome them.

As a corollary to the use of advisory councils and a sympathetic approach to Indian and non-Indian organizations, there should be a strong emphasis on public relations. The necessity for this is inherent in the responsibilities of the Branch. The statutory duty of the Branch to administer the Indian Act is only part of its wider responsibility for increasing the effective participation of Indians in the general society and economy of Canada. If its efforts are to succeed it needs the support, understanding, and co-operation of Indians, the general public, provincial governments, employers, and service organizations. An effective public relations programme constitutes therefore a basic weapon in the successful pursuit of Branch objectives.

Traditional assumptions about the appropriate division of labour between public servants and politicians are no longer acceptable, except in the sense that the final say does, as it should, continue to reside with the politicians. Not only is it necessary to accept the fact that effective policy-making is impossible without the contributions of experience and understanding possessed by the public service, but it can also be said that in particular circumstances members of the public service have, and should assert, a legitimate right to represent certain segments of the community who, for a variety of reasons, find few articulate spokesmen in legislatures, cabinets, and pressure groups. In such circumstances the alternative to a particular branch of the public service constituting itself a spokesman for an interest or group with little political backing is for that group or interest to obtain less attention from government than it needs and probably less than simple notions of equity would consider reasonable.

The case of Indians constitutes a classic proof of the above proposition. As a group, Indians are a special segment of the disadvantaged poor who are usually unskilled in the arts of applying pressure, possess few organizational means of effectively doing so, and who, until recently, were deprived of the franchise. Such groups are almost inevitably underrepresented in the overt political system. In such cases it is especially legitimate for a public agency of government specifically charged with the responsibility of Indian affairs to so conduct itself that it counterbalances political underrepresentation with a forceful calling of governmental attention to the needs of its clients. If the logic of this is unacceptable, then the Canadian people are implicitly saying that Indians can only direct attention to their needs by the weapons of the agitator and the revolutionary.

NOTES

1. C. T. Loram and T. F. McIlwraith, eds., *The North American Indian Today* (Toronto, 1943), pp. 4–5.
2. Annual Report, 21 November 1964.
3. Joint Committee, 1961, p. 343. See also ibid., p. 328.
4. Joint Committee, 1947, p. 1405, complaint of the Garden River Band. See also the complaints of the Union of Ontario Indians and the general statement of Professor T. F. McIlwraith, ibid., pp. 1302, 1942–43.
5. See, for example, Joint Committee, 1947, pp. 2050–51; Joint Committee, 1960, pp. 569, 612–13; Joint Committee, 1961, p. 183.

6. See F. E. LaViolette, *The Struggle for Survival: Indian Cultures and the Protestant Ethic in British Columbia* (Toronto, 1961), pp. 87, 92–93 for the interest of members from British Columbia in the interwar years. See also Joint Committee, 1947, pp. 893, 1411 for additional examples.

7. LaViolette, p. 166. One member informed the first joint committee that "many members whom I have known have just ignored the Indian" (Joint Committee, 1947, pp. 1048–49).

8. See the statement of the director of Indian Affairs Branch, Colonel Jones, to the Joint Committee, 1960, pp. 403–4; LaViolette, pp. 184–85; and Joint Committee, 1959, pp. 151, 154 for the views of Rev. Peter Kelly and R. P. Clifton of the Native Brotherhood of British Columbia.

9. This excludes 1,270 Indians whose ages were not known.

10. The attempt to overcome Indian feelings of distrust and suspicion is partially behind the proposed establishment of an Indian Claims Commission.

11. See, for example, Joint Committee, 1960, pp. 15–23, 134, 347, 777, 993–94, 1025.

12. Ontario Hansard, 17 June 1965, p. 4363.

13. Vol. 7, no. 2 (March-April, 1966).

Section II

Native Responses to Changing Relations and Circumstances

1

Alcoholism, Indians, and the Anti-Drink Cause in the Protestant Indian Missions of Upper Canada, 1822–1850

F. L. Barron

Fundamental to the European presence in North America was an inordinate use of alcohol. Jacques Cartier, on the Island of Orleans in the St. Lawrence River, reportedly celebrated his first formal meeting with Donnaconna and his warriors by providing a feast of bread and wine.[1] At the time, the use of alcohol was little more than a measure of European custom; however, as the course of history would reveal, it was emblematic of what would become a North American "drink culture," not only poisoning white-Indian relations but also threatening to disrupt the societies of the European and Indian alike.

Perhaps nowhere were the problems of alcoholism more evident than in the Indian communities of Upper Canada during the early decades of the nineteenth century. This was a feature of Indian life that generated considerable comment by contemporary travellers and settlers. Although their accounts normally betray an underlying ethnocentrism and sternness of morality that cannot properly be applied to the various tribes, they nevertheless testify to the very real existence of a drink problem for many of the colony's eight thousand Indians.[2] In 1820, John Howison observed that, subsequent to the distribution of annual presents at Grand River and the head of Lake Erie, "the Indians spent all the money they received in this way upon spirits; hence drunkenness ensues — fatal combats take place — and shocking scenes of outrage, intoxication, and depravity, continue until the actors are stripped of all they possess."[3] Alfred Domett's tour of the province in the early 1830's included a trip to Brantford where his carriage "narrowly escaped running over some drunken Indians who were lying in the muddy road."[4]

Likewise in 1860, the Reverend John Carroll vividly recalled the state of the Mississaugas in the vicinity of York: "They were drunkards to a man," he said, "their women totally divorced of virtue — and the whole of them sunk in poverty and filth beyond expression. At the time of their receiving their annuities and presents . . . a bacchanalian revel took place, which usually lasted days, and issued in squandering every copper of money and selling or pawning every article they had received, for the deadly 'firewater.'"[5]

To place these accounts in perspective, it is important to note that, by the 1820's, white society perceived the Indian as only a marginal and unimportant segment of the community. With the rapproachement between Great Britain and the United States in the aftermath of the War of 1812, the one-time military importance of the Indian was rendered null. Moreover, given the migration of the fur trade to the far west, neither the Indian's labour nor his wilderness technology had any relevance to the larger community. Indeed, the province had already entered a stage of development which, in many of its essentials, prefigured the emergence of twentieth-century Ontario. By 1850, the colony had a population of nearly a million, and this was accompanied by the introduction of industry, the commercialization of agriculture, a system of formal education, as well as other features of an emerging capitalist society.[6] All spoke to a process of "modernization" which, in addition to intensifying the contact between Whites and Indians, ushered in an era that would little tolerate an Indian culture born of wilderness. In 1828, an Indian agent named Colonel Givens advised one pagan Indian to embrace a Christian and sedentary way of life because "in a few years the hunting would be destroyed by the white settlers who were constantly extending back into the country."[7] Likewise, according to the Methodist *Christian Guardian,* the colony had entered an age whose main characteristic was untold change and motion, "almost at telegraphic speed," within which "the Anglo-Saxon approached; the war-whoop died away . . . [and] the wilderness itself fell prostrate before him."[8] Both accounts denote the passing of the frontier stages of development and the beginning of a new era in which the Indian and his culture were deemed anachronistic and negligible.

Reinforcing this perception was the apparent inability (or unwillingness) of the Indian to adapt. Unsupported by the new environment, and yet doggedly refusing to be remade in the image of white society, Indian culture often was forced into a kind of limbo. In 1834, Catherine Parr Traill noted that the "Indians appear[ed] less addicted to gay and tinselly [sic] adornments than formerly and rather affect[ed] a European style of dress."[9] Somewhat later, Major Strickland affirmed that many of the old Indian customs were falling into disuse and that the Indians, both Christian and heathen, were gradually adopting the manners of the white man.[10] Yet, despite these trimmings of cultural surrender, John Howison, an astute observer of Canadian society as it existed in 1820, asserted that the Indians "obstinately refuse[d] to assimilate . . . except in so far as they acquire a number of vicious propensities" from the white man.[11] Similarly in 1841, Sir Richard Bonnycastle noted that although the Indians living in the narrows of Lake Simcoe were in a state of cultural transition, the abandonment of their traditional way of life was incomplete.[12] The fact was that, not unlike earlier attempts to "Francicize the Amerindians,"[13] the pressures of cross-cultural contact had served, not to assimilate the Indian into white society, but to relegate him to a peripheral and inferior position, plagued by social and cultural dislocation.

According to the conventional wisdom of the day, most of the ills which afflicted Indian communities could be traced to the evils of alcohol. This view assumed special meaning for the Protestant missionaries, who, in attempting to "Christianize and civilize" the colony's natives, were quick to endorse temperance principles. The anti-drink crusade, which enjoyed its widest support in Great Britain and her colonies, as well as in the United States, had been imported into Upper Canada in 1828 as part of an international humanitarian movement addressed to wide-ranging societal abuse. While it won some sympathy among Conservatives and high churchmen, it was most warmly embraced by sectarian and low church groups, especially by the Methodist Episcopal Connection and other reformist elements who were susceptible to American influence.[14] Like the reformation of prisons, Sabbatarianism, or the abolition of slavery, the temperance movement was predicated on the utilitarian understanding of progress and human perfectibility; and, although the Indian often figured as an impoverished and contemptible creature in the eyes of white society, that in itself made him a fit subject for Christian benevolence and temperance reform.

The response of the Protestant churches to the Indian drink problem was led by the Methodists. Prior to 1850, the Presbyterians injected little enthusiasm or insight into the field of Indian missions; and, while the Moravians and Baptists made a realistic effort to bridge the gap between the Indian and white societies, the scope of their activities was localized and limited.[15] By the same token, despite the initial advantages offered by early Church of England contact with the Iroquois, the potential of Anglican missions among the Indians was allowed to lapse. One problem was that school masters, placed on the reserve to teach the catechism and a rudimentary level of education, were often of dubious character with little appreciation of the Indian culture.[16] Another was that clergy of the Church of England were in short supply — even for the parishes in the settled areas of the colony — and commonly exhibited lofty cultural pretensions which alienated settler and Indian alike.[17] Then too, because the clergyman's responsibilities extended to many areas other than the mission, he rarely dwelt among the Indians or understood their language, with the result that his contact with the native culture was only cursory at best.[18]

By contrast, the genius of the Methodist organization was its ability to develop a far more enduring and reciprocal relationship with the Indian community. As early as 1822, when Methodists under Alvin Torry and Edmund Stoney began work among the Six Nations on the Grand River, thoughtful leaders realized that, if they were to come to any understanding of the complex values governing the Indian existence, they would have to systematize the numerous Indian dialects and approach the Indian through his own language.[19] It was for this reason that Egerton Ryerson, who was familiar with the structure of language, received the charge in 1826 to open a mission among the Mississaugas on the Credit River. Within a year, the youthful Ryerson was not only preaching in the native tongue, but had also introduced the Pestalozzian system, a method of education which combined lessons with work and other physical activity.[20] It was also under Methodist auspices that the Reverend Peter Jones, a Mississauga half-breed, translated the Gospels into Indian dialect and rendered a book of Wesleyan hymns into his native language.[21] The result was Methodist pre-eminence in the field of Indian missions, a fact underscored in the alarm sounded by rival religious groups. As one Anglican lamented in 1841, "pestered by the peddling preachers from that go-ahead people, who wander all over Canada, the poor Indians did not know which way to turn; and a clergyman, either of England or Rome, has little chance against these coster-mongers of our faith, who with a borrowed horse, and a pair of saddle-bags, dispense grace, and resistance to monarchy, with equal fervor and untiring zeal."[22]

From its inception, the temperance programme of the Methodists represented an *a priori* condition of effective contact with the Indian. Apart from the personal and social tragedies attendant on alcoholism, the use of intoxicants by the Indian was seen as a massive barrier to the conversion process through which civilization was to be achieved. Drunkenness was interpreted less as an offence against society than as a sin transgressing the laws of God, and for that reason, abstinence represented the road to salvation. As one account said of an Indian who had experienced conversion, "he found the Great Spirit, when he immediately re-nounced his magical acts and drunkenness, and was now determined to be a Christian as long as he lived."[23] Similarly, according to the explanation given by Peter Jones for the conversion of the Indians at the Credit and a number of other Methodist missions, "they had forsaken their destroyer, the firewater, so that now instead of getting drunk, quarrelling, and fighting; they love the Great Spirit, and one another, and prosper in many things."[24]

In teaching the virtues of abstinence, Methodist preachers placed a great emphasis on the school and pulpit, but this approach was soon supplemented by the organization of mission temperance societies replete with a constitution and pledge cards. They also assumed a stance which, in any other contemporary setting, would have been dismissed as radical enthusiasm. Almost from the beginning, the literal meaning of "temperance" was discarded in favour of the demand for total abstinence from all intoxicants.[25] To reinforce this demand, in the early 1830's several Indian missions, under the guidance of Methodist clergy, petitioned the colonial assembly for a legislative ban on the sale of liquor to the Indians.[26]

As an agent of Christian evangelicalism, the Indian temperance programme bore little direct relationship to the larger Upper Canadian community. It was, in most ways, an esoteric solution to a peculiar problem, and although the Methodists also carried the temperance banner into the white and settled areas of the province, the goals they attempted to impose upon their Indian charges were very different from those applied elsewhere. Fundamental to Methodist missions among the Indians was a racial bias that reflected the value structure of white society from which the Methodists and their anti-drink campaign received their commission. The fact was that for all their genius in dealing with Indians, those who sought to Christianize and civilize the Indian through sobriety could not escape the racial assumptions that governed provincial social development.

Serving as a frame of reference for the Indian programme, the larger Upper Canadian temperance movement was largely a Protestant and white crusade in which the non-white minorities were either relegated to a separate society or openly debarred from membership by deep-seated prejudices. In 1850, for example, the National Division of the Sons of Temperance of North America passed a resolution recommending that it be "improper and illegal to admit into our Order persons of Colour."[27] In reaction, the Ontario Division, located in Toronto, was quick to protest such blatant discrimination.[28] However, as laudable as the Toronto response may have been, it ignored a longstanding, if somewhat subtle and informal, tradition of black segregation in Upper Canada, and it might well be imagined that it was not well received in all quarters. In many older churches, segregated pews and slave galleries were very much a part of the setting. While it was only in the 1820's that all Wesleyan churches permitted Blacks to take communion with the white congregation,[29] all-black churches survived that period in a number of racially mixed communities.[30] And the same prejudice was true of anti-drink societies. As one reformer noted in regard to the reorganization of the all-black Amherstburg temperance association in 1840, "it is unfortunate that the state of feeling respecting colour is such in Canada, that the coloured people are not invited to join the societies formed by whites."[31]

An analogous situation existed for the Indian population. In general, the so-called savage was often the brunt of contempt and ridicule. In 1850, the Barrie *Magnet* carried an editorial for "the amusement of the readers" in which the names of some Sioux who had signed the temperance pledge were cited in jest. The fact that references to "kills-the-Spirit" or "Stands-and-Looks" were thought to be appropriate copy was itself an indication of where the Indian stood in relation to the wider temperance movement.[32] Moreover, in communities that were in close proximity to an Indian settlement, temperance societies seldom were organized on an interracial basis, and where there was an exception, the association was often divided into separate branches. In Coldwater there was a biracial society, but the segregation was denoted in two separate committees, one for Coldwater proper, the other for the Narrows where the Indians lived.[33] In both cases, the committee was dominated by a white majority, apparent evidence that the Indian was not always accepted as an adult capable of directing his own affairs.

Within the confines of the mission, the Indian also found himself co-opted into a temperance association predicted on the assumption that he was a child-like figure, unable to curb his passion for intoxicants or detect the adulteration of lesser alcoholic drinks, such as cider or beer.[34] It was for this reason that the Methodists endorsed an extreme definition of temperance, as well as a legislatively imposed solution to the Indian drink problem at a time when the principles of total abstinence and prohibition were completely antipathetic to what the white community or even the Methodists were prepared to apply to themselves. In fact, it was only after 1835 that teetotalism became the gospel of the wider temperance movement and well into the 1840's before the idea of state intervention became an acceptable formula for sobriety in the settled areas.[35] What made the double standard especially suspect, of course, was that drunkenness was not only characteristic of Indian society, but a province-wide phenomenon. By 1850, there were some forty-nine breweries in Upper Canada, producing in excess of 3.4 million litres of beer; there were 100 distilleries manufacturing close to 13.5 million litres of hard liquor, at a time when the alcoholic content of spirits was about 50 per cent greater than now; and, in addition, Upper Canada annually imported perhaps 1.8 million litres of wine and spirits.[36] Remarkably, these millions of litres of alcohol were destined for local consumption by a population of only 952,004 people, including women and children. Even assuming that the native population, which represented 8 per cent of the total, consumed an amount of alcohol disproportionate to its number, these figures attest to an all-pervasive drink problem in the white communities of the colony. Indeed, it was in recognition of that fact that the temperance movement was first called into being — not because alcohol represented a barrier to Indian proselytism, but because in the eyes of many it threatened to undermine the foundations of white society. Nevertheless, despite that revelation it was the Indian — and only the Indian — who was singled out for a legislatively imposed solution.

That settlers and missionaries alike supported a "radical cure" for Indian drinking was underscored in the enactment of a liquor ban in 1835. Rationalized as a response to petitions from the Indians, particularly those at the Grand, Credit, and Muncey Rivers, the act (5 Will. IV, c. 9) was designed ostensibly for the better regulation of Indians, as well as "to promote [their] peace, comfort, prosperity and happiness."[37] Although a ban on beer and wine was rejected by the legislators as being too radical — even for Indians — the act strictly prohibited the sale, barter, exchange, or gift of any distilled spirituous liquors to any Indian man, woman, or child.[38] On violation of the law, attested to by one or more credible witnesses, justices of the peace were authorized to impose fines not in excess of £5, plus costs, for each and every offence. As in the case of other "petty trespasses," part of the fine was to be paid to the informer, while the remainder was to be applied to the improvement of roads in the area where the violation had been committed. And as a lingering monument to the medicinal properties thought to be true of alcohol, medical men who prescribed alcohol as a remedy for illness were specifically exempted from the terms of the act.[39]

In 1840, the provisions of the act were amended and made permanent, the only change of importance being an increase in the maximum fine to £20 for each offence.[40] In substance, the legislation represented an act of paternalism which sought to make the white community accountable for Indian abstinence by making the delivery of spirits a misdemeanour punishable by law. By contrast, the Indian — apparently seen as a child-like ward of the state — was not required to assume any responsibility for his actions. His consumption of fermented and distilled intoxicants, even to the point of inebriation, in no way constituted a breach of law. In fact, the only aspect of the legislation that related to the behaviour of the Indian was an unwritten assumption, the understanding that by implication Indian drinking carried with it a certain stigma.

As a representative feature of the Indian temperance programme, the legislation did little to solve the problem of alcoholism. In 1841, the secretary of the Brantford Temperance Society noted with grave disapproval that, despite the law, the Indians living on the edge of town were still found intoxicated in great numbers.[41] This was an observation echoed throughout much of the province, and two years later, the *Canada Temperance Advocate* concluded that, for all practical purposes, the act was a dead letter "daily violated with impunity."[42]

One explanation of the failure is that the use of liquor was a time-honoured component of Indian-white relations, and as such, not readily abandoned at the urging of distant legislators. John Langton recalled the time when, during a steamboat trip to Mud Lake, some three dozen Indians were invited on board and, as was expected, provided with wine glasses according to their rank. It turned out, however, that there was not enough wine to go around, necessitating the concoction of an admixture that included a bottle and a half of brandy.[43] Another problem, as Sir Richard Bonnycastle succinctly noted, was that those who lived among the Indians were not always "the best sample of [their] race,"[44] often exhibiting a propensity for alcohol that did little to reinforce the intent of the legislation. From the earliest days, Egerton Ryerson and others had complained of the embarrassment occasioned by the immoral and drunken behaviour of those sent out by the Indian Department. Among the most notorious was a Coldwater Indian agent, charged with incompetence and intemperance by the local school teacher, Samuel Rose.[45] Equally disturbing to temperance advocates were those who bartered whisky in order to strip the Indians of their possessions, especially after the distribution of annual presents. This was true of the plethora of tavern keepers who found it both convenient and profitable to exchange alcohol for Indian game and blankets. It was even more true of the many Indian traders, from both the United States and Canada, who, according to one source, fell upon the Indians "like a hungry set of sharks."[46] Enforcement was also a problem. Although convictions under the liquor ban were not unknown, normally the liquor trade was carried on without any interference from the law whatsoever. Indicative of the weaknesses of liquor regulation in general, there was only one unassisted licensing inspector, responsible for the regulation of taverns throughout the entire Home District, populated by some sixty thousand.[47] Then too, there was a general reluctance to report violations to the authorities, while those who were brought before the court almost invariably received only a trifling fine. In October 1842, for example, one William Augustus was found guilty of selling liquor to Indians, but he was fined only £3 and then the amercement was never collected because he left the country.[48]

Apart from these problems, the real fallacy of the legislation — and one which explains the failure of the Indian temperance programme in general — was that it was based on a system of values that imperfectly related to the Indian culture. The ultimate goal of Indian missions, the civilizing and Christianizing of the "savage," was laced by definition with an ethnocentrism that did not go unnoticed, least of all by the Indian people themselves. There are a number of passages in the journals of Peter Jones which suggest that the Indian discerned a double standard in the white man's Christian and temperance message. Especially revealing is an 1828 entry which related the story of "Kanootong," head chief of a tribe of Chippewas settled north of the Thames River:

> Now I suppose if the Great Spirit had intended the Indian to worship like the white man he would have made him white instead of red, etc. Our forefathers have told us that when an Indian dies, his spirit goes to a place [prepared] for him toward the setting-sun, where Indians dwell for ever in dancing and feasting; and should I become a Christian and throw away the religion of my fathers, I am not sure that the Great Spirit would receive me into heaven. And how should I look after worshipping like the white man? Perhaps when I come to die my soul might go up to heaven, and the Great Spirit would ask me, "what have you come up here for, you Indian? This is not your place; you must go where your forefathers have gone; this place is only made for white people, not for Indians, therefore begone." How foolish then should I look to be driven from Heaven; therefore I think I can not become a Christian, and throw away my old ways; and more than this, I do not see that the white men who are Christians are any better than the red men, for they "make firewater," get drunk, quarrel, fight, murder, steal, lie, and cheat.[49]

To the same extent that the spiritual message ran against the grain of Indian tradition, the appeal to materialism that crept into the temperance programme fell on deaf ears. In the white communities of Upper Canada, the temperance movement grew up as a companion of industry and commerce, and it was supported by the middle, lower middle, and established artisan classes often as a means of disciplining a regular labour force.[50] As champions of that cause, the Methodists preached the harmony of interest between capital and labour in accumulating "real capital" for the benefit of the general community. To that end, thrift, punctuality, industry, and other Methodist ascetic values became an essential component of the temperance message.[51] This not only provided many of the ethical foundations for capitalist enterprise but also defined the means to middle-class status in a competitive and achievement-oriented society. For the ambitious and aspiring Canadian, abstinence and sobriety became the touchstone of respectability, while membership in a temperance society represented the road to social mobility. Likewise in the native communities the same *raison d'etre* was carried over as a rationale for Indian abstinence. It was no accident that in Peter Jones's account of the conversion of the Indians at the Credit River and elsewhere, he claimed that sobriety led the Indians to "prosper in many things";[52] nor was it out of character that the Indian liquor legislation, in addition to promoting the peace and comfort of the Indian, was rationalized as an attempt to increase his "prosperity."[53] What was being peddled was a concept of materialism — a concept that was a creature of the evolving capitalist organization of white society and one that had no meaning whatsoever for the pre-industrial culture of the Indian. Respectability, middle-class status, social mobility — these were goals that were extraneous to Indian society, and for that reason, they had little impact as a rationale for temperance. Indeed, the feature of Indian society that most often invited comments of bewilderment and contempt by contemporary Whites was the apparent imperviousness of the Indian culture to social improvement, the inability and unwillingness of the Indian to share the white man's nineteenth-century reverence for human perfectibility.[54]

And so, the temperance programme aimed at the Indians of Upper Canada proved ineffectual. It was, perhaps, as a final commentary on that fact that Major Strickland related the story of one Mississauga Indian, "Old George" Kishcow or "Captain George" as he was generally known at the Credit River. As one of the most notorious drunkards, George seemingly was prevailed upon by an itinerant minister to attend a meeting in a school house in Whitby township, the intent being "to convert him from the error of his ways."[55] During the meeting, "in the midst of a powerful appeal to his uncivilized audience," the minister suddenly laid his hand on George and exhorted, "Brother, have you [got] religion?" "Oh yes," George was quick to reply, "me got him here" — and to prove the point, he produced a flask of whiskey.[56]

NOTES

1. Ernest H. Cherrington, *The Evolution of Prohibition in the United States* (Ohio, 1920), p. 10.
2. Because the first provincial census was not taken until 1850, it is impossible to ascertain the exact number of Indians. James Buckingham estimated that in 1839 the Indian population was not more than 8,000 and this was supported by Major Strickland, who placed it at 7,490. By 1845, according to a report on Indian affairs submitted to the legislature in March of that year, the total had increased to 8,862 (James S. Buckingham, *Canada, Nova Scotia, New Brunswick, and other British Provinces of North America* [London, 1839], p. 47; Major Samuel Strickland, *Twenty-Seven Years in Canada West: or the Experience of an Early Settler* [London, 1853], 2:80–81. For the report on Indian affairs, see the *Toronto Star*, 13 September 1845).
3. John Howison, *Sketches of Upper Canada, Domestic, Local and Characteristic* (Edinburgh, 1965), pp. 150–51.
4. Alfred Domett, *The Canadian Journal of Alfred Domett. Being an Extract from a Journal of a Tour in Canada, the United States and Jamaica 1833–1835*, ed. E. A. Horsman and L. R. Benson (London, Ontario, 1955), p. 34.
5. John Carroll, *Past and Present, or a Description of Persons and Events Connected with Canadian Methodism for the Last Forty Years by a Spectator of the Scenes* (Toronto, 1860), p. 57.
6. In 1850, the population of the colony stood at 952,004. There were some 3,300 service industries, employing an average of 3.32 workers in each shop. The province also boasted over 1,000 schools and a student population of 152,000, representing 59 per cent of all the children between the ages of five and sixteen. For a more comprehensive discussion of the modernization process prior to 1850, consult F. L. Barron, "The Genesis of Temperance in Ontario, 1825–1850" (Ph.D. Diss., University of Guelph, 1976), pp. 80–92.
7. Colonel Givens, cited in *Life and Journals of Kal-Ke-Wa-Quo-Na-By: The Reverend Peter Jones* (Toronto, 1860), p. 165.
8. *Christian Guardian*, 31 May 1848.
9. Catherine Parr Traill, *The Backwoods of Canada: Being Letters from a Wife of an Emigrant Officer, Illustrative of the Domestic Economy of British America* (Toronto, 1929), p. 292.
10. Strickland, 2:66.
11. Howison, p. 147.
12. Sir Richard Bonnycastle, *The Canadas in 1841* (New York, 1968), 2:22.
13. During much of the French regime, the Indian figured prominently as a subject of Christian conversion as well as a source of labour and a potential consumer of French manufactured goods. For these reasons, early missionary and imperial policy aimed at the "Frenchification" of the Indian, a scheme based upon the naive assumption that the Amerindian could be assimilated into the French fold through a concerted contact with the European and his "superior" culture. As the Jesuits and French officials came to realize, however, Indian exposure to the European rarely resulted in a positive acculturation to white society and, more often than not, led the Indian to adopt only the worst features of that society, especially the white man's fondness for alcohol. For detailed discussion of French attempts to assimilate the Indian, see Cornelius J. Jaenen, "Problems of Assimilation in New France, 1603–1645," *Canadian History before Confederation*, ed. J. M. Bumsted (Georgetown, 1972), pp. 58–77. Also consult G. F. G. Stanley, "The Policy of 'Francisation' as Applied to the Indians during the Ancien Régime," *Revue d'Histoire de l'Amerique Française* 3 (1949–50):333–48.
14. The importance of American influence is discussed in F. L. Barron, "The American Origins of Temperance in Ontario, 1828–1850," *Canadian Review of American Studies* 11 (Fall 1980):131-50.
15. William H. Elgee, *The Social Teachings of the Canadian Churches. Protestant. The Early Period, before 1850* (Toronto, 1964), p. 32.
16. Ibid., p. 170.
17. S. D. Clark, *Church and Sect in Canada*, (Toronto, 1965), pp. 108, 110, 125–27.
18. Elgee, p. 170.
19. C. B. Sissons, *Egerton Ryerson: His Life and Letters* (Toronto, 1973), 2:61.
20. Ibid., pp. 62–63.
21. Strickland, 2:35. Known in the Mississauga tongue as "Sacred Waving Feathers," Peter Jones was

the son of an Ojibwa Indian mother and Welsh father who became the deputy provincial surveyor. Born in Burlington in 1802, he was brought up as an Indian by his mother until, at age fourteen, he was taken to live on his father's farm along the banks of the Grand River, where he learned the English language as well as the ways of the white man. Six years later, at his father's insistence, he was baptized in the Church of England, but apparently he never internalized any religious conviction until he became a convert to Methodism during a camp meeting in Ancaster in 1823. As a Methodist missionary, principally identified with the Credit River, his efforts centred on an attempt to eradicate the Indian characteristics of the mission and to introduce white codes of behaviour — to make the Indians "brown Englishmen," according to his Indian critics. On behalf of the Methodist Episcopal Church, he also conducted very successful fund raising tours of England where he was feted and honoured as a colonial Indian, including being granted an audience with Queen Victoria in 1838. Subsequent to his first visit to England, he caused a sensation both in London society and in Upper Canada when he married Eliza Field, the daughter of a well-to-do London businessman. He died in 1856. See Donald B. Smith's three-part series on Peter and Eliza Jones in *The Beaver* (Summer, Autumn and Winter 1977).

22. Bonnycastle, 2:22–23.
23. *Life and Journals of Kal-Ke-Wa-Quo-By*, p. 120. It might be noted that the same rationale was used in the temperance movement in the white communities of the province. As one Methodist argued, "little prosperity can be hoped for the cause of religion wherever strong drink is predominant. But where the light of temperance has shone, the blessings of religion have often been consequent" (Letter from Eli Walker to the Wesleyan Conference, reprinted in the *Canada Temperance Advocate*, 1 December 1846).
24. *Life and Journals of Kal-Ke-Wa-Quo-By*, p. 123.
25. See the Report of the Canada Conference Missionary Society for Conversion and Improvement of the Indians, *Kingston Gazette and Religious Advocate*, 30 April 1830.
26. Report of the Brantford Temperance Society, *Christian Guardian*, 7 May 1834.
27. Letter from J. M. Ross of the Ontario Division of the Sons of Temperance, *Toronto Examiner*, 7 August 1850.
28. Ibid.
29. Elgee, p. 174.
30. See the 1839 reference to a Baptist church "for coloured persons only" in Buckingham, p. 17.
31. This comment was made by John Dougall, a temperance lecturer, who travelled through much of Upper Canada on behalf of the Montreal temperance society. His account is taken from the *Canada Temperance Advocate*, February, 1840.
32. *The Barrie Magnet and District of Simcoe General Advertiser*, 25 April 1850.
33. *Christian Guardian*, 20 June 1832.
34. In 1830, the Canada Conference Missionary Society for the Conversion and Improvement of the Indians recommended a stringent enforcement of total abstinence for the Indian, even from lesser alcoholic drinks. This was made on the grounds that the consumption of beer or cider predisposed the Indian to imbibe stronger intoxicants and, at the same time, exposed him to the danger of adulteration by "those who have an interest in his drunkenness," a reference to the white whiskey traders. "For the Indians at least," concluded the society, "it is their safety and happiness to abstain wholly from the use of all fermented liquors." The Report of the Missionary Society was carried in the *Kingston Gazette and Religious Advocate*, 30 April 1830.
35. The first teetotal society in Upper Canada was organized in St. Catharines in June 1835. It was only in August 1850, when the Hincks Act (13–14 Vict., c. 65) and the Cameron Act (13 and 14 Vict., c. 27) received royal assent, that temperance legislation in Upper Canada became a reality. For a discussion of the transition to teetotalism and state intervention, as well as the terms of the Hincks-Cameron legislation, consult Barron, "Genesis of Temperance," pp. 198–240.
36. In 1851, the 25 breweries submitting census returns produced 439,315 gallons of beer (almost two million litres), or an average of 17,573 gallons (79,387 litres), bringing the total production for all 49 breweries to 861,077 gallons (3,914,456 litres) (see the *Census* . . *1851–52*, 2:265). John Moir cites distillery production in 1851 at 1.17 million gallons (5.3 million litres), while James Talman places it at about 2,159,268 gallons (9,816,537 litres) (see John Moir, "The Upper Canadian Religious Tradition," *Profiles of a Province* (Toronto, 1967), p. 193; and James Talman, quoted in Margaret K. Zieman, "When Whiskey Went Round with the Waltz," *Globe Magazine*

12 April 1969, p. 9). Both these estimates, however, are low. According to the *Census . . . 1851–52*, 2:263, the 68 distilleries that submitted census returns collectively produced 1,986,768 gallons (9,021,757 litres) of whiskey, or an average of 29,217 gallons (132,820 litres) for each establishment. Assuming that this average was also true of the 32 distilleries that did not send in returns, the annual production for all 100 distilleries in the province would have been 2,921,700 gallons (13,282,048 litres). This total, expressed as an adult (sixteen and over) per capita consumption, is 4.4 gallons (20 litres), which compares favourably with Bonnycastle's opinion that the adult consumption stood at 5 gallons (22.73 litres) per capita. (Sir Richard Bonnycastle, *Canada and the Canadians in 1846* (London, 1849), 2:264). The estimate of imported wine is taken from James Talman, cited in Zieman, p. 9.

37. The text of the 1835 Act was cited in the *Christian Guardian*, 2 March 1842.
38. Ibid.
39. Ibid.
40. *The Provincial Statutes of Canada 1849* (Kingston, 1849), pp. 1012–13.
41. John Tupper, quoted in the *Canada Temperance Advocate*, May 1841.
42. *Canada Temperance Advocate*, 16 May 1843.
43. *Early Days in Canada: Letters of John Langton from the Backwoods of Upper Canada and the Audit Office of the Province of Canada*, ed. W. A. Langton (Toronto, 1926), p. 28.
44. Bonnycastle, *Canada and the Canadians in 1846*, 2:62.
45. Sissons, 1:149, and 149n.
46. Strickland, 2:69.
47. "Report on the Public Departments of the Province by a Commission Appointed by His Excellency the Lieutenant Governor in Conformity with an Address of the House of Assembly of Upper Canada, in 1839," *Journal of the Legislative Council of the Province of Upper Canada, Appendix 1839–40* (Toronto, 1840), p. 46.
48. *Chatham Journal*, 5 November 1842.
49. *Life and Journals of Kal-Ke-Wa-Quo-Na-By*, p. 124.
50. Barron, "Genesis of Temperance," p. 260. See also James M. Clemens, "Taste Not; Touch Not; Handle Not; A Study of the Social Assumptions of the Temperance Literature and Temperance Supporters in Canada West Between 1839 and 1859," *O.H.* (September 1972): 145.
51. Barron, "Genesis of Temperance," pp. 260–61.
52. See above, p. 194.
53. See above, p. 196.
54. In 1830, the Anglican Bishop of Quebec visited Upper Canada in order to attend the inaugural meeting of a new missionary society in York. During his address, he found it necessary to reassure the audience that there was no truth in the longstanding notion that the Indian was incapable of temperance reform and that there was something in the Indian mind "that must render every effort for improving his condition utterly hopeless." The contemporary pessimism about Indian reform was also implicit in Lord Sydenham's criticism that the Christianized (and presumably reformed) Indians were ten times worse in character than their heathen brothers. Bishop Stewart's address may be found in the *Christian Guardian*, 6 November 1830. Lord Sydenham's comment is taken from Elgee, p. 170.
55. Strickland, 2:71.
56. Ibid. According to Donald Smith, of the University of Calgary, the central figure in Strickland's account was really George Keshegoo, born of a family from the Lake Scugog area. He eventually settled at the Credit Mission and converted to Christianity in 1827.

2

The Tragedy of the Loss of the Commons in Western Canada

Irene M. Spry

This is an account of the transition in western Canada from common property resources, to open access resources, and finally to private property. In essentials, it is a story of the tragedy of the disappearance of the commons on the Prairies after 1870.

When in 1870 Rupert's Land and the Indian territories were transferred to Canada, nearly all the inhabitants (apart from the people of Red River Settlement) were wandering bands of Indians and groups of Metis hunters. The few settled communities consisted of fur trade personnel at the scattered Hudson's Bay Company posts; a handful of mission-based settlements, notably White Horse Plain (St. François Xavier) and other communities on the Assiniboine River as far west as Portage la Prairie; Lac Ste. Anne and St. Albert, near Edmonton; Isle-à-la-Crosse; Lac la Biche; White Fish Lake; Victoria (later Pakan); and, lower down the North Saskatchewan, Prince Albert. As well there were two or three semi-permanent clusters of cabins at Tail Creek on the Red Deer River; in the Qu'Appelle Valley; and in the Cypress Hills; and, perhaps, at the forks of the Red Deer River and the South Saskatchewan. Even the inhabitants of such settlements spent much of their lives travelling in pursuit of buffalo or as tripmen and freighters.

Revised and Reprinted from C.P.R.C. publication no. 6, *Man and Nature on the Prairies*, ed. Richard Allen.

Most of the population depended for its basic subsistence on the natural products of the country over which they roamed and hunted. Those products were open to use by the Indian bands that claimed the territory as their hunting grounds and by anyone else who could gain access to that territory.

Tribal boundaries were by no means rigid.[1] They shifted as the strength of one tribe or another waxed or waned with greater or less effective access to European technology, and as pressures of population altered — for example, when epidemics took devastating toll. However, there seem to have been, at any one time, well-recognized boundaries, separated in some cases by "neutral zones" into which few but war parties ventured to go and which became effective wildlife reserves.[2]

Within their own hunting grounds each tribe lived off the land, using space, shelter, water, game, fish, timber, and wild plants in accordance with customary patterns, well understood and respected by the members of the tribe. Decisions by band councils and enforcement by tribal authority, such as the "soldiers" of the Blackfoot Confederacy and other tribes, regulated individual activity and provided the necessary organization for communal hunting efforts, especially the use of buffalo pounds and concerted running of buffalo herds in the plains hunt.[3] The rules of the hunt were strictly observed. They included restrictions on hunting in the calving season and the take of "parchment" hides, as well as rules that prevented an individual getting an advantage in the hunt at the expense of others.[4] Within a tribe's hunting grounds, game was the common property of all, and everyone had a chance to share in this gift of nature. This common use of natural riches was reinforced by the tradition that the stronger and more skillful or more fortunate shared their plenty with those in need.

To some extent recognized tribal boundaries protected and preserved resources within them for the use of each tribe, but the exclusion of outsiders, though it seems to have provided a basis for the pattern of economic organization, was by no means absolute. Friendly tribes on occasion hunted in each others' territories, and friendly travellers and traders were allowed to move about the country using space, wood, water, forage, game, and fish as need arose. Enemies could not always be kept out of the territory claimed by a tribe.[5] The great Metis buffalo hunt, notably, organized with military precision, penetrated, season after season, into hostile Sioux territory in search of migrant herds. Besides the powerful Metis, less formidable groups, such as the Kootenay, who had been pushed across the Rocky Mountains by their foes, and the Mountain Stoneys made annual forays out on to the buffalo plains to hunt in Blackfoot territory, despite the ever-present danger of attack by their enemies should they be discovered. The plains tribes, too, made long journeys often beyond the limits of the tribal territories.

Islands among these tribal hunting ranges had been established; the Hudson's Bay Company had established tentative and fragmentary claims to property in land within the pickets about its posts, to fenced and planted fields around them, and to pastures in the company's "horse-guards." The fields were often trampled, horses on occasion stolen from the horse-guards, and a post left empty, torn down by a people who had no notion of exclusive and permanent property rights in land or the other gifts of the Great Spirit.

These free gifts all had a right to use on their tribal lands, while outsiders who could gain access to those lands by friendship or by force might also use the riches that they offered. Indian, Metis, missionary, and traveller could and did pitch their camps or build their cabins wherever they saw fit outside the range of raids by hostile groups. They took water from any lake or stream they came upon for themselves and their horses. They cut wood for fuel, for lodge poles, for cabin logs, or for Red River carts from the bluffs out on the plains, from the trees along the waterways, from the "edge of the woods," where plain and forest met, and from the Cypress Hills. Berries and edible roots were free for the picking and digging. Fish swarmed in the lakes and rivers where anyone might catch them. Fur-bearing animals, especially beaver, muskrat, and rabbit, and, in season, wildfowl and their eggs were plentiful. Most important of all, vast herds of buffalo and other game were available, within the disciplines of Indian customs, communal authority, and, in the case of both Indians and Metis, the regulations that governed the buffalo hunt, to any hunter capable of making a kill.

The prosperity of the native peoples depended, therefore, basically on the size and richness of the area to which they had access. This, in turn, depended on their prowess in war. Prosperity depended also on the people's knowledge of the country and on their skill, endurance, and pertinacity as travellers, hunters, fishermen, and foragers. Such knowledge was the first essential — knowledge of the whereabouts of water sources and of sheltered camping places, with access to a supply of wood and forage; knowledge of localities where roots, berries, or wild rice might be looked for; knowledge of the habits and haunts of the buffalo, moose, and other game; or of fish and wildfowl. Skill was needed as well — the skill to track down, come up with, and capture or kill the wild beasts, fish, or birds on which life depended. Energy, courage, and endurance were essential, too, for success in the hunt. The bounty of nature could not be purchased. It could only be won by those with high human qualities and by concentrated human effort. Outsiders coming into the country were soon aware of this. Even such "mighty hunters" as John Palliser and Lord Dunmore and other eager young sportsmen who travelled to the Prairies in search of adventure and heavy game, had need of native guides and hunters to provide their parties with the intimate local knowledge and skills that were essential to success in the hunt and without which it was impossible to survive for long out on the plains.[6]

The utmost knowledge, skill, and persistence did not always yield a good living. In some years, in some localities, and in certain seasons nature proved "niggardly." The movements of the great buffalo herds were of an "utterly irregular character."[7] At times they did not appear in their accustomed range. At times, other game or fish might fail. Then even the most cunning and untiring of hunters or fishermen might not make a catch. Seasonal shortages, moreover, especially in a severe winter, were a recurrent danger. Chief Dan Kennedy wrote: "Under ordinary circumstances the chase was sufficient to give the tribesmen [an] abundant living, but in winter the elements were unpredictable."[8]

In general, apart from such periods of spasmodic shortage, the buffalo Indians and the Indians and Metis of the parklands that fringed the open plains along the edge of the northern forests and western mountains had at their disposal a range of nature-given produce that provided sufficient material means for a good life. Peter Erasmus, for example, commented in his reminiscences on the easy living of "the Prairie buffalo hunting days."[9] Alexander Sandison, in similar vein, remembered that people in the buffalo hunting days were "contented and happy; they had no licenses of any kind to pay either for hunting game or fishing or making beer."[10] Due allowance must be made for the nostalgia of old men looking back at the golden days of their youth, but the impression of abundance is confirmed by other men (John McDougall[11] and Sir Cecil Denny,[12] for example) whose lives spanned the transition from the buffalo hunting days of common property resources to the days of private property. On the other hand, the contrast between earlier plenty and a growing scarcity was noted by mid-nineteenth century visitors such as Milton and Cheadle, who wrote of the passing of "the days when it was possible to live in plenty by the gun and net alone,"[13] while David G. Mandelbaum's careful study of the Plains Cree indicates that the buffalo "was a reliable source of food and the Cree flourished."[14] The great herds provided food, shelter, clothing, coverings, containers, thread, rope, implements, toys — all that the Indians and Metis needed except lodge poles (which served also as travois poles) and materials for constructing carts and cabins; motive power, for which the people had to rely on their own muscles and those of their dogs and later horses, as well as tobacco and pipe stems, tea, and, of course, liquor. The herds even provided fuel in the form of "buffalo chips" that out on the plains supplemented the scarce supply of firewood, though it was not enough to meet the requirements of a northern winter when sheltered camping places accessible to stands of trees had to be found.

The buffalo herds and other natural produce of the plains and parklands provided the basis, if not for an easy life, at least for a good life, so long as the pressure on those products remained in balance with the supplies available. J. G. Nelson's book, *The Last Refuge*, concludes: "No evidence has been found in this study which would indicate that the Indians were hunting any animal so heavily as to cause severe depletion and possible extinction prior to the arrival of the white man."[15] Whether any pressures of population did in fact develop, and, if not, how and why they were kept in check does not emerge with unquestionable clarity from such scattered and partial evidence as is available. Perhaps periodical seasons of scarcity corrected any incipient imbalance; perhaps the rigours of a roaming life were sufficient to curb any tendency to expansion of population beyond the limits of the available means of subsistence.

The wandering life led by the plains and woodland Indians certainly allowed little scope for the accumulation of material possessions, except such as were themselves mobile, notably horses and dogs. The constraints of a roving life, therefore, set a limit to any urge to an increasingly intensive exploitation of the natural products available to the wandering Indians.

Whether or not these constraints were reinforced by a conservationist attitude among those Indians is a controversial question. We have no means of knowing clearly what was the practice of the native peoples before the coming of the white man. Such fragments of evidence as exist from Indian sources are largely in the form of reminiscences and material collected by anthropologists and historians from old people. Such memories may well be coloured by time and by revulsion against such evidently wanton exploitation by white men as the slaughter of the buffalo. They must be considered in relation to references in the records left by fur traders and other early travellers to heedless and improvident slaughter by Indians and Metis far in excess of any possible requirements for use. However, there are, as well, contrary comments such as those of Pierre Esprit Radisson that the "wild men kill not except for necessary use,"[16] and later statements such as that of R. B. Marcy that "the Indian, who supplied himself with food and clothing from the immense herds around his door would have looked on it as sacrilege to destroy more than barely sufficient to supply the wants of his family."[17] It is true that all the animals trapped in a buffalo pound were killed, but this was because the Indians believed that such as might escape would warn their fellows in future against getting caught in a similar trap.[18] The careful and systematic regulation of the buffalo hunt among plains Indians and, later, Metis was at least in part conservationist in effect and probably in intention, which is surprising when there seemed as yet to be no danger of scarcity. There would appear to be small reason for conserving a resource that appears to be abundant beyond any conceivable need. "What level of killing is excessive if bison are incredibly numerous and believed to be supernatural in origin and inexhaustible?"[19]

F. G. Roe, in his great work entitled *The North American Buffalo*, after reviewing a wide range of assertion and counter-assertion, rejects the idea that Indians were "wasteful" in killing buffalo. Many of the observers whom he cites agree with Mandelbaum's statement about the Plains Cree that "they used every part" of their mainstay, the buffalo.[20]

The animals that were killed were killed for use so that the inroads made on the great herds by the Indians' hunt were limited by the peoples' needs. Even after the white man's arrival game was at first still killed only for use within the country. Fur-bearing animals, and especially beaver, were killed for the export trade. Buffalo and other game began also to be killed for exchange for the white man's goods at the fur trade posts, but this was basically to supply the needs of the post personnel and of the voyageurs who manned the brigades of canoes, York boats, and Red River carts that carried pelts out of the country and brought the trade goods into it.

Even so, as population increased, pressures on the natural produce of the country began to build up. The mixed-blood offspring of Indian women and white fur traders and voyageurs were multiplying, and outsiders began to filter into the western plains. The population of Red River Settlement was rising according to the Red River Census from a total of 2,427 in 1831 to 4,459 in 1846,[21] and, according to the "Statistical Account of the Red River Colony" contained in one of the papers delivered by Sir George Simpson to the Select Committee of the House of Commons on the Hudson's Bay Company in 1857, from 5,291 in 1849 to 6,623 in 1856.[22] By 1870 the Census of Manitoba (which, of course, included other settlements that were spreading westward up the Assiniboine, and to the north and east from those in the Red River Valley) gave a total population of 12,228 and an estimated aboriginal population of 500.[23] Besides the natural increase in population, there had been since 1841 an inflow of outsiders — missionaries, big-game hunters, gold-seekers, explorers, surveyors, traders, and settlers.[24] From 1870 onward this inflow was reinforced by increasing numbers of public servants, notably the North West Mounted Police in 1874, and by a swelling tide of settlers and enterprising men intent on seizing business opportunities and the opportunities for making money offered by the wide plains and parklands of this new land rich with as yet unappropriated resources. As the population increased, so did the drain on the natural products of the country. More food — and so more game and fish; more wood — for fuel and for increased construction; more hay; more water; and more space was needed.

By degrees, too, buffalo robes and buffalo tongues were beginning to acquire value in export markets. Chief Factor Robert Campbell, for example, reported that the Fort Pelly returns for 1864 included over 4,000 robes,[25] as well as the pemmican required for local use. The number of carts going out from Red River for the buffalo hunt, according to Alexander Ross, had increased from 540 in 1820 to 1,210 in 1840,[26] and perhaps these numbers may have increased further in later years.[27] This increased pressure of the biennial Red River hunt was intensified by parallel hunts made out on the plains not only from Hudson's Bay Company posts inland, but also from the new settlements that were springing up at Lac Ste. Anne, St. Albert (Big Lake), Victoria, White Fish Lake, and elsewhere.[28] Further, in the late 1860's and early 1870's whisky traders from Fort Benton and elsewhere in U.S. territory traded buffalo robes and hides in increasing quantities for shipment down the Missouri River.[29] All this meant a higher rate of depletion of the buffalo herds.

Despite their extraordinary numbers, their powers of regeneration could not keep pace with the increased intensity of hunting that came about as a result of a final, fatal combination of a new demand for buffalo hides, an increasingly efficient means of slaughter, and easier access to the plains. The new demand arose from the discovery in 1871 of a method of tanning buffalo hides that would make them strong enough for use as belting for power transmission in the new factories that were multiplying in the eastern United States.[30] This innovation coincided with improvements in the technique of shooting buffalo when long range, breach-loading, repeater rifles were introduced into the West.[31] A new means of transporting the hide hunters to the buffalo range and of carrying out thousands upon thousands of hides to markets in the East was provided with the construction of transcontinental railroads across the plains, starting with the Union Pacific in 1867 and culminating with the Northern Pacific between 1870 and 1873.[32] The massive destruction in American territory of the buffalo in which these three innovations played a part swept away the great southern herd by 1875; by 1883 the northern herd had gone as a means of subsistence for the Indians and as a commercial resource.[33] In Canada the herds had disappeared by 1879, though a few stragglers were recorded from time to time during the next decade,[34] and a handful of the wild cattle had been tamed and preserved by private owners such as the Honourable James McKay of Deer Lodge, who built up a herd that on his death in 1879 was acquired by Colonel Samuel Bedson of the Stony Mountain Penitentiary.[35]

The destruction of the buffalo appears to have been an object of deliberate policy in the United States. Despite a series of attempts at conservation[36] nothing effective was done, and when, for instance, the Texas Legislature was considering a bill for the preservation of the buffalo, General Phil Sheridan dissuaded them from accepting the measure on the grounds that the hide hunters were doing more to settle the Indian question than the entire army had done in thirty years, by destroying the Indian's commissary. He urged the legislators to let them kill, skin, and sell until the buffalo was exterminated, as this was, he maintained, the only way to bring about a lasting peace.[37] Charles MacInnes asserted that in 1878 "the United States Government decided to starve Sitting Bull and his followers into surrender. A cordon of half-breeds, Indians, and American soldiers was therefore formed, and ordered to drive the buffalo back whenever the herds started to come north."[38] Certainly, a line of prairie fires flared along the border, heading the buffalo southward, while the despairing efforts of the Canadian Indians and of Sitting Bull's refugee Sioux to find the remnants of the great herds played a part in turning the buffalo away from their old range north of the forty-ninth parallel.[39]

Long before the great herds had finally vanished, some, at least, of the Indians had made resolute efforts to prevent overhunting by strangers on their lands and increasing overuse of other natural riches. Such efforts took the form both of attempting to keep out intruders and of imposing limits on their hunting. In American territory resistance to white intrusion led to long and bloody Indian warfare. Further north the Cree with whom Henday travelled to the Blackfoot country in 1754 had refused to take more than a limited number of beaver and game on the ground the Archithinues (Blackfoot) "would kill them if they trapped in their country."[40] The Rainy Lake Indians expected to be paid for right of way if S. J. Dawson built roads through their country.[41] The Metis buffalo hunt won access to the buffalo plains only by developing sufficient military strength to face down the hostility of the Sioux. Hind reported in 1858 "that the Plain Crees, in council assembled, had last year 'determined that in consequence of promises often made and broken by the white men and half-breeds, and the rapid destruction by them of the buffalo they fed on, they would not permit either white men or half-breeds to hunt in their country or travel through it, except for the purpose of trading for their dried meat, pemican [sic], skins and robes.' They wished to establish a sort of toll of tobacco and tea for permission to pass through their country threatening that if it were not given they would . . . stop us by force."[42] Travellers in general were well aware of the need to carry presents for the Indians through whose country they passed, but Hind's experience is one of only a few known instances of attempts to levy specific payments for the use of right of way and other natural resources. Dr. John Rae, for example, recorded in 1861 that the "Young Dogs" (Piapot's part-Cree, part-Assiniboine band)" act in a very oppressive manner towards the few half-breeds who have made a home for themselves in this part of the prairies [south of the Qu'Appelle Lakes]. They do not allow them to kill the buffalo for food, without levying a heavy fine for every buffalo they kill."[43] The following year Lord Dunmore's party of big game hunters encountered between the Qu'Appelle Lakes and the Coteau some Assiniboines whose chief complained bitterly of white men who came from a rich country "to rob my meat stores." He allowed the half-breeds to take half of the game that lived in the country, but wanted more than the very small presents offered by the rich young pleasure seekers for the privilege of hunting his people's game.[44] These shrewd initiatives, which foreshadowed the contention of such modern economists as R. H. Coase and John Dales that the cure for over-rapid depletion of open-access resources is to charge for their use a price that will induce the users to economize them,[45] did not find favour with the authorities once government had been established after 1870. In 1877, in the course of negotiations for the Blackfoot Treaty, one of the Blood chiefs, Button Chief, said: "We want to be paid for all the timber that the police and whites have used since they first came to our country. If it continues to be used as it is, there will soon be no firewood left for the Indians." Lieutenant-Governor Laird replied that this request seemed to him "so unreasonable" that, if there was to be any payment, it ought not to be for the little wood that the Indians' benefactors had used, but "from the Indians to the Queen for sending them the police."[46] The laughter with which the chiefs received this sally obscured the essential problem: that the drain imposed on its natural products by outsiders moving into the country was upsetting the traditional balance between what was available and its use. As Chief Sweet Grass of the Plains Cree had said in 1871, "our country is no longer able to support us."[47]

In the years before the negotiations for the Treaties of 1871 to 1877 the Indians from Rainy Lake westward had been becoming increasingly uneasy and anxious about strangers coming into their country.[48] Parties of surveyors and telegraph men were turned back;[49] settlers were prevented from cutting wood and, if given permission to occupy land, were in some cases given only temporary permission for a defined period of time.[50] As the 1870's wore on, Indian bands that had not yet made a treaty made representations to the governor about their concern that strangers were coming into their country without leave and without payment. The principal Indians of Portage la Prairie, for example, protested in 1871 that they had never received anything for the land that belonged to them "that settlers use to enrich themselves."[51]

The emphasis was on the use of the lands — indeed, it seems probable that the Indians thought of the problem as that of the right to *use* their lands when they entered into negotiations for a treaty. The outright *sale* of those lands was a concept entirely unfamiliar to them. How could interpreters find words for the Indians' meaning when they discussed white men's ideas of "property" and "sale" and those terms had to be translated? Poundmaker's protest at the Carlton Treaty negotiations in 1876 sums up the difference between their point of view and that of the white man: "This is our land. It isn't a piece of pemmican to be cut off and given in little pieces back to us. It is ours and we will take what we want."[52] Before the negotiations began Chief Sweet Grass had sent a message to Governor Archibald welcoming him but stating: "We heard our lands were sold and we did not like it; we don't want to sell our lands; it is our property, and no one has a right to sell them."[53]

In the course of the treaty negotiations, the commissioners were at pains to give the Indians assurances that certainly strengthened the expectation that they would continue to be able to use the resources of their lands. Morris records that he said in 1876: "Understand me, I do not want to interfere with your hunting and fishing. I want you to pursue it through the country, as you have heretofore done. . . . What I have offered does not take away your living, you will have it then as you have now." The commissioners would not interfere with the Indians' daily lives, except to assist them in farming. As for the reserve land, this was to be marked off "so you will know it is your own, and no one will interfere with you." The commissioners had not come "to barter or trade with you for the land," nor, they said, had they come "to take away anything that belongs to you."[54] A clause in the Blackfoot Treaty specifically stated that "Her Majesty the Queen hereby agrees with her said Indians, that they shall have right to pursue their vocations of hunting throughout the tract surrendered . . . subject to such regulations as may, from time to time, be made by the Government of the country" except for such tracts as might be required and taken up from time to time "for settlement, mining, trading or other purposes by her Government of Canada, or by any of Her Majesty's subjects duly authorized therefor."[55] It is not surprising that the Indians did not foresee the significance of those exceptions. At Fort Pitt they made it clear that they wanted to be at liberty to hunt on any place as usual. They wished to be free to take wood as well as game: "When timber becomes scarcer on the reserves we select for ourselves, we want to be free to take it anywhere on the common."[56]

One chief still thought in 1876 that "the land is wide, there is plenty of room,"[57] but increasing pressures on space and resources were being felt. The arrival of the NWMP to enforce law and maintain order had one effect that is seldom recognized: the Indians were no longer to be permitted to keep intruders out of their country by force.[58] It is true that the lure of "fire-water" had induced the Blackfoot to allow into the country whisky traders from Fort Benton to set up trading posts at Fort Whoop-Up and elsewhere, to their ruin. The police suppressed this whisky trade, but now other strangers might come freely into the tribal hunting grounds. The perspicacious Blood chief who had raised the question of wood in the treaty negotiations of 1877 also asked that the Crees and half-breeds should be sent back to their own country. Lieutenant-Governor Laird replied that "the Commissioners could not agree to exclude the Crees and Half-breeds from the Blackfoot country; that they were the Great Mother's children as much as the Blackfeet and the Bloods, and she did not wish to see any of them starve."[59] Their competition for the few remaining buffalo increased the rate of depletion. Hunting by Sitting Bull's Sioux refugees added to the drain. The Blackfoot and other Indians ranged further and further afield in their search for the dwindling herds, but by 1879 the great herds of buffalo had gone from the Canadian Prairies, and all the plains tribes faced starvation. The old balance between a limited human use of the gifts of nature held as common property by each tribe and the natural regeneration of those gifts was finally destroyed when they were thrown open to all comers, including those intent on commercial exploitation. The disappearance of the buffalo was a classic instance of the "tragedy of the commons,"[60] when a common-property resource was transferred into an open-access resource.

Not only the buffalo, but other game and other natural products were threatened too. Game in general was becoming scarce. Edgar Dewdney, then Indian commissioner, reported in 1880 that "the country [to the] south is entirely destitute of game (that is, of small game)."[61] Other observers predicted that game would disappear just as the buffalo had disappeared. In 1889, Superintendent Griesbach of the NWMP, for example, stated: "If something is not done and done quickly to prevent the wholesale destruction of game, a few years must see the end, and the halfbreeds and Indians of the north must lose a source of income and food which has hitherto been their greatest standby."[62]

A similar disaster threatened the Woods Indians, for whom fish was a very important staple food that had been a self-renewing resource provided by nature, on which they could depend so long as the lakes and rivers were not fished beyond the limits of the regenerative capacity of the fish population. The influx of strangers meant an increasing drain on fish stocks, especially of sturgeon and whitefish. Fishing in the spawning season was blamed for the depletion of the fisheries, but it seems to have been the pressures of new population and the emergence of an export fishery, carried on, for example, by a Detroit firm using 10.5 kilometres of seine in Lake Winnipeg, that caused specially acute alarm.[63] Because it was difficult to establish rights of private property in the fisheries, an attempt was made to meet the problem by instituting a system of licences, mesh regulations, and a closed season while the fish were spawning. Since many Indians and half-breeds depended for winter food on the fishery, strict enforcement of the regulations caused hardship to the local people. Dewdney petitioned for a relaxation of the new Fisheries Act in 1884 to allow limited fishing by half-breeds in the Qu'Appelle Lakes during the closed season as the harvest had failed. Permission was given to each family to use one gillnet each. The diary of F. C. Gilchrist, fisheries overseer for the Qu'Appelle River and the adjoining lakes from 1884 to 1891 and fisheries inspector for the Northwest Territories from 1891 to 1896, records a number of cases of exceptions being made to allow individuals to fish when they were in extreme want.[64] It was not so much local individuals fishing for their own use that was the cause of the trouble, but fishing for sale to make a profit, especially when more efficient — and so more destructive — gear was used.

New uses for the waters of the country also played a part in the process of exhaustion. It was reported that steamboats on rivers were destroying the sturgeon fishery.[65] There is also a case recorded of a water mill being set up at a traditional Indian fishing place on Red River, by leave of an Indian who had no real authority to grant such a right to the miller. This mill, like the steamboats, posed a threat to the sturgeon fishery.[66]

Besides game and fish, the wood supply was endangered. Settlers moving into the country required wood for fuel, for building, and for fencing.[67] More and more travellers used firewood, as did the police. Broad-axes were introduced by groups of 1859 and 1862, "Overlanders" from New Brunswick.[68] Sawmills followed in due course,[69] and commercial logging operations began to carry off timber which had been an essential and customary source of supply on which Indians and mixed bloods alike depended. Joseph Royal (later to be lieutenant-governor) wrote in great concern begging Lieutenant-Governor Archibald to stop the "pillage" of timber on crown lands on the upper Assiniboine and Sale Rivers. These were almost the only places where the local population could get wood for fuel and construction for the next few years. "Jusqu'ici, ces bois étaient une *commune* où chacun allait se couper ce qu'il lui fallait pour son propre usage." The "exaggerated cuts by speculators" had upset the Metis, whose lands would be of little use if all the wood had gone.[70]

Commercial logging operations elsewhere threatened Indian wood supplies. The Roseau River Reserve, south of Winnipeg, had not been surveyed when in March 1872 lumber men started woodcutting operations. The customs officer at

Pembina — the only government official within reach — intervened and, on the lieutenant-governor's authority, posted notices forbidding the felling of trees, but as soon as he had gone, the lumberers set to work again, laughing at the Indians' protests. The Indians themselves were not allowed to sell their wood, which they had started to do to supplement their diminishing means of livelihood. This prohibition was intended to conserve supplies of firewood and wood for essential construction for the Indians of the reserve. Yet although cutting and sale of wood by the Indians was prohibited — and dealers like Andrew McDermott in Winnipeg were forbidden to buy wood from them — the Indians had no means of preventing outsiders from pirating their wood.[71]

The Hudson's Bay Company, too, had drawn on stands of timber, for fuel and building purposes, and also for the construction of the great York boats for the annual transport brigades; now they introduced steamboats on the lakes and rivers of the West, and for these a great deal of wood was needed as fuel. The Indians were alarmed at this new drain on their wood supply. One recorded clash over the issue occurred when Broken Finger's band in 1872 refused to allow the company to cut wood at Big Sandy Point near Manitoba House for the steamers. He was sure that the point had been promised as part of the reserve, but this had not yet been surveyed. In this case the company won out; the reserve was held not to include the Point with its good harbour — a "most excellent wooding station."[72]

There were other protests over wood. Half-breeds claimed that Canadian settlers were knocking down fences they had built and carrying off logs they had cut and piled ready to build cabins.[73]

There were similar problems about the waters of the country. Some concerned conflicting uses of those waters — such as the cases mentioned earlier of navigation harming the fishery and the construction of a mill taking over a traditional Indian fishing site. A more general problem was that of drinking places in a thirsty land. Under common law, water could not itself be claimed as anyone's property. Before the needs of mining and irrigation compelled the creation of special property rights in water, the only way to secure control of a water source was to acquire the land around it and to prevent any approach to it by other would-be users. The problem became acute in ranching country where hundreds of square kilometres of good grazing were useful only if there was a sufficient opportunity for watering stock. Attempts to gain control of watering places were frowned on by those who were concerned with the needs of a wider range of users. John R. Craig in *Ranching With Lords and Commons* wrote, "Neither settlers nor cattle companies should be permitted to monopolize the water front of the grazing country."[74] The land itself was useless without access to a supply of water, and, as Craig maintained, "a statute prohibiting them [settlers] from taking up land along the stream or enclosing springs . . . practically excluded settlement."[75] There was thus a conflict between the need to preserve a common right to water sources for all using the open range and the requirement for settlement of identifiable, exclusive rights to an essential supply of water.

The wide grasslands themselves, on which for so long buffalo and other game had thrived in untold millions, were open to use, once Indian claims had been extinguished, by anyone who wished to pasture cattle.

For a couple of decades after 1874 beyond the limits of occupied land and surveyed land, any passer-by could still use grass and hay as he pleased — or at least what had been left by close-grazing herds of buffalo or predatory swarms of grasshoppers. Wandering bands of Indians and of mixed bloods and casual travellers pastured their horses and cattle freely as they moved across the country. The herds of the Hudson's Bay Company grazed under the watchful eye of the "horse-guard" in the vicinity of each post. The few scattered mission and mixed-blood settlements drew on surrounding grasslands for forage and hay as they had need. Even in "the early days of the [ranching] industry the number of operators was so small, compared to the grazing area available, that a man could homestead a quarter-section and turn his cattle loose in hundreds without having any shade or title to any of the land on which his cattle grazed." But later, "owing to the rapid multiplication of ranching enterprises, large and small," it became "necessary for the rancher to protect himself from encroachment of neighboring ranchers by leasing large areas adjoining his homestead. . . . The anxiety to control grazing areas has resulted among large ranchers in the straight purchase of lands."[76]

Besides pasture freely open to access by the still limited number of users, the right to make hay on unclaimed land within reach of transient and permanent settlements was of great importance wherever, from the Red River Settlement westward, multiplying horses and cattle required winter feed. Mrs. John Norquay described a characteristic hay-cutting situation in Red River in the days before the West became a part of Canada. Up to a day fixed by proclamation towards the end of July, 3.2 kilometres of hinterland behind each river lot was known as "the hay privilege" of the owner of the lot, "but in actual practice the whole prairie back of the Selkirk settlers' lots was common ground for hay-cutting. Before the day fixed for the beginning of hay-cutting each year, the best hay meadows were spied out and each man had planned where he was to cut hay. In dry years when there was a scarcity of hay it was usual for the men to go out and be in readiness to start hay-cutting on the stroke of midnight." A man "pre-empted his hay area by making a circle around it with a scythe." Each man's ownership of his hay circle was always respected, but "if a prairie fire destroyed the hay-stacks of a family the neighbours always supplied the deficiency."[77]

When the new "postage stamp" province of Manitoba was created in 1870, there were problems of assimilating such rights of common into the new system of property rights in land that were systematized as the formal land survey expanded. Commissioners were appointed in Manitoba in 1873 to work out a means whereby the old hay privilege and rights of common might be transformed into some equivalent that could be fitted into the new framework of property rights based on the comprehensive land survey and land ownership founded on it.[78] Traditional hay commons were to be a recurring problem as the frontier of private property moved westward, transforming the untamed wilderness into identifiable land lots held as exclusive private property, not only on Red River but gradually right across the prairies and parklands into the foothills of the Rocky Mountains.

As private ownership of specific parcels of land extended, customary common rights to hay and wood and other resources were squeezed out. Unclaimed open-access wood, water, grass, and land dwindled. Space itself began to be a problem. The Indians had been accustomed to camping wherever they saw fit within the untamed wilderness that was their home, while Metis and other travellers had done the same. As the land began to be progressively occupied, old camping grounds were threatened. The Hudson's Bay Company had early found it necessary to reserve a camping ground of 200 hectares about Fort Garry for plains traders when they came in from the West to trade.[79]

A life based on free access to a variety of common resources scattered over a wide territory had involved continual movement from one base of operations to another according to the season, the migration of game, and traditional ceremonial meeting places. Such a life was highly space-intensive and required free access to wide areas and use of the resources on them.

It became evident, as private property rights expanded, that the only hope of Indians or Metis to retain some of the space to which they were accustomed would be by securing from the government recognition of their claim to the extensive areas over which they wished to be free to roam as they had always done.

The Indians and metis were still thinking in terms of the space that was needed for their accustomed way of living, of hunting and trapping. They were ignorant of agricultural criteria and failed to envisage the limited amount of land thought to be necessary for a sedentary life. The extent of the reserves for which they asked seemed unreasonable and was unacceptable to white men thinking of agriculture. For example, Yellow Quill (Oo-za-we-kwun) in 1874 "asserted very large pretensions as to the extent of his Reserve" but was finally persuaded to accept the area agreed under the terms of the Treaty of 1871 to so much land on the south and east side of the Assiniboine River above the Portage as would furnish 96 hectares for each family of five and "a further tract enclosing said reserve to compromise an equivalent to twenty-five square miles of equal breadth, to be laid out round the reserve" though with due regard to the claims of any settlers already established at the date of the Treaty within these bounds.[80]

Bishop Grandin submitted a request on behalf of his Metis flock at St. Albert for a land reserve that seemed to Lieutenant-Governor Archibald entirely unrealistic in its amplitude.[81]

A conflict of ideas developed and a failure of understanding on both sides when the requirements of a wandering life impinged on the claims of new settlers, whether Metis or white, farmers or traders. The case of the treaty ground at Fort Qu'Appelle was a classic instance of the clash of ideas and interests — and of the confusion that arose from imperfect identification of land boundaries and administrative uncertainties. Here Treaty 4 had been negotiated in 1874, and here the Cree and Saulteaux Treaty Indians expected to camp each year when they received their treaty payments. They had a "great regard" for the site and were likely to assemble there for many years to come. Meanwhile, the buffalo were becoming very scarce, and a number of half-breed hunters began to look for land to settle on. They came to the Qu'Appelle Valley and the Indians, finding that the treaty ground was likely to be occupied, applied to the Indian agent for an assurance that they would always have their treaty money paid at this point. Accordingly, the Indian agent asked that the land might be reserved, and the Department of the Interior approved the application, subject to a stipulation that the land might be resumed by the minister if this was required in the public interest and provided that care was taken to exempt any land to which a prior claim might have been established by settlement or cultivation. The half-breeds were headed off, but a small portion of the 600 hectares at issue, stretching from the eastern boundary of the Hudson's Bay Company reserve to the lake, had already been applied for by a Mr. Smith representing "the Honourable Mr. Bowen of Winnipeg" (probably Walter Bown, John Christian Schultz's partner). The Indian agent had asked that some other arrangement be made with him. The following spring the North West Trading Company, a Schultz-Bown enterprise, asked that information should be forwarded to the surveyor-general, so that land claimed by the company at Qu'Appelle Lakes might be located on the map. Schultz, as president, had applied to the surveyor-general for a patent covering almost the same ground as that reserved by the Indian agent. Schultz had heard of this application and represented to the surveyor-general the difficulties that it might cause the company. The Indian agent explained that he had no wish to interfere with the company's claim and would be satisfied if the company would give permission for the treaty ground to be used for the annual ceremonies of annuity payment until these could be transferred to the Indian reserves in accordance with the policy that the Indian Department had been attempting to persuade the Indians to accept.

Schultz, no doubt happy that such a promising occasion for trade with the Indians should be brought to the company's doorstep, gave permission for the Indians to use any unimproved land — land of which Dewdney had written that what the Indians had been promised should be kept for them, a promise that ought to be regarded as sacred, just as much as if the land was a reserve. Earlier, in 1879, one William Daniels had squatted on Section 5, Township 21, Range 13, west of the second meridian. On his death this plot was claimed on the basis of a quit claim deed by a certain Cameron. Further to confound confusion, Cameron's lawyer had a letter from the Department of the Interior asserting that the land belonged to the

Hudson's Bay Company, with which terms must be negotiated. Cameron's claim was supported by Alex Petit Didier and pressed by Archbishop Taché. Yet another claimant, a man of action named Jackson, having purchased the northwest half of the disputed township, without more ado surveyed it into town lots which he sold in spite of an express warning from Dewdney both to Jackson and the Hudson's Bay Company and threatening posters displayed on the land to deter trespassers. Jackson had gone into the speculation, so Dewdney claimed, with his eyes open, depending on political friends to pull him through. When the Indians arrived, Pie-Pot (Piapot) refused to stay on the high land above the treaty ground flat. He led the Indians down and planted his flag there, stating that this was where he would receive his treaty payment. The agent, having summoned the NWMP to his support, persuaded him to adjourn to the office, and the affair bogged down in interdepartmental altercation.[82]

This was not the only case in which a spot held in veneration by Indians passed into white men's hands. Already in Red River the Kirk of Kildonan had been "erected on a piece of land long desecrated by the idolatrous revels of the Indians," according to the Rev. Dr. John Black's account;[83] in other words, a site where they had encamped every year and held their annual Dog Feast before they separated for the winter.

The Indians' interest in other disputed land was of immediate practical significance. A controversy developed over the allocation to the Hudson's Bay Company of six hectares at each end of Portage la Loche (Methye Portage) and of twenty hectares at each end of the Grand Portage on the Saskatchewan River — including the whole of the portage track. John Schultz drew the attention of the secretary of state to the danger of allowing the Hudson's Bay Company to retain the exclusive use of landing places at these points, which would give the "infernal company" virtual control of the carrying trade of the Saskatchewan, Mackenzie, and Peace Rivers, to the disadvantage of "other mercantile interests."[84] He did not mention the possibility of even greater "disadvantage" to the Indians.

Such struggles for key property rights were symptomatic of the third cataclysmic change that was now taking place in the economy of the plains and parklands of the West: the establishment of exclusive private property instead of the traditional common property of the native peoples. Not only had the coming of the white man built up population and commercial pressures on the natural riches of the country; not only had the Indians' tribal territories been opened to use by newcomers — so that the buffalo had been destroyed, other game woefully depleted, once-rich fisheries endangered, and wood lots ruthlessly cut out; but the native peoples found that they might no longer help themselves to what they needed in the country through which they had been accustomed to wander. Such dwindling riches as remained might not now be used except by the owner of a homestead, a railway right of way, a grazing lease, or a timber-cutting licence. As the wide plains were progressively surveyed and taken up by private owners, as homesteads were fenced in and grazing rights leased; as the right to cut wood was appropriated to lumbermen; as fences closed in hay meadows and drinking spots; as railroad rights of way cut across Indian trails and game trails, the age old rights of common gave way before the advance of exclusive saleable property rights. Only the private owner, supported by the police, might now use the gifts of the Great Spirit.[85] Gradually, the full implications of the treaties became clear. Assurances as to continued freedom to hunt over tribal lands as usual until those lands were settled or appropriated for other uses faded into insignificance. It became clear that the true meaning of the treaties lay in the clauses which provided (for example, in the words of Treaty 6) that the Indians had ceded, released, surrendered, and yielded up forever "all their rights, titles and privileges, whatsoever, to the lands" within the treaty limits.[86] The country and the nature-given riches of that country that had been shared by the members of the tribe which ranged it and their cousins of mixed blood, its spaces, its grass, its waters, its woods, and its other natural products now belonged to private owners who were entitled to keep other people out of their property.

This final tragedy was a tragedy of the loss by the native peoples of their customary "commons" to private owners of exclusive property rights, rights which only those who had money and understood the strange new laws could hope to make their own. The Indians had their reserves and the Metis were allocated — and quickly lost — half-breed land or scrip, but nothing in the experience, character, or point of view of either people made it possible for them to come to terms with the, to them, disastrous new institution of private property in land and its riches. They had been urged and cajoled to take up reserves. Once settled on them they found that the narrow boundaries of those reserves — small plots of land marked off from the wide wilderness that had once been free to them — had become the limits of the land whose natural produce they might count on using. The Indians who had in 1871 agreed at Lower Fort Garry and Lake Manitoba to Treaties 1 and 2,[87] for instance, were warned in a proclamation that from the dates of those treaties they had "no right to cut any wood or timber on any land except within the Limits of the reserves allotted to them under the said Treaties."[88] No one, White or Indian, might cut wood outside a reserve unless he had a licence from the Crown to do so; a white man who had such a licence was entitled to cut wood and must not be molested by the Indians. The Indians negotiating Treaty 6 in 1876 asked specifically to be allowed to continue to cut timber on crown lands,[89] but do not appear to have had any answer.

When the buffalo had gone and ranchers complained that starving Indians were killing their cattle, the Indians were kept more rigidly to their reserves.[90]

The question of what exactly the boundaries of those reserves included became increasingly important as the Indians found themselves more and more strictly limited to the use of the resources on them. In the early stages of land and resources appropriation a variety of clashes occurred over reserves that were not yet surveyed nor identified. In some cases the Indians believed that the reserve to which they had agreed included certain specific land features and resources which, upon the survey's being made, turned out not to be within its limits. Misunderstandings were very hard to avoid when the treaty commissioners did not know the local lie of the land and the Indians had little conception of what survey measurements meant. Further, reserves were not always surveyed immediately after the treaty had been signed, and until the survey had been completed, no one knew just where the boundaries of the reserve might lie. Such uncertainty was an element in both the Sandy Point and Roseau River imbroglios described above.

Some constraint on the use of the natural riches of the country was certainly becoming essential with the increased pressure on its products that built up with the influx of strangers after 1870. Unaccustomed demands were creating unprecedented scarcities. The constraints of private property and a system of market prices was one way of rationing the use of the newly scarce resources and of safeguarding them against overuse to the point of exhaustion. The alternative was some sort of conservation legislation. A belated and ineffective attempt had been made to save the buffalo by such means. An ordinance passed by the North-West Council in 1877 proved impossible to enforce[91] and came to nothing, despite Morris's hope that the law made to protect them would "save the buffalo."[92] He was "satisfied that a few simple regulations would preserve the herds for many years,"[93] but within three years they were gone. Similar efforts were made to save the fisheries, especially the whitefish and sturgeon fisheries. Regulations made under the Fisheries Act of 1876 were enforced at least to some extent, as F. C. Gilchrist's diary shows. He seems to have thought that the measures taken had increased the catch of fish, but they were difficult to enforce as concessions had to be made when those who broke the law, many of whom seem to have been mixed bloods, were apparently so dependent on the fishery that on occasion Gilchrist waived the fines and gave limited permission to fish during the close season.[94] To devise conservation measures that would be effective without penalizing the native peoples, who had always lived by the hunt and the fishery, was a puzzle.

The dramatic disappearance of the buffalo herds and other products of the land created such havoc in the subsistence of the native peoples that it overshadowed the more slowly acting but in the end still more disruptive impact on the native peoples of the new order based on private ownership of all natural resources outside the reserves.

Hugh Dempsey gives a vivid picture of the disastrous effect on the Blackfoot of the loss of the buffalo and of the new order:

Nothing was the same in the old land. The formerly neat lodges of the Blackfeet were ragged and torn, the once-gallant warriors were subdued, and even the children had lost the spark of life. The buffalo were gone, the old life was gone. Scores of fresh graves dotted the countryside from the Oldman

River to the Missouri. Warriors who had defeated every enemy in battle were reduced to bony derelicts before starvation and disease carried the life from their bodies. No one knows exactly how many people from the Blackfoot tribe died during those starvation years, but from 1879 to 1881 at least one thousand members [out of some 6,000] of the nation in Canada perished. . . .

What remained? A small plot of land in the middle of their domain. Here they would camp in the river bottoms and receive the beef and flour of the white men. They would scratch the earth and grow turnips and other vegetables.[95]

The *Edmonton Bulletin* carried the sad story on, in its reports of misery on the reserves in 1881 and the years that followed. There was no food, there were few clothes, and the lodges were wretched.[96]

The long-run effect was described twenty-five years later by the Reverend John McDougall, himself a great advocate of "civilization" and settlement, who had personally witnessed and taken part in the change from the old common-property economy of the Indians to the system of reserves in the midst of the private-property/market economy of the white man. In the old days, he wrote of the Indian:

Millions of cattle [buffalo], millions of deer, and countless millions of fowl; the trout in the streams and lakes, the whitefish and sturgeon filling great inland oceans, and myriad lakes and streams were his, all his. The bracing winters made him strong, and the warm fruitful summers made him glad. . . . He gratefully accepted things as they were and did not ask for more and better.

Civilization with its permanent home life and dwelling in houses and fixed habitations and multiple insanitation, has been cruel and full of disease-breeding to the Indian peoples. While their former life gave them pure air and constant change of camp and scene, the steadily demanded need of a permanent residence on the reserve has thrust the Indians into crude cabins full of foul atmosphere and surcharged with germs of terrible disease. Then the change of diet from meat and fowl and fish to cereals and vegetables and salt and sugar and syrup, etc., has come so suddenly, especially with all our western Indians, that nature herself has been taken by surprise and is unable thus hurriedly to adapt herself to these sudden and radical changes.[97]

Part of the contrast was, of course, attributable to the transition from a nomadic economy to a settled economy, which, as Professor V. C. Fowke has noted,[98] cannot succeed on a subsistence basis in the geographical conditions of the Canadian Prairies. A very large part, however, was owing to the transition from the old common-property system — by way of a disastrous and destructive interlude of open access to natural riches — to an economy based on the purchase and sale of property rights, with the Indians remaining in an uneasy limbo on their reserves, part way between the old institutions of shared resources and the new institutions of private personal property. They had neither the experience, nor the acquisitive skills, nor the will to prosper under a system of private property, but, in any case, in a laudable attempt to prevent the dangers of an "unprotected encounter"[99] with newcomers engaged in buying and selling to make a profit — unfamiliar, as they were, with the idea of making money by shrewd speculation in land values — the Indians were made wards of the Crown, as represented by the Department of Indian Affairs, and a reserve system developed that was neither fully a matter of common property nor fully a matter of individual private property. The reserves and their resources were intended to provide for the members of the bands that held the reserves and their descendants. They were to use them in perpetuity, though where it was considered that the reserve that had been set aside was bigger than was needed, arrangements might be made for the sale of the excess land on agreement of the adult males of the band. The proceeds were paid into a trust fund, and interest from this fund was to be used for the benefit of the band; in rare cases part of the capital sum might be applied to some specific purpose, such as the acquisition of agricultural machinery on the Blackfoot Reserve.[100] The results of probably well-intentioned controls may have added to the difficulties of the Indians in the new regime. To quote McDougall again:

> If he is a treaty Indian he cannot visit a friend on a neighbouring reserve without a permit. He cannot go to the nearest market town without a permit. In what was his own country, and on his own land to which he was born, out of the centuries, he cannot travel in peace without a permit. He cannot buy or sell without a permit. He can raise cattle, but he cannot sell them unless the Government official allows. He may cultivate the soil, but is not the owner of his own produce. He cannot sell firewood or hay from the land that is his by divine and citizen right, and thus reap the result of his own industry, unless subject to the caprice and whim of one who often becomes autocratic.[101]

The Indians' economic activities were, thus, subject to other constraints than those of the market, the constraints of administrative controls, often clumsy and ill-judged, imposed by the Indian Act under the vigilant surveillance of the Indian agent and the farm instructor.

The process of readjustment to the new state of affairs was slow and painful, and standards of living on the reserves remained at a low level. The abundance of the buffalo days had gone forever. In those days the Indians had been, in the words of the commissioner of the NWMP, "self-supporting, almost rich, and certainly contented."[102] Now all they had was a share in the limited resources of the reserve, a few dollars each a year by way of treaty annuities, and any other treaty benefits that were due them, such as education and medical assistance under the controversial "medicine-chest" clause, and, as time went on, something from income that was earned as interest by trust funds accumulated through the surrender of supposedly surplus reserve land. As well, there were government rations — often grudgingly given — to stave off starvation. The Indians were now supposed to learn to support themselves by farming or cattle-raising — both unfamiliar exercises. Some of them learnt very fast to farm efficiently, as witness evidence that was given in 1887 to the Senate Committee on Natural Food Products,[103] but returns to gardening and agriculture were uncertain[104] and the problem of securing housing and sanitation adequate for a sedentary life remained acute. Moreover, a people used to a meat diet and a wandering life in the open air and sunshine were desperately vulnerable to malnutrition and disease when their basic food changed overnight to saltpork and flour, and the children began to be cooped up in school rooms. Government rations by no means made up for the loss of real income from the lost commons, and the humdrum life of the sedentary agriculturalist was a poor substitute for the varied and exciting life of the wandering hunter and horse-raiding warrior.

The economic basis of the life of the Metis, too, had been the abundant common resources to which they had had access. Few of them understood the significance of property in land. Much of the half-breed land reserve of 565,000 hectares set aside in 1870 in Manitoba (or scrip that represented a claim to that land) slipped from the hands of its mixed-blood recipients at prices far below its market value.[105] The mixed bloods, having disposed of their claims, moved further west into still unsettled lands, hoping to continue to live the wandering life they were used to and enjoyed. Civilization, settlement, and private property caught up with them.[106] The rising of 1885 was a last despairing attempt to protect the commons on which they depended for their way of life. With those commons gone, they faced economic disaster, especially as supplementary opportunities for earning an income as tripmen were disappearing at the same time as the buffalo. Steamboats and then railways replaced the traditional "brigades" of York boats and Red River carts that had been manned by mixed-blood and Indian voyageurs.

In the old life a good hunt, a good catch of fish, a plentiful wild rice or berry crop had meant for both Indians and Metis leisure for dancing, feasting, horse-racing, gambling, visiting, and ceremonies. Alexander Sandison remembered with pleasure the dancing and week-long wedding feasts of old Red River.[107] The shared gifts of nature had provided the means, not for the accumulation of material wealth for its own sake, but for a good life as the Indians and Metis saw it. It was a happy life on the whole, albeit at times a precarious one, subject to periodic shortages if the game or the fisheries failed, and one that was vulnerable to alcohol. Still, Captain (later Sir Cecil) Denny judged that "with plenty of meat in the lodges, no happier people might be found anywhere" than the people of the Blackfoot Confederacy in the old days.[108]

Now the abundance of those days had given place to a new kind of poverty from which there seemed to be no prospect of escape, as the pressures on the resources of the country, of new people, new demands, and new technology increased and the native peoples lost control of those resources to the newcomers.

A bitter turn of the screw was added to this new indigence by the enrichment of successful new white neighbours. At one end of the economic scale the strangers who now owned the gifts of the Great Spirit — if they were shrewd or lucky — became rich on the basis of the newly created property rights, while at the other end of the scale the native peoples found themselves sunken in abject and persistent poverty. Feverish land booms, speculation in half-breed scrip, control of key points on transport routes or the sites of burgeoning towns all gave rise to new wealth based, not on a steady and sustainable use of the productivity of the Indians' ancestral lands, but on the rising value of those lands themselves, as well as on using up stocks of such natural riches as timber.

The Indians and Metis had been used to a notably egalitarian society in which all had access to the common riches provided by nature, and in which, if disparities in skill, strength, and luck gave some more wealth than others, the difference had been to a considerable extent offset by sharing by the more fortunate of their material means with those in need, in accordance with the strong native tradition. Now they were shouldered aside by wealth-accumulating new-comers, sinking to the lowest position in an unfamiliar order characterized by wide disparities in economic and social status.

The abundance of natural riches in the days before 1870 had given way to a new and increasing scarcity. Some mechanism had become essential to secure the rationing of the newly scarce nature-given resources. So long as these were open-access resources, free to all comers, they were used without stint and beyond their natural power of renewal. Once they became private property, with the price rising as scarcity increased, that rising price compelled some limitation of their use. Farming and cattle-raising, more labour and capital intensive than hunting and fishing, replaced those older ways of getting a living, with their spacious require-ments of territory. Even so, private property in land did not prevent the "soil mining" that nearly turned the Prairies into a dust bowl by the 1930's. Whatever the effectiveness of private property as a means of securing the rationing and husbanding of scarce natural resources, its effect in terms of the redistribution of wealth played a part in creating an extreme of deprivation among a people unused to its constraints alongside new wealth among the new property owners. It provided a means whereby the resources of the West were mobilized for the peopling of the plains, but in so doing it contributed to the economic degradation of the original peoples of the plains and to a new inequality in the economic and social system.

NOTES

1. A. S. Morton, *A History of Canadian West to 1870-71* (Toronto, 1935), pp. 5–21; F. G. Roe *The North American Buffalo*, 2d ed. (Toronto, 1970), pp. 650–51.
2. Irene M. Spry, ed., *The Papers of the Palliser Expedition* (Toronto, 1968), pp. 143, 145–46; J. G. Nelson, *The Last Refuge* (Montreal, 1973), pp. 110–11; Isaac Cowie, *The Company of Adventurers* (Toronto, 1913), pp. 303–4; F. G. Roe, p. 650.
3. E. Walker, "The Seasonal Nature of Post-Altithermal Communal Bison Procurement on the Northwestern Plains," *NAPA'O: Saskatchewan Anthropological Journal 4* (April 1974): 1–6; Roe, pp. 630–49.
4. Roe, pp. 116–18, 374–75, 658; Nelson, p. 29.
5. Alexander Henry the Elder, for example, commented that the cause of the perpetual war between the "Chipeways" (Ojibwa) and Sioux was "that both claim, as their exclusive hunting ground, the tract of land which lies between them" (See Alexander Henry (the Elder), *Travels and Adventures in Canada and the Indian Territories Between the Years 1760 and 1776* [New York, 1809; reprint Edmonton, 1969], p. 189).
6. There are, for example, many references to guides and hunters in the Palliser reports. Though some proved "expensive and useless," the skill of others was most impressive, notably that of the Stoney hunter Nimrod. See also John Rae, "A Visit to the Red River and the Saskatchewan, 1861," ed. Irene M. Spry, in *The Geographical Journal* 140, Part I (February 1974); and "Log of the Wanderers on the Prairies in Search of Buffalo Bear Deer etc.," 1862, Dunmore Papers, for comments on the skill of the great plainsman and guide, James (later the Honourable James) McKay.
7. Roe, p. 654.
8. Saskatchewan Archives, Regina.
9. Peter Erasmus, "Buffalo Days and Nights," 1928, MS Glenbow-Alberta Institute, p. 65. Subsequently published, Calgary, 1976.
10. PAM, Schultz Collection, Box Ia, Misc. MSS, Alexander Sandison, Reminiscenses.
11. For the long list of his books, see Spry, "Early Visitors to the Canadian Prairies," in Brian W. Blouet and Merlin P. Lawson, eds., *Images of the Plains* (Lincoln, Nebraska, 1975).
12. Sir Cecil E. Denny, *The Law Marches West* (Toronto, 1939; reprint 1972) has many references to the days of plenty in the 1870's in what is now Alberta.
13. Viscount Milton and W. B. Cheadle, *The North-West Passage by Land* (London, 1865), p. 160.
14. David G. Mandelbaum, *Anthropology and People: "The World of the Plains Cree"* (Saskatoon, 1967), p. 7.
15. Nelson, p. 189. However, he adds that it has been claimed by some archaeologists and other scientists that man contributed to the extinction of the mammoth and other giant fauna of the plains some 11,000 years ago.
16. Cited in Roe, pp. 292, 655.
17. R. B. Marcy, *Exploration of the Red River of Louisiana, in the Year 1854* (Washington, 1854), p. 104.
18. John McDougall, *Saddle, Sled and Snowshoe* (Toronto, 1896; reprint), p. 282.
19. Nelson, p. 152. Roe, pp. 654–59.
20. Mandelbaum, p. 7.
21. PAM, Red River Census.
22. *Report* of the Select Committee of the House of Commons, 1857, Appendix B, p. 363. There were also settlements of Metis south of the American Border at Pembina on the Red River, at St. Joseph (now Walhalla, North Dakota) on the Pembina River, and later, further west in Montana.
23. *Census of Canada, 1870–71*, 4:380, lxxii and lxxxiv. The first official map of Manitoba gives the population in 1871 as 5,707 French half-breeds, 4,083 English half-breeds, 1,565 Whites, and 533 Indians (A. L. Russell, Map of the Province of Manitoba, 1871; original in Public Archives of Canada, reproduced in J. Warkentin and R. I. Ruggles, *Historical Atlas of Manitoba* [Winnipeg: Manitoba Historical Society, 1970], p. 249).
24. See footnote 11 above.
25. Robert Campbell (chief factor), Memoirs (typescript kindly loaned to me by Professor Donald MacGregor), p. 182.

26. Alexander Ross, *The Red River Settlement: Its Rise, Progress and Present State* (London, 1856; reprint 1972), p. 246; Roe, ch. 14.

27. But see Roe, pp. 412–13, for a critique of some estimates of the number of carts.

28. See Spry, ed., *Papers of the Palliser Expedition*; Erasmus, see footnote 9 above; and Rae, for references to these hunts. See also Roe, pp. 467–75.

29. For this see Paul F. Sharp, *Whoop-Up Country: The Canadian-American West 1865–1885* (Minneapolis, 1955); and Roe, pp. 467–75. Roe has also a detailed discussion of estimates of the whole process of depletion of the southern and northern herds in the American West and in Canada in chapters 15, 16, and 17.

30. R. A. Billington, *Westward Expansion: A History of the American Frontier* (New York, 1919; 3d ed., 1967), p. 670; Nelson, p. 166; Ralph K. Andrist, *The Long Death, The Last Days of the Plains Indian* (London, 1964), p. 179.

31. Billington, p. 670; Roe, pp. 432, 449–50.

32. Roe, pp. 430–31, 449; Billington, pp. 645–52, 670.

33. Roe, chs. 15 and 16.

34. Ibid, ch. 17; Erasmus.

35. PAM, Inkster Papers, 4, "The Honourable James McKay." The wood buffalo of the forested northern plains still survived, as they do to this day by dint of careful management and protection in Wood Buffalo National Park.

36. Roe, p. 870 and Appendix H; Alexander Morris, *The Treaties of Canada with the Indians of Manitoba and the North-West Territories* (Toronto, 1880), pp. 188, 193, 195, 227, 228, 237, 241, 259, 267–68, 271. Denny records that the North-West Territories law was a dead letter, being impossible to enforce.

37. Martin S. Garretson, *The American Bison* (New York, 1938), p. 128. Charles M. MacInnes, *In the Shadow of the Rockies* (London, 1930), p. 146.

38. The Hon. Edgar Dewdney reported that "prairie fires, however, were started at different points almost simultaneously, as if by some preconstructed arrangement, and the country north of the boundary line was burnt from Wood Mountain on the east to the Rocky Mountains on the west, and nearly as far north as the latitude of the Qu'Appelle" (*Annual Report* of the Department of Indian Affairs for 1880). See also Roe, p. 477.

39. Hugh A. Dempsey *Crowfoot: Chief of the Blackfeet* (Norman, Oklahoma, 1972), p. 114 says that "the Indians had no doubt that the American hide hunters had started the fires to prevent the main herds from returning to Canada" in 1879.

40. See Lawrence J. Burpee, ed., "York Factory to the Blackfoot Country: The Journal of Anthony Hendry, 1754–55," *Proceedings and Transactions of the Royal Society of Canada*, 3d series, 1 (1907), sec. 2, pp. 307–60. The passage quoted is on p. 344.

41. PAM, Archibald Papers, 25.

42. Henry Youle Hind, *North-West Territory. Report of the Assiniboine and Saskatchewan Exploring Expedition* (Toronto, 1859), p. 52.

43. Rae, p. 11.

44. "Log of the Wanderers," p. 14, Dunmore Papers.

45. John H. Dales, *Pollution, Property and Prices* (Toronto, 1968); Ronald Coase, "The Problem of Social Costs," *Journal of Law and Economics* (October 1960); P. Crabbé and Irene M. Spry, eds., *Natural Resource Development in Canada (Ottawa, 1973), session 4*.

46. Morris, pp. 257–58, 270–71.

47. Ibid., p. 171.

48. Palliser reported on the disquietude in 1857 of the Rainy Lake Ojibwa (see Spry, ed., *Papers of the Palliser Expedition*, pp. 76–79). S. J. Dawson had submitted a memorandum dated 17 December 1869, about the Indians on the Red River (Dawson) Route and in subsequent correspondence stressed the importance of securing the right of way from the Indians (Archibald Papers, 1–3). The following, among others, reported on the growing anxiety of the western plains Indians: the Rev. George McDougall (1875), C. F. Wm. J. Christie, from Edmonton (1871), and the Rev. Father Constantine Scollen (1876). See Morris, pp. 169–70, 173–75, 247–49.

49. PAM, Morris Papers, Ketcheson Collection, 69; Morris, pp. 173–75.

50. Wm. Fletcher reported from Portage la Prairie, 25 October 1870, that for about 12.8 kilometres from the Portage to Rat Creek, land might be occupied only for three years by permission of the

Indians, granted only by the intervention of the "Late Governor," James McKay (Archibald Papers, 58). See also Morris, pp. 128, 136–37.

51. Archibald Papers, 332.
52. Erasmus.
53. Morris, p. 170.
54. Ibid., pp. 95, 186, 204, 205, 211, 212. In Manitoba, Indians still have the right to hunt on private land.
55. Ibid., p. 369.
56. Ibid., p. 215.
57. Ibid.
58. As Turner puts it, "the road to an enormous territorial promise had been opened" (John Peter Turner, *The North-West Mounted Police, 1873–1893* [Ottawa, 1950], 1:210).
59. Morris, pp. 157–58.
60. G. Hardin, "The Tragedy of the Commons," in *The Environmental Hand Book*, ed., G. De Bell (New York, 1970).
61. Dewdney, *Annual Report*, 1880, p. 94.
62. Cited in Turner, 2:464.
63. Evidence given before the Select Senate Committee on Natural Food Products, 1887 (Schultz Papers, Misc. MSS II, pp. 16–17, 28).
64. Material concerning the regulation of the fisheries is based largely on the diaries of F. C. Gilchrist. See D. H. Bocking, "The Gilchrist Diaries," *Saskatchewan History* 20 (Autumn 1967): 108–13.
65. Report by S. J. Dawson, 19 December 1870, Archibald Papers, 153.
66. Letter from Archdeacon Cowley, 21 March 1871, enclosing a letter from a Mr. Phair dated 17 March 1871, Archibald Papers, 226.
67. The Gilchrist Diaries give a vivid impression of how much wood was needed.
68. Colin Inkster, *Winnipeg Free Press* 30 June 1934, in Inkster Papers.
69. See, for example, Denny, p. 132, on a sawmill set up at Fort Macleod where "hundreds of spruce logs were cut and driven down to it from the hills some miles away."
70. Royal to Archibald, 15 February 1871, Archibald Papers, 193, 198 (original letter is in French); see also Chief Moosoo's complaint, ibid., 150.
71. Treaty No. 1 (1871) in Canada, *Indian Treaties and Surrenders* (Ottawa, 1891), 1: 282–84; Bradley correspondence with the lieutenant-governor, 1872, Archibald Papers, 586–89, 601, 603, 621, 622, 628, 632, 651, 652–54.
72. Archibald Papers, 582, 583, 592, 593, 600, 650.
73. Morris Papers, Ketcheson Collection, 243.
74. John R. Craig, *Ranching with Lords and Commons* (Toronto, 1903; repr. 1971), p. 258.
75. Ibid., p. 293.
76. Ibid., p. 236.
77. W. J. Healy, *Women of Red River* (Winnipeg, 1923), p. 150.
78. Morris Papers, Ketcheson Collection, 50.
79. Healy, p. 139.
80. *Indian Treaties and Surrenders*, 1:283; Morris Papers, Ketcheson Collection, 153. Other attempts to secure large reserves were those of James Seenum (Chief Pakan) and Toma on behalf of Red Pheasant in the Fort Pitt and Fort Carlton Treaty negotiations. Toma asked for a grant of sixteen kilometres of land round the reserves in a belt (Morris, p. 186). Seenum's request for a large reserve led to subsequent long drawn-out misunderstandings; the issue was not settled until 1884 (Erasmus). In the view of the Department of Indian Affairs, the "chief held for many years a very exaggerated idea of the quantity of land to which his band was entitled" (Report for the year 1884, xlvi).
81. See correspondence of Bishop Grandin, C. F. Wm. J. Christie, and the lieutenant-governor in 1871, Archibald Papers, 523, 544, 559, 655.
82. Memorandum re treaty ground at Fort Qu'Appelle and ensuing correspondence, Schultz Papers, Misc. MSS, II.
83. Healy, p. 68.
84. Schultz to McDougall, 1869, Schultz Papers, Misc. MSS, III; and draft of letter to Secretary of

State re lands to be retained by the Hudson's Bay Company, 29 March 1873, VI, Correspondence, etc., 130.

85. "The Great Spirit, and not the Great Mother, gave us this land" (Morris, p. 270).
86. *Indian Treaties and Surrenders*, 1891, 2:36.
87. Treaties No. 1 and 2, 1871, ibid., pp. 282–85, 291–94.
88. Archibald Papers, 573.
89. Morris, pp. 185, 215.
90. Denny, pp. 138, 143, 168–69, 195–96, 200.
91. Ibid., p. 102; Morris, pp. 188, 193, 195, 228, 236, 241, 258–59, 267–68, 271.
92. Ibid., p. 267.
93. Ibid., p. 195.
94. F. C. Gilchrist, Diaries 1859–96, Saskatchewan Archives Board, Regina, Personal Papers, A/382; Bocking.
95. Dempsey, p. 134; see also Dempsey, *Red Crow*, (Saskatoon, 1980).
96. *Edmonton Bulletin*, 17 January 1881.
97. John MacDougall, "The Future of the Indians of Canada . . . , a Paper read before the Missionary Convention at Edmonton, *Methodist Magazine and Review* (March 1905): 244–48.
98. The papers of the late V. C. Fowke. It is possible that the plains Indians had moved from an attempt at agricultural life back to a wandering life for this reason on the coming of the horse.
99. A phrase used by Archdeacon Cowley with reference to contacts between the aboriginal peoples and incoming white settlers (Archibald Papers, 282).
100. Lucien M. Hanks Jr., and Jane Richardson Hanks, *Tribe Under Trust. A Study of the Blackfoot Reserve of Alberta* (Toronto, 1950), ch. 2.
101. McDougall, pp. 245–46.
102. Quoted in Denny, p. 168.
103. Evidence given before the Select Committee of the Senate on Natural Food Products, Schultz Papers, Misc. MSS, II, 61.
104. Hanks, pp. 63–65.
105. See A. S. Morton and Chester Martin, *History of Prairie Settlement* (Toronto, 1938), pp. 237–38. Concern about problems arising in connection with the half-breed land grant is evident in the Archibald, Morris, and Schultz Papers. See, for example, Archibald Papers, 740.
106. On this see George F. G. Stanley, *The Birth of Western Canada* (London, 1936; 2d ed., Toronto, 1960, 1963).
107. Sandison, 1914, Schultz Papers, Box Ia, Misc. MSS, I.
108. Denny, p. 49.

3

A Witness to Murder: The Cypress Hills Massacre and the Conflict of Attitudes towards the Native People of the Canadian and American West during the 1870's

*Robert S. Allen**

The development of the American West in the 1860's produced a calamitous cultural shock for the northern plains tribes, who viewed with mounting anger the loss of their traditional lifestyle of the buffalo hunt and nomadism. The Minnesota Sioux War of 1862 and the Red Cloud War, which began in 1864 to the southeast of Montana Territory, had been major new items in Benton, Montana. But it was not until the time of Appomattox, April 1865, that a series of reciprocal murders took place in Montana that hardened the white population of that territory, indeed conditioned and encouraged them to kill Indians in the interest of future white "peace, prosperity and progress." Often the killers were hailed as heroes, contributing to a stable society and helping to protect innocent and defenceless white women and children.[1] This attitude provides the key to understanding the Cypress Hills Massacre of 1873 and the angry bewilderment of the Americans in Montana over the subsequent proceedings of the Winnipeg Trial by Canadian authorities.

This tragedy was exacerbated by the atmosphere of violence and bloodshed which swept the American western frontier in the 1860's and 1870's, particularly in Montana, the home of most of the whisky traders, wolfers, and adventurers who were the perpetrators of the Cypress Hills Massacre. The exchange of atrocities

Deputy chief, Treaties and Historical Research Centre, Department of Indian and Northern Affairs, Ottawa.

began in the spring of 1865 when Peigan and Blood* war parties, frustrated by white intrusion and the whisky trade and further encouraged by traditional horse-stealing stole about forty horses from Whites in Benton and later killed several miners and traders. In revenge, a group of Whites left Benton on an "Indian hunt," captured three innocent Peigan and hanged them. During the same week, inspired and bolstered by a plentiful consumption of liquor, a party of Whites fatally mauled three Blood Indians in the streets of Benton. Two days later, a Blood war party under Calf Shirt caught ten woodcutters on the Marias River, twenty kilometres out of Benton, and slaughtered them all[2]

In 1866 Little Dog, a Peigan band chief, recognized the danger and futility of continuing the "Blackfeet War" and generously gave food to starving miners in the Sun River valley in an effort to initiate peace. But the animosity between Indian and White was so great that even the Peigan considered this peacemaking chief a traitor, and just outside of Benton a party of drunken warriors killed Little Dog and his son because he was "too friendly to whites and had returned stolen horses."[3] The killings and mounting bitterness persisted. Charles Carson, nephew of Kit Carson, was ambushed and slain near Benton by Blood warriors. John Morgan and a group of friends retaliated by inviting four Blood Indians to his ranch and killing them. In the late spring another Peigan revenge party, under Bull Head, attacked and destroyed the experimental farm at Sun River and killed the farm instructor.[4] The incidents continued to increase until the campaign of 1869–70, which ended the Blackfeet depredations, but not the senseless killing of Indians by Whites.[5]

In response to the demands of the citizens of Montana for action against the Blackfeet raids, the United States army conducted a winter campaign against Mountain Chief, a leading chief of the south Blackfoot. The local military commander, Colonel E. M. Baker at Fort Shaw, was ordered "to strike them hard."[6] Baker surprised and attacked a Peigan village of thirty-seven lodges along the Marias River on a cold winter morning in January 1870. It was a smashing victory; the soldiers killed 173 Indians and captured 300 horses. Remarkably, the Whites suffered only two casualties, one killed and one classified as wounded, although he had broken his leg when he fell off his horse. Immediately, conflicting reports began to circulate that the affair was not a battle, but a wholesale massacre. The majority of the Indian dead were women and children. Most revealing was the discovery that the camp was not that of Mountain Chief (who had escaped across the "medicine line" to safety in Canada), but the friendly and smallpox-riddled village of Heavy Runner, who had been slain while running towards the advancing troops frantically waving his identification papers.[7]

---

*Blood and Peigan, along with the Blackfoot proper made up the Blackfoot Confederacy. In the U.S. the term "Blackfeet" is used to indicate this combination of tribes.

Eastern reaction to the Marias Massacre was generally negative. *The New York Times* asked whether "the wholesale slaughter of women and children was needed for the vindication of our arms."[8] Montanans, however, were jubilant about the affair, and regarded the destruction of the village as yet another victory of civilization over savagery. The battle became a symbol of victory and success, and its participants were praised as frontier heroes. William Wheeler asserted that: "Ever since January 1870 the Blackfeet tribes have been peaceable and quiet, and it has been safe to travel in their country. Very few white men have been murdered by them."[9] For the white settlers of Montana the Blackfeet menace appeared over, but the memories of victory, glory, praise, respect, and hero-worship continued. Montana adventurers, eager for excitement and recognition, soon found other Indian tribes to provoke.

To the north, there remained a vast, fertile and unpopulated region largely ignored by the Canadian government. In Montana, the Indian whisky trade had been rigidly enforced and largely suppressed by the late 1860's. The American free traders, hounded by the authorities in Montana, saw an unhindered and easy profit for their whisky trade in the "British Possessions." By the early 1870's the Americans had established a number of "whisky forts" north of the border, such as those along the Belly River with such colourful names as Slide-out, Standoff, Whiskey Gap, and Robber's Roost. The centre of this trading traffic was Fort Whoop-Up (near-present day Lethbridge, Alberta), and the entire area became popularly known as Whoop-Up country. Business was good in 1872, proclaimed the *Helena Daily Herald*:

> the traders at Whoop-Up, in the British possessions, are doing well this winter. They have a good trade with the Indians, and no U.S. detective or spy dare invade their quiet rendezvous; nor is whiskey even confiscated when it gets to that "happy hunting ground."[10]

It was reported that Whoop-Up country was inhabited by a class of persons whose sole occupation "is trading whiskey to the Indians, and as they are in British America no notice will be taken of their crimes by the United States authorities." This lawlessness and anarchy had resulted in the killings of several traders who were all "directly or indirectly engaged in the trade of whiskey to the Indians."[11]

In addition to the killings, the Americans were embroiled in a short and bitter civil war in Whoop-Up country. The two warring factions were both American — wolfers and traders. The wolf-hunters killed their prey by poisoning buffalo meat. This practice angered the Indians both because it spoiled valuable meat and because Indian dogs also often ate the poisoned meat. The wolfers resented the traders selling whisky, repeating rifles, and ammunition to the Indians; drunken and well-armed Indians were dangerous foes. Although the wolfers had entrenched themselves at Spitzee post on the Highwood River under the leadership of John Evans, who was prominent a year later at Cypress Hills, and Harry "Kamoose" Taylor, they nonetheless protested loudly against the whisky traders and organized the "Spitzee cavalry" in an attempt to drive the traders out of Whoop-Up country. The effort failed, although compromises were made and both groups continued their respective businesses, but the whisky posts predominated.[12] The reports by Hudson's Bay Company representatives, missionaries and travellers of lawlessness, increasing violence, and the demoralizing effects of the whisky trade on the northern plains Indians finally prompted Ottawa to take some overt action to ascertain the state of affairs in the Canadian West. In 1870 Lieutenant William Francis Butler of the British army was commissioned to investigate the conditions for the Canadian government. Butler toured for about three months and found the Saskatchewan District "without law, order or security for life or property . . . robbery and murder . . . have gone unpunished . . . and all civil and legal institutions are entirely unknown."[13] The American traders at Whoop-Up cared only for a quick profit in furs through an illegal trade in whisky.

In 1872 a second reconnaissance of the Canadian West was conducted by Colonel Patrick Robertson-Ross, commander and adjutant-general of the Canadian Militia. His instructions were to recommend the necessary action for providing law and order. During his four-month tour, Ross was appalled at the rampant lawlessness in the West and the strength and influence of the American whisky posts in Canadian territory. He reported on good authority that eighty-eight Blackfeet had been murdered in drunken brawls in the past year and that "the demoralization of the Indians and injury resulting to the country from this illicit traffic is very great."[14] Whisky was sold openly to the Blackfeet bands and Plains Cree by American "smugglers," who derived large profits and showed a complete disdain for the Canadian sovereignty. When HBC officials remonstrated, the Americans replied coolly that as there was no force in the country to prevent them, "they would do just as they pleased."[15] Like Butler, Ross recommended the establishment of a well-equipped, mounted force which would be sufficient to police the region, and "support Government in establishing law and order in the Saskatchewan, preserving the peace of the north-west territory, and affording protection."[16]

The recommendations of Butler and Robertson-Ross, coupled with the urgent solicitations of various HBC officials and missionaries, resulted in "An Act respecting the Administration of Justice, and the Establishment of a Police Force in the North West Territories" in May 1873.[17] But in Ottawa, the political entanglements of the Pacific Scandal meant that Macdonald and the Conservative government could devote little time to affairs in the West. The force, therefore, did not reach Whoop-Up country to crush the whisky trade and the violence in the region until the late summer of the following year.

On Sunday afternoon, 1 June 1873, a camp of Assiniboine was virtually annihilated in the Battle Creek valley in the Cypress Hills of southwest Saskatchewan, a few kilometres north of the international boundary. Although the Cypress Hills Massacre was not the reason for the creation of the North West Mounted Police, the event hurried their despatch to the West.

Along the banks of the Teton River near Benton, Montana, a group of wolfers had their horses stolen by a raiding party of Plains Cree. Incensed, the wolfers followed their tracks but lost the trail in the Cypress Hills. Tired and angry, the wolfers arrived at the trading posts of Moses Solomon and Abel Farwell along Battle Creek to rest, complain, and drink. Solomon was a veteran Montana whisky trader before he established his small post across the Creek from Farwell's in 1872. Records of the T. C. Power Bro. and Company, wholesalers and distillers, show that Solomon had been buying from that company since 1867 and that his main purchases for the Indian trade were "Red Jacket Bitters" and "Shawban" whisky."[18] Abel Farwell was thirty-five years old in 1873 and was originally from Fort Peck, Montana. He was married *à la façon du pays* to Big Mary, a Crow woman.[19] Farwell had established his post in the Cypress Hills in 1871, but not before eliminating the Indian trade of John Kerler of Winnipeg, who had established a post just south of the Canadian border. Farwell reported Kerler to the United States authorities, who arrested him and ended his trading operations. Farwell was complimented for his "good citizenship," whereas in fact he had neatly eliminated the competition and continued to operate his own post with similar trade goods.[20] The T. C. Power Company orderbooks show that on 28 August and 18 October 1872, Farwell bought his winter stock of Indian trade goods and that in addition to beads, blankets, and other common trade items, he also purchased nearly $100.00 of strychnine (for wolfing); and considerable quantities of Bitters, Vinegar, and "Shawban" whisky worth almost $300.00. Farwell denied at the Winnipeg Trial in June 1876 that he was wolfing or selling whisky, but the Power accounts indicate otherwise. Also, Farwell meekly confessed that he had bought out the whisky stock of trader William Rowe, but only "to keep him out of the business."[21]

While resting at the trading posts, the Benton wolfers were told that the local Indians were taking shots at the windows of Solomon's post and making regular threats to kill the white occupants.[22] These annoyances were accentuated by the loud complaint of George Hammond, a Farwell employee, that the Assiniboine had stolen his horse. Consisting of about forty lodges under Little Soldier, the Indians were camped just south of Solomon's post. The previous winter had been bitterly cold for these Indians on the barren prairie lands, and they had survived only by trekking south to the Cypress Hills. In an effort to prevent starvation, they had eaten most of their horses and had been reduced to boiling buffalo hides to make soup. Tired and edgy, they used their few remaining skins and robes to purchase whisky and commenced to drink heavily.[23]

While the Indians revelled, Hammond persuaded the Benton group, as well as some from Solomon's post, to assist him in recovering the missing horse, which was apparently casually grazing on a nearby hill, and harassing the Indians. The wolfers, about sixteen in number, approached the Assiniboine camp, but stopped at a breast-high coulee which commanded a clear, yet protected view of the Indians. These veterans, hardened frontiersmen, shared the common Montana attitude that killing Indians was justified. Many were ex-soldiers, either from the Civil War or from countless frontier skirmishes. They included Thomas W. Hardwick, aged twenty-nine, who was considered somewhat of a hero in Montana, for he had led a party of wolfers in an unprovoked attack on the Assiniboine in April 1872 that became known as the Sweetgrass Hills Massacre. This "victory" was joyfully detailed in the *Helena Weekly Herald*, although Hardwick's account differs markedly from that of A. J. Simmons, Indian agent for the Upper Milk River country, who characterized Hardwick and his group as "lawless desperadoes" who "kill and destroy game and poison the carcasses for wolf-baits." The initial account by Hardwick was that the fight was provoked by a Blackfoot raiding party. Later, however, after Simmons had inspected the Indian clothing on the field, it was discovered that they were friendly Assiniboine, attached to a nearby agency, and that Hardwick and the wolfers had fired without warning.[24] Of particular importance was that the Sweetgrass Massacre, like the Marias Massacre and the other atrocities, had produced no arrests or convictions.

Also among the Benton and Solomon groups was the black-bearded James Hughes and Philander Vogle, who was recovering from a crippling case of frostbite to his feet. George M. Bell, an ex-soldier of the 13th Infantry, which had been stationed at Fort Shaw, was Solomon's trading partner. These were the only three participants in the massacre to stand trial at the June Assizes in Winnipeg in 1876. In addition, the group included Canadian wolfers George Hammond, Elijah Jefferson Devereaux, S. Vincent, and Ed Le Grace, the only white fatality at the Cypress Hills Massacre; all of these men were either Canadian Metis or French Canadian.[25] Others known to have participated in the massacre are: John Mac-Farlane, a hunter just arrived from the plains whom Farwell identified as having killed two Indian women during the massacre with "an American needle-gun;"[26] Trevanion Hale, a thirty-two-year-old Iowan; and John Evans, C. Harper, C. Smith, J. Duval, J. Marshall, J. Lange, Xavier Faillon, and Moses Solomon.[27]

In a desperate bid to avert bloodshed, Abel Farwell quickly entered the now alarmed Assiniboine camp and assumed the role of peaceful mediator. He began to explain the situation about the stolen horse to the Indians, but in order to prevent any misunderstanding, he decided to seek out his interpreter, Alexis Le Bombard. As Farwell departed, firing began either from the coulee or from the Indian camp and soon became general. Years later, Eashappie, who was a twelve-year-old boy at the time of the massacre, recalled that in the Assiniboine camp "whiskey flowed like water . . . and by mid-day the tribesmen were all hopelessly drunk."[28] Eashappie's father lay in a stupor inside the tent, and every artifice, including herbs, failed to revive him. Into this defenceless Assiniboine camp the Benton and

Solomon groups poured a murderous fire. Another Indian survivor, "The Man who took the Coat," later recounted how the "Americans" killed an old man in the camp and then proceeded to "take up a pole and run it through him from his backside to his head," and left him dangling as a grisly trophy or reminder.[29] A-pas-teen-in-cha-co, the mother-in-law of Little Soldier, stated that when the shooting started she "was asleep, drunk." When she awakened she heard Little Soldier scolding the attackers: "White men, you will know what you have done today. You never knew a Woody mountain Assineboine [sic] Indian to harm a white man." At that moment he was shot through the heart.[30] "The woman who eats grizzly bear," the wife of Little Soldier, recounted that she was inside her lodge when the firing started. The Whites pulled up the pins and collapsed the tent. She clung to her husband until he was killed, but she was then dragged away to Solomon's post by a white man who "remained with me all night and had connection with me many times . . . he told me I would not live till morning."[31]

The fighting lasted until the late afternoon, when the death of Ed Le Grace, "a Canadian of great bravery," sobered the Whites. They returned to Solomon's where they remained until the next morning.[32] The Assiniboine survivors fled into the nearby woods and were eventually sheltered by a camp of friendly and sympathetic Plains Cree. Big Mary boldly went to Solomon's in the morning and successfully argued for the release of four captive Assiniboine women.[33] The next day Farwell and Solomon packed up their goods, burned their small posts, and departed the Cypress Hills — they never returned. The Benton group quickly divided; some returned immediately to Montana, while others travelled west directly into Whoop-Up country to continue the futile search for their stolen horses.

News of the fight with the Assiniboine soon reached Benton, where the story was circulated in the saloons. The first published report appeared on 11 June in the *Helena Daily Herald* under the headline:

> Indians on the Horse Steal. Whites on the War Path. Forty Lodges wiped out by sixteen Kit Carsons. Ed Grace shot through the heart and buried at Cypress Mountain.

The *Herald* recounted how the heroic and noble frontiersmen "effectively wiped out the forty lodges" and taught the Indians a costly but necessary lesson.[34] Fort Peck Indian agent, A. J. Simmons, heard a very different version of the affair from Abel Farwell and, already concerned at the lack of action taken after the Sweet-grass Hills Massacre of a year before, wrote a stinging account of the tragedy to his superiors. These wolfers and whisky traders, he stated, had attacked "a camp of 40 lodges of peaceful Assiniboines attached to this agency, who were almost entirely defenceless, and killed 16 of their number, men, women, children, and mutilated their bodies in a most outrageous and disgusting manner."[35] From the

Crow Agency, Indian agent Felix R. Bonnot wrote to Washington giving the facts regarding the murder of the Assiniboine and added that in his opinion the general reputation of Hardwick and Evans "is that of horse thieves and traders in whiskey to Indians, and that the party was made up of persons of the worst class in the country."[36] By the middle of August all the reports had been forwarded to Hamilton Fish, the American secretary of state. As the affair had taken place in "British Territory," Fish sent the entire file over to Sir Edward Thornton, the British minister to Washington, hoping that the entire matter would be drawn to the attention of the "Canadian authorities for such action in the premises as they may see fit to take."[37]

The dossier from Thornton on the Cypress Hills Massacre, as well as a worried report from Alexander Morris, lieutenant-governor of Manitoba and the Northwest Territories, and a detailed statement by Edward McKay, "a loyal British subject and a friend of the Indians," reached Ottawa in early September 1873. In his letter, Morris warned the dominion government that it would "soon find itself involved in Indian difficulties of the gravest character" unless an immediate enquiry and severe action were taken to ensure no repetition.[38] Of even greater interest was the statement of McKay, a hunter who wrote on behalf of the Plains Cree, Assiniboine, and Saulteaux. McKay stated that a band of Plains Cree had stolen the horses of the Benton group, but that these Whites had taken their revenge on the Assiniboine after making them drunk. The Whites had killed twenty-two men, women, and children besides burning all their effects. McKay wished to know if "nothing can be done to put law in force [in the region]." More important, the Indians were very uneasy "in consequence of this affair," and they were "anxious to know whether the Government intends to take away their land without paying them for it, as they fear."[39] Later in September another report on the massacre was received in Ottawa in the form of an affidavit by Narcisse Lacerte, a Metis hunter from St. Norbert, Manitoba. Lacerte was at the Cypress Hills site five days after the massacre; he also told a story of an unprovoked attack by the Americans on drunken Indians.[40]

The implications of the Cypress Hills Massacre alluded to by Morris, McKay, and others and the resultant Winnipeg trial were a watershed in the history of the Canadian West. The federal government had successfully negotiated Treaties 1 and 2 in 1871 with the Chippewa (Ojibwa) and Swampy Cree in the Red River-Lake Manitoba region. But in the Saskatchewan District the warlike and more numerous Blackfoot Confederacy, Sarcee, Plains Cree, Assiniboine, and Saulteaux would provide much more serious and expensive difficulties unless a quick and severe example was made of the white participants at Cypress Hills. The government of Canada was anxious to expand and settle in the northwest Prairies. Yet Alexander Morris knew that the magnitude of the task of preserving order, suppressing crime, creating the institutions of civilization, and maintaining "peaceful relations with the fierce tribes of the vast plains beyond Manitoba" was not fully appreciated by the government and people of Canada.[41] The financial burden of building the Pacific railway and the woefully inadequate military force in the northwest meant that the delicate and sensitive question of treaty and aboriginal rights, indeed the whole question of land title, would have to be settled economically and peacefully.

The plains tribes of the Canadian West were most suspicious of white settlement, and Ottawa recognized the need to make a symbolic example of the Cypress Hills tragedy through a well-publicized trial which would show the tribes that Canadian justice was honourable and racially equitable. There must be no repetition of the Cypress Hills Massacre, and there must be a total rejection of the policy of violence, bloodshed, and broken treaties which had characterized American-Indian relations. The Winnipeg Trial was thus to be a positive indication to the Canadian plains tribes that Indians were to receive the same protection as the Whites. The trial clearly combined humanitarian ideals with practical self-interest.

The Canadian government therefore undertook to apprehend the perpetrators and bring them to trial. An enquiry was launched in Winnipeg by Gilbert McMicken, the dominion police commissioner and a political adviser to Macdonald and Morris. The difficulty of travel to Montana in the winter forced the affair to languish until the summer of 1874, when McMicken's orders were cancelled and the investigation was taken over by the North West Mounted Police, who had just completed their epic trek across the Prairies.[42] Not until the late spring of 1875 were the police able to take action on the information in their possession. Police officers A. G. Irvine and James F. Macleod travelled to Benton, Montana, with warrants for the arrest of most of the members of the Benton and Solomon parties. Officials in Washington had instructed Governor Benjamin F. Potts of Montana Territory to co-operate. Assisted by U.S. marshalls, Irvine and Macleod arrested seven of the wanted men on 21 June. Immediately, mob violence and public indignation erupted throughout Montana, and local sheriffs refused to co-operate with the Canadian police. In a bitter tirade the *Fort Benton Record* asserted that the "savage cut-throats and brutes" at Cypress Hills were taught a lesson like the one Baker had given the Peigan at the Marias in 1870. If Whites were to be punished for protecting themselves against Indians, warned the paper, renewed hostilities and depredations would soon erupt again.[43] The *Bozeman Times* argued that there was but one way to treat the "savages" and that was "to pursue and punish them according to their own method of warfare."[44]

The seven Benton men, who included Hardwick and Evans, were transferred to the slightly less hostile Helena for an extradition hearing before United States Commissioner W. E. Cullen, held on 7 July. William F. Sanders of the North West Mounted Police presented the Canadian case with a firm determination, denouncing the Benton men as "Belly River wolfers, outlaws, smugglers, cutthroats, horse thieves, and squaw-men."[45] The chief witness for the Canadians was Abel Farwell, who contradicted his testimony upon cross-examination by Mr. Shober and a horde of Montana lawyers who had been hired on behalf of the Benton men. In his evidence Farwell admitted that "he did not see any of the accused men kill an Indian," although he "saw one white man carrying around on a pole an Indian head." He could not determine which side had fired first.[46] A witness for the defence, John Jo, a Metis who worked for Farwell, testified that Farwell traded whisky, and the defence council trouped through a number of witnesses who implicated Farwell in selling whisky, engaging in sex scandals, cheating, and committing perjury.[47] George Powell and another defence witness called Doncan testified that Farwell had told them that "the Indians began the fight," but that "he fired the first shot."[48] Yet another defence witness, a Mr. Murray, damaged his testimony by stating that Farwell had said the Indians started the fight, but then he continued, I "never heard a man speak well of Farwell for the last two years."[49]

Commissioner W. E. Cullen gave his decision on the extradition on 29 July. Objectively and succinctly he reiterated the events leading up to the massacre in which the Whites foolishly menaced the Indians, who "with all their savage fierceness intensified by drink would require but little provocation to induce them to commence hostilities." If the defendants had gone to the Indian camp with the premeditated design of attacking and killing the Indians, then this act would constitute murder. But, reasoned Cullen, the prosecution was unable to establish this intent clearly. In addition, the testimony on both sides was conflicting and unsatisfactory. Cullen concluded that an impartial jury in Canada or the United States would undoubtedly have difficulty in finding the defendants guilty of the charge of murder, and he was therefore "constrained to discharge the defendants from further custody."[50]

The news of Cullen's decision was greeted with glee throughout Montana, embellished with bands, flags, and haranguing anti-British speeches. John Evans opened his own establishment, which became the financially profitable "Extradition Saloon." Farwell was physically threatened and treated with "silent contempt." His life in Montana eventually became so unpalatable that he moved to Canada where he gained employment as a mail carrier between Fort Mcleod and Benton for the North West Mounted Police.[57]

In the Canadian West the police doggedly continued their investigation, and in September 1875, Philander Vogle and James Hughes were arrested at Fort Macleod and George M. Bell in the Cypress Hills. Accompanied by A. G. Irvine, the three accused men were removed to Winnipeg to stand trial for the murder of Little Soldier. Irvine knew that "there was not an Indian in the Northwest who was not aware of the enterprize in which I was engaged." He echoed the thoughts of the Canadian government: "These arrests will do more to establish confidence in the government by the Indians than any quantity of presents, promises or pow-wowing."[52]

Vogle and Hughes received preliminary hearings at Fort Macleod, but Bell did not have his day until 15 September, after the three accused had arrived in

Winnipeg. All three were committed to stand trial for murder at the October Assizes. However, the trial was postponed until February, and it was finally held in June 1876, giving the esteemed and astute American consul in Winnipeg, James Wickes Taylor, time to gather laboriously all the evidence he could for the defence.

In frequent correspondence with Governor Potts and a number of members of the Benton group in Montana, Taylor became convinced that the Cypress Hills "massacre" was in reality no more than a "frontier fight" in which the Indians were as much to blame as the Whites. A severe setback for the defence resulted when key witnesses such as John Evans and Trevanion Hale, also under indictment for murder, were refused immunity from arrest in Canada if they came to testify.[53] Evans stated that he could prove the innocence of the three charged Montanans, but without safe passage he could not testify. Taylor was incensed at the Canadian attitude and expressed fears that the three Americans were to be sacrificed as a token to the new "friendly" Canadian Indian policy for the West. Taylor had to be content with collecting a number of depositions from various Metis and white eyewitnesses to the Cypress Hills affair.[54]

The testimonies of Trevanion Hale and John Evans, probably protecting themselves as much as the three accused, completely exonerated the defendants. Hale stated that Hughes had stayed near the fort and did not participate, Vogle was lame with frozen feet and scarcely able to walk, and Bell, the night watchman at Solomon's post, was asleep when the firing started.[55] Evans also affirmed that when they went to the Assiniboine camp, "the Indians fired several shots in the air, called us white dogs and repeatedly threatened to kill all of us." Although some of the Indians did not want to fight several "advanced toward us in a very hostile manner talking and yelling," and as the situation was "desperate," the Whites fought in self-defence. Yet Hughes was not in the coulee, and Bell and Vogle were at Solomon's and did not participate.[56]

Under Francis Cornish the prosecution was also busy collecting evidence and statements. In addition to Farwell, Big Mary, and Le Bombard, the Crown collected the statements of five Assiniboine survivors, who gave their accounts orally to A. G. Irvine, who copied the statements and forwarded them to Winnipeg.[57] After "a great deal of trouble," a jury of twelve white, English-speaking males from the Winnipeg area was chosen; some were recent arrivals from Ontario.[58] On 19 June 1876, the Winnipeg Trial, which became a microcosm of the divergent Canadian and American attitudes towards the native people of the West, finally began, with His Lordship Chief Justice Wood presiding.

On the first morning of the trial the case was formally opened for the Crown by the calling of the key prosecution witness, Abel Farwell. According to Farwell, George Hammond initiated the events which led to the massacre by insisting that the Assiniboine had stolen his horse and by suggesting to the recently arrived and angry Benton group that they should "go and clean out the camp." At this critical juncture Farwell went to the Assiniboine camp to act as a peaceful mediator and to seek an explanation. The chief informed Farwell that Hammond's horse "is on the hill back of your fort with two other horses." While this parlaying was in session, the Whites had advanced to the coulee overlooking the Indian camp. The menacing position of the Whites made the Indians increasingly agitated, and in a last effort to avert violence Farwell went to the coulee to explain the situation to the Whites. Thomas Hardwick was annoyed and shouted at Farwell that "if you had come out [of the camp] when we first told you, we would have had a good shot." Farwell pleaded with the Whites to wait until he fetched Le Bombard to confirm his story, as they did not believe that Farwell was sufficiently bilingual to understand the Souian dialect. They promised to wait, but as Farwell started toward his fort, George Hammond fired at the camp, and the shooting became general.[59]

The details of the massacre were then carefully outlined by Farwell. He saw S. Vincent shoot Little Soldier and later noticed that the chief's head "was cut off and stuck on a lodge pole." The bodies of women and children, as well as men, were scattered about the camp and in the timber beyond. In regard to the three accused, when the firing started, "Hughes was in the coulee; Bell and Vogle were near it; I saw Hughes shooting in the direction of the camp." The Solomon party, which included Bell and Vogle, was also shooting into the camp. Upon the completion of Farwell's examination by the Crown, Mr. Biggs for the defence attempted a vigorous cross-examination, but Farwell was unshakable except for one moment of doubt when he was not sure "if any arrows were fired by the Indians" before Hammond commenced firing. The cross-examination continued the next morning but nothing of importance was extracted. Thus ended the Farwell examination, and Messrs. Cornish, Walker and Crown could not help but be pleased.[60]

However, by mid-morning on 20 June, the case began to turn against the prosecution when Alexis Le Bombard surprisingly contradicted the Farwell account. Le Bombard confirmed that Hammond's horse was indeed not in the Assiniboine camp, but safely among a herd near Farwell's post. Then Le Bombard rocked the courtroom and Farwell's veracity when he testified that he saw:

> Farwell in the Indian camp, surrounded by Indians, and seeming as if trying to make himself understood; I knew from my relations with Farwell and the Indians that he could not understand them, and that there was none in the Assiniboine camp who understand any English, except a few words about trade.[61]

Whether Farwell could or could not speak the Indian language was not important. Eashappie, when interviewed years later recalled that both Solomon and Farwell "could speak the Assiniboine tongue, not fluently, but well enough to carry on their wicked trade."[62] What was vital to a jury which was not unsympathetic to the prisoners was that Farwell might have perjured himself in other aspects of his story, which stood uncorroborated and apparently contradicted. Le Bombard concluded by stating that he did not notice Vogle and Bell participating in the fight, although Vogle had seemingly recovered from his frozen feet ordeal because "when the fight took place; he could walk very well." Le Bombard's final remark was that "for all I know to the contrary the Indians may have fired first."[63]

The second day of the trial ended with the examination of Big Mary, Farwell's wife. She contributed little because, as she readily admitted, "I was so frightened that I did not look much." She did not see Vogle, Bell, or Hughes on the day of the massacre. Various details of the position of dead Indians were outlined, and she pointed out that Farwell was on reasonably good terms with the Assiniboine, as opposed to Solomon's bad relations with them.[64] Following Big Mary's testimony, the court adjourned until 21 June. For Cornish and the prosecution, the day had been discouraging.

On the third and final day Cornish rested the Crown's case. Biggs opened the defence by calling George M. Bell, who was examined on behalf of Vogle and Hughes. When the fight started, Bell stated, he was in one of the bastions of Fort Solomon and was looking out of the port-hole, "when I saw the Indians stripping to fight." Vogle was in the Indian trading room, noted Bell, when the firing commenced. During the afternoon, while the massacre was in progress, Bell saw Vogle in the kitchen and "off and on during the rest of the day." Bell could not swear positively that "Vogle was in the fort all the time, but I saw him in the kitchen and Indian room and I know the gate was locked." As for Hughes, Bell "did not see him with the men in the coulee."

Prosecutor Cornish, in a valiant effort to rally the case for the prosecution, vigorously cross-examined Bell on his whereabouts and those of Vogle during the massacre, but was unable to shake his testimony.

The next defence witness, Philander Vogle, stated that when the fight started, Bell was in the bastion and never left the fort.[65] The two prisoners from Solomon's party thus neatly covered for each other, stating that neither left the fort during the whole affair. Hughes was not called. His defence rested on the assertion by Bell that he was not among the Benton men in the coulee, an assertion which was substantiated by the written affidavits of Trevanion Hale and John Evans.

Biggs next called three Metis who had been brought to Winnipeg by the Crown as prosecution witnesses. Joseph Vital Turcotte testified that two days before the battle he overheard an Indian say: "It is a pity you half-breeds are here now, for we have determined to clean out the whites and take all their stock." The defence next called Baptiste Champagne, who explained to the court that his "memory was very defective" since he received a violent blow on the head two years ago. Nonetheless, he stated that the Indians had fired first. A final Metis witness also testified for the defence. Joseph Laverdure stated that an Indian told him "as soon as those Americans come out we intend to attack them and take what they have." Laverdure further testified that he saw the beginning of the fight and that the

"Assiniboine fired at random, giving out cries of contempt and provocation." These three Metis witnesses added considerable strength to the defence case by providing clear, and seemingly unbiased, evidence which showed that the Assiniboine had intended two days before the arrival of the well-armed Benton group to the Cypress Hills to slaughter the white traders, at least those at Solomon's post.[66]

A final and well-known witness for the defence was the Honourable James McKay, a Scottish half-breed who had provided invaluable service to the Canadian government during the Indian treaty negotiations in Manitoba in 1871. McKay clearly possessed some personal vendetta against the Assiniboine, and particularly against Little Soldier, whom he had known in the past. McKay testified that:

> from what I know of the Assiniboine Indians I have no hesitation in saying that they would rob, pillage and murder if they had the opportunity; this is the general character of the Assiniboines, more particularly of the camp of Little Soldier.[67]

Although the bitter remarks of McKay, "given with fervor," were immediately ordered struck from the record by a furious Chief Justice Wood, the evidence presented by the defence was overwhelming. McKay's outburst, the testimonies of the three Metis and of Bell and Vogle, Le Bombard's revelation of Farwell's lack of linguistic ability, and an impassioned address to the jury by Mr. Biggs resulted in a verdict of not guilty. Indeed, the jury had retired for only a short time before they returned with the foreman remarking that "the jury thought it unsafe to convict for want of sufficient evidence of actual participation by the parties under trial."[68]

A disappointed Francis Cornish wrote a detailed report of the trial to the minister of justice in Ottawa. The three prisoners were charged with the murder of Little Soldier, Cornish explained, and he had impressed upon the jury the fact that it was not necessary to prove that any of the three had killed the chief, but merely that they had acted in criminal concert with the Benton and Solomon groups and that the killing constituted murder. This, of course, the jury refused to do. As for the Metis, Cornish was convinced that they were "being tampered with" by Taylor and the defence. Also surprising to Cornish was the considerable amount of sympathy for the prisoners generally, since they were not key participants in the affair like Hardwick and Evans. Indeed, the interest and feeling on their behalf "was not confined to any particular class, and did not appear to proceed from a belief that the prisoners were not participants, but that the attack was justifiable." Finally, Vogle, Bell, and Hughes were arraigned on three indictments but were brought to trial only for the murder of Little Soldier. However, Wood discharged them on their own recognizance to appear when summoned.[69] The three quickly left the province and never returned. The Cypress Hills affair was not finally ended until 1882, when writs of *nolle prosequi* were issued and the case was legally closed.

The Winnipeg Trial of June 1876 was unquestionably significant in the development and settlement of the Canadian West. Though it resulted in no convictions, it produced a profound effect, not so much on the American western frontier but rather on the minds of the northern Plains Indians of Canada and the United States, who came to believe that a genuine attempt was being made by the Queen's government in Ottawa to establish a just and racially equitable system of law, order, and authority. This belief inspired a confidence among the Canadian tribes; Treaty 6 (1876) and Treaty 7 (1877) were peacefully negotiated with the Plains Cree and Blackfoot Confederacy. Even the irascible Sioux felt that native rights would be guaranteed north of the "medicine line," providing they obeyed the Queen's laws. This feeling contrasted sharply with the continued violent confrontations between Indians and Whites in Montana and the western states. The relatively peaceful settlement of the Canadian Prairies, uncomplicated by costly Indian wars, attests in large measure to the effects of the Winnipeg Trial on the Indian mind.[70] Indeed, events in June 1876 clearly illustrated the conflicting attitudes which had evolved in Canada and the United States toward native people. At almost the same time as white men were on trial for murdering Indians in Winnipeg, in the valley of the Little Big Horn in Montana, Sioux and Cheyenne warriors were in the process of annihilating George Armstrong Custer and the American Seventh cavalry.

NOTES

1. In particular, see editorial comments in the *Fort Benton Record, Helena Daily Herald, Helena Weekly Herald*, and *Bozeman Times*, 1872–76.
2. These incidents are chronicled in Report 18, Cypress Hills Massacre (Ottawa, n.d.) and John C. Ewers, *The Blackfeet: Raiders of the Northwestern Plains* (Norman, 1958), esp. pp. 238–40.
3. *Montana Post*, 9 June 1866.
4. Report 18, Massacre; and Bradley Papers, Montana Historical Society, Helena, vol. 9 (1923), pp. 251–54.
5. For a lengthy, detailed, and biased account of the 1869 campaign, see William F. Wheeler, "The Peigan War of 1869–70," *Helena Daily Herald*, 1 January 1880.
6. Ewers, p. 249.
7. Ibid., pp. 250–2; Ralph K. Audrist, *The Long Death: The Last Days of the Plains Indian* (New York, 1964), p. 171; and Report 18.
8. *New York Times*, 24 February 1870.
9. *Helena Daily Herald*, 1 January 1880. Although it was true that the Blackfeet tribes never raided in force again, horse-stealing, threats, and violence on a small scale was still common in Montana throughout the 1870's, particularly by Peigan and Blackfoot bands. For a lively and bawdy accounting of these times, see the reminiscences of Andrew Garcia, *Tough Trip Through Paradise*, ed. B. H. Slein (New York, 1967).
10. *Helena Daily Herald*, 12 February 1872.
11. Ibid., March 1972.
12. See Paul Sharp, *Whoop-up Country* (Minneapolis, 1955).

13. PAC, MG11, CO42, vol. 698. *Report* on the North West Territories, 10 March 1871, by William Butler. See also Sir William Francis Butler, *The Great Lone Land* (Toronto, 1919).
14. PAC, MG11, CO42, vol. 715. *Report* on the North West Provinces and Territories, 17 March 1873, by Patrick Robertson-Ross.
15. Ibid., and Robertson-Ross, "Report of a Reconnaissance of the North-West Provinces and Indian Territories of the Dominion of Canada," *Journal of the Royal United Service Institution* 17, no. 74 (1873): 563.
16. Robertson-Ross, *1873 Report*, p. 565.
17. See S. W. Horrall, "Sir John A. Macdonald and the Mounted Police Force for the Northwest Territories," *CHR* 53 (1972): 179–200.
18. See T. C. Power Papers (Helena). Moses Solomon, Petty Ledger Books 1867–68, and no. D 1872–74; also Orderbooks, 1872–74.
19. *The Winnipeg Trial*, taken from *The Standard* (Winnipeg), 19 June 1876. Testimony of Abel Farwell.
20. See *Helena Daily Herald*, 15 November 1871; and *Sun River Sun*, 22 January 1885, in Hugh A. Dempsey Papers, Glenbow Archives.
21. Power Papers, Orderbook 3 (1872–73), purchases by Abel Farwell; and *Winnipeg Trial*, 20 June 1876, testimony of Abel Farwell.
22. PAC, MG27, H2, James Wickes Taylor Papers. Deposition of Trevanion Hale, 15 December 1875.
23. Report 18, Massacre; and Dan Kennedy (Ochankugahe), *Recollections of an Assiniboine Chief* (Toronto, 1972), pp. 42–45.
24. *Helena Weekly Herald*, 9 May 1872, provides details on the Sweetgrass Hills Massacre, and Simmons's reaction.
25. *Winnipeg Trial*, 20 June 1876. Examination of Alexis Le Bombard, Farwell's interpreter — "I spoke to Hammond in French; he speaks better French than I do; I think he is a French Canadian."
26. Ibid., 19 June 1876. Farwell testimony.
27. *Winnipeg Trial*, 19 June 1876, Farwell testimony. P. B. Waite, *Canada, 1874–1896: Arduous Destiny* (Toronto, 1971), p. 11, realistically and succinctly summarizes the wolfers and traders, both American and Canadian, by pointing out that they were tough-minded and that among them were probably some desperadoes, but that they did business in the fastest, most efficient and most ruthless frontier fashion; they traded whisky for skins.
28. Kennedy, p. 45; and Report 18, Massacre. The recollections of Eashappie and Ochankugahe (D. Kennedy) were taken by the R.C.M.P. historian John Peter Turner during a visit to the Assiniboine reserve at Sintaluta in the summer of 1940 at the time of the annual Sun Dance.
29. PAM, Alexander Morris Papers, file 1177. Statement of "The Man who took the Coat," Fort Walsh, Cypress Mountains, 20 December 1875.
30. Ibid., Statement of A-pas-teen-in-cha-co, 20 December 1875.
31. Ibid., Statement "The woman who eats grizzly bear," 20 December 1875.
32. The intricate details and movements regarding the Cypress Hills Massacre and the various interpretations subsequently put forward by a host of scholars and historians have been analysed effectively by Philip Goldring, "The Cypress Hills Massacre — A Century's Retrospect," *Saskatchewan History* 26 (Autumn 1973): 81–102.
33. *Winnipeg Trial*, 20 June 1876. Testimony of Mary Farwell.
34. Ibid., and Sharp, *Whoop-Up Country*, p. 66.
35. PAC, MG27, C8, Alexander Morris Papers, Simmons to Fort Peck, 12 July 1873.
36. Report 15, Extracts from the Department of Justice Files (Ottawa, n.d.), Felix Bonnot to Department of the Interior (Washington), Crow Agency, 5 August 1873.
37. Ibid., Hamilton Fish to Sir Edward Thornton, Washington, 15 August 1873.
38. PAC, MG27, C8, Alexander Morris Papers, A. Morris to minister of the interior, Fort Garry, 20 August 1873.
39. PAM, Morris Papers, file 1945, Edward McKay to A. Morris and the North-West Council, 24 August 1873.
40. Ibid., file 1947, affidavit of Narcisse Lacerte, Winnipeg, 8 September 1873. See also, ibid., file 1950, Deposition of John Wells, Fort Garry, March 1874. Wells was also a plains hunter, but his story proved biased and inaccurate. He maintained that Farwell had come to his camp after the massacre to hire carts to take his goods to Benton, and that Farwell had said "that the assiniboines

had commenced the affair." Also, stated Wells, Farwell told him that "they had killed twenty-six Indians."

41. PAC, MG27, C8, Morris Papers, A. Morris to minister of the interior, Fort Garry, 4 December 1873; see also: Waite, p. 11.

42. PAC, MG26, A1, Sir John A. Macdonald Papers, vol. 246 (Gilbert McMicken); see also Sharp, p. 68; and John Peter Turner, *The North West Mounted Police*, 2 vols. (Ottawa, 1950), 1:84–85, 101–2.

43. *Fort Benton Record*, 26 June 1875.

44. *Bozeman Times*, 6 July 1875.

45. See Sharp, pp. 77, 69–73.

46. *Helena Weekly Herald*, 8 and 15 July 1875. Various Montana newspapers were incensed that Farwell attempted to implicate persons who were not on trial, and some of whom were in their grave. This reference refers most notably to Moses Solomon, who, living recklessly to the end, died following an "altercation with S. J. Perkins" (*Fort Benton Record*, 1 March 1875).

47. See especially, *Helena Daily Independent*, 16 July 1875; and *Helena Daily Herald*, 17 and 22 July 1875.

48. *Helena Weekly Herald*, 22 July 1875.

49. *Helena Daily Herald*, 17 July 1875.

50. *Helena Weekly Herald*, 29 July 1875, Cullen Decision.

51. *Fort Benton Record*, 7 August 1875; and Sharp, pp. 72–73; see John Clarke Papers, Glenbow-Alberta Institute. The strain of the Cypress Hills Massacre, and the Helena and Winnipeg Trials had a telling effect upon Farwell, and he died in 1886 at Clark's Ford, Montana from "a congestion of the brain, the result of chronic alcoholism." *The River Press* (Benton), 19 May 1886, concluded his obituary with: "Abel Farwell leaves no friends in Montana, where he was well, but unfavourably known. It was through his lying representations and turning state's evidence that caused the arrest of a number of reputable citizens of Fort Benton for alleged complicity in the so-called Cypress Hills Massacre." During the Helena Trial, "Farwell made himself famous by his lying statement to secure the conviction of his former friends."

52. *Manitoba Free Press*, 18 September 1875.

53. Report 15, John Evans to B. F. Potts, governor of Montana, n.d. (probably late 1875).

54. PAC, MG27, H2, James Wickes Taylor Papers, depositions of Louis Bellegarde, Laula Doney, and François Desgarlot, 15 December 1875; these three, Metis from Red River, gave little evidence that implicated the accused, and Doney asserted that the Indians told him that "they had come to clean out the whites."

55. Ibid., deposition of Trevanion Hale, 15 December 1875.

56. Ibid., deposition of John Evans, 20 December 1875.

57. PAM, Morris Papers, file 1177, statements of Mis-ko-ta-ki-ko-ti-na ("the man who took the coat"), Kees-ka-san (Cutter), The Sitting Blue Horn, A-pas-tun-in-cha-co (an Indian woman), and Wa-ki-us-ke-mo ("the woman who eats grizzly bear"), Fort Walsh, Cypress Mountains, 20 December 1875.

58. Report 15.

59. Winnipeg Trial, 19 June 1876, examination of Abel Farwell.

60. Ibid., 19 and 20 June 1876, examination and cross-examination of Abel Farwell.

61. Ibid., 20 June 1876, examination of Alexis Le Bombard.

62. Kennedy, p. 42.

63. Winnipeg Trial, 20 June 1876, examination of Alexis Le Bombard.

64. Ibid., 20 June 1876, examination of Mary Farwell (Big Mary).

65. Ibid., 21 June 1876, examination of Philander Vogle.

66. Ibid., 21 June 1876, examination of Joseph Vital Turcotte, Baptiste Champagne, and Joseph Laverdure. Paul Sharp, p. 76, contends that these Metis visited a priest before they appeared at the trial and were cautioned to tell the truth under their sacred oath, and as a result testified for the defence, rather than the Crown. This claim is unsubstantiated.

67. Ibid., 21 June 1876, examination of the Honourable James McKay. Isaac Cowie, *The Company of Adventurers* (Toronto, 1913), was also familiar with the Assiniboine and traded east of the Cypress Hills in the early 1870's as a representative of the HBC. Like McKay, Cowie had an aversion for the Assiniboine and indicated that they were renowned horse thieves. Cowie maintains that the affair at

Cypress Hills was begun by the Assiniboine, who received the "white demands with contempt, mockery, and signs of challenge toward the post." But "the effect of this bloody lesson on the natives of what a few whites could do was far reaching," pp. 259, 452–53. For a more positive side to the Assiniboine, see, Kennedy, esp., p. 47.

68. Report 15, Cornish to minister of justice, June 1876.
69. Ibid.
70. The North West Rebellion of 1885, which was inspired by the Metis and Louis Riel but which included the Frog Lake Massacre by Wandering Spirit and Big Bear's band of Plain Cree, and the Almighty Voice affair of 1896 were two notable and rare exceptions to the peaceful settlement of the Canadian West.

4

Louis Riel and Aboriginal Rights[1]

Thomas Flanagan

The central theme of native politics in Canada is the affirmation of aboriginal rights. The government's attempt in the White Paper of 1969 to end recognition of such rights only strengthened native people's adherence to them.[2] The issue is of great practical importance, as most of Canada's land mass has never been formally ceded by native peoples through treaty or other agreement. Only Ontario and the three prairie provinces, and perhaps part of the Northwest Territories, have been surrendered in this way. In all other provinces and territories, native spokesmen claim that aboriginal title still exists.

Negotiations over aboriginal rights, or "comprehensive claims" as the government of Canada prefers to call them,[3] have not progressed quickly. A major reason is that native spokesmen often do not accept the underlying theory of aboriginal rights, which has been developed in the decisions of Canadian and British courts and which now structures the government's negotiating proposals. This difference of outlook is not new. As far back as the historical record provides information, native leaders have operated on premises about their rights which diverge from official opinions. This chapter focuses on the views of Canada's most famous native leader, Louis Riel. An exposition of how he saw aboriginal rights will help tell the story of what native people have thought about this question.

The working title of this chapter, "Louis Riel's Theory of Aboriginal Rights," was based on the misconception that Riel had such a theory. He did not. As Jean Morisset has shown, the concept of "aboriginal people," with its limited sphere of "aboriginal rights," is something projected onto Canada's native peoples from the outside.[4] Aboriginal status carries with it a network of assumptions in British and Canadian jurisprudence: that the colonizing power could unilaterally establish its sovereignty without consulting the people who already lived there; that their consent was not required because they were not civilized; that sovereignty carried with it underlying title to land; that aboriginal title was the right to subsist on the land but not the full ownership of it. Riel accepted none of those paternalistic assumptions. He developed a theory of the rights of Indians and Metis as nations existing alongside the English, French, or Spanish under the law of nations (*droit des gens*). The rights of Indians or Metis were not qualitatively different from the rights of other nations. Indians and Metis were aboriginal peoples in the descriptive sense of being prior inhabitants of the land, but their rights to the land were not legally affected by this fact. Aboriginality was for Riel a historical description but not a separate legal status.

Riel's theory can only be appreciated against the background of the events of 1869–70 and their aftermath, which he interpreted quite differently than official circles in Ottawa or London. The "official view" of aboriginal rights was not articulated until the *St. Catherine's Milling Case*, decided in 1889. The theory of aboriginal rights developed in this case was implicit in the practice of the previous decades, including the acquisition of Rupert's Land by Canada and subsequent dealings with Indians and half-breeds in that territory. Hence the official view, here contrasted with Riel's, was not yet fully worked out in Riel's day. Naturally, there is room for debate over the exact contours of an implicit, unarticulated view.

To the rulers of Britain and Canada as well as to the proprietors of the Hudson's Bay Company, the acquisition by Canada of Rupert's Land and the Northwestern Territory was a complicated real estate conveyance. In return for compensation from Canada, the company surrendered its land to the Crown, which in turn passed it to Canada by act of Parliament and royal proclamation. The whole transaction was founded on the property rights conferred on the company by the royal charter of 1670:

> the sole trade and commerce of all those seas, straights, bays, rivers, creeks and sounds in whatsoever latitude they shall be that lie within the entrance of the straights commonly called Hudson's Straights together with all the lands and territories upon the countries, coasts, and confines of the seas, bays, lakes, rivers, creeks, and sounds aforesaid that are not already actually possessed by or granted to any of our subjects or possessed by the subjects of any other Christian prince or state.[5]

It is true that Canada had accepted the company's ownership rights only reluctantly and after years of protest, putting forward the alternative theory that most of Rupert's Land ought to belong to Canada because of the explorations undertaken from New France.[6] But the Colonial Office refused any measures that might diminish the company's rights, and in the end the sale went through on the assumption that the company was the rightful owner of this immense territory.

When the Metis of Red River, who had never been consulted about the sale, showed signs of resistance, the Canadian government refused to take possession, much as a purchaser might refuse to take possession of a house which had undergone damage in the period between signing of contract and date of transfer. The imperial government doubted the legality of Canada's position but did not force the issue. Canada invited the inhabitants of Red River to send a delegation to Ottawa to make their concerns known. Having discussed matters with Riel's delegates, Father Ritchot, Alfred Scott, and John Black, the Canadian government drafted the Manitoba Act to respond to the desires of Red River: provincial status, responsible government, official bilingualism, and protection of customary land rights among others. Importantly, the Manitoba Act was a unilateral action of the Canadian Parliament, not a treaty between independent partners (although it was probably *ultra vires* of the Canadian Parliament and had later to be confirmed by imperial statute).[7] Payment for Rupert's Land was made in London after the company delivered the deed of surrender to the Colonial Office; and the imperial government, by order-in-council of 23 June 1870, annexed Rupert's Land to Canada, effective 15 July 1870.

It was always assumed by both governments that aboriginal rights of the Indians would be respected. Indeed, section 14 of the order-in-council specified that "any claims of Indians to compensation for lands required for purposes of settlement shall be disposed of by the Canadian Government in communication with the Imperial Government."[8] The Metis were not explicitly mentioned, but the Canadian government had already recognized their aboriginal status in the Manitoba Act.

Aboriginal title was not seen as sovereignty in the European sense. Only a state could claim sovereignty, and the North American natives had never been organized as states and therefore could not possess the validity of claims to sovereignty made by European states on the basis of discovery, settlement, and conquest. Nor was aboriginal title understood as ownership in fee simple, for the nomadic tribes of North America had never marked off plots of land in a way compatible with European notions of private property. Aboriginal title was interpreted as an encumbrance upon the underlying title to the land held by the sovereign. Natives had a real and enforceable right to support themselves on this land as they had from "time immemorial." This right could be surrendered only to the sovereign, not to private parties; and compensation had to be paid for surrender according to the ancient principle of common law that there should be no expropriation without compensation.

When the courts developed a definitive theory of aboriginal title later in the century, they resorted to the Roman Law concept of usufruct to clarify the situation. Usufruct was the right to use and enjoy the fruits of property — usually slaves or a landed estate — without actually owning it. The holder of usufructuary rights could enjoy the property undisturbed during the life of those rights but could not sell or otherwise alienate the property, because usufruct was a personal right of enjoyment, not full title of ownership. At the expiration of the usufruct, the property reverted to the owner. The Canadian and British courts, seeking to interpret aboriginal title as it had developed over the centuries, used this concept as an analogy. They cast the sovereign in the role of owner and the natives in the role of holders of usufructuary rights. Title was vested in the Crown. The aboriginal right to use the land was a usufructuary encumbrance on that title which had to be extinguished before the Crown could alienate the land to private owners. Extinguishment required compensation, which might take the form of such requirements as land reserves, money payments, and educational or medical services. Logically, the situation was not different from other real estate conveyances where an encumbrance existed upon a title, as from mortgage or other debt. Title had to be cleared before alienation through sale or donation was possible.[9]

The Canadian government acted on this basis to extinguish aboriginal rights in Rupert's Land. The Indians were dealt with in the numbered treaties of the 1870's, and a land grant of 565,000 hectares was divided among the Metis of Manitoba. The only anomaly concerned the Metis of the Northwest Territories, where delay had ensued for various reasons. But on the eve of the Rebellion, the government announced that it would also deal with them, although the precise form that compensation would take was apparently still undecided. This sequence of actions should have wiped the slate clean, according to the official view. All encumbrances to title would have been removed, all aboriginal rights extinguished. Without injustice to Indian or Metis, the government could open the land for homesteading, make land grants to railways or colonization companies, and in general act as a landlord with a clear title.

It is crucial to appreciate the intellectual framework within which the government acted. From offer to purchase through taking possession and finally clearing title, everything was based on the validity of the Hudson's Bay Company's charter and on the contemporary understanding of aboriginal title. The quarrel with Riel arose in large part because he had a view of the situation which diverged at fundamental points. At least, after the Rebellion he explicitly denied the validity of the Hudson's Bay charter. He did not quite reach the position that a European power could not unilaterally declare sovereignty over inhabited territory, a position which would have forbidden the king to grant something that was not his to grant. Rather Riel attacked the charter for its monopolistic provisions. The company's sole right to trade "unjustly deprived the Northwest of the advantages of international trade and the rest of humanity, especially neighboring peoples, of the benefit of the commercial relations with the North-West to which they were entitled."[10] The result was impoverishment and oppression of the native inhabitants, both Indians and Metis. Riel coined the term *haute trahison internationale*[11] to describe the situation, which might translate into today's idiom as "a crime against humanity." Thus, the charter was void, as was any sale based upon it; for the company could not sell what it did not own. The most Riel would admit was that the company had an interest in the land which it had sold to Canada,[12] thus neatly reversing the official position. In Riel's mind, the natives had the underlying title while the company possessed a limited right to carry on the fur trade. The sale by the company of its commercial rights did not affect the natives, who were the true owners of the land. In Riel's mind Indian and Metis title was clearly not a mere encumbrance on the sovereign's title but sovereignty plus full ownership — not individual ownership in fee simple, perhaps, but a collective ownership by the Metis as a nation and by the Indians as tribes.

Riel stood in the tradition of Metis nationalism which stretched back to the conflict with the Hudson's Bay Company over the Selkirk Settlement. Traders of the North West Company had suggested to the Metis that the land was theirs, not the company's, and the idea had persisted across the generations.[13] For Riel, it was axiomatic that the Metis were a distinct people with ownership rights separate from those of the Indians. He never dealt with any of the difficult questions that can be posed on this subject. If aboriginal rights arise from habitation from "time immemorial,"[14] are the Metis an aboriginal people, since by definition they did not emerge until the coming of the white man? What makes the Metis aboriginal, their Indian blood or the fact that they were living in the northwest before its acquisition by Canada? If the former, why should the Metis be in a different category from Indians? If the latter, how do they differ from descendants of white employees of the Hudson's Bay Company or of the Selkirk Settlers? Unfortunately, the government of Canada accepted the Metis as an aboriginal people in the Manitoba Act without answering or even asking these hard questions. Many subsequent anomalies in Metis history have arisen from the hasty and ill-considered decision, made under intense political pressure in the spring of 1870, to buy off the Metis with a land grant.

When he established the Provisional Government of 8 December 1869, Riel had skirted the question of Metis title. His "Declaration of the People of Rupert's Land and the North-West" took another path to contesting the Hudson's Bay Company's right to sell the land, while remaining silent about Metis ownership rights:

This Company consisting of many persons required a certain constitution. But as there was a question of commerce only their constitution was framed in reference thereto. Yet since there was at that time no government to see to the interests of a people already existing in the country, it became necessary for judicial affairs to have recourse to the officers of the Hudson's Bay Company.

Thus inaugurated that species of government which, slightly modified by subsequent circumstances, ruled this country up to a recent date.

Although this government "was far from answering to the wants of the people," the Metis "had generously supported" it. But now the company was abandoning its people by "subjugat[ing] it without its consent to a foreign power"; and according to the law of nations, a people abandoned by its government "is at liberty to establish any form of government it may consider suitable to its wants."[15] Thus, the Provisional Government was legitimate according to the law of nations, and the Hudson's Bay Company had no right to transfer to Canada the land and people it had abandoned. Canada would have to deal with the Provisional Government if it was going to annex Rupert's Land.

Riel's original position of 1869 was that it violated the law of nations (or "international law") to transfer a population without seeking its consent. In 1885 he added the argument that the company did not own Rupert's Land because its charter was void. Both arguments lead to the same conclusions — that the sale to Canada is invalid until the inhabitants of Rupert's Land give their consent and that, living in a political vacuum, they have the right to form their own government to negotiate the terms of sale on their behalf.

Riel not only sought to demonstrate the legitimacy of the Provisional Government through abstract reasoning, he also tried to show that the Provisional Government had been recognized by both Britain and Canada. He formulated the facts slightly differently on various occasions, but the main line of argument was always the same: ministers of the Canadian government had invited the insurgents to send delegates to Ottawa and had conducted negotiations with them. An amnesty had been promised by the governor general himself, both directly and through intermediates. Thus, both Canada and Britain had recognized the Provisional Government *de facto*, even if there had not been a formal exchange of ambassadors according to international protocol.[16]

The legitimacy of the Provisional Government was essential to Riel because it determined his interpretation of the Manitoba Act and of the entry of Manitoba into Confederation. His frame of reference was the law of nations (*droit des gens*), because he held that negotiations had been carried out between independent entities, Canada and Red River. Rupert's Land had not been purchased; rather its inhabitants, acting through their government, had decided to join Canada. The £300,000 paid to the Hudson's Bay Company did not purchase the land but only extinguished the company's interest. Union with Canada was not the result of unilateral action in Ottawa; it had required the assent of the Provisional Government, which was formally given after Father Ritchot returned from Ottawa to report on the terms offered by Canada. After the vote, Riel's "secretary of state" wrote to Canada's secretary of state to inform him that the Provisional Government and the Legislative Assembly, in the name of the people of the North-West, do accept the "Manitoba Act," and consent to enter into Confederation on the terms entered into with our delegates . . . The Provisional Government and the Legislative Assembly have consented to enter into Confederation in the belief, and on the understanding, that in the above mentioned terms a general amnesty is contemplated.[17]

Riel saw the arrangement as a "treaty" in the sense of an international agreement between states. The treaty had two parts: the written text of the Manitoba Act and the oral promise of amnesty for all actions committed over the winter of 1869–70. This explains the final lines of Riel's pamphlet on the amnesty question:

Ce que nous demandons, c'est l'amnistie" c'est l'exécution loyale de l'acte du Manitoba. Rien de plus, mais aussi rien de moins.[18]

Riel literally meant that the annexation of Rupert's Land was the result of a "solemn treaty"[19] which, like all treaties, would become void if it was not observed. The annexation was reversible. The people of Rupert's Land, which had become the Province of Manitoba and the Northwest Territories, could remove themselves from Canada if the treaty was broken in either of its branches: the amnesty or the Manitoba Act.

In Riel's view, Canada had betrayed its obligations under both headings. It had not conferred a full amnesty on him and the other leaders of the resistance, and it had not executed the Manitoba Act, particularly section 31, as he interpreted it. Section 31 of the Manitoba Act authorized the half-breed land grant. At the time of entry into Confederation, Manitoba consisted of approximately 3,800,000 hectares, of which 565,000 hectares were set aside by section 31 to be distributed to the "children of half breed heads of families."[20] It appears that the government of Canada thought to equip each young Metis with an amount of land so as to make him economically self-sufficient. It was the same principle as the one by which Indian reserves were calculated at the rate of a quarter-section of land per family of five. The government was thinking in terms of the future needs of a special group among the population.

Riel, on the contrary, viewed the 565,000 hectares as the sale price of the 3,800,000 hectares comprised in Manitoba. This ratio set a precedent for the rest of the land of the northwest. As subsequent areas were opened for settlement, the Metis of those areas should receive a similar price, in order to extinguish their title, namely one-seventh of the land or the financial value of the one-seventh, which would amount to about 70,400,000 hectares for the northwest outside the original boundaries of Manitoba.[21]

Note that Riel's position implicitly contradicted the official theory that Metis title was "a personal and usufructuary right" to draw subsistence from the land. If aboriginal title is a usufruct, compensation for extinguishment is logically proportional to the number of natives who relinquish the right to gather food on a given territory because a number of personal claims are being satisfied. But if Metis title is a form of collective ownership, compensation for extinguishment must logically be proportional to the value of the asset expropriated. If a provisional government were expropriating a farmer's land for an electric transmission line, he would be paid according to the amount of land taken, not according to the size of his family.

Riel's single best explanation of this theory was given in his final trial speech. It must be read carefully, for his phrasing in English is sometimes awkward, even though the ideas are clear and logically developed:

But somebody will say, on what grounds do you ask one-seventh of the lands? In England, in France, the French and the English have lands, the first was in England, they were the owners of the soil and they transmitted to generations. Now, by the soil they have had their start as a nation. Who starts the nations? The very one who creates them, God. God is the master of the universe, our planet is his land, and the nation and the tribes are members of His family, and as a good father, he gives a portion of his lands to that nation, to that tribe, to everyone, that is his heritage, that is his share of the inheritance, of the people, or nation or tribe. Now, here is a nation strong as it may be, it has its inheritance from God. When they have crowded their country because they had no room to stay anymore at home, it does not give them the right to come and take the share of all tribes besides them. When they come they ought to say, well, my little sister, the Cree tribe, you have a great territory, but that territory has been given to you as our own land, it has been given to our fathers in England or in France and of course you cannot exist without having that spot of land. This is the principle God cannot create a tribe without locating it. We are not birds. We have to walk on the ground, and that ground is encircled of many things, which besides its own value, increases its value in another manner, and when we cultivate it we still increase that value. Well, on what principle can it be that the Canadian Government have given one-seventh to the half-breeds of Manitoba? I say it must be on this ground, civilization has the means of improving life that Indians or half-breeds have not. So when they come in our savage country, in our uncultivated land, they come and help us with their civilization, but we helped them with our lands, so the question comes: Your land, you Cree, or you half-breed, your land is worth today one-seventh of what it will be when the civilization will have opened it? Your country unopened is worth to you only one-seventh of what it will be when opened. I think it is a fair share to acknowledge the genius of civilization to such an extent as to give, when I have seven pair of socks, six, to keep one. They made the treaty with us. As they made the treaty, I say they have to observe it, and did they ooserve the treaty? No.[22]

The statement accepted and justified the surrender of land by aboriginal peoples in return for compensation. To that extent, it was compatible with the official Indian policy of Britain and Canada. However, beyond that lay some marked differences. Riel seemed to challenge the unilateral assumption of sovereignty which was the foundation of British rule in North America; and he certainly did not accept the principle of unilateral extinguishment of aboriginal title through legislation. The land grant of section 31 was valid compensation for surrender of land only inasmuch as it was part of a treaty approved by both sides. Furthermore, the basis of compensation was a *quid pro quo* as in any sale. Because the advantages of civilization could multiply the value of land seven times or more, the Metis would be at least as well off by surrendering six-sevenths of their land and adopting civilized ways while retaining one-seventh (or its money equivalent). It was decidedly not a matter of government allocating a certain amount of land to each Metis individual. In another text, Riel derided the latter approach as a "sophism" designed to let the government "evade its obligations" and "frustrate the Métis, as a group or nationality, of their seventh of the lands."[23]

Although Riel did not express himself in precise legal terms, his ideas can be readily translated. He was saying that Metis and Indian rights were not merely an encumbrance upon the sovereign's underlying title, not merely the right to gather produce from the land as long as the sovereign allowed. Metis and Indian rights were full ownership of the entire land by the tribe or nation which inhabited it. This position, which is currently espoused by native rights activists in Canada's North, is still unacceptable to the Canadian government, which is why negotiations in the North have been stalled for years.

It should now be apparent why Riel's demands could not be satisfied by any actions which Canada was likely to take. The government grudgingly agreed to a new issue of scrip to provide for the relatively few Metis who had not participated in the Manitoba land grant, but in Riel's mind, the whole northwest outside Manitoba still belonged to the Metis. The Hudson's Bay Company had sold whatever interest it had, and the Indians, at least in the fertile belt, had signed land surrender treaties. It was still necessary to extinguish the Metis title, and that could not be done with a few pieces of scrip. It would require payment of the value of one-seventh of the whole northwest, following the precedent solemnly established in the "Manitoba Treaty." And if that treaty continued to be broken, the Metis would no longer be part of Canada. According to the law of nations, they could once again form a Provisional Government and undertake negotiations with other governments. There might be a new treaty with Canada, or perhaps the northwest would become a separate colony within the Empire, or perhaps it would ask for annexation to the United States, as Riel did after his trial. Everything was possible. It is this train of thought, and only this, which makes the North-West Rebellion intelligible.

Riel had a concrete plan for capitalizing the value of the one-seventh of the Northwest Territories which was the due of the Metis. When Bishop Grandin visited St. Laurent in early September 1884, Riel read him a list of demands which included the following points:

> 5. That two million acres be set apart by the government for the benefit of the half breeds, both Protestant and Catholic. That the government sell these lands; that it deposit the money in the bank, and that the interest on that money serve for the support of schools, for the construction of orphanages and hospitals, for the support of institutions of this type already constructed, and to obtain carts for poor half breeds as well as seed for the annual spring planting.
> 6. That a hundred townships, selected from swampy lands which do not appear habitable at the moment, be set aside by the government and that every eighteen years there take place a distribution of these lands to the half breed children of the new generation. This to last 120 years.
> 7. The Province of Manitoba has been enlarged since 1870. The half breed title to the lands by which it was enlarged has not yet been extinguished. Let that title be extinguished in favour of the half breed children born in the province since the transfer [i.e., since 15 July 1870] and in favour of the children born there for the next four generations.[24]

Item 5 amounted to a trust fund for the Metis designed to promote their economic and social advancement, while item 6 would have ensured the availability of land to several new generations of Metis. Item 7, although vague, had the most radical implications, for it hinted at Riel's theory that Metis ownership rights to the northwest were still alive. All three points flowed from his idea of collective ownership of the northwest by the Metis nation. Riel was asking for a 800,000-hectare reserve, plus a hundred townships (921,600 hectares), plus something for the expansion of Manitoba in 1881: a considerable amount in all, but far less than one-seventh of the northwest. Yet these demands were moderate because they were only a first instalment, as shown by Riel's postscript to the document:

> This is what we ask while we wait for Canada to become able to pay us the annual interest on the sum that our land is worth and while we wait for public opinion to agree to recognize our rights to the land in their fullest extent (*dans toute leur étendue*).[25]

Grandin gave a copy of Riel's text to Lieutenant-Governor Dewdney, who forwarded an English translation to Sir John A. Macdonald. The bishop stated that he supported the traditional demands of the Metis but that he could not speak to the political questions of responsible government and aboriginal title.[26] Macdonald received additional information about Riel's postscript from A. E. Forget, clerk of the North-West Territorial Council, who had accompanied Grandin. Forget reported that Riel's document

> only purports to contain such requests as need an immediate settlement. In addition to these advantages, they claim that their right to land can only be fully extinguished by the annual payment of the interest on a capital representing the value of land in the Territories estimated to be worth at the time of transfer twenty-five cents an acre [ten cents per hectare] for the halfbreeds and fifteen cents [six cents] for the Indians. This is the claim alluded to in the postscriptum of Riel's memo to His Lordship.[27]

Forget added that the Metis were planning to draw up a memorial on this basis and send it to the House of Commons. He tried to persuade them to direct it to the governor general-in-council through Dewdney.

A draft of such a memorial exists in Riel's hand, addressed to "votre excellence en conseil." The heading suggests it was written after the conversation with Forget on 7 September, although earlier drafts must have preceded this neatly written text. Unaccountably, this document was overlooked by all students of Riel until Gilles Martel pointed out its importance.[28] It is an invaluable statement of Riel's true objectives.

The text begins by denouncing the Indian treaties as a swindle because they "are not based on a reasonable estimation of the value of their lands." The Indians would not be content until they receive this value. "It is the opinion of your humble petitioners that the land in its uncultivated state, with its natural wealth of game, fish, and berries cannot be worth less to the Indians than twelve and a half cents per acre." The same principle applies to the Metis, except that the land is worth ten cents per hectare to them because their usage of it is "passablement civilisée." There follow some calculations, based on certain assumptions:

— 440,000 hectares of land in the North-West
— 100,000 Indians
— 100,000 Metis
— 5 per cent interest rate

The result of these assumptions is an annuity of $68.75 for each Indian and $137.50 for each Metis. However, not too much importance was attached to these calculations, which were "only approximate." They were offered only to give "a fair idea" of Metis rights and to suggest "the profound distress in which the

Dominion of Canada plunges us by taking possession of our lands and not giving us the adequate compensation we expect of it.''[29]

The line of reasoning embodied in this petition was not a temporary aberration on Riel's part. He reproduced exactly the same argument in his last major piece of writing, published posthumously as "Les Métis du Nord-Ouest," except that he used figures of six cents per hectare for the Indians and twelve cents per hectare for the Metis.[30] Furthermore, the total amounts of money involved are of the same magnitude as the value of the one-seventh of the northwest demanded at the trial.[31] The notion of a trust fund based on the value of the land surrendered flows directly from Riel's conception of native title as collective ownership, not a mere encumbrance on the sovereign's title, and is in direct contrast to the official policy of calculating compensation proportionally to numbers of individuals rather than to the area of land involved.

Why this petition dropped from sight is one of the riddles of the agitation. One may conjecture that its radical theory of Metis and Indian rights was unacceptable to the white settlers whose support was indispensable to a joint movement. Evidence along this line comes from the story of the clash between Riel and the white secretary of the movement, William Henry Jackson. The two, who had worked closely together for months, had a heated quarrel in February 1885, after which Riel kept Jackson under virtual arrest. After the Rebellion was over and Jackson had been sent to a lunatic asylum, he briefly explained what had caused the argument. He had enraged Riel by maintaining

> that the particles of matter composing the Earth were the property of whosoever first chose to develop them into articles of utility except in case of the express allocation of land as in the case of Canaan, while Mr. Riel, was, if I remember, pursuing the argument which I see he advanced on the occasion of his trial of Regina — that *every* nation is allotted its means of existence in the shape of *land*.[32]

Since it hinges on the idea of uniting one's labour to the land to form property, Jackson's view may loosely be called Lockean. More precisely, it resembles the position of the noted publicist Emer de Vattel that agricultural peoples could rightfully appropriate lands on which nomads were accustomed to roam. Nomads "occupy more land than they would have need of under a system of honest labor, and they may not complain if other more industrious Nations, too confined at home, should come and occupy part of their lands."[33] Since the human race could not survive in its present numbers without tilling the soil, the rights of agriculture could not be denied.

From another source, we know that Jackson was skeptical of the whole idea of aboriginal title. He wrote:

Why should God give a whole continent to 40,000 Indians and coop up 40,000,000 Englishmen in on a little island? The Indians are the same race; they, too, once lived in Europe. America was once without a man in it, why should a part of the human race go into that empty continent, and as soon as they have got there, turn around and forbid any more to come in, unless they pay for the privilege?[34]

It is easy to see why Jackson's views irritated Riel so much, for they contradicted the implications of his own position: that native peoples were sovereign masters of their land and had full ownership rights which they could voluntarily exchange for compensation but of which they could not rightfully be deprived by unilateral action of any government.

Riel's theory of aboriginal rights is an interesting intermediate position between the official government doctrine, which is still held by Canadian courts, and the emerging view of the native community. The official position, to recall it briefly, is that British sovereignty was established by discovery, settlement, and conquest. The sovereign has the underlying or radical title to all lands in his realm. Aboriginal title consists of usufructuary rights which are an encumbrance on the sovereign's title. These rights are legally enforceable until they are extinguished by the sovereign, which may occur through proclamation, legislation, or agreement ("treaty"). In any case, compensation should be paid for expropriation of the usufructuary rights.

Riel certainly rejected the unilateral aspects of the official view, as shown by his insistence that the Manitoba Act was a treaty according to the law of nations. He did not make an unambiguous assertion about sovereignty, but the rest of his theory makes sense only if unilateral imposition of sovereignty by a European state is not rightfully possible. In this respect, Riel's thinking is aligned with that of contemporary native spokesmen who have criticized the unilateral aspect of the traditional theory. William Badcock writes, for example, about John Marshall's decisions which formulated the legal doctrine of aboriginal rights in North America:

It seems, then, that non-Indian claim to North America is based on the preposterous proposition that only civilized Christians could have any claim to land and that, therefore, a Christian from one side of the world, if he should "discover" land on the other side of the world inhabited by uncivilized heathens, assumed rights which, if they ever did exist for the original inhabitants, were thereby annulled.[35]

C. Gerald Sutton writes in the same vein: "It was that initial denial of sovereignty that denied to the Indian the right and opportunity to negotiate his place in

Canadian society."[36] Riel would have agreed to the sentiments of both writers.

However, he differed from the new view with respect to extinguishment. Native spokesmen are now demanding not "extinguishment" but "enhancement" or "entrenchment" of aboriginal title.[37] That is, they do not seek compensation for surrender of usufructuary rights; they want legal recognition of full ownership to the lands they once roamed. The ultimate in this direction comes from the Declaration of Rights of the Native Council of Canada: "We have the inalienable right to the land."[38] If this is meant literally, extinguishment is impossible, because an inalienable right is by definition one that can never be surrendered. This mode of thinking is a revolutionary departure in native claims which, although understood by native spokesmen and government negotiators, is not sufficiently appreciated by the Canadian public. In this instance Riel is on the side of the traditional or orthodox view. His proposal for an endowment fund capitalizing the value of one-seventh of the northwest was a proposal for extinguishment — generous to be sure, but still extinguishment. In that sense, it was more like the Alaska or James Bay agreement than like the proposals of the Dene.

Far from a mere legal technicality, this difference about extinguishment is the central practical issue. Extinguishment of aboriginal title was a mechanism for native peoples to enter white society. The compensation paid for extinguishment, whether the reserves allocated to Indians or the land grant given to the Metis, was understood as a transitional device to make the natives independent and self-supporting farmers. Riel wanted more generous compensation negotiated on terms of sovereign equality, but he did not reject the ultimate goal of social assimilation.

On this point, a careful distinction must be made. Riel was an ardent Metis nationalist who wanted the Metis to conserve a separate identity as a people or nation. But different nations can participate in the same society. English-Canadians, French-Canadians, and Americans are distinct nations but are all equally part of western society and do not differ radically in their way of life. Riel's goal was for the Metis to join the community of nations in western society. In contrast, the current symbolism of the "Fourth World" popularized by George Manuel suggests that western society is in such urgent need of reform that native peoples must create something fundamentally different. Manuel addresses the white man:

> We cannot become equal members in *your* society. We *can* become a member of a new society in which everyone chooses to share. But that cannot happen until you begin to reconsider and reformulate your understanding, and your view of the world, as we have begun to reformulate ours.[39]

Enhancement of aboriginal rights is the means by which the native will preserve his separation from white society so that he can develop a better way of life. Riel, although estranged from the British and Canadian governments, had not arrived at such a thoroughgoing critique of western society and so remained content with the concept of extinguishment.[40]

NOTES

1. A rather different paper bearing a similar title was presented at Brandon University, 15 November 1979, and afterwards distributed in A. S. Lussier, ed., *Pelletier-Lathlin Memorial Lecture Series Brandon University 1979–1980* (offset), pp. 28–46.
2. Sally Weaver, *Making Canadian Indian Policy: The Hidden Agenda 1968–1970* (Toronto, 1981).
3. Indian and Northern Affairs Canada, *1977–78 Annual Report* (Ottawa, 1978), p. 36.
4. Jean Morisset, "The Aboriginal Nationhood, The Northern Challenge, and the Construction of Canadian Unity," *Queen's Quarterly* 88 (1981): 37–240.
5. Cited in Peter A. Cumming and Neil H. Mickenberg, *Native Rights in Canada*, 2d ed. (Toronto, 1972), p. 138. I have modernized the orthography.
6. George F. G. Stanley, *The Birth of Western Canada*, 2d ed. (Toronto, 1961), pp. 27–28.
7. D. N. Sprague. "Government Lawlessness in the Administration of Manitoba Land Claims, 1870–1887," *Manitoba Law Journal* 10 (December 1980): 415–16.
8. Cumming and Mickenberg, p. 148.
9. See ibid., pp. 13–50.
10. Louis Riel, [Mémoire sur les troubles du Nord-Ouest], *Le Canadien*, 26 December 1885. Ms. missing.
11. Ibid.
12. Interview with C. B. Pitblado, Winnipeg *Sun*, 3 June 1885.
13. Marcel Giraud, *Le Métis canadien* (Paris, 1945), pp. 533–34.
14. Cumming and Mickenberg, p. 3.
15. Thomas Flanagan, ed., "Political Theory of the Red River Resistance: The Declaration of December 8, 1869," *Canadian Journal of Political Science* 11 (1978): 154.
16. *Le Canadien*, 26 December 1885; and petition "To His Excellency [Grover] Cleveland." [? August–September 1885], National Archives and Records Service, Washington (NARS), despatches from U.S. consuls in Winnipeg, no. 441.
17. Cited in Stanley, 124.
18. Louis Riel, *L'Amnistie* (Montréal, 1874), p. 22.
19. Ibid.
20. The most recent review of Metis scrip in Manitoba is D. N. Sprague.
21. Louis Riel to J. W. Taylor, [2–3 August 1885], NARS, despatches from U.S. consuls in Winnipeg, 1869–1906, no. 433; [Manifeste à ses concitoyens américains], [? August–November 1885]; PAC, MG27, I, C4, 2150–56, 2159–60.
22. Desmond Morton, ed., *The Queen v. Louis Riel* (Toronto, 1975), pp. 358–59.
23. Riel, [Manifeste].
24. Louis Riel to J.-V. Grandin, Archives of the Chancellery of the Archdiocese of Edmonton (ACAE), Correspondence of Vital Grandin.
25. Ibid.
26. PAC, MG26, A, 42897–905, Edgar Dewdney to J. A. Macdonald, 19 September 1884. The English translations are in ibid., 42935–41.
27. Ibid., 42921–34, A. E. Forget to Edgar Dewdney, 18 September 1884.
28. Gilles Martel, "Le Messianisme de Louis Riel (1844–1885)" (Thèse de doctorat, Ecole des Hautes Etudes en Sciences Sociales, Paris, 1976), p. 393.
29. PAC, RG13, B2, 42–43, petition "à votre excellence en conseil," [? September 1884].

30. "Les Métis de Nord-Ouest," *Montreal Daily Star*, 28 November 1885.
31. Riel's petition requested a total compensation to natives of 37½ cents per acre (about 15 cents per hectare), slightly more than one-seventh of the current pre-emption price of $2.00 per acre (80.9 cents per hectare).
32. PAM, Selkirk Asylum Medical Records, MG3, C20, W. H. Jackson to "My dear Family," 19 September 1885.
33. Emer de Vattel, *The Law of Nations* (1758), in *The Classics of International Law* (Washington, 1902; reprinted, New York, 1964), p. 38.
34. Cited in T. E. Jackson to the Toronto *Globe*, 2 July 1885. Original missing.
35. William T. Badcock, *Who Owns Canada?* (Ottawa, 1976), p. 11.
36. C. Gerald Sutton, "Aboriginal Rights, in *Dene Nation — The Colony Within*, ed. Mel Watkins (Toronto, 1977), p. 154.
37. See, for example, a statement originated by Chief Sol Sanderson of the Federation of Saskatchewan Indians and adopted by the National Liberal Convention 4 July 1980 (Delia Opekokew, *The First Nations* [Saskatoon, 1980], p. 92).
38. Harry W. Daniels, *We Are the New Nation* (Ottawa, 1979), p. 54.
39. George Manuel and Michael Posluns, *The Fourth World* (Don Mills, Ontario, 1974), p. 261.
40. This point is perhaps more subtle than appears in this paragraph. As shown in Thomas Flanagan, *Louis "David" Riel: "Prophet of the New World"* (Toronto, 1979), Riel was a harsh critic of western society. He felt that it had become individualistic, hedonistic, and "liberal." The Metis would take the lead in its moral reformation by establishing an exemplary theocracy. In a sense, this is similar to the current judgment of many native spokesmen that western society is too materialistic and obsessed with power, and that natives are going to build a better future. However, Riel wished to recall western society to what he considered its true principles, while Manuel et al. seem to say the western world is on the wrong track altogether.

5

A Parting of the Ways:
Louis Schmidt's Account of Louis Riel
and the Metis Rebellion

Raymond Huel

On 10 April 1885, Louis Schmidt, a Metis employed in the Land Office in Prince Albert, sent a handwritten document to Archbishop Taché of St. Boniface. It was entitled "Notes: Mouvement des Métis à St. Laurent, Sask., T.N.O. en 1884."[1] In a letter appended to these notes, Schmidt stated that Taché must be very disheartened to learn that it was one of his "privileged protégés" who was the driving force behind the North-West Rebellion. Schmidt was grateful that he himself had not been involved in these events and declared that he had condemned the agitation as early as August 1884, because he was convinced that Riel's principles were "false and dangerous."[2]

This source is unusual because it is a contemporary account written by a literate Metis. Furthermore, the author personally knew the principals involved, and he was cognizant of the discontent and agitation that culminated in rebellion. Schmidt witnessed the early developments surrounding Riel's return, and while he never saw Riel after 17 August 1884, he communicated with people who were in contact with the Metis leader. In his notes, Schmidt attempted to be as accurate as possible and always indicated the source of his information. His initial optimism for the Metis cause quickly deteriorated into outright condemnation of and contempt for Riel. He did not provide an overall synthesis of the events he

Paper given at the Pelletier-Lathlin Memorial Lecture at Brandon University, March 1981.

264 As Long As The Sun Shines And The Water Flows

recorded, but he included his personal comments and always made it very clear that these were personal observations.[3]

Louis Schmidt was born at Old Fort on Lake Athabaska in 1844. His father was a fisherman employed by the Hudson's Bay Company; his mother, the daughter of a Red River guide. In 1854, Schmidt moved to Red River, and four years later he, Louis Riel, and Daniel McDougall were selected by Bishop Taché to further their education in Lower Canada. Schmidt attended the Collège de St. Hyacinthe but abandoned his studies in 1861 and returned to St. Boniface. During the Red River Insurrection, Louis Schmidt served as assistant secretary of state to the Provisional Government. He was later elected to the Legislative Assembly of Manitoba and served as secretary-treasurer of the St. Boniface School Board before moving to the District of Saskatchewan in 1880, where he established himself at St. Louis on the east side of the South Saskatchewan River. In 1884, Schmidt left his homestead and moved to Prince Albert, where he later obtained employment as a French-speaking assistant in the Land Office.

Schmidt began his account by commenting on the difficulties the Metis experienced with rectangular surveys and registering their homesteads. Petitions outlining grievances had been sent from St. Louis and other neighbouring lo-calities, but the authorities did nothing to eliminate the sources of complaint.[4] Consequently, in the winter of 1884 Charles Nolin and Maxime Lépine began to organize a "mouvement général" to force the government to undertake positive action. Emissaries were also sent among the English-speaking mixed bloods of Prince Albert, who responded favourably to the invitation. In April, a large meeting was held in St. Laurent and various resolutions were passed. The last one dealt with the nomination of delegates to confer with Riel. Schmidt remarked that Riel's name, which had struck such a discordant note among the English since 1869, was becoming more favourably received by the English mixed bloods who, in a subsequent meeting, agreed to support the proposal to send a delegation.[5]

On 8 July 1884, Riel spoke at Charles Nolin's home in St. Laurent and announced his intention of creating a "mouvement général" encompassing all the people of the northwest. In keeping with Riel's request, a public meeting was held at Lindsay school on 11 July. According to Schmidt, Riel made a good impression on the audience and was invited to address the residents of Prince Albert on 19 July.[6]

Despite these sympathetic responses, Schmidt noted that there was opposition to Riel's movement. In Prince Albert, Lawrence Clarke, the Hudson's Bay factor, Colonel Sproat, and a few others feared that Riel's return would bring about unrest. Since they had been unable to prevent Riel from speaking in Prince Albert, Clarke and Sproat advised the authorities to take imprudent measures. For-tunately, Lieutenant-Governor Edgar Dewdney did not heed their advice and sought a more precise appraisal of the situation from Father André, the parish priest in Prince Albert. For his part, André informed Dewdney that, as yet, there was nothing to fear, and Riel should be left alone because he exercised a moderating influence on those who were overly excited.[7]

According to Schmidt, Riel's name was a synonym for trouble-maker in the minds of many English-speaking residents. Consequently, Riel's arrival caused uneasiness among the moderate element and enthusiasm among the radically minded. On the other hand, the Metis regarded Riel as a powerful person who could force the authorities to redress outstanding grievances. Furthermore, the Metis believed that Riel's return could not but result in positive consequences. Although Riel spoke only of peaceful means, Schmidt recorded that the agitation was beginning to cause concern to many moderate, serious-minded Metis.[8] Despite their confidence in Riel, they suspected that he had not divulged all his intentions. The fact that he was an American citizen convinced some that his real motive was to annex the northwest to the United States.[9]

However, it was the clergy who adopted the most reserved stance. At first they tended to be defiant, but Riel's peaceful declarations and religious piety made them observe the strictest neutrality. According to Schmidt, the clergy would not hinder the movement so long as it remained within legal limits. Schmidt noted that Riel had made a good impression on Father André, and while the clergyman feared a hidden machination that might alter the objectives of the movement, he openly sympathized with Riel's cause and energetically condemned the actions of Prince Albert's "petty aristocracy," Clarke, Sproat, and associates.[10]

In the meantime, Dewdney informed André that the minister of the interior would consider Metis complaints upon his return from England. This news caused Schmidt to write: "Jusqu'ici tout marche donc pour le mieux." Even the Prince Albert *Times*, which had not demonstrated any sympathy for Riel or the movement, was making few comments, and the same was true of the town's "petty aristocracy." Since everything was calm, Schmidt reflected that the storm was not long in coming.[11]

The first cloud appeared on the horizon after mass on 10 August when Riel spoke to the people of Batoche. His words left no doubt that he was offended by the defiant attitude which the clergy displayed toward him.[12] A few days later, Schmidt went to Duck Lake and noted that Riel's presence was making the Indians very confident. They were saying that since the government had not fulfilled its treaty obligations with them, the treaty was null and void, and a new one had to be negotiated. The Indians had sought Riel's advice, but Schmidt noted that Riel did not want to become openly involved in their affairs. However, Riel had asked one of his associates to arrange a meeting with the Indian chiefs of the area.[13]

In the meantime, Riel and Father André met in St. Laurent, and the clergyman reiterated his intention to remain neutral so long as the agitation was constitutional. This declaration did not satisfy Riel, who desired the active support of the clergy. Riel argued that since he was working in the interests of justice, the clergy were obliged to assist him. He declared that he had no hidden motives and that his objectives were not revolutionary. These affirmations did not entirely convince André, who remarked that Riel's ideas bordered on revolution. Despite these differences of opinion, they parted on good terms.[14]

This amicable relationship was not to last. On 17 August, Riel, Lépine, and André met in Louis Schmidt's home in Prince Albert. The discussion was often animated. According to Schmidt, Riel cast discretion aside and openly professed revolutionary and heretical ideas. Riel stated that he did not have complete confidence in the clergy because they were "natural flatterers" of those in authority, and, hence, their dogmatic decisions could not be accepted with certitude. This came as quite a revelation to Father André, who declared that Riel was a "veritable fanatic" who associated religion with all things.[15]

The first point of discussion focused on Riel's conception of the Metis identity in the northwest. Riel wanted to create a distinct Metis nationality which would be known as "métis-canadiens-français." He argued that French Canadians who immigrated to the northwest would have to abandon their nationality, associate themselves with this new Metis collectivity, and adopt its name. For his part, André replied that this was a utopian dream. The Metis would remain Metis where they found themselves in sufficient numbers, but if they were submerged in the tide of French-Canadian immigration they would have to identify with them if they wished to live in peace and harmony and obtain their share of public offices. As the argument progressed, André stated that it was fanaticism on Riel's part to think that he was always in harmony with the desires of Providence. Riel replied that he was a statesman with a special and divine mission to fulfil.[16]

Schmidt's own views on the role of the Metis in Canadian society had more in common with André's comments than Riel's. Schmidt felt that the Metis should be proud to identify with the French-Canadian nation which, after all, was their father. Furthermore, French Canadians had supported, encouraged, and contributed to the success of the Metis movement in 1869–70.[17] French Canadians had always regarded the Metis as their brothers, and, hence, Schmidt argued that it would be "unreasonable, imprudent and impolitic" to make a distinction between the two groups. While most French Canadians might regard the Metis as an inferior race, Schmidt argued that they were not. They were inferior only in the sense that they lacked education, and given the lifestyle of the Metis, one could not expect a different state of affairs. Schmidt felt that if the Metis wanted to be a factor in Confederation, they had to "unite body and soul" with the French. For their part, the French would have to treat the Metis "as their equals, their brothers."[18]

Although André had been dumbfounded by Riel's remarks, he did not speak out against him when officials of the territorial government sought his advice.[19] Nevertheless, the rift between Riel and the clergy was widening. This became apparent in Schmidt's account of the meeting between Bishop Vital Grandin of St. Albert and Riel at St. Laurent on 1 September. In replying to an address presented by Riel, Grandin recommended moderation and submission to authority. This advice did not please Riel or Lépine, who accused the prelate of being under the tutelage of his clergy.[20] Describing Riel as a tenacious individual, Schmidt stated that he pressured Grandin constantly to obtain his approbation. In an attempt to impress the bishop, Riel convoked a large assembly at St. Laurent on 5 September, but Schmidt was not overwhelmed by the proceedings. He noted that Moïse Ouellette made a speech which no one could understand, and when Riel attempted to provide explanations, Ouellette prevented him, stating he was capable of doing so himself. For his part, Gabriel Dumont wondered why the clergy was becoming hostile to the movement. Charles Nolin then gave the audience a sample of his "overwhelming eloquence" by repeating the term "Monseigneur" ten times in each sentence![21]

In bringing the discussion to a close, Riel proposed that the Metis constitute themselves in a distinct entity under the guidance of and with the blessing of their clergy. Grandin replied that the Metis would need a patron saint, and after consulting those present, Riel suggested St. Joseph, which the prelate accepted. Standing before Grandin and his clergy, Riel then dramatically held hands with a French Canadian and a Frenchman. Schmidt stated that these theatrics greatly impressed "nos pauvres Métis" but occasioned only a chuckle from the priests who were present. Grandin, who was tired, raised no objections and gave his blessing to the proposal. The meeting ended with everyone being convinced that, since the bishop had listened to their speeches and given his benediction to those present, he approved everything the Metis were doing. This naïve interpretation provoked Schmidt to make the following judgement:

> Pauvre gens! qu'est-ce ce pauvre évêque et tous les prêtres peuvent con-damner dans leur conduite jusqu'à présent? Ce serait peut-être un peu trop de crédulité et de bonne foi naïve qui leur fait prendre Riel pour un petit dieu, voilà tout.[22]

While Schmidt was willing to excuse the Metis because they were gullible, he was not as forgiving toward Riel and his more zealous partisans. Schmidt argued that Riel should cease to accuse the clergy of servility and begin to question his own sincerity. According to Schmidt, Riel was motivated by an "unbridled ambition," and he possessed none of the qualities of a statesman. Furthermore, only the uneducated and illiterate found Riel's arguments convincing. For his part, Schmidt had no difficulty in discerning the object of Riel's agitation. Riel wanted the authorities to think that he was a formidable individual in order to obtain an important position from them. When Grandin had proposed that Riel be appointed to the territorial council, the latter replied that he would be dishonouring himself by accepting such a position. This convinced Schmidt that Riel wanted nothing less than a federal portfolio.[23]

Schmidt previously had voiced little sympathy for Riel's plans, which he described as impractical and utopian.[24] His opinion did not change when Riel presented his demands during the meetings at St. Laurent. Schmidt felt that the eleven items in Riel's memorandum were exaggerated and that the authorities would reject them. In particular, he felt that the sections dealing with land grants for Metis were indefensible and extravagant and that only the Metis would support them. Schmidt qualified this remark by adding that the Metis "demanderaient la lune si Riel la demanderait avec eux."[25]

Turning to Riel's associates, Schmidt stated that the very individuals who had refused to meet and present their grievances to the lieutenant-governor during his visit to the district were now prostrating themselves before him and asking for lucrative positions. They asked Grandin and André to use their influence with the authorities to have Riel appointed to the territorial council and Charles Nolin appointed Indian agent. For his part, the egotistical Maxime Lépine was humbly asking his compatriots to elect him to the territorial council next spring. In the meantime, not one word was voiced concerning Metis grievances. This shameful conduct caused Schmidt to write: "Voilà donc ce beau movement national à la voierie! Des places pour les agitateurs et rien de plus. Quelle farce!"[26] In his assessment of the contemporary scene Schmidt stated that despite earlier reverses, Riel was "master of the situation" because his private disputes with the clergy were enhancing his popularity among the Metis. The Metis were convinced that Riel had been able to influence Bishop Grandin and, hence, that his cause must be just and there would be no risk in supporting him. According to Schmidt, Riel was cunning and ingratiating, and there was nothing surprising about the prestige he enjoyed. His exemplary conduct and his speeches imbued with religiosity made him appear as an inspired person. Schmidt affirmed that Riel displayed all the mannerisms of fanatics who led revolutions.[27]

In the meantime, the first mass in honour of St. Joseph was celebrated in Batoche on 24 September, and Schmidt recorded two humorous incidents that took place. To begin with, Father Moulin, the parish priest, wanted to speak on this special occasion, but he was ignorant of the developments that had culminated in the naming of a patron saint for the Metis. Thus, he spoke on St. John the Baptist, thinking that that saint was also the patron of the Metis. According to Schmidt, it was a curious misunderstanding because it could easily have been regarded as intentional. However, another priest quietly informed Moulin of the error, and the latter abandoned St. John in favour of St. Joseph and continued his sermon. For his part, Father Fourmond of St. Laurent, an amateur poet and musician, wished to sing a song he had composed. Unfortunately, in his enthusiasm, he sang one octave too high, and, furthermore, no one else knew the words. After mass, Riel spoke for three-quarters of an hour. Charles Nolin, in his own style, elaborated on Riel's plea that the Metis should not adopt ostentatious ways. Nolin urged Metis women to always remain covered and to replace stockings with the more traditional gaiters. A sarcastic Schmidt noted that Nolin almost went as far as to ask males to wear a loincloth.[28]

Despite Riel's popularity, Schmidt noted that the Metis were not in complete agreement. While they had full confidence in Riel, many Metis did not like his close advisers. Lépine and Nolin, for example, were notorious because of their unabashed actions and ambitions. The fact that the petition which Riel had been preparing was not yet ready in late October was also a source of consternation. Public opinion was vacillating, and no one knew whether the English element would support Riel.[29]

More than a month went by before Schmidt made another entry in his notes. On 5 December he recorded that a committee of the parishes in the District of Lorne was deliberating in St. Laurent. Schmidt felt that this committee was vested with a grave responsibility because ultimately it would decide whether the movement would be constitutional or not. Given the division within the different elements of the population, Schmidt felt that Riel would have to mount a *coup d'état* to rally a majority behind him. In Schmidt's view, it was only the uneducated Metis and hard-core revolutionaries who expected great things from Riel. The better educated and moderate Metis, who sought a solution to outstanding grievances, welcomed Riel's leadership but were disconcerted by his inactivity and extravagant schemes.[30] In Schmidt's estimation, opposition to Riel was increasing, and this would have beneficial effect because it would create a clear distinction between Riel's supporters and opponents.[31]

In attempting to explain Riel's behaviour Schmidt would not accept André's contention that Riel was truly deranged. According to Schmidt, Riel was confident in his destiny, and since he had always been regarded as a formidable person, he would lose his prestige and stature if he resorted to ordinary means. Since the Metis looked upon Riel as a god, he had to act accordingly to maintain their support. Schmidt advanced another theory to explain Riel's actions. The press had not mentioned Riel for quite some time, and this lack of publicity was eroding his influence in administrative circles. Thus, Riel put on an act to impress André, hoping that the priest would inform the government that Riel was still obsessed with impractical plans. Upon learning this, the government would become worried and would hasten to come to terms with Riel. However, André was not deceived by Riel's tactics and remained indifferent to his inopportune outbursts.[32]

By 12 December Schmidt was beginning to have second thoughts about Riel's sanity, and he wrote: "Pauvre Riel! il me fait réellement pitié! Son cerveau serait-il réellement malade?" Schmidt went on to relate another meeting between Riel and André. After having expounded his impractical plans and heterodox doctrines for some time, Riel admitted that he was in an impossible situation and that he wanted to extricate himself at any cost. Riel asked André's assistance to obtain some money from the government to enable him to leave the district. Riel would then pretend that he was being sent as a delegate to negotiate with the federal authorities. Schmidt hoped that this scheme would succeed because he feared that if

Riel did not leave, many Metis would become apostates. Schmidt was convinced that Riel was the instrument of Satan:

> Il est en guerre ouverte avec le clergé, tout en prêchant la foi et la religion au peuple. Il se montre au peuple dévot, mystique, plein de simagrées pieuses qui fait croire à un grand nombre qu'il n'est rien moins qu'un saint. Ce grand nombre le suivrait partout; il se ferait schismatique avec lui.[33]

Schmidt then cited the celebration of a wedding in Moïse Ouellette's family as an example of Riel's monomania. Prior to the meal, Riel had ordered that an extra chair be placed at the end of the head table. Informing those present that they had to transport themselves spiritually to the wedding at Cana, Riel affirmed that the empty chair would be occupied by the Saviour. He also advised the newlyweds to abstain from dancing for a few hours in memory of the Virgin and St. Joseph. Claiming that these proceedings bordered on sacrilege, Schmidt stated that no one contradicted Riel because they felt that he surpassed the clergy in knowledge and piety. Schmidt also claimed that Riel was no longer content with having lengthy discussions with the clergy and would utilize any means to demonstrate that they were in error. For their part, Riel's close associates were impertinent toward the clergy and were accusing Bishop Taché of every conceivable indignity. An exasperated Schmidt declared that Riel, Nolin, and Lépine "sont véritablement fous avec leur politique."[34]

By January 1885, Schmidt was no longer using the term "insane" in a figurative sense. He was convinced that Riel was mentally deranged. According to Schmidt, Riel imagined that someone was trying to kill him. Schmidt then related an incident in the Jackson home in Prince Albert where Riel was having a meal. Riel suddenly left the table, rushed outside, and forced himself to vomit because he felt that he had been poisoned. Schmidt noted that Riel often succumbed to such frightening experiences, and that even when he was in his own residence Riel believed there were people outside who were waiting to pursue or to assassinate him.[35]

According to Schmidt, Riel's frame of mind was obviously causing concern to Nolin and Lépine, who were becoming aware that he was utterly impractical. To substantiate this contention, Schmidt stated that everyone in the locality was organizing school districts in accordance with recent amendments to the territorial school ordinances. Some sought Riel's advice on the erection of districts in French parishes, but Riel could offer no assistance because he understood nothing about the legislation. In Schmidt's words, the matter was "en dehors de sa sphère."[36] In another instance, Nolin and Lépine wanted to submit a tender for work on the telegraph line. Since there were some calculations involved, they sought Riel's help, but he was unable to assist them, and they had to approach Father André. Riel later prevailed upon Nolin and Lépine not to tender on government projects because this would harm his movement. Schmidt stated that Riel was a burden on

Nolin and Lépine, who were obliged to take up collections to ensure that he did not starve to death.[37]

In addition, Riel was exasperated because the authorities still paid no attention to him. When the government announced that a commissioner would be sent out to negotiate with those Metis who had not yet received a grant of land to extinguish their aboriginal claim, Riel retaliated by stating that he would form a provisional government. While such pronouncements seemed to excite only the idle and curious, Schmidt felt that the situation was critical, and the proverbial spark was all that was necessary to start a conflagration. According to Schmidt, Father André was the only person who could counter Riel's influence among the Metis.[38]

Since the government continued to ignore Riel, Schmidt wrote that the latter decided on a bold strategy to refurbish his waning influence. Consequently, on 25 February 1885, Riel convened a large meeting in the parish church in Batoche. He informed the assembly of his decision to return to the United States because his presence was impeding the settlement of Metis grievances. According to Schmidt, a large number in the audience would have been happy to witness Riel's departure, but a more audacious element shouted that he was their leader and, hence, he must remain. Members of the district clergy were present and spoke, but Schmidt was at a loss to explain why Father Fourmond of St. Laurent congratulated the Metis on their patriotism and praised Riel.[39]

A few days later, Riel informed a gathering in St. Laurent that, since peaceful means had not resolved outstanding issues, he would now show the authorities how powerful he was. Hinting that "a large multitude" was waiting for his signal, Riel declared that he was prepared to act vigorously, and the Metis must follow him. Announcing that the English would be meeting in a few days at Halcro, Riel urged as many Metis as possible to attend and to arm themselves as a sign of strength. Schmidt noted that Riel used "*mots couverts*" to designate firearms.[40]

The meeting at Halcro on 3 March was attended by more Metis than English mixed bloods. Schmidt said that its outcome was similar to that of the 25 February assembly in Batoche, and he limited his comments to what he perceived to be the more comical aspects of the proceedings. On the one hand, Riel argued that until their grievances were redressed, the Metis should refrain from voting and have nothing to do with government departments. For his part, Mr. Betts, a Prince Albert merchant, spoke of the forthcoming elections to the territorial council and the qualifications desired of potential candidates. William H. Jackson, Riel's "intimate advisor," made a speech that was well received and then dramatically announced that he was resigning as secretary of the Settler's Union in order to fully devote himself to the salvation of his soul. He also declared that he wanted to become a Catholic. This revelation surprised the English-speaking members of the audience.[41]

In the meantime, Father André visited St. Laurent and conferred with the leading Metis of the district, who had sought his advice. Reiterating the church's position on obedience to duly constituted authority, André declared that in the event that a warrant were issued against Riel, those that continued to support him would be regarded as criminals by the Church and the authorities. These affirmations impressed the Metis, and Nolin, whom Schmidt described as "le vieux capon," declared that he would follow the dictates of his conscience and that if he entertained any doubts he would seek André's advice and follow whatever action the clergyman recommended. At this point Riel arrived and turned the discussion with a tirade against the clergy and Archbishop Taché; André asked him to leave. Schmidt reported that Riel's outburst had not made a good impression on the Metis who were present.[42]

Two days later, Riel returned and resumed the animated discussion. André did not hesitate to state that Riel was mad when he discussed politics. As he left, Riel stated that he was departing for the United States but that he would return with thousands of men who would ravage the countryside, and André would have to bear the responsibility for the consequences. Riel argued that malice on André's part prevented the clergyman from understanding his purpose, whereas Fathers Fourmond and Touze of Duck Lake were as ignorant as five-year-olds and could not understand him. These exchanges caused Schmidt to reflect that if the district were to emerge from this malaise without misfortune it would owe a large debt of gratitude to Father André. According to Schmidt, André was the only person who exposed Riel for what he really was and who could counter his impractical schemes.[43]

Schmidt then reported that Riel had sent Gabriel Dumont to speak to Lawrence Clarke, who had recently returned from Winnipeg and Regina. Clarke stated that military reinforcements were on the way and that all talk of revolt had to cease or there would be severe repercussions. Instead of heeding this prudent advice, Riel and Dumont, whom Schmidt referred to as "ces deux maniaques," decided to muster men in Batoche and raise the standard of revolt. Emissaries were sent among the Metis urging them to come to Batoche and protect Riel, but many Metis, fearing the consequences of armed revolt, did not heed Riel's call. Charles Nolin was prudently among their number, but an armed band of Metis brought him back by force, and he was tried by a council. Riel desired the death penalty but would have left the sentence in abeyance so that the clergy might intercede on Nolin's behalf and save his life by giving their approbation to the Rebellion. However, the council decided that if Nolin took his place among Riel's followers, the matter would be resolved.[44]

Schmidt noted that the news of the capture of Mitchell's store by Riel's men reached Prince Albert on 20 March and that reinforcements were sent to Fort Carleton and volunteers called up. Schmidt was among those who volunteered. Schmidt felt that nearly half of Riel's supporters in Batoche were there against their will, and he felt that many would leave if they heard of Major Crozier's proclamation that those who left the rebel camp would be treated well by the authorities.[45]

While these developments were taking place, English mixed bloods were holding meetings in which they deplored Riel's resort to arms but, nevertheless, continued to sympathize with him. They expressed their desire to remain neutral, but, in the present circumstances, Schmidt affirmed that this attitude was suspicious to say the least. He qualified his remarks by stating: "nos gens du moins, ont dans leur folie montré une espèce de bravoure, mais ceux-la attendant qu'on leur tire les marrons du feu."[46] When Riel sent some armed men to force the mixed bloods to join him, Schmidt felt that they were receiving that which they deserved: "ils sympathisent avec lui, eh! bien qu'ils aillent le défendre."[47]

Like other residents of Prince Albert, Schmidt was relieved when Colonel Irvine's column arrived on 24 March. Schmidt felt that Riel could easily have intercepted Irvine and delayed his arrival. The psychological effect of such an act would have increased Riel's forces considerably.[48] While Irvine's presence was reassuring, Prince Albert feared a surprise attack by the rebels or Indians. For his part, Schmidt did not believe that Riel would risk a confrontation when so many of his men were coerced into supporting him. Schmidt feared that Riel's more violent associates would gain the upper hand and force the issue and possibly even defeat the inexperienced troops marching towards them.[49]

During the evening of 26 March, Schmidt had visited with Father André. After returning to his residence, he was awakened by a loud knock and ordered to present himself to the barracks. While on his way there, Schmidt met a sentry who recognized him and told him to proceed. However, instead of going directly to his destination, Schmidt decided to return to Father André's in order to confess himself. He had taken only a few steps when the sentry, thinking that Schmidt was running away, ordered him to halt. Schmidt was then brought to the barracks as a prisoner, and it was there that he heard of the attack on Crozier's men near Duck Lake.[50] While some English residents suspected Schmidt, the officer in command did not and sent for André. A few hours later, Schmidt was released and put to work with other residents building a rampart around the Presbyterian Church which was to serve as the centre of refuge for Prince Albert.[51]

On 28 March, Schmidt learned that Charles Nolin had arrived in Prince Albert after having escaped from the rebels moments before they left to attack Crozier's column. Nolin was later placed under detention and complained to André that the guards were mistreating him. Schmidt was not moved by Nolin's lamentations:

Pauvre Nolin, on peut dire qu'il est puni par où il a pèché. N'est-il pas le principal instigateur des troubles d'aujourd'hui! Il est vrai qu'il a reconnu son erreur, mais il était trop tard.[52]

While Nolin was being questioned, news arrived that Fort Carleton had been abandoned and that the police and troops were returning to Prince Albert. That same afternoon, the population enthusiastically greeted the arrival of these men, and the town felt a great sense of security. In returning to his home, Schmidt discovered that numerous friends from the countryside had taken refuge there. He was in the midst of retiring when the alarm was sounded. He returned to the fortified church, obtained a firearm and ammunition, and took his place on the ramparts. Shortly after midnight the defenders were informed that it had been a false alarm. Everyone returned home, and Schmidt noted later that five women gave birth on that "terrible night."[53]

On 1 April 1885, Schmidt received news of conditions in Riel's camp. The Metis were dirty and disheveled and looked like demons, while the Indians had put on warpaint. Riel had stopped attending mass and had openly declared that he no longer adhered to the Church of Rome and that it was not the source of true Christian doctrine. Schmidt stated that he would not be surprised if the Metis came to revere Riel in an idolatrous manner. According to Schmidt, Riel was blinded by arrogance, and his religiosity had deluded the Metis, who were now being manipulated by him. Schmidt also lamented the fact that his uncle, Baptiste Boucher, was among Riel's followers despite the fact that a week before the outbreak of the Rebellion, Father André had exhorted him not to take up arms in support of Riel.[54]

In the meantime, Prince Albert lived under a state of siege, and provisions, grain, and hay were carefully rationed out to the inhabitants. On Good Friday, 3 April, Schmidt reported that there were no new developments, and he profited from the relative calm to record details of the encounter near Duck Lake on 26 March. He wrote that Crozier erred in leaving with so few men. Furthermore, Crozier wanted the honour of striking the first blow against Riel and underestimated the strength and determination of the Metis. The Prince Albert volunteers were equally naïve in thinking that the Metis would retreat after the first volley had been fired. Schmidt was not impressed with Riel's use of the crucifix during the battle: "Toujours de la comédie dans ce démon hypocrite." Schmidt claimed that Riel had broken one of the arms on the crucifix and later told his men that it had been damaged by gunfire.[55]

On Easter Sunday, Schmidt recorded that a courier from Battleford had arrived during the night bringing news that Indians had seized the industrial school and other government buildings outside the fort. These events did little to relieve tensions among Prince Albert's population. Schmidt wondered whether these Indians would join forces with Riel and bring even more havoc and destruction to the district. In attributing all the present misfortunes to Riel, Schmidt could not help but state:

Et c'est sous le couvert de la religion, de la piétié qu'il a médité et préparé ces plans infameux! C'est là sa mission divine, à cet homme d'état éminent![56]

Upon hearing that Riel's men had abandoned Fort Carleton and returned to Batoche, Schmidt wrote that Riel continued to mislead the Metis with his prophetic revelations. However, Schmidt could not ascertain whether the Metis still had as much confidence in Riel because many were deserting. Schmidt noted that Riel had informed his followers that he had experienced an extraordinary dream in which St. Joseph appeared and predicted that Riel would be king. According to Schmidt, this was not the first time that Riel revealed his dreams and commented on them. Riel used these charlatan acts to create the impression that he was a prophet, and the Metis, in their sincerity and blind faith, accepted them as signs of divine inspiration. Again, Schmidt's judgement was severe: "C'est ainsi qu'il a entamé tant d'innocents à l'abyme."[57]

On 9 April, Schmidt made the last entry in his notes. He recorded that Riel was in Batoche and that tranquility reigned in St. Laurent. There were desertions from Riel's camp, but no one seemed willing to inform these Metis that they would be well treated if they surrendered to the authorities. In discussing this matter with Father André, Schmidt expressed surprise that Father Fourmond had refused to accept such a mission. André replied that even if Fourmond had accepted, no one would believe him because the Metis listened only to Riel. While Schmidt did not wish to question the motives of the clergy, he felt that they should not abandon their responsibilities so quickly. He remained convinced that a large number of Metis would lay down their arms if they were assured that they would be dealt with fairly. According to Schmidt, the Metis had no alternative but to surrender: "C'est leur seule planche de salut."[58] The following day, Schmidt sent his notes to Taché.

After the fall of Batoche, Schmidt wrote Taché and stated that famine would compound the sorrow and desolation which the Metis presently faced. Predicting that the Metis would pay dearly for their apostasy, Schmidt described the extent to which the Metis had been deluded by Riel:

> ils le croyaient véritablement prophète comme il le disait et qu'il faisait des miracles. A preuve que le jour de la bataille de Batoche, les femmes en entendant le roulement des détonations de la mitrailleuse, s'écriaient "voici donc le miracle, écoutez le tonnerre qui tombe sur les soldats de Middleton."[59]

According to Schmidt, the Metis were convinced that they could win victory after victory and destroy the forces that had been sent against them. He explained this irrational behaviour by affirming that God rendered mad those whom he desired to destroy. Instead of listening to the clergy, the Metis had insulted and persecuted them and consequently had fallen into a hideous chasm. Schmidt concluded by stating that the district clergy had been severely shaken by the rebellion.[60]

In assessing Schmidt's manuscript, two questions immediately come to mind: Why did he keep such a lengthy account? Although a Metis and close friend, why was Schmidt so critical of Riel? Schmidt himself commented on the question of motivation in the letter he appended to his notes. Schmidt felt that individuals, whom he described as enemies of the French race and Catholic religion and jealous of his position in the Land Office, might attempt to discredit him by implying that since he had been involved in the Red River Insurrection, he must also be one of the instigators of the contemporary agitation. Thus, Schmidt compiled these detailed observations and sent them to Taché, who could then use them to defend him should the need arise.[61] As events were to prove, Schmidt's apprehensions were not without substance. His detention during the night of 26 March indicates that some in Prince Albert thought that he was a rebel agent. When the North-West Rebellion was being debated in Parliament in July 1885, M. C. Cameron, the Liberal member for Huron West, charged that Louis Schmidt, a Conservative, while in his capacity as "a paid official of the Tory Government, was private secretary and Secretary of State to Louis Riel."[62]

In addition to their use as a means of proving his loyalty, there was another reason why Schmidt wrote his account. He suggested that Taché might wish to prepare a resumé of the manuscript and release it to the press to make the public aware of the origins of the agitation. Schmidt believed that the Rebellion would be attributed to factors other than the real ones and that an attempt might be made to implicate the clergy. Schmidt affirmed that perhaps he had not sufficiently stressed the fact that influential people in Prince Albert had encouraged Riel. It was this support that had rendered Riel so bold.[63] Schmidt later sent a long memorandum to the deputy minister of the interior in which he related the numerous, but futile, attempts by the Metis to inform the authorities of their problems.[64]

Schmidt's critical assessment of Riel is a more complex matter, and a satisfactory explanation entails an examination of his role in the community, his religious convictions and his concept of the Metis identity. Schmidt has been accused of being indecisive, a man who remained aloof from the events of 1884–85 because he did not want to jeopardize his employment.[65] This appraisal is not only inaccurate but unjust. Schmidt took an active part in the early period of agitation. He sent petitions to Ottawa on behalf of the Metis of St. Louis and served as secretary of local meetings in which Metis grievances were voiced. It was Schmidt who suggested that Riel should be asked to come to the northwest. Schmidt felt that Riel would unite the Metis and that his influence would contribute to a satisfactory settlement of the difficulties.[66] Schmidt was secretary of the committee responsible for selecting the delegation which would confer with Riel. Schmidt was selected as one of the delegates, but on 12 May 1884, he received his appointment in the Land Office, and Father André dissuaded him from going to Montana.[67] In the meantime, Schmidt publicized the plight of the district in the French-language press. Riel later admitted that had it not been for Schmidt's articles in *Le Manitoba*, the agitation of the Settler's Union would not have been publicized. Riel urged his associate, W. H. Jackson, to credit Schmidt for his efforts without compromising his position.[68] Shortly after Riel's arrival in St.

Laurent, Schmidt went to see him and offered his services, but Riel urged Schmidt to remain in the Land Office where he could make a significant contribution to the Metis cause.[69] The collaboration between Schmidt and Riel appears to have ended in mid-September 1884 when Riel sent Schmidt a copy of the memorandum containing Metis demands and asked him to forward it to the press. Schmidt, who felt that the demands were extravagant, informed Riel that he was not prepared to add a commentary to the memorandum.[70]

It was not the fear of losing his employment that caused Schmidt to withdraw his support but the realization that Riel was not the same person he had collaborated with in Red River. Although Schmidt initially had been very optimistic, shortly after Riel's return he had a premonition that the protest movement might get out of hand.[71] Early in his notes Schmidt wrote that the object of Riel's agitation was to gather the people of the northwest into a common front and make their views known to Ottawa by means of a memorial. Schmidt felt it necessary to qualify his remarks with the statement, "Voilà ce que Riel dit aujourd'hui."[72] In August 1884, Schmidt's premonition had become a deep suspicion as a result of the encounters between Riel and Father André. A short time later, Schmidt became convinced that Riel was an arrogant hypocrite who was utilizing religion to further his own interests. According to Schmidt, Riel's religiosity was not sincere; it was a façade to manipulate the gullible Metis.

In all probability Schmidt could have forgiven Riel's opportunism had Riel not donned the mantle of the prophet. Schmidt was an intensely devout person, and he could not tolerate any deviation from orthodoxy. In addition to fulfilling his religious obligations, Schmidt also had great admiration for the clergy. When Riel challenged the doctrines of the Church and the authority of its clergy, Schmidt could not but harshly condemn him. So great was Schmidt's disgust and contempt for Riel that the latter's name was never mentioned in the Schmidt household. Schmidt's diary, of which fifty-one years are still extant, mentions Riel only four times: one entry notes the time of his execution, and the three subsequent ones recall the anniversary of Riel's death.[73]

Schmidt's reaction to Riel provides us with valuable insights into his concept of the Metis identity. Schmidt had very little in common with the defenders of Batoche. He never denied that he was a Metis and took great pride in his mixed-blood ancestry. In his writings, he makes a clear distinction between Metis and Indian, but the same demarcation does not exist between Metis and French Canadian. In his comments on Riel's proposal to create a new nationality in the West, Schmidt implies that the difference between the Metis and French-Canadian races is that the former have less education than the latter. It is also implied that as the Metis alter their lifestyle, they will be in a position to obtain an education and be no different from French Canadians. Schmidt could base this observation on his own experience. For all practical purposes, Louis Schmidt had been absorbed into the French-Canadian community. He did not have to strive for this transition to take place; it came about naturally because of his education and Catholicism, and he was not ostracized because of his mixed blood.

In the final analysis, history has been more generous to Riel than it has been to Schmidt. To the Metis, Riel became a martyr and a hero, whereas Schmidt, if he were remembered at all, was regarded as a person who had abandoned or betrayed the Metis in 1885. So strong was this conviction that a quarter of a century later in 1909, Schmidt felt compelled to make a solemn declaration outlining his activities during the Rebellion.[74] Scholars have tended to dismiss Schmidt as a person who lacked imagination because he did not fulfil a leadership role in Metis society. In fact, Schmidt provided leadership but not in the society his critics examined. Schmidt was a pillar in the French-Canadian community, and he played a significant role on the school board, municipal council, parish council, the movement to organize French-speaking Catholics in Saskatchewan, and the efforts to promote and enhance French language instruction in schools. Thus, it was fitting that the following inscription should appear on his tombstone: "Chrétien Convaincu Ardent Patriote."

NOTES

1. Archives of the Archdiocese of St. Boniface [hereafter cited as AASB], Louis Schmidt, "Notes: Mouvement des Métis à St. Laurent Sask. T.N.O. en 1884," T29781–840.
2. Ibid., Schmidt to Taché, 8 avril 1885, T31062–063.
3. Ibid., T29806.
4. Ibid., T29781–782.
5. Ibid., T29783.
6. Ibid., T29784.
7. Ibid.
8. Ibid., T29785.
9. Ibid., T29786.
10. Ibid.
11. Ibid., T29787–788.
12. Ibid., T29788.
13. Ibid.
14. Ibid., T29789.
15. Ibid.
16. Ibid., T29790.
17. Ibid., T29791.
18. Ibid., T29792.
19. Ibid., T29790–791.
20. Ibid., T29793.
21. Ibid., T29796.
22. Ibid., T29797.
23. Ibid., T29795.

24. Ibid., T29794.
25. Ibid., T29798.
26. Ibid., T29794.
27. Ibid., T29798.
28. Ibid., T29901–802.
29. Ibid., T29802–803.
30. Ibid., T29803–804.
31. Ibid., T29806.
32. Ibid., T29804–805.
33. Ibid., T29808.
34. Ibid., T29808–810.
35. Ibid., T29811.
36. Ibid.
37. Ibid., T29812.
38. Ibid.
39. Ibid., T29813.
40. Ibid., T29813–814.
41. Ibid., T29815.
42. Ibid., T29815–816.
43. Ibid., T29816.
44. Ibid., T29817–819.
45. Ibid., T29820.
46. Ibid.
47. Ibid., T29821.
48. Ibid.
49. Ibid., T29824.
50. Ibid., T29825.
51. Ibid., T29827.
52. Ibid., T29832.
53. Ibid., T29830–831.
54. Ibid., T29833–834.
55. Ibid., T29836–837.
56. Ibid., T29837–838.
57. Ibid., T29838–839.
58. Ibid., T29840.
59. Ibid., Schmidt to Taché, 27 mai 1885, T31420.
60. Ibid., T31420–421.
61. Ibid., Schmidt to Taché, 8 avril 1885, T31063–064.
62. *Debates of the House of Commons, Canada*, 1885, p. 3155.
63. AASB, Schmidt to Taché, 8 avril 1885, T31065.
64. Ibid. Schmidt to Burgess, 26 mai 1885, T31401–404, copy.
65. George Woodcock, *Gabriel Dumont: The Métis Chief and His Lost World* (Edmonton, 1975), pp. 120, 127.
66. *Le Patriote de l'Ouest*, "Les Mémoires de Louis Schmidt," 16 mai 1912.
67. Ibid., 23 mai 1912.
68. Archives of the University of Saskatchewan, W. H. Jackson Papers, Riel to Jackson, 2? August 1884.
69. Louis Schmidt, "Déclaration," 16 décembre 1909.
70. Saskatchewan, Archives Board, Louis David Riel R298, Schmidt to Riel, 19 septembre 1884.
71. AASB, Schmidt to Taché, 8 avril 1885, T31064.
72. Ibid., "Notes," T29785.
73. Le Journal de Louis Schmidt.
74. Schmidt, "Déclaration."

6

La Conquête du Nord-Ouest, 1885–1985:
or
The Imperial Quest of British North America*

Jean Morisset

Committed under the juridicial patronage of the Queen of England,[1] the hanging of Louis Riel in Regina on 16 November 1885 stands out as the virtual assassination of the Métis canadien. In fact the very name Regina — latin for Queen — had three years before been substituted for the Cree name Oskana (pile of bones), thus symbolizing the geographical conquest of the northwest land by the British Crown.

The year 1885 is one of the foremost dates of British North American history. Not only does it mark the official completion of the northwest conquest, but it also tolls the death knell of the idea of a Métis country north of the United States of America. As a matter of fact, Louis Riel embodied in his single person the two nationalities — the *nationalité canadienne* and the *nationalité autochtone* — that the state recently created through the BNA Act (1867) set forth to eradicate at the onset from its socio-political matrix. The consequences of such a political action are still with us to this day and indeed for the cornerstone of the so-called "Canadian" problem.

The persistent endeavor to eliminate from the British North America statehood both the *dimension canadienne* (referred to nowadays as the Québec syndrome) and the *dimension autochtone* (otherwise known as the native land claim issue) summarizes a century of efforts on the part of British Americans. If anyone were not certain on that matter, the events that took place during the night of 5 November 1981 left no doubt as to the spirit that has commanded the confederation predicament for more than a century, when the nine partners (the nine English-speaking provinces) against one (the non-English-speaking province) announced that they had reached a constitutional arrangement. So what is the total one may ask? It cannot be "ten," for if "nine" partners have coalesced into "one," it is not nine against one, but rather it is One against One. The nine-that-make-one also originally excluded from their constitutional package deal any aboriginal right's clause. So obviously one is faced again with a One-to-One ratio. What do we end up with then? We have the nine-that-makes-one English-speaking provinces, we have the one-that-makes-one French-speaking province, and we have the aboriginal-People throughout the provinces.[2] And it could hardly be more evident that such a triangular relationship, once termed "les Canadiens," les Sauvages," and "les Anglais" brings us back exactly to the situation that has existed in this country since the Conquest.[3] In turn, this led to the conquest of the northwest or the imperial conquest of British North America.

Throughout this text I use the appellation British North America to refer to what is actually known as Canada. It is not a matter of fortuitous policy that the act issued by the British Parliament in 1867 was not called the Canadian Act but the British North America Act. The country and people of Canada are a conquered people and country. And they were conquered by newcomers who have come very reluctantly at first but more gradually afterwards to call themselves under the proper name of the conquered ones, the "canadiens." This is a unique fact in the history of the Americas.[4] The land known as Canada can only be called such under a straightforward process of usurpation and henceforth cannot really be referred to, in geohistorical terms by any other appellation than British North America. The whole question of appropriation thus leads me to the question of the founding principles, that is the "founding myths" whether explicit or implicit, upon which the British North American state has built itself.

There can hardly be a more revealing way to decipher the basic nature of this state than to examine its political and symbolic behaviour with respect to the issue of *métissage*, whether somatic or cultural. For what matters above all is to know what type or political entity, what type of "American country" or, in other words, what kind of "new world country" British North America has wanted to be throughout its development.[5] Such a question cannot be put forward without a reinterpretation of history (and history does not exist outside its interpretation), namely from the viewpoint of the conquered ones.

British North America is the result of three historical periods:

1. the Conquest of Canada, 18th century,
2. the Conquest of the Northwest, 19th century,
3. the Conquest of the Far North, 20th century,

during which three groups were present:

1. the "Indians,"
2. the "Canadians,"
3. the "British Americans."[6]

Not only were the Indians politically present throughout these periods, but from a *canadien* viewpoint the fact that a country called Canada could exist was obviously less owing to France's efforts than to the sociological and strategical alliances of the *canadiens* with the Indians. And besides, without the *canadiens* there cannot be any *Canada*. I think that one can go as far as to say that the *canadiens* as a people would have ceased to exist sometime in the eighteenth century if it had not been for the *Indians*. And this is precisely why the settlers of the English colonies referred to the wars that led to the Conquest of Canada as the French and Indians wars rather than as the Seven Years' War. This bespeaks the Indians permanent geopolitical importance. To maintain that the Indians were in such a state of defeat after the eighteenth century that they only remained witnesses to their own nonexistence while passively attending the political process that built British North America is nothing but a conqueror's phantasm:[7] if we now turn to the second conquest, that of the northwest which immediately followed Confederation, the Métis appears by all accounts, as the main political force that enabled British North America to secure territories that would otherwise have been annexed to the United States of America.[8] To thank the Métis for such loyalty, the state found no better solution than to arrange their dispersion by all sorts of measures similar to those the Acadiens had to suffer a century and a half before. Remember the words of John A. Macdonald: "Should these miserable half-breeds not disband, they must be put down. . . . These impulsive half-breeds have got spoiled by this emeute and must be kept down by a strong hand until they are swamped by the influx of settlers."[9] The point that must be stressed here is that those people that ought to be swamped kept reappearing continuously in the minds of the conquerors' heirs. If we only take for instance Margaret Laurence's *The Diviners*, the Métis/Native appears as the overall hero of British North American literature. And if you scratch the skin of the Métis, you will find the Indian's long shadow haunting the soul of the conqueror, who is desperately searching for his own identity, again through usurpation and appropriation. In this respect John Newlove's poem *The Pride* comes to mind.

> At last we become the Indians
> And they become our true forebearers . . .
> And in this land *we are their people*. . . .[10]

It would be difficult indeed to find a clearer case of intellectual hijacking if Northrop Frye himself had not overbid him through his own spiritual abduction. Frye's statement comes out in non-equivocal terms: "It seems clear that for

Canadian culture the old imperialist phrase going native has come to roost. We are no longer an army of occupation, and the natives are ourselves."[11] To put the above in a true perspective, only a short time ago an oil company's representative declared in Yellowknife "[forget about the native claims] we should develop and enter the North as an army of occupation."

This makes it all the more obscene that everything was possible in the northwest during the 1870–85 period and afterwards. All the conditions were there for the development and growth of a North American Métis/Native country comparable to what the New World has produced in parts of Middle America, the Caribbean, or Brazil. There were then about 10,000 Métis (roughly 55 per cent were Métis canadiens and 45 per cent Métis Orcadians)[12] and there were of course many more indigenous people in the rest of the unincorporated territory. It is revealing to compare that situation with the one that prevailed in Canada at the time of the Conquest.

In 1713, there were about 10,000 canadiens, and 60,000 in 1760. They have become the 6 million "Canadiens" of today, a number that should be increased to 15 or even 20 million if all those who have been assimilated in North America could be added up. Now if we apply the same ratio to the northwest, it is obvious that there would exist today a Métis/Native Nation totalling at least 3 to 4 million people had they not been swamped by the influx of the state. The first political act of the British North American state was indeed to erase such possibility, and this is why the execution of Riel and the others must be understood, in present day terms, as a deliberate political assassination to prevent the development of such a Métis/Native country in the northwest of the Americas. Such a possibility did exist at the time and still exists, all things being equal, today in the North. And it is now clear that such a country was at the time eradicated by an imperial dictator by the name of John A. Macdonald.

The prime minister of British North America, John A. Macdonald, said something that tells everything about his conception of the New World: "I was born a British subject, I shall die a British subject." The first and last principle of a British North America is therefore a colonial one. "I want to produce a British Nationality out of America," he emphasized elsewhere.[13] He did not say "I want to produce an American Nationality out of the British." And this is why he had to kill Louis Riel, whose very essence was the antithesis of his own, whereas Esprit-Errant (Wandering Spirit), Gros-Ours (Big Bear), and Faiseur-d'Enclos (Pound Maker) conveyed the image of America he most highly despised and set forth to destroy.

So Macdonald, the revered father of the so-called "Canadian Confederation," never wanted to be a Canadian to begin with. He was not born in Canada. He was an immigrant who was never part of Canada. Far from being a "canadien," Macdonald is precisely the *anti-canadien par excellence*. He just could not be otherwise. And further, Macdonald was also an *anti-americain* in the sense that he never wanted to produce an American nationality of any kind. He rather wanted to produce an European type of identity into the New World. And most of all, Macdonald was *anti-métis* and *anti-native*. I think I should finally add a last distinction; John A. Macdonald has been essentially an anti-liberator.

What is meaningful to remember is that Macdonald's visions were put forward in the late nineteenth century at a time when all the countries of the Americas had obtained their independence from Europe and were telling the whole world how different they wanted to be from the Old World. Macdonald's concept of the New World society was the Canadian Pacific Railway, that is, a bridge to cross from Britain to British Columbia and onwards to British India and British Australasia via British America. Oddly enough, this colonial/imperial geography was being boosted at the same historical period in which Simon Bolivar in Venezuela, José Martí in Cuba, Emiliano Zapata in Mexico, Toussaint l'Ouverture in Haiti, Tupac Amarú in Peru, and Louis Riel in the northwest were shaping the image of the Americas against the old realities of Europe. And they were doing so basically by calling upon a single parameter: the *Other*, that is the *Autochtone*, the *Native* — the very being without which the New World could not really be "New." In many corners of the Americas, the Black was of course called upon as an "element de métissage" without which an american identity could not exist, but he was no more a native American than the European was. As a matter of fact, it is practically impossible, everywhere in the Americas, to build up an *american identity* outside of Native America. And it is further impossible to contemplate such an identity without some sort of "founding métissage."

The word "métissage" does not exist in English, and there is simply no social philosophy based on such process. Rather the English colonial mind is the genitor of the "apartheid policy" and of the "Indian reservation." Born out of the United Empire Loyalists' desire to remain faithful to colonial Britain, and thus to colonial and monarchistic Europe, British North America had no choice but to build a set of values completely different from what was taking shape elsewhere in the Americas, and even in the United States. One only has to compare Jefferson's thinking with that of Macdonald to encounter two worlds that could not be further apart: the first one being democratic and republican, the second one imperialistic and monarchistic. And it is evident that the whole anti-republican ideology that followed the Confederation was a mere political exercise devised to show how different the USA was from British North America. It is therefore all the more revealing to realize that as soon as British North America was given an opportunity to state its differences from the United States, the sons of the United Empire Loyalists found no better idea than to borrow at once from those same Americans a machine gun to show the Métis the right way at Batoche, in the purest Custer tradition. The contradiction thus comes to a full turn.

This tells us much about the true principles upon which British North America would enshrine its ongoing development. The history of the northwest is indeed a mirror reflecting the philosophical and political beliefs of British North America. Why is there to this day such a thing as the "Northwest Territories?" If one looks upon a map, the Northwest Territories point directly to the northeast. Why such an anomaly? My underlying question becomes, Where do the Northwest Territories come from?

There is a revealing assertion made by Riel about the northwest. He noted, "The North-West is . . . my mother, it is my mother country . . . and I am sure that my mother country will not kill me."[14] As Riel's mother was not British, it is obvious that the northwest did exist long before British America came into being. If one reads the map of North America, the northwest does appear a century and a half or so before the British North America Act was signed, and therefore not only can it not be British American at all, but is a translation from something else — a translation from another time and from another universe — a translation from another language. In fact the name northwest comes from the *canadien* "nord-ouest" and refers to the Métis/Native country extending somewhere beyond Canada and Louisiana. A country that my forefathers had called *le nord-ouest*, that is north and west of the Mississippi and Missouri, at the time when they were mixed with the people and the land of this country. But this country, *le nord-ouest*, has never existed as a recognized political entity. The northwest has remained and shall always remain an invisible country, a ghost-country, a country that only existed to be wiped out through the provincialization of its land. And the provincialization of the land was realized through the treaty-making process according to the principles, the schemes, the law and order of the British conquerors. And where the conquerors did not see fit to push this process upon the autochtones, the northwest still exists, as is the case in the present day Far North.

The Métis plea for a special Métis/Native type of jurisdiction had resulted in the formation of the province of Manitoba in 1870. But instead of working out a new type of provincehood, British North America set up a provincial status for Manitoba that was somewhat like Quebec's, with provisions for the use of French as under the federal jurisdiction. In reality, the dominant language of the northwest was called *le metiff*. Indeed, French did not become an official language of Manitoba as a European language but as a Métis language. It is that language which was made outcast by the provincial legislature in 1890. And so was it with the creation of Saskatchewan and Alberta in 1905. By the turn of the twentieth century, the old southern northwest had entirely disappeared under the province-making process of British North America.

The conquerors were skillful indeed in accepting native names, such as Manitoba or Saskatchewan. In so doing they co-opted the aboriginal people into being assimilated under a name of their own. For a "Manitoban" was not only a "son of the *Land of the Manitou*," he was also a product of the British North American state. The gradual disappearance of the northwest, the creation of non-contiguous reservations so as to destroy the unity of the land, and the formation of alien provinces brought about a geographical duality that remains at the heart of the British North American policy of assimilation to this very day. The fact that we can hold a Métis Symposium without simultaneous translation (even if I know that a Métis is a simultaneous translation by himself) is meaningful enough, and is indeed only possible because we all tacitly agree to speak the language of the conqueror.

At his trial, Riel was condemned as a traitor to the country that was not his country. The answer to Riel's plea for his mother, *le nord-ouest*, came from John A. Macdonald in rather blunt and violent terms: "He shall hang though every dog in Quebec bark in his favour." In 1885, Riel and his mother-land, *le nord-ouest*, were hanged together. According to British North America state policy, there would not be such a thing as a new nation in North America — there would not be a Métis/Native country. As Buffy Sainte-Marie has so bitterly pointed out in a poem:

> Now that the pride of the sires receive charity,
> Now that we're harmless and safe behind laws,
> Now that my life's to be known as your heritage,
> Now that even the graves have been robbed,
> Now that our own chosen way is a novelty,
> Hands on our hearts, we salute you your victory,
> Choke on your blue-white-and-scarlet hypocrisy . . .
> My Country Tis of Thy People You're Dying.
>
> Buffy Sainte-Marie, 1966.

If we look towards the coming years, it is obvious that the government of British North America (otherwise known as "Canada") intends to have settled by 1985 the case of the Dene and the Inuit people in the Northwest Territories (the present day *Nord-Ouest.*) Will the British North America founding principles lead only to a re-enactment of the 1885 parody? And will Dènèndeh and Nunavut be inexorably driven towards the same political fate as that experienced by Manitoba and the former Northwest Territory? The night of 5 November 1981 in Ottawa and the ongoing renewed constitutional pilfering herald a rather gloomy future. But it is not at all obvious that British North America will escape unscathed if it chooses to celebrate the end of the twentieth century by a new conquest of the northwest based on the nineteenth-century model.

NOTES

* Je suis on ne peut plus reconnaissant envers Denis Demontigny du Collège communautaire de la Montagne-à-la-Tortue (Dakota-Nord) de m'avoir transmis l'enregistrement de ma communication. Autrement je n'aurais pu rédiger ce texte qui a profité egalement des conseils éditoriaux de Ian Getty. Je remercie egalement Antoine S. Lussier de m'avoir invité à la conference de Brandon. I would also like to mention that his paper is not a translation and was written in a language that is not mine.

1. See Desmond Morton, ed., *The Queen v. Louis Riel* (Toronto, 1974), p. 383.
2. I have expanded slightly these ideas in a text called "Le maraudage constitutionnel renouvelé" and re-titled by *Le Devoir* (6 janvier 1982) as "Quand le Canada triomphe des Indiens et des Québécois."
3. For another aspect of the same geopolitical interplay, see my article "The Aboriginal Nationhood, The Northern Challenge and the Construction of Canadian Unity" in *Queen's Quarterly* 88, no. 2 (Summer 1981): 237–50.
4. It is not impossible to forsee the day when Quebec will abandon its present name (which was imposed by the conquerors anyhow) of Quebec to go back to its real name of Canada, and the English-speaking provinces will then have to find a name of their own rather than usurping from the conquered country of Canada. These questions are documented at length in my forthcoming book, *L'identité usurpée. La fabrication du Canada* (Montréal, 1983).
5. I use here the term "American" in its identical meaning that is as opposed to "European."
6. I have first suggested this interpretation in my essay "Miroir indogène/reflet eurogène. Essai sur l'américanité et la fabrication de l'identité canadienne," in *Recherches Amérindiennes au Québec* 9, no. 4 (1980): 285–313.
7. The fact that a man like George Erasmus (president, Dene National Office and by far the greatest political leader that the West and the North have produced in the twentieth century) could emerge is meaningful enough.
8. See amongst other sources A.-G. Morice, *Histoire abrégée de l'Ouest Canadien* (Saint-Boniface, 1914), in particular p. 91. See also Joseph Howard's *Strange Empire* (Toronto, 1952, 1974).
9. Quoted by Stanley-Bréhaut Ryerson in *Unequal Union, Roots of Conflict in the Canadas, 1815–1873* (Toronto, 1968) from Joseph Pope's *Correspondence of Sir John Macdonald*, pp. 388–89.
10. Quoted by Northrop Frye in "Haunted by Lack of Ghosts," in David Staines, ed., *The Canadian Imagination* (Cambridge, 1977), pp. 22–46, 39–40. Emphasis is my own.
11. Excerpt from "Canadian Culture Today," an address read to the *Twentieth Century Canadian Culture Symposium* (Washington, D.C., 2 February 1977) and reprinted under the title "Sharing the Continent," in Northrop Frye, *Divisions on a Ground: Essays on Canadian Culture* (Toronto, 1982). See p. 69. Emphasis is my own.
12. See Alexandre-Antonin Taché, *Equisse sur le Nord-Ouest de l'Amerique* (Montréal, 1869).
13. This quotation and the one above are mentioned in Mason Wade, *The French Canadians, 1760–1945* (Toronto, 1955).
14. See Desmond Morton, p. 312.
15. Quoted in George F. G. Stanley, *Louis Riel* (Toronto, 1963), p. 367.

7

Native People and the Justice System

Don McCaskill

Given the frequency with which native people come into conflict with the law in this country and the immeasureable human suffering entailed, one would assume that there would be in existence a large body of theoretical and empirical literature on the topic. Such is not the case. The area of native people and the justice system, and the law generally, has been a neglected area of scholarly enquiry in Canada. This is despite the fact that the relationship between native people and the justice system is, in at least two ways, of fundamental importance to both Indians and Canadians generally.

The first and most pressing in the immediate sense is the issue of native people and the criminal justice system. The situation is nothing short of a national disgrace. A study of native offenders conducted in 1970 discovered that the number of Indians in correctional institutions was shocking, especially west of central Ontario. For example, in Manitoba in 1968 the proportion of imprisoned native people varied from 30 per cent in federal and provincial institutions near Winnipeg to almost 100 per cent of the inmate population in rural correctional institutions.[1] Even more serious is the fact that since that time the situation appears to have worsened. In 1978, 34 per cent of all inmates admitted into correctional institutions in Alberta were native. The figure for Saskatchewan is 61 per cent.[2] Similarly, in northwestern Ontario in 1978, native male admissions to provincial jails constituted 24 per cent in Thunder Bay, 32 per cent in Fort Frances, and 48 per cent in Kenora.[3] The percentages are even higher for female offenders.[4] Clearly, the law and justice system are ineffective in their dealings with native people.

The conventional explanation for this phenomenon views native offenders as members of a pathological community characterized by extensive social and personal problems. The focus is inevitably on the individual offenders. They are seen as simply being unable to adjust successfully to the rigours of contemporary society. They are part of a larger "Indian problem" for which various social service agencies have been created to help Indians meet the standards of the dominant society. The long-range goal is that, in time, with sufficient help, Indians will lose most of their culture, adopt the values of the larger society, become upwardly mobile, and be incorporated into mainstream society. In short, Indians will assimilate.

This is a misleading and inaccurate way of understanding the conflict between native people and the justice system. Viewed in a different way, when patterns of behaviour seem unresponsive to attempts by the legal system to affect them, it might be more useful to focus attention on the legal system itself to explain why the law is ineffective.[5] The issue becomes one of the "justness" or "fairness" of the system. It is analyzed as a structural problem addressing questions of social injustice based on inequalities in society as they are reflected in the legal system.

The second, and broader, issue, is the application, legitimacy, and meaning of the justice system as it affects native people in Canada. In order to comprehend the meaning of the justice system for native people, it is important to understand the colonial relationship which exists between native people and the larger Canadian society. Colonialism involves a relationship which leaves one side dependent on the other to define the world. At the individual level, colonialism involves a situation where one individual is forced to relate to another on terms unilaterally defined by the other.[6] The justice system becomes a central institution with which to impose the way of life of the dominant society.

This relationship grew out of the Canadian government's policy toward Indians in the nineteenth century. After Indians were no longer useful for economic or military purposes, the government established a system of reserves designed to "protect and civilize" native people in order that they might eventually assimilate. The policy was to settle the Indians on the land and, over time, develop them into "productive citizens." In theory, Indians were to learn to exercise self-determination and assume responsibilities for their own affairs. Missionaries, educators, Indian agents, judges, and police were sent to the reserves to facilitate the transition from savagery to civilization. The Indians themselves had little to say about the process, because there was no political structure within which they could operate effectively. The reserve system, to some degree, replaced the Indians' traditional authority structures with the paternalistic authoritarianism of the dominant society's agents. As Chamberlain points out.

The exercise of choices and of responsibilities was urgently demanded; and when it was not forthcoming, the illusion was fostered that choices had been made and responsibilities accepted. But it was nothing more than an illusion; and when the illusion was shattered, a deep disillusion set in, which in many cases continues still.[7]

Encouraged to become self-sufficient, the Indian was prevented from being so in almost every area — economic, political, and administrative. He was being asked to give up his traditional culture but was given little sense that he had any control in the process of change. In time, the colonial policy was partially successful as Indians became dependent upon the political, economic, and legal structures of the dominant society.

In this way the Canadian legal and judicial system become a mechanism of social control which functioned to legitimate the reality of the dominant society. Legitimation in this colonial context can be seen in the government's attempt to "explain" and "justify" to native people the values and institutions of Canadian society. Agents of legitimation such as teachers, Indian agents, police, and judges had the responsibility to inform native people why they should perform one action and not another, all in the interest of civilizing the Indian. Deviation from the law was not to be tolerated since it represented a threat to the authority of the government over native people, indeed, at times, even a threat to its tenuous hold over the country itself. Thus, when the Metis assumed political control of the Red River settlement in 1869 and established their own judicial system, retribution of the most serious kind was evoked by the Canadian government.

Viewed with the benefit of hindsight, it can be seen that the policy of attempting to protect and civilize the Indian was bound to fail. This failure continues to have serious implications for the relationship between native people and the justice system today. Much of the failure can be traced to contradictions inherent in the policy itself. Placing Indians on isolated reserves away from meaningful contact with the larger society did indeed "protect" them from significant encroachments, but, in fact, it also functioned to thwart any substantive "civilizing" effects. For the government to assume that they could replace Indian authority structures with a foreign value system simply through the individual efforts of educators, government agents, and others was naive. Civilizing the Indian with an eye to eventually assimilating them did not, and could not, occur.

Viewing the situation as a problem of legitimation (including legitimation of the legal system), we can see that while government agents attempted to justify the values and norms of Canadian society, they made little efforts to explain the institutional order by affording Indians any meaningful experience with the institutions themselves. It is important to understand that any legitimation effort involves a cognitive as well as normative element.[8] In other words, legitimation is not just a matter of values; it always implies knowledge as well. Legitimation not only tells the individual why he should perform one action and not another; it also tells him why things are the way they are. For this to occur, individuals need to acquire extensive first-hand experience with the institutional structure. With native people isolated on reserves and rural settlements away from contact with white society, this could not occur. Native people, therefore, could have no understanding of the structure and functioning of the legal and judicial systems.

In many instances this situation still exists. In research among native inmates it is not uncommon to find individuals in jails who do not understand what happened to them from the time of arrest until incarceration.[9] This was particularly the case for native people from isolated northern regions. As Judge Ian Dubienski, a magistrate with extensive experience in the North with cases involving native people, states:

> The futility of some cases is striking. How do you judge an accused who truly doesn't know he has done wrong, who knows nothing of the rules of evidence, who is completely mystified by the court procedure.[10]

But if the legal and judicial systems have not, to any large degree, been adequately applied, or even legitimated, for native people, and if they have not assimilated, how did native people come to terms with their situation? One response, of course, is to become a victim of the system. There is no doubt that this is the case for an extremely large number of native people who come into conflict with the law and end up in correctional institutions. But it would be simplistic and misleading to suggest that this has been the only response Indians have made to the intolerable circumstances they find themselves in with regard to their relationship with the judicial system. Even in a situation of colonial oppression, individuals not only respond to their circumstances but also create them. Native people developed a number of adaptive strategies which involved the formation of a strong minority community on reserves and rural settlements, as well as particular patterns of interaction with the larger society. A central feature of this pattern involved avoiding meaningful contact with members of the larger society. Specifi-cally, this entailed a lack of participation in the institutions of the dominant society, formation of ethnic-specific kinship and friendship networks, and con-tinued involvement in Indian cultural activities. From the point of view of native people, these patterns can best be understood as attempts to legitimate a coherent sense of self in response to the treatment inherent in the colonial situation. The isolated reserves provided an ideal geographical base to maintain this response, especially after the 1930's when government attempts to civilize the Indians began to dissipate in many parts of the country. After that it is perhaps accurate to characterize government policy as to "protect and forget" native people.

It is also important to remember that in any interaction situation, no matter how oppressive, individuals retain knowledge of and attachment for their old society and way of life, especially when the new standards of behaviour have little meaning and are not seen to be legitimate in the first place. This is particularly pertinent for native people and the law and justice system. There is general agreement among anthropologists and legal scholars that virtually all societies have something that can reasonably be termed "law" in the sense of some collective enforcement of norms; and a "judicial system" viewed as specialized machinery for general settling of disputes.[11] Adamson Hoebel provides a definition of law as follows: "A social norm is legal if its neglect or infraction is regularly met, in threat or in fact, by the application of physical force by an individual or group possessing the socially recognized privilege of so acting."[12] In his study of the law of traditional native cultures, Hoebel makes it clear that virtually all Indian societies possessed functioning legal and judicial systems. For example, the tribal council of the Pueblo Indians and the Cheyenne military societies carried out in their pursuit of justice similar duties and responsibilities to those of our modern courts.[13] Similarly, Judge Jack Sissons, first magistrate of the Territorial Court of the Northwest Territories, discovered that the Inuit possessed a functioning set of laws and customs which, he felt, should be recognized by the Canadian justice system:

> Through the bland subterfuge of making white man's law apply to Eskimos, the department was illegally taking away from these people the protection of their ancient rights and customs. . . . I held that the marriage . . . was a marriage in accordance with Eskimo custom and was a legal marriage under the laws of the Northwest Territories.[14]

This situation is recognized as a central legal problem inherent in colonial law where "subcultures in such a society may create vast problems of law's being out of phase with the customs and mores of parts of the society."[15] The problem occurs because there are in existence two legal systems, the colonial government's and the Indian's. The response of governments in dealing with the situation is usually (as in the Canadian case) to ignore the sub-culture's legal system and impose a unicentric power system. The result is inevitably unsatisfactory.

> The mark of a colonial situation might be said to be a systematic misunderstanding between the two cultures within the single power system, with constant revolutionary proclivities resulting from what is, at best, a "working misunderstanding."[16]

Thus if the justice system of a society "depends essentially on how fundamental rights and duties are assigned and on the economic opportunities and social conditions in the various sectors of society,"[17] and if the preceding analysis of the colonial experience as it affected native people is valid, then it can be justifiably concluded that the Canadian justice system is, in fact, in many ways, not "just" at all as it applies to native people.

Perhaps the most serious consequence of the colonial experience in human terms has been the disproportionately large number of native people coming into conflict with the law and their subseqent incarceration in correctional institutions in this country. It is interesting to note that the high incidence of conflicts with the law have occurred only within the last twenty years since native people have begun to extend their participation beyond the boundaries of the reserve and compete within the structures of the dominant society. Therefore, native crime can be viewed as the consequence of increased interaction with institutions of the larger society where the pressures to assimilate are acute. In Manitoba, the reserves exhibiting the highest rates of crime are those closest to white towns and cities.[18] Conversely, the lowest crime rates are in isolated reserves.

With increased interaction with the dominant society, native people often find themselves categorically excluded. The colonial experience of the reserve extends itself to their relationship with members of the white community where they are treated as members of an inferior category, without respect to their individual merits. They are distinguished from the dominant group by physical and cultural traits in a way that can be described as a "minority situation," characterized by a lack of full participation in the institutions of the dominant society.[19] Members of the minority remain visible by virtue of their disadvantageous position and are further hampered by their lack of access to dominant values. Finally, the consequences of such treatment are characteristics that set the minority further apart and debar it from participation.

The social and psychological characteristics of a minority group then develop as a consequence of its disadvantaged position. The inferior power position of native people in the colonial situation is thus perpetuated.

> Minority groups are thus the product of the dominant group's power to establish its way of life as normative and to pass on the eligibility of its participants. Those who are defined as ineligible become as unequal as they are treated. Minority status becomes self-perpetuating as exclusion extends itself over time; deprivation of access to dominant values leads to lack of qualification for them.[20]

At the individual level, native people must come to terms with their categorically ascribed inferior status. They do so often at considerable social and psychological costs. Patterns of native criminality can be usefully understood as a response to these intolerable frustrations inherent in the minority situation. This is supported by the dissimilarity between the patterns of criminal activity of native people and those of non-native offenders. It can be argued that Indian and Metis people presently incarcerated in correctional institutions should not be considered "criminals" in the stereotypical sense of the word. A 1970 study revealed three characteristics of Indian and Metis criminal activity which supports this contention. First, to a large extent, native people commit only two types of crime — theft and assault.[21] Among native inmates of federal and provincial correctional institutions, over 90 per cent of all crimes fell into these categories. Of the crimes against property almost all were committed against the property of a non-Indian (usually the "white" store on the reserve or in a nearby town), whereas all crimes against the person were committed against other Indians. Secondly, the vast majority (63 per cent) of native offences were impulsive in motivation and unpremeditated.[22] Finally, a large proportion of violations involved alcohol, either directly (70 per cent) or indirectly (85 per cent).

These criminal patterns of the early 1970's can be interpreted in light of the model described earlier as characteristic of minority groups which consider themselves excluded from participation in the dominant society. Thus, stealing from Whites becomes a way of "getting back" for exclusion, or at least it is condoned by native society because it is against outsiders, whereas to assault a white person directly would be too threatening for people in such an inferior position. On the other hand, the violence felt as a result of the frustration and anger of their minority position is turned inward toward self or members of the minority. Elliot Liebow discerned similar criminal patterns among Blacks in the U.S. in the late 1960's.[23] Research is now needed to determine whether these criminal patterns have continued or whether native offences are less characteristic of people in the minority situation. Preliminary statistics indicate that little has changed. In 1978 in Manitoba nearly 80 per cent of all crimes committed by native people were of the types mentioned earlier — theft and assault.[24]

Given the preceding contentions that the judicial system is unjust in its dealings with native people and that this injustice is manifest in the large numbers of Indian people incarcerated in correctional institutions, there appears to be no alternative but to address seriously the question of reforming the legal and judicial systems. There can be no question that this is a legitimate task. John Rawls, a noted legal scholar, declares that when a judicial system is unjust it should be changed:

> it might be still better in particular cases to alleviate the plight of those unfairly treated by departures from existing norms. How far we are justified in doing this . . . is one of the tangled questions of political justice. In general, all that can be said is that the strength of the claims of formal justice, of obedience to system, clearly depends upon the substantive justice of institutions and the possibilities of their reform.[25]

It would appear that native people have at least three options available to them in this important task of developing a more equitable system of justice. All three have been forcibly presented by leaders of the native movement. It remains our task as Canadians to overcome our narrow cultural ethnocentrism and carefully consider what is being proposed.

Much of the misunderstanding and intransigence of government and Canadians generally results from the fact that we do not take seriously (even if we say we do) the traditional cultural viewpoint as it is expressed today. Indeed, when we speak about Indian culture, we are accused of trying to turn the clock back to an outmoded past of moccasins and igloos; of taking a position based on unreality and naivety. We, therefore, inevitably approach issues such as reform of the justice system as it affects native people exclusively in terms of western political culture.[26] For the westerner, even those who are sympathetic and involved with native people, the political question is obvious: it is that of social justice understood in the sense of respect for the rights of man, and, in the case of native people, of their aboriginal rights, their right to political self-determination, and their right to equality before the law. It never occurs to us that for native people the political question might be a different one. Robert Vachon gives us an example of this fundamentally different approach.

Native people do not raise the social question uniquely or even primarily in terms of rights and social justice, but in terms of duties, responsibilities and consciousness. The problem today, in their view, is not primarily the lack of respect for the rights of man, but the lack of consciousness that man has of the role that nature has assigned to each thing in life, the forgetfulness of his natural place, the ignorance of the "spirits" of things.[27]

The worldview implied in these ideas is inherent in the first option available to native people in their coming to terms with the legal and judicial system. It involves simply denying the legitimacy of the justice system of the dominant society and calling on native people to recognize and follow the "true" laws of native society. This position is articulated by the Hau de no sau nee, or the Six Nations Iroquois Confederacy, who are stating the fact of their continued existence as "a distinct people, with our own laws and customs, territories, political organization and economy."[28] Similarly, the Dene in the Northwest Territories reject the colonial experience and demand the right to be recognized as a nation in order to preserve their traditional culture. As one Dene leader put it, "The land claim is our fight to gain recognition as a different group of people — with our own way of seeing things, our own values, our own life style, and own laws."[29]

The second strategy available to native people involves more middle-range goals. It addresses the issue of the justice system being out of phase with the customs and values of native society and seeks to establish judicial institutions which are more consistent with those values. The development of a separate Indian court system is an example of an institution of this kind. In the United States a system of Indian courts has been in place on many reservations since 1882.[30] Other examples of initiatives in this direction can be seen as part of an overall cultural revitalization that is presently occurring in many native communities. Indians are discovering traditional authority structures such as elders and cultural ceremonies and restoring them to positions of former importance. A dramatic example of this phenomenon occurred recently in Manitoba. The reserve which formerly had the highest crime rate of any native community in Manitoba now possesses a crime rate which is among the lowest in the province. This is a direct result of the implementation of former cultural traditions. Similarly, a recent National Crime Prevention Conference held in Winnipeg devoted several sessions relating to native crime prevention to the revival of Indian spiritualism as a mechanism to strengthen Indian identity, restore self-confidence, and thereby effectively reduce crime.

The principle of native communities assuming "greater responsibility for the delivery of criminal justice for their people"[31] has been accepted by native people and government representatives alike. Indeed, the rhetoric of numerous conferences extols the virtue of adapting "the judicial system to the particular needs of the Native peoples."[32] But when the implementation of these principles is discussed, the government usually backs off. For example, native people at the federal-provincial Ministerial Conference on Native People and the Criminal Justice System in 1975 recommended the establishment of a system of "peace-maker" courts in native communities as an alternative to aspects of the existing court system. This recommendation was the only one the ministers refused to accept, even in principle. This was despite the fact that the Law Reform Commission had made a similar recommendation. The reasons given for the refusal were the classic political putdowns; that the idea needed more study and that native people should concern themselves with more limited measures of improving the delivery of justice. Alexander Macdonald, attorney-general of British Columbia, expressed this latter view when he stated "that Native communities should concern themselves with diversion and rehabilitation instead."[33] This attitude subtly expresses the moral superiority and cultural ethnocentrism inherent in the colonial situation described earlier. Governments continue to define the problem as one of individuals' inability to cope with the demands of the dominant society, rather than examining their own assumptions and biases and looking at the issue as a problem of the judicial system itself.

Despite this intransigence, it is at this level that native people should place the greatest emphasis in their attempts to reform the justice system, because it is here that the government is most vulnerable. Public awareness of the seriousness of the problem and recognition of the blatant inability of the justice system to respond will, with sufficient political pressure, lead to a willingness to examine alternative justice systems based on values and procedures more compatible with native culture.

The third option available to native people is to work within the existing justice system and to attempt to reform it. This has been the most common response because it involves the least challenge to the system itself. Most of the recommendations of the National Conference on Native People and the Justice System are at this level. Orientation of lawyers and judges to the special needs of native people, court worker programmes, education of Indians about the law, diversion programmes, more effective interpreters, holding court in native communities, alcohol education programmes, and more native people working in the justice system are typical programmes operating at this level. I believe that, in the long run these efforts will be unsuccessful in reforming the justice system because they address the issue by "patching up" the existing system rather than viewing the situation as a problem of the system itself. In addition, these approaches do not take into consideration the differing values and customs of native culture.

Whatever approach native people take on the issue, there can be no doubt of its seriousness. As long as native youth between the ages of sixteen and twenty-four in some prairie provinces have a 60 per cent chance of spending some time in a correctional institution, the cost in terms of human potential is staggering. Native associations and communities need to set this problem high on their list of priorities if the justice system as it relates to native people in this country is to become truly just.

NOTES

1. McCaskill, p. 9
2. The figure for British Columbia is 16 per cent and for the Yukon 51 per cent. Implementation Work Group on Justice Information and Statistics, 1981, pp. 253, 224, 282, and 300.
3. Jolly, p. 22.
4. Ibid.
5. Friedman, p. 44.
6. Watkins, p. 108.
7. Chamberlain, p. 55.
8. Berger and Luckmann, p. 93.
9. McCaskill, p. 3.
10. Dubienski, p. 34.
11. Schur, p. 75.
12. Hoebel, p. 28.
13. Llewellyn, p. 38.
14. Sissons, p. 140.
15. Friedman, p. 948.
16. Ibid., p. 949.
17. Rawls, p. 43.
18. McCaskill, p. 23.
19. Kramer, p. 4.
20. Ibid., p. 5.
21. The category of theft included robbery, break and enter, and theft. The category of assault included murder, manslaughter, attempted murder, wounding, and assault (McCaskill, p. 27).

22. Ibid., p. 28.
23. Liebow, p. 89.
24. The crimes included in these categories are the same as above.
25. Rawls, p. 59.
26. Vachon, p. 39.
27. Ibid., p. 47.
28. Hau de no sau nee, p. 17.
29. Watkins, p. 120.
30. Washburn, p. 169.
31. Canadian Intergovernmental Conference Secretariat, p. 2.
32. Ibid., p. 3.
33. Ibid., p. 11.

REFERENCES

Berger, Peter L., and Thomas Luckmann. 1966. *The Social Construction of Reality*. New York.
Canadian Centre for Justice Statistics. 1978. *Correctional Institutions Statistics*. Ottawa.
Canadian Intergovernmental Conference Secretariat. 1975. "Federal-Provincial Ministerial Conference on Native Peoples and the Criminal Justice System: Summary of Proceedings." Edmonton.
Chamberlin, J. E. 1975. *The Harrowing of Eden*. Toronto.
Daniels, Harry. 1977. "Metis and Non-Status Indian Crime and Justice Commission Report." Ottawa.
Dubienski, Ian V. 1974. "How Can You Break A Law If You Don't Know the Law Exists?" Toronto.
Friedman, Lawrence, and Stewart Macauly. 1969. *Law and the Behavioral Sciences*. New York.
Hau de no sau nee. 1978. *A Basic Call to Consciousness*. Rooseveltown.
Hoebel, E. Adamson. 1964. *The Law of Primitive Man*. Cambridge.
Implementation Work Group on Justice Information and Statistics. 1981. *Correctional Services in Canada*. Ottawa.
Irvine, M. J. 1978. "The Native Inmate in Ontario: A Preliminary Survey." Toronto.
Jolly, Stan. 1980. "Annual Report and Financial Statements: Ontario Native Council on Justice." Toronto.
Kramer, Judith. 1970. *The American Minority Community*. New York.
Liebow, Elliot. 1967. *Tally's Corner*. Boston.
Llewellyn, Karl, and E. Adamson Hoebel. 1941. *The Cheyenne Way*. Norman.
McCaskill, Donald N. 1970, "A Study of Needs and Resources Related to Offenders of Native Origin in Manitoba." Ottawa.
Obonsawin, Roger, and Stan Jolly. 1980 "Review of the Ontario Native Court Worker Programme." Toronto.
Rawls, John. 1971. *A Theory of Justice*. Cambridge, MA.
Rheaume, Gene. 1967. *Indians and the Law*. Ottawa.
Schmeiser, Douglas. 1974. *The Native Offender and the Law*. Ottawa.
Schur, Edwin. 1968. *Law and Society: A Sociological View*. New York.
Sissons, Jack. 1968. *Judge of the Far North*. Toronto.
Solicitor General of Canada. 1975. *Native Peoples and Justice*. Ottawa.
Vachon, Robert. 1979. "Political Self-Determination and Traditional Native Indian Political Culture." *Monchanin Journal* 12, no. 3.
Washburn, Wilcomb. 1971. *Red Man's Land — White Man's Law*. New York.
Watkins, Mel, ed. 1977. *Dene Nation — The Colony Within*. Toronto.

8

Becoming Modern: Some Reflections on Inuit Social Change

Lance W. Roberts

Contrary to the stereotypes perpetuated in the schools and mass media of southern Canadians, the Inuit are no longer a simple hunting and gathering society. They are, in most important respects, a "modern" people who share many characteristics with other Canadians. The salient social forces that have recently turned the Inuit into a fundamentally modern people must be understood in order to appreciate the present Inuit condition and discuss their future realistically.

Observers of Canadian native people regularly use the term "sociocultural" in their discussions. This concept is useful because it emphasizes that any meaningful discussion of human groups must take into account both societal and cultural phenomena (Kroeber and Parsons 1958). However, there is a drawback in using this term which results from its blending of two quite distinct components of social life. For analytical purposes it is important to distinguish the two terms.

Kornhauser identifies the essence of culture and social structure:

> Culture . . . is restricted to the realm of meaning; it refers to the *shared meanings* by which people give order, expression, and value to common experiences. . . . In the grand tradition of cultural analysis, the distinctively cultural refers to those symbols by which a people apprehend and endow experience with *ultimate human significance*. . . . If culture is manifested in those aspects of behaviour enjoined by ideal patterns of belief, social structure is manifested in those aspects of behaviour enjoined by *patterns of interrelationships among social positions*. Social structure refers to the stabilization of

> co-operative efforts to achieve goals, by means of the differentiation of a
> social unit according to positions characterized by a set of activities, re-
> sources, and links to other positions and collectivities (1978:6–7, emphasis
> added).

In other words, culture resides in the realm of the ideal; it contains the norms and
values that comprise a shared symbolic blueprint which gives life meaning. Social
structure, on the other hand, signifies the constraints on individual action arising
from the interdependent roles and statuses that connect individuals in any
organized system. With these distinctions in mind, attention can be focused on the
idea of modernization.

Modernization refers to the process that transforms simple (sometimes called
"primitive") societies into complex ("modern") ones. The transformation involved in becoming modern is, fundamentally, a *social structural* change (Caudill
1973:240). The change is social structural because it centres on the way in which a
group of people organize themselves to meet the challenges of their environment.
Simple societies are "simple" because they rely on a relatively unsophisticated
division of labour to meet their goals. For much of human history most people
have operated under such a social system. It is only within the past 150 to 200 years
that we have witnessed the development of what we now call "modern" societies
for this change followed the spread of the industrial revolution. As new technologies were used to control and exploit the environment, the scale of economies
multiplied, and, concurrently, the social world became increasingly differentiated
(Weiner 1979). New occupations and specialized social structures emerged to
replace the traditional ways of conducting social affairs, and the world became
more complicated.

The reason for asserting that the modernization process is fundamentally social
structural rather than cultural should now be clear — for any group can become
"modern" by establishing or accommodating the complex division of labour
necessary to employ advanced technologies for the production and distribution of
goods and services. This is why it is accurate to describe the Canadian Inuit as a
modern people for they, like southern Canadians, not only employ the products of
our continuing industrial revolution in their quest for survival but have changed
their traditional social arrangements to accommodate this achievement.

There is no doubt that whatever might be defined as "traditional" Inuit culture
was not homogenous in nature (Jenness 1964; Brody 1978). However, as Graburn
and Strong (1973:138) note, although the differentiation between various pre-
contact Inuit cultures "involved technological and demographic adaptation to
vastly differing ecological niches within the Arctic," these led only to "superficially different social and physical structures." Consequently, if attention is
focused on the underlying similarities between different Inuit groups rather than

on the unique characteristics of each, it is possible to describe, as Hughes (1964:13–14) has done, a traditional "pan-Eskimo" culture:

all the principal elements of pan-Eskimo culture were found in pre-contact Canada. The orientation to sea mammal hunting, alternating (where conditions warranted) with inland caribou hunting; fishing as a seasonal pattern; collecting and gathering of various food items; migratory settlement patterns; ingenious technology; highly animistic, relatively unformalized religious institutions, with many taboos and ritual prescriptions and the shaman often the most important sociopolitical leader as well as religious figure; relatively "loose" social organization in the sense of few sharply specified behaviour patterns or kinship political social units; and the development of hunting and sharing partnerships of various types.

From such synthetic descriptions derives the subsistence hunting and gathering stereotype most southerners have of the Inuit today — complete with igloo, kayak, dog team, blubber, and fur coat.

However quaintly comforting this stereotype of the Inuit may be, it is simply no longer accurate. As Hugh Brody (1978:21) reminds us, modern Inuit society is anything but "a candidate for preservation as a simple subsistence economic system." Nor was it a preserver of ancient Inuit traditions even a decade or two or three ago, when it was still possible to find Inuit families living in semi-nomadic hunting camps (Matthiason 1967). Even then the white whalers, missionaries, policemen, and traders had left an indelible imprint on traditional Inuit society.

For present purposes it is unnecessary to detail how and when these various white agencies transformed the Inuit from an independent to a dependent people in various regions of the Arctic. It is sufficient to make the following general remarks about the influence each of these groups had.

During the nineteenth century the whalers provided the Inuit in several arctic regions with their first reliable contact with westerners. Through such contact many Inuit became effective barterers for white goods (Mutch 1906) and developed a conception of the white economic system. Trading with whalers affected the material and economic life of the Inuit for, by the latter 1800's, some had acquired rifles, ammunition, and other trade goods which increased their interest in the ways of white foreigners (Matthiasson 1967). Direct and indirect contact also allowed many new iron and wooden material objects to enter the Inuit system, while sexual and social intercourse exposed them to a foreign nonmaterial culture (Tremblay 1921). In short, the changes introduced by the whalers left a substantial imprint on many Inuit by the time the whaling industry collapsed in the first decade of this century (Bissett 1967).

The decline of the whaling industry was followed by the rise of another foreign economic system among the Inuit, that of the fur traders. The history of Inuit culture contact with this second wave of western Whites is the story of increased dependence on western technology and exposure to white culture.

By the 1920's the Hudson's Bay Company had established an active network of trading posts throughout the Arctic (Usher 1971), and dealing with these centres, "systematically encouraged Eskimos to spend more time hunting animals with skins most highly prized in the southern market and less time hunting animals that merely offered a supply of food" (Brody 1975:21). For a while during the 1920's, the fur market brought substantial material benefits to the Inuit (Bissett 1967). Per capita incomes improved dramatically, and money could be exchanged for steel traps, rifles, non-local foods, and a variety of other items (Hughes 1964). But this short-term gain was to be followed by considerable pain, for the "commercial world of the white man had caught the Eskimos in its mesh, destroyed their self-sufficiency and independence, and made them economically its slaves" (Jenness 1964: 203). When southern fur prices slumped during the 1930's, the Inuit were at the mercy of the market, and harsh social and economic circumstances quickly followed (Kleiven 1966).

Brody (1975:23) parallels the influences of the traders and missionaries in the eastern Arctic between 1900 and 1940: "If the Hudson's Bay Company may be said to have established an economic serfdom, then the missionaries sought to establish a moral serfdom." In many respects, the missionary ideological influence during this period legitimized the changes being effected by the traders. The common trend in both instances was toward a system of Inuit dependence on a foreign economic system and incorporation of western morals. One book, *The Eskimo's Book of Knowledge*, translated for the Inuit by the missionaries, contains a conclusion that exemplifies the desired self-image of dependence on western Whites:

> Take heed, Inuit, for the future will bring even greater changes than have taken place in your country in the past twenty years. There will be white trappers who will trap the foxes out of your country; strange ships will visit your harbours and strange traders will come among you seeking only your furs. Many white men will explore your lands in search of precious rocks and minerals. These traders and these trappers and these wanderers are like the drift-ice; today they will come with the wind, tomorrow they are gone with the wind. Of these strangers some will be fairer than others, as is the nature of men; but whosoever they be, they cannot at heart possess that deep understanding of your lives through which our traders have learned to bestow the care of a father upon you and upon your children (Binney et al. 1931:234).

Many of the Anglican and Roman Catholic missionaries were energetic evangelists, and combined with the syllabic translation of the Bible, their efforts effectively introduced a competing value system into the traditional animistic, shaman-based religious system of many Inuit (Jenness 1964). As Morice (1943:52) reports, this new moral outlook dovetailed with the local traders' belief that "only religion could make the Eskimos good hunters, men of action, and honest enough to pay their debts."

During the trapping period between the world wars, a third contact agency, the RCMP, generally increased its influence on the Inuit. As trading companies were expanding their contact in the Arctic, the Canadian government decided it needed to establish a police presence in the region to monitor their activities (Craig 1923:8). In most of its outposts the RCMP carried out an impressive variety of functions. Van Norman (1951:111), himself an officer, describes his duties:

> At the post RCMP is the only Government department stationed, and consequently upon its personnel fall the duties which other Government departments require performed. Family allowance and old age pension administration, reporting on game conditions, registration of births, deaths, and marriages, post office, issuing coal mining permits, collecting royalties on exporting furs, issuing general hunting licenses, recording weather, plus the normal duties involving enforcement of the Northwest Territories Ordinances and Criminal Code, patrolling by dog teams to various Eskimo camps to determine native living conditions, and such remaining duties which the Government deems advisable to enforce.

This quotation supports the conclusion drawn by other northern observers (Crowe 1974), that the RCMP, like other white agencies of culture contact, promoted and extended a variety of foreign services and values onto the people.

The point to be emphasized from this overview is that early Inuit cultural contact acted as a leveller and homogenizer; for by the time of World War II, the Inuit found themselves in a common situation: dependent on a fur trade operated by and for white interests, which were legitimized and enforced through foreign religious and social control systems. The collapse of the fur markets caused a shared economic and social crisis, with widespread starvation in many areas (Hughes 1964). Concurrently, Inuit in many regions experienced drastic declines in the availability of caribou, so that the people not only experienced depletion of their market resources but of traditional subsistence resources as well. It was into such a situation that the federal government, for humanitarian and sovereignty reasons, began active intervention in the Arctic. In doing so, the federal government became one of the continuing progression of southern white influences that increased Native dependence on a foreign way of life.

All of this suggests a first proposition that must be understood in any discussion of the present Inuit situation and their future: By 1950, traditional Inuit culture was so irredeemably transformed by contact that their future was dependent on some form of relationship with southern white society. The effects of the federal government's rescue operations comprise the most significant factors that have shaped the predicament that the modern Inuit find themselves in. An understanding of these forces is essential to our discussion of the Inuit future.

The present predicament facing the Canadian Inuit results from their modernization; that is, from recent rapid changes in their social structure. Before 1950, the modernization process had been started by whalers, missionaries, policemen, and traders, but the Inuit at least retained many aspects of their hunting and trapping organizational forms. This bond to the land was quickly, though not cleanly, severed shortly after the federal government began active, large-scale intervention in the Arctic.

The central feature in this change involved the rapid shift of the Inuit from a nomadic land-based people to a sedentary, settlement-based population (Graburn and Strong 1973). An anthropologist who lived in one of the last hunting camps in the eastern Arctic during the early 1960's comments on the magnitude of the social change:

> In the intervening decade the Inuit of Pond Inlet had experienced what were almost cataclysmic changes. During the earlier period almost all of them lived "on the land," making their living from seal hunting and trap lines. . . . By 1973 the camps were virtual ghost towns, visited only by the occasional weekend hunter (Matthiasson and Matthiasson 1975:2).

The primary reason for the government encouraging this rapid concentration of people was administrative; centralized populations were much more effectively and efficiently serviced by the programmes they were about to offer. The establishment of Distant Early Warning line sites also helped concentrate the people, with results similar to those of the social programmes. However well-intentioned this strategy was, it initiated a series of major social changes among the Inuit, changes that radically altered their future possibilities and which must be understood in order to appreciate the present situation. Some of these changes are more fundamental than others and we shall outline those most salient.

DEMOGRAPHY

One feature which drew Inuit to the newly formed settlements were nursing stations providing modern medical attention. Before World War II the Inuit population had high fertility and mortality rates characteristic of "underdeveloped" groups (Graburn and Strong 1973). Tuberculosis, measles, influenza, and other epidemics regularly took high tolls (Shaeffer 1972; Simpson 1953). With easy access to the curative and preventative medical attention in the settlements, Inuit mortality was sharply reduced (Nicholson 1969). The result was that Inuit population growth exploded.

The approximate population figures for the past three decades reveal this trend: 1951 — 6,800; 1961 — 8,000; 1971 — 12,000; 1981 — 17,000. Such growth rates, approaching 50 per cent increases per decade, are extraordinarily high. Freeman (1971: 215–16, emphasis added) points out the classical problems these rates cause:

> Some people argue that less developed regions having large land areas and small populations (e.g., Brazil, Newfoundland, and the N.W.T.) are in no way faced with a population problem, unless it be too few people. However, the *crucial factor is not density of people, but too great a ratio of people to capital resources*. This imbalance can be remedied by increasing capital, usually through borrowing or attracting investment, but to convert these potential gains into actual increase in wealth takes time, as well as skill. *The question for underdeveloped regions therefore becomes one of growth of capital versus growth of population*, and because of the accelerating demands in these regions today for improved education, health, communication, housing, and other material facilities, a rapid rate of population growth generally prevents any successful attempt to remedy the prevailing unfortunate economic situation.

Where fertility rates are high, the base of the population pyramid becomes disproportionately large, and the number of potential producers to consumers (the "dependency ratio") shifts in a direction unfavourable to economic development. Where there are too many dependents, communities find it difficult to mobilize development capital. This is the situation in many Inuit communities. For example, Barclay (1958:267) suggests that the proportion of the population between ages fifteen and sixty-four provides a good indicator of economic development potential from a demographic viewpoint, with economically well-off areas having over 60 per cent of their population in the "producing" ages. In many Inuit communities, it is common to find only about 45 per cent of the population in these ages.

All of this points out a central social fact that must be accounted for in discussing the Inuit future. With such large numbers of young people, it is going to be difficult to generate the sizeable amounts of capital required to develop particular communities and regions, especially where the federal government has and continues to hold an attitude of limited subsidization (Lesage 1955: Chrétien 1972, 1973).

EDUCATION

Besides modern medicine, the federal government also established schools in settlements throughout the North after 1950 and began the task of educating the

Inuit, who were only 5 per cent literate at the time (Nicholson 1969). The guiding policy of these schools was one of "cultural replacement" (Hobart and Brant 1966), characterized by the use of non-native teachers, the exclusive use of English, and curriculum materials almost entirely oriented to southern Canadian values.

This educational programme had a series of specific adverse effects on Inuit students (Hobart and Brant 1966). Besides these consequences, the available evidence suggests that this educational exposure did manage to introduce the young Inuit to a set of values, attitudes, and behaviours that were very different from more traditional one held by their parents. These programmes set the stage for young persons to belong to an ideological world very different from their elders.

Surveys of native students demonstrated that their expectations and aspirations were similar to those found in southern Canada (Smith 1975). In one eastern Arctic settlement, for example, almost 100 per cent of the youth had job expectations and aspirations oriented in non-traditional directions (Bissett 1967:132–133).

When these educational effects are combined with the demographic facts, a picture of discontent emerges. Large proportions of young people make it difficult enough for a region to develop economically; but when these youths have modern expectations and are placed in circumstances where there are few economic opportunities to fulfil their aspirations, dissatisfaction, discouragement, and frustration follow (Chance 1960; Davies 1962).

Drastic changes in the native curriculum have recently occurred (Robinson, 1974b), although the extent that these changes have affected classrooms remains debatable (Robinson, 1974a).

SOCIAL AND ECONOMIC CONDITIONS

The Inuit were generally in dire economic circumstances when they moved from a semi-nomadic hunting and trapping existence to the settlements after the collapse of the fur trade and the decline of caribou herds. The federal government provided them with considerable relief from their pressing circumstances through housing programmes, welfare and education subsidies, and medical facilities. However, the acceptance of such relief was purchased at a considerable social cost.

A first social cost occurred simply because efficiency of administration required the concentration of people in settlements — a drastic structural change from the hunting-camp existence. This was a new form of existence for the Inuit and one that was initially disorienting. Immediately, for instance, status distinctions occurred between those who were latterly of the land and those who were of the settlements (Vallee 1962). Establishing this new form of social organization was compounded over time as the white-dominated educational institutions also produced divisions between young, more modern Inuit and their older, more traditional parents. In short, the transition from the land to the settlement-based existence left the Inuit in a state of organizational ambiguity, and under such conditions they were exceptionally susceptible to external influence.

The primary instrument of influence during this period was the federal government which administered the various social programmes. Brody (1975:167) captures the social and psychological effect of this government intervention on the Inuit:

> Once made, the central feature of the move was a new relationship to Whites and their institutions; to move was acknowledgment both of the Eskimos' dependence on the Whites' goods and services, and White hegemony over social, economic, and moral life. The move was made in full consciousness that, whereas camp life offered privacy and some sense of integrity and independence, settlement life must be lived under White domination — this consciousness at once described the terms of settlement life and assumed that the fundamental responsibility for them was in the hands of White administrators.

This theme of Inuit dependence and loss of autonomy pervaded all of the government initiatives. For instance, the settlements were governed by appointed area administrators (Sparham 1974). Welfare and transfer payments in many areas provided over half of the total available income (Polar Record 1954) and did little to promote self-sufficiency (Parker 1964). Moreover, in the most newly formed communities, there were very few employment opportunities, and, in addition, the settlement life brought a new orientation to traditional subsistence activities. In this regard, the Hudson's Bay store played an important role since it was a storehouse of ready-made and modern food, clothing, tools, and machines. This source of immediate gratification provided a powerfully attractive alternative to the traditional means of subsistence.

This short description of the major changes following World War II leads to the following conclusion: whereas federal government intervention alleviated the drastic economic plight of the Inuit, it also introduced modern structures that led to significant social changes which left the Inuit both dependent and somewhat in disarray. Their intimate and daily bond to the land was replaced by congregation in settlements. Controlled population growth was replaced by accelerating increases. Formal education exposed young people to a set of expectations that divided them from their parents, yet gave them little chance of fulfilment within existing opportunity structures. Welfare systems, stores, and other settlement offerings fostered dependence on the southern, white means of existence and further divorced the people from their traditional habits. On balance, many Inuit found their new condition to be a marginal one filled with conflicts — conflicts that manifested themselves in various forms of deviance and disorganization, including excessive gambling, drinking, prostitution (Clairmont 1963), lying, stealing, aggressiveness in and out of school (Hobart and Brant 1966), suicide, (Balicki 1960), marital discord (Yatsushiro 1962), and several related phenomena (Gemini North 1974; Van Stone 1960; Murphy 1968).

The social structure the Inuit inhabit has become increasingly segmented as more specialized agencies have developed to meet specific concerns. From the situation of a simple, family-oriented existence which handled most important issues, their condition has evolved toward one where nurses address medical problems, teachers educate the young, social workers handle cases of individual and collective welfare, other agencies govern, and so forth. In many respects, these changes have improved the Inuit condition, a result the people themselves recognize.

However, a fundamental problem has resulted from these changes; namely that the process is incomplete. As previously stated, the thrust of modernization is toward differentiation and specialization of social functions, but the process does not stop there. In the final analysis, modernization affects individuals, and its result is to extricate them from the web of the close-knit traditional community. The modern condition is one where an individual has to relate to several specialized structures in order to fulfil his needs (Coser 1975). This is effectively a liberating experience since it separates individuals from the guidance of the more homogeneous collective and forces them to deal with a variety of distinctively different constraints. In handling such a modern social world, individuals become more autonomous and learn that they can and must control their own situations in order to acquire their desired ends.

It is precisely at this stage that the dilemma of the modern Inuit occurs. Traditionally, the Inuit have been a relatively "open" and flexible people who have valued self-reliance, adaptability, and personal initiative; and the historical record documents that they have adapted to a variety of circumstances (Jenness 1964). Recently, most have accepted and are adjusting to the new world of settlement life as it has been constructed largely by southerners. Moreover, a significant and growing proportion, especially among the young, have adopted a mental outlook associated with their modern social situation. These attitudes centre on self-control, of oneself and one's surroundings, in order to achieve personally defined goals. But here's the rub: because so much of modern Inuit existence has been fashioned by southerners or their representatives, the modernization of the people has not been completed. These people, although modern in outlook, are not afforded the opportunities to fulfil themselves in the structures created and controlled by foreigners. The result is a frustrating and tragic situation.

The situation is frustrating because newly acquired and desired goals cannot be achieved, for the means of self-determination and fulfilment are lacking. The situation is tragic, for there are many reasons to believe that the Inuit people can and do perform very capably when provided with appropriate opportunities to participate in modern forms of government, industry, and the like. There are many examples that illustrate this latter assertion, but one recent and emphatic one is the Inuit adaptation to the industrial wage-employment opportunities provided by oil and mining exploration activity.

The case of industrial adaptation is particularly salient since it represents one of the few recent large-scale opportunities that Inuit people have had to demonstrate their competence in what is arguably the most important sector of modern life, the world of work. Recent studies by Roberts (1977) and Hobert (1981) of workers with Gulf Oil in the western Arctic, Panarctic Oils in the eastern Arctic, and at the Nanisivik mine all point out that the Inuit employees have adapted well both on and off the job.

For instance, Roberts's (1977) investigation found that native employees, on balance, performed as satisfactorily on their oil exploration jobs as southern white workers did. Moreover, in their home communities of Pond Inlet and Arctic Bay, the potentially great adverse effects of such a large-scale employment programme were very capably managed and, on the whole, contributed more to community growth and solidarity than it did to disintegration. This conclusion is corroborated by both a recent follow-up study in these two Inuit communities and a longitudinal study of the impact of similar employment experiences on the Inuit from the Coppermine region.

In his recent summary of these results, Hobart (1981:23) notes a point that follows the theme of this article:

> There is an interesting contrast between the Coppermine and the Arctic Bay and Pond Inlet employment data. The Coppermine data show that during the period of Gulf employment there was a steadily increasing involvement. By contrast, in both Arctic Bay and Pond Inlet there appears to be a pattern of declining involvement. . . . An explanation may be that Gulf appears to have provided more encouragement and opportunities for advancement than Pan Arctic did.

This is an intriguing hypothesis, for it suggests that, where other variables are held approximately constant, expanding opportunities to participate in more complex levels of modern employment are important to the Inuit. Where their opportunities are restricted, their motivation to participate decreases — all of which suggests a readiness and eagerness to participate in modern employment structures that leads to frustration and withdrawal when thwarted.

While discussing these data there is another general point that deserves emphasis. This concerns the conditions under which these Inuit workers and their communities were best able to adjust to the effects of modernity. Such a discussion leads us back to a consideration of how modernization and culture are related.

Among other things, these studies of natives in modern employment situations suggests the following conclusion: Inuit workers perform best in industrial settings where they have great control over the organization and execution of required tasks. In other words, where the Inuit were allowed to work together, using their own system of organization and language, they generally do well; if they are forced to function in a system designed by and for southern white mentalities and staffed primarily by the same types, Inuit workers do not do so well. This, interestingly enough, is precisely what one would expect from a people who have modern mentalities; where they can control the environment, they are more satisfied and perform accordingly.

The analagous case to the situation of native workers can be found at the level of community adjustment. There are too many arctic examples that demonstrate unsuccessful Inuit community adjustment to southern modernization forces. By contrast, the Inuit of Coppermine, Arctic Bay, and Pond Inlet appear to have adapted remarkably well and hold exceptionally favourable attitudes toward their development experience. What accounts for this distinctive difference? The answer suggested by Chance (1960) and Roberts (1977) centres on community control. Unlike the experience of so many other natives, the Inuit in these communities have had a better chance to meet the challenges of modernization on their own terms. In all cases, the industrial operations where the Inuit were employed were located at sufficiently distant places that their home communities remained relatively isolated. Workers were rotated to and from work sites at regular intervals, with the consequence that native community life was spared immediate immersion in a new way of life controlled by foreigners; their contact was buffered and indirect, "at arm's length," so to speak. To have native workers employed and bringing home regular paycheques from industrial operations located away from the community is an experience qualitatively different from having an industry operated largely by southern Whites located in the community itself. In the latter case the natives' chance of being overwhelmed and dominated by the Whites and their ways is greatly increased.

Mention is made of these points in order to reiterate that culture and social structure are different aspects of reality and that the modernization process occurs primarily in the realm of social structure. In other words, there are many means by which the new structures associated with modernization can be assimilated, and the specific route a particular group uses can be coloured by their culture. The failure to take this fact into account is a central problem in far too many development proposals, which assume that the only way to become modern is through the route taken for granted by southern Whites.

Let there be no mistake, the Canadian Inuit do embody a distinctive culture, sufficiently so that some observers argue they constitute a unique ethnic group (Matthiasson and Matthiasson 1975). To be sure, this culture is hardly a replica of that held by even their nineteenth-century ancestors; rather, it is as Brody (1978:30) describes: "when Eskimos worry about the loss of their tradition, they are thinking of the passing of the fur trade way of life." It is essential not to underestimate the importance of the Inuit bond to the land when contemplating their future, especially since this link with tradition is so different from that of most southern Whites. For the Inuit, their hunting and trapping heritage is the essential benchmark of their identity and, if preserved, can be an important bridge to a successful future. Moreover, this cultural experience deserves to be considered in the modernization process since it is not essential that it be discarded in order to modernize.

A strong sense of identity is essential to personal integration and self-esteem and derives largely from social sources. To know that one is part of a meaningful tradition, that one understands the surrounding world, and that one can take an active part in shaping the future; these provide a feeling of personal control and worth. When social circumstances are rapidly changing, as they have for the Inuit since World War II, the threats to a strong identity are manifestly increased. Paradoxically, it is precisely under these changing conditions that strong identities are required in order to struggle against disorganizing events and adjust in a fulfilling manner.

The modernization process has exacted a considerable toll from the Inuit. A "psychology of dependence" has developed in several areas because of well-intentioned, but paternalistic, government control. Among other groups, modern expectations without adequate opportunities have sown the seeds of frustration and discontent. In other cases, culture contact has been so rapid and total that adjustment proved impossible and disorganization followed. These are the saddening consequences of modernization as it has happened so far.

On the other hand, it must be conceded that many Inuit have accepted and enjoy the products and benefits of living under more modernized social conditions. As well, it can be argued that what has occurred so far, though hurtful in some respects, was the result of a required response to the dismaying circumstances many Inuit were in after the fur trade collapsed and caribou populations declined.

Given these circumstances, a fundamental question emerges: How can the Inuit become "modern" in a manner that preserves their self-identity and minimizes social disorganization? We have suggested that this result is most likely under conditions where the Inuit have both modern opportunities and a considerable measure of control over how they wish to manage these structures for their own interests. Their individual performances and community adjustments to recent oil exploration activity illustrates these conditions in action and gives the ideas behind them credence.

Oil exploration and other industrial employment has been beneficial in providing a considerable source of funds and limited employment opportunities for the Inuit; both have enriched the people materially and helped to satisfy some of the wants created by exposure to education, mass media, and the like. However, the extent of this influence has to date been meagre compared to what looms on the horizon. The Inuit are in a crucial period in their history because the forthcoming scale of impact, including both modern peoples and structures, is greater than it ever has been.

It is simply a matter of time, and probably sooner rather than later, before there is full-scale development of northern natural resources. This means potentially massive influxes of southern personnel, technology, ideas, and modes of organization. Such circumstances are just those least conducive to successful Inuit development, for under these conditions the people of the land will have neither the resources nor time to adjust.

The Inuit appear to be at the crossroads now, since choices made in the immediate future will have a lasting and irreversible impact. There is little doubt that the Inuit will increasingly be affected by the social forces of modernity in the future. The relevant question involves only the form these changes will take. If the people are able to maintain a considerable degree of control over their future, there is good reason to believe that they shall be able to modernize in a manner that suits their own view of themselves and their future, one that permits the maintenance of personal integrity and the opportunity to pick and choose among modern structures in such a way as to create a genuine contribution to the Canadian multicultural mosaic. If not, their future as a distinctive and vital ethnic group looks bleak.

In this context, it is crucial that the land-claims issue be settled before more modernization proceeds. For the way this one issue is resolved will provide the frame in which the pieces of their puzzling future will be set. Without a sufficiently generous settlement in terms of land, money, opportunities, and control, it is unlikely that future social change will be influenced by Inuit culture in a way that suits their visions. Such a result is essential if the Inuit are to inhabit a modern world that is meaningful to them, since the maintenance of culture is a primary source of all meaning.

There are some signs for optimism which suggest that events are moving in directions favourable to the Inuit. One principal player, the minister of Indian affairs and northern development, John Munro, appeared to recognize the importance of the land-claims issue. In an interview he remarked: "There is a feeling in the North that they're not going to have the political evolution that would come close to their expectations or the economic development that usually comes with greater political autonomy until you settle land claims. . . . The settlement will provide the underpinning of the whole economic situation up there" (*Financial Post*, 17 October 1981:S27). Native northerners are also playing an important role by working diligently to take charge of their own affairs (Jull 1981). This has resulted in some encouraging developments like the two million tax free dollars paid to the Inuvialuit Development Corporation which has invested in a variety of business ventures with Inuit interests in mind. However, the general outcome of the land claims issue is far from determined. Both major interests, the government and the Inuit, have a long road of difficult bargaining yet to travel.

If there is one thing the audience of southern Canadians should remember as they watch the process proceed, it is this: the most productive forms of social organization are not necessarily the most satisfying. Although there is no doubt that the modernization model followed by southern Whites yields high material rewards, the cost is that many find themselves operating in a system they neither understand nor control. Their work is experienced as alienating and meaningless, a qualitative cost not to be taken lightly. Remembering this, southern Whites should not be too quick to judge the Inuit as they strive to create a system aligned with their own cultural interests. After all, their quest is essentially similar to ours — to search for a system that blends meaning and modernity. It is clear that we do not possess the definitive answer to this curious mixture, while they are at a point where such a result may not be an impossible dream. We should watch with interest, for we may learn something from the outcome.

REFERENCES

Balicki, A. 1960. "Ethnic Relations and the Marginal Man in Canada." *Human Organization* 19 (Winter): 170–71.

Barclay, G. W. 1958. *Techniques of Population Analysis*. New York.

Binney, George, et al. 1931. *The Eskimo Book of Knowledge*. London.

Bissett, Don. 1967. *North Baffin Island: An Area Economic Survey*. 2 vols. Ottawa.

Brody, Hugh. 1975. *The People's Land*. Markham, Ont.

———— 1978, "Ecology, Politics, and Change." *Development and Change* 9: 21–40.

Caudhill, W. A. 1973. "The Influence of Social Structure and Culture on Human Behaviour in Modern Japan." *Journal of Nervous and Mental Disease* 157: 240–57.

Chance, Norman. 1960. "Culture Change and Integration: An Eskimo Example." *American Anthropologist* 62: 1028–44.

Chrétien, Jean. 1972. "Mackenzie Corridor: Vision Becomes Reality." *North* 19 (July–August): 1–4.

———— 1973. *Northern Policy for the Seventies*. Ottawa.

Clairmont, D. 1963. "Notes on the Drinking Behaviour of the Eskimos and Indians in the Aklavik Area." Ottawa.

Coser, R. L. 1975. "The Complexity of Roles as a Seedbed of Individual Autonomy." In *The Idea of Social Structure: Papers in Honour of Robert K. Merton*, ed. L. Coser. New York.

Craig, J. D. 1923. *Canada's Arctic Islands: Log of the Canadian Expedition: 1922*. Ottawa.

Crowe, Keith. 1974. *A History of the Original Peoples of Northern Canada*. Montreal.

Davies, J. C. 1962. "Towards a Theory of Revolution." *American Sociological Review* 27: 5–19.

Freeman, M. M. R. 1971. "The Significance of Demographic Changes Occurring in the Canadian Eastern Arctic." *Anthropologica* 13: 215–36.

Gemini North. 1974. *Social and Economic Impact of the Proposed Arctic Gas Pipeline in Northern Canada*. 4 vols. Calgary.

Graburn, N., and B. S. Strong. 1973. *Circumpolar Peoples: An Anthropological Perspective*. Pacific Palisades, CA.

Hobart, C. W. 1981. "Impacts of Industrial Employment on Hunting and Trapping among Canadian Inuit." Unpublished.

————, and C. S. Brant. 1966. "Eskimo Education, Danish and Canadian: A Comparison." *Canadian Review of Sociology and Anthropology* 3 (May): 47–66.

Hughes, C. C. 1964. "Under Four Flags: Some Recent Trends in Culture Change among the Eskimos." *Current Anthropology* 6 (February): 3–69.

Jenness, D. 1964. "Eskimo Administration II." Montreal.

Jull, Peter. 1981. "Diplomats of a New North." *Policy Options* 2(2): 21–26.

Kleiven, H. 1966. *The Eskimos of Northeast Labrador: A History of Eskimo White Relations: 1771–1955.* Norsk Polarinstitute Skrifter, no. 139.

Kornhauser, R. 1978. *Social Sources of Delinquency: An Appraisal of Analytic Models.* Chicago.

Kroeber, A., and T. Parsons. 1958. "The Concepts of Culture and of Social System." *American Sociological Review* 23: 582–83.

Lesage, Jean. 1955. "Enter the European." *The Beaver:* 3–9.

Matthiasson, John S. 1967. "Eskimos Legal Acculturation: The Adjustment of Baffin Island Eskimos to Canadian Law." Ph.D. diss., Cornell.

———, and C. Matthiasson. 1975. "A People Apart: The Ethnicization of the Eastern Canadian Arctic Inuit." Paper delivered at the Canadian Ethnic Studies Association.

Morice, A. G. 1943. *Thawing out the Eskimo.* Translated by Mary T. Loughlin. Boston.

Murphy, Jane. 1968. "The Use of Psychophysiological Symptoms as Indicators of Disorder among the Eskimos." In *Approaches to Psychiatry,* ed. Jane Murphy. New York.

Mutch, James S. 1906. "Whaling in Ponds Bay." In *Boas Anniversary Volume, Anthropological Papers Written in Honour of Franz Boas.*

Nicholson. 1969. "The Problem of the People." *The Beaver* 289: 20–24.

Parker, S. 1964. "Ethnic Identity and Acculturation in Two Eskimo Villages." *American Anthropologist* 66: 425–40.

Polar Record. 1954. "Eskimo Affairs in Canada." 7: 58–70.

Roberts, L. W. 1977. "Wage Employment and Its Consequences in Two Eastern Arctic Inuit Communities." Ph.D. diss.

Robinson, P. 1974. "Pardon Me I've Lost My Rose Colored Spectacles." *Arctus* (Winter).

——— 1974. *Elementary Education in the Northwest Territories: A Handbook for Curriculum, Development.* Yellowknife.

Schaeffer, Otto. 1972. "Further Comments on Northern People and Northern Development." In H. B. Hawthorn, ed. *Science and the North.* Ottawa.

Simpson, R. N. 1953. "Epidemics in the Eastern Arctic during 1953." *Arctic Circular* 6, no. 5: 53–55.

Smith, Derek. 1975. "Occupational Aspirations and Expectations of Native Students in the Canadian North." Paper presented at the Canadian Ethnic Studies Conference.

Sparham, R. 1974, "Report on Pond Inlet." Manuscript.

Tremblay, A. 1921, *The Cruise of the Minnie Maud.* Québec.

Usher, Peter. 1971. *Fur Trade Posts of the Northwest Territories, 1870–1970.* Ottawa.

Vallee, Frank. 1962. *Kabloona and Eskimo in the Central Keewatin.* Ottawa.

Van Norman, R. D. 1951. "Life in an Eastern Arctic Detachment." *Royal Canadian Mounted Police Quarterly* 17.

Van Stone, J. W. 1960. "A Successful Combination of Subsistence and Wage Economics on the Village Level." *Economic Development and Cultural Change* 8, 2: 174–191.

Weinir, M. 1979. *Modernization.* New York.

Yatsushiro, T. 1962. "The Changing Eskimo: A Study of Wage Employment and its Consequences among the Eskimos of Frobisher Bay." *The Beaver* 293 (Summer): 19–25.

Reprinted from *Journal of Canadian Studies* 16, no. 2.

9

The Inuit and the
Constitutional Process:
1978–1981

Simon McInnes

INTRODUCTION

This article discusses the recent involvement of the Inuit in the reform of Canada's constitution up to the period of the reference of the Patriation Resolution to the Supreme Court of Canada in April 1981.[1] The main purpose is to illustrate how the Inuit related to the federal, provincial, and territorial governments, at ministerial and official levels, showing which methods of interaction proved successful in gaining the rights aboriginal peoples achieved in the Patriation Resolution. In order to establish a context for the discussion, it will be necessary to consider the constitutional status of the Inuit and federal-provincial-territorial relations in the period under consideration.

PATRIATION RESOLUTION 1981: ABORIGINAL PROVISIONS

The provisions of direct concern to the aboriginal peoples contained in the Patriation Resolution referred to the Supreme Court in April 1981 were a negatively drafted reference in the Charter of Rights and Freedoms, the positive affirmation and recognition of aboriginal and treaty rights, and the right of

Reprinted from *Journal of Canadian Studies* 16, no. 2.

participation in first ministers' conferences. Part I, s. 25 of the Resolution states that the Charter of Rights and Freedoms shall not be construed so as to abrogate or derogate from any aboriginal, treaty, or other rights or freedoms that pertain to the aboriginal peoples of Canada. Part II recognizes and affirms the traditional aboriginal and treaty rights of the Indian, Inuit, and Metis peoples of Canada. Part IV, s. 36 (2) [now S.37(2)] stipulates that the prime minister shall invite representatives of the aboriginal peoples to participate with first ministers in discussions on matters directly affecting them and their rights. These first ministers' conferences are slated to take place each year for two years after Part VI comes into force. The details of these provisions will be expanded upon below.

A BRIEF SYNOPSIS OF EVENTS 1978–81

Although contemporary attempts to revise Canada's constitution began in the early 1960's and continued intermittently until the recent push in 1980–81, aboriginal peoples were not involved and expressed few ideas on the subject. The Inuit presented a brief to the Joint Senate-House of Commons (Molgat-Mac-Guigan) Committee in 1978. In February 1979, upon the urging of Prime Minister Trudeau, the first ministers agreed to place the item, "Canada's Native People and the Constitution," on the agendas of future constitutional conferences. A subcommittee of the Continuing Committee on the Constitution (CCMC) chaired by the Hon. Bill Jarvis, federal-provincial relations minister in the nine-month Clark government, and by the Hon. Roy Romanow, Saskatchewan's attorney-general, met in December 1979 with the National Indian Brotherhood [now superseded by the Assembly of First Nations], the Native Council of Canada, and the Inuit Committee on National Issues for preliminary discussions on the constitutional status of aboriginal peoples.

The CCMC again met with the three national aboriginal associations in August 1980 for further discussions. The first ministers' conference of September 1980, which followed on the heels of the summer meetings of federal and provincial justice ministers trying to hammer out constitutional agreements in the wake of the Quebec referendum on sovereignty-association, failed to produce tangible evidence of progress. On 2 October 1980 Prime Minister Trudeau unveiled his Patriation Resolution. A Joint Senate-House of Commons Committee was struck to examine the resolution and heard witnesses from 14 November 1980 to 9 January 1981. The committee hearings were extended by nearly five weeks because of rigorous opposition by the Tories, who objected to the speed with which the prime minister wished to proceed. The committee reported on 13 February 1981, having heard four premiers, both territorial governments, and 104 groups and individuals as witnesses. The resolution, as referred to the Supreme Court of Canada, was a substantially revised version of the original, including those provisions affecting Canada's aboriginal peoples.

CONSTITUTIONAL DOCUMENTS PERTAINING TO THE INUIT: A CHRONOLOGICAL
SURVEY[2]

Before addressing in detail the events of 1978–81, it is necessary to sketch the
legal bases of Ottawa's constitutional responsibilities towards the Inuit.[3] Section
91 (24) of the British North America Act, 1867[4] confers jurisdiction on the federal
parliament over all matters coming within the class of subjects "Indians, and
Lands reserved for the Indians." A Supreme Court of Canada decision in 1939
held that the Inuit of northern Quebec are "Indians" within the meaning of that
section,[5] and doubtless the reasoning in that decision applies to the Inuit in the rest
of Canada. It may be noted in passing, however, that the Inuit are not "Indians" for
the purposes of the Indian Act.[6]

Several documents of constitutional importance have bearing on the Inuit.
First, and most importantly, the Royal Proclamation of 1763 enunciated a number
of measures to protect Indians and their lands which had not been ceded to or
purchased by the Crown. There is high judicial support for the view that the
Proclamation has not been repealed in its material provisions.[7] Brian Slattery
argues that the Proclamation "encompasses all indigenous groups occupying
territories claimed by the British Crown in North America in October 1763,"[8] and
that therefore the term "Indians" used in the Proclamation includes the Inuit. As
Cumming and Mickenberg note, while the Proclamation clearly recognizes the
pre-existing land rights of aboriginal peoples, an important question is whether it
constitutes the exclusive source of aboriginal rights.[9] A number of judicial
decisions[10] have answered that "the law of Canada recognizes the existence of an
aboriginal title independent of the Royal Proclamation."[11] There is some doubt as
to whether the Proclamation applies to Rupert's Land (roughly the lands surrounding the Hudson and James Bay areas), but it has been forcefully argued by several
scholars that the Inuit of Rupert's Land, northern Quebec and Labrador are all
beneficiaries of the Proclamation provisions.[12] Thus, until these scholarly contributions are authoritatively rejected by the Supreme Court, the Proclamation must
be regarded as a document of constitutional import for Canada's aboriginal
peoples, including the Inuit, a fact which the Patriation Resolution of 1981
recognized.

The second constitutional document is the order-in-council of 23 June 1870,
pursuant to which Rupert's Land and the Northwestern Territory became part of
Canada. In this legal instrument the dominion government gave various undertakings to the imperial government. These were, in broad terms, that the claims of the
Indian tribes to compensation for lands required for purposes of settlement were to
be considered and settled in conformity with the equitable principles which had
uniformly governed the British Crown in its dealing with the aborigines; and that
(at any rate in relation to Rupert's Land) these claims were to be disposed of by the
Canadian government in communication with the imperial government.[13] In light
of these undertakings Professor Hooper has argued that "the existence of aborigi-

nal title received not only executive, but also legislative affirmation.''[14] Under contemporary (though not necessarily current) constitutional theory,[15] the Parliament of Canada could not unilaterally amend this order-in-council. Thus it is one basis on which the Inuit can fix legal obligations on Ottawa to deal with their land claims, and it is therefore a significant constitutional document as the Patriation Resolution 1981 also recognized.

There are a number of other legislative acts (such as the Quebec Boundaries Extension Act, 1912),[16] which have implications for aboriginal rights, but these are not universally considered to be part of what is known as the "fundamental law,"[17] that is, those documents which are safeguarded by law against repeal or amendment by the unilateral action of any legislative body in Canada. Until the advent of the Patriation Resolution of 1980, a broad interpretation was taken of which documents were part of that fundamental law.[18] However, the narrower interpretation in the Patriation Resolution excludes all pre-1867 documents, and all others which do not have a direct bearing on matters such as the division of powers between Parliament and the legislatures and acts creating new provinces.

In short, the federal government assumed various obligations towards the Inuit prior to the Patriation Resolution 1981. Under the law, they were recognized as having a homeland within Canada as a birthright preceding the two constitutional documents above, and which reflected that right in law. The Patriation Resolution of 1981 recognized and affirmed those rights, as will be discussed later.

FEDERAL-PROVINCIAL TERRITORIAL RELATIONS AND THE INUIT

No article on the constitution is complete without at least a brief mention of core aspects of Canada's federal system. The BNA Act refers to matters of federal jurisdiction under s. 91, and to those of provincial jurisdiction under s. 92. Since 1867 provincial power has increased substantially more than may originally have been intended by the Fathers of Confederation, while federal power has been limited (although not sufficiently, according to some provinces).

In any federal system, relations between the federal and regional governments will be an important ingredient in national politics and policy-making has been characterized by a considerable interlocking of responsibilities, owing in large measure to the variety of cost-shared programmes (as in the health and social security fields) and federal economic expenditures initiated largely at its own behest.[19] Suffice it to say that today Canadians face a bewildering honeycomb of policies and programmes resulting partly from the entanglement of both levels of government. The inability to disentangle these increasingly complex intergovernmental arrangements has, of course, been one (although not necessarily the most important) reason for the drive to patriate the BNA Act with an amending formula.

For the Inuit, intergovernmental entanglement is of comparatively more recent origin. In the Northwest Territories (NWT), where 17,000 Inuit live, the federal government was not strongly present until the creation in 1953 of the Department of Northern Affairs and National Resources. The territorial government was established in Yellowknife in 1967, and in 1979, following territorial elections, the Territorial Council began to assume the semblance of authority of a provincial assembly. Despite the fact that the NWT is under federal jurisdiction, the devolution of some responsibilities to the government of the NWT (GNWT) has resulted in some confusion among NWT residents as to which government (federal or territorial) has immediate policy responsibility in certain areas. In the health area, for instance, responsibility for delivery of health services has recently been transferred to the GNWT from Ottawa. But treatment of seriously ill patients may require referral to larger hospitals in the south, and in the case of the Keewatin region, "its" hospital is in Churchill, Manitoba.[20]

Intergovernmental entanglement affecting Inuit is particularly evident in Northern Quebec, the home of 6,500 Inuit. Until 1963 delivery of nearly all services to Quebec Inuit communities was carried out by Ottawa because of lack of interest in Quebec City. With the advent in 1960 of the "Maîtres chez nous" policy of Premier Jean Lesage, Quebec began to compete with Ottawa for the provision of services. Inuit complaints in the late 1970's and today are that Quebec City has not provided services at the same level as Ottawa, nor even at the level enjoyed by Quebecers south of 55 degrees.

Matters are further complicated by a secretariat, SAGMAI,[21] which reports to the premier's office and co-ordinates all aboriginal matters of interest to the provincial government. Far from being a mere agency, the Inuit argue that SAGMAI is becoming a provincial DIAND.[22] Often attempts by Inuit to present views and demands to other governmental departments are routinely referred to SAGMAI and its director, where, in the view of the Inuit, little adequate action is taken.[23]

The situation is also complicated by the fact that the Inuit signed the James Bay and Northern Quebec Agreement in 1975, the first modern comprehensive land claims settlement between Ottawa, a province, and aboriginal groups (in this case the James Bay Cree and the Inuit of Quebec). Owing to disagreements between Ottawa and Quebec as to the provision of services, housing and municipal services, to name two areas, have, in the eyes of the Inuit, deteriorated since the land claims negotiations commenced in the early 1970's. One community, Port Burwell, which is located on an island just off the northeast coast of Quebec (and therefore by definition in the NWT), has been abandoned because of the failure of Ottawa to provide adequate health and social services. Implementation problems of the James Bay and Northern Quebec Agreement and the resultant intergovernmental entanglement remain to be solved,[24] even as general withdrawal of the federal government from provision of services to the region is taking place.

In northern Labrador, where 1,500 Inuit live, similar problems regarding entanglement and poor services arise. A recent report cited the lack of regular medical and dental services, unsanitary water supplies, refuse problems, and a low standard of services supplied by the province.[25] In the housing sector, an excellent example of intergovernmental entanglement detrimental to the Inuit, new houses have not been delivered to the Inuit communities for two years, despite the severe shortage of housing.[26] The problem seems to have been that the surplus left from funds spent under a federal-provincial agreement which were usually diverted to housing needs have not been so allocated since the end of the 1978 building season. Despite federal promises, this matter remains unresolved to date.[27]

In sum, the impact of federal-provincial-territorial policy entanglements on the Inuit has been significant. Despite the fact that the federal government has constitutional responsibility for Inuit, their interventions on constitutional revision attempt to accommodate not only those jurisdictions within which the Inuit live, but also those in which they do not live. Provinces with no Inuit population still have a strong influence on the constitutional processes touching aboriginal rights.

THE INUIT, THE GOVERNMENTS, AND THE CONSTITUTIONAL PROCESS 1978–81: A STEP IN THE RIGHT DIRECTION

The events leading to the recognition of aboriginal rights in the Patriation Resolution have their roots in the historical position of Canada's aboriginal peoples. Clearly they used and occupied this continent in societies organized after their own fashion.[28] As mentioned above, this was recognized and given a certain legal status. But the actions of federal and provincial governments often belied that status, undermining the ability of aboriginal peoples to retain their traditions in the face of general technological challenges. In 1969 a federal white paper tacitly endorsed the assimilation of the aboriginal peoples into Canadian society and the abolition of whatever remaining particular rights they had.[29] Outrage greeted this policy, spurring aboriginal peoples to argue their case more coherently and with more publicity. In British Columbia the Nishga tribe went to court to protect its rights. The Supreme Court of Canada dismissed the Calder case on a technicality, but the court split evenly on whether the Nishga had aboriginal rights. The dissenting opinion (including that of Bora Laskin, now chief justice) argued that until subsisting private title was legally changed by a new sovereign, existing aboriginal rights would continue.[30]

The Calder case persuaded the federal government to open serious land claims discussion with the aboriginal peoples, resulting, for example, in the agreement with the Inuit of Northern Quebec in 1975 and in negotiations with the Inuit in the NWT and Labrador. The government recognized, however, that land claims negotiations would cover only that portion of aboriginal rights pertaining to land.

In June 1978 the federal government released a paper, *A Time for Action*, which included the possibility of the aboriginal peoples expressing their constitutional views.[31] Bill C-60 included recognition in its preamble of the contribution of "Canada's original inhabitants" and also a clause in its Charter of Rights and Freedoms that nothing therein would derogate from existing rights and freedoms of the native people under the Royal Proclamation. In addition, the explanatory document accompanying Bill C-60 referred to those rights.

In August 1978, the Inuit Tapirisat of Canada, the national Inuit association, in a presentation to the Special Joint Senate-House of Commons Committee on the Constitution of Canada (the Molgat-MacGuigan Committee), called upon the government of Canada to provide a forum which "would offer us a fair opportunity to research, discuss and present our [constitutional] position."[32] In September, the government responded by proposing to the provinces that the aboriginal peoples be invited to make their views known at the First Ministers' Conference on the Constitution, by speaking and circulating briefs. However, the aboriginal peoples were to be accorded observer status only on non-aboriginal matters. The Inuit, on the other hand, felt that they should sit as equals with the eleven governments when matters pertaining to aboriginal rights were being discussed.

Government meetings with national aboriginal associations began in November 1978. The major governmental actor was the Federal-Provincial Relations Office (FPRO). The advisors liaising with the aboriginal groups included Gordon Robertson, Nick Gwyn and Peter Jull. On the government side, while matters were handled at the first instance by FPRO, other departments or agencies with aboriginal or policy control concerns were involved in a "Working Group on the Natives Item." These included the Privy Council Office (the bureaucratic arm of cabinet, primarily the prime minister's advisory staff, and pre-eminent among central agencies); DIAND; the Department of the Secretary of State (through which core-funding for the aboriginal groups was ultimately channelled); and the Department of Justice. On the aboriginal side in 1978, in addition to the Inuit Tapirisat of Canada, were the National Indian Brotherhood representing Canada's 300,000 status Indians, and the Native Council of Canada, representing 750,000 Metis and non-status Indians.

The first major step toward placing aboriginal rights in the constitution came at the First Ministers' Constitutional Conference held in February 1979. Prime Minister Trudeau and Premier Davis of Ontario persuaded the premiers to place on the agenda of future first ministers' conferences an item on "Canada's Native Peoples and the Constitution" and to initiate discussions with the aboriginal groups at the deputy-minister level to clarify their concerns. However, the May 1979 federal election intervened, and the aboriginal groups had to wait several months while the Clark government tried to find its feet. To its credit, it was as keen as had been Mr. Trudeau to pursue discussions, and on 29 June 1979 the Hon. Bill Jarvis wrote to the aboriginal groups that he was willing to meet with them.

In one year, from the June 1978 *Time for Action* paper to Mr. Jarvis's June 1979 letter, the government of Canada had gently prodded the provinces in the right direction and the Progressive Conservatives had picked up where Mr. Trudeau had left off. By mid-1979 momentum appeared to be building.

The Inuit were especially interested in these constitutional developments. By the winter of 1978–79, the Inuit of Northern Quebec in particular were beginning to discover some limitations to their land claims agreement, and they felt that other matters not dealt with in the agreement could only be addressed in constitutional discussions. The Inuit Tapirisat of Canada (ITC) had its hands full with the land claims negotiations for three of the NWT regions. The fourth region, the western Arctic, had severed its land claims negotiations from the ITC after the withdrawal by the ITC of the 1976 agreement-in-principle. Labrador Inuit too felt somewhat isolated from the ITC.

At the urging of Charlie Watt, the leader of the Quebec Inuit, a resolution was passed at the 1979 Annual General Meeting of the ITC held in Igloolik, NWT, setting up the Inuit Committee on National Issues (ICNI) which, reporting to the annual general meeting, was given responsibility to represent Inuit views on the constitution and on other issues of national significance. The committee was composed of two co-chairmen chosen by the annual general meeting (one of whom was Charlie Watt), and one representative from each of the six Inuit regions, usually the presidents of: the Committee for Original Peoples' Entitlement (Western Arctic); the Kitikmeot Inuit Association (Central Arctic); the Keewatin Inuit Association; the Baffin Region Inuit Association; the Makivik Corporation (Quebec), and the Labrador Inuit Association. The M.P. for Nunatsiaq (the federal riding above the tree-line in NWT), Peter Ittinuar, and the president of the ITC became ex officio members. From September 1979 to August 1980 ICNI had no funds of its own and had to rely on financial support from Makivik and the ITC.

The first Inuit priority in the fall of 1979 was to press the governments of Canada to take action on aboriginal constitutional participation. In early October the Continuing Committee of Ministers on the Constitution (CCMC) met in Halifax to discuss this item and general constitutional reform. A steering committee of the CCMC was set up to meet with the three national aboriginal organizations, and in November Mr. Jarvis, co-chairman of the CCMC, invited them to meet the CCMC.

The steering committee was composed of the federal government and the provinces of Saskatchewan and Quebec. At the federal level FPRO handled liaison with the aboriginal groups, but the other departments remained involved. The federal government, because of its constitutional responsibility for aboriginal peoples, spoke for the steering committee of the CCMC in handling arrangements for a CCMC-aboriginal groups meeting. In Saskatchewan, as Roy Romanow was both attorney-general and minister of intergovernmental affairs, interdepartmental co-ordination was fairly straightforward and intergovernmental affairs was the primary provincial actor. Quebec, like Saskatchewan, contributed two actors: the ministère des affaires intergouvernementales (Claude Morin), and SAGMAI (see Figure 1).

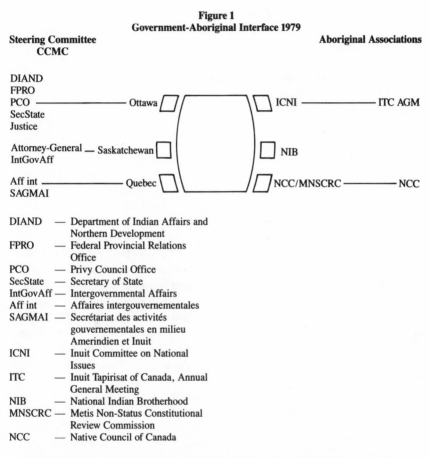

Figure 1
Government-Aboriginal Interface 1979

Steering Committee   **Aboriginal Associations**
    CCMC

DIAND
FPRO
PCO ——————— Ottawa   ICNI ——————— ITC AGM
SecState
Justice

Attorney-General — Saskatchewan   NIB
IntGovAff

Aff int ——————— Quebec   NCC/MNSCRC ——————— NCC
SAGMAI

DIAND	— Department of Indian Affairs and Northern Development
FPRO	— Federal Provincial Relations Office
PCO	— Privy Council Office
SecState	— Secretary of State
IntGovAff	— Intergovernmental Affairs
Aff int	— Affaires intergouvernementales
SAGMAI	— Secrétariat des activités gouvernementales en milieu Amerindien et Inuit
ICNI	— Inuit Committee on National Issues
ITC	— Inuit Tapirisat of Canada, Annual General Meeting
NIB	— National Indian Brotherhood
MNSCRC	— Metis Non-Status Constitutional Review Commission
NCC	— Native Council of Canada

Throughout November 1979 the federal working group and the three aboriginal associations met to discuss both the format and content of the 3 December meeting between the steering committee of the CCMC and the aboriginal associations. The meetings were of two types — informal and formal. The NIB initiated a series of informal meetings between the federal officials and the three national aboriginal associations. Three of these meetings, one at each of the headquarters of the associations, took place.

The first, at the NIB, was successful in initiating dialogue. Arnold Goodleaf, then special assistant to the president of the NIB, Noel Starblanket, chaired the meeting and suggested three items for the agenda of the 3 December meeting: an opening statement by each party, a discussion of the meeting of "direct legal impact," and the extent of the subject "Canada's Native Peoples and the Constitution." The second and third items reflected the fact that the governments had no clear idea as to whether or not aboriginal rights could be entrenched in the constitution nor of the extent of those aboriginal rights. The question was, did aboriginal rights pertain simply to land and hunting, or did they cover the full range of sociocultural and economic issues?

The phrase "clear legal impact" had slipped from Prime Minister Clark's lips at an earlier meeting with the NIB. He had been seeking to explain to the NIB Executive Council that aboriginal views on constitutional matters should most properly be limited to those items with "clear legal impact" on native peoples.[33] The Indians viewed this phrase as an opportunity to open debate on a large number of issues. The federal officials, however, were nervous of just such an interpretation, and downplayed its breadth of meaning by insisting the prime minister meant "direct legal impact." Federal officials underlined the government's position that the aboriginal peoples would have no privileged access other than in the forum, "Canada's Native Peoples and the Constitution," although their views on general constitutional topics would be welcomed.

The second and third meetings, between federal officials and the aboriginal associations, at the NCC and ICNI offices respectively, dealt further with the agenda of the forthcoming meeting between the steering committee of the CCMC and the aboriginal associations. At the ICNI meeting, Inuit representatives distributed a list of twenty-one items they wished to bring forward for discussion to the steering committee. The federal officials frankly explained that general policy issues such as fisheries or transportation which have an indirect impact on aboriginal groups could not be the subject of discussion. As one federal official admitted, the ICNI list would "probably scare the hell out of the Governments." The representatives from the aboriginal associations interpreted the federal officials' views as indicating that the government was trying to narrow the field of constitutional discussion. They were determined to keep the process as wide open as possible.

A formal meeting took place on 27 November 1979, immediately preceding the December meeting. Held in the Conference Centre, the meeting reviewed the agenda, the order of speaking, and a host of other minor details. Officials from Quebec and Saskatchewan participated. The informal meetings had established a working relationship between the federal government and the aboriginal associations, while the formal meeting merely confirmed prior logistical understandings. Both types of meetings, however, did not dispel the unease of the associations that the governments' promise of constitutional participation might be empty.

The 3 December meeting between the aboriginal associations and the steering committee of the CCMC was an historic occasion of sorts. It was the first time that government and aboriginal leaders met to discuss formally the aboriginal position towards Canada's constitution. The meeting was co-chaired by Jarvis and Romanow. Claude Morin (Québec) and Senator Jacques Flynn, federal minister of justice, were also present. The three aboriginal associations' views were similar in that they spoke of the need to embrace a broad range of constitutional matters of concern to them. The Inuit emphasized that aboriginal rights had to be affirmed and protected through entrenchment in the constitution, but they went on to discuss offshore resource development and coastal zone management, and Inuit representation in Parliament and the legislatures. ICNI also read into the record eleven items it wished to discuss at future meetings.

The 3 December meeting was inconclusive. The steering committee of the CCMC indicated that it considered the meeting only the first in a possible series. It also said in no uncertain terms that it could only report to the CCMC and that it had no authority to act on anything presented to it by the aboriginal associations. Roy Romanow in particular went to some lengths to explain to the aboriginal associations how the federal-provincial constitutional process worked (see Figure 2). It became clear that constitutional reform involving aboriginal peoples would be a very lengthy process. As Figure 2 shows, had the process initiated in December 1979 continued, several working groups of officials could have been established to explore certain issues (4th level). The fruits of their labours would have then been reviewed by the 3rd level, thence to the full CCMC (2nd level) and finally by the first ministers. Even though accorded participant status on aboriginal matters at that level, there was little guarantee that accords struck at lower levels would have been acceded to at the top. There was always hope, but aboriginal leaders had learned through long experience that hope rarely produced concrete results. They left the December meeting with a mixture of satisfaction at having finally opened discussion with the government of Canada and of weariness at the long patch before them.

The Clark government was defeated in the House on 13 December 1979 and subsequently lost the February 1980 election. Prime Minister Trudeau decided not to appoint a minister of federal-provincial relations, and instead the day-to-day responsibility of handling constitutional reform fell to the minister of justice, Jean Chrétien, while the prime minister guided its overall direction. Mr. Trudeau's interest in the constitution, his earlier commitment of February 1979, and Chrétien's background as a well-liked former minister of Indian affairs and northern development boded well for the aboriginal peoples. On 29 April 1980, the prime minister made a major speech to a national meeting of Indian chiefs renewing that commitment. He announced funding for constitutional research for each of the three national aboriginal associations at $400,000 each. He also believed attention should be focused on four areas in particular: aboriginal and treaty rights, aboriginal self-government, aboriginal representation in political institutions, and the responsibilities of the federal and provincial governments for the provision of services.

Figure 2
Hypothetical Constitutional Process 1979–80
(process cut-off by February 1980 Federal Election)

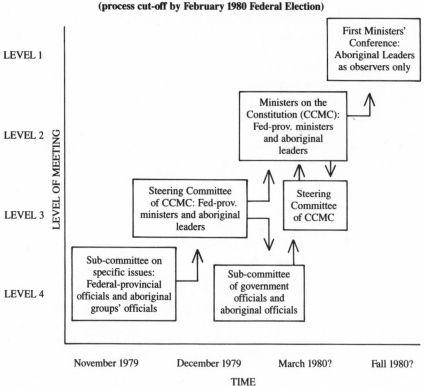

The announcement of funding had been long delayed from the perspective of the aboriginal associations. ITC had originally put in a request for over $600,000 to Hugh Faulkner, minister of IAND, in late 1978, then withdrew it. ICNI submitted a request for $1.2 million in the fall of 1979. This request was examined closely by the federal "Working Group on the Natives Item." At the 3 December meeting Jarvis had intimated that the government had in mind $1.5 million for all three aboriginal associations. For the Inuit the sum announced by Mr. Trudeau was woefully inadequate, given the ambitious research programme and vast territory in which they lived. From the federal government's perspective, however, it was a considerable sum, and each group received a similar amount despite differences in membership. The smallest group, the Inuit, received an identical amount to the NIB and NCC because of the expense of northern travel and the fact that ICNI had to cover one-third of Canada's land mass, the area in which its people lived. For the government, an identical amount to each group was administratively and politically the simplest solution. The funds, announced in April, were not received until August 1980.

The funding by the federal government also recognized the possibility of the provinces contributing funds for provincial aboriginal associations. To encourage them, Ottawa pledged funds for the aboriginal groups north of 60 degrees, that is, for those in the Yukon and NWT. The ICNI received $60,000 for constitutional work on behalf of regional associations in the NWT. The provinces were not uniformly responsive. Both Makivik Corporation (Québec) and the Labrador Inuit Association applied to their respective provincial governments with no luck. However, some provinces such as Ontario and Saskatchewan were fairly generous in their support of some provincial associations.[34]

During May 1980 the federal government concentrated on the Québec referendum on sovereignty-association. The referendum issue was keenly felt by the Quebec Inuit. They were adamantly opposed to the "Oui" forces. In addition to voting in the province-wide referendum, the Inuit organized their own referendum in their communities. The Inuit were asked whether they endorsed the position of Makivik Corporation supporting federalism. Held two weeks prior to the Quebec referendum, Makivik received an overwhelming 95 per cent endorsement. The efforts of Charlie Watt, Makivik's president, and the Inuit referendum result did not go unnoticed in Ottawa. In an emotional moment in the Québec referendum campaign, Prime Minister Trudeau, in reply to Premier Lévesque's charge that as an "Elliott" he was not a good Québécois, invoked Watt's name:

> And what about the Inuit, whose chief is called Charlie Watt, and they're disposed to vote No in the referendum. They've been here since the stone age. Are they not good Quebecers?[35]

This personal warmth between Trudeau and Watt became useful later in furthering Inuit objectives both in the constitutional and other policy spheres.

The victory of the "Non" forces in the Quebec referendum led the prime minister to urge the provincial premiers to tackle once again the thorny subject of constitutional reform. The prime minister had committed Ottawa during the referendum to find solutions to the problems of federalism. He therefore dispatched Jean Chrétien to meet his provincial counterparts. Throughout the summer of 1980 the CCMC met and considered twelve subjects[36] and attempted to produce position papers acceptable to all governments. However, the item "Canada's Native Peoples and the Constitution" was not one of the subjects, and the aboriginal peoples were invited only as observers to the September 1980 First Ministers' Conference.

In late August 1980 the aboriginal associations met with a sub-committee of the CCMC, consisting of Mr. Chrétien, Mr. Romanow, Gerry Mercier, attorney-general from Manitoba, and Dick Johnston, minister of federal and intergovernmental Affairs from Alberta. Also in attendance were Thomas Wells, minister of intergovernmental affairs, Ontario; Gerald Ottenheimer, attorney-general of Newfoundland; Garde Gardom, minister of intergovernmental relations, British Columbia; and Claude Morin. The meeting was not a good forum for aboriginal contributions to constitutional reform. It was more an opportunity to express views on the twelve items being discussed by the governments of Canada. Among other things, the Inuit called for "adequate reference" to their special status as an aboriginal people; entrenchment of aboriginal rights; provisions for the collective and individual nature of Inuit property rights; Inuit language rights; aboriginal participation in the future constitutional amendment process and recognition of Inuit family law practices.[37] However, as with the December 1979 meeting, the August meeting had no power to make decisions. Mr. Chrétien indicated that the constitution could be changed in light of the aboriginal peoples' views, but that the September 1980 meeting of first ministers would not be discussing the aboriginal aspects of the constitution. The Inuit pointed out that aboriginal participation in constitutional talks was hampered by the unavailability of many provincial position papers. As a result of the meeting, the leaders of the ICNI, NIB and NCC issued a joint press release condemning the discussion because the CCMC had failed to commit the governments of Canada to "full, equal and ongoing participation" of aboriginal peoples in first ministers' constitutional talks and because there was no assurance that the item "Canada's Native People and the Constitution" would be placed on the September agenda.[38]

As is now well known, the September First Ministers' Conference on the Constitution was a failure. The reasons for this need not be discussed here. In any event, the Inuit felt that no conference could be a success without aboriginal involvement. The decision of Prime Minister Trudeau to patriate Canada's constitution unilaterally in early October 1980, with a Charter of Rights and Freedoms and an amending formula, without provincial consent, threw the three national aboriginal associations, let alone the provinces, into a flurry of activity. The ICNI presented a report in late October 1980 to the annual general meeting of the ITC on constitutional developments to date. But thorough analysis of the Patriation Resolution did not commence until November. During that month the legal staff of the three national aboriginal associations met on several occasions to discuss the shortcomings of the Patriation Resolution.

At first glance, the resolution seemed harmless, or so federal officials were at pains to assure the aboriginal associations. First, s. 15 of the Charter of Rights and Freedoms, pertaining to non-discrimination rights, contained a subsection which excluded from the section programmes or activities designed to ameliorate the conditions of disadvantaged persons or groups. Federal officials felt that this subsection would leave room for special programmes for aboriginal peoples. Second, s. 22 indicated that provisions protecting the official languages of Canada would not abrogate or derogate from any legal or customary right or privilege with respect to languages other than French and English. Third, s. 24 indicated that the charter would not be construed as denying the existence of any other rights or freedoms existing in Canada, "including any rights or freedoms that pertain to the native peoples of Canada."[39]

At a meeting on 31 October with Michael Kirby, secretary to cabinet for federal-provincial relations, the federal government view, as revealed in a letter from the prime minister, was that the resolution was perfect and that aboriginal concerns could be dealt with more adequately in the post-patriation period, although there might be a slim possibility of amendments. This attitude of the government officials at this and subsequent meetings with staff of the aboriginal associations only served to heighten their unease with the Patriation Resolution. To their credit, government officials encouraged the aboriginal associations to take their case to the parliamentary committee.

The three associations had, by early November, decided to oppose the resolution and to lobby British parliamentarians. At a press conference in London, England, 7 November 1980, the three indicated that their rights had been ignored and they appealed to the British Parliament to protect those rights.[40] In a joint brief submitted on 20 November to the Foreign and Commonwealth Affairs Committee of the British House of Commons, the three associations stated that they were seeking to be "self-governing nations within Canadian Confederation"; that they wished to maintain their special relationship to the imperial Crown, and that in their view the Crown had an obligation to protect them under the provisions of the Royal Proclamation of 1763.[41] On 3 December 1980 the ICNI placed a half-page advertisement in the *Times* of London explaining that Inuit, while dissatisfied with the Patriation Resolution, viewed their future within Canada.

The London lobbying by the aboriginal associations generated some sympathy among a number of M.P.'s. For the federal government, a slight danger was that the Patriation Resolution might be treated by these M.P.'s as a debatable bill rather than one receiving automatic dead-of-night passage as had been the case with previous amendments to the BNA Act passed at Westminster. Given the packed schedule of the UK Parliament, any threat of disruption to regular business could have deterred Prime Minister Thatcher from proceeding with the resolution until assured of a smooth passage. Naturally, Ottawa was keen to avoid any obstacles to patriation.

Having addressed the British, the aboriginal groups turned to the task of presenting their views to the Special Joint Committee of the Senate and House of Commons. Considerable effort was made by each association to voice common criticisms of the resolution. After several meetings, the flaws of the resolution pertaining to aboriginal matters were agreed upon. The presentation of the Inuit, the first aboriginal group before the Committee, on 1 and 2 December 1980, covered the major points.[42]

Before detailing their criticisms, the Inuit reviewed their own historical status and position. They argued that the Patriation Resolution should not entrench the incremental erosion of aboriginal rights which had occurred since before Confederation. Rather, they argued, it should at least respect their aboriginal status to the extent that it had been recognized by the Royal Proclamation of 1763. Specifically, the Inuit proposed the following changes to the resolution.

1. Change to s. 6 regarding mobility rights: to permit reasonable laws and practices to mitigate adverse environmental and social impacts on a community, culture, economy or society of the aboriginal peoples of Canada (e.g., to allow actions, which would otherwise contradict general mobility rights, to protect the north from sudden influxes of southern workers to exploration and mining camps).
2. Re equality before the law and equal protection of the law (s. 15): to permit laws, programmes, or activities whose object is to recognize aboriginal and treaty rights of the aboriginal peoples of Canada (i.e., to ensure that aboriginal and treaty rights are not seen as discriminatory).
3. Re Aboriginal Rights and Freedoms (new section):
   i) aboriginal peoples mean Indian, Inuit and Metis;
   ii) right to self-determination within the Canadian federation;
   iii) negotiation of rights and protections in a number of areas, including aboriginal and treaty rights;
   iv) no extinguishment of aboriginal rights;
   v) right to collective property, no confiscation except in a national emergency and for reasonable compensation.
4. Re s. 24, Undeclared Rights and Freedoms: mention of rights acquired under or confirmed by the Royal Proclamation of 1763.
5. Participation of Aboriginal Peoples at first ministers' conferences (s. 32): a new section including direct participation of Indian, Inuit and Metis representatives, as promised in prime minister's letter of 30 October 1980.
6. Aboriginal consent (new section): to obtain aboriginal consent for amendments referring to any of the aboriginal people.
7. Schedule 1 (list of constitutional documents): to include the Royal Proclamation, and the Order-in-Council re Rupert's Land and the Northwestern Territory.

The reaction of the parliamentary committee was a mixture of surprise at the thoroughness of the ICNI brief and sympathy for the Inuit position. The committee had a pivotal role to play. Formally their job was to report to Parliament on its deliberations, with Parliament having final say before the resolution was passed to the Queen. However, everyone understood that the battle lay in convincing the committee to adopt suitable amendments. In actual fact, of course, the ICNI had to convince the Liberal majority on the committee, that is, convince Trudeau and Chrétien who would then instruct that majority how to vote.

The ICNI enlisted the support of one primary actor, one other actor, and an important go-between. Peter Ittinuar, NDP M.P. for Nunatsiaq, an Inuk from Rankin Inlet, persuaded the NDP caucus to support the ICNI's basic position and in particular the key amendments of the several it had put forward. This was no mean feat. The leader of the NDP, Ed Broadbent, had indicated his support for the Patriation Resolution in October provided an amendment was moved giving provinces the right "to control and manage their natural resources, and to tax these resources for the general benefit of the people of the province."[43] Broadbent had to be persuaded to broaden his *quid pro quo* for supporting the Trudeau package. Fortunately Ittinuar, with the aid of some of his caucus colleagues, was able to do so.

Another figure was Warren Allmand, Liberal M.P. for Notre Dame de Grace. Allmand, a former minister of IAND and in 1980–81 no longer a cabinet member, spoke frequently in caucus and to the Liberal members of the parliamentary committee. Allmand's counsel was important in helping to further the credibility of the aboriginal position. The go-between was Senator Jack Austin, who was a committee member, and as the government member of the committee's "steering committee" was the "team leader" for the Liberal majority on the committee. He also had close contact with the prime minister. Several meetings took place in January 1981 between the ICNI leaders and Austin. Austin relayed the ICNI views to Chrétien and Trudeau, leading finally to the government agreeing to three major amendments.

Evaluating why the government changed its mind on the aboriginal positions requires mentioning a fourth actor, Sir Anthony Kershaw, who chaired the British Foreign and Commonwealth Affairs Committee which undertook to examine informally the question as to whether the prime minister's resolution required provincial support. Sir Anthony's report in late January concluded that the Canadian Parliament could not act alone to patriate the constitution with a Charter of Rights. This conclusion was a blow to the government as it had the potential of persuading a significant number of British parliamentarians to attempt to block passage and of dissuading Prime Minister Thatcher from introducing it in Westminster unless smooth passage was assured. Certainly a factor for Ottawa to consider was the maximization of support from Canadians; and the endorsement of 1.25 million aboriginal people was not insignificant.

On 30 January 1981 the government therefore agreed to the following points, all of which received unanimous support from the three federal parties:

1. In Part II of the Patriation Resolution, 1981, the aboriginal and treaty rights of the Indian, Inuit and Metis peoples of Canada were recognized and affirmed;

2. In s. 25 of the Charter of Rights and Freedoms, it was guaranteed that the Charter cannot be interpreted so as to abolish or detract from the aboriginal, treaty, or other rights or freedoms pertaining to the aboriginal peoples including those recognized by the Royal Proclamation of 1763, and those acquired by way of land claims settlements.

3. In Part IV, s. 36 (2), the first ministers' conference convened in the first two years after patriation would include on their agenda an item respecting constitutional matters that directly affect the aboriginal peoples of Canada. Those were to include the identification and definition of those rights to be included in the constitution. It was also provided that aboriginal people would participate in the discussion on their rights.

4. The Order-in-Council admitting Rupert's Land and the Northwestern Territory was added to the list of constitutional documents contained in Schedule A of the Constitution Act.

The government would not agree to any restrictions on mobility rights nor to the idea of aboriginal consent being required for amendments to provisions related to aboriginal rights contained in the resolution. The ICNI agreed to accept the government concessions as it felt that these amendments were a good basis for futhering aboriginal rights. In return for these provisions, the ICNI agreed to visit London at a later date to inform British parliamentarians of the Inuit support for patriation and the aboriginal provisions.

Third reading of the Patriation Resolution commenced on 17 February 1981. The government was in a buoyant mood. Their faith in the Patriation Resolution had been upheld by a 3 February decision of the Supreme Court of Manitoba which, upon reference from the provincial government, upheld the legality of the Resolution 3-2. The debate continued intermittently until 19 March when the government House Leader proposed a time allocation to end the debate. The Progressive Conservatives, who had long opposed unilateral patriation, were angered by the attempt to close debate, and on 24 March commenced a filibuster. The unusual weapon they chose was the raising of points of order and points of privilege after each daily Question Period (except on the so-called allocated "Opposition Days"), thereby preventing the orders of the day from proceeding. On 30 March the Tories' filibuster received a boost from the Newfoundland Court of Appeal, which, upon a reference from the provincial government, ruled 3–9 against Ottawa.

Faced with the complete breakdown of regular parliamentary business, Prime Minister Trudeau offered to refer the Patriation Resolution to the Supreme Court. Finally on 8 April after intense three-party negotiations, the House, followed by the Senate, agreed to refer the resolution to the Supreme Court after three further days of debate with final amendments. One of these amendments, introduced by the NDP, brought Part II of the resolution affirming the aboriginal and treaty rights of the Indians, Inuit and Metis, under the general amending formula.

The reasons for this particular amendment lie in earlier events. Very soon after the 30 January unanimous approval of the three amendments relating to the aboriginal peoples, the government proposed to the Special Joint Constitution Committee that Parliament and individual legislatures be allowed to make changes in the constitution concerning the right of aboriginal peoples in their provinces. This meant that in any province these rights would be subject to the decree of Ottawa and that province, and in any territory these rights could be unilaterally amended by Parliament. The three aboriginal associations vigorously opposed this as it reduced constitutional recognition and affirmation of their treaty and aboriginal rights to mere legislative fiat. While this amendment was withdrawn in the committee on 4 February, it was not until the final days in April that the House and Senate unanimously approved placing these rights under the general amending formula.

The ICNI and Peter Ittinuar tried unsuccessfully to persuade the government to accept the notion of aboriginal consent to amendments regarding treaty and aboriginal rights, but the government would agree only to Part II being brought under the general amending formula. While this means that changes to aboriginal rights would require the consent of the federal Parliament and the appropriate number of provinces, thereby making change difficult, it also means that Part II could not be eroded easily.

By April 1981, then, the aboriginal peoples had achieved constitutional recognition and the opportunity to elaborate further the meaning and extent of aboriginal rights at first ministers' constitutional conferences in the two years following patriation. It was a small but significant step towards the ultimate goal of establishing a Charter of Aboriginal Rights and other protections designed to ensure a stronger voice for aboriginal peoples in Canada

THE POST-PATRIATION PERIOD

Assuming the Supreme Court supports the Patriation Resolution, and further assuming that the resolution is passed in Britain, the Inuit plan to raise a number of issues in the two year post-patriation period at the annual first minister's conferences. Among the items to be discussed will be those raised by the prime minister in his letter to the ICNI on 30 October 1980, repeating his 29 April speech.

The first item is aboriginal and treaty rights, and under that the ICNI will be raising sub-items such as cultural, economic, and linguistic rights. The second item the prime minister mentioned was aboriginal self-government. This has always been a strong priority for the Inuit. In the NWT the concept of a Nunavut government meets the need to give its arctic residents a form of responsible government suitable to their needs. In Northern Québec and Labrador strong regional governments could meet the needs of northern residents. The ICNI will be supporting the desires of the permanent northern residents in this regard.

A third item raised by Trudeau was aboriginal representation in Parliament. While Nunavut is fortunate to have its own M.P., Peter Ittinuar, and its own senator, Willie Adams, neither northern Québec nor Labrador have members in either House. The ICNI believes that Inuit need more representation in Ottawa in order that the Inuit voice from all regions is heard. A related question to discuss with the provinces of Québec and Newfoundland is the representation the Inuit have in the provincial assemblies of those provinces. (Strong representation by the Inuit in Québec during 1980 did not prove successful.)

A fourth item mentioned by the prime minister was the responsibilities of the federal governments in relation to the provision of services to aboriginal peoples. These cover many areas such as health, housing, municipal services, and social services. A question is how each level of government should share the provision of services, and to what extent aboriginal people should manage and design such services themselves.

In addition, the Inuit are keen to ensure that their land use, hunting, fishing, and whaling rights are not infringed by resource development. Accordingly, the ICNI plans to put forward its views on rights it feels the Inuit have in securing their adequate participation in all aspects of northern life, present and future. The major problem will be how these views can be given constitutional import. The tradition in most western democracies does not encourage the view that a constitution should be a type of "operators manual" or detailed blueprint for societal development. Yet what the Inuit may be pressing for is closer to that view than tradition has allowed. However, the hope may be that special constitutional provisions for aboriginal peoples could establish principles of Inuit participation in Canadian society which could serve to guide more clearly than have past consitutional practices both the decisions of the courts and the passage of federal and provincial legislation. The two years following patriation may very well be the proof of the constitutional "pudding" set in the winter of 1980–81.

One certainty may be the process itself. It will likely follow the pattern of multi-level constitutional discussions which have been the practice of the federal and provincial governments (see Figure 2 above). As such, it seems rather unlikely that the aboriginal peoples will be able to discuss with the governments in two years all the items they wish to. Therefore, it can be anticipated that the aboriginal peoples will begin to press the governments after the first year for an extension of negotiations on further entrenchment of aboriginal rights in Canada's constitution. Should that be the case, it is to be hoped that the governments will not prematurely end these fine constitutional beginnings.

NOTES

* I am grateful to Peter Jull and Geoff Lester for their comments on an earlier draft.
 1. At time of writing (June 1981), the future of the resolution is not known, so the reader is cautioned to place this article in the appropriate context. See Special Joint Committee of the Senate and the House of Commons on the Constitution of Canada, *Report*, 13 February 1981.
 2. I am indebted to Geoff Lester for assistance in re-drafting this section.
 3. On a strict view of the law, plenary jurisdiction over the Northwest Territories (and also the Yukon Territory), and hence over their residents, is derived from s. 4 of the British North America Act, 1871 (34–35 Vict., c. 28 [U.K.]), which enables the Parliament of Canada from time to time to make provision for the administration, peace, order, and good government of any territory not for the time being included in any province. However, because there are Inuit in Québec and Newfoundland-Labrador, and also because of the limitations imposed on the power of the commissioner-in-council by s. 14(1) of the Northwest Territories Act (R.S.C., 1970, c. N-22), the effect of which is not discussed in this article, it is relevant to begin with the Constitution Act of 1867.
 4. 30–31 Vict., c. 3 (U.K.).
 5. *Re Eskimos* (1939), S.C.R. 104.
 6. R.S.C., 1970, c. I-6, s. 4(1).
 7. For example, *Calder et al v. A.G. British Columbia*, 1973 S.C.R. 313 at p. 395, per J. Hall.
 8. Brian Slattery, "The Land Rights of Canada's Indigenous Peoples, as Affected by the Crown's Acquisition of their Territories" (D. Phil. diss., Wadham College, Oxford, 1979), p. 243.
 9. Peter A. Cumming and Neil H. Mickenberg, *Native Rights in Canada*, 2d ed. (Toronto, 1972), p. 30.
10. See for instance *Regina v. Koonungnak* (1964), 42 C.R. 143, at p. 160 (1963–64), 45 W.W.R. 282, at p. 302 (N.W.T. Terr. Ct.).
11. *Baker Lake et al. v. Minister of IAND et al.* (1979), as cited in *Musk-Ox*, vol. 26 (1980), p. 71.
12. Kenneth M. Narvey, "The Royal Proclamation of 7 October 1763, the Common Law, and Native Rights to Land within the Territory Granted to the Hudson's Bay Company," *Saskatchewan Law Review* 38 (1974): 123–233; Slattery, pp. 14–18; Jack Stagg, *Anglo-Indian Relations in North America to 1763, and an Analysis of the Royal Proclamation of 7 October 1763* (Ottawa, 1981), pp. 382–85, 389–90.
13. See R.S.C., 1970, Appendices, no. 9, pp. 8, 11, 12, 14, 18.
14. Anthony Hooper, "Aboriginal Title in the Northwest Territories," in Cumming and Mickenberg, p. 149.
15. See s. 146, B.N.A. Act, 1867, and s. 2 of the Colonial Laws Validity Act, 1865 (28–29 Vict., c. 63 [U.K.]).
16. S.C. 1912, c. 45.
17. See Paul Gérin-Lajoie, *Constitutional Amendment in Canada* (Toronto, 1952), ch. 1.
18. RSC 1970, Appendix II, pp. 121–22, "Constitutional Acts and Documents," lists 38 whereas the Patriation Resolution 1981 lists only 30.
19. A good summary of these developments is contained in Donald Smiley, *Canada in Question*. 3d ed. (Toronto, 1980).
20. However, this may change to Rankin Inlet. For a good review of health problems in the Keewatin see *Report of a Study of Inuit Health and Health Services in the Keewatin Zone of the Northwest Territories 1980* (Ottawa, 1981).
21. Secrétariat des activités gouvernementales en milieu Amerindien et Inuit.
22. The federal Department of Indian Affairs and Northern Development.
23. For an analysis of administration in Northern Quebec, see G. R. Weller, "Local Government in the Canadian Provincial North," *Canadian Public Administration* 24, no. 1 (1981): 44–72.
24. For further details, see *Brief to the Standing Committee on Indian Affairs and Northern Development*, submitted by Makivik Corporation, on behalf of the Inuit of Quebec, 20 March 1981.
25. "Poorest of the Poor, Labrador Looking for a Fair Shake," Toronto *Globe and Mail*, 23 January 1981.
26. A recent housing survey found only 68 sq. ft. pp (per person) (6.31 m²) in Nain, to 149 sq. ft. pp (13.84 m²) in Postville, well below the national standard of 225 sq. ft. pp (20.9 m²); Inuit Non-Profit Housing Corporation, *Labrador Coast Housing Survey* (1979).

27. Correspondence, and memoranda.
28. In the case of the Inuit in NWT, see *Report, Inuit Land Use and Occupancy Project* (Ottawa, 1976), three vols.
29. DIAND, *Statement of the Government of Canada on Indian Policy* (Ottawa, 1969).
30. *Calder v. A.-G. B.C.* (1973), S.C.R. 313.
31. Ottawa, 1978.
32. Inuit Tapirisat of Canada, "Presentation," 30 August 1978.
33. See text of "Meeting with Prime Minister Clark/Cabinet Ministers and the National Indian Brotherhood Executive Council September 28, 1979," Ottawa.
34. For example, the Ontario Metis-Non Status Indian Association received a grant from the Davis government. Saskatchewan funded Saskatchewan aboriginal groups $80,000 in 1980.
35. L. Ian MacDonald, "A 'Restored' Trudeau Weaves His Old Magic on the Crowds," Montreal *Gazette*, 16 May 1980.
36. These were: 1) A Statement of Principles: 2) Charter of Rights, including language rights; 3) Equalization and Regional Disparities; 4) Patriation and an Amending Formula; 5) Resource Ownership and Interprovincial Trade; 6) Offshore Resources; 7) Fisheries; 8) Power affecting the economy; 9) Communications, including broadcasting; 10) Family Law; 11) Upper House; and 12) Supreme Court.
37. Inuit Committee on National Issues, *Submission to the CCMC*, 26 August 1980.
38. *Joint Press Release*, NIB-NCC-ICNI, 26 August 1980.
39. *Proposed Resolution for a Joint Address to Her Majesty the Queen respecting the Constitution of Canada*, 2 October 1980.
40. "Canadian Indians Appeal to Britain for Protection." *Manchester Guardian Weekly*, 9 November 1980.
41. Inuit Committee on National Issues, *Brief to the Joint Senate and House of Commons Committee on the Constitution*, 1 December 1980, Appendix II, p. 4. The British committee, however, rejected the view of an obligation by the imperial Crown to Canada's aboriginal peoples.
42. Ibid.
43. For a detailed exposition of his views, see Ed Broadbent, "A Formula for Ending the Resource Impasse," Toronto *Globe and Mail*, 8 December 1980, p. 7.

A Declaration of The First Nations

We the Original Peoples of this land know the Creator put us here.

The Creator gave us laws that govern all our relationships to live in harmony with nature and mankind.

The laws of the Creator defined our rights and responsibilities.

The Creator gave us our spiritual beliefs, our languages, our culture, and a place on Mother Earth which provided us with all our needs.

We have maintained our freedom, our languages, and our traditions from time immemorial.

We continue to exercise the rights and fulfill the responsibilities and obligations given to us by the Creator for the land upon which we were placed.

The Creator has given us the right to govern ourselves and the right to self-determination.

The rights and responsibilities given to us by the Creator cannot be altered or taken away by any other Nation.

Assembly of First Nations Conference
December, 1980

Chief, Charles Wood
Chairman, Council of Chiefs

Delbert Riley, President
National Indian Brotherhood

TREATY AND ABORIGINAL RIGHTS PRINCIPLES

1. The aboriginal title, aboriginal rights and treaty rights of the aboriginal people of Canada, including:
   (a) all rights recognized by the Royal Proclamation of October 7th, 1763;
   (b) all rights recognized in treaties between the Crown and nations or tribes of Indians in Canada ensuring the Spiritual concept of Treaties;
   (c) all rights acquired by aboriginal peoples in settlements or agreements with the Crown on aboriginal rights and title;
are hereby recognized, confirmed, ratified and sanctioned.

2. "Aboriginal people" means the First Nations or Tribes of Indians in Canada and each Nation having the right to define its own Citizenship.

3. Those parts of the Royal Proclamation of October 7th, 1763, providing for the rights of the Nations or tribes of Indians are legally and politically binding on the Canadian and British Parliaments.

4. No law of Canada or of the Provinces, including the Charter of Rights and Freedoms in the Constitution of Canada, shall hereafter be construed or applied so as to abrogate, abridge or diminish the rights specified in Sections 1 and 3 of this Part.

5. (a) The Parliament and Government of Canada shall be committed to the negotiation of the full realization and implementation of the rights specified in Sections 1 and 3 of this Part.
   (b) Such negotiations shall be internationally supervised, if the aboriginal peoples parties to those negotiations so request.
   (c) Such negotiations, and any agreements concluded thereby, shall be with the full participation and the full consent of the aboriginal peoples affected.

6. Any amendments to the Constitution of Canada in relation to any constitutional matters which affect the aboriginal peoples, including the identification or definition of the rights of any of those peoples, shall be made only with the consent of the governing Council, Grand Council or Assembly of the aboriginal peoples affected by such amendment, identification or definition.

7. A Treaty and Aboriginal Rights Protection Office shall be established.

8. A declaration that Indian Governmental powers and responsibilities exist as a permanent, integral fact in the Canadian polity.

9. All pre-confederation, post-confederation treaties and treaties executed outside the present boundaries of Canada but which apply to the Indian Nations of Canada are international treaty agreements between sovereign nations. Any changes to the treaties requires the consent of the two parties to the treaties, who are the Indian Governments representing Indian Nations and the Crown repre-

sented by the British Government, the Canadian Government is only a third party and cannot initiate any changes.

Joint Council of the National Indian Brotherhood
November 18, 1981

Chief Charles Wood
Chairman, Council of Chiefs

Delbert Riley,
President, N.I.B.

The Indian in Canadian Historical Writing, 1972–1982

James W. St.G. Walker

The picture of the Indian as a human being which emerged from the initial version of this study was confusing, contradictory, and incomplete.[1] There was a long string of epithets used to describe Indians, the most common being "savage" and including such corresponding terms as cruel, treacherous, bloodthirsty, dirty, fiendish, superstitious, and fickle. Some of the nouns used included thief, ogre, butcher, and vagabond. There were some contrary adjectives — brave, hospitable, devoted, and faithful — and the occasional appearance of a "bronzed stalwart" or a "copper-hued patriot," but not enough to reverse the negative impression. The most common illustration of savagery was the treatment of prisoners and the method of waging war, with some extremely gory descriptions of the Jesuit martyrs of 1649 and the Lachine massacre of 1689. Indians were portrayed as inferiors, at a lower level of evolution, living like animals amidst disease and squalor. Indian women were immoral, "proved" by the facts that they wore immodest clothing or even went naked and tended to be free with their sexual favours. This was explained by the absence of any religion among them and the disorganized nature of their society. The final impression was one of a childish, uncivilized people whose only salvation lay in conquest and conversion by Europeans.

The Indian's allotted place in Canadian history was in keeping with his personal qualities, or lack of them. Indicative of the Indian's historical position was the way in which he was first introduced into Canada's story. The typical history began with geography, then the Vikings, then John Cabot, and then Cartier, when the first reference to Indians would be made. They would appear suddenly to greet Cartier, or they would be introduced to explain some of the hardships faced by the early settlers. Indians were treated as part of the setting, the environment in which the history of the European newcomers could unfold. Once the Whites arrived, the Indian was given a role of subservience: supplying food to settlers, teaching skills which enabled Whites to adapt, guiding explorers, and above all in the fur trade. The Iroquois, in particular, were an obstacle for New France, but usually Indians were allies in white men's wars. The American Revolution and the War of 1812 were given special attention. After 1812, the Indian almost totally disappeared. He emerged fleetingly during the various Red River disturbances to commit a few murders, and the occasional historian mentioned the treaties. The final curtain call was 1885. Most books were sympathetic to the Indians, but they were definitely pictured as "also rans" with Louis Riel. After 1885 there is an almost total neglect of Indians in Canadian society.

In 1971 there were several problems affecting the treatment of Indians by historians: the uncritical use of biased sources; a double standard which could call Indians savage when European punishments at the time — including breaking on the wheel, burning at the stake, and sentences to 1,000 lashes — would by any honest standard by equally savage; the urgent quest for heroes — Champlain, the Jesuits, Dollard — whose adversaries had to be portrayed as evil; and the preoccupation with political affairs, especially between French and English and Canadians and Americans. Nevertheless, there was cause for hope in the fact that the most careful and scholarly accounts, those with the greatest depth of research and use of published material from related disciplines such as anthropology and archaeology, contained an improved and more complete image of the Indian's historical position. What was lacking at that time was more specialized works in native studies, which would contribute to the background material for the more careful and scholarly general histories of Canada.

The past decade has been very rich for native studies. The period began with Robert Surtees's *The Original People* (1971),[2] followed a year later by Palmer Patterson's *The Canadian Indian*, both of them offering broad interpretive insights. In the same category fell George Manuel's *Fourth World* (1974), Howard Adams' *Prison of Grass* (1975), and Harold Cardinal's *Rebirth of Canada's Indians* (1977). All these books gave an Indian perspective on Canadian history and illuminated new aspects of the native experience in Canada, and they were supplemented by several of the articles in Del Muise, ed., *Approaches to Native History in Canada* (1977).

In addition, there have been several scholarly or semi-scholarly accounts of individual Indian nations, personalities, and issues. Moving geographically from east to west there was Rowe on *The Beothuks* (1977), and on Quebec that most fruitful combination of archaeology and anthropology by Pendergast and Trigger, *Cartier's Hochelaga* (1972). On Huronia we had Heidenreich's *History and Geography* (1971) and Trigger's *History to 1660* (1976), two works by non-historians which have made a great contribution to historical understanding. Barbara Graymont's *The Iroquois in the American Revolution* (1972), despite its title, is another broad contribution to the ethnohistorical literature. Johnson on *The Ojibway Heritage* (1976) and Schmalz on *The Saugeen* (1977) provide intimate group portraits, while Barker's reminiscences in *Forty Years a Chief* (1978) go beyond his personal story. Adolf Hungry Wolf gave much of historical significance in *The Blood People* (1977), and Chief John Snow's *These Mountains Are Our Sacred Places* (1977) is a useful history of the Stoney Indians. Much new material on the western Indians appeared in the papers edited by Getty and Smith, *One Century Later* (1978). In prairie biography there was Hugh Dempsey on

Crowfoot (1972) and MacEwan's *Portraits from the Plains* (1971), the latter a series of biographical sketches. Finally, for the educated general reader, there was George Woodcock's *Peoples of the Coast* (1977).

These books all dealt with native history in itself, that is, they did not rely on episodes in white history to give them relevance. Of course, no one will deny that since about 1600, in the east, the white presence has been a fundamental influence on Indian life, and the past decade has supplied some major works to help us understand that influence. Allen's *The British Indian Department* (1975) and Chamberlin's *The Harrowing of Eden* (1975) together give a very full picture of the evolution of government policy towards Indians in both Canada and the United States. The Department of Indian Affairs has itself published several pieces on Indian policy throughout the decade, including Leslie and Maguire, eds., *The Historical Development of the Indian Act* (2d ed., 1978). Leslie Upton's *Micmacs and Colonists* (1979) is a model study on the Maritimes, supplemented by some of the historical essays in McGee's collection on *The Native Peoples of Atlantic Canada* (1974), by Dickason's *Louisbourg and the Indians* (1976), and by Daugherty's *Maritime Indian Treaties in Historical Perspective* (1980). Another model, and a widely recognized one, is Cornelius Jaenen's prizewinning *Friend and Foe: Aspects of French-Amerindian Cultural Contact in the Sixteenth and Seventeenth Centuries* (1976). Moving further west, we have Stuart Hughes's collection of personal narratives, including Indian ones, on *The Frog Lake Massacre* (1976), and Richard Price, ed., *The Spirit of the Alberta Indian Treaties* (1979). British Columbia has been especially blessed. Robert Cail's *Land, Man, and the Law* (1974) will long be the definitive study on Indian land, and Robin Fisher's *Contact and Conflict* (1977) has fully as much to say about native history as it does about Indian-white relations. Also of value on British Columbia land policy is LaViolette's *The Struggle for Survival* (1973). Mention should be made of the Coles Reprint series, which has made available in inexpensive paperback reprints several highly valuable nineteenth-century documents and first-hand accounts of Indian affairs.

Because the fur trade has figured so prominently in the general histories, it is worth mentioning separately several books which almost amount to a new literature on the subject. Taken together, these books show how the Indians organized their part in the trade and during several important phases actually controlled it, and they describe the impact of the trade on Indian society not just in terms of destruction and assimilation but through cultural adaptation and deliberate change. Significantly, several of these works come from the pens of ethnohistorians and historical geographers. The kind of book I refer to includes Bishop's *The Northern Ojibway and the Fur Trade* (1974), Ray's *Indians in the Fur Trade* (1974), Baldwin's *The Fur Trade in the Moose-Missinaibi River Valley* (1976), Martin's *Keepers of the Game* (1978), Ray and Freeman's *Give Us Good Measure* (1978), and Judd and Ray's *Old Trails and New Directions* (1980). The implications for our understanding of the entire fur trade from these and similar works is immense.

Then there has been a body of works produced in other disciplines which contribute to our historical as well as our contemporary knowledge of Indian issues. Some of the essays in Jean Elliott's *Minority Canadians: Native Peoples* (1971) fall in this category, as do most of the sections in Bowles et al., *The Indian: Assimilation, Integration or Separation* (1972). Legal studies have given us Roman Komar's *Royal Proclamation of 1763: A Legal Enquiry into Indian Land in Canada* (1971), Cumming and Mickenberg's *Native Rights in Canada* (2d ed., 1972), the booklet *Indian Life and Canadian Law* (1973) from the Canadian Civil Liberties Education Trust, another booklet from the London-based Minority Rights Group, *Canada's Indians* by James Wilson (1974), Derek Smith's *Canadian Indians and the Law* (1975), and the Indian Claims Commission's *Indian Claims in Canada* (1975), which contains an excellent bibliography covering this question. Current events, and the natives' entry into the political arena as well as the courts, have inspired another group of works which have sought to explain the historical context of several of these contemporary conflicts. René Fumoleau's *As Long as This Land Shall Last* (1975) is a fine example of the genre, giving the historical and treaty background to the Mackenzie pipeline debate. Mel Watkins' *Dene Nation* (1977) also begins with the Mackenzie enquiry and goes on to explain the native response and the native solution to the dilemma. Across the continent, the James Bay project provoked two studies by Boyce Richardson, *James Bay: The Plot to Drown the North Woods* (1972) and *Strangers Devour the Land* (1976). Hugh and Karmel McCullum, *This Land Is Not for Sale* (1975), deals with several points of Indian-government conflict, while Salley Weaver's thorough and brilliant *Making Canadian Indian Policy* (1981) goes behind the scenes to enlighten the public on the government's reconsideration of native issues at the time of the 1969 White Paper.

Most of the books just mentioned have been readily available in paperback, and the problems they deal with have been reflected in widespread newspaper coverage as native people have been articulating and pressing their demands ever more forcefully on the Canadian and provincial governments. Once again Indians have been in possession of lands wanted by Whites, but this time the natives have been using the political and judicial process to bargain for a just solution. Most recently the constitution and the confrontation at Restigouche over salmon fishing rights have put Indian affairs into our newspapers regularly. The general public in Canada, which includes the historians, cannot have failed to recall the Indian presence in Canada today and the unresolved issues of historical origin which continue to face Canadians. The increase in specialized research has been paralleled by an increase in native activity, making Indian affairs more apparent than at any period during this century.

More obscure, perhaps, from the general public, but quite accessible to the professional academic, have been a host of articles appearing in the scholarly journals.[3] As every undergraduate knows, one place to look for the latest scholarship on any topic is in the academic journals, and there is no absence of Indian material there. Another place to look is in the graduate schools, where each M.A. or Ph.D. candidate is expected to produce an original contribution. There have been scores of theses submitted on topics of relevance to Indian history.[4] While the majority of these come from anthropology, the latest edition of the Canadian Historical Association's *Register of Post-Graduate Dissertations in Progress* (1981) names thirty-five titles on Indian history.

Specialists and graduate students have, quite clearly, been producing an excellent range of material in recent years. However, it would be entirely unrealistic to expect this research to find its way into the general histories in the same decade that it is written. Even if a renewed public interest in Indians might have attracted historians to the subject, it is not until the 1980's that there will be major revisions. But at the same time there are several major bibliographies which list thousands of titles published *before* 1971, indicating both the amount of information already available and the ready access to it in any major university library. The serious historian would not have found it difficult to obtain Indian material even before the burst of scholarly activity in the 1970's, and anyone writing since 1971 has had bibliographical guides to facilitate the search. The telling point, as always, has been the historian's interest and thoroughness, not the presence or absence of suitable material. Among the many reference guides available the most complete is probably Abler and Weaver, *A Canadian Indian Bibliography, 1960–1970* (1974), which annotates over 3,000 entries including books, articles, theses, and forty-three other bibliographies published during the 1960's. Don Whiteside's *Aboriginal People* (1973) lists over a thousand items, and there are supplementary bibliographies by Joan Ryan (1972), Arlene Hirschfelder (1973), Jack Marken (1973), the Department of Indian Affairs (3d ed., 1975), the Indian Claims Commission (1975), Dwight Smith (1974 and 1980), and some provincial ministries of education. Any one of these would direct the generalist to more than enough material. Mention should also be made of the Newberry Library's bibliographical series, which now contains over a dozen volumes, almost all of them with content relevant to Canada.[5]

Despite the normal time-lag between a specialized study and its incorporation into more generalized accounts, one might therefore expect to find a new and more complete image of the Indian in our textbooks published since 1971. This has not always been the case. In the preface to his *Canada: The Heroic Beginnings* (1974), Donald Creighton quite conveniently sets out the themes for his book, which he tells us are "the principal themes in Canadian History": "the occupation of the Atlantic seaboard, the Anglo-French conflict, the drive to the Pacific, the settlement of the west, the defence of the coasts and the frontier, and exploitation of the north."[6] The selection of these themes effectively excludes the Indians from any meaningful place in Creighton's history. There is a prologue, "The Earliest Canadians," with some minimal impressions of pre-contact native society, but chapter one begins with the Vikings. Since they could not fit into the thematic framework, the original inhabitants had to be dealt with before the history of Canada begins. They return briefly to teach Cartier a cure for scurvy and to help Champlain's settlers "adjust to their environment," but never do they have an independent role to play.[7] The Iroquois "harried and terrorized" the early French settlements on the St. Lawrence and "menaced the very existence of New France," thus necessitating "two punitive military expeditions" in 1666. But before long the Iroquois, though they "retained their terrible skill in surprise attacks," "gradually became the clients and auxiliaries of the potentially far more powerful colony of New York."[8] Full stop to any significance for the Iroquois, positive or negative.

Subsequently, the Indians are useful in helping to extend the French fur trade into the North and West, a tendency not lost on the British fur-traders, who with presents and alcohol acquired Indian co-operation. But if they assisted with the extension of European interests, the Indians could also be obstacles. David Thompson, for example, was defeated by the Americans in his race for the Columbia mouth in 1810–11 because of "the hostility of the Indians, and the difficult detour he had to make to avoid their threats." Of course, their role in the American Revolution and the War of 1812 was beneficial. "The brilliant Shawnee chief Tecumseh," in particular, died to keep Canada British.[9]

From central Canada in 1812 the focus next shifts to the West in the 1870's, where "an unhappy restlessness" appeared among the Indians as a result of the disappearance of the buffalo and the restrictive life of the new reserves. By 1885 grievances were being expressed as the "ineffectual farming" practices of the Indians failed to replace the buffalo hunt and the fur trade. This situation provided a following for "the able and influential Poundmaker" and "the sullen and inveterate" Big Bear, who, inspired by the Duck Lake massacre, were prompted to pillage Battleford and massacre nine people at Frog Lake.[10]

Creighton sums up the Indian situation after 1885 in these words: "The Indians remained an anxious concern for future generations, but henceforth the problems of their adjustment to the new order were incidental to the main issues of western development."[11] This is at least an honest statement, and it is quite consistent with the main themes in Creighton's introduction, but this most influential of Canadian historians has reduced the Indian presence in Canadian history to that of a problem and, after 1885, to a minor annoyance. This is almost the last word on Indians in Creighton's book. The final reference is to Skookum Jim and Tagish Charley, who are mentioned for their part in the Klondike gold discovery in 1896.[12] But there is one further passage in this book which deserves attention. In a discussion of the settlement of provincial boundaries Creighton adds this very revealing sentence: "Beyond [the provincial boundaries] lay the far north and the Arctic, into which only a relatively small number of people — trappers, Hudson's Bay Company traders, missionaries, teachers, Indian agents, and scientists . . . had so far ventured."[13] There is no more eloquent witness in this entire book to illustrate the almost total disregard of natives as people; they are an assumed presence, no more, a job to be done or a problem to be solved, not dignified as worthy of consideration in a study of our national history. The Indians are not even minor actors in the Canadian drama, simply stage-props against which others work out their roles.

This book serves as a model, an entirely typical product of the 1970's historical writing. Moreover, this book was published by Macmillan in co-operation with the Department of Indian Affairs, and it has a foreword written by the Hon. Judd Buchanan, then minister. The historical profession, entrusted to interpret our national heritage, and the government department which exists to further the interests of native people, have in this instance denied any meaningful role for the natives in the development of Canada.

Progress has been made in the 1970's. There is, for example, much more sensitivity in the language used to describe Indians and their activities. You will have noticed that "savages" are absent from Creighton's account, and there are no more ogres and vagabonds. Though the Iroquois are a "menace" and French wars against them are "punitive expeditions," the Jesuit martyrs, Long Sault, and Lachine are not even mentioned. Creighton's attitude is typical of that expressed in other general works of the 1970's.[14] Indian warfare and methods of fighting still receive the occasional reprobraton,[15] torture is sometimes mentioned,[16] and Indian victories can be labelled "massacres,"[17] but the bloody, prurient descriptions of earlier works are no longer to be found. A white Canadian schoolchild would not get nightmares from reading the histories now being written. Even the evils of alcohol appear only rarely.[18] The entire image of childishness and lack of civilization has, by and large, passed from the scene.

As has always been the case, the Iroquois continue to attract the most attention, and a term still used to describe them is "menace."[19] However, opportunities to engage in a detailed description of Iroquois-induced hardships are avoided. The Jesuit martyrs are rarely mentioned, or if they are, it is pointed out that the Jesuits deliberately sought their own deaths, that in any case as French nationals they were legitimate belligerants, and that the *Jesuit Relations* inclined to exaggerate Iroquois ghoulishness in order to glorify the martyrs.[20] Dollard's heroics at Long Sault receive only the briefest of references,[21] and Lachine has disappeared as a symbol of habitant survival in the face of native savagery.

The benefit of the new and more sensitive treatment has been that the negative portrait of Indian society and the derogatory image of the Indian as a human being are not longer being perpetuated. However, the cost has been that there is no longer any image at all. Instead of revising the previous impressions, historians have simply cut them out. Measured in column inches of print, histories written in the 1970's pay less attention to Indians than ever before. The exceptions to this generalization can quickly be pointed out. Most of the books which attempt to correct earlier images with new information, or which pay any attention to the fact that there is an Indian history apart from Indian-White relations, are provincial histories. This betrays something about the problems of our national histories. Provincial histories, freed from the self-imposed restraints of national interpretation, are allowed to explore what really happened. MacGregor's *History of Alberta* (1972) is perhaps the most noteworthy example of this. Pre-contact society and the changes that were occurring before the arrival of the white man are carefully described by MacGregor. Even after the white presence is established, Macgregor continues to acknowledge Indian activities, and if there is perhaps too much attention paid to white "firsts" (the first white man to see this, the first white baby born there), the history does reflect the statistical fact that until almost the end of the nineteenth century, natives outnumbered Whites in Alberta and therefore produced much of the history.

National histories, on the other hand, and some of the provincial histories as well, have followed the pattern of Creighton's *Heroic Beginnings*. Indians are treated exclusively in terms of the history of the European in Canada, with perhaps a nominal reference in a prologue or introduction to the prior existence of human beings on this continent. As was the case before 1971, the Vikings and the European explorers continue to be the humans most commonly introduced in opening chapters. Indians appear only when the Whites meet them: when the European fisherman encounter the Beothuks,[22] when the Micmacs trade with Cartier,[23] when Captain Cook is greeted by Indians[24]; in one account Indians do not appear until the War of 1812.[25]

To be brief, there is no improvement in the last decade's acknowledgement of pre-contact native history. As soon as a single white man sets foot on Canada, the Indian's historic role is to assist him with forest lore, new food crops, and methods of survival,[26] or the Indian presence is used to explain the nature and extent of European settlement patterns.[27] Very quickly, the Indians are reduced to being clients and allies of the Europeans, their subsequent activities explained in terms of the interests of their white sponsors. The fur trade, quite expectedly, retains its place as the chief example of how Whites were helped by Indians. Indians supply the furs,[28] they supply the pemmican without which the traders would have starved,[29] and they supply the wives and consorts so necessary for their comfort.[30] Fernand Ouellet acknowledges that the Indians sometimes used their fur supply to gain political concessions from the Whites,[31] and Trudel shows that native groups used sophisticated tactics to ensure optimum advantages from their supply monopoly,[32] but rarely is the Indian participation in the trade actually described. MacGregor, once again, is an exception, explaining the early reluctance of some groups such as the Blackfoot to engage in this doubtful activity in the first place, the existing trading system among Indian groups which formed the basis for the exchange of furs, and the impact on Indian society of the conversion to commerce in furs.[33] Generally, the impression from the recent histories is simply that the fur trade inspired the European occupation of Canada, and the Indians co-operated in the venture.[34]

Once a white presence is firmly established, the Indians are allowed to drift out of historical consciousness, returning only occassionally but always in the role of client or problem. The pattern followed is the one already recognized in Creighton and established well before 1971. The American Revolution and the War of 1812 typically receive a brief mention. Most accounts are favourable, and there are even hints that the Indians were not simply allies but had motives of their own for wishing to fight the Americans.[35] Pierre Berton's *Invasion of Canada* (1980) may represent the strengthening of this trend. Certainly, the book pays ample attention not only to Indian activities during the War of 1812 but to the Indians' independent purposes, so that the reader understands that what in fact was happening was an Indian war and a British-Canadian war which coincided but did not entirely overlap. Among the non-specialized treatments of native history, Berton's is the most realistic. However, so far, no Canadian history treats the consequences of the war for the Indians. Once Tecumseh is dead the interest in the Indian lapses.

Without so much as a pause for Red River, the new histories follow Creighton to the West of the 1870's when white settlement made the Indians a problem once again. Compared to the treatment given in histories written during the few decades prior to 1971, there is a slight but discernible increase in attention paid to the treaty process. Peter Waite's contribution to the Canadian Centenary series, for example, describes the treaty system in considerable detail and criticizes the policies adopted by Ottawa. The removal of the Indians for the sake of white settlement is acknowledged as a significant theme in Canada's national history during that period.[36] Similarly, the problems created for the Indians by the removal to the reserves and by the diseases and other consequences of white contact are now being described in such a way that government responsibility is indicated.[37] But unlike the War of 1812, there is as yet no treatment of 1885 which would suggest that the Indians were fighting their own war. Riel still has the spotlight, and Indian participation receives the briefest of references. The significance of 1885 remains cemented in traditional political themes. The Riel Rebellion is listed in the index of one widely used textbook as a sub-heading under "English-French relations,"[38] reflecting the fact that any importance of this event must derive from Ottawa, not from the Indians or the Metis or even the West.

Up to 1971 only about half a dozen Indians were mentioned personally in Canadian histories. In the last decade, the names have remained the same, but the individual references have become less frequent. Donnacona has virtually lost his place in history. Perhaps that is no bad thing, for his image was never very good. In one of the rare surviving references to this St. Lawrence chief, Marcel Trudel describes the kidnapping by Cartier of Donnacona's sons with these words: "Cartier had brought off a masterly coup by means of a very simple trick, arousing

Donnacona's greed with the offer of an axe."[30] Pontiac and Joseph Brant get one or two mentions apiece, but no descriptions. Even Tecumseh gets only a mention, though more frequently than Brant. The flowing, patriotic adjectives are no more.[40] Big Bear and Poundmaker, by and large, get sympathetic treatment but limited description. Poundmaker's trial is being recognized as a "mockery of justice" and Big Bear is "a sincere Indian patriot," but Crowfoot is considered the wiser man.[41] As an individual none of these men is representative of anything. Their names simply appear, stripped of savagery but lacking any other human characteristics as well. Coverage of Indian women in relation to the fur-traders are provided by Jennifer S. H. Brown in *Strangers in Blood* (1980) and Sylvia Van Kirk, *"Many Tender Ties"* (1980).

Once again the trend is slight, but there is some evidence that Indians are creeping back into Canadian history after 1885. Sometimes they come back in the old "problem" context, as in an account of northern Ontario which states that the native population of 23,000 occupies hundreds of thousands of hectares. But, since the reserves are all in the far north, the reader is reassured that "They offer no barriers to settlement."[42] In one of the few genuine attempts to revise an earlier book in the light of recent events, Hodgins and Page have added a fifty-page section dealing with the Berger enquiry and the whole issue of native land claims to the 1979 edition of their work.[43] More pervasive and encouraging are generalized references to native revival and resurgence, both in terms of population recovery and in artistic, religious, and political self-expression.[44] At the very least this implies the rediscovery of the Indian in Canada, an acknowledgement that they did not disappear entirely with the deaths of Big Bear and Poundmaker, and that they are defining their own issues. An initiative is at last returning to the Indian, though the trend is still no more than a hint, for the first time since the fur trade.

Apart from these indications that the nineteenth-century treaties and the 1970's revival are gaining some notice, the major change in the last decade's historical writing on Canada has been an improvement in the language used to describe Indians. Even this improvement has been at the price of a general reduction in Indian content. In the important area of Indian participation, and in giving adequate attention to an Indian contribution to Canada, the recent writing is no better than the older works. Indians are still being presented as peripheral to "real" Canadian history, and their place is mentioned only when Indian affairs overlap — and more typically conflict — with the progress of white society. Scholarly research has not in itself produced any notable changes, thus revealing that general historians have not been availing themselves of the new material being written by specialists in native history. With the exception of Hodgins and Page, "revised" editions appearing in the 1970's do not reflect any increase in knowledge about the Indians. McNaught's *Pelican History of Canada*, for example, contains identical Indian content in its 1969 and 1976 editions, and there is still no

Indian material in the Suggestions for Further Reading.[45] Otherwise careful historical studies — in particular McClelland and Stewart's Canadian Centenary series — have failed to build a more realistic impression of Indian participation in Canada's historical development. One of the most impressive volumes in that admirable series, Brown and Cook's *Canada, 1896–1921*, omits the Indian entirely.[46] Despite its depth of research and its consideration of social issues, this book stands as an example of the fact that something other than scholarship is necessary. Another book from the same series, Trudel's *Beginnings of New France*, does contain Indian content, but no account has been taken of the new research on St. Lawrence and Huron history by Trigger and Pendergast and Heidenreich. Even Zaslow's *Opening of the Canadian North*,[47] though replete with Indian and Inuit content, has relatively little on the natives' autonomous activities and is more about the treatment of the native than about native life.

One continuing problem with the new writing is that there exists a fixed set of themes in Canadian historiography, a basic developmental line which is common to almost all our histories. Canadian historians writing in English have been seeking to explain how Canada evolved as an independent North American nation, and to prove that it deserves to exist not just *vis à vis* Britain and/or the United States, but as a single political entity uniting English- and French-language groups. This line implies a series of touchstones which mark and illustrate the national evolution: the European occupation of Canada, of which the Iroquois Wars and the fur trade form a part; English-French relations, including the Conquest, Quebec Act, Confederation, Riel, Manitoba Schools, Conscription, the Quiet Revolution, and Separatism; the progress of dominion status and independence from Britain, featuring the 1837 Rebellions, Durham Report, responsible government, Rebellion Losses Bill, Galt Tariff, Confederation again, World War I and the Imperial Conferences, the Chanak Crisis, Halibut Treaty, and Statute of Westminster; and survival against American pressures, where the American Revolution, War of 1812, railways, Confederation once more, monarchical institutions, industrialization, the "French fact," and the "mosaic" can all be considered. Apparently, every general history of Canada feels obliged to touch each or most of these stones in passing, with the result that anything else gets treated in terms of these episodes; that is, it is measured by its contribution to or detraction from the standard plot, or it is ignored.

Revisions, as they appear, have a tendency to re-examine the old touchstones.[48] Over the years we have had a wide variety of interpretive schools in Canadian history,[49] but the material being examined by each successive school has been remarkably similar. And so was the goal: to explain Canada's existence as a nation state and to define Canadian identity. Given this preoccupation, it is not surprising that so much Canadian history has been political and constitutional. Since information relative to the Indian could not be slotted in without damaging the plot, no amount of new scholarship on Indians could produce an accurate assessment of the

Indian contribution to Canadian history. Indian history therefore supplies a case study to reveal that the standard plot is a fiction. What is necessary is the abandonment of the old plot, the search for new significant episodes, and an entirely original school of historical interpretation which begins with recognition that the inevitable evolution of a coherent and politically definable Canadian identity is a myth.

There is some sign that this is occurring. An increasing body of monographic literature is departing from the old interpretive strictures and breaking new ground in fields long ignored.[50] In a 1970 article entitled "Metaphor and Nationality in North America,"[51] Allan Smith argued that the long-sought homogenizing Canadian identity should be set aside while historians recognize the plural nature of the Canadian heritage. Maurice Careless has written of "Limited Identities in Canada"[52] and has noted elsewhere that "the Canadian Endless Quest for identity has obscured the very real existence of these individual identities that still mark the country."[53]

There exists in Canada a plural society, a variety of identities and particularisms. Geography has encouraged pluralism, and so has a French Quebec with political power, and so has immigration. And so have the native peoples. Once it is recognized that a plural Canada is the modern result, then the Indian role in the country's history becomes fundamental. Pre-contact and non-contact native history provide an element in a decentralized vision of Canada. It is not just the way Indians have been treated by Whites that is of importance to national self-understanding, but the way Indians have survived with a distinct identity in the face of forces, both circumstantial and deliberate, to obliterate it. In 1971 Prime Minister Trudeau acknowledged in the House of Commons that there is no single Canadian culture, that the nation is socially complex.[54] Any attempt to explain how this came about is going to have to take a new look at Indian history and assess the native fact in the evolution of modern Canada. Along with the many other factors now being considered by professional historians, the Indian's accommodation into the general interpretations must eventually dismantle the old touchstones and bring us closer to the historical forces underlying the events we examine. A new Canadian historiography lies in the decade ahead, but it will not happen automatically, and it cannot be done without the active collaboration of those specializing in native studies. Their research has made possible the reconstruction of the Indian past. A new challenge for the 1980's is the opportunity to contribute to the understanding of the entire shape of Canadian history and society.

NOTES

1. James W. St. G. Walker, "The Indian in Canadian Historical Writing," Canadian Historical Association, *Historical Papers* (1971):21–51.
2. Full titles for this and all subsequent books mentioned in this section are given in the accompanying bibliography.
3. To mention only a few of direct historical relevance, articles have been published over the past decade in *Acadiensis*, the *Alberta Historical Review, Alberta History*, the *American Review of Canadian Studies, Anthropologica, BC Studies*, the *Canadian Geographer*, the *Canadian Geographical Journal*, the *Canadian Historical Review*, the *Canadian Review of Sociology and Anthropology*, the *Dalhousie Review, Ethnohistory*, the *Journal of Canadian Studies*, the *Newfoundland Quarterly*, the *Nova Scotia Historical Quarterly, Ontario History, Saskatchewan History*, and the *Western Canadian Journal of Anthropology*.
4. See, for example, Alexander Malycky et al., "University Research on Canada's Indians and Metis," *Canadian Ethnic Studies* 2(1970):95–107 and 5(1973):pp. 153–82, and D. M. Tupling, *Canada: A Dissertation Bibliography* (Ann Arbor, 1980).
5. The first volume devoted exclusively to Canada in this series is Robert J. Surtees, *Canadian Indian Policy: A Critical Bibliography* (Bloomington, 1982).
6. Donald Creighton, *Canada: The Heroic Beginnings* (Toronto, 1974), p. 7.
7. Ibid., pp. 30, 35.
8. Ibid., p. 42. These references appear in a chapter entitled "The Anglo-French Conflict."
9. Ibid., pp. 72, 74, 79, 88, 127, 136, 139, 143.
10. Ibid., pp. 157–58, 161–63, 167–68.
11. Ibid., p. 170.
12. Ibid., p. 232.
13. Ibid., p. 241.
14. The discussion that follows is based on a survey of books published in the English language. Since 1971 there have been too few French language studies to justify generalizations, since most Quebec historians have been concentrating on examinations of intimate aspects of French-Canadian history or have dealt with the more recent period when the Indian presence has been deemed less significant. The works by Ouellet and Trudel included in this survey are translations or summations of books originally written in French. For an excellent treatment of the subject to its date of publication see Donald B. Smith, *Le Sauvage: The Native People in Quebec Historical Writing on the Heroic Period (1534–1663) of New France* (Ottawa, 1974).
15. Donald Creighton, *The Story of Canada*, rev. ed. (London, 1971), pp. 19, 26–29, 41; W. J. Eccles, *France in America* (New York, 1972), p. 21.
16. J. L. Finlay and D. N. Sprague, *The Structure of Canadian History* (Scarborough, 1979), p. 27; June Callwood, *Portrait of Canada* (New York, 1981), p. 31; Eccles, *France in America*, p. 21.
17. Ramsay Cook et al., *Canada: A Modern Study*, rev. ed., 1971), p. 131; Creighton, p. 41; George Woodcock, *The Canadians* (Don Mills, 1979), p. 41–43; W. L. Morton and L. F. Hannon, *This Land, These People: An Illustrated History of Canada* (Agincourt, 1977), p. 233; Margaret A. Ormsby, *British Columbia: A History*, rev. ed. (Vancouver, 1971), pp. 204–7.
18. Callwood, *Portrait*, p. 9; James G. MacGregor, *A History of Alberta* (Edmonton, 1972), p. 40; G. P. de T. Glazebrook, *Life in Ontario: A Social History* (Toronto, 1971), p. 15; Eccles, *France in America*, p. 55.
19. E.g., Creighton, p. 26; Finlay and Sprague, *Structure*, p. 29; Eccles, *France in America*, pp. 51, 96.
20. Finlay and Sprague, p. 25; Marcel Trudel, *The Beginnings of New France, 1524–1663* (Toronto, 1973), p. 219; Eccles, *France in America*, pp. 44–46.
21. Callwood, pp. 19–20; Trudel, p. 271.
22. Callwood, p. 3.
23. Creighton, p. 13; Finlay and Sprague, pp. 9–10; Trudel, pp. 15–16.
24. Ormsby, p. 9.
25. Cook, *Canada*, p. 25.
26. Morton and Hannon, p. 51; Trudel, p. 153 ff; Eccles, *France in America*, p. 58; Glazebrook, pp. 8, 13–14.

27. Creighton, p. 26; Finlay and Sprague, pp. 29, 42; Ormsby, p. 127.
28. Jacques Monet, "The 1840s," in *Colonists and Canadiens, 1760–1867*, J. M. S. Careless, ed. (Toronto, 1971), p. 220; Creighton, p. 18; Morton and Hannon, p. 51; James A. Jackson, *The Centennial History of Manitoba* (Toronto, 1970), p. 20; Glazebrook, p. 8.
29. S. F. Wise, "The 1790's," in Careless, *Colonists and Canadiens*, p. 74; MacGregor, p. 43; Jackson, p. 20.
30. Jackson, pp. 22–23; Ormsby, p. 52.
31. Fernand Ouellet, *Lower Canada, 1791–1840. Social Change and Nationalism* (Toronto, 1980), pp. 31, 55.
32. Trudel, pp. 140–41.
33. MacGregor, pp. 27, 29, 40, 51.
34. But see W. J. Eccles, "A Belated Review of Harold Adams Innis, *The Fur Trade in Canada*," *Canadian Historical Review* 60 (1979); 419–41, in which it is argued that the fur trade was a means rather than an end of French imperial activity in North America and of Franco-Indian relations.
35. E.g., Jean-Pierre Wallot, "The 1800s," in Careless, *Colonists and Canadiens*, p. 98.
36. Peter B. Waite, *Canada 1874–1896. Arduous Destiny* (Toronto, 1971), pp. 67–73.
37. Waite, p. 68; Finlay and Sprague, p. 200; Callwood, p. 203; MacGregor, pp. 102, 111.
38. Cook, *Canada*.
39. Trudel, p. 17.
40. Alan Wilson, "The 1810s," in Careless, *Colonists and Canadiens*, p. 143; Cook, *Canada*, pp. 25–26; Glen Frankfurter, *Baneful Domination: The Idea of Canada in the Atlantic World, 1581–1971* (Don Mills, 1971), pp. 108–9; Woodcock, pp. 59, 136; Callwood, pp. 71, 99–101; Morton and Hannon, p. 51.
41. Waite, pp. 161–62; MacGregor, pp. 103, 145, 161–62; Callwood, pp. 188, 203; Morton and Hannon, p. 51; Woodcock, p. 173.
42. Glazebrook, p. 277.
43. Bruce Hodgins and Robert Page, eds., *Canadian History Since Confederation. Essays and Interpretations*, rev. ed. (Georgetown, 1979), pp. 630–87.
44. Woodcock, p. 26, 243; Morton and Hannon, p. 51; Joseph Schull, *Ontario Since 1867* (Toronto, 1978), pp. 349–50; MacGregor, pp. 305–7; Ormsby, p. 492; Frankfurter, p. 298; Callwood, p. 335; Robert Bothwell et al., *Canada Since 1945: Power, Politics and Provincialism* (Toronto, 1981), pp. 33, 453.
45. Kenneth McNaught, *The Pelican History of Canada* (London, rev. ed., 1976).
46. R. Craig Brown and Ramsay Cook, *Canada 1896–1921. A Nation Transformed* (Toronto, 1974).
47. Morris Zaslow, *The Opening of the Canadian North, 1870–1914* (Toronto, 1971).
48. E.g., see K. A. MacKirdy et al., *Changing Perspectives in Canadian History. Selected Problems*, rev. ed. (Don Mills, 1971), which reveals that new questions are being asked but the problems and episodes selected for analysis remain the same.
49. See Carl Berger, *The Writing of Canadian History: Aspects of English-Canadian Historical Writing, 1900–1970* (Toronto, 1976); Carl Berger, ed., *Approaches to Canadian History* (Toronto, 1967); Robin W. Winks, *The Relevance of Canadian History* (Toronto, 1979); W. L. Morton, "Some Thoughts on Understanding Canadian History," *Acadiensis* 2(1973): 100–107; Patricia E. Roy, "The National Perspective: Survey Texts of Canadian History," *Canadian Historical Review* 57(1976): 180–88; N. J. Hanham, "Canadian History in the 1970s," *Canadian Historical Review* 58(1977): 2–22.
50. A mere sampling of the books which have appeared in the multicultural field alone will illustrate this point: Ken Adachi, *The Enemy That Never Was: A History of the Japanese Canadians* (Toronto, 1976); G. M. Anderson and D. Biggs, *A Future to Inherit: The Portuguese Communities in Canada* (Toronto, 1976); Leo Driedger, ed., *The Canadian Ethnic Mosaic: A Quest for Identity* (Toronto, 1978); Frank Epp, *Mennonites in Canada, 1786–1920: The History of a Separate People* (Toronto, 1974); Wsevolod Isajiw, ed., *Identities: The Impact of Ethnicity on Canadian Society* (Toronto, 1977); K. Ishwaran, *Family, Kinship and Community: A Study of Dutch Canadians* (Toronto, 1977); Z. Keywan and M. Coles, *Greater Than Kings: Ukrainian Pioneer Settlement in Canada* (Montreal, 1977); H. Radecki and B. Heydenkorn, *A Member of a Distinguished Family: The Polish Group in Canada* (Toronto, 1976); Harold Troper and Lee Palmer, *Issues in Cultural*

Diversity (Toronto, 1976); Robin W. Winks, *The Blacks in Canada: A History* (Montreal, 1971). This same phenomenon can be witnessed in local, economic, labour, and women's history, among others. For a broad discussion of new departures in specialized historical monographs see Ramsay Cook, "The Golden Age of Canadian Historical Writing," *Historical Reflections* 4(1977): 137–49.

51. Allan Smith, "Metaphor and Nationality in North America," *CHR* 51(1970): 247–75.
52. Maurice Careless, "Limited Identities in Canada," *CHR* 50(1969): 1–10.
53. Careless, *Colonists and Canadiens*, p. viii.
54. *House of Commons Debates*, 8 October 1971, pp. 8545–46, and opposition responses, pp. 8546–48.

BIBLIOGRAPHY

Abler, Thomas S., and Sally M. Weaver. *A Canadian Indian Bibliography, 1960–1970*. Toronto, 1974.
Adachi, Ken. *The Enemy That Never Was: A History of the Japanese Canadians*. Toronto, 1976.
Adams, Howard.*Prison of Grass: Canada from the Native Point of View*. Toronto, 1975.
Allen, Richard, ed. *Man and Nature on the Prairies*. Regina, 1976.
Allen, Robert S. *The British Indian Department and the Frontier in North America, 1755–1830*. Ottawa, 1975.
Anderson, G. M., and D. Higgs. *A Future to Inherit: The Portuguese Communities in Canada*. Toronto, 1976.
Archer, John H. *Saskatchewan. A History*. Saskatoon, 1980.
Armour, Leslie. *The Idea of Canada and the Crisis of Community*. Ottawa, 1981.
Armstrong, F. H., H. A. Stevenson, and J. D. Wilson, eds. *Aspects of Nineteenth Century Ontario: Essays Presented to James J. Talman*. Toronto, 1974.
Bailey, A. G. *Culture and Nationality*. Toronto, 1972.
Barker, George. *Forty Years a Chief*. Winnipeg, 1978.
Bercuson, D. R. "Recent Developments in Prairie Historiography." *Acadiensis* 4 (1974): 138–48.
Berger, Carl. *The Writing of Candian History: Aspects of English-Canadian Historical Writing, 1900–1970*. Toronto, 1976.
———· ed. *Approaches to Canadian History*. Toronto, 1967.
Bergeron, Léandre. *The History of Quebec. A Patriote's Handbook*. Rev. ed. Toronto, 1975.
Berton, Pierre. *Invasion of Canada*. Toronto, 1980.
Bishop, Charles A. *The Northern Ojibwa and the Fur Trade: An Historical and Ecological Study*. Toronto, 1974.
Bolger, Francis, ed. *Canada's Smallest Province: A History of PEI*. Charlottetown, 1973.
Bothwell, Robert, Ian Drummond, and John English. *Canada Since 1945: Power, Politics and Provincialism*. Toronto, 1981.
Bowles, R. P., J. L. Hanley, G. A. Pawlyk, and B. W. Hodgins, *The Indian: Assimilation, Integration or Separation*. Scarborough, 1972.
Brown, Jennifer S. H. *Strangers in Blood: Fur Trade Company Families in Indian Country*. Vancouver, 1980.
Brown, R. Craig, and Ramsay Cook. *Canada 1896–1921. A Nation Transformed*. Toronto, 1974.
Brumble, H. David, III. *An Annotated Bibliography of American Indian and Eskimo Autobiographies*. Lincoln, NE, 1981.
Cail, Robert E. *Land, Man, and the Law: The Disposal of Crown Lands in British Columbia, 1871–1913*. Vancouver, 1974.
Callwood, June. *Portrait of Canada*. New York, 1981.
Canada, Department of Indian Affairs and Northern Development. *About Indians: A Listing of Books*. 3d ed. Ottawa, 1975.
———· *Atlas of Indian Reserves and Settlements*. Ottawa, 1971.
———· *History of Indian Policy*. Ottawa, 1973.
———· *Indian Status: What is the Present Law?* Ottawa, 1973.
———· *Native Claims: Policy, Processes and Perspectives*. Ottawa, 1978.

Canadian Civil Liberties Education Trust. *Indian Life and Canadian Law.* Toronto, 1973.

Cardinal, Harold. *The Rebirth of Canada's Indians.* Edmonton, 1977.

Careless, J. M. S. "Limited Identities in Canada." *CHR* 50 (1969): 1–10.

———' ed. *Colonists and Canadiens, 1760–1867.* Toronto, 1971.

Chamberlin, J. E. *The Harrowing of Eden: White Attitudes toward North American Natives.* Toronto, 1975.

Cook, Ramsay. "The Golden Age of Canadian Historical Writing." *Historical Reflections* 4 (1977): 137–49.

———' with John Ricker and John Saywell. *Canada: A Modern Study.* Rev. ed. Toronto, 1971.

Creighton, Donald G. *The Story of Canada.* Rev. ed. London, 1971.

———· *Canada: The Heroic Beginnings.* Toronto, 1974.

Cumming, Peter, and Neil Mickenberg, eds. *Native Rights in Canada.* 2d ed. Toronto, 1972.

Daugherty, Wayne. *Maritime Indian Treaties in Historical Perspective.* Ottawa, 1980.

Deer, A. Brian. *Bibliography on the History of the James Bay People relating to the Cree People.* Rupert House, 1974.

Dempsey, Hugh A. *Crowfoot: Chief of the Blackfeet.* Edmonton, 1972.

Dickason, Olive P. *Louisbourg and the Indians: A Study in Imperial Race Relations, 1713–1760.* Ottawa, 1976.

Driedger, Leo, ed. *The Canadian Ethnic Mosaic: A Quest for Identity.* Toronto, 1978.

Eccles, W. J. *France in America.* New York, 1972.

———· "A Belated Review of Harold Adams Innis, *The Fur Trade in Canada.*" *CHR* 60 (1979): 419–41.

Elliott, Jean L., ed. *Minority Canadians: Native Peoples.* Scarborough, 1971.

Epp, Frank. *Mennonites in Canada, 1786–1920: The History of a Separate People.* Toronto, 1974.

Erasmus, Peter. *Buffalo Days and Nights.* Calgary, 1976.

Finlay, J. L. *Canada in the North Atlantic Triangle. Two Centuries of Social Change.* Toronto, 1975.

———· and D. N. Sprague. *The Structure of Canadian History.* Scarborough, 1979.

Fisher, Robin. *Contact and Conflict: Indian-European Relations in British Columbia, 1774–1890.* Vancouver, 1977.

Frankfurter, Glen. *Baneful Domination. The Idea of Canada in the Atlantic World, 1581–1971.* Don Mills, 1971.

Frideres, James S. *Canada's Indians: Contemporary Conflicts.* Scarborough, 1974.

Fumoleau, René. *As Long as This Land Shall Last.* Toronto, 1975.

Getty, Ian, and Donald B. Smith, eds. *One Century Later: Western Canadian Reserve Indians Since Treaty Seven.* Vancouver, 1978.

Glazebrook, G. P. de T. *Life in Ontario. A Social History.* Toronto, 1971.

Gough, Barry. *Canada.* Englewood Cliffs, NJ, 1975.

Graymont, Barbara. *The Iroquois in the American Revolution.* Syracuse, 1972.

Hamelin, Jean, ed. *Histoire du Québec.* Toulouse, 1976.

Hanham, H. J. "Canadian History in the 1970s." *CHR* 63 (1977): 2–22.

Hardwick, Francis C. *When Strangers Meet: North American Indian Contribution to Canadian Society.* 2d ed. Vancouver, 1973.

Harris, Richard C., and John Warkentin. *Canada Before Confederation: A Study in Historical Geography.* New York, 1974.

Heidenreich, Conrad. *Huronia: A History and Geography of the Huron Indians, 1600–1650.* Toronto, 1971.

Henderson, William B. *Land Tenure in Indian Reserves.* Ottawa, 1978.

———· *Canada's Indian Reserves: Pre-Confederation.* Ottawa, 1980.

———· *Canada's Indian Reserves: The Usufruct in Our Constitution.* Ottawa, 1980.

Hiller, James, and Peter Neary. *Newfoundland in the Nineteenth and Twentieth Centuries: Essays in Interpretation.* Toronto, 1980.

Hirschfelder, Arlene B. *American Indian and Eskimo Authors: A Comprehensive Bibliography.* New York, 1973.

Hodge, William. *A Bibliography of Contemporary North American Indians.* New York, 1976.

Hodgins, Bruce, and Robert Page, eds. *Canadian History Since Confederation. Essays and Interpretations.* Rev. ed. Georgetown, 1979.

Hughes, Stuart, ed. *The Frog Lake "Massacre": Personal Perspectives on Ethnic Conflict.* Toronto, 1976.
Hungry Wolf, Adolf. *The Blood People: A Division of the Blackfoot Confederacy.* New York, 1977.
Indian Claims Commission. *Indian Claims in Canada: An Introductory Essay and Selected List of Library Holdings.* Ottawa, 1975.
Isajiw, Wsevolod, ed. *Identities: The Impact of Ethnicity on Canadian Society.* Toronto, 1977.
Ishwaran, K. *Family, Kinship and Community: A Study of Dutch Canadians.* Toronto, 1977.
Jackson, James A. *The Centennial History of Manitoba.* Toronto, 1970.
Jaenen, Cornelius J. *Friend and Foe: Aspects of French-Amerindian Cultural Contact in the Sixteenth and Seventeenth Centuries.* Toronto, 1976.
Johnston, Basil. *Ojibway Heritage.* Toronto, 1976.
Judd, Carol M., and Arthur J. Ray, eds. *Old Trails and New Directions: Papers of the Third North American Fur Trade Conference.* Toronto, 1980.
Keywan, Z., and M. Coles. *Greater than Kings: Ukrainian Pioneer Settlement in Canada.* Montreal, 1977.
Komar, Roman. *The Royal Proclamation of 1763: A Legal Enquiry into Indian Land in Canada.* Ottawa, 1971.
Lamb, W. Kaye. *Canada's Five Centuries: From Discovery to Present Day.* Toronto, 1971.
LaViolette, Forrest E. *The Struggle for Survival: Indian Culture and the Protestant Ethic in British Columbia.* Toronto, 1973.
Leslie, John, and Ron Maguire, eds. *The Historical Development of the Indian Act.* 2d ed. Ottawa, 1978.
Lower, J. A. *Canada: An Outline History.* Rev. ed. Toronto, 1973.
McCullum, Hugh and Karmel. *This Land Is Not for Sale.* Toronto, 1975.
MacEwan, J. W. Grant. *Portraits from the Plains.* Toronto, 1971.
McGee, Harold F. *The Native Peoples of Atlantic Canada: A Reader in Regional Ethnic Relations.* Toronto, 1974.
McGee, H. F., S. A. Davis, and M. Taft. *Three Atlantic Bibliographies.* Halifax, 1975.
MacGregor, James A. *A History of Alberta.* Edmonton, 1972.
MacKirdy, K. A., J. S. Moir, and Y. F. Zoltvany. *Changing Perspectives in Canadian History.* Rev. ed. *Selected Problems.* Don Mills, 1971.
McNaught, Kenneth. *The Pelican History of Canada.* Rev. ed. London, 1976.
Manuel, George, and Michael Posluns. *The Fourth World: An Indian Reality.* Don Mills, 1974.
Marken, Jack W. *The Indians and Eskimos of North America: A Bibliography of Books in Print through 1972.* Vermillion, SD, 1973.
Martin, Calvin. *Keepers of the Game: Indian-Animal Relationships and the Fur Trade.* Berkeley, 1978.
Marr, William L., and Donald G. Paterson. *Canada: An Economic History.* Toronto, 1980.
Morton, Arthur S. *A History of the Canadian West to 1870-71.* Toronto, rev. ed., 1973.
Morton, W. L. "Some Thoughts on Understanding Canadian History." *Acadiensis,* II (1973), 100-107.
——— and L. F. Hannon. *This Land, These People: An Illustrated History of Canada.* Agincourt, 1977.
Muise, D. A., ed. *Approaches to Native History in Canada.* Ottawa, 1977.
National Indian Brotherhood of Canada Library. *Annotated List of Holdings.* Ottawa, 1973.
Nagler, Mark. *Perspectives on the North American Indians.* Toronto, 1972.
Ojibway — Cree Resource Centre. *Bibliography.* Timmins, 1978.
Ormsby, Margaret A. *British Columbia: A History.* Rev. ed. Vancouver, 1971.
Ouellet, Fernand. *Lower Canada, 1791-1840. Social Change and Nationalism.* Toronto, 1980.
Owram, Douglas. *Promise of Eden: The Canadian Expansionist Movement and the Idea of the West, 1856-1900.* Toronto, 1980.
Patterson, E. Palmer. *The Canadian Indian: A History Since 1500.* Don Mills, 1972.
Pendergast, James F., and Bruce Trigger. *Cartier's Hochelaga and the Dawson Site.* Montreal, 1972.
Ponting, J. R., and R. Gibbins. *Out of Irrelevance: A Socio-political Introduction to Indian Affairs in Canada.* Toronto, 1980.
Price, Richard, ed. *The Spirit of the Alberta Indian Treaties.* Montreal, 1979.
Radecki, H., and B. Heydenkorn. *A Member of a Distinguished Family: The Polish Group in Canada.* Toronto, 1976.

Ray, Arthur J. *Indians in the Fur Trade: Their Role as Hunters, Trappers and Middlemen in the Lands Southwest of Hudson Bay, 1660–1870.* Toronto, 1974.
———— and Donald B. Freeman. *Give Us Good Measure: An Economic Analysis of Relations between the Indians and the Hudson's Bay Company before 1763.* Toronto, 1978.
Reader's Digest. *Heritage of Canada.* Toronto, 1978.
Richardson, Boyce. *James Bay: The Plot to Drown the North Woods.* Toronto, 1972.
———— *Strangers Devour the Land: The Cree Hunters of the James Bay Area versus Premier Bourassa and the James Bay Development Corp.* Toronto, 1976.
Rowe, Frederick W. *A History of Newfoundland and Labrador.* Toronto, 1980.
———— *Extinction: The Beothucks of Newfoundland.* Toronto, 1977.
Roy, Patricia E. "The National Perspective: Survey Texts of Canadian History." *CHR* 57 (1976): 180–88.
Ryan, Joan, ed. *Bibliography on Canadian Indians 1960–72.* Calgary, 1972.
Saskatchewan Provincial Library. *Indians of the Americas: A Bibliography.* Regina, 1973.
Schmalz, Peter S. *The History of the Saugeen Indians.* Ottawa, 1977.
Schull, Joseph. *Ontario Since 1867.* Toronto, 1978.
Sharpe, Errol. *A People's History of Prince Edward Island.* Toronto, 1976.
Smith, Allan. "Metaphor and Nationality in North America." *CHR* 51 (1970): 247–75.
Smith, Derek G., ed. *Canadian Indians and the Law: Selected Documents, 1663–1972.* Toronto, 1975.
Smith, Donald B. *Le Sauvage: The Native People in Quebec Historical Writing on the Heroic Period (1534–1663) of New France.* Ottawa, 1974.
Smith, Dwight L. *Indians of the United States and Canada: A Bibliography.* Santa Barbara, 1974.
Snow, Chief John. *These Mountains Are Our Sacred Places.* Toronto, 1977.
Surtees, Robert J. *The Original People.* Toronto, 1971.
———— *Canadian Indian Policy. A Critical Bibliography.* Bloomington, IN., 1982.
Thomas, Lewis G., ed. *The Prairie West to 1905. A Canadian Source book.* Toronto, 1975.
Thomas L. H., ed. *Essays on Western History in Honour of Lewis Gwynne Thomas.* Edmonton, 1976.
Trigger, Bruce G. *The Children of Aataentsic: A History of the Huron People to 1660.* 2 vols. Montreal, 1976.
Troper, Harold, and Lee Palmer. *Issues in Cultural Diversity.* Toronto, 1976.
Trudel, Marcel. *The Beginnings of New France, 1524–1663.* Toronto, 1973.
Tupling, D. M. *Canada: A Dissertation Bibliography.* Ann Arbor, 1980.
University of Saskatchewan Indian and Northern Education Program. *Annotated Bibliography of Articles pertaining to Native North Americans.* n.p., 1972.
University Microfilms International. *The North American Indians: A Dissertation Index.* Ann Arbor, 1977.
Upton, Leslie. *Micmacs and Colonists: Indian-White Relations in the Maritime Provinces, 1713–1867.* Vancouver, 1979.
Waite, Peter B. *Canada 1874–1896. Arduous Destiny.* Toronto, 1971.
Walker, James W. St. G. "The Indian in Canadian Historical Writing." Canadian Historical Association, *Historical Papers.* Ottawa, 1971.
Walsh, Gerald. *Indians in Transition.* Toronto, 1971.
Watkins, Mel, ed. *Dene Nation: The Colony Within.* Toronto, 1977.
Weaver, Sally. *Making Canadian Indian Policy. The Hidden Agenda, 1968–1970.* Toronto, 1981.
Whiteside, Don. *Aboriginal People: A Selected Bibliography Concerning Canada's First People.* Ottawa, 1973.
Wilson, James. *Canada's Indians.* London, 1974.
Wilson, Keith. *Manitoba: Profile of a Province.* Winnipeg, 1975.
Winks, Robin W. *The Blacks in Canada. A History.* Montreal, 1971.
———— *The Relevance of Canadian History. U.S. and Imperial Perspectives.* Toronto, 1979.
Woodcock, George. *Peoples of the Coast: The Indians of the Pacific Northwest.* Edmonton, 1977.
———— *The Canadians.* Don Mills, 1979.
Zaslow, Morris. *The Opening of the Canadian North, 1870–1914.* Toronto, 1971.

Suggestions for Further Reading

PART I

Much of the recent scholarship on British Indian policy and Canadian Indian policy and Canadian Indian administration still remains in unpublished theses, but increasingly this research is found in various journals, and in anthologies of conference papers. A useful bibliographical aid to Indian history was compiled by Thomas S. Abler and Sally M. Weaver, *A Canadian Indian Bibliography, 1960–1970* (Toronto, 1974), and most recently by Robert J. Surtees, *Canadian Indian Policy: A Critical Bibliography* (Bloomington, 1982). Also the Department of Indian Affairs and Northern Development, Government of Canada, periodically updates a listing of books entitled "About Indians." For the respective land purchases and treaties, see Canada *Indian Treaties and Surrenders*, 3 vols. (Ottawa, 1891–1912) reprinted by Coles Publishing, Toronto, in 1971. The following selections dealing with Indian-white relations generally, and with aspects of Indian policy and administration subsequent to the Proclamation of 1763, are listed alphabetically by author and not chronologically or geographically.

I.A.L.G.

A.S.L.

Brody, Hugh. *The People's Land. Eskimos and Whites in the Eastern Arctic*. Harmondsworth, England, 1975.

Cox, Bruce, ed. *Cultural Ecology: Readings on the Canadian Indians and Eskimos*. Toronto, 1973. Carleton Library no. 65.

Crowe, Keith J. *A History of the Original Peoples of Northern Canada*. Montreal, 1974.

Cumming, P. A., and Neil H. Mickenberg. *Native Rights in Canada*. Toronto, 1972 (2d ed.).

Duff, Wilson. *The Indian History of British Columbia*. Volume 1, *The Impact of the White Man*. Victoria, 1964. Anthropology in British Columbia, Memoir no. 5.

Fisher, Robin. *Contact and Conflict: Indian-White Relations in British Columbia*. Vancouver, 1977.

Fumoleau, René, O.M.I. *As Long as This Land Shall Last: A History of Treaty 8 and Treaty 11, 1870–1939*. Toronto, 1973.

Getty, Ian A. L., and Donald B. Smith. *One Century Later: Western Canadian Reserve Indians since Treaty 7*. Vancouver, 1978.

Jenness, Diamond. *Eskimo Administration:* II. *Canada*. Arctic Institute of North America Technical Paper no. 14. Montreal, 1964.

Leslie, John, and Ron Maguire, eds. *The Historical Development of the Indian Act*. Ottawa, 1978.

McGee, H. F., Jr. *The Native Peoples of Atlantic Canada: A Reader in Regional Ethnic Relations*. Toronto, 1974.

Morris, Alexander. *The Treaties of Canada with the Indians of Manitoba, the North-West Territories and Kee-Wa-tin*. Toronto, 1971 (originally printed 1880).

Muise, D. A., ed. *Approaches to Native History in Canada: Papers of a Conference held at the National Museum of Man, October, 1975*. Ottawa, 1977.

Patterson, E. Palmer, II. *The Canadian Indian: A History since 1500*. Don Mills, 1972.
Ponting, J. Rick, and Roger Gibbons. *Out of Irrelevance. A Socio-Political Introduction to Indian Affairs in Canada*. Toronto, 1980.
Price, A. Grenfell. *White Settlers and Native Peoples*. Melbourne, 1950.
Upton, Leslie F. S. *Micmacs and Colonists: Indian-White Relations in the Maritimes, 1713–1867*. Vancouver, 1979.
Weaver, Sally M. *Making Canadian Indian Policy: The Hidden Agenda, 1968–1970*. Toronto, 1981.

In addition to the above texts, there have been a number of articles and chapters written on British Indian policy and Canadian Indian administration. The following is a selection of the significant readings.

Allen, R. S. "The British Indian Department and the Frontier in North America, 1755–1830." In *Canadian Historic Sites*, Occasional Papers in Archaeology and History, no. 14. (Ottawa)
Harper, Allan G. "Canada's Indian Administration: The Treaty System." *América Indigéna*, no. 5 (April 1945): 129–48.
———. "Canada's Indian Administration: Basic Concepts and Objectives." *América Indigéna*, 5 (April 1945): 119–32.
———. "Canada's Indian Administration: The 'Indian Act.'" *América Indigéna*, 6 (October 1946): 297–314.
———. "Canada's Indian Administration: The Treaty System." *América Indigéna*, 7 (April 1947): 129–48.
Hodgetts, John E. "Indian Affairs, The White Man's Albatross." In *Pioneer Public Service, An Administrative History 1841–1867*. Toronto, 1955, chapter 8.
Jenness, Diamond. "Canada's Indians Yesterday: What of Today? *C.J.E.P.S.* 20, no. 1 (February 1954): 95–100.
Laird, David. "Our Indian Treaties." Transaction no. 66 of the *Historical and Scientific Society of Manitoba*. Winnipeg, 1905.
Loran, C. T., and T. F. McIlwaith, eds. *The North American Indian Today*. University of Toronto-Yale University Seminar Conference, Toronto, September 4-16, 1939. Toronto 1943.
MacInnes, T. R. L. "History of Indian Administration in Canada." *C.J.E.P.S.* 12 (1946): 387–94.
Patterson, E. Palmer, II. "The Colonial Parallel: A View of Indian History." *Ethnohistory* 18, no. 1 (Winter 1971): 1–18.
Rousseau, Jacques, and George W. Brown. "The Indians of Northeastern North America." *Dictionary of Canadian Biography*, vol. 1. Toronto, 1966.
Scott, Duncan C. "Indian Affairs, 1763–1841." In *Canada and Its Provinces*, ed. by A. Shortt and A. G. Doughty, vol. 4, Toronto, 1913.
———. "Indian Affairs, 1840–1867." Ibid., vol. 5.
———. "Indian Affairs, 1867–1912." Ibid., vol. 8.
Stanley, G. F. G. "The First Indian 'Reserves' in Canada." *Revue d'histoire de l'Amerique française* 4 (1930): 178–210.
———. "The Policy of 'Francisation' as Applied to the Indians during the Ancien Régime." *R.H.A.F.* (1950): 333–48.
———. "The Indian Background of Canadian History." Canadian Historical Association *Annual Report* (1951–52): 14–21.
Surtees, Robert J. "The Development of an Indian Reserve Policy in Canada." *Ontario History* 61 (1969): 87–98.
Taylor, John L. "Canada's North-West Indian Policy in the 1970's: Traditional Premises and Necessary Innovations." In *Approaches to Native History in Canada*, ed. D. A. Muise. Ottawa, 1977.
Trigger, Bruce G. *The Indians and the Heroic Age of New France*. Canadian Historical Association Booklet no. 30, 1977.
Upton, L. F. S. "The Origins of Canadian Indian Policy." *Journal of Canadian Studies* 8 (November 1973): 51–61.
———. "Indian Affairs in Colonial New Brunswick." *Acadiensis* 3 (Spring 1974): 6–26.
———. "Colonists and Micmacs." *Journal of Canadian Studies* 10, no. 3 (August 1975): 44–56.

————· "Indian Affairs in Colonial Nova Scotia, 1783–1871." *Acadiensis* 4 (Autumn 1975): 3–31.
Wise, S. F. "The Indian Policy of John Graves Simcoe." Canadian Historical Association *Report* (1953): 36–44.
————· "The American Revolution and Indian History." In *Character and Circumstance*, ed. J. S. Moir. Toronto, 1970, pp. 182–200.

PART II

In recent years there has been extensive documentary research conducted into native land claims and into moral, as well as legal, implications of the treaties signed with Canada's Indians. Dozens of research projects have been conducted by national and provincial native organizations, and even by many individual Indian bands across Canada, in order to document their aboriginal and treaty rights and land claims. Some of this research and the oral testimony of tribal elders is now surfacing, and more Indian and Inuit writers are presenting their views in native newspapers, journals, magazines and in several excellent autobiographies.

Ahenakew, Edward. *Voice of the Plains Cree*. Ed. Ruth M. Buck. Toronto, 1973.
Berger, Thomas R. *Northern Frontier. Northern Homeland: The Report of the Mackenzie Valley Pipeline Inquiry*. Vol. I. Ottawa, 1977.
Brody, Hugh. *Maps and Dreams. Indians and the British Columbia Frontier*. Vancouver, 1981.
Cardinal, Harold.*The Unjust Society: The Tragedy of Canada's Indians*. Edmonton, 1969.
————· *The Rebirth of Canada's Indians*. Edmonton, 1977.
Dosman, Edgar J. *Indians: The Urban Dilemma*. Toronto, 1972.
Gros-Louis, Max. *First among the Hurons*. In collaboration with Marcel Bellier. Montreal, 1974.
Frideres, James S. *Canada's Indians. Contemporary Conflicts*. Scarborough, Ont., 1974.
Hanks, Lucien M., and Jane R. Hanks. *Tribe Under Trust: A Study of the Blackfoot Reserve in Alberta*. Toronto, 1950.
Hawthorn, H. B., ed. *The Indians of British Columbia: A Study of Contemporary Social Adjustment*. Toronto, 1958.
————· *A Survey of the Contemporary Indians of Canada. A Report on Economic, Political, Educational Needs and Policies*. 2 vols. Ottawa, 1966.
Helm, June, ed. *Subarctic. Handbook of North American Indians*. Vol. 6. Washington, 1981.
Kennedy, Dan. *Recollections of an Assiniboine Chief*. Ed. J. R. Stevens. Toronto, 1972.
Johnston, Basil. *Ojibway Heritage*. Toronto, 1976.
Jones, Peter. *History of the Ojibway Indians*. London, 1861.
LaViolette, F. E. *The Struggle for Survival: Indian Culture and the Protestant Ethic in British Columbia*. Toronto, 1961.
McCallum, Hugh, and Karmel McCallum. *This Land Is Not for Sale*. Toronto, 1975.
Manuel, George, and Michael Posluns. *The Fourth World: An Indian Reality*. Don Mills, Ont., 1974.
O'Malley, Martin. *The Past and Future Land. An Account of the Berger Inquiry*. Toronto, 1976.
Pelletier, Wilfrid, and Ted Poole. *No Foreign Land: The Biography of a North American Indian*. Toronto, 1973.
Price, Richard, ed. *The Spirit of the Alberta Indian Treaties*. Montreal, 1979.
Richardson, Boyce. *Strangers Devour the Land: The Cree Hunter of the James Bay Area versus Premier Bourassa and the James Bay Development Corporation*. Toronto, 1975.
Ryan, Joan. *Wall of Words: The Betrayal of the Urban Indian*. Toronto, 1978.
Snow, Chief John. *These Mountains Are Our Sacred Places: The Story of the Stoney Indians*. Toronto, 1977.

Thompson, Chief Albert Edward. *Chief Peguis and His Descendents*. Winnipeg, 1973.
Tootoosis, John. *A Biography of a Cree Leader*. Ed. Norma Sluman and Jean Goodwill. Ottawa, 1982.
Trigger, Bruce G., ed. *Northeast. Handbook of North American Indians*. Vol. 15. Washington, 1978.
Waubageshig, ed. *The Only Good Indian: Essays by Canadian Indians*. Toronto, 1970.
Watkins, Mel, ed. *Dene Nation: The Colony Within*. Toronto, 1977.
Wuttunee, William I. C. *Ruffled Feathers: Indians in Canadian Society*. Calgary, 1971.
Zaslow, Morris, ed. *A Century of Canada's Arctic Islands 1880–1980*. Ottawa, 1982.

Resource materials about the Metis people have also continued to grow to such an extent that they now have their own publications outlet, Pemmican Publications, in Winnipeg, and their own research institute, the Gabriel Dumont Institute of Applied Research and Native Studies in Regina. A comprehensive annotated reference book on historical, sociological, and educational sources of the Metis people was recently compiled by John W. Friesen and Terry Lusty, *The Metis of Canada: An Annotated Bibliography*. Toronto, 1980. The following books are the basic reference texts for Metis history.

Adams, Howard. *Prison of Grass: Canada from the Native Point of View*. Toronto, 1975.
Brown, Jennifer S. H. *Strangers in Blood: Fur Trade Company Families in Indian Country*. Vancouver, 1980.
Campbell, Maria. *Halfbreed*. Toronto, 1973.
De Tremaudan, A. H. *La Nation Métisse dans l'Ouest Canadien*. Translated by E. Maguet: *Hold High Your Heads* (History of the Metis Nation in Western Canada). Winnipeg, 1982.
Dobbin, Murray. *The One-and-a-Half Men*. Vancouver, 1981.
Giraud, Marcel. *Le Métis Canadien*. Paris, 1945.
Gould, G. P., and A. J. Semple, eds. *Our Land: The Maritimes*. Fredericton, 1980.
Howard, Joseph. *Strange Empire: Louis Riel and the Metis People*. Toronto, 1974. (First published 1952.)
Long, John. *Treaty No. 9: The Half-Breed Question, 1902–1910*. Cobalt, Ont., 1978.
Lussier, Antoine S., and D. Bruce Sealey, eds. *The Other Natives: The/les Metis*. Vol. 1: 1700–1885; Vol. 2: 1885–1975; Vol. 3: Winnipeg, 1978.
Macleod, Margaret A., and W. L. Morton. *Cuthbert Grant of Grantown*. Toronto, 1963.
Sawchuk, J. *The Metis of Manitoba*. Winnipeg, 1978.
Sawchuk, J., P. Sawchuk, and T. Ferguson. *Metis Land Rights in Alberta: A Political History*. Edmonton, 1981.
Slobodan, R. *Metis of the Mackenzie District*. Ottawa, 1966.
Stanley, G. F. G. *Louis Riel*. Toronto, 1963.
Van Kirk, Sylvia. *"Many Tender Ties." Women in Fur-Trade Society in Western Canada, 1670–1870*. Winnipeg, 1980.

Notes on Contributors

Robert Allen is the deputy chief at the Treaties and Historical Research Centre of the Department of Indian and Northern Affairs. His publications include "The British Indian Department and the Frontier in North America, 1755-1830" and *Canadian Historic Sites, Native Studies in Canada: A Research Guide.*

Laurie Barron is associate professor of Native Studies at the University of Saskatchewan and has published in the fields of Canadian social history, Canadian art and native studies.

Tom Flanagan is now professor and head, Department of Political Science, University of Calgary. He is deputy editor of the Louis Riel Project, University of Alberta, and has published several articles and books, including *Louis "David" Riel: Prophet of the New World.*

David Hall has been with the Department of History, University of Alberta, since 1969. He is currently working on the second volume of his biography of Clifford Sifton.

Raymond Huel is a volume editor for the Louis Riel Project and is currently associate professor and chairman, Department of History, University of Lethbridge.

Diamond Jenness (1886–1969) was born in New Zealand and studied at Oxford University. He joined the Canadian Arctic Expedition in 1913 and went on to become chief of the Anthropology Division of the National Museum. He wrote a classic study on *The Indians of Canada* in 1932 and his volumes on "Eskimo Administration" are a standard reference.

Douglas Leighton is an associate professor of History at Huron College. His articles have appeared in *Ontario History* and the *Dictionary of Canadian Biography.* He is currently preparing a book-length study of the Canadian Indian Department in the nineteenth century.

Don McCaskill is associate professor and chairman of the Department of Native Studies, Trent University. He is articles editor for the *Canadian Journal of Native Studies* and has carried out research on urban native affairs, native education and training, and correctional services for native people.

Simon McInnes is a constitutional advisor to the Inuit Committee on National Issues. His principal field of study is the political consequences of Northern development.

David McNab taught Canadian history from 1973–1978 (Wilfrid Laurier University,

Memorial University of Newfoundland, and Brandon University), and since 1979 he has been senior Indian land claims researcher with the Ontario Ministry of Native Resources. He has published several articles on nineteenth-century British Indian policy.

John Milloy taught in the Department of History, University of Winnipeg from 1976–1982 and is currently associate professor, Department of Native Studies, Trent University.

Jean Morisset is professor in the départment de géographie, Université de Québec de Montréal. He is author of several articles on natives in Northern Canada and is currently working on a major treatise, *L'identité usurpée! Canada — Québec: Les masques de la Conquête.*

Lance Roberts is assistant professor of Sociology at the University of Manitoba, Winnipeg. As a social psychologist, he has published cross cultural studies on the relationship between social structure and personality.

Irene Spry is professor emeritus in Economics at the University of Ottawa. Well known for her studies on western Canadian history, her publications include *The Papers of the Palliser Expedition* and the papers of Peter Erasmus, *Buffalo Days and Nights.*

George F. G. Stanley was director of Canadian Studies, Mount Allison University until his retirement in 1975. He is presently general editor of the Riel Project, University of Alberta and lieutenant-governor of New Brunswick. He is author of *The Birth of Western Canada, Louis Riel, Canada's Soldiers, New France: The Last Phase,* and other works.

Robert Surtees is associate professor of History at Nipissing University College, North Bay. His publications include *The Original People* and *Canadian Indian Policy: A Critical Bibliography.*

John Tobias worked with the Federation of Saskatchewan Indians as research consultant (1972–1974) and as director of Research (1975). Since 1976 he has been history instructor at Red Deer College.

James Walker joined the University of Waterloo in 1971 and is currently chairman of the Department of History. He has written three books: *The Black Loyalists, Identity: The Black Experience in Canada,* and *A History of Blacks in Canada.*